SANCTUARY
of the
DIVINE PRESENCE

"This is a major piece of literature in the Jewish canon. . . ."
STANLEY KRIPPNER, PH.D., PROFESSOR OF
PSYCHOLOGY AT SAYBROOK UNIVERSITY

"To enter the *Sanctuary of the Divine Presence* is to traverse layer upon layer of ever deepening mystery. This is the temple of hidden secrets where each letter of the Hebrew alphabet is imbued with sacred meaning, where words intertwine and dance with the song of the universe, where story and metaphor render the unspeakable. Herein lies the inner sanctum of wisdom, a blueprint for enlightenment that is indispensable for all who seek to become a dwelling place for the divine."
PAUL RADEMACHER, AUTHOR OF
*A SPIRITUAL HITCHHIKER'S GUIDE TO
THE UNIVERSE* AND FORMER EXECUTIVE
DIRECTOR OF THE MONROE INSTITUTE

"In her latest book, Zohara Meyerhoff Hieronimus has made a monumental contribution to the literature of the Kabbalah. For centuries—perhaps even for millennia—attempts to demonstrate the spiritual riches in the Kabbalah have been the prerogative of men. Now, thanks to this book, we have an opportunity to catch a glimpse of a different approach to Kabbalah that offers a more feminine vision of our relationship to God through contemplation, song, and good deeds. There can be no doubt that the wisdom of the Kabbalah and the wisdom within the countless commentaries on this secret tradition have both been strengthened by the contributions in this most remarkable book."

"*The Sanctuary of the Divine Presence* is both traditional and uniquely innovative. The book's ecumenical tone will appeal to readers of all faiths. Based on fully orthodox Chasidic sources, this work offers a personal and sorely needed feminine vision of Jewish mysticism reaching from Luria to modern Chasidism that will inspire women and men of the current and coming generations. The author's language combines the theoretical and the embodied and stimulates thought-provoking insights while offering practical guidance for those who seek to follow the Jewish path of universal compassion and righteousness."

SANCTUARY
of the
DIVINE PRESENCE

Hebraic Teachings on
Initiation and Illumination

J. ZOHARA MEYERHOFF HIERONIMUS, D.H.L.

Inner Traditions
Rochester, Vermont • Toronto, Canada

Inner Traditions
One Park Street
Rochester, Vermont 05767
www.InnerTraditions.com

Text stock is SFI certified

Library of Congress Cataloging-in-Publication Data
Hieronimus, J. Zohara Meyerhoff.
   Sanctuary of the divine presence : Hebraic teachings on initiation and illumination / J. Zohara Meyerhoff Hieronimus.
     p. cm.
   Includes bibliographical references and index.
   ISBN 978-1-59477-375-4 (pbk.) — ISBN 978-1-59477-951-0 (e-book)
   1. Cabala. I. Title.
   BM525.H4935 2012
   296.1'6—dc23

                                                              2011040324

Printed and bound in the United States by Lake Book Manufacturing
The text stock is SFI certified. The Sustainable Forestry Initiative® program promotes sustainable forest management.

10 9 8 7 6 5 4 3 2 1

Text design and layout by Priscilla Baker
This book was typeset in Garmond Premier Pro with Tiepolo, Delphin, and Gill Sans used as display typefaces

To send correspondence to the author of this book, mail a first-class letter to the author c/o Inner Traditions • Bear & Company, One Park Street, Rochester, VT 05767, and we will forward the communication, or contact the author directly at **www.zoharaonline.com**.

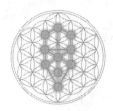

Contents

Acknowledgments

Each of us benefits in our lives from both those living and those who have passed through to the World to Come. This book is dedicated to our ancestors, who whisper in our ears; to my late mother, Lyn P. Meyerhoff, who encouraged independence and bravery, who showed me mothering and love of nature; to my father, Harvey M. Meyerhoff, for insisting on thoroughness, service to others, and fairness in our lives; to my sisters, Terry M. Rubenstein and Lee M. Hendler, and brother, Joseph Meyerhoff II, for loving me, challenging my ideas, and appreciating all of our differences as talents added to our shared charitable work, which is guided by Judaic principles; and to all of our children and theirs, who bring delight to our shared lives; to my daughter, Anna, who was born on Pesach 1987, for setting my heart free to love unconditionally; and to my stepchildren, Mare and Plato, for adding rich relationships to my life; most of all, to my husband, Robert R. Hieronimus, Ph.D., for his enduring love and support, for sharing in the pursuit of universal truths and the effort to put them into action in the world.

Also, I would like to acknowledge Rabbi Elchonon Lisbon and Rabbi Noah Shavrick for their Chassidic counsel while editing the first of three drafts of this book, but especially to Rabbi Shavrick, for his ongoing guidance in my research; and Rabbi Moshe Shualy, for giving me my first copy of Sefer HaAggadah. I acknowledge with heartfelt gratitude Rabbi Avraham Brandwein of Jerusalem (Rosh Kol Yehudah Yeshiva) and Samuel Avital of Colorado, who helped prepare me over the years with their lives and their teachings for this work.

And to Inner Traditions International—their wonderful staff, including freelance editor Margaret Jones, who helped assure consistency in the structure of the work and clarity of meaning in what can be a difficult field of study; and to Inner Tradition's founder and president, Ehud Sperling, I extend my deepest appreciation for the beauty of your publications and the team that made this book possible: Jon Graham, acquisitions editor; Jeanie Levitan, managing editor; and Jamaica Burns Griffin, project editor. It has been a journey of several years with these "makers" of the published word. It is the second book we have produced together. It is a blessing to have shared in this devotional service of creating *Sanctuary of the Divine Presence,* as described by the People of the Book.

Finally yet foremost, were it not for God (HaShem) and the people of the biblical period, these teachings would not be ours to use. I regard the ancient Israelites' lives and their stories as proof of God's divine guidance; it is an amazing journey to be their student and a privilege to write about them. Their love of God and disciplined spiritual devotion shows us what we are capable of in our relationship with divinity. May God bless all of our journeys with His presence as He did theirs.

The Priestly Blessing, Birkat Kohanim ברכת כהנים
(Numbers 6:24–26)[1]

24 *The LORD bless thee, and keep thee;*
25 *The LORD make His face to shine upon thee,*
and be gracious unto thee;
26 *The LORD lift up His countenance upon thee,*
and give thee peace. Amen.

---

[1] Shefa Tal, Hanau, 1612. Hebraic Section, Library of Congress.

Preface

Sanctuary of the Divine Presence springs from a single momentary vision I had in 2008/5768, on the first night of the Jewish festival of Sukkot. Sitting in our family's sukkah (a temporary booth used for eight days to commemorate the glory of God's presence, which protected the Israelites during their Exodus), I had a revelatory experience, similar to what occurred to me in 2004 and which became the impetus for my first work on prophecy, *Kabbalistic Teachings of the Female Prophets* (Inner Traditions, 2008).

This time I was shown a new map of correspondences, between Kabbalah's Tree of Life, the Etz Chayim; certain Hebrew Bible texts sometimes referred to as the Ten Songs of Creation; and the five distinct stages of an initiatic process affecting the human body and soul that takes place inside the Tent of Meeting and its Tabernacle, which Moses and the Israelites built and used, and from which the design of today's synagogue is based. What I did not know when I was called to write this book is that the subject in general—that of the Tent of Meeting, often referred to as the Tabernacle (though technically the Tent encloses the Tabernacle), and its meaning—is a vast topic in both the Judaic and Christian traditions. Christian rituals, church hierarchy, and church architecture all spring in some way from the Israelites' First Temple, which originates in this archetypal holy design called the Tent of Meeting, the sacred place we are each to build within for God's presence to dwell in. This is the directive God gave the Israelites about 3,500 years ago as a covenant lasting a thousand generations.

In writing *Sanctuary of the Divine Presence,* I have used only references on the subject itself, from the tradition of which I am a student, the Chassidic tradition of classical Kabbalah and Judaism. Of these references I used very few books, as there are only a few on this particular topic. Yet to the issue of self-refinement and self-mastery, the heart of the initiatory path, all of Torah (the teachings of the People of the Book) and all of Kabbalah (the inner teachings of this tradition) apply. In this sense, *Sanctuary of the Divine Presence* expresses the interior process each person experiences in coming to this holy place of being illuminated by the Divine Presence. My interest is more as a phenomenologist than as a Bible scholar, looking for the method the ancient Hebrews practiced to reach these elevated states of being. For if the Kabbalistic system's truths are universal, as I believe they are, every human being can benefit by using them.

Looking for the authentic perspective of the Hebrews as passed down through the generations, I have relied almost entirely on the Hebrew Bible and the Mishnaic teachings of Judaism, the oral tradition for which the Jewish people have a vast and glorious library. The biblical quotes in this work are derived from several sources: the Art Scroll Tanakh, and the Jewish Publication Society Bible (1917), as well as an electronic source of JPS (1917) available at www.mechon-mamre.org, which was used for the biblical texts sung by the prophets and the Israelites, and, in some instances, for other biblical quotes presented throughout this work (these various text sources are not cited individually). Due to the fact that every Bible translation from the Hebrew Bible has variations based on the translator's background and bilingual training, I suggest each person use the Bible text translated from Hebrew that they are most comfortable with. My preference is the Stone Edition Tanakh (the twenty-four books of the Hebrew Bible), an Art Scroll Series published by Mesorah Publications, Ltd., 2003; it is the one I used in preparing the initial draft of this work. In addition, I used two primary compendiums that have collected many of the oral tradition's teachings (except for Jewish law, Halacha, a category of its own): R. Ibn Yaakov's *Ein Yaakov,* compiled in the sixteenth century and translated into English in 1990 by Rabbi Yaakov Finkel; and the *Sefer HaAggadah (The Book of Legends),* translated and compiled by Hayam Nahman Bialik and Yeshoshua Hana Ravnitzky (translated by William G. Braude), published in 1992. Another wonderful resource is the *Encyclopedia of Biblical Personalities: Anthologized from the Talmud, Midrash, and Rabbinic Writings,* by Yishai Chasidah, published in 1994.[1] Readers can enrich their own libraries and continue their explorations into this and other subjects in life and in the Hebrew Bible with just these three references. With these as the primary reference tools, I hope to have articulated the very traditional and classical view of this rich and holy topic from the Jewish people's own writings and teachings, the root of my own illumination.

As to the name of the Creator used throughout this book, in the schools of teachings I have drawn from, the word *HaShem* (lit. "the name") would be used, but for the comfort of the majority of readers, the word *God* has been used instead. However, this work represents the classical teachings and terminology of the ancient Hebrews' teachings. It has been an amazing journey discovering and writing about this sacred system, thousands of years old, talked about for centuries, designed for humanity's overall benefit.

I pray that this book assists others in making their lives a holy place for the Divine Immanence and the Holy Spirit to rest in. This is what the People of the Book show us how to do.

> *Happy is the man that findeth wisdom, and the man that*
> *obtaineth understanding.*
>
> PROVERBS 3:13

---

[1] See bibliography for complete publishing information.

Introduction

The Tent of Meeting and Prophecy

*So Moses finished the work [of making and setting up
the Tent of Meeting]. Then the cloud covered the Tent of
Meeting, and the glory of the LORD filled the Tabernacle
. . . For the cloud of the LORD was upon the Tabernacle
by day, and there was fire therein by night, in the sight of
all the house of Israel, throughout all their journeys.*

EXODUS 40:34, 38

All of humanity shares a common destiny, that of self-refinement, self-mastery, and unity consciousness. Human beings are designed to complete the task that the first man and woman began, which is to reach Godliness and peace, within and without. The sacred traditions and practices of the world offer us many paths. As a woman of Jewish ancestry, I believe human beings are made in God's image. If so, what does this mean to each one of us making the effort to contribute to the world's well-being?

After the Israelites leave Egypt, God tells the prophet Moses to make a sanctuary for His presence to dwell in. The process for individual initiation to revelation and Godliness can be found within the rituals and design of the sacred dwelling place the Israelites build. It is called the Tent of Meeting, or Ohel Moed as named in the Hebrew Bible, as it starts out literally as Moses' tent. It is a sanctuary of illumination, divine inspiration, and prophecy.

1

All humans are designed to receive the holy light of the Creator. The rituals of the ancient Hebrews were created to accomplish this, and God's emanation in the form of the Cloud of Glory, which is visible while guiding the Israelites' entire Exodus, also visibly fills the Tent of Meeting, demonstrating His constant presence. Exodus 29:43–45 comments: "And there I will meet with the children of Israel; and [the tent] shall be sanctified by My glory. And I will sanctify the Tent of Meeting, and the altar; Aaron also and his sons will I sanctify, to minister to Me in the priest's office. And I will dwell among the children of Israel, and will be their God."

The Tent of Meeting and the Tree of Life

Sanctuary of the Divine Presence explores how the Hebrew Tent of Meeting and its holy Tabernacle, in which are housed the Ark and the Ten Commandments, is an archetypal pattern reflecting our body and soul. When the Tree of Life is superimposed on this holy meeting place, one discovers a concealed method for approaching each person's spiritual development. It is the pattern on which the ancient Temple of the Hebrews is based, as well as many of today's synagogues and churches. This pattern is also a hidden structure in some of the rituals and practices of the Jewish and Christian faiths, as well as in the practices of other traditions, including those of the Mennonites, the Freemasons, and the ancient alchemists.

In offering a description of our bodies as sacred sanctuaries, and particularly in showing us how the way we act in the world can be a form of ritual practice, the ancient methods of the Hebrew Bible provide a lesson for our own self-refinement today. For instance, in Exodus (30:37) our prayers are described as being like the incense in the Tabernacle's Holy Place, in that both rise up and are said to be pleasing to God: "And the incense which thou shalt make, according to the composition thereof ye shall not make for yourselves; it shall be unto thee holy for the LORD." Refining our emotions, like the water rituals of the priests in the Outer Court of the Ohel Moed, is a daily task we are each required to perform, as Aaron and his sons are instructed: "Whenever they come to the Tent of Meeting, they shall wash with water and not die, or when they approach the Altar to serve to raise up in smoke a fire offering to God. They shall wash their hands and feet and not die. It shall be for them an eternal decree, for him and his offspring for their generations" (Exodus 30:20–21). When we give up selfish traits such as bullishness, we are performing the animal sacrifices of the priests in the courtyard: "And you shall bring the bull near before the Tent of Meeting; and Aaron and his sons shall lean their hands upon the head of the bull. You shall slaughter the bull before the LORD, before the entrance of the Tent of Meeting" (Exodus 29:10–11). Even our feet, like the Tent of Meeting itself, stand in the world, while the brain, like the Ark in the Holy of Holies, is concealed in a hidden chamber: "And the LORD spoke unto Moses, saying: 'On the day of the first new moon, on the first of the month shalt thou rear up the Tabernacle of the Tent of Meeting. And thou shalt put therein the Ark of the Testimony, and thou shalt screen the Ark with the veil'" (Exodus 40:1–3).

For the People of the Book, ever since the destruction of the Second Temple by the Romans in 70 CE, studying the Tabernacle and the later Temple rituals and reciting the specific prayers associated with those rituals takes the place of actually performing them. This devotional practice adds specific spiritual influences to one's life, affecting different parts of the soul's five components and associated functions in the body. For example, the water ritual in the Outer Court influences the part of our soul that is called the Ruach, or spirit, while lighting the menorah in the Holy Place elevates the Neshamah, that part of the soul that is both physical and nonphysical, and which represents our higher sense of hearing or intuitive understanding. These examples reveal how the initiatory rites of the Mosaic tradition are preserved for all generations to use: "Know therefore that the LORD thy God, He is God; the faithful God, who keepeth covenant and mercy with them that love Him and keep His commandments to a thousand generations. . . . Observe therefore the words of this covenant, and do them, that ye may make all that ye do to prosper" (Deuteronomy 7:9, 29:8).

The basic Hebrew words and explanations used throughout *Sanctuary of the Divine Presence* describe our physical and spiritual constitutions according to the ancient Israelites' tradition, which includes Kabbalah, a received tradition that was for centuries an entirely oral transmission. Memorizing these terms is not as important as understanding how the hermetic axiom "As above, so below; as within, so without" is being gradually revealed. The portals to our physical and spiritual sanctuary come with a set of keys, which are aspects or qualities of ourselves as expressed in the Kabbalistic Tree of Life. When used properly, these qualities—crown, wisdom, understanding, love, strength/judgment, beauty, victory, majesty/glory, foundation/covenant, and kingdom/sovereignty—open the ten secret chambers that exist within each of us. In Kabbalah these chambers are called Sefirot (enumerations, luminous spheres or vessels of measured light); they are the ten parts of the Tree of Life and are reflected in the sanctuary's functions. The Tree of Life thus describes the qualities of the Creator we endeavor to emulate. When any one of us masters the Tree of Life, we become co-creators—we become God-like.

Each chapter in this book explores one of the various parts of the Tent of Meeting and the Tabernacle contained within it, as well as the corresponding stage of personal and communal development it represents. There are five different aspects to reaching Godliness, just as there are five different fields of activity within the Tent of Meeting: initiation, consecration, elevation, illumination, and revelation or Godliness. These five stages of a person's growth are an ascending journey, from the bottom of the Tree of Life, our feet, to the top of the Tree, our head. In the same way we construct a building by creating its foundation and then the first floor and so forth, so will we build our personal holy sanctuary in this logical, progressive fashion, proceeding from the entry gate, the feet, to the most hidden upper chamber, the Holy of Holies, our brain.

Each of the biblical narratives revealed in *Sanctuary of the Divine Presence* revolves around a tool the ancient Hebrews offer us. Specific moments in their lives, as told in the words of the prophets and prophetesses, reflect the Tree of Life's hidden story, concealed in the Tent of Meeting's inner alchemy. Altogether we will use ten different sets of correspondences overlaid on one another to experience the initiatic path of the Israelites and their prophets. Thus as an integrated system of transformational alchemy, the mystery teachings of the ancient Israelites come alive for us today.

The Coming Ascent of the Light

Practical Kabbalah teaches a person how to ascend and descend the Tree of Life like a ladder, rung by rung. Most of recorded history has been the story of the descent of the light through the generations. The Chassidic tradition says that after the very challenging present time we live in now we will begin a thousand-year messianic period of peace—the long-awaited age of Moshiach (meaning "the anointed one," the term from which *Messiah* comes from), which coincides with the very bottom Sefirah of the Tree of Life, Malchut. At that point civilization will begin its spiritual ascension. The teachings of many other ancient traditions seem to agree with this prophecy.

At this present time of 2012/5772, the world is in its final descent from the current age of Yesod. Sometime during the next 230 years, on or around the year 2230/6000 (though the potential for divine revelation by all of humanity exists now), we will enter the age of Malchut, signaling the returning light, in which we will begin a thousand-year period of global peace as a planetary community. Each person who attains the self-mastery that the Tree of Life describes and prescribes adds to this prophesied time on earth. Just as each Sefirah holds some of the light of every other Sefirah, so too our current age already holds some of the returning light of Malchut. We will each climb the Tree of Life, just as all of humanity will eventually ascend this "ladder of light" for centuries to come. According to predictions that go back many centuries, the present time is said to be the beginning of an age of prophecy, when God will speak primarily through women, children, and even some of those thought to be mentally unstable, all three considered to possess the requisite humility for being a divine vessel of prophecy.

To climb the Tree of Life from the bottom to the top as we do in this book requires looking at biblical history in reverse chronological order, just as following a road in one direction on a journey and returning by the same route one sees things anew, but in reverse order. (For this reason, the reader will benefit from reading the book a second time from the last chapter to the first.) This method of study is also a spiritual practice one can use each night as a form of self-evaluation, to look at one's day in reverse order. It is also described as the process each of us experiences as part of the soul's afterlife journey, which includes a review from the end of one's life to its beginning.

Peace, shalom, from the Hebrew word *shalem,* means wholeness. To be whole, something must be balanced and include all parts in harmony, in proper measure. So sacred is peace that when God created the world

He looked for the proper vessel to hold the blessings He wanted to give Israel. He chose peace, for only peace is able to contain the highest light of the Creator's loving emanations.[1] Peace, then, is the outcome of the fully self-realized human, our God-given inheritance.

As we each grow in our love of and reverence for the divine, we improve our own lives and are thus better able to contribute to the world's spiritual development and maturation. Prophecy is the ability to bring people back to a love of God, to facilitate healing, to know the future, to read others' minds, to avert natural and national disasters, and to speak with and for God. All of these abilities are the outcome of making oneself a dwelling place for the Divine Immanence, called the Shechinah, as well as for God's Holy Spirit, the Ruach HaKodesh. These manifestations of God are experienced both physically and spiritually; they can induce altered states of awareness through the mind and the senses that in turn can inspire elevated emotions and awareness of other realities beyond the physical world.

Creating conditions for God's presence to illuminate a person is said to be a hallmark of the age we are now the midwives to, the age of Moshiach and messianic (unity) consciousness. Every person alive today is part of this holy plan to become masters of our own natures and agents of God's supreme love. What is said of the messianic leader of the Davidic bloodline can be said of all human beings of the new age that is dawning: "The spirit of God will rest upon him—a spirit of wisdom and understanding, a spirit of counsel and strength, a spirit of knowledge and fear [i.e., awe] of God" (Isaiah 11:2).

Sanctuary of the Divine Presence describes how the Israelites communicate with God and God with them, and how their story of preparing and using a specific place of meeting God is the story of the journey to holiness of each individual and all of us who dwell in the world.

---

[1] "God will bless His nation with peace." R. Ibn Yaakov Chaviv, *Ein Yaakov,* Uktzin, 803.

1

The Architecture of Light

The Creation of Humankind and the Tree of Life

Then God said, "Let us make man in our image, in our
likeness, and let them rule . . ." So God created man in his
own image, in the image of God he created him; male and
female He created them. God blessed them and said to
them, "Be fruitful, and multiply, and replenish the earth,
and subdue it; and have dominion over the fish of the sea,
and over the fowl of the air, and over every living thing
that creepeth upon the earth."

GENESIS 1:26–28

The Purpose of Life

The blessed sage R. Moshe Chayim Luzzatto (1707–1746 CE), known as the Ramchal, writes in *The Path of the Just* that our very first step on the path of spiritual development is to clarify our purpose. When asked why we have been created, he writes: "Our Sages of Blessed memory have instructed that man was created for [the sole purpose of] reveling in the Eternal and delighting in the splendor of the Divine Presence, this being the ultimate joy and the greatest of all pleasures in existence." This sublime state of being is fully realized as pleasure in the World to Come (Olam HaBa), which in the classical tradition of Judaism is defined as the spiritual realms in which a person's soul continues its existence and learning, eventually leading to the soul's complete return to Gan Eden (the Garden of Eden), the realm of eternal perfection. The Ramchal goes on to explain that "this world [i.e., our earthly existence] resembles a corridor before the World to Come,"[1] and that our good deeds, our mitzvot, are the measures of light we should occupy ourselves with, for the good we do now is repaid in kindness later.

The Ramchal reiterates that incarnating multiple times into this world is necessary for humankind to return to the splendor of the Garden. But we do not arrive at this ultimate destination by attaching to things of this world; rather, it is by attaching to God. "If you delve further into this matter," the Ramchal reminds us, "you will realize that cleaving to the Eternal alone is absolute perfection."[2] In conclusion, he says, "A person was not created for his position in this world, but rather his position in the world to come."[3] This is to diminish neither the purpose and benefit of incarnating in this world, nor the good things we do in life; rather, it is to point out that by residing in a physical body where we can learn to refine our character, control our desires, and help others, the soul can reach a higher level than had it never incarnated at all. Thus it is by incarnating into physical form that we prepare our place in the World to Come, so that we may reach our ultimate, ineveitable destination, the perfected state of Gan Eden.

In the Chassidic tradition, we learn that all souls are rooted in Adam Kadmon, the primordial "man of earth," our template. Then Adam committed the sin of eating from the Tree of Knowledge of Good and Evil. After this event, his perfect and whole self shattered into 600,000 pieces, from which all souls are hence derived. According to the Hebrew mystics, this is the rectification we each take part in as we ascend the "ladder of light," the metaphor Kabbalists use to describe the stages of self-mastery as depicted by the Tree of Life.

So, if the greatest pleasure a person can experience is to revel in the

---

[1] R. Moshe Chayim Luzzatto, *Mesillat Yesharim, Path of the Just,* 8.
[2] Luzzatto, *Mesillat Yesharim,* 8.
[3] Ibid., 10.

Divine Presence, wouldn't everyone want to know how to experience this? Human beings are always seeking pleasure, whether through food, sex, power, consumption, fame, wealth, or relationships, and are never satisfied. What if more people knew that the greatest pleasure, the one that satisfies every need, is bound up in our ability to make ourselves a vessel for the presence of God to rest in? If the Creator made us out of love, then we must be designed to experience the ultimate pleasure of divine love now, on earth.

This is the purpose of Kabbalah: to bring humankind close to God and to our own innate Godliness. All of the elements of the Tree of Life are designed to bring each person to his or her divine perfection. This is also the purpose of the Tent of Meeting, or Ohel Moed, the holy Tabernacle of the ancient Israelites: for those of us living in the modern era it provides a detailed description of the rituals and processes that allow each of us to reach this illuminated state of being.

Kabbalah: Keys to Wisdom

Kabbalah is the Hebrew term for "received tradition," referring to the fact that for many centuries it was an oral transmission passed down directly from teacher to student before it was ever written down. It is a school of thought and a spiritual discipline concerned with the hidden or esoteric teachings of rabbinic Judaism. As such it is a guide to understanding all of Torah's concealed wisdom.

Kabbalah's primary map is the Etz Chayim, the Tree of Life. It is a guide for living and helps to decode the written and oral teachings of Torah. In so doing, it delineates a system of correspondences between the eternal, mysterious Creator and His creation as it manifests in the finite universe. It thus offers us a precise road map that shows the descent of the light of God to all aspects of His creation; in so doing, it reveals the path of spiritual ascension, so that we may fully realize and embody our inherent Godliness.

That humans are made in God's image explains why Kabbalah's holy map is a sacred tool for humanity's spiritual development and refinement. Each of us reflects this sacred pattern in our spiritual and physical composition. By thus using Kabbalah for self-refinement, we unite with God and His Holy Spirit, making our lives meaningful, joyous, and full of peace.

The Ten Sefirot of the Tree of Life

In the beginning God created the heaven and the earth. Now the earth was unformed and void, and darkness was upon the face of the deep; and the spirit of God hovered over the face of the waters. And God said: "Let there be light." And there was light. And God saw the light, that it was good; and God divided the light from the darkness. And God called the light Day, and the darkness He called Night. And there was evening and there was morning, one day.

GENESIS 1:1–5

The People of the Book believe that God created the world "using ten things": "wisdom, understanding, knowledge, strength, rebuke, might, righteousness, judgment, kindness, and compassion."[4] These ten elements correspond to the ten Sefirot of the Tree of Life, which are described as luminous spheres or "measures of light" that are specific sources of vitality: Keter (crown), Chochmah (wisdom), Binah (understanding), Chesed (loving-kindness), Gevurah, (strength/judgment), Tiferet (beauty), Netzach (victory), Hod (majesty/glory), Yesod (foundation), and Malchut (kingdom/sovereignty). The Sefirah Daat, which is knowledge, is considered a part of Keter (in a self-realized state), the outcome of wisdom (Chochmah) and understanding (Binah) combined. Daat generally plays a role in discussions only when Keter is excluded, as much of Kabbalistic study omits Keter as an unknowable realm of God's light. Instead, Daat, as the third part of the intellect, as in the triad of Chochmah, Binah, and Daat (or ChaBaD for short) is discussed. However, since this work not only includes Keter but focuses specifically on this Sefirah as the pinnacle of human potential, Daat, for the most part, is omitted from this book's discussion; however, it is implied in our discussions of the intellect and the upper Sefirot in the Tree of Life.

In figure 1.1, listed from the top of the Tree (crown/Keter) to its bottom (kingdom/Malchut), are the ten "measures of light" involved in our spiritual evolution, which we will be studying in reverse order, from the

---

[4] "The Maharsha explains that these ten things parallel the ten sefirot and the ten Divine utterances with which the world was created" (R. Yaakov Ibn Chaviv, *Ein Yaakov*, Chagigah, 342).

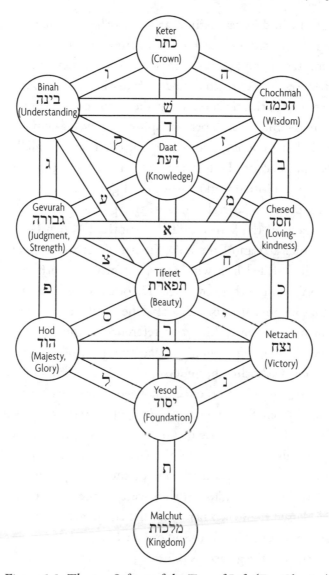

*Figure 1.1. The ten Sefirot of the Tree of Life (Etz Chayim)
and its twenty-two pathways*

bottom to the top, beginning with Malchut. In this way we will climb the ladder of light rung by rung.

These measures of light are emanated from the moment of Creation. They are also the spiritual progressions represented in the rituals of the Tent of Meeting, or Ohel Moed, the holy sanctuary that God asks the Israelites to build for Him in order to refine themselves through worship. In this way, the Tree of Life and its ten Sefirot, as well as the ten emotions expressed in the songs associated with each of the Sefirot, are keys to understanding the different stations and processes involved in the ceremonial arts that the ancient Hebrews used to reach divine illumination and revelation.

These ten sefirotic attributes are qualities possessed by the Creator. As such they are the root of each person's spiritual as well as physical anatomy, for each Sefirah has not only a corresponding emotional or intellectual quality, but also an associated body part to which our life is connected in both the material and spiritual worlds, as seen in figure 1.2.

Scholars point to several verses in the Hebrew Bible that show us the arrangement of the Sefirot and their powers. When God appointed Betzalel as chief artisan of the holy Tabernacle of the ancient Israelites, He said: "I have filled him with the spirit of God, with wisdom, with understanding, and with knowledge" (Exodus 31:3). Betzalel's position required that he possess knowledge of alchemy, the art of combining the elements of nature, hence this was a reference to the four upper Sefirot of the Tree of Life when including Daat: the spirit of God, the crown, is Keter; wisdom is Chochmah; understanding is Binah; and wisdom combined with understanding produces knowledge, or Daat.[5]

The next seven Sefirot below these upper Sefirot are named in 1 Chronicles 29:10–11. This occurs after the Jewish people have come forward to help build the First Temple with contributions of gold, silver, copper, precious stones, and materials for the priestly garments and curtains used in the Temple, just as they were in the Tabernacle: "Wherefore David blessed the LORD before all the congregation; and David said: 'Blessed be Thou, O LORD, the God of Israel our father, for ever and ever. Thine, O LORD, is the greatness [Chesed], and the power [Gevurah], and the glory [Tiferet], and the victory [Netzach], and the majesty [Hod]; for all that is in the heaven and in the earth is Thine [Yesod]; Thine is the kingdom [Malchut], O LORD, and Thou art exalted as head above all.'"[6]

---

[5] As explained, in this work, since we deal with ten Sefirot and not eleven, Daat is implicit as the outcome of wisdom and knowledge, and we instead focus our attention on the top three Sefirot excluding Daat as we will examine Keter instead. Though Keter is regarded as unknowable, in the context of the Tabernacle it is very much the source of divine transformation, which the Tent of Meeting facilitates.

[6] R. Aryeh Kaplan, *Sefer Yetzirah*, 25.

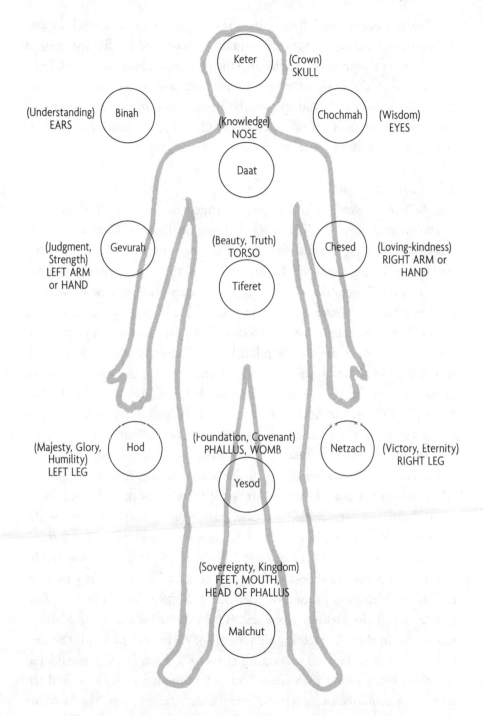

Figure 1.2. The human body and the Tree of Life

The ten Sefirot, which combine various qualities of our intellect and our emotions, reflect the very same qualities possessed by the first man of earth, Adam Kadmon. In Kabbalah, this primordial human is considered the source of the design for our human composition, completely integrated both physically and spiritually. By focusing our attention on the inner nature of each Sefirah, we can become more integrated ourselves, our body and soul in conscious partnership.

The Flow of Light

The Sefirot of the Tree of Life are arranged in three vertical columns, as shown in figure 1.3. The original limitless light of Creation travels downward in a zig-zag fashion, as the arrows indicate, like a lightning strike. Beginning with the Keter/crown, at the top, it proceeds from right to left: Chochmah/wisdom; Binah/understanding; Chesed/loving-kindness; Gevurah/strength and judgment; Tiferet/beauty (in the middle of the Tree); Netzach/victory; Hod/majesty and glory; Yesod/foundation (after Hod on the middle pillar below Tiferet); and ending in Malchut/kingdom. Then from kingdom, at the bottom, the light begins an upward pattern in reverse order, from Malchut, to Yesod, to Hod, then Netzach, Tiferet, Gevurah, Chesed, Binah, Chochmah, concluding in Keter. Going in the reverse order of the descending light is the progression this book explores, which is the same path of self-mastery described in the Hebrews' sacred rituals in the Tent of Meeting. It is the same path all of humanity shares. It is the journey of the soul awakened to its divinity and power while inside the body, participating in the return of the earth and all of humankind to an Edenic, paradisiacal, perfected state.

As shown in figure 1.1 (see page 11), the ten Sefirot are connected by twenty-two pathways. These pathways correspond to the twenty-two letters of the Hebrew alphabet, or Alef-Bet, אלף-בית (named after the first two letters of the Hebrew alphabet). The ancient Hebrews and Kabbalists maintain that the Hebrew alphabet is of divine origin and is the tool God uses in creating and sustaining the world. Each letter is considered an actual living power with special qualities unique to the individual letter or to a combination of letters. Sometimes referred to as "the heavenly alphabet" and "the celestial writing," the Alef-Bet is a powerful vehicle enabling communication between God and humans—a kind of language

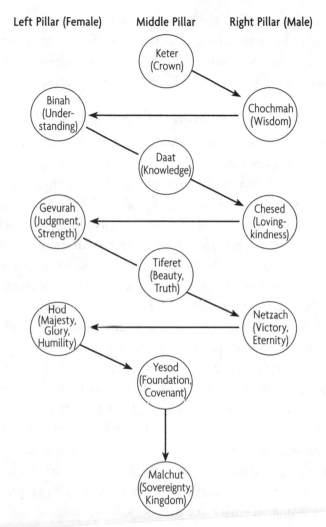

Left Pillar (Female)   Middle Pillar   Right Pillar (Male)

Figure 1.3. The Tree of Life with its three pillars showing the descent of the light, as indicated by the arrows

between heaven and earth, in which is concealed and revealed all of God's holy wisdom.

The twenty-two pathways of the Tree of Life, as expressed by the Alef-Bet, plus its ten Sefirot make for a total of thirty-two pathways of wisdom one aspires to master. The descending light of God that fills each of the ten Sefirot means they are interconnected. The light from the upper Sefirot, or vessels, a metaphor often used in Kabbalah to signify that which holds the light, filters down to all of the Sefirot below in a gradual way, following the pathways, each of which is governed by a letter of the Hebrew alphabet. Thus the lower Sefirot have some of the light from the upper Sefirot within their makeup, in the same way that a grandchild is said to have some of his ancestors' qualities.

Ten-Dimensional Cosmogenesis

According to the Jewish sages, the number 10, as in the ten Sefirot of the Tree of Life, expresses a pattern of "ten-ness" that recurs throughout the universe.[7] In general, ten signifies something that is complete, whole, containing all its parts in harmony. One of Kabbalah's most ancient sources, the Book of Formation, or Sefer Yetzirah, attributed by some scholars to the patriarch Abraham, says that many aspects of life are made of ten elements, reflecting humankind's ten-dimensional existence as posited by the ancient Hebrew mystics. By observing the recurrence of this pattern based on the number ten—for example, our hands and feet, which each have ten digits—it is evident that God creates using a decalogue, a ten-part formula.

The Hebrew sages posited the significance of the number ten on the physical plane in many other ways: the universe is made of three elements (fire, air, water) and seven planets; the agricultural year in Israel is composed of two major seasons (summer and winter), alternating with two shorter half seasons (creating a numerical value of one) plus the seven days of creation; the living soul is contained in a body made with three primary parts (head, chest, and stomach), and seven apertures in the head (two eyes, two ears, two nostrils, and one mouth). The prophets whose lives and teachings we study in this book are known by ten different names: "envoy, man of faith, servant, messenger, missionary, sentinel, seer, angel, prophet, man of God." Likewise, the teachings that come from the two forms of God's emanation that facilitate divine insight or the various levels of prophecy, the Divine Immanence (or Shechinah) and the Holy Spirit (or Ruach HaKodesh), are also known by ten names: "parable, metaphor, riddle, speech, saying, call, command, pronouncement, prophecy,

---

[7] "Just as the Book of Psalms was composed by ten men [with David], so was it composed in ten different forms of song [zemer and mizmor are analogous]: Zemer, nitzuach, nigun, mizmor, shir, hallel, tefillah, beracha, hoda'ah, halleluyah, and ashrei. The greatest of all is halleluyha (lit. 'praise of God')." (Shocher Tov 1:6; R. Yisrael Yitzchak Yishai Chasidah, *Encyclopedia of Biblical Personalities*, 140.

vision."[8] Prophecy itself is said to have ten aspects; six are described as "gentle" and four as "stern": "Prophecy, seeing, watching, parable, metaphor, and Holy Spirit are gentle; vision, pronouncement, preaching, and riddle are stern. God spoke with the patriarchs through seeing, prophecy, and vision; with Moses, our teacher, through prophecy, seeing, and the Holy Spirit. With the other prophets, he communicated through most or some of these means."[9]

Kabbalah integrates its ten-dimensional cosmology into a framework that guides us into alignment with our divine nature, our archetypal anatomy, as seen in figure 1.2 (see page 13). It is thus a blueprint for physical and spiritual integration, a map that guides us to mastery of the temple of the body and the soul, the successful integration of which leads one to becoming a dwelling place, a sanctuary, for the Divine Presence—which brings prophecy and peace.

The Ten Commandments

The Ten Commandments, given to Moses orally and inscribed on two sets of stone tablets he brought down from Mt. Sinai, contain the light of the ten aspects of Creation as well. The Commandments serve as holy guidance for societal and personal order and have their roots in the ten unique attributes described by the Tree of Life. God commanded Moses and the Israelites to build a dwelling place for Him, a place that would house the final set of the Ten Commandments, and later the Torah,[10] the manna, and other instruments.[11] Betzalel, the chief artisan of the Tabernacle, built a special Ark as instructed by God, which was housed at first inside of the portable Tent of Meeting the Hebrews used during their Exodus and then later in the First Temple of Jerusalem.

---

[8] Hayim Nahman Bialik and Yehoshua Hana Ravnitzky, *Sefer Ha-Aggadah*, 8:68, 475. In addition, Maimonides (Rabbi Moshe ben Maimon, a.k.a. the Rambam, (1135–1204 CE) in his *Guide of the Perplexed,* lists thirteen different kinds of prophetic experiences (see book 2, chapter 45, 396, 403). See also J. Zohara Meyerhoff Hieronimus, *Kabbalistic Teachings of the Female Prophets,* 19–20.

[9] Bialik and Ravnitzky, *Sefer Ha-Aggadah,* 8:68, 475.

[10] Torah, from the Hebrew word *Yoreh,* means "to teach." Torah can mean the five books of Moses, as it does in this instance, or all twenty-four books of Hebrew scripture, or all the written and oral teachings of Judaism combined.

[11] It is taught that a Torah scroll written by Moses was also hidden inside the Ark along with its two stone (sapphire) tablets.

And so we see that the ten songs (or utterances), the Tree of Life, the Ten Commandments, the Torah, and the Tent of Meeting with its Tabernacle, which houses the Ark and its contents, are all connected through the act of Creation itself. They all share the common root of a ten-dimensional cosmogenesis, or cosmic origin.

The Jewish sages, or Chazal (an acronym meaning "Our Sages, may their memory be blessed"), teach that in addition to the ten utterances that made the world, there were ten things created on the first day of Creation: heaven and earth; chaos (*tohu*) and desolation (*bohu*); light and darkness; wind and water; and the twelve hours of day and the twelve hours of night.[12] The Hebrew Creation story reveals how these elements comprise the material universe and the manner in which we human beings have a place in it. These instruments of Creation are emanations from the Creator and are encoded in each of us, whether in our thoughts, speech, or actions. In this way it can be said that we are each made in His image.

The Singing Tree: The Ten Songs of Creation

Prayer, study and meditation, Kabbalah tells us, are tools for facilitating the holy union between human beings and God, but equal to these is music and song. Sound, as we know from science and metaphysics, is vibration; it animates and shapes matter. The twenty-two letters of the Hebrew alphabet, as seen in the twenty-two pathways of the Tree of Life in figure 1.1 (see page 11), are said to be God's tools for creating and sustaining the world. Each letter is a living vessel of energy animated by its essence, shape, and function. When letters form words that are read, sung, chanted, listened to, and contemplated, we experience a profound effect in our bodies, minds, and souls. Thus the root of all Hebraic ritual and discipline is to harmonize the human being to the Word (i.e., the sound, or vibration) of God.

In Kabbalah it is said that music and prophecy share the same spiritual source. Rabbi Chayim Vital (1543–1620 CE) tells of the ancient prophets being accompanied by musicians until reaching a level of prophecy when the music would cease.[13] In Torah, the connection between music and prophecy is made explicit: "And you shall meet a band of

---

[12] R. Yaakov Ibn Chaviv, *Ein Yaakov,* Chagigah (near 11b), 341.
[13] Sharie Kedusha 4:2 (Zohar 3:223b).

prophets coming down from the high place with a lyre, a timbrel, a flute and a harp [being played before them]; and they shall prophesy" (1 Samuel 9:5).

The prophets used different types of music that expressed different moods as a means of elevating their awareness. The ten songs we will examine in this book, which correspond to texts from the Hebrew Bible, along with their corresponding Sefirot, and the ten different emotional qualities expressed by each song comprise a body of teachings that guides us in increasing our own awareness. By absorbing the stories of the prophets and the ancient Hebrew people along with the songs that embody certain states of awareness the Israelites gained during their Exodus journey, we can learn how to speak with and for God.[14]

All ancient texts connect us to those who have studied and lived the teachings throughout the centuries. The resulting resonant field of life is a timeless continuum that is the fabric of what is sometimes called eternity—a field that goes on recording and reordering itself with every new event and vibration that takes place in the universe. Nothing is ever lost from it. A prophet's text and song connect us to that prophet. In the same way, an ancient sage's wisdom, repeated in his name as is the custom of the People of the Book, bring the living close to the soul of the sage who first spoke those words. Physicists would describe this association in terms of waveforms in the field of consciousness and in the field of life itself. In this way, unaltered holy texts can serve as a lifeline between generations, as fields of physical and spiritual continuity that, like customs and traditions, unite families, communities, and even entire nations. This is one reason why the Jewish people were instructed by God through Moses at the end of his life by these words:

> Hear, O Israel: the LORD our God, the LORD is one. And thou shalt love the LORD thy God with all thy heart, and with all thy soul, and with all thy might. And these words, which I command thee this day, shall be upon thy heart; and thou shalt teach them diligently unto thy children, and shalt talk of them when thou sittest in thy house, and when thou walkest by the way, and when thou liest down, and

---

[14] For a more complete exploration of the subject of prophecy, see *Kabbalistic Teachings of the Female Prophets*.

when thou risest up. And thou shalt bind them for a sign upon thy hand, and they shall be for frontlets between thine eyes. And thou shalt write them upon the door-posts of thy house, and upon thy gates. (Deuteronomy 6:4–9)

Ten Types of Song and Ten Emotional Qualities

In the Tikunei Zohar ("the garments of the Zohar"), a collection of seventy Kabbalistic writings on the first verse of the Hebrew Bible, it is said that there are ten different kinds of songs, and that the emotions they express correspond to the Sefirot of the Tree of Life.[15] Each of these songs is a description of an aspect of our emotional composition and thus represents our spiritual roots. Each quality points us toward areas for personal development. Together these ten emotional qualities are a template of our spiritual anatomy.

The ten types of song and associated emotional qualities of each of the Sefirot, from the top of the Tree of Life to the bottom, are:

- Sublime insight (ashrei) אשרי
- Jubilant song (shir) שיר
- Drawing down blessings (beracha) ברכה
- Soaring melody (nigun) נגן
- Breaking through (zemer) זמר
- Radiating praise and joy (hallel) האליל
- Song of victory (nitzuah) ניטזה
- Majestic humility (hodu'ah) הדיה
- Song of devotion (ranenu tzaddikim) רנה צדיקים
- Self-reflection, prayer (tefillah) תפלה

These ten qualities are expressed through the experiences of the Israelites, who collectively, and a few individually, experience to varying degrees divine revelation and union with the Holy Spirit (Ruach HaKodesh, רוח הקדוש) and the Divine Immanence (Shechinah, שכינה), two forms of God's presence. We will be studying these qualities in the stories of prophets and prophetesses in the coming chapters. Studying them brings us into rapport with the spiritual essence of the Sefirah from which each emanates.

Note that while certain generations as well as specific time periods in

---

[15] Tikunei Zohar, 3:223b.

an individual's life might be dominated by one or more of the Sefirot, all of the Sefirot operate in our lives all of the time to one degree or another. For example, the current generations (the twentieth- and twenty-first century) are in the age of Yesod, a time for reaffirming our covenant with God, a time for crying out of one's heart with devotion. Moshiach (משיח), the age of Malchut, will come when humanity collectively cries out for divine assistance, for a change from within.

The following are the Hebrew Bible texts associated with the ten types of song, which, as Targum Yonatan[16] teaches, represent each of the ten Sefirot of the Tree of Life and their corresponding emotional quality. It is easy to see why these texts could also be called the Ten Songs of Creation or the Ten Songs of the Sefirot, because of the deeper meaning attached to these powerful moments in biblical history, which correspond to each person's spiritual journey as mapped by the Tree of Life. By following the lessons contained within these songs, one is guided on the middle path, the path that leads to peace and unity with the divine in all life, which culminates in revelatory union with God and one's own original divinity.

The ten Hebrew Bible texts we will be studying are:

- Keter: Adam after Expulsion from the Garden (Psalm 92); ashrei
- Chochmah: Song at the Sea (Exodus 15:1–29); shir
- Binah: People Sing to the Well (Numbers 21:1-20); beracha
- Chesed: Moses' End of Life Song (Deuteronomy 32:1–43); nigun
- Gevurah: Joshua Stopping the sun and moon (Joshua 10:1–14); zemer
- Tiferet: Devorah and Barak (Judges 5:1–31); hallel
- Netzach: Chanah's Song (1 Samuel 2:1–10); nitzuah
- Hod: David Delivered from Saul (2 Samuel 22:1–51); hodu'ah
- Yesod: King Solomon (Song of Songs); ranenu tzaddikim
- Malchut: The Moshiach and each person (Shemoneh Esrei); tefillah

Ten Inner Qualities of the Sefirot

In addition to the ten songs, which are emanations of the ten Sefirot and which are expressed through the journey of the ancient Hebrews as recorded in Torah, Kabbalah also teaches that each Sefirah of the Tree of

---

[16] Pesachim 10:117a.

Life has an inner quality that imparts a lesson that is an important component of physical and spiritual development.[17] They are: **faith** (*emunah*); **self-nullification** (*bitul*); **joy** (*simcha*); **love** (*ahavah*); **fear** (*yira*); **mercy** (*rachamim*); **confidence** (*bitachon*); **sincerity** (*temimut*); **truth** (*emet*); and **lowliness** (*shiflut*). Figure 1.4, illustrating the layers of correspondences we will be studying, shows the workings of the Kabbalistic process for uncovering deeper teachings in basic stories of Torah. The ten Sefirot, the ten songs, the ten emotions, and the ten inner qualities all correspond to the progression of a person through the structure of the original Tent of Meeting and its holy Tabernacle rituals. By using this Kabbalistic method of integrating various systems, a person is able to explore the essence and action of each Sefirah from which we draw our divine design.

Chassidut, the teachings of the Chassidic lineage beginning with the wisdom of its progenitor, Baal Shem Tov (Rabbi Yisroel ben Eliezer, 1698–1760), states that English is the last language to be elevated, that is, to be used for holy instruction. This may explain the expansive efforts that are being made to translate into English and publish not only many great Hebrew classics, but the holy books of other wisdom traditions from around the world as well.

How can studying ancient Hebrew texts, especially those translated into English, bring us peace and well-being, even illumination? The simple answer is that by studying the words of the sages and prophets, we can change our behavior. By using our mind to overcome emotional imbalances, we eventually overcome selfish desires. In the *Zohar*, also known as the *Book of Splendor*, the central framework of Kabbalah's mystical interpretation of the Torah, it is said that the person attached to the Tree of Life is called a penitent, for the congregation of Israel, which is Malchut, is also called penitence, or repentance. Such an inner change in a person is said to be even greater than the status achieved by an already completely righteous person, a *tzaddik*. Coming to a place of sincere humility and wanting to change is what initiates a person into all schools of holy teachings. We cannot buy an entry ticket; we cannot borrow someone else's privilege of access. Entry into the deeper mysteries of any of the world's sacred wisdom teachings is accomplished through personal self-refinement; so, too, in Judaism's Kabbalah and Torah wisdom tradition.

---

[17] See also the work of Rabbi Yitchak Ginsburgh at Gal Enai, www.inner.org.

Sefirah/ Partzuf	Text /Prophet	Type of Song	Inner Emotion	Soul Path
Keter crown Adam Kadmon	Adam Psalm 92	sublime insight / ashrei	faith/emunah	**Revelation** Source of light between the cherubim on the Ark
Chochmah wisdom Father/Abba	Israelites' Song at the Sea Exodus 15:1-29	jubilation/shir	self-nullification/ bitul	**Illumination** The Ark and the Holy of Holies
Binah understanding Mother/Imma	Israelites sing to the well Numbers 21:1-20	drawing down blessings/ beracha	joy/simcha	**Elevation** The Holy Place: incense, menorah and shewbread
Chesed loving-kindness the Son/Zeir Anpin (ZA)	Moses' end of life song (Hazeinu) Deuteronomy 32:1-43	soaring melody/ nigun	love/ahavah	**Consecration** Outer Court fire rituals, water purification
Gevurah strength/ judgment ZA	Joshua stopping sun and moon Joshua 10:1-14	breaking through/zemer	fear, awe/yira	Outer Court (as above)
Tiferet beauty ZA	Prophetess Devorah & Gen. Barak Judges 5:1-31	radiating praise and joy/ hallel	mercy/ rachamim	Outer Court (as above)
Netzach Victory ZA	Prophetess Chanah 1 Samuel 2:1-10	victory/nitzuah	confidence/ bitachon	Outer Court (as above)
Hod majesty ZA	King David 2 Samuel 22:1-51	majestic humility/ hodu'ah	sincerity/ temimut	Outer Court (as above)
Yesod foundation ZA (completion of the Son)	King Solomon Song of Songs	devotion/ ranenu tzaddikim	truth/emet	Outer Court (as above)
Malchut kingdom Daughter/ Nukvah	Moshiach and each person Shemoneh Esrei/ Standing Prayer	self–reflection/ tefillah Prayer	lowliness/ shiflut	**Initiation** Place where Tent of Meeting Stands

Figure 1.4. Correspondences of the Sefirot, songs, and sanctuary progression

When spoken and contemplated, English translations derived from Hebrew portions of the Torah show us emanations from God. When they are presented in a particular order, from the lowest rung of the Tree of Life to the highest—the pattern of the returning light that is the structure of this book—they afford us the opportunity of spiritual ascension, of "going up," or in Hebrew, *aliyah,* עליה (Ayin Lamed Yod Hay).

Building our Personal Sanctuary

Figure 1.4 depicts the Sefirot, their associated emotional qualities and inner nature, and their role in our spiritual maturation, which is the goal of practical Kabbalah. When considered as steps in creating our own Tent of Meeting, from the bottom (Malchut) to the top (Keter), this system helps us make our life a holy process of gradual and clearly delineated spiritual development. These ten steps are essentially a blueprint for spiritual development, which includes specific tools needed to build our individual sanctuaries for God to inhabit.

The Limitless Light and Revelation

It is said that humankind does not directly experience the limitless light, the Or En Sof, or light from the infinite and formless Creator (En Sof), from where all light is issued, though it is this light that is said to shine inside the Holy of Holies once a year, on Yom Kippur. This is when the High Priest enters the Holy of Holies, where the Ark is located. Here the light of the primordial man, Adam Kadmon, shines on the integrated person, making him or her an illuminated one who can then bestow the light of God on others. This describes a process each soul experiences at the exit of the body at death, when the enraptured illumination of knowing that we are each part of the divine body of God, cosmic love, is experienced. Yet this bliss is available to us now while we live in the body and is part of the sacred literature of all wisdom-keeping traditions of the world. It is referred to as revelation—when one revels in the light of God and is united with His presence, with the very fabric and essence of the cosmos.

Adam, representing the Sefirah of Keter, was illuminated by this brilliant light (*bahir*) as he stood outside the gates of Eden. The Israelites were enwrapped in this ecstatic frequency of the limitless light shining in the Sefirot of Chochmah and Binah. The prophet Joshua was enraptured by it; so was his teacher, Moses, each respectively representing Gevurah and Chesed. The great warrior-judge and prophetess Devorah was full of this Holy Spirit in Tiferet, and Chanah the prophetess as well, in the Sefirah of Netzach. King David, in Hod, composed all of his holy writings through the infusion of the Holy Spirit, and his son Solomon built the First Temple, standing for our foundation and covenant in Yesod, under its influence. Each of us receives this shine of the Almighty when we pray, which is the activity of the Sefirah of Malchut.

Each of us is a potential vessel for God's Holy Spirit to fill. When in prayer, in Malchut, the physical world, we open our hearts to song and surrender. We are embraced by the divine life within and without, always around us, always interacting with us in the fields of life. At the dedication of Solomon's Temple, representing Yesod (the age in which we live today, explored more fully in chapter 4), we see how each person is designed to be filled with the holy glory of God.

The Five Levels of Spiritual Development

Behold the LORD our God hath shown us His glory and His greatness,
and we have heard His voice out of the midst of the fire; we have seen
this day that God doth speak with man, and he liveth.

DEUTERONOMY 5:24

In Kabbalah, the world of the human being includes both the physical realm that we can experience through our sensory faculties as well as realms that are not physical but just as real. As we shall see, there are five distinct worlds or levels of existence, and they each have their correspondence in the various parts of the physical body as well as in the five distinct aspects of the human soul, including its nature and development, as well as in the five progressive stages of development in the Tabernacle of the Tent of Meeting. Briefly described here are the correspondences this book uses to explain the method of each person's self-refinement in ascending to divine revelation.[18]

---

[18] It is also important to know that there are many traditional schools of thought about these Kabbalistic elements, just as there are considered to be seventy points of view for any interpretation of the Torah. The elements detailed in this book are based on the author's effort to explain in a more simplified fashion what is traditionally presented in the Zohar and Lurianic Kabbalah.

The Five Spiritual Worlds

One of the Tree of Life's set of keys involves Kabbalah's delineation of the five worlds, or realms. From the bottom of the Tree of Life to the top, these are:

Asiyah, the realm of action in the world, the realm of our physical, observable deeds, which include what we say and do;

Yetzirah, the realm of formation, which corresponds to our emotions and our mastery of our own impulses;

Beriyah, the world of creation, where our intellect is used to express the divine in life;

Atzilut, the realm of emanation, where one experiences complete enlightenment in body and soul and being enveloped in the direct shine of the Creator's presence;

Or En Sof, the ultimate and highest realm of experience and being, the light without end that shines from the En Sof, His limitless light, the dominion of Adam Kadmon, the first man of earth, said to be the perfect template from which each person is created. Equated with total revelation in the divine presence, which is beyond intellect or feeling, it is the root of the possibility of the final Resurrection.

The Body and the Worlds

As figure 1.5 shows (see page 31), the five worlds have anatomical correlations in the human body:

The world of **Asiyah** represents the feet and the mouth, our walking, talking, and what we do.

Yetzirah corresponds to the sense of smell, which uses both the nose and the lungs, but also corresponds to the generative organs, torso, and our two arms (including the hands) and two legs and the form of our emotions that is invested in our worldly conduct.

Beriyah corresponds to hearing and to the heart and one's intuitive understanding and use of it in life to benefit the world.

Atzilut is the source of our eyes and seeing and the intellectual processes by which we consciously direct our lives.

The **Or En Sof,** the light without end, is the source of our ability to achieve sublime consciousness and to act independently, and it is from here that our free will and divine soul originate.

The Five Levels of the Soul

Just as the body, the senses, the emotions, and the intellect reside within the five worlds, the soul also has five analogous components, which when added to these correspondences show us how Kabbalists are able to discern the spiritual root of physical ailments—the physical body being the last in the descent of the light from above—as well as prescribe physical and spiritual remedies that address these problems.

In Kabbalah, the subject of the soul of man guides our understanding of how the transcendent experience is grounded in our material existence and vice versa. While some sages say that various levels of the soul are acquired over time through self-development, others, with whom I agree, suggest that all five levels of the soul are inherent in each composite soul, but they remain unconscious until we reach certain levels of self-mastery. Still others speak of people receiving new soul components or having them taken away based on conduct, as well as being dependent on the health of the person or the grace that Sabbath and other sacred holy days bring, when it is said that elevated souls may enter the living temporarily.

The five components of the soul, in ascending order, are:

The **Nefesh,** which is the vital force in the blood of each person, corresponds to the world of Asiyah, to action, to walking and talking.

The **Ruach,** spirit, is related to our ability to smell and is the source of all of our emotions; it corresponds to the realm of Yetzirah, or formation.

The **Neshamah** corresponds to both hearing and heart-centered knowing, to our capacity for understanding. It derives its vitality from the realm of Beriyah, or creation, it being the "soul" breathed into each person at birth.

The **Chayah,** that part of the soul related to our ability to see, to acquiring wisdom, is also called the "living presence," "life essence," or "life force" and is not rooted within the body but remains connected to the body from its supernal root.

Finally, the very apex of the soul's makeup, which is eternal and outside of the body though part of the person's nature, is called **Yechidah;** it is also known as the divine spark of God in each one of us, and is also called "singularity" and "unity," showing us that all souls come from the same eternal Creator of us all, making each of us part of the whole of God's divine creation.

This book does not present in detail all the varying Kabbalistic beliefs about the nature of the soul, nor does it give the special attention generally shown to the unity of the Nefesh, Ruach, and Neshamah aspects; rather, this work assumes that all five aspects of the soul are each person's inheritance, which can be accessed by gradual self-refinement in this life, or through a series of lifetimes. In fact, it is said that in the time of Moshiach, the Nefesh, Ruach, and Neshamah aspects will be experienced consciously by each person, but until then most people only become conscious of their Nefesh, some their Ruach, and fewer still the Neshamah.

The Five Partzufim

Another Kabbalistic system of correspondences that this book uses refers to the five partzufim, or archetypes (sometimes called personas or masks, such as those the Creator puts on for our benefit), as reflected in the Tree of Life. These archetypes describe a complete family and are represented by the Sefirot of the Tree of Life. At the top of the Tree is **Adam Kadmon**, also called Primordial Man,[19] which corresponds to the Sefirah of Keter. The Father, or **Abba,** corresponds to Chochmah; while the Mother, or **Imma,** corresponds to Binah. The next six Sefirot below, Chesed through Yesod, comprise **Zeir Anpin** ("small face"), or the Son. The final Sefirah of Malchut is represented by **Nukvah,** the Daughter, or woman/female. These five components are an additional interrelated system by which we can learn about individual, familial, and societal balance and well-being.

The Five Stages of the Tabernacle Progression

The following is an overview of the five stages of spiritual development involved in climbing up the Tree of Life as expressed in the architecture and rituals of the Tent of Meeting's Tabernacle (seen in figures 1.4 [p. 23] and 1.5 [p. 31]). These five levels of spiritual development, like

---

[19] Adam Kadmon is composed of two aspects not elaborated on in this work: an inner nature called the Ancient One (Atik Yomin or "Ancient of Days") and an outer expression called the Long Face (Arich Anpin, or "Long Face"); these two aspects together correspond to Keter.

the five levels of the soul, represent the fundamental progression of each person—and the Israelites as a nation—as shown to me in 2008 while in my sukkah. This progression in life and in prayer and its relationship to the Tree of Life and to the other systems outlined above is the premise of dynamic interrelatedness on which this book is based. All of life is interconnected, and this Kabbalistic mapping gives humanity tools for optimal design and function in any enterprise.

Initiation

Self-reflection, in Malchut, also known as the kingdom and referring to the sovereign being, is the first step in initiation. We must be honest about who we are and what we need to change about ourselves, and we must ask God and others for help in our efforts to change. Asking for help is the first step in getting it. As self-refinement is ultimately obligatory for each soul, prayer is given to us as a lifelong tool; it is the foundation of all spiritual development. Prayer and meditation offer a direct line to the God center. Here in Malchut, we are asked to refine the physical world by refining ourselves. In the process of doing so, we learn how to speak to the divine in all of life.

Consecration

In the next stage of growth, consecration involves our deep love of divinity, our enduring service, and our humility, which reflect the basic qualities of the six Sefirot ruling the emotions: Chesed, Gevurah, Tiferet, Netzach, Hod, and Yesod. Here, just like a person in love, we are eager to share everything, to give everything to the One we love, to the world around us, to the divine. The Tent of Meeting's Outer Court is the area of consecration where the grain and animal sacrifices are made; similarly we can elevate every action in our ordinary life to an act of devotion through our intention to benefit others by our own refinement and our desire to unite with God. This stage of spiritual growth encompasses all of sexuality, spiritual devotion, and surrender. It engages all of our emotions, hence the fire and water rituals of purification, as well as the capacity for love, balanced judgment, and truth. Consecration asks us to use our hearts and hands in all that we do, sanctifying everything with disciplined strength and compassionate love.

Elevation

Elevation is that aspect of ourselves that allows us to arouse the souls of others in complete harmony, enticing the desire of oneself and others for understanding, for giving nourishment to the generation. Here, in Binah (understanding), like the Mother that is this Sefirah's archetype, we are no longer for ourselves alone but for the benefit of the whole world. Refining the soul's faculties of seeing, hearing, smelling, and tasting, we are able to apply our entire being, body and soul, to divine service. As the essence of faith, this stage of elevation of the individual and the community prepares a person and his or her society for complete illumination. In the Tabernacle, this spiritual progression is akin to the Holy Place and its rituals of menorah, incense, and shewbread.

Illumination and Bestowal

This arena of spiritual growth completely engages the emotions, the intuition, and the intellect, giving us a heart of wisdom. Here great illumination leads to an overflow of light from God, making the person a vessel of the Shechinah and the Ruach HaKodesh and enabling higher forms of prophecy. The Holy of Holies, the most sacred place of the Tabernacle, is where the High Priest offers prayers once a year, on the Day of Atonement, Yom Kippur. This is for the benefit of the entire community. We embody and share divine wisdom and compassion with others for the welfare of all life, now and in the future. In this most holy part of the Tabernacle, the special incense fills the air, and the light of God illuminates the person's body and soul.

Revelation

This final aspect of the Tabernacle experience is beyond words or concepts. It describes the experience of the soul unencumbered by the body, yet a vehicle the soul can animate at will. Here is the source of the light, which the cherubim on the Ark conduct. Here the initiate gains access to all wisdom, all knowledge, and the tools of Creation itself. Humanity is designed for this revelation, wherein the soul gains the knowledge of life and death—its own immortality—and hence the purpose and method of Resurrection.

Sanctuary	Body	Soul	World	Sefirot	Partzufim	Soul Paths
Mercy Seat	Crown/ Skull	Spark of Divine Soul Yechidah	Limitless Light Or En Sof	Crown/Keter	Adam Kadmon Ancient One	Godliness At-One- Ment Revelation
Holy of Holies	Eyes	Living Presence Chaya	Emanation Atzilut	Wisdom Chochmah	Father Abba	Illumination
Holies	Ears Heart	Soul Neshamah	Creation Beriyah	Understanding Binah	Mother Imma	Elevation
Outer Court	Nose Arms/ Hands, Torso, Legs	Spirit Ruach	Formation Yetzirah	Beauty/Truth Tiferet (Chesed– Yesod)	Son Zeir Anpin	Consecration
Place	Feet/ Mouth	Vital Force Nefesh	Action Asiyah	Kingdom Malchut	Woman (female) Nukva	Initiation

Figure 1.5. Correspondence chart of the sanctuary, body, soul, worlds, Sefirot, partzufim, and soul path

Five Parts of the Sanctuary

As we have seen thus far, the Tree of Life of the ancient Israelites is an informing archetypal pattern reflected in various systems of ten: the ten Sefirot, the ten songs, and ten types of emotions all have correspondences in the body, in the realm of the soul, in the five worlds, and in the many corresponding systems of five that we are made of and exist in. This dynamic pattern is also reflected in the elements and rituals that comprise the Tent of Meeting and its holy Tabernacle, which chart the soul's progressive path of ascension, as we shall see in the coming chapters.

The interrelated elements we shall be studying in this book, as shown in figure 1.5 in columns from left to right, include: the Tent of Meeting, the body, the five aspects of the soul, the five worlds, the ten Sefirot, the five partzufim, and the five stages of the Tabernacle ritual that constitute the soul path. By reading the horizontal rows, one is shown the way the Tree of Life contains *all* of these systematic elements in a pattern of relationship. For example, the Mercy Seat in the Tabernacle represents the skull of the person, which is animated by the divine spark of God; this is the uppermost Sefirah of our being, Keter (crown), and it represents Adam Kadmon and revelation.

Gematria: A Kabbalistic Tool for Uncovering Spiritual Roots

As noted earlier, each letter of the Hebrew alphabet is considered an actual living power with a numerical value; therefore it stands to reason that any combination of letters making a word also has a numerical value expressing certain powers and meaning. A valuable tool used in Kabbalah and Hebrew meditation, study, and teaching to facilitate spiritual development relies on the use of gematria, a numerological system whereby words and whole sections of Torah are converted into numbers, thereby revealing the sympathetic and varied correspondences between even seemingly unrelated topics or events.

Kabbalists say that words and phrases sharing the same numerical value share the same spiritual root. Gematria gives us the key to understanding the concealed nature of anything through the deeper levels of meaning associated with roots of words and phrases. By observing trees in nature, we know that roots are primary, superior to branches, and that branches are superior to fruit, yet all three are necessary for the fulfillment of the tree's purpose: to bear fruit, seed, and regenerate. Similarly, numbers express potencies that are spiritual roots, and words with the same number value share a single root. By finding the number value of a letter, word, or phrase, we can tune in to its essence and thereby extrapolate deeper meaning (a Hebrew alphabet chart can be found in appendix 1). Kabbalists have used gematria for centuries to find the connection between seemingly unrelated words, letters, and even sentences, and to thereby discover the timeless correspondences between events, places, and people.

To give an example of how this works: The number 410, the numerical value of the Hebrew word for Tabernacle, **Mishkan, משכן** (Mem [40] Shin [300] Caf [20] Nun [50]), where the holy Ark, the resting place of the Divine Immanence, is housed, has the same number value as the word **Ararat, אררט** (Alef [1] Reish [200] Reish [200] Tet [9]), the name of the place where Noah's ark comes to rest. Both words involve places where vessels built according to God's instructions rest, and both are given God's protection. Both involve arks. Each contributes to humanity's survival and well-being. It is noteworthy that 410 is also the number of years the First Temple stood before being destroyed. Other words with this same numerical value include the Hebrew word for holy, **kadosh**, קדוש, as when the Israelites are told "And ye shall be unto me a kingdom of priests, and a holy nation" (Exodus 19:6); the word meaning to dwell, rest, or settle, **l'shechin**, לשכין, as in "And they shall know that I *am* the LORD their God, that brought them forth out of the land of Egypt, that I may dwell among them: I *am* the LORD their God" (Exodus 29:46); **v'kadosh**, וקדש, which means to conscreate or sanctify, as in "Speak unto Eleazar the son of Aaron the priest, that he take up the censers out of the burning, and scatter thou the fire yonder; for they are hallowed [sanctified]" (Numbers 16:37); the word for love, **b'ahavat**, באהבת, referring to God's love of Israel, as in "Blessed be the LORD thy God, who delighted in thee, to set thee on the throne of Israel; because the LORD loved Israel for ever, therefore made He thee king, to do justice and righteousness" (1 Kings 10:9); **c'shamin**, כשמן, referring to oil and ointment, as in Aaron's initiation: "It is like the precious oil upon the head, coming down upon the beard; even Aaron's beard, that cometh down upon the collar of his garments" (Psalms 133:2); and the word for peace, **shalom**, שלום, as found in Deuteronomy 23:6: "Thou shalt not seek their peace nor their prosperity all thy days for ever." Putting all of this together, we find that all these words with the value of 410 refer to aspects of the holy Tabernacle and what occurs inside it.[20] Here we can see clearly from these words with a common numerical root of 410 that inside the Tabernacle, or *Mishkan,* we are made holy. The Shechinah rests there. God's love for Israel and His anointing oil are rooted in it, as is the most precious possession of all, peace, shalom.

With the advent of computerized databases of correlated Hebrew words, any word whose meaning and spelling can be found in Hebrew can be easily examined through gematria's method of comparing it with other like-valued words with the same or similar vibration and spiritual

---

[20] One method is to select a key word associated with any one of the Sefirot. For example, **tefillah,** תפילה, "prayer," is associated with Malchut and is equal to 515—the same value as **HaShir,** השיר, the word for "the song." This is a good method for finding many concealed teachings associated with each Sefirah.

root. This valuable tool affords spiritual practitioners a powerful method of contemplation that enhances prayer, ritual, and meditation.

Summary:
Integrating Ten Kabbalistic Teachings

*The spirit of man is the lamp of the LORD, searching
all the inward parts.*

PROVERBS 20:27

Just as the God of the Hebrew Bible guides the children of Israel in building and using the Tent of Meeting and its holy Tabernacle for their collective elevation, the ten elements we will weave together in this book will allow us to travel, one step at a time, into the ten dimensions of a mystical inner journey of spiritual elevation. These ten components are:

1. **The Tree of Life and the ten Sefirot,** a map of self-mastery with ten corresponding systems
2. **The ten inner qualities** of the Sefirot[21]
3. **The partzufim,** or family archetypes
4. **The five worlds**
5. **The five aspects of the soul**
6. **The human body**
7. **The ten songs** of the Zohar[22]
8. **The ten texts' historical exemplars,** each associated with certain prophets or moments of collective enlightenment
9. **The ten sefirotic qualities** described in the Tikunei Zohar
10. **The Tent of Meeting (Ohel Moed)** and its structure, holy rituals, and processes as a sacred five-part journey

All ten of these categories together create a comprehensive map for self-refinement, healing, and spiritual development. The illustrations provided in this chapter and others in this book are useful adjuncts to the

---

[21] Tikunei Zohar, The Ten Emotions, 3:223b.

[22] The ten texts of Torah representing the ten Sefirot are found in the Aramaic Targum ("translation," "interpretation") to the Song of Songs. Targum Yonatan, Song of Songs (Shir haShirim) 1:1.

progression we are about to explore in the chapters to come. The reader is thus in possession of an integrated system for spiritual development that allows him or her to ascend the Tree of Life, and inversely, descend the Tree as well. The tools needed to fulfill our divine purpose, to be a living Tabernacle, are at our fingertips. By practicing in this way, following in the footsteps of the ancient Hebrews, we can make ourselves and the world a living holy place, a sacred sanctuary in which the architecture of spirit structures our lives.

Conjoining body and soul, mind and heart, to create a meeting place between God and ourselves is exactly what we are designed to do. This is the process *Sanctuary of the Divine Presence* endeavors to describe.

2
The Tent of Meeting
Creating a Dwelling Place for God

I love them that love me, and those that seek me earnestly shall find me.

Proverbs 8:17

The First Tabernacle

During the years 1522 BCE to 1313 BCE, the Jewish people lived in Egypt, where they had originally gone to seek relief from famine in the land of Canaan, but where they became enslaved. They were at that time a loosely knit group of tribes united by a belief in an invisible, imageless God. During the year 1312 BCE, the Hebrews, emancipated through divine intervention from Egypt, were led by their tribal leaders and prophets, the three siblings Moses, Miriam, and Aaron. After the miraculous crossing of the Red Sea (a.k.a. Sea of Reeds), their final step in leaving Egypt, they camped in the desert at Mt. Sinai, where more divine revelations took place. One of these events was the bestowal of the Ten Commandments.

The story of the Ten Commandments is first presented in Exodus 24:1–7, when Moses is directed "to go up to God, you, Aaron, Nadab and Abihu, and seventy of the elders of Israel, and you shall prostrate yourselves from a distance and Moses alone shall approach God, but they shall not approach, and the people shall not go up with him." Receiving, then, the holy instructions as an oral teaching, "Moses returns and tells the people all the words of God and all the ordinances, and the entire people respond with one voice and they said, 'All the words that God has spoken we will do.'" Moses then writes the words of God down. Rising early in the morning the next day, Moses builds an "altar at the foot of the mountain, and twelve pillars for the twelve tribes of Israel." Moses sends the youth of the camp out to gather sacrifices "of burnt offerings, and they slaughtered bulls to God as peace-offerings . . . He took the book of the Covenant and read it in earshot of the people and they said 'Everything that God has said we will do and we will obey!'"

Afterward, Moses is once again called to Mt. Sinai, where God visibly manifests in the form of a luminous cloud:

> And Moses went up into the mount, and the cloud covered the mount. And the glory of the LORD abode upon mount Sinai, and the cloud covered it six days; and the seventh day He called unto Moses out of the midst of the cloud. And the appearance of the glory of the LORD was like devouring fire on the top of the mount in the eyes of the children of Israel. And Moses entered into the midst of the cloud, and went up into the mount; and Moses was in the mount forty days and forty nights. (Exodus 24:15–18)

After this description of Moses receiving the Ten Commandments, the next passage in Torah recounts God's instructions for building a holy sanctuary to house them, which will be a formal meeting place for the Lord and His people:

> And the LORD spoke unto Moses, saying: "Speak unto the children of Israel, that they take for Me an offering; of every man whose heart maketh him willing, ye shall take My offering. And this is the offering which ye shall take of them: gold, and silver, and copper; and blue, and purple, and scarlet, and fine linen, and goats' hair; and rams' skins dyed red, and sealskins, and acacia-wood; oil for the light, spices for the anointing oil, and for the sweet incense; onyx stones, and stones to be set, for the ephod, and for the breastplate. And let them make Me a sanctuary, that I may dwell among them." (Exodus 25:1–8)

So begins Torah's record of God's lengthy instructions regarding the creation of a holy sanctuary, known in the Hebrew Bible as the Mishkan,[1] a word that has variations: Ohel Moed, or Tent of Meeting (sometimes called the Tent of Congregation or the Tent of Communion) between God and man; *Mishkan HaShem,* Sanctuary of God; *Mishkan HaEdut,* Sanctuary of Testimony; and *Mikdash HaShem,* the Holy Temple of God. More chapters in Torah are dedicated to this particular subject than any other aspect of the Israelites' journey, and the descriptions are detailed and vivid. "They shall make a Sanctuary for Me, so that I may dwell among [i.e., within] them" is the outcome of making and using the specifically prescribed architecture, rituals, sacred vestments, and furnishings that God prescribes: "According to all that I show thee, the pattern of the tabernacle, and the pattern of all the furniture thereof, even so shall ye make it." (Exodus 25:9)

From here, the arena's contents, including specific details, from hooks, to pillars, to curtains needed for making the sacred place operational; to its sacred tools—the altar, laver, menorah, incense, shewbread, anointing oil, and the holy Ark and its contents and how to make them—are given. These lengthy instructions end with a description of the eight articles worn by the High Priest, or *Kohen Gadol:* the breeches, tunic, girdle, turban, ephod [richly ornamented vest or apron], breast piece, and the turban with gold crown attached are all worn so that "when they enter the Tent of Meeting or when they approach the Altar to serve in holiness . . . they should not bear a sin and die; it is an eternal decree of him and his offspring after him" (Exodus 28:43).[2] Finally, we learn that everything together in this place is called the Ohel Moed, the Tent of Meeting.

The term *Ohel Moed* is often used interchangeably with *Tabernacle,* but in fact there is a distinction, as we shall see later in this chapter. In one sense, the word *ohel,* אהל (Alef Hay Lamed), simply means a tent whose poles extend outward. *Ohel* can also mean "to radiate in all directions," making a ritual tent—much like a person such as Moses, who is able to radiate in all

---

[1] The three-letter root of the Hebrew word for Mishkan, שכן, is Shin Chaf Nun, which means "dwelling," reflecting the concept of a dwelling place for God on Earth.

[2] Exodus 29:29–30 is a description of the succession of High Priests: "The holy vestments of Aaron shall belong to his sons after him to become elevated through them, to become inaugurated through them. For a seven day period, the Kohane who succeeds him from his sons, who shall enter the Tent of Meeting to serve in the Sanctuary, shall don them."

directions. The Ohel Moed is described in Numbers 2 as standing in the middle of the Israelites' encampment, like the hub of a twelve-spoke wheel, with the twelve tribes arranged around it.[3] The Hebrew word *moed* is also used to highlight an appointed time and place for meeting, signifying the appointed times and seasons for the Sabbath and the Hebrews' feast celebrations. And so, to put it quite simply: the Ohel Moed is a tent of radiating light where at certain times one meets God.

The Tent of Meeting is at one point mentioned as Moses' own tent: "Moses would take the Tent and pitch it outside the camp, far from the camp, and call it the Tent of Meeting. So it was that whoever sought God would go out to the Tent of Meeting, which was outside the Camp" (Exodus 33:7).[4] Thus while Moses' personal tent was also a place of meeting God, the Ohel Moed is the Israelites' formal ritual tent, which marked the beginning of regulated worship practices based on the seasons and historical events, assuring the Sabbath as the central timekeeper for the People of the Book.

The length of time the Ohel Moed stays in its various historical locations is well documented in the Mishnah, the first major written redaction of the Jewish oral traditions: "We learned in a Baraita: The Tabernacle in the wilderness lasted thirty nine years; the Tabernacle at Gilgal lasted fourteen years, namely the seven years of conquest [of Eretz Yisrael] and the seven years of apportioning the Land [to the tribes]. The Tabernacle of Nob and that of Gibeon lasted fifty-seven years. Thus for Shiloh there are left three hundred and seventy years; less [part of] one year."[5] After Shiloh, the Tabernacle rested in a more formal structure for 369 years until the First Temple was built by King Solomon, where it stood for 410 years. Figure 2.1, illustrating the basic components of the

---

[3] At the center of the Israelites' encampment was the Tabernacle and its furnishings, around which was grouped Moses and Aaron and the sons of Levi (Gershon, Kehat, and Merari), who were each responsible for a part of the Tabernacle and its implements. Surrounding the Ohel Moed were the twelve tribes arranged in four groups: Judah, Issachar, Zebulun, Reuben, Simeon, Gad, Ephraim, Manasseh, Benjamin, Dan, Asher, and Naphtali. The later division of the lands to the tribes was consistent with their size and importance of placement in the camp.

[4] Moses' seclusion of his tent came after the sin of the golden calf. Once the Ohel Moed was erected as a formal sanctuary, it was protected by being in the center of the people's encampment, but when they traveled it was in the front of the camp with the family of Kehath, from the tribe of Levi, who bore it on their shoulders.

[5] Zevachim (after 118b). See also R. Yaakov Ibn Chaviv, *Ein Yaakov*, 755–56.

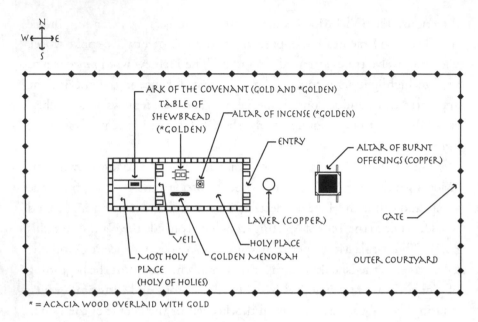

*Figure 2.1. The Hebrew Bible's Tent of Meeting and Tabernacle
(Based on Torah description, drawn by Amy Ford)*

Tent of Meeting, is an approximation of the scale of the holy sanctuary overall.

The Ten Commandments and the Ten Sefirot

After descending the mountain and finding his people worshipping the golden calf, Moses throws down the God-given holy tablets, then gives directives that lead to a massive, camp-wide elimination: "Then Moses stood in the gate of the camp, and said: 'Whoso is on the LORD's side, let him come unto me.' And all the sons of Levi gathered themselves together unto him. . . . And the sons of Levi did according to the word of Moses; and there fell of the people that day about three thousand men" (Exodus 32:26, 28). Later, God calls to Moses again:

And he hewed two tables of stone like unto the first; and Moses rose up early in the morning, and went up unto mount Sinai, as the LORD had commanded him, and took in his hand two tables of stone. And the LORD descended in the cloud, and stood with him there, and proclaimed the name of the LORD. And the LORD passed by before him, and proclaimed: "The LORD, the LORD, God, merciful and gracious, long-suffering, and abundant in goodness and truth; keeping mercy unto the thousandth generation, forgiving iniquity and transgression and sin; and that will by no means clear the guilty; visiting the iniquity of the fathers upon the children, and upon the children's children, unto the third and unto the fourth generation." (Exodus 34:4–7)

Moses receives the second set of tablets, but when he descends to recite them to the people, they are frightened by the prophet's shining countenance, which is so brilliant that he must veil his face: "And it came to pass, when Moses came down from mount Sinai with the two tables of the testimony in Moses' hand, when he came down from the mount, that Moses knew not that the skin of his face sent forth beams while He talked with him. And when Aaron and all the children of Israel saw Moses, behold, the skin of his face sent forth beams; and they were afraid to come nigh him" (Exodus 34: 29–30).

The final reference to the Decalogue occurs in Deuteronomy 5:6–18, when Moses reviews for the Israelites all the teachings God requires of them for their inheritance of the Holy Land. Here Moses recounts how he received the Ten Commandments on the mountain, when all the people heard the voice of God, who "sealed a covenant with us at Horeb. Not with our forefathers did God seal this covenant, but with us—we who are here, all of us alive today. Face to face did God speak with you on the mountain from amid the fire. I was standing between God and you at that time, to relate the word of God to you—for you were afraid of the fire and you did not ascend the mountain."

The drama of this event is underplayed in Torah relative to its climactic significance, but its purpose is glorified in the sanctuary of our lives and in the nature of our actions from generation to generation. As the Tree of Life suggests, all orders of ten are rooted in the ten Sefirot, which shine through the Ten Commandments, just as they do the ten songs and the ten emotions and all of their correspondences, which we will study in the coming chapters.

And Moses turned, and went down from the mount, with the
two tables of the testimony in his hand; tables that were written

> *on both their sides; on the one side and on the other were they*
> *written. And the tables were the work of God, and the writing*
> *was the writing of God, graven upon the tables.*
>
> EXODUS 32:15–16

The story of returning to Keter, the crown, or the Garden, Gan Eden, is the story of each person's emancipation from inner darkness to achieve divine revelation on the mountaintop of self, looking out over the horizon of consciousness. The Ten Commandments are the principal guideposts on that landscape of free will, reflecting the emanations of the ten Sefirot and the ten utterances of Creation. Many people are familiar with those biblical ten ordinances, but most human beings are unfamiliar with the ten Sefirot that they embody and how they relate to the ten numbered systems of the body and soul, the exploration of which is the task of this book.

The Bestowal of the Ten Commandments (Exodus 20:1–22)

1 *And God spoke all these words, saying:* **2** *I am the* LORD *thy God, who brought thee out of the land of Egypt, out of the house of bondage. Thou shalt have no other gods before Me.* **3** *Thou shalt not make unto thee a graven image, nor any manner of likeness, of any thing that is in heaven above, or that is in the earth beneath, or that is in the water under the earth;* **4** *thou shalt not bow down unto them, nor serve them; for I the* LORD *thy God am a jealous God, visiting the iniquity of the fathers upon the children unto the third and fourth generation of them that hate Me;* **5** *and showing mercy unto the thousandth generation of them that love Me and keep My commandments.* **6** *Thou shalt not take the name of the* LORD *thy God in vain; for the* LORD *will not hold him guiltless that taketh His name in vain.* **7** *Remember the Sabbath day, to keep it holy.* **8** *Six days shalt thou labour, and do all thy work;* **9** *but the seventh day is a Sabbath unto the* LORD *thy God, in it thou shalt not do any manner of work, thou, nor thy son, nor thy daughter, nor thy man-servant, nor thy maid-servant, nor thy cattle, nor thy stranger that is within thy gates;* **10** *for in six days the* LORD *made heaven and earth, the sea, and all that in them is, and rested on the seventh day; wherefore the* LORD *blessed the Sabbath day, and hallowed it.* **11** *Honour thy father and thy mother, that thy days may be long upon the land which the* LORD *thy God giveth thee. Thou shalt not murder. Thou shalt not commit adultery. Thou shalt not steal. Thou shalt not* *bear false witness against thy neighbour.* **13** *Thou shalt not covet thy neighbour's house; thou shalt not covet thy neighbour's wife, nor his man-servant, nor his maid-servant, nor his ox, nor his ass, nor any thing that is thy neighbour's.* **14** *And all the people perceived the thunderings, and the lightnings, and the voice of the horn, and the mountain smoking; and when the people saw it, they trembled, and stood afar off.* **15** *And they said unto Moses: "Speak thou with us, and we will hear; but let not God speak with us, lest we die."* **16** *And Moses said unto the people: "Fear not; for God is come to prove you, and that His fear may be before you, that ye sin not."* **17** *And the people stood afar off; but Moses drew near unto the thick darkness where God was.* **18** *And the* LORD *said unto Moses: Thus thou shalt say unto the children of Israel: Ye yourselves have seen that I have talked with you from heaven.* **19** *Ye shall not make with Me—gods of silver, or gods of gold, ye shall not make unto you.* **20** *An altar of earth thou shalt make unto Me, and shalt sacrifice thereon thy burnt-offerings, and thy peace-offerings, thy sheep, and thine oxen; in every place where I cause My name to be mentioned I will come unto thee and bless thee.* **21** *And if thou make Me an altar of stone, thou shalt not build it of hewn stones; for if thou lift up thy tool upon it, thou hast profaned it.* **22** *Neither shalt thou go up by steps unto Mine altar, that thy nakedness be not uncovered thereon.*

Rabbi Elazar, the son of Rabbi Shimon Bar Yochai, whose dialogue fills the Zohar, says that

in the Ten Commandments were engraved all the laws of the Torah, all the decrees and punishments, all the laws concerning purity and impurity, all the branches and the roots, trees and plants, heavens and earth, seas and depths, for this Torah is the Name of the Holy One, blessed be He. As the Name of the Holy One, blessed be He, is engraved in the Ten Commandments, the Ten Commandments are then the Name of the Holy One, blessed be He. So is the whole Torah engraved in them, and the Whole Torah is thus one Name, the holy Names of the Holy One, blessed be He, indeed.[6]

From this perspective, the Tabernacle is the dwelling place of God's holy name; the Ten Commandments are the instruments through which His

---

[6] Zohar 10:497.

presence is illumined to the world; and His name is this vessel, which all of Torah represents. The 304,805 letters (or approximately 79,000 words) in Torah are a vibratory engine, which is encased inside a special Ark consisting of three layers of gold-covered boxes made of acacia (shittim wood), one inside the other, containing and conducting specific energy for the purpose of divine revelation and divine protection: "And thou shalt put the ark-cover above upon the ark; and in the ark thou shalt put the testimony that I shall give thee. And there I will meet with thee, and I will speak with thee from above the ark-cover, from between the two cherubim which are upon the ark of the testimony, of all things which I will give thee in commandment unto the children of Israel" (Exodus 25:21–22).

This shows the deep inner connection between receiving the Ten Commandments and Torah, and the need to protect them and house them in a sacred place where the Cloud of Glory, the visible evidence of the presence of God, is clear, thus facilitating direct contact with Him. So too the sacredness of receiving a human incarnation and our obligation to house it properly in holy actions is described in the ancient Hebraic traditions of initiation, self-mastery, and illumination.

"There I Will Meet with You"

The Ark that contains the Ten Commandments within the holy Tabernacle is a continuation of the revelation of Mt. Sinai as well as a facilitator of perpetual illumination. God makes this very clear, telling Moses, "It is there I will set my meeting with you and I shall speak with you from atop the Cover [i.e., from above the Mercy Seat], from between the two Cherubim that are on the Ark of the Testimonial tablets everything that I shall command you to the Children of Israel" (Exodus 25:22).

The Tent of Meeting, we quickly discover, is not just a place where the Israelites come to worship and honor God, an arena for sacrifices and repentance as well as thanksgiving and rejoicing; it is the place of God's presence. This is not a metaphor; it is an actual physical manifestation (which includes the implicit and stated threat of death to anyone who dares enter the Holy of Holies who is not a qualified High Priest). Thus the people of the Sinai could visit and dwell with the energy of God's presence in a very physical way because it was actualized on the physical plane.

A portable place of holy ritual accompanying the Exodus' 600,000 men plus their families engaged this nation in something other than worldly affairs or the personal needs of its members; it demanded a legion of tribal members to disassemble and pack it up for transport during the thrity-nine (of forty) years of wandering after the Tent of Meeting was first established. As the community's religious setting, it was the place through which consciousness could be altered. It set aside a specific arena as holy ground, making a distinction between the sacred and the profane, a constant reminder for each person of these two distinct yet connected qualities in life. The sanctuary enabled ritual devotion, purification, and unification. It was a house of prayer and sacrifice, a place of joy and repentance. Above all, it became the house of the Lord: the very place where the Divine Immanence, the Shechinah, and the Holy Spirit, the Ruach HaKodesh, would manifest.

It is said that with Adam's sin of eating from the Tree of Knowledge of Good and Evil, the Shechinah withdrew from the earth. Over the centuries, through the various patriarchs beginning with Abraham, this aspect of the Creator, referred to in feminine terms, was successively brought back to the material world from each of the seven heavens, above which God, as King, rules. This is a deeply esoteric subject discussed in the Talmud,[7] which describes the spiritual universe as comprised of seven heavens, with earth beneath them. We also have seven holy vehicles of the soul within our body in our senses of sight, hearing, smell, and taste (these are the seven holy "gates," including the two eyes, two ears, two nostrils, and the mouth). It is said that it was Moses who brought the Shechinah into full embodiment on the physical plane, making the Tent of Meeting the archetypal model for uniting our lives with the Divine Immanence.

Today we are charged with redeeming the light of God within and without, knowing that divinity is everywhere. Our body and soul combined is a Tent of Meeting. It is the place where the material and spiritual orders are integrated. How we live life either makes room for God's presence or fails to reflect this holy light. The inner sanctuary that we each possess is made sacred through what we give to others and to the world. In this context, sacrifice means what we give up from our own behavior and temperament that does not serve holiness, purifying our natures through constant return

---

[7] Chagigah 12b.

to God. The Ark and its contents, like the essence of the soul and mind of a person, are inscribed with God's divinity.

As we shall see in the coming chapters, we are each a portable Tent of Meeting; within each of us is the structure, the holy instruments, and the levels of awareness that can lead to direct contact with God, to speaking with Him as one does a friend. The mind, as the inner sanctum of the Ark, combined with the inner teachings of truth found in the heart, awakens the holy cherubim, who in turn facilitate communication with the divine. It seems that this is a description of an actual alchemical process we can each experience when in a state of illumination; this leads to revelation. In the illustration of this pattern of the Tabernacle as shown in figure 2.2,

SANCTUARY OF THE DIVINE PRESENCE

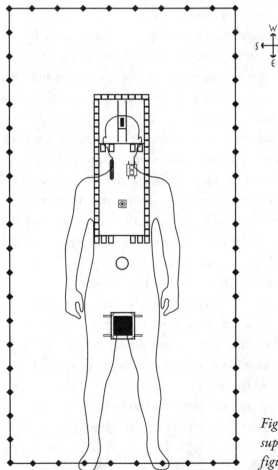

Figure 2.2. The Ohel Moed superimposed on the human figure (Drawn by Amy Ford)

one begins to see the overall manner in which this Kabbalistic system of correspondences is applied.

A Sanctuary of Re-Creation

Described in Torah as a sanctuary, the Tent of Meeting and the Tabernacle contained within it is the prototype for all future Hebraic places of worship. Why, though, does God instruct the Israelites to build a sanctuary when the people had already reached a level of communal revelation at Mt. Sinai?

> All the people perceived the thunderings, and the lightnings, and the voice of the horn, and the mountain smoking; and when the people saw it, they trembled, and stood afar off. And they said unto Moses: "Speak thou with us, and we will hear; but let not God speak with us, lest we die." And Moses said unto the people: "Fear not; for God is come to prove you, and that His fear may be before you, that ye sin not." And the people stood afar off; but Moses drew near unto the thick darkness where God was. (Exodus 20:14–17)

They all heard the voice of God. They all experienced His brilliance, His fire, His thundering approach. The Cloud of Glory had shone on them all, uniting them. Surely they did not need to be reminded of the collective, life-altering experience they had already chronicled in their recorded history, as well as in their very bones!

At face value one can say that having a formal sanctuary would remind the people of the giving of Torah at Mt. Sinai; it would house the Ten Commandments, the culmination of the escape from Egypt and the forty-year Exodus that followed; it would contain the directives for keeping and guarding the Sabbath. During the next thirty-nine years after the establishment of the sanctuary, many of those born in Egypt would pass away before having a chance to enter the Holy Land. Thus, by having a formal dwelling place for God, the Hebrews' collective memory was institutionalized to enable them to guide future generations out of personal and communal exile.

And so the Tent of Meeting, the Ohel Moed, is a divine sanctuary whose design incubates the field for the presence of God, which the People of the Book describe in their writings and can attest to. This portable sanctuary is also a repository of the elements within ourselves that we can use to overcome our sense of separateness from God, from one another, and from the world. It is a model reflecting the spiritual and physical anatomy of human beings as represented by the Tree of Life. The holy Tent of Meeting is thus the outer model of the inner human, the cosmic human—Adam Kadmon—as well as being the place where the earthly embodiment of the Shechinah dwells.

If the human being reflects the Tree of Life, which itself is said to reflect the attributes of the Creator and the act of Creation, then the Ohel Moed is a sanctuary of re-creation, with each and every act or encounter reflective of some aspect of Creation and renewal. Here is where the eternal, limitless light of God, the Or En Sof, filters down through the worlds, and where the Sefirot are housed in Malchut, the physical world, among the people. The eternal light of God is housed within each one of us when we make a place for the flame of devoted love inside our personal place of meeting, where the two tablets of stone turned to flesh, the living Word of God, becomes inscribed in our hearts.

Since the fall of the Second Temple, the Jewish people are said to be in the Roman exile, which will end, it is said, with the appearance of Moshiach and the development of messianic awareness. In this context, exile, *galut,* גלות (Gimel Lamed Vav Tav), also called the "exile of the Shechinah," suggests the necessary, ongoing efforts being made by people to free themselves of the *kelipot* קלפה (Kof Lamed Pey Hay), that is, the "husks" (of evil) that cover over everything divine, within and without, that conceal and obscure the light of God.

The Temple rituals and the Torah on which they are based, along with the Ten Commandments, which summarize all the primary monotheistic teachings, bring a person to the one Word of God, to inner unity. Together these sacred elements comprise the river of light and truth flowing out of the Ohel Moed as radiant streams of glory. As we will see in chapter 8 on Joshua, the Tent of Meeting is the place of initiation, the place of holy consciousness in our own lives. The God of the Hebrews makes it clear that the Shechinah is anywhere we invite Her in. Thus the ancient Israelites institutionalized the act of God imparting His Ten Commandments by establishing a sanctuary and imparting to humanity a fundamental ten-step program for sanctification of divinity in our lives.

And the LORD said unto Moses: Thus thou shalt say unto the
children of Israel: Ye yourselves have seen that I have talked with
you from heaven. Ye shall not make with Me—gods of silver,
or gods of gold, ye shall not make unto you. An altar of earth
thou shalt make unto Me, and shalt sacrifice thereon thy burnt-
offerings, and thy peace-offerings, thy sheep, and thine oxen;
in every place where I cause My name to be mentioned
I will come unto thee and bless thee.

EXODUS 20:19–21

Developing a regular personal practice oriented to service of holy values is essential to re-creation, to making life itself a sanctuary. The Ten Commandments, housed inside the Ark of the Tabernacle, which are housed inside the Holy of Holies, all held within the Tent of Meeting, reflect the Tree of Life and its ten Sefirot, whose essence represents the act of Creation itself. In it are the lessons for daily re-creation of our lives, Sefirah by Sefirah—one rung of the ladder of light after another, one particular holy text after another—until reaching Adam, just outside the Garden of Eden.

The Self-refinement of the Individual

In a beautiful writing called *Basi LeGani* ("I have come to my garden"), Rabbi Yosef Y. Schneersohn (1880–1950),[8] the sixth rebbe of the Chabad Lubavitch Chasidic movement, explains that

the ultimate purpose for the creation of the [spiritual and physical] worlds was that God desires to have a dwelling place in the lower worlds. He desired that Divinity be revealed [even on the material plane] below—by means of man's divine service of subordinating and transforming his physical nature; He desired that the divine soul descend from its spiritual heights and become enclothed in a body with an animal soul, which could conceal and obscure the divine soul's light; and despite all this, [through the study of Torah and the

---

[8] Delivered on the 10th of Shevat (January), 1950 (5710) by R. Yosef Y. Schneersohn of Lubavitch. It was his last Chassidic discourse as well as the first Chassidic discourse given by his son and successor, R. Menachem M. Schneerson of Lubavitch, in 1951.

observance of the commandments], the divine soul would refine and purify the body and the animal soul as well as its portion in the world, i.e., its environment.[9]

This, Rabbi Schneersohn tells us, is the meaning of God's commandment to "make me a sanctuary and I shall dwell within them." This means that God dwells within "each individual . . . The individual brings about [revelation of the divine presence within his personal sanctuary] through his divine service of sifting and refining materiality by subordinating and transforming his physical nature. In this spirit it is written, 'When the sitra achra [literally, "the other side," i.e., the cosmic force opposing holiness] is subdued, the Glory of God rises thereby [and is diffused] throughout all the worlds.'"[10]

The saintly Arizal, Rabbi Yitzchak Luria (1534–1572), affectionately known as the Ari, a central figure of Kabbalah, explains that if a person steals in the physical world, he causes the forces of evil to steal in the spiritual worlds, which then attach to certain souls being born into the world.[11] Thus our failure to do good deeds and in fact to do harmful acts affects souls entering the world, not just ourselves or those already born. Therefore, refining ourselves, learning how to make the right decisions in life, is a gift not only for our own well-being but also for the world's. This is the great work all of humanity is assigned to do together: to do good works wherever we are, whenever we can, for the entire planet depends on it.

When we overcome the desire for the follies of the body and instead refine our physical, emotional, and spiritual temple through proper nourishment, we make it an equal partner in divine service. This elevates us to heights greater than before we incarnated. Thus by the use of humility and joyful will, Hod and Netzach (the left and right legs respectively); love and strength, Chesed and Gevurah (the right and left hands respectively); with balanced mercy and truth in Tiferet (the place of the heart), divine service becomes a daily engagement, something we do with our

---

[9] R. Yosef Y. Schneersohn, R. Menachem M. Schneerson of Lubavitch, *Basi Legani*, 3.

[10] Schneersohn, *Basi Legani*, 4.

[11] R. Yitzchak Luria, R. Moshe Wisnefsky, trans., *Apples from the Orchard: Gleanings from the Mystical Teachings of the Rabbi Yitzchak Luria (The Arizal) on the Weekly Torah Portion*, 618–19.

entire being. Its purpose is to create a resting place in our lives, a place of balance from which the Shechinah can emanate.

As we are already a vessel created to be full of God's glory, designed to host the Divine Presence, we can either obscure it or reveal it. God dwells in each one of us, in all aspects of our soul to greater or lesser degrees, just as there are small candles and big torch lights. Both are lights of varying intensities. So too are souls like this. In this way it becomes clear that each person is a Tent of Meeting for the Shechinah to be at home in and for God's Holy Spirit to touch. Each person has the holy Ark, with its holy seal of truth, illuminating his or her body; having a personal conscience is evidence of this inner judge of truth.

Aspects of Re-creation: The Divine Immanence and the Holy Spirit

God's indwelling presence, the Divine Immanence, or Shechinah as it is called in the rabbinic literature, is to be distinguished from the Holy Spirit, the Ruach HaKodesh. The Shechianic quality of God's presence is an indwelling presence made of surrounding light, *Or Makif,* God's transcendent light and glory; the Ruach aspect of God functions more like a divine messenger.

After the Ohel Moed is erected for the first time, Exodus 40:34 recounts how "the cloud covered the Tent of Meeting, and the glory of the LORD filled the Tabernacle." This Glory Cloud is the physical manifestation of the Shechinah. In the very next verse we are told that so great is this illumination that even the greatest prophet of all, who earlier was enveloped by this very same Cloud of Glory on top of Mt. Sinai, cannot go in: "And Moses was not able to enter into the tent of the congregation, because the cloud abode thereon, and the glory of the Lord filled the Tabernacle" (Exodus 40:35).[12] We know from Exodus 33:9 that whenever Moses would enter the Tent, the Cloud of Glory would descend and stand at the entrance of the Tent: "And it came to pass, when Moses entered into the Tent, the pillar of cloud descended, and stood at the door of the Tent; and [the Lord] spoke with Moses." In addition, Numbers 1:1 recounts how "the Lord spoke to Moses in the Tent of Meeting in the

---

[12] As well, 1 Kings 8:11 says, "The priests could not stand to minister because of the cloud, for the glory of the LORD filled the house of the LORD."

Desert of Sinai on the first day of the second month of the second year after the Israelites came out of Egypt." It was on this very day that the Ohel Moed was erected and consecrated.

Torah includes many examples of how the Cloud of Glory fills the Tent of Meeting, affirming that the phenomenon is not simply a metaphor, but an actual facilitator of divine influence. For example, before Moses' death, God tells him, "'Now the day of your death approaches. . . . Call Joshua and present yourselves at the Tent of Meeting, where I will commission him.' So Moses and Joshua went and stood in the Tent of Meeting. Adonai appeared in the tent, in a pillar of cloud, and the pillar of cloud stood by the entrance of the Tent" (Deuteronomy 31:14–15). During the time of the Temple we are again shown that the Glory Cloud, the Shechinah, is an actual physical reality with a discernable presence. "And it came to pass, when the Kohanim [priests] left the Sanctuary, that the cloud filled the Temple of the LORD. The priests could not stand to minister because of the cloud; for the glory of the LORD filled the house of the LORD" (1 Kings 8:10–11).

The Shechinah is like a tentlike skirt of a mother (Mother, the Sefirah of Binah) spread over her children; like the wings of the eagle protectively covering the chicks in her nest; or like the sukkah dwelling on Sukkot, which is also reminiscent of the portable sanctuary marking the path of the Israelites. In terms of the five worlds or realms, this is the Or Makif, the surrounding light, the light that shines to us from the Or En Sof, the Creator's limitless light, which filters down through the worlds, down through each Sefirah, into the dominion of the material world. Like the portable sanctuary where we are one with God, we travel under the protective glory of this surrounding light. What we do determines the amount of illumination filling each of us, as each action, prayer, or holy thought is a vessel capable of being filled with divine essence, making a person conscious of the unity in all of life.

Historically, the Cloud of Glory is the essence or medium facilitating God's protection of the children of Israel, His communication with Moses, and His initiation of priests and tribal leaders. We too are made of His immanent light, the *Penimi,* the face of the presence of God that is a filling light, the inner light, which differs from the surrounding light that all of life is embraced by. We are, in a sense, inside the God-body, in the process of becoming conscious of it. The holy indwelling presence is aroused when our soul desires unity with the field of divine being-ness. This desire activates the reciprocal shine from above to below, from within to without, from the soul to its source. The holiness of the Divine Presence that dwells within us and around us is attained whenever people prepare a place for it: when a person studies holy teachings, when one's heart is devoted to the teachings of truth, when one acts charitably with compassion, love, and mercy.[13] The ten Sefirot and their associated emotional qualities prepare us for this spiritual engagement. When we create an environment in our inner life for God's presence, we, like the prophets, benefit from His merciful protection, communication, spiritual initiation, elevation, and illumination. These are all aspects of our spiritual growth, central elements of the Tent of Meeting in our lives.

"It is from the Shechinah," Rabbi Schneur Zalman (1745–1812), (also called the Baal HaTanya), founder of Chabad Chassidism, writes, "which is clothed in the shrine of the Holy of Holies of each and every general or particular world, that light and vitality are extended and diffused to the whole world and the creatures contained therein, the souls, angels and so forth, for all of them were created by the ten fiats in the act of creation, these being the 'word' of God, which is termed Shechinah."[14]

The Holy Spirit, or Ruach HaKodesh, is the transformative spirit of God that comes and goes much in the manner of the winds. It is quick but knowable and imparts a specific message or duty particular to each person or group it visits. As an aspect of God, it is distinguished from the Shechinah, which is the Divine Presence in all of God's created world. While said to be in exile when a person is ignoring their own inherent goodness and hence distanced from spiritual truths, the Shechinah is with us when we are nurturing that aspect of life that brings us closer to God. The Shechinah is concealed within us and around us; we need only reveal it and prepare a place for it. This is why engaging the Shechinah is likened to courtship, seduction, lovemaking, and procreation. The Ruach HaKodesh is similarly given a place around a person through the surrounding light of God, the Or Makif. When we refine our own vessel,

---

[13] For full exploration of the Shechinah, see J. Zohara Meyerhoff Hieronimus, *Kabbalistic Teachings of the Female Prophets*, 353–71.

[14] R. Schneur Zalman of Liadi (Baal HaTanya), *Lukkutei Amarim Tanya*, 277.

the Ruach HaKodesh is given its rightful place and becomes a filling light, the Penimi, sparking a person's imagination such that it holds an image, message, or other God-given information. The person then becomes the receiver of divine answers to personal or collective petitions.

While the Shechinah, like sunlight, illuminates anything not shaded from it, the Ruach HaKodesh, a tool of the Creator that heals the sick, raises the dead, and enlightens minds and hearts everywhere in the world, guides us. While the Shechinah, seen as a more feminine expression of the Creator's being, is the surrounding light animating the entire cosmos, like an all-nurturing mother principal, the Ruach represents the divine as messenger, a prophetic tool to actively help in humanity's development, and is thus a more masculine principle. Thus She is the vessel, the Shechinah; He is the filling light, the Ruach. Both of these aspects of the divine are reflected in humans as well: we each have both a receptive nature and an emanatory quality. In this way we are designed to receive and give different kinds of holy lights, just as we can eat foods from different realms of creation: mineral, plant, and, for non-vegetarians, animal.

The Composition of the Tent of Meeting

The Israelites' adoption of formal worship and the Hebraic traditions that arose from it are rooted in the deliberate cultivation of a place for God's presence as recorded by Moses after his illumination on Mt. Sinai. The patterns are hidden in every part of the Ohel Moed, from the interior makeup of the altars, the incense mixture, and the design of the curtains, to its sacred Ark of the Covenant and Mercy Seat. All are vital to its powerful function of cultivating a place in which God can dwell.

The Tent of Meeting is divided into three primary sections and corresponding fields of activity: the Outer Court, the Holy Place, and the Holy of Holies (or Most Holy Place). Each arena leads sucessively to a more profound level of spiritual transformation. Within these three fields are five basic types of activities:

1. The place and overall structure of the Tent contains the entire field of activity.

2. The Outer Court, which is not covered, is where the priests offer the people's sacrifices and perform water purifications.

3. The Holy Place is where the priests go to offer incense, light menorah, and place and bless shewbread.

4. The Holy of Holies, housing the Ark of the Tabernacle, contains the Word of God.

5. The ultimate purpose of the Tent and all its contents is the Ark's cover, known as the Mercy Seat, or Kapporeth. Made of two golden cherubim positioned face to face, with their wings touching to form a canopy, this is the place where communication between God and the High Priest takes place.

The following is an introduction to the various components of the Tent of Meeting, which will be explored in greater detail in the coming chapters, as we look at how each element of the Tent relates to the revelation of divinity in our own daily lives.

The Components of the Tent of Meeting

As approximated in figure 2.1 (see page 40), the overall Sanctuary structure, in which the Tabernacle was housed, was 100 cubits[15] long at its northern and southern walls, and 50 cubits wide at its eastern and western walls; it was divided between the Outer Court and its inner sanctum. The Tent's perimeter consisted of ten posts at the eastern and western sides, and twenty pillars on the northern and southern sides. Each pillar had a base of copper and a top (capital) of silver. The area of this arena that was occupied by the Mishkan and its two inner chambers, the Holy Place and the Holy of Holies, was 30 by 10 cubits. The first inner chamber was 20 by 10 cubits, and the most inner chamber, the Holy of Holies, was 10 by 10 cubits. In this way the Outer Court was designed to service the Tabernacle and its components. The open entryway was oriented to the east, allowing the rising sun to illuminate it.

More elaborate details on the construction of the Ohel Moed and the Tabernacle can be found in Exodus 25–31.[16] Those interested can pursue

---

[15] A cubit is an ancient unit of measure based on the length of the forearm from the elbow to the tip of the middle finger, usually anywhere from twelve to eighteen inches.

[16] See R. David Meyers, *The Mishkan Illuminated*, 2010.

deep and meaningful studies based on gematria and the measurements found inside the Tent of Meeting, as Jewish sages and others have done for centuries in their studies and writings.

The Outer Court, HaChetzor, החצר *(Hay Chet Tzadee Reish)*

> *And thou shalt set up the court round about, and hang up the screen of the gate of the court. And thou shalt take the anointing oil, and anoint the tabernacle, and all that is therein, and shalt hallow it, and all the furniture thereof; and it shall be holy. And thou shalt anoint the altar of burnt-offering, and all its vessels, and sanctify the altar; and the altar shall be most holy.*
>
> EXODUS 40:8–10

There was only one gate by which people could enter; it was placed just outside the Outer Court and it is omitted from the drawings in this book. The entry gate into the Outer Court itself, by which the priests entered, was thirty feet wide and was located directly in the center of the Outer Court, on the east side. A curtain screen (*masach*) made of finely twisted linen in blue, purple, and scarlet covered the gate. It was here that the priest would bring the people's offerings, to consecrate, and express individual requests for forgiveness and give thanks to God. It was in this area just outside the gate and all around the outside of the Ohel Moed, that the people likely spoke or sang their prayers to God:

> R. Joshua ben Levi said: he who utters song [in praise of God] in this world will merit uttering it in the world-to-come, as is said, "Happy are they that dwell in Thy house now; they will be praising Thee forever, Selah" (Psalms 84:5). R. Hiyya bar Abba said in the name of R. Yohanan: All the prophets are destined to utter song with one voice, as is said, "Hark, Thy watchmen raise their voices: as one they shout for joy" (Isaiah 52:8).[17]

---

[17] B. Sanhedrin 91b. See also, Hayim Nahman Bialik and Yehoshua Hana Ravnitzky, *Sefer Ha-Aggadah*, 8:144, 485.

The Altar of Burnt Offerings, or Mizbe'ach, מזבח (Mem Zayin Bet Chet)

And thou shalt set the altar of burnt-offering before the door of the
tabernacle of the tent of meeting.

EXODUS 40:6

At the entrance to the Outer Court, on the east side of the rectangular domain, was where this copper-covered acacia-wood altar, used for penetitents' sacrificial offerings, was located. A grating or network of copper with a ring at each of its four corners hung in the middle of the top of the altar, on which was placed the wood for the fire that consumed the offerings (*korbanot*). Rings of copper were on two sides of the altar, through which were laid shittim-wood staves, each overlaid with copper, by which the altar could be carried from place to place. All of the other service vessels—the pots, shovels, basins, flesh hooks, and fire pans—were also made of copper (as described in Exodus 27:1–8, and 38:1–7). The altar, which was also copper, was kept burning day and night. It represents the densest of the temple elements and processes, telling us that before we can reach higher states of awareness and greater refinement in the inner sanctums of the Tabernacle we must first burn off the ego, the selfish animal nature we can be so preoccupied with. We have to make this sacrifice of our ego and make offerings of forgiveness, extending peace toward others and joy in divine service.

The Laver, or Kiyyor, כיור (Caf Yod Vav Reish)

And thou shalt set the laver between the tent of meeting and the
altar, and shalt put water therein.

EXODUS 40:7

Closer to the curtain of the Holy Place was the laver, or *kiyyor*, of purification. Here the priests anointed themselves with water and prayers before entering the Holy Place for the ritual offering of incense, menorah, and twelve weekly shewbreads. The laver consisted of a copper upper bowl holding the water, which the priests used for personal ritual purification, resting on a lower copper base. The laver had an upper and a lower spigot, allowing easy washing of both hands and feet. Tradition states that it was lined with the metal mirrors of the women of the twelve tribes of Israel who brought them as their contributions for the holy sanctuary: "And he made the laver of brass [i.e., copper], and the base thereof of brass [copper], of the mirrors of the serving women that did service at the door of the tent of meeting" (Exodus 38:8). As a vessel of purification, we learn at this station of the Tabernacle that we must be pure in body and heart before achieving higher aspects of awareness. Purifying our emotions, refining them, is the work we do in the outer court of life before we can access the higher aspects of ourselves and the Creator's holy wisdom.

The Tabernacle, or Mishkan, מִשְׁכָּן (Mem Shin Caf Nun)

You shall make the Tabernacle of ten curtains—linen, twisted,
with turquoise, purples, and scarlet wool—with a woven design
of Cherubim shall you make them.

EXODUS 26:1

Mishkan comes from the root word *shechin,* which means to settle, dwell in, or inhabit; it is from this that the word *Shechinah,* the indwelling Divine Immanence, is derived. As the place of physical and spiritual transformation, the Mishkan is where the soul and body unite in serving the divine will of God. It is within its framework that we participate in the holy rituals leading to our elevation, illumination, and revelation in life. As the human body, with all its various parts, is mirrored in the structure of the Tent of Meeting, the Holy Place, the Holy of Holies (Tabernacle proper), represents our head and heart. Our physical incarnation, the body our soul occupies in any given lifetime, is the holy meeting place between oneself and God.

The curtained Tabernacle measured 30 by 10 cubits and stood in the western side of the courtyard. It contained two hidden sanctums: the Holy Place and the Holy of Holies, which were each the same width; however, the Holy Place, which measured 20 by 10 cubits, was twice as long as the Holy of Holies, which was a perfect cube, 10 by 10 by 10 cubits. The walls of the centrally placed Tabernacle were made of acacia boards overlaid with gold and carried by the use of four golden rings attached at the Ark's four corners (Exodus 26:15–25). Priests who entered the Mishkan to minister received the Ohel Moed's physical and spiritual light, which they transmitted to the entire community. Overhead was a "covering for the tent of rams' skins dyed red, and a covering of badgers' skins above that" (Exodus 36:19). The animal-skin covering makes it clear that the supernal realms' effluences are for the elevation of the material realm. In the life of humankind as a global sanctuary, the holy soul of man is covered over by the human body's flesh; in the process of refinement, our souls elevate our bodies and we each elevate the world.

The Golden Menorah מנרה (Mem Nun Reish Hay)

> And thou shalt hang up the veil under the clasps, and shalt bring
> in thither within the veil the ark of the testimony; and the veil
> shall divide unto you between the holy place and the most holy.
> . . . And thou shalt make a Menorah [candlelabra] of pure gold: of
> beaten work shall the Menorah [candlelabra] be made, even
> its base, and its shaft; its cups, its knops, and its flowers,
> shall be of one piece with it. . . . And thou shalt make
> the lamps thereof, seven; and they shall light the
> lamps thereof, to give light over against it.
>
> EXODUS 26:33, 25:31, 25:37

In the Holy Place, along the south side of the chamber, stood the golden menorah, a seven-branched candelabra that is the symbol of Creation and the Sabbath. The priests trimmed the wicks daily and refilled the bowls with oil so that the menorah would be a constant source of light, twenty-four hours a day, as recounted in Leviticus 24:1–4: "And the LORD spoke unto Moses, saying: 'Command the children of Israel, that they bring unto thee pure olive oil beaten for the light, to cause a lamp to burn continually. Without the veil of the testimony, in the Tent of Meeting, shall Aaron order it from evening to morning before the LORD continually; it shall be a statute forever throughout your generations. He shall order the lamps upon the pure Menorah before the LORD continually.'" We learn that through prayer and good deeds we keep the flame of divine service renewed each day. As a symbol of divine enlightenment through self-refinement of the seven "gates" in our head—our two eyes, two ears, two nostrils, and mouth—the menorah is an agent of the Holy Place within ourselves, which we minister to daily. It is the light of the heart and its devotional attachment to Godliness that is renewed each day.

The Shewbread, or Lechem Painim, לחם פנים *(Lamed Chet Mem Pey Nun Yod Mem)*

> *And thou shalt set upon the table shewbread before Me always.*
>
> EXODUS 25:30

On the north side of the Holy Place stood the *shulcan,* שלחן (Shin Lamed Chet Nun), a table of gold-covered acacia wood the top of which included a crown around its perimiter. It was here that the twelve loaves of unleavened bread (as recounted in Exodus 25:23–30 and Leviticus 24:5–9) were placed. Called shewbread, or *lechem painim,* also known as the Bread of the Presence, these cakes or loaves of bread were always present in the Holy Place of the Ohel Moed. Representing manna, the shewbread stands for God's presence and ongoing nourishment of humanity and His blessings from Sabbath to Sabbath, for which new shewbread is placed each week. The shewbread also represents the holiness of our soul: just as it is renewed from week to week through its presence in the Tabernacle, our souls are enlivened by immersion in God's commandments. By refining ourselves, we maintain access to this illuminating manna, the bread of the wilderness that sustained the Israelites during their Exodus.

The Sweet Incense, or Ketoret, קטרת *(Kof Tet Reish Tav)*

> *And thou shalt make an altar to burn incense upon. . . . And thou shalt put it before the veil that is by the ark of the testimony, before the ark-cover that is over the testimony, where I will meet with thee. And Aaron shall burn thereon incense of sweet spices.*
>
> EXODUS 30:1, 6–7

Sweet incense, *ketoret* (Exodus 25:6), was placed on a special altar, also made of gold-covered acacia wood (Exodus 30:1–3); this rested against the ornate veil that separated the Holy Place from the Holy of Holies. This altar was much smaller than the altar in the courtyard. Covered in gold, it contained a copper pot that held hot coals from the brazen altar of burnt offerings. It was here that the priest burned a special blend of incense, filling the sanctuary with a sweet-smelling cloud. Just as the menorah is symbolic of the Pillar of Fire, and the shewbread symbolic of the manna, and each corresponds to a different world and its related Sefirah, so the incense represents the presence of God in the form of the pillar of smoke. The Arizal writes that the soul experiences life in the body through the senses: he correlates Keter (crown) with the sense of sight, Chochmah (wisdom) with taste, Binah (understanding) with smell, the middot (the six emotions) with our sense of touch, and Malchut (kingdom) with hearing.[18]

Another component of ritual items used in this arena was the holy anointing oil (Exodus 30:31–33) used to consecrate the Tent itself and everything in it (Exodus 30:26 and 40:9), including the Ark, the table and its vessels, the lampstand, the altars, and Aaron and his sons, the High Priests of the Tabernacle.

Holy of Holies, or Kadosh HaKadoshim, קֹדֶשׁ הַקֳּדָשִׁים (Kof Dalet Shin Hay Kof Dalet Shin Yod Mem)

And they shall make an ark of acacia-wood . . . And thou shalt overlay it with pure gold. . . . The staves shall be in the rings of the ark; they shall not be taken from it. And thou shalt put into the ark the testimony which I shall give thee. . . . And thou shalt put the ark-cover upon the ark of the testimony in the most holy place. . . . On the first day of the first month shalt thou rear up the tabernacle of the tent of meeting. And thou shalt put therein the ark of the testimony, and thou shalt screen the ark with the veil.
EXODUS 25:10–11, 15–16; EXODUS 26:34; EXODUS 40:2–3

The length, width, and depth of the Holy of Holies, the Tabernacle's most sacred chamber, were all an equal 10 cubits, making this part of the sanctuary a perfect cube, reflecting the inherent "ten-ness" of creation discussed earlier, and representing wholeness. It is here that the Ark of the Covenant (or Ark of the Testimony, as it is often called), the sacred chest where the ancient Hebrews kept the two tablets of the Ten Commandments, rested.

---

[18] Luria, *Apples from the Orchard*, 206.

The Holy of Holies (and the Ark and its contents) represent the unity of the human soul and the physical body in its function in the six directions in space, which in turn represents the Tree of Life and the process of creation.[19] The special veil at the entrance to the Holy of Holies acts as the divider between the spiritual station of elevation and that of bestowal, much as a bridal veil divides the bride and groom before their being united. Only High Priests such as Moses and Aaron were permitted to lift the veil, just as the bride's veil is lifted only by the groom to identify her before the ceremonial vows.[20]

The Ark of the Covenant, or Aron HaBrit, ארון הברית (Alef Reish Vav Nun Hay Bet Reish Yod Tav)

> And Betzalel made the ark of acacia-wood: two cubits and
> a half was the length of it, and a cubit and a half the
> breadth of it, and a cubit and a half the height of it.
> And he overlaid it with pure gold within and without,
> and made a crown of gold to it round about.
>
> EXODUS 37:1–2

Inside of the Holy of Holies, which the High Priest enters annually on the Day of Atonement, is "the Ark of the Covenant of the Lord of all the earth" (Joshua 3:11). Measuring 2½ cubits long by 1½ cubits wide and 1½ cubits high, and constructed of three gold-covered acacia boxes, one inside the other, like a child's nesting boxes, are the Ten Commandments, Aaron's budded rod, and a small container of manna.[21] As instruments of power, testimony, and witness, these sacred instruments are conductors and vessels of holy light. The Ark and its contents, with its special top made of two winged cherubim, represent alchemical processes in the upper realms between the Creator and the hierarchy of angels. On this level, the cherubim are the outer face of this inner conduction—

---

[19] Luria, *Apples from the Orchard,* 201. The six directions, reflecting Zeir Anpin, are: Sunday, Chesed, right; Monday, Gevurah, left; Tuesday, Tiferet, front; Wednesday, Netzach, up; Thursday, Hod, down; Friday, Yesod, back. These culminate in Shabbat, Malchut, or time.

[20] In many Orthodox weddings, the bride's veil is lifted during the procession to the altar, when the groom verifies that this is the woman he intends to wed.

[21] It is also said that a Torah scroll written by Moses is kept there.

the innocent heart of a child who is also a fierce protector of vessels for divine revelation on earth.[22]

The Mercy Seat, Kapporeth, כפורת (Caf Pey Vav Reish Tav)

> And thou shalt make an ark-cover of pure gold: two cubits and a half shall be the length thereof, and a cubit and a half the breadth thereof. And thou shalt make two cherubim of gold; of beaten work shalt thou make them, at the two ends of the ark-cover. And make one cherub at the one end, and one cherub at the other end; of one piece with the ark-cover shall ye make the cherubim of the two ends thereof. . . . And there I will meet with thee, and I will speak with thee from above the ark-cover, from between the two cherubim which are upon the ark of the testimony, of all things which I will give thee in commandment unto the children of Israel.
>
> EXODUS 25:17–19, 22

The lid of the Ark, the Mercy Seat, or Kapporeth, was made of two shining, radiating cherubs, which are like the two hemispheres of the brain as represented by Chochmah and Binah. The heart's wisdom and understanding is a symbol of the throne of God and the presence of the Almighty in heaven. It is suggested that the fire from the Ark between the wings of the cherubim represents or even causes a physical alchemical engagement of the High Priest's brain (the pineal, hypothalamus, and pituitary glands), which are stimulated to a point of divine realization. The priest is thus "crowned" with divine illumination. That our two hemispheres of the brain touch in

---

[22] As representatives of the pairing between the divine Father and Mother (Abba and Imma) of our emotions and earthly body (Zeir Anipin and Nukvah), the cherubim also correspond, as do each of the personas and worlds, to a letter in the name of God, pronounced Adonai, called HaVaYaH, and spelled Yod Hay Vav Hay. The realm of emanation (Atzilut) is the Yod and Chochmah of pure divine consciousness. Divine intellect is the first Hay, the realm of creation, or Beriyah, and the persona of Binah, the Mother. Our divine emotions, or the partzuf of the Son, are in the realm of formation, or Yetzirah, and the letter Vav. Finally, divine expression, the realm of action, or Asiyah, is in Malchut, the partzuf of the Daughter/Woman and the final Hay. In this way, we can see how the cherubim activate the entire workings of God's name and His full embodiment above the Ark, between the wings of the cherubim. Just as we find the surrounding light (Or Makif) in the Holy of Holies, we also experience the indwelling aspect of God's presence, the Penimi, or filling light.

this fashion, illuminating us with divine insight, suggests an inner alchemy resulting from great personal effort.[23]

Synagogues of Today Reflect the Ohel Moed

Historical as well as modern Jewish sanctuaries reflect the general pattern just described. Most modern synagogues have a menorah and symbolic eternal flame (called the *Ner Tamid*), generally placed above or near the holy Ark, or *Aron HaKodesh,* in which the Torah scrolls are housed. These elements are comparable to the original menorah, Holy of Holies, and Ark of the Covenant holding the Ten Commandments. At the center of the synagogue is an elevated area known as the *bimah,* where the Torah is read. This is equivalent to the Tabernacle's altars, where historically animal and grain sacrifices were offered and where water purifications occurred and incense was offered. On the main holidays, the lineage of priests, descendants of Moses, Aaron, and their sons, gather at the front of the synagogue to bless the congregation, as did their priestly ancestors. Called the Birkat Kohanim, ברכת כהנים, this written blessing is the same as that given by Moses to Joshua, and down through the ages it is recited by parents over their children on Sabbath eve:

> May Adonai bless you and guard you—
> May Adonai make his face shine upon you and be gracious unto you—
> May Adonai lift up his face onto you and give you peace—Amen.

Included in the Ohel Moed and the function and rituals of the Israelites are other items used historically for special functions and holidays and for purifications of the community. Each item serves both an exoteric function as well as an inner function. For example, the shofar calls people to prayer and is also our own declared trumpeting of His glory. The mortar and pestle is used for grinding incense, which is also the process of self-refinement that we experience in prayer and self-management of our actions. The stone vessel for carrying water from the springs to mix with the ash of the red heifer—for purifying those contaminated by contact with the dead or open graves, bones, or objects on the dead—tells us of the importance of living

---

[23] Other Bible references to the Kapporeth include Exodus 25:17–22, Leviticus 16:2, and Psalms 80:1.

waters, of studying holy teachings as the ultimate purifying remedy. A silver decanter and silver trumpets, as well as the shofar and lyre, each play a role in community ritual as well as personal development according to the meaning the reader may extract from research and contemplation on these and other elements not addressed in this work.[24]

Creating One's Personal Tent of Meeting

Moses was told by God to make a house for him. The prophets show us how the Holy Spirit facilitates this kind of relationship between humans and God: specifically, the Ruach HaKodesh (Holy Spirit) is for certain levels of prophecy, while direct immersion in the Divine Immanence, the Shechinah, is for other forms of prophecy.[25] We human beings are asked to make a holy resting place for God in our hearts. We are asked to remember who we are. In the same way that the Israelites' Tent of Meeting with its Tabernacle traveled with them everywhere they went, we are each a similar portable sanctuary. As some have observed, the Tent of Meeting is not only a meeting ground for God and humanity, it is the place where the human being is truly at home. Likened to Adam's holy abode, Gan Eden, with its specifically defined areas, our personal sanctuaries also contain certain defined areas of worship and holy vessels within our physical temples, our bodies.

The Stages of Self-Refinement

Once a person has become an initiate and committed himself to divine right order, the stages of self-refinement of the inner sanctuary reflect the very same rituals present in the outer sanctuary—an illustration of the universal esoteric principle "As above, so below; as within, so without," which is so central to Kabbalah.

Entering the path of initiation requires self-nullification and making a sincere effort to become close to God in the realm of Asiyah (action). Through prayer, good works, sacrifices, and refinement of one's words,

---

[24] As a departure point for extrapolating further meaning, see Numbers 10:1–10. Also, there are numerous components and details pertinent to servicing the Tabernacle and creating it, which this book does not detail. The reader is encouraged to follow up with: R. Dovid Meyers, *The Mishkan Illuminated;* and R. Shalom Dov Steinberg, *The Mishkan and the Holy Garments* (see bibliography for complete details).

[25] See appendix 2, "Eleven Degrees of Prophecy."

thoughts, and deeds, the person graduates to the next stage, that of consecration and the realm of Yetzirah (formation). Here, entering into the service of the limbs, of the applied will, we consecrate everything we do, informing it with our purposeful intent. This is where we find the symbolic animal and water rituals, in which we burn off those qualities of the self that are animalistic as we continually purify our emotions and intentions before we say or do anything.

At this point, the soul, known through the faculties of hearing, sight, smell, and taste, is elevated—just as the menorah, shewbread, and incense represent different aspects of our awareness. This is the realm of creation, or Beriyah, which is found inside the Holy Place, where we listen to the voice of God's divine spirit.

Finally, after we are in complete repentance (Yom Kippur, the Day of Atonement), we enter the Holy of Holies, where we are exposed to the full glory of God's presence in what is seen and experienced through divine illumination of the heart. This corresponds to the realm of Atzilut, or emanation, where, enveloped in the direct shine of the Creator's presence, the initiate experiences complete enlightenment.

If our entire life and all that we do with our body *is* the Tent of Meeting, the place in which God dwells, it follows that the Divine Presence is always available to us. It is around us and within us at all times; all we need do is honor it. As Moses made clear when Torah was given to Israel:

> For this commandment that I command you today, it is not hidden from you, and it is not distant. It is not in heaven [for you to say], "Who can ascend to the heaven and take it for us, so that we can listen to it and perform it?" Nor is it across the seas [for you] to say, "Who can cross to the other part of the sea for us and take it for us, so that we can listen to it and perform it?" Rather the matter is very near to you—in your mouth and in your heart—to perform it. (Deuteronomy 30:11–14)

The Illusion of Duality

If God is in every existing thing, animate and inanimate, then God's divinity is everywhere. So why, then, do we sometimes feel so far from anything holy or enlightened or spiritually awake to the glory we exist in? Because we cover it up with our consciousness of separateness, our focus on other things—needs, feelings, and ideas—rather than allowing ourselves to experience the unity in all of life and the blessings in every moment.

The Shechinah, the Divine Immanence, the presence of the Creator, is always surrounding us and therefore always available to our awareness as we begin to peel off the layers of illusion that obstruct our inner vision and create this feeling of separation. When we come into rapport with this divine essence, which is an all-pervading field of love throughout the universe, we experience the eternal spark, the Yechidah from which our soul originates in this God-body we call the world and the universe. Then we know that the soul is always aligned with and present to the renewed creation of His splendor and glory. And so it is the mind and heart of each person that either conceals or reveals this holy light. When we allow the Shechinah to rest, we are at peace; all is one (Alef); all is unity (Echad), אחד (Alef Chet Dalet). This is the emanation of the Shechinah, the emanation of the divine. This is the illumination that Moses and the other prophets we are about to meet experienced in varying degrees.

When the self is no longer observing the world, when the self dissolves into being *of the world,* we become conscious co-creators; then the Shechinah is said to rest within us. And when does She emanate? When our highest goal is the desire to receive in order to give; when we glorify the unity of all creation of which we are a part; when we unite the material and spiritual components of our makeup and become emanators whose sole purpose is celebrating in joy all of creation; when we each know that our purpose is for the betterment of others and all life in the world. It is then that we awaken to the path of peace, the one path we all share as our common root and final destiny.

Our life is the appointed place and time of meeting. It is always here, now, for we are individually and collectively the Tent of Meeting where holy activities take place. We awaken to the divine that is within and without. This is the journey our ancient Israelite guides describe through their lives and teachings.

Initiation

3
United in Prayer
Malchut • Self-reflection and Return

My House shall be called a house of prayer for all people.
                   ISAIAH 56:7

Tenth Sefirot: Malchut
Meaning: Kingdom, sovereignty, world
Rung on the Ascending Ladder: One
Archetype: Woman/female (Nukvah)=daughter
Symbol: Book of Psalms
Spiritual World: Asiyah/action
Spiritual Anatomy: Feet and mouth
Inner Quality: Lowliness (shiflut)

Historical Personage: Moshiach, the Davidic bloodline, and all of humanity
Text: Eighteen Benedictions (Shemoneh Esrei)
Key Words: Prayer and penitence/repentance/connecting with God
Key Emotion in Song: Deep self-reflection, aroused devotion (tefillah)

Tent of Meeting: The world we stand in
Spiritual Stage: Initiation; one who is doing or initiating action

Spiritual Practice: Return to God and prayer
Illumination: The illumination of speech and action

> In Malchut, at the bottom of the Tree of Life, one begins
> one's ascent toward divine awareness by "doing" prayer, thus
> contributing to divine revelation on earth.

The Sefirah Malchut: The Descending Light Becomes the Ascending Light

In Kabbalah, the light of the Creator coming down to us from above is followed by our ascension, which acts in terms of the returning light that goes back up the Tree of Life, where we unite with Adam at the threshold of Gan Eden. This corresponds to each of the ten Sefirots' texts from the Hebrew Bible, which are historical settings that weave together the story of humanity's creation and ultimate redemption as seen through the journey of the children of Israel (B'nai Yisrael). More than just history, these texts describe a spiritual process we must undertake if we are to make our lives a Tent of Meeting, a sanctuary in which the holy presence dwells. And so we begin in reverse historical order, at the bottom of the Tree of Life, in Malchut, with action (the world of Asiyah), engaging in the activity of praying—an appropriate beginning of our ten-dimensional odyssey, for it is said to be the level closest to us at this point in the world's history. By thus preparing ourselves for divine awareness and emanation (the highest realm, that of enlightenment, Atzilut), each person contributes to the time of divine revelation on earth.

The Tree of Life is often referred to as a ladder of light that we climb, rung by rung. Rabbi Yehuda Leib HaLevi Ashlag (1885–1954) named his twentieth-century masterpiece, a translation of the Zohar from Aramaic into Hebrew, the *Perush HaSulam* (*Commentary of the Ladder*). As a result of writing his magnum opus, Rabbi Ashlag became known as the Baal HaSulam, the "Owner (Master) of the Ladder." Using this imagery of the ladder, we too will explore how prayer is the first rung of the ladder of life that leads to union with God and a life of spiritual and physical refinement.

The tenth and last song of Creation corresponds to the Sefirah of Malchut, the kingdom or world we live in, which is both material and spiritual (as are all of the Sefirot and corresponding worlds). In the Zohar, Malchut is also referred to as the Throne, the Queen, the Bride, Israel, the moon, Shabbat, and, in the nomenclature of the *partzufim,* the Daughter, or Woman/Nukvah. Like the moon that circles our earth, Malchut has no light of its own; rather, it reflects all the light that has filtered down the Tree of Life from the nine luminous spheres, or vessels, above it. In this way, some scholars are of the opinion that the tenth song is not yet known—that it will be the song sung by humanity when the Moshiach (or Messiah), meaning "Anointed One," and the corresponding messianic, perfect consciousness and action manifests.

Each Person: Creating the Conditions for Moshiach

It is said that today humanity is currently in the age of Yesod; because we have not yet reached the age of Malchut and Moshiach, the beginning of the ascent of the light, we must use our prayers to create the conditions for this eventuality, making the tenth song one of prayer, or in Hebrew, *tefillah.*

The word *tefillah* (תפלה) comes from the root HLL (Hay Lamed Lamed), from *l'hitpael,* meaning to judge oneself. It also means connection, thus expressing its basic function between man and God, between a person and his soul. Prayer is how the heart speaks openly. Prayer connects our hearts and our mouths, our feelings and our intellect. Traditionally it is said that prayer is the service of the heart. Essentially, talking with God in prayer is the language of the soul and the joy of the heart. When we stop the noisy mind chatter and humble ourselves in prayer, we can settle down into the innermost place in our hearts, the sanctuary of the self where God and all life are reflected and where compassion is cultivated. From here we are open to welcoming the Divine Immanence, the Shechinah; as well it is here that we experience the Holy Spirit, or Ruach HaKodesh, an elevating force experienced in prayer and the lower forms of prophecy. As the first rung of the ladder on our path to illumination, prayer is the fundamental practice for a successful spiritual journey. Prayer makes it possible to go through life with greater intuition and keener sensory awareness. King David is said to have written his Psalms under the influence of the Holy Spirit, or Ruach HaKodesh, sometimes referred to as the essence that illuminates our minds and hearts in prayer.

"To Do Prayer"

In Kabbalah, the human is sometimes called the speaking human, to distinguish the power of speech possessed by human beings as being the greatest gift bestowed by God. Malchut corresponds to our feet, how we walk on the earth, and to our mouths, how we talk on the earth (see chapter 1, figure 1.2, page 13). Speech is an act of creation. A primary lesson of Malchut, then, is for us to do what we say we are going to do—to "walk our talk," in modern parlance. Prayer unites the heart and the feelings that arise in the act of praying with the mind and the thoughts and ideas expressed in prayer; the mouth then speaks the prayer. Thus prayer uses the creative forces inherent in the act of speaking holy words. Each word, composed of letters, becomes a vessel for light to animate. According to Chassidic teachings, each time we speak holy words we give the angels attached to them an opportunity to endow us with the Creator's light. Just as each angel is called to a specific task, each one of us creates a vessel of light when we pray. In this way prayer connects us with His legions. When we pray to God, we immerse ourselves in the field of life, surrendering our will to divine unfoldment.

When we pray for divine right order rather than for some particular outcome, research shows that our prayer is more effective.[1] Through self-nullification we make it possible for the spiritual hierarchies to work with us for the betterment of others and the greater good of the world. Each word in prayer has a governing angelic presence associated with it, as every letter is an animated spiritual being. In this way, prayer is humanity's method of spiritual co-creation. Just as God spoke Creation into being through His Word, we too have the ability to influence life through the spoken word. We are thus taught that prayer is "the ladder standing on earth, with its head reaching the heavens" (Genesis 28:12).

The sages teach that the world began with prayer.[2] Until Adam communicated with God, there was no fulfillment of Adam's needs for survival and

---

[1] See the work of the Spindrift Institute. Their experiments in directed and non-directed prayer showed that whether a person focused on mung beans growing or fruit flies multiplying, if the prayer focused not on a specific result but rather on "Thy will be done," the outcomes were more beneficial. Also, the many books and studies by Dr. Larry Dossey show clearly the benefits of prayer in healing.

[2] Rabbi Avrohom Chaim Feuer, *Shemoneh Esrei,* 11.

glorifying God. In fact, God's created universe stood waiting for humanity's birth on the sixth day. It was only after Adam prayed for rain that the earth came forth with her bounty. Prayer is therefore the first lesson of service that Adam learned, the first act of initiation—an act we emulate in the Sefirah of Malchut, as we stand at the entryway to the Ohel Moed. It can therefore be said that Adam, representing the highest rung (Keter) of the Etz Chayim, shines his light on us at the very start of our journey. Thus our first lesson in service, that is, initiation-in-doing, is "to do prayer."

Until we ask for God's help, we cannot receive it. We understand, then, why the sages have said that the world rests on a foundation of prayer. One could even say that God created human beings for the express purpose of prayer, to make it possible for His creations to speak directly to Him. Just as prophecy is the Creator's speech to humans, prayer is our way of speaking to Him. So if we enter the path of spiritual initiation, prayer must hold a primary place in our lives. If prayer reflects the manner in which God created the world—through the spoken word and with a heart of love—it also shows us the importance of our own words, which are the basis of the human being's inheritance as God-like creative beings.

The Transformative Power of Prayer

Prayer nurtures the body and soul, invigorating the higher subtle body. In prayer the blood is sealed with the teachings of truth. The higher vibration that is created by speaking holy words is felt throughout the body, demonstrating the importance of speech in shaping matter, and how each word we speak is first deposited in the body and then in the outer physical world around us. This is why the use of sacred words for holy purposes elevates a person and why coarse, profane language is a devolving influence.

Modern research confirms the positive, transformative power of prayer.[3] It harmonizes and refines the body, helping us heal. The body is our foundation, like the grounding wire in an electrical appliance; it facilitates the ecstatic experience certain spiritual disciplines can lead to. This kind of sublime union with God that we are designed to experience can occur when we direct our attention to unity with all. At the end of life, when we are about to leave the body, we are told it requires not will

---

[3] See the work of Dr. Larry Dossey.

but acknowledgment as we return to the field of unity consciousness that is innate within the soul. Similarly, when we no longer experience a sense of separation from the rest of life in our mind and heart, it is said we become illuminated.

Malchut, as the realm of initiation in the physical world or kingdom, reminds us that elevating the sparks of light is the human task. This is the realm of action, Asiyah, of working in the world, doing our part in the community. This is why this Sefirah stands for the world in which the Ohel Moed stands, as action in the physical world prepares for a response from the spiritual realms. This natural calling from below and bestowal from above is the designed relationship between the physical and the immaterial, spiritual realms. Words, thoughts, and actions are like a baker's molds, waiting for spiritual substance to be poured into them.

Words, Kabbalah makes clear, are more than simply names to identify things or ideas. They are living formations of creative power. Each letter has a distinct nature. Our prayers are made of letters and words that build realms together. This is why there are centuries-old formulae for the order of prayers or for the making of talismans or even for making golems (artificial beings created by certain words and rituals, made to serve their creator's will). Numerically, the word for **prayer** in Hebrew, *tefillah,* תפלה, is equal to 515, a number shared by the Hebrew words for **gathering,** יקהת (Yod Kof Hay Tav); **seek,** דרשהו (Dalet Reish Shin Hay Vav); and **song,** שירה (Shin Yod Reish Hay). All these words express the essential nature of prayer: to gather spiritual forces together.

Of the benefits of prayer, Rabbi Shimon bar Yochai (Rashbi, 80–160 CE), the great first-century Mishnaic scholar, says, "Through prayers, man's body and Nefesh [the vital force of the soul] are mended and become whole. Prayer consists of corrections carried out together, four corrections in all. The first correction is mending oneself so one may become whole, the second is correcting the world. The third is to correct the heavenly armies, the fourth is the correction of the holy Name by means of the holy Chariots and all the worlds, properly corrected above and below."[4] Nefesh circulates in the blood of the body as the vital life force that permeates a person's entire anatomy, which is invigorated by prayer. This energy corresponds to the

---

[4] Zohar, Vayak'hel, 12:409.

realm of action, Asiyah, the lowest realm in which material life occurs (see chapter 1, figure 1.5, page 31). Therefore prayer provides spiritual sustenance to the body and to the world.

To initiate positive change in the world, we must constantly refine ourselves. Like a garden shovel, prayer is a tool that digs deep into the soil of the heart, so that by turning it over we can return, again and again, to closeness with God. As Rabbi Eleazar ben Azariah, another great first-century Mishnaic sage, comments, "Why are prayers of the righteous compared to a shovel? [The verb *atar*, 'to pray, to plead,' is derived from *eter*, 'shovel.'] To teach you that just as the shovel turns the grain from one place to another in the barn, so the prayers of the righteous turn the mind of the Holy One, blessed be He, from the attribute of harshness to that of mercy."[5] Prayer elicits the energy of loving-kindness from God's universe. We should never underestimate the power of our prayers for the well-being of natural systems, others, or ourselves.

The Song of Malchut: Deep Self-reflection in Prayer (Tefillah)

When the 120 prophets, sages, and scribes of the Great Assembly[6] created the Shemoneh Esrei,[7] commonly called the Amidah, Tefilat HaAmidah (תפילת העמידה), or the Standing Prayer, the central prayer of any Jewish religious service, it was for the many generations of people in exile that continue to this day. The composition of this prayer, which is the song of Malchut, is said to reflect various passages in the Hebrew Bible. It is said that if a person recites the Standing Prayer every day, it is as if he had read all of Torah.

The Amidah is a source of enjoyment for God and His spiritual hierarchy. The eighteen benedictions bestowed by this prayer (Shemoneh Esrei means "The Eighteen") ensures Israel's life while her people are in

---

[5] Sukkah, 14a. See also R. Yaakov Ibn Chaviv, *Ein Yaakov*, 221.

[6] According to Jewish tradition, the Anshei Knesset HaGedolah (אנשי כנסת הגדולה), "The Men of the Great Assembly," also known as the Great Synagogue, was an assembly that existed in the period from the end of the biblical prophets to the time of the development of Rabbinic Judaism, marking a transition from an era of prophets to an era of rabbis. They lived during the two-century period ending around 70 CE.

[7] For the entire Shemoneh Esrei text and discourse, see R. Avrohom Chaim Feuer, *Shemoneh Esrei*.

exile and while the Third Temple (and our own corresponding inner tabernacles) awaits us.[8] Note that the number 18 also represents the Hebrew word for **life,** *chai,* חי (Chet Yod).

As a formula for prayer, the Shemoneh Esrei provides a three-stage process that facilitates our uniting with the Creator and hence with our own inner source of divinity. This is the essential ground of the initiate's practice in Malchut: coming to union with God in prayer. Chanah, the fourth of the seven prophetesses (when named chronologically), whose own prayer is one of the Ten Songs of Creation, as we shall see in chapter 6, is credited with having taught the Jewish people how to pray in this proper three-part fashion.[9] In her petitions to the Creator to bear a child (the prophet Samuel), she discovered this sacred formula, and it became the basis for the structure of the song of Malchut, the Shemoneh Esrei, as composed by the sages of old.

In the Zohar the person who prays is called "the penitent," expressing the cornerstone of humility on which all prayer is based. When one recites the Standing Prayer, one is engaged in a deep process of work (*avodah*). Our own repentance, our honesty about our flaws, and our thanksgiving for our blessings are hallmarks of the balanced path of the middle pillar. Thus the initiate's path is called the middle path, for when we learn how to do things in balance, a mixture of parts in perfect proportion, we rectify ourselves and elevate the heavenly armies (the angels and their community), the Chariots (our heavenly spiritual bodies), and all the worlds in which our ten-dimensional existence takes place. In terms of one's personal Tent of Meeting, prayer is the field on which all other activities are based. By perfecting one's speech, clarifying one's heart, and expressing the mind's glory, the soul and body become ready for the next level of spiritual development.

Reciting the Standing Prayer

The Standing Prayer, which is called simply "The Prayer" in the Talmud, is recited while in a stationary standing position. It begins by beseeching

---

[8] For those in exile from their divine natures, this story is for them as well. Israel as both a place and state of awareness is a promise the entire world will see fulfilled.

[9] For a comprehensive study of Chanah the prophetess, see chapter 6 of this author's *Kabbalistic Teachings of the Female Prophets,* 196–233.

the Creator: "My Lord, open my lips, that my mouth may declare Your praise." It is noteworthy that at the bottom rung of the ladder we begin with the action of the lips, as a speaking human being, a person who prays, for it is through prayer, it is taught, that we ascend the rungs of the ladder, one realm at a time. So to begin we ask for permission to pray by asking for God's participation.

What a radical notion—that before we begin our praise, requests, and thanksgiving, we must first ask God for permission to speak to Him, as though we are calling Him on a spiritual cell phone! Indeed, the very cells of our body proclaim, "Receive us into your unity consciousness." Our lips (Malchut) call out to His Or En Sof (limitless light of Keter) to shower light on us. Beseeching God in this way shows us that the foundation of prayer is humility and attachment to God; only then can we use the power of speech properly. One sees this in the prayer sequence, which begins with an orderly progression of bows to express this humility before the glory of Creation.

In an earlier book of mine, *Kabbalistic Teachings of the Female Prophets,* I noted that by standing in prayer we emulate the patriarchs who, it is said, were able to rouse the angels as they chanted the eighteen benedictions to the Creator. The Amidah is comprised of eighteen praises to the Creator; that number corresponds to the eighteen times God's name is found in Psalm 29 and the eighteen times it is found in the recitation of the Shema, the primary daily prayer of a Jewish person (said at least two times a day), as well as the last words one speaks before dying.[10]

The simple, three-part structure of the Shemoneh Esrei as shown by Chanah the prophetess formalizes the method for contacting God: first, we praise the Creator; then we ask for help or guidance; finally, we thank Him for having delivered us from whatever it is that we are challenged by. This method, which is the secret of prayer, is a gift from the ancient Hebrews to each one of us.

When, in praising God, we act out of selflessness, our needs can be fulfilled—a great truth regarding the manifest world. Humility, we learn, makes us an empty vessel for spirit to fill, explaining in part why humility is crucial to the inner workings of prayer. The three-part progression of prayer

---

[10] See appendix 3 for the full text of the Shema.

reflects Chesed (loving-kindness), when we call on God's mercy; Gevurah (strength), when we ask for particular personal and communal needs that require self-refinement as well as self-sacrifice and repentance (*teshuvah*); and Tiferet (beauty, truth), the source of healing, when we thank God for having healed us. In the schemata of the Tree of Life, these three Sefirot are what is known as the Upper Chariot; they represent our ability to refine our actions with mercy, discernment, and truth. It is therefore clear that prayer leads to the spiritual elevation of a person, or *aliyah* (which also refers to a person returning to the land of Israel or going up to read the Torah during religious services). Prayer is thus the spine of our spiritual anatomy.

The Shemoneh Esrei (שמנה עשרה)

Blessing One: Binding with God

Invoking our Forefathers (Avot) אבות *(Alef Bet Vav Tav)*

The first three blessings of the Shemoneh Esrei, or Amidah, are those of praise.[11] We begin with:

> Blessed are you God, our God and the God of our forefathers, God of Abraham, God of Issac, and God of Jacob; the great, mighty, and awesome God, the supreme God, Who bestows beneficial kindness and creates everything, Who recalls the kindness of the Patriarchs and brings a Redeemer to their children's children, for His Name's sake, with love. O King, Helper, Savior, and Shield, Blessed are You, God, Shield of Abraham.

The Aramaic word *d'avuhon*, "of our fathers," mentioned in the opening few lines of the Amidah, has been translated as "davening," the Yiddish word used by Orthodox Jews to connote praying. Both meanings show us that a Jewish person alive today prays as their Hebrew forefathers did. This is a common theme in holy traditions: reverence for the elders and wise ones of ancient and modern times, who merit being remembered every day in Jewish prayer. Acknowledging that we are entering a tradition that has a long line of human and Godly efforts, our first step in initiation is to bind ourselves to our ancestors.

Here, in the first of eighteen blessings, we become united with the

---

[11] Text for the Shemoneh Esrei from R. Avrohom Chaim Feuer, *Shemoneh Esrei*. See bibliography for complete publication details.

three patriarchs named; just as they received the supernal light of the Creator in their lifetimes, so do we. Focusing on the lineage to which we are each connected to, we appreciate that we pray just as our ancestors have. Receiving Torah is tantamount to receiving the tools and the tradition of prayer as developed throughout humankind's journey. The ten songs reflecting Creation are a distillation of all of Torah.

On a deeper level, the three patriarchs of this first blessing represent the Sefirot of Chesed (Abraham), Gevurah (Isaac), and Tiferet (Jacob). While each patriarch plays an individual role, both in Torah and in the Etz Chayim, it is through their collective energy that we experience the greatest understanding and the deepest personal connection with God. When we can balance our love (Abraham) and discrimination (Isaac) with beautiful order (Jacob), we elevate everyone and everything, thus encouraging messianic awareness, Moshiach. In this book, the prophets Moses, Joshua, and Devorah represent the Sefirot of Chesed, Gevurah, and Tiferet (in other traditional teachings the three patriarchs named above fill these stations), emanating to each of us, standing as we do in the material world in Malchut.

Prayer requires our heartfelt love of the Creator (Chesed) as well as strength in self-refinement and self-evaluation (Gevurah). Only then can we join God in the Tent of Meeting—the sanctuary in our hearts—in the halls of truth (Tiferet).

Blessing Two: Recognizing our Holiness

Praising God's Might (Gevurot) גבורות *(Gimmel Bet Vav Reish Vav Tav)*
The second blessing praises God with notice of His eternal might (Gevurah) and His many ways of saving life and resuscitating the dead:

> *You are eternally mighty, my Lord, the Resuscitator of the dead are You;*
> *abundantly able to save. (He makes the wind blow and He makes the rain*
> *descend), He sustains the living with kindness, resuscitates the dead with*
> *abundant mercy, supports the fallen, heals the sick, releases the confined,*
> *and maintains His faith to those asleep in the dust. Who is like You, O*
> *Master of mighty deeds, and who is comparable to You, O King Who*
> *causes death and restores life and makes salvation sprout! And You are*
> *faithful to resuscitate the dead. Blessed are you God, Who resuscitates*
> *the dead.*

After asking God for permission and the ability to speak in prayer, binding us to the patriarchs, we proceed to praising Him for His amazing ability to give life, to elevate our awareness, to restore us. Here in the second phase of the Shemoneh Esrei we are reminded that nothing is beyond the Creator's abilities, and that as we approach divinity we become more aware of His awesome powers, thus awakening to our own.

What is striking to many people upon reflecting on this passage is the specific reference to the ability of the God of Abraham to bring the dead back to life. This theme of resuscitation, also called Resurrection of the Dead, has been debated for centuries. Some scholars suggest this means the resuscitation of a person who has suddenly died, whereby God restores them immediately to life. To the student of the deeper mysteries, however, it connotes the entire range of powers associated with the final Resurrection in the time of Moshiach and messianic awareness—the ability to raise the dead en masse, both physically *and* spiritually, literally and metaphorically.

Being in Malchut, the place of Moshiach, shows us how vital humanity's spiritual refinement is for the entire physical world. When we as individuals or our entire generation is "dead" to God's Word and divinity's holy presence in our lives, and then we awaken, we are "resurrected," as though from actual physical death. The return to awareness of the divine is the beginning of emulating divinity. This includes the facet of eternity, thus making resurrection a literal description about messianic times, when the dead will literally rise up from their graves, fully restored as living beings.

The Chazal make it clear that while on earth we are engaged in a struggle between our animal soul, the *yetzer hara* (or evil inclination), and our divine soul, the *yetzer tov* (or good inclination). When this struggle is over and the soul returns to the "World of Souls" and it is "purged of any taint left from its earthly sojourn, it is then exposed to intense Divine light, which fortifies it against any mundane influence forever." Yet while the body is interred in the grave, like a seed being planted to flourish later, "a dramatic transformation takes place and a new body is sculpted to conform perfectly to every desire of the soul." After being judged "for their past actions in this world," the harmonized body and soul goes on to reside in eternal bliss.[12] All of us who incarnate on the earth share in the same journey of bringing

---

[12] Feuer, *Shemoneh Esrei,* 69–70.

wholeness, and therefore peace, to our body and soul through right action and proper restraint.

The Judaic teachings on Resurrection are derived from Daniel 12:2: "Many of those who sleep in the dusty earth shall awaken, some of these for everlasting life [the righteous], and some of these for shame, for everlasting abhorrence." The Talmud tells us of various masters who, with the assistance of God, revived the dead. In scripture, Elijah the prophet raises the dead once, Elisha twice, and Ezekial an entire valley of dry bones. The Talmud records that even Cleopatra believed in the Resurrection of the Dead. The Egyptian queen posed the following to Rabbi Meir (the Baal Ha'nes, "Master of the Miracle," one of the great rabbinic sages who lived after the Second Temple was destroyed in 70 CE): "I fully believe that the dead are destined to be resurrected, but I would like to know if they will emerge from the earth naked or clothed?" The master replied, "The dead will arise fully clothed, and this can be logically proved by observing nature. A naked kernel of wheat is planted in the ground, yet it emerges fully clothed as a stalk of wheat, covered with husks and wrappings. Certainly man, who is clothed in shrouds at his burial, will emerge from the earth covered with garments."[13]

In the next passage in the Talmud[14] we are told that at the time of the Resurrection all people with handicaps will be healed of their infirmities. So too are we reminded that while we are still alive all of our character defects can be perfected through sincere effort at self-refinement and by entreating God's help. This is the foundation of all of the modern 12-step recovery programs: one must first affirm one's faith in a higher power. We see this element of faith, *emunah,* as the bottom rung of our ladder—our faith in God's mighty powers and our soul's attachment to that source. Initiation asks that we sanctify everything we do in the world as an act of faith in something greater than ourselves.

However one interprets the levels of meaning in the Second Blessing of the Amidah, it is clear that God is responsible for the living and the dead. His nature is eternally mighty. We too are ultimately designed for eternal life. Thus, so far, in two simple steps, we are told to bind to God through

---

[13] Sanhedrin 90b.
[14] Ibid., 91b.

our forefathers and to meet Him on His own terms. Here we find a teaching from the Sefer Yetzirah, or Book of Formation, the ancient Kabbalistic book some attribute to Abraham, which says in its opening passages that the end is contained in the beginning. In other words, the bottom rung of the ladder of light holds the potential outcome of the highest rung: reunion with the eternal Creator and with our primordial template, Adam Kadmon. Thus the light of the Or En Sof, filtered through the realm of emanation (Atzilut) and the Sefirah of Keter/crown, is held within the body of the person as the effluence of his own soul.

When we are in prayer, the soul is strengthened and the body is harmonized; we come into greater alignment with our spiritual design from above, which our body below expresses. Our words, thoughts, and deeds (as in the very act of praying) carry out the will of the soul's Nefesh, or vital force, bringing it into rapport with the other soul components: the Ruach (spirit), the Neshamah (pneuma, or breath), and those aspects of the soul outside of the body: the Chayah (life force) and Yechidah (spark of God). Prayer is indeed the ladder on which we stand, with our heads reaching heavenward. And thus the second step in initiation recognizes our return to holiness through God's power to sustain the living and raise the dead.

Blessing Three: Proclaiming the Source of All
Recognizing the Holiness of God's name (Kedushat HaShem)
קדשת השם *(Kof Dalet Shin Tav Hay Shin Mem)*
By now we have joined with the ancestors and acknowledged the eternal nature of the body and soul and God's power to raise the dead. Here, in the third blessing, the petitioner recognizes and proclaims the holiness of God's name. Accordingly, we recite:

> *You are holy and Your Name is holy, and holy ones praise you everyday, forever. Blessed are You, GOD, the holy God.*

There are many teachings concerning the names of God. One is that all of Torah is His name. Another says that there are seventy-two names by which the Creator and His powers and dominions can be known.[15] Regardless of which names we may invoke in prayer and meditation, they

---

[15] See appendix 4, "The Seventy-two Names of God."

all act as a vehicle on which the consciousness of the person can focus. By contemplating in this manner on specific Hebrew letters, one can move into more subtle realms of awareness.

The third blessing, the holiness of God's name, concludes the first section of the Standing Prayer, the opening praises of the Creator, which are likened to the third patriarch, Jacob, the grandson of Abraham and the son of Isaac. While Abraham represents loving-kindness (Chesed), and Isaac, justice and strength (Gevurah), Jacob stands in the place of truth, *emet,* corresponding to the Sefirah of Tiferet. In Hebrew, truth is comprised of the first, middle, and last letters of the holy Alef-Bet, the Hebrew alphabet: אמת Alef Mem Tav. Truth is balanced from start to finish, just as combining loving-kindness and justice in proper measure brings about a moral, beautiful, and true person or society.

And so, completing the three-part phase of the Amidah called praise (Shin Bet Chet), the holy sage Pinchas ben Yair, the father in-law of Rabbi Shimon bar Yochai, who wrote the Zohar, explains the acquisition of holiness represented by this third blessing associated with Jacob: "Holiness leads to acquisition of the Divine Spirit and acquisition of the Divine Spirit leads to the revival of the dead."[16] In the same way, Torah begins with Creation and ends with Moses' prophetic superiority to all humanity, telling us that we are created to speak for and with God. But not only speak with and for him, for here we learn that we are also designed to raise the dead (with God's help). The Kabbalistic interpretation is that we can raise (elevate, aliyah) ourselves from being dead to God and the divinity in and around us, to being fully alive in Godliness.

And so, with the first three elements of the first rung of the ladder of ascent, we are given the keys to understanding the purpose of our lives in the material world. It is in the realm of Asiyah, action, where the body and soul unite and where we can elevate ourselves to the perfection of being One and eternal. All of humanity shares in this journey of returning to unity with God. Like the patriarchs, we too are influenced by God's emanations from the Tree of Life, including the Sefirot of Chesed (loving-kindness), Gevurah (judgment and strength), and Tiferet (truth

---

[16] Avodah Zarah 20b.

and beauty). We are all offered the path to righteousness. By emulating these qualities of the Creator, knowing that they are emanated to us whenever we recite these blessings, we become awakened to their transformational power.

Blessing Four: Requesting the Bestowal of the Holy Spirit

Drawing Down Knowledge (Daat) דעת (Dalet Ayin Tav)

Blessing Four, which begins the middle section of the Amidah, is comprised of a series of explicit requests to God to provide all of life's necessities so that we can serve Him; six pertain to the individual in general and six to the community of Israel, confirming that we are born not for ourselves alone, but for the entire world. When we pray, everyone benefits. The initiate learns that service is the foundation of devotion in action; prayer is the heart of that service.

> You graciously endow man with intellect and teach insight to a frail mortal. Endow us graciously from Yourself with intellect, insight, and wisdom. Blessed are You, GOD, gracious Giver of intellect.

Here we are thanking God for His emanations to our intellect, which are invoked when we pray for knowledge, insight, and wisdom. Some traditions say our intellect (*sechol,* שכל) is comprised of Chochmah, Binah, and Daat (known by the acronym ChaBaD); other traditions refer to the intellect as consisting of the uppermost three Sefirot of Keter, Chochmah, and Binah. Both views are valid. The medieval French scholar Rashi, Rabbi Schlomo Itzhaki (1040–1105), says that Daat (knowledge, דעת)[17] is the Ruach HaKodesh (רוח הקודש), "the holy spirit, that permeates the human mind."[18] Thus when we invoke ChaBaD, we are calling down the Holy Spirit, the Ruach HaKodesh, in a few specific words.

---

[17] Daat (knowledge) is the outcome of combining Chochmah (wisdom) and Binah (understanding). As explained in chapter 1, Daat is included as one of ten Sefirot when Keter is omitted. Many classical teachings do this. This work, however, like the act of Creation, issues from Keter (Or En Sof), the limitless light, and it is based on teachings that omit mention of Daat from the primary structure.

[18] Feuer, *Shemoneh Esrei.* See the commentary on Exodus 31:3, 98.

Blessing Five: Repenting to Receive the Divine Emanation of Bestowal

Offering Daily Repentance (Teshuvah) תשובה *(Tav Shin Vav Bet Hay)*

> *Bring us back, our Father, to our Torah, and bring us near, our King, to Your service, and influence us to return in perfect repentance before You, Blessed are You, GOD, Who desires repentance.*

Teshuvah, repentance, represented by the Sefirah of Gevurah (strength/judgment) on the left pillar of the Tree beneath Binah (understanding) and above Hod (glory), is a daily duty incumbent on the petitioner. Teshuvah is the regular way in which we return to closeness to God through self-examination. Perfect repentance suggests the drawing up of all ten Sefirot of one's makeup in the act of acknowledging what we have done wrong. This recognition brings personal change. After we receive the fourth blessing's influx of light from above (ChaBaD), illuminating our mind, we must humble ourselves in order to use this influx properly; we must come to perfect repentance in order to change our behavior.

Blessing Six: Cultivating Humility and a Sincere Heart

Asking for Forgiveness (Selichah) סליחה *(Samech Lamed Yod Chet Hay)*

> *Forgive us, our Father, for we have erred; pardon us, our King, for we have willfully sinned; for You pardon and forgive, Blessed are You, GOD, the gracious One Who forgives abundantly.*

Here the petitioner personally takes on communal errors while acknowledging God's mercy to forgive (*selichah*) them all. After the intellect is illuminated, we must nullify the ego and acknowledge our flaws and shortcomings as we recommit ourselves to what is true in life, what is eternal and universal. By binding one's heart to God and His creation, forgiveness of oneself and others becomes a gentler process, making our hearts softer and suppler. This is a process of refining the light we have received from above. After we first acknowledge our errors, God's forgiveness cleanses the heart and soul of the effects of wrong action.

Blessing Seven: Seeing All People's Redemption as One's Own

Affirming our Redemption (Geulah) גאילה *(Gimmel Alef Yod Lamed Hay)*

> *Behold our affliction, take up our grievance, and redeem us speedily for Your Name's sake, for You are a powerful Redeemer, Blessed are You, GOD, Redeemer of Israel.*

Here we continue our exercise of personal redemption, or *geulah*, cleansing our heart and soul, knowing that the Creator will redeem us. This act affirms our collective experience of difficulties and the unity consciousness that comes with communal redemption. Simply put, we are all in this life experience together.

Blessing Eight: Asking God to Bless Us with Health and Healing

Opening to Healing (Refuah) רפואה *(Reish Pey Vav Alef Hay)*

> *Heal us God—then we will be healed; save us—then we will be saved, for You are our praise. Bring complete recovery for all our ailments, for You are God, King, the faithful and compassionate Healer. Blessed are You, GOD, Who heals the sick of His people Israel.*

It is noteworthy that a person does not request healing, *refuah*, until they have first asked for forgiveness and redemption. Thus our first healing must be rooted in self-awareness, consciously recalling one's own actions. Then the physical body receives the healing illumination of Tiferet, of God ministering to us directly through prayer.

Blessing Nine: Asking God to Bless the Year and Our World with Bounty

Requesting Prosperity (Birchat HaShaNim) ברכת השנים *(Bet Reish Caf Tav Hay Shin Nun Yod Mem)*

> *Bless on our behalf, O God, our God, this year and all its kinds of crops, for the best, and give (blessing/dew and rain for a blessing) on the face of the earth, and satisfy us from Your bounty, and bless our year like the best years, Blessed are You, God, Who blesses the years.*

Now we turn our attention to the bounty of the earth, for the benefit of the entire world and ourselves: we request a year of prosperity, or *Bircat*

HaShahNim. With this ninth blessing we have moved from personal repentance to communal redemption; we now arrive at communal welfare. Our world is composed of both personal and communal responsibilities. Just as the Ohel Moed is composed of its various parts, each of which contributes to the spiritual elevation of the community, here in the outer world in which the Tabernacle stands each of us participates in personal and communal refinement. So it is interesting to note that the next petition is a precise "calling in" of all those who choose to come into union with God.

Blessing Ten: Assembling Others of Like Mind and Heart in Service to God

Ingathering of the Exiles (Kibbutz Galuyot) קיבוץ גלויות *(Kof Yod Bet Vav Tzadee Gimel Lamed Vav Yod Vav Tav)*

> *Sound the great shofar for our freedom, raise the banner to gather our exiles, and gather us together from the four corners of the earth. Blessed are you, God, Who gathers in the dispersed of His people Israel.*

After participating in personal teshuvah, forgiveness, and healing, we become part of the ingathering of the righteous. The abundance of Chesed and Tiferet leads to the restoration of justice in the world. Prayer can accelerate the ingathering of the exiles, *Kibbutz Galuyot,* and the restoration of justice on earth. In the Zohar, this is Knesset Yisrael, all of Israel (those on the straight path to El, or God the powerful), in unity to hold the light of God and to be illuminated by the Shechinah.

Blessing Eleven: Becoming Agents of Justice in Our World

Restoring Justice (Din/Birkat HaDin) ברכת הדן *(Bet Reish Caf Tav Hay Dalet Nun)*

> *Restore our judges as in earliest times and our counselors as at first; remove from us sorrow and groan; and reign over us—You, GOD, alone—with kindness and compassion, and justify us through judgment. Blessed are You, GOD the King Who loves righteousness and judgment.*

Before justice can be restored, *Birkat HaDin,* "as in earliest [i.e., biblical] times," the ingathering must occur. This means that before we can be truly just participants in society, we must have a strong union with the divine. In Kabbalistic thought this means that all of the person's (i.e., the physical body, Malchut) "ministers" (i.e., the hands, heart, head, feet) must be brought to devotion.

Blessing Twelve: Eliminating All Separateness from Holiness

Uprooting Heretics (Birkat HaManim) ברכת המנים *(Bet Reish Caf Tav Hay Mem Nun Yod Mem)*

> *And for slanders let there be no hope; and may all enemies be cut down speedily. May You speedily uproot, smash, cast down, and humble the wanton sinners speedily in our days. Blessed are You God, Who breaks enemies and humbles wanton sinners.*

At this stage of the Standing Prayer we turn our attention to those who would undermine communal refinement—"heretics." This is also a call for us to be mindful of our thoughts, words, and deeds, and for us to uproot those habits or practices that, like an enemy, undermine unity and closeness with divinity.

Blessing Thirteen: Honoring One's Teachers

Recognizing Righteousness (Tzaddikim) צדיקים *(Tzadee Dalet Yud Kuf Yod Mem)*

> *On the righteous, on the devout, on the Elders of Your People the Family of Israel, on the remnant of their scholars, on the righteous converts and on ourselves—may Your compassion be aroused, GOD, our God, and give goodly reward to all who sincerely believe in Your Name. Put our lot with them forever, and we will not feel ashamed, for we trust in You. Blessed are You, GOD, mainstay and assurance of the righteous.*

Having dealt directly with that part of oneself that doubts, we now recognize righteousness and the people who are righteous, the tzaddikim, that we are inherently designed to become. Collectively this will result in the building of Jerusalem's future Third Temple, a symbol of bringing peace to the world. In the same way, our own body and soul are refined when we are gathered into our faith and trust in God. Then His holy city—the "city" of our own life, wherever we may live—is like Jerusalem, full of His glory. In this way we are the holy city and its occupants.

Blessing Fourteen: Building Our Tent of Meeting through Greater Humility

Rebuilding Jerusalem (Binyin Yerushalyim) בנין ירושלים *(Bet Nun Yod Nun Yod Reish Vav Shin Lamed Yod Mem)*

> And to Jerusalem, Your city, may You return in compassion, and may You
> rest within it, as You have spoken. May You rebuild it soon in our days as
> an eternal structure, and may You speedily establish the throne of David
> within it. Blessed are You, God, the Builder of Jerusalem.

Here the petitioner becomes part of the promised building of the Third Temple, *Binyin Yerushalyim,* which is synonymous with Jerusalem and esoterically means that Jerusalem becomes the world's temple. This is to remind us of our participation in the royal bloodline of David, whose song, sung after his escape from King Saul, is one of the Ten Songs of Creation, falling in the Sefirah of Hod.

Blessing Fifteen: Salvation Flourishes as the Outcome of Prayer

Joining the Kingdom of David (Malchut Beit David) מלכות בית דוד *(Mem Lamed Caf Vav Tav Bet Yod Tav Dalet Vav Dalet)*

> The Offspring of your servant David, may You speedily cause to flourish,
> and enhance his pride through Your salvation, for we hope for Your
> salvation all day long. Blessed are You, GOD, Who cause the pride of
> salvation to flourish.

The petitioner recognizes the Davidic bloodline and the quality of Hod, or glory and majesty, which is the royalty we are part of when we become humble. When we accept this royalty along with its obligations, as the prophet-king David shows us, we give up what is precious to us. Generally, one's ego is held dearly; therefore, surrendering personal desire to divine will elevates one's actions and leads to peace within and without because our divine partner is working with us.

This, then, concludes the second portion of the Amidah, in which personal and communal requests are stated. These requests are not only for our own personal needs, but for the world and the future as well.

We see, then, that the Amidah's structure reflects the descent of the light through the Sefirot: from the intellect, composed of wisdom (Chochmah), understanding (Binah), and knowledge (Daat); to the emotions (*middot*), or measured flows, in the lower Sefirot; finally ending and returning upward again from Malchut (the world of Asiyah, the material plane), the Sefirah in which the returning light originates. It is from our feet that our body has its motion to move, to act in the world. It is through our mouth and from the use of speech that we can inspire others to action. Like a mirror, we reflect back to the Creator the universal stream of creative, unifying love energy. When we pray, we elevate the essence contained in the person, place, or moment by tapping into this stream of God energy. This is why prayer elevates the sparks that remain on earth from the original breaking of the vessels, or Sefirot, during the creation of the Tree of Life.

Blessing Sixteen: Speaking Directly to God to Accept Our Prayers

Accepting Our Prayer (Kabbalat Tefilah) קבלת תפלה *(Kof Bet Lamed Tav Tav Pey Lamed Hay)*

The third part of the Shemoneh Esrei is composed of three blessings in which we thank God for the opportunity to serve Him. Recall that we began this three-part process by asking God for permission to speak to Him, to pray to Him. Here we close our eighteen-part prayer (actually nineteen parts when the closing blessing is included), which is a step-by-step investigation of the aspects of initiation, by once again asking God to hear our words and allow us to serve in the Temple and bring peace to earth. As seen in the description in chapter 2 concerning the components of the Tent of Meeting, the Outer Court is where the highest peace offerings are brought; this arena signifies consecration. Here in Malchut, initiation, where we stand at the gateway to the Ohel Moed, we first gain peace, and then we take into the courtyard as an offering in the next step of our journey, where we consecrate our lives to divine service.

> *Hear our voice, God, our God, pity and be compassionate to us, and accept—with compassion and favor—our prayer, for God who hears*

prayers and supplications are You. From before Yourself, our King, turn us not away empty-handed, for You hear the prayer of Your people Israel with compassion, Blessed are You, God, Who hears prayer.

We have praised God and asked for His help; now we beseech Him to hear our voice, to fulfill our needs, to be compassionate with us, *Kabbalat Tefillah*. We know that it is God "Who hears prayers." This final statement makes it clear that prayer is our way of speaking to and being heard by God.

Blessing Seventeen: Uniting Our Hearts and Minds in Preparation for Aliyah

Restoring Temple Worship (Avodah) עבודה *(Ayin Bet Vav Dalet Hay)*

Be favorable, God, our God, toward your people Israel and their prayer and restore the service to the Holy of Holies of Your Temple. The fire-offerings of Israel and their prayer accept with love and favor, and may the service of Your people Israel always be favorable to You. May our eyes behold Your return to Zion in compassion. Blessed are You, God, Who restores His Presence to Zion.

The seventeenth passage of the Standing Prayer summarizes the People of the Book's relationship to God as revealed in Torah. Worship becomes the service, the work, avodah, we do to perfect ourselves and the world. We near the close of the Amidah with God's eternity, the Sefirah Netzach; our thanksgiving, the Sefirah Hod, which is our inherited royalty and majesty, the offspring of humility; our covenant, Yesod; and our recognition of God in everything and every season, Malchut. We thank Him for His return to Zion (Malchut) and the Holy of Holies (Keter), telling us this union between humanity and the Creator in Jerusalem is the meeting place of the heart and mind in each individual life.

Blessing Eighteen: Thanking God for His Beneficence

Expressing Gratitude (Hoda'ah) הודאה *(Hay Vav Dalet Alef Hay)*

We gratefully thank You, for it is You who are GOD, our GOD and God of our forefathers for all eternity; Rock of our lives, Shield of our

salvation are You from generation to generation. We shall thank You and
relate your praise—for our lives, which are committed to Your power and
for our souls that are entrusted to You; for Your miracles that are with
us every day; and for Your wonders and favors in every season—being
morning, and afternoon. The beneficent One, for Your compassions were
never exhausted, and the Compassionate One, for Your kindnesses never
ended—always have we put our hope in You. For all these, may Your
Name be blessed and exalted, our King, continually forever and ever.
Everything alive will gratefully acknowledge You, Selah! And praise Your
Name sincerely, O God of our salvation and help, Selah! Blessed are
You, God, Your name is "The Beneficent One" and to you it is fitting to
give thanks.

Reflecting the essence of humility and thanksgiving, *hoda'ah,* the final blessing reminds us of the centrality of these qualities in our relationship to the divine. The petitioner learns that thanksgiving and service are one and the same, and that in messianic times all the Temple sacrifices will be unnecessary except for the offering of thanksgiving, which will continue. Without humility, there cannot be sincere thanksgiving. Thus humilty before the divine is our form of Temple service.

Closing Blessing
Granting Peace (Sim Shalom) שִׂים שָׁלוֹם *(Shin Yod Mem Shin Lamed Vav Mem)*

Establish peace, goodness, blessing, graciousness kindness, and compassion
upon us and upon all of Your people Israel. Bless us, our Father, all of
us as one, with the light of Your countenance, for with the light of Your
countenance You gave us, GOD, our God, the Torah of Life and a love of
kindness, righteousness, blessing, compassion, life, and peace. And may
it be good in Your eyes to bless Your people Israel, in every season and
in every hour with your peace. Blessed are You, God, Who blesses His
people Israel with peace.

While the closing prayer brings the count of the blessings in the Shemoneh Esrei to nineteen, it is considered the culmination of the journey that prayer enables. Peace, we are shown, is the end result of each person's unity with God.[19] Being at peace is the purpose of one's spiritual practice and devotion.

Summary of the Shemoneh Esrei

We begin our recitation of the eighteen blessings of the Shemoneh Esrei by asking God to open our lips, asking for permission to pray, for the ability to pray with the right intention (*kavanah,* כונה). Then we praise God for the patriarchs, for God's might, and for the Holiness of His name. This tells us how to pray: to surrender our speech to holiness and to bind our hearts to our ancestors and to revere God's holy name, for truth is hidden in it. Then our requests, which cover the necessities of life and spiritual welfare—our intellect, repentance, forgiveness, personal salvation, health and healing, and prosperity—are made. Next we petition for six communal needs—the ingathering of the exiles, restoration of justice, disavowal of heretics, following of the righteous, rebuilding Jerusalem, and the restoration of the Davidic reign, all said to occur during the messianic times. Then we ask God to accept our prayer. Finally, we close our prayer, an encounter with God's Holy Spirit, by praying with thanksgiving for the restoration of the Temple, for all the blessings in our lives, and for peace. We do all of this with the emotional expression of deep personal commitment and a welling up of devotion to this service. This deep, heartfelt longing to unite with God and restore our soul through love is a state the practitioner develops each time he or she prays.

As we can now see, the Shemoneh Esrei is an anthology of beliefs in God as the Father aspect of Creation—protector, provider, and administrator of Israel. Using this three-part prayer of praise, petition, and gratitude as a preparatory conditioning in order to reach revelation now makes total sense. In reciting this holy prayer, one commits to self-refinement and to communal participation, aligning one's will with God's cosmic will for the welfare of the world. One sees how the elders who composed

---

[19] "[The Gamara asks:] Why did they arrange the berachah 'establish peace' after the Priestly blessing? [The Gemara answers:] For it says, '[the prophets] will thus link My names with the children of Israel, and I will bless them' (Numbers 6:27). This verse follows after the verse of the priestly Blessing: 'And the blessed One, the holy One, blessed be He, is peace, as it says, "God will bless His nation with peace" (Psalms 29:110.'" Source: Megillah, before 17b, in Chaviv, *Ein Yaakov,* 280.

this prayer deliberately built into it a progressive topical development that the petitioner experiences each time the prayer is recited, which for the observant means at least two times a day.

Ritual: The Importance of Proper Intention

Just as in biblical times the Israelites would make a journey to tithe at the Temple, so too must we walk the path of devotion with the intention of making our lives an offering to holiness. The feet and mouth, as Malchut, stand for the physical world. In the schemata of the Tent of Meeting, this corresponds to the gateway to the Outer Court as well as being the very earth on which the sanctuary stands. It is for this reason that prayer is the ground of one's life and serves as the agent of inner transformation.

The third-century Talmudic sage Rabbi Simlai teaches, "One should never deviate from this procedure—first recount God's praises and afterwards make your requests."[20] Rabbi Moses ben Nachman (1119–1270), who was called the Ramban—not to be confused with Rabbi Moshe ben Maimon, or Maimonides (1135–1204), a revered Jewish scholar, philosopher, and physician of the middle ages (called the Rambam)—tells us in his *Iggeress HaRamban* (*A Letter for the Ages*) that we must cast all worldly matters from our mind when we pray, as we are preparing our hearts for the presence of the Holy One. He adds, "One who prays must direct his heart to heaven" with devoted intention.[21] How do we achieve clear intention? The Talmud recounts how the pious men of earlier generations would spend an hour in meditation and prayer before even beginning formal prayer, so that they might be able to pray properly when the morning service (Shachrit) began. They show us that having the proper intention, or kavanah, in prayer is fundamental to the act of praying; it literally determines the quality of the prayer.

Using the mind and heart through creating proper intention to guide the body in the act of praying for the purpose of spiritual service for the benefit of all demonstrates why prayer is a spiritual devotion that develops the self-correcting, resourceful tendencies that are inherent in our nature. What we do defines who we are. How we do what

---

[20] Berachot 32a.
[21] Ibid., 31a.

we do clothes our body and soul through action. The Tent of Meeting stands in the world as a place of uniting human consciousness and God's presence. Illumination, the state of union between the two, is why self-refinement is necessary. In Deuteronomy, Moses describes how the people, after crossing over the Jordan River under Joshua's leadership to the land promised them by God, will leave Torah, only to later return in earnest to its teachings:

> And the LORD shall scatter you among the peoples, and ye shall be left few in number among the nations. . . . But from thence ye will seek the LORD thy God; and thou shalt find Him, if thou search after Him with all thy heart and with all thy soul. In thy distress, when all these things are come upon thee, in the end of days, thou wilt return to the LORD thy God, and hearken unto His voice. (Deuteronomy 4: 27, 29–30)

When all of humanity comes to know His presence, that of the one God, the story of the Israelites will be the witness to this power, a reality to which prayer opens the door.

> *Out of heaven He made thee to hear His voice, that He might*
> *instruct thee; and upon earth He made thee to see His great fire;*
> *and thou didst hear His words out of the midst of the fire. . . .*
> *And thou shalt keep His statutes, and His commandments, which*
> *I command thee this day, that it may go well with thee, and with*
> *thy children after thee, and that thou mayest prolong thy days*
> *upon the land, which the LORD thy God giveth thee, for ever.*
> DEUTERONOMY 4:36, 40

When the great second-century Mishnaic sage Rabbi Eliezer ben Hurcanus was dying, his disciples came to visit him and asked, "Our master, teach us the proper pathways of life so that we may reach the World to Come." Rabbi Eliezer responded, "When you stand in prayer, know before Whom you are praying, and through that you will merit the World to Come."[22] The Amidah is the sacred formula for speaking

---

[22] Berachot 28b. See also Feuer, *Shemoneh Esrei*, 48.

to God directly. When followed by a person of any faith who loves the Creator and His Holy Spirit, it will increase the opportunities for experiencing health, love, peace, and closeness to God.

The Nature of Blessings

When prayers begin with the Hebrew word *baruch* (plural *berachot*), commonly translated as "blessed" or "praised," it means to increase, expand, and intensify.[23] When we praise our Lord, we increase the emanation of His glory to us and to the world. Prayers said by the individual benefit the entire community, in the same way that prophecy by the individual prophet is for communal welfare, to bring the people back to God.[24] This is one reason why we praise what we want to emulate or encourage in another person or in the world, as it brings that quality to the forefront of one's awareness, intensifying the impact and positive effects of praise in the world. *Baruch* also refers to the Hebrew root of the word *knee,* or *barak* ברכ (Bet Reish Caf), which manifests in the custom of bending one's knees as one bows forward in supplication while reciting the Amidah as a sign of humility before the Creator.

In general, there are three types of blessings, or *berachot:* those said before enjoying a material pleasure (*berachat ha-na'ah*); those recited before performing a mitzvah, or commandment (*berachat ha-mitzvot*); and blessings recited at special times and events (*berachat hoda'ah*). The saying of berachot is part of a Jewish person's daily life, from the moment one awakens in the morning, thanking God for restoring the pure soul within, to the last prayer before retiring at night, in which one praises God for forgiving our errors, in this or any other lifetime. The sages tell us to recite at least one hundred blessings a day, the number 100 signifying holiness. (The letter Kof, which has the numerical value of 100, begins the word **kadosh,** קדוש, the Hebrew word for holy: Kof [100] Dalet [4] Vav [6] Shin [300].)

When a person recites these special blessings, they are actually describing a state of God's presence in the world. We praise God at various times throughout the day and year: for example, "restoring a pure soul" within

---

[23] Feuer, *Shemoneh Esrai,* 53.

[24] For more on prophecy, see this author's *Kabbalistic Teachings of the Female Prophets,* 24.

us is said upon waking each day; "bringing forth fruit from the vine" is a blessing on the wine; bringing forth "bread from the earth" is a blessing on bread; and we also bless before performing a mitzvah (a good deed or commandment). In each instance we are praising the Creator for giving us these things: a pure soul, the wine, the bread, the opportunity to help someone in need. The berachot help us focus our attention on the act we are performing, reminding us that each act serves to bring us closer to God and divine life. The blessings then become part of the actions themselves, a convocation of intention, which is the holy essence that fills the action of one's prayer. While action is the key word of Malchut and the world of Asiyah, intention is the power, the engine, in that movement.

Spiritual Development:
Conditioning the Field through Prayer

The first three statements comprising the opening praises of the Amidah connect us to the covenant God made with Israel, to God's mighty ability to give life and raise the dead, and to the fact that His very name conceals and also reveals truth.[25] We are designed to be immortal beings who, like God, can create vessels of life using our words, thoughts, and deeds, the garments of the soul in the World to Come. As incarnate souls in physical bodies, we have the opportunity to refine the body and soul and come into self-mastery and illumination. Fundamentally, this is what Malchut teaches. This is what is meant in Genesis when we learn that the entire world was made for humanity's intelligent and compassionate engagement, where we accept that our dominion is a sacred honor and responsibility of reverent stewardship.

The next six statements of the Standing Prayer, which form the second part of this three-part formula, are petitions for God's help with our worldly needs—for refinement of the intellect, repentance, forgiveness, personal salvation, health, and a year of prosperity. There are also prayers for six communal categories: the ingathering of the exiles, the restoration of justice, our displeasure with our own heretical nature, our love for the righteous, our hope for rebuilding Jerusalem and the world,

---

[25] The names of God and various permutations of HaVaYaH, a sacred name of HaShem are used in Kabbalistic meditative practices.

and the return of the Davidic reign in the person of the Moshiach. In other words, prayer, tefillah, represented by the Amidah, reflects the light of the crown (Keter) in its descent through all of the Sefirot, depositing some essence from each of them in the final Sefirah of the material world, Malchut, the kingdom.

All that is prophesied to happen, the perfection of the material world, is reflected in our requests that come from below, in Malchut. Here, as we begin our ascent to union with God, we state with clarity our dependence on the divine for personal and collective success. Recalling that Malchut is also the mouth as well as Moshiach means that all the world will declare that God is One. Until then, each of us participates in conditioning earth for unity consciousness through prayer. In modern parlance we could say that we are conditioning the field, meaning we are laying the vibratory foundation for the material to manifest, which will reflect the quality of the spiritual work we have done—like preparing organic soil before planting our seeds, where the soil becomes the foundation of the garden's future success.

Prayer is the essential use of speech for elevating the world. It conditions the field for the eventual manifestation of the prophesied holy thousand years of peace. This is why we can say that prayer is the work of the initiate, and why every person is able to pray; this will bring the thousand years of messianic peace (after which time it is said there will be a thousand-year period without life on earth, as stated in some prophecies, which suggest that the earth will go through a period of a thousand years devoid of human inhabitants, but it should also be noted that these prophecies suggest a graduation for humans, not an elimination of human life).

Rabbi Yochanan ben Zakai (30 BCE–90 CE), an important sage of the era of the Second Temple and a primary contributor to the Mishnah, says, "In the generation when the son of David [i.e., the Moshiach] will come, the number of Torah scholars will dwindle, and as for the rest of the people, their eyes will be weakened through anguish and grief. Every day will bring new adversities and harsh decrees. No sooner is one trouble over than another one appears." He then goes on to tell us that the

Rabbis taught in a Baraita: In the seven-year cycle at the end of which the son of David will come, in the first year, this verse will be fulfilled,

"I will make it rain on one town, and not on another" (Amos 4:7) [i.e., abundance in one region, famine in another]. In the second year, the arrows of famine will be sent forth [i.e., there will not be abundance anywhere] (Rashi). In the third year there will be a great famine, men, women and children, pious people and men of good deeds will perish, and the Torah will be forgotten by its students [for lack of food] (Rashi). In the fourth year there will be some degree of affluence. In the fifth year there will be great abundance, people will eat, drink, and rejoice; and the Torah will return to its students. In the sixth year there will be the sounding [of the shofar, heralding the coming of Moshiach]. In the seventh year there will be wars [between the heathen nations and the Jews] (Rashi). At the close of the seventh year [i.e., in the eighth year], the son of David will come.[26]

Prayer as the Foundation of Peace

The Shemoneh Esrei draws down the heavenly light of peace to the world. When reduced to its opening and closing elements, it is a prayer for peace. In Kabbalah it is said that the Amidah draws down from the highest realm of Atzilut, emanation, and from the crown, Keter, in the Tree of Life, which is illuminated by the Or En Sof, the limitless light of God. Thus the initiate in prayer in Malchut, the bottom of the Tree, receives light from the top of the Tree. This tells us how significant it is when a person stands in prayer—why it is the foundation of peace. The Shemoneh Esrei is a formula for creating peace within and without. As the foundation for the returning light, it suggests that as God chose peace as the vessel for the blessings He wanted to bestow on Israel, then all of Torah must be for the creation of peace in the world of Asiyah, the physical world. The returning light, our upward-reaching efforts, and the advancement of humankind depends on this peace, for it is the only vessel capable of holding the highest (Keter) of God's blessings: illumination for all the world. Ultimately, prayer leads to peace in the individual's kingdom just as it will in the world.

---

[26] Sanhedrin, "The Advent of Mashiach," in Chaviv, *Ein Yaakov,* 661.

The Path of Initiation

Initiation as the practice of prayer is the stage at which a person is motivated to change, to refine one's life in some way—to find a sense of peace in life, to find balance between family, work, pleasure, spiritual pursuits, and inner needs. More importantly, when one tires of being controlled by one's emotions—anger, lust, desire, frustration, arrogance, depression— change becomes possible. It happens to any person who enters the path of intiation. Prayer makes personal change possible and allows the soul the joy of speaking to God every day. One doesn't need formal prayers to talk to God; you only need a sincere heart that calls out to God with genuine faith. This is the place of the Tent of Meeting.

Following the sages' guidance on how to pray, we leave the first rung of our ladder of light knowing that when we want to speak to God, we prepare ourselves by reaching a state of lowliness, or *shiflut,* which humbles us to receive all that is being bestowed on us through prayer, through our conversation with God. Next, we praise His greatness before stating our requests and petitioning for His help. We close by offering thanksgiving for His having helped us, knowing that He has already fulfilled our requests in the supernal realms—itself an expression of our faith. Thus when we pray, we pray not only for ourselves, but for the entire world.

All of the blessings of the Amidah are aspects of self-refinement that bring us into unity with God and our ancestors and create a Tent of Meeting for God's Holy Spirit to dwell in. A person could take these eighteen steps as a general template and compose his or her own words in place of the formal ones of the text.[27] But regardless of whether the initiate follows the actual text of the Shemoneh Esrei or uses it as a departure point for words of their own chosing, the crucial elements are: cultivating sincerity of one's heart, a desire for greater self-refinement, and an expectation that God hears our prayers. Prayer brings peace within and peace without. Bringing peace, shalom, is the foundation of illumination and Moshiach. Peacemaking is the work of the human being both on the individual level and in the world, for peace brings unity, which is the completion of the rectification of the world (Malchut).

---

[27] See appendix 5 for a suggested template for creating one's own eighteen-part prayer.

The Power of Prayer

One sees why Kabbalists associate both the feet and the mouth with the bottom Sefirah of the Tree of Life. Our words are the foundation of our action in the world (the realm of Asiyah). Our use of words for prayer elevates the very act of speaking to an act of holy creation. The speaking human being elevates anything that is prayed for, which is why we must never underestimate the importance of our prayers for one another and for all beings—for the hungry, the poor, for the world's nations, for our families, for the trees, for the oceans, for the animals. Binding our hearts and minds to the Creator in our petitioning and being grateful for having our prayers answered is the innermost secret of prayer and the benefit of initiation. It is understood that what we pray for is granted in the act of speaking the prayer itself.

And so, with the foundation of prayer firmly established, we now reach for the second rung of the ladder and the ninth Song of Creation on the singing Tree of Life. Having prayer as the primary tool of self-refinement, as the foundation of one's life in Malchut, we now proceed to the next song in our ascent of the Tree of Life, King Solomon's Song of Songs, representing Yesod. We will embark on our journey upward, from the Standing Prayer of self-reflection, repentance, thanksgiving, and praise in Malchut, to a song of love in Yesod. Here we will experience union with God, as though with a lover. We cry out in joy and we consecrate our bodies and hearts in service to the divine in all life.

Consecration

4
Love Song of Devotion
Yesod • Joyous Song, Crying Out in Joy

My beloved is mine and I am his.

SONG OF SONGS 2:16

Ninth Sefirot: Yesod
Meaning: Foundation, covenant
Rung on Ascending Ladder: Two
Archetype: The Son (Zeir Anpin)
Symbol: The First Temple
Spiritual World: Yetzirah/formation
Spiritual Anatomy: Generative organs
Inner Quality: Truth (emet)

Historical Personage: King Solomon
Text: Song of Songs (Shir HaShirim)
Key Words: Devotion to proper action and restraint
Key Emotion in Song: Crying out in joy (ranenu tzaddikim)

Tent of Meeting: Outer Court
Spiritual Stage: Consecration; sanctifying one's life through devotion
Spiritual Practice: Heartfelt devotion to God; dedication of one's life to
　　divine service

Illumination: The illumination of conjugality of body and soul

> *Meeting King Solomon in the arena of consecration, the Outer Court of the Tabernacle, one learns how to devote one's personal and communal life to service of the divine.*

The Sefirah Yesod: Softening One's Heart to the Pulse of the Divine

In our ascent of the Tree of Life, the Sefirah of Yesod marks our entry into the Outer Court of the sanctuary. In the Tabernacle this is where the agricultural and animal sacrifices, burnt on the altar, and water purifications take place. Anatomically Yesod corresponds to the generative organs and the ability to procreate and dedicate.

In Kabbalah, Yesod, while its own field, is also considered part of a larger construct of six Sefirot that in terms of the partzufim, or family personas, is called the Son, or Zeir Anpin (also referred to as "the small face" or "the impatient one," as seen in chapter 1). When we are young we learn to master our emotions as part of a developmental process, as impatience can inhibit a person's greater capacity for good by failing to honor the truth that everything has its own time and season. Patience—allowing something to mature properly, be it a relationship, a project, or a devotional service—is the result of overcoming the desire for immediate gratification. By comparison, the highest Sefirah of Keter is called "the long face" (of HaShem), as well as *Arich Anpin,* a reference to an external aspect of Keter, and *Atik Yomin,* "the Ancient One," which refers to Keter's internal nature. Just as the Father (i.e., Chochmah) is more mature than the Son (Zeir Anpin), so Keter, the Grandfather or Ancient One, by analogy, is made of the light closest to the source of God. In terms of our own development, this means that as one refines one's character and ascends the ladder of light, it ultimately becomes possible to see into the future and the past, uncovering the relationships between things that only the long view and patience make possible.

The Son refers to the six Sefirot of Chesed (loving-kindness), Gevurah (strength), Tiferet (truth and beauty), Netzach (eternity and victory), Hod (glory and majesty), and Yesod (covenant and foundation). Together these Sefirot represent the Outer Court rituals of earth, fire, and water. In this part of the practice the individual is doing the work (avodah) of burning off pride and the various selfish desires of the ego, as well as purifying the emotions through right action and self-correction.

Yesod stands for our foundation, our union with deity. Anatomically it represents what we do with our organs of conjugality. The light coming down the Tree of Life from the head, in order to reach our foundation in Malchut (the Sefirah representing Earth, the kingdom, and everything we do in the world), must go through Yesod, our generative organs. This tells us that sexual energy and our ability to procreate is part of our dedicated service to God; it is essential, in fact, to life on earth. Clearly we are designed to be co-creators.

Yesod is where we balance our desire for sexual pleasure with our desire for spiritual union or spiritual pleasure, there being no separation between the two. It introduces the elements of dedication to one's personal spiritual practices and surrender to the vitality of desire. Desire, when focused on one's divinity, brings a person into rapport with the divine body of God. The devotional service of joyful love, of crying out with this enthusiasm, is what brings one to consummate love on the spiritual level.

Yesod represents the covenant, or *brit,* God makes with the Hebrews through the practice of the circumcision, called *brit milah;* in another way it directs each person to the brit, or covenant, of the heart, the symbolic circumcision of the heart, or removal of the covering of the heart. For example, arrogance, anger, and deceit are all states of being that express a heart covered over. Humility, compassion, and honesty express the divine nature of the heart. The brit milah, therefore, of the Hebrew male child at eight days of age is a covenant of duty in relationship to honoring God. The brit of the heart, incumbent on all human beings, is the lifelong process of arriving at complete joy in loving God and therefore all of His creation. This informs us that spiritual union, either with the beloved on earth or the beloved Creator, is through the heart, the joyful and delighted heart, one that cleaves to God. King Solomon,[1] in his

---

[1] Traditionally, the word *king,* when used as a title as in *King Solomon,* is lowercase in the Hebrew Bible and other Chassidic source material (i.e., "king Solomon"), the uppercase treatment being reserved for the one King of all, HaShem (God). However, in this book I am following the regular convention of using the uppercase when referring to worldly kings such as King Solomon.

Song of Songs, with its emotional crying out with joyous purity, exemplifies this crucial step in our development on the middle path of truth.

King Solomon: The Wisest of All Men

And the days that David reigned over Israel were forty years: seven
years reigned he in Hebron, and thirty and three years reigned
he in Jerusalem. And Solomon sat upon the throne of David his
father; and his kingdom was established firmly.

1 KINGS 2:11–12

Born in 848 BCE to King David and Bathsheba, Solomon reigned for forty years as the third king of Israel before his death at the age of fifty-two.[2] His reign brought the nation and the people peace, economic stability, and international power. He was known as *chacham mi'kol ha'adam,* "the wisest of all men." Torah relates how kings from all over the world came to hear his wisdom, which included not only Torah but science and all other secular subjects:

> For he was wiser than all men: than Ethan the Ezrahite, and Heman, and Calcol, and Darda, the sons of Mahol; and his fame was in all the nations round about. And he spoke three thousand proverbs; and his songs were a thousand and five. And he spoke of trees, from the cedar that is in Lebanon even unto the hyssop that springeth out of the wall; he spoke also of beasts, and of fowl, and of creeping things, and of fishes. And there came of all peoples to hear the wisdom of Solomon, from all kings of the earth, who had heard of his wisdom. (1 Kings 5:11–14)

When only a boy, Solomon was anointed by his father after considerable family politicking by Solomon's older brothers, who each claimed rights to the throne.[3] Despite the brothers' underhanded and even

---

[2] Solomon's forty-year reign began ca. 967 BCE while David was still alive but infirm. Their co-regency thus lasted only a short time.

[3] Solomon, also named Jedidiah, "beloved of the Lord" (2 Samuel 12:25), was anointed king when his older brother, Adonijah, the first in line for the throne, attempted to proclaim himself ruler while David was still alive (1 Kings 1:5ff). Solomon's mother, Bathsheba, as well as the prophet Nathan and others convinced King David that his younger son should wear the crown (1 Kings 1:11).

murderous schemes, King David selected his youngest son as his successor. "When Solomon became king his father David placed one [of Solomon's] hands in the hand of Benaiah, son of Jehoiada [the head of the Sanhedrin] and the other hand in [that of] the prophet Nathan.[4] Then his mother [Bathsheba] stood and kissed him on the head."[5]

Yesod's song, King Solomon's prophetically inspired Song of Songs, expresses Yesod's greatest quality: the desire to become one with God. This longing for divine consummation is suggested in the words of advice King David offers the twelve-year-old boy-king at his anointing:

> I am going the way of earth: be strong and become a man. Safe-guard the charge of God, your God, to walk in His ways, to only serve His decrees, commandments, ordinances and testimonies, as written in the Torah of Moses, so that you will succeed in all that you do and wherever you turn; so that God will uphold His word that He spoke regarding me, saying, "If your children will safe-guard their way, to walk before Me sincerely with all their heart and with all their soul, saying 'No man of yours will ever be cut off from upon the throne of Israel.'" (1 Kings 2:2–4)

Yesod, as the place of intercourse between a man and a woman and between the initiate and God, is the Sefirah of coupling. It is noteworthy that the word *coupling* (חבר) has several other connotations: it refers to the way the loops on the Tabernacle curtains are attached to the structure; to Solomon's hair locks, which are like the loops of the curtain; and to the rainbow as being God's covenant and His coupling with earth in proclaiming that humankind would never again be destroyed by a worldwide flood (Genesis 9:15).[6] When we couple with the divine, uniting body, mind, heart,

---

[4] The prophet Nathan told David he would build the Temple, and then later informed him that he would not actually build it, but makes the plans and provisions for it.

[5] Yishai Chasidah, *Encyclopedia of Biblical Personalities,* 497.

[6] In a gematriatic practice called Stones and Houses, from the Sefer Yetzirah, the Book of Formation, one takes the three letters of any word (its root), and by rearranging these into six various possibilities one finds other meanings in each word, thus seeing a deeper story. As an example, the Hebrew letters that make up the word **coupling** (חבר) also make up the Hebrew words for **choose** (בחר, Exodus 17:9); the word **breadth** (רחב, Exodus 26:16); and the Hebrew word for **flee** (ברח, Genesis 27:43). See also this author's *Kabbalistic Teachings of the Female Prophets,* appendix 2, 393.

and soul, it is guaranteed that we, like King Solomon, will sit on the throne of the world (Malchut). To walk the path of truth, the middle pillar on which Malchut, Yesod, Tiferet, and Keter all sit (see the arrangement of the Sefirot in chapter 1, figure 1.1 on page 11), which is the path the prophets and the righteous walk, guarantees our success. What is expected of humanity is clear: we must be righteous, kind, fair, honest, self-correcting, eager to help others, and we must love God sincerely.

A Young Prophet

Shortly after Solomon is anointed king, God appears to him in a dream in which He asks the young king to make a request for himself. Solomon responds, "I am but a small child; I know not how to go out or come in. . . . Give Thy servant therefore an understanding heart to judge Thy people, that I may discern between good and evil; for who is able to judge this Thy great people?" His request pleases God, who tells him, "Because you have requested this thing, and you have not requested length of days and have not requested riches, and have not requested the life of your enemies, but you have requested understanding, to comprehend justice . . . I have given you a wise and understanding heart, such that there was never anyone like you before, nor will anyone like you arise" (1 Kings 3:7–12).

Though only a boy when he becomes king, Solomon, like his father, is called a prophet.[7] The second-century Talmudist Rav Huna says that David, Samuel, and Solomon "are the first prophets."[8] Just as Joshua is nurtured and trained by his predecessor, Moses, Solomon is schooled by his father, King David. "[In his youth,] Solomon would sit at the entrance of king [David's] gate, and when anyone came to be judged by the king, [Solomon] would ask what he wanted."[9] His love of Torah and his passion for its teachings are said to be responsible for the "hundred and fifty thousand proselytes converted by him."[10] Having a teacher is a necessary part of the prophetic tradition. As prophecy runs in bloodlines, oftentimes a parent, grandparent, or great-grandparent becomes the guardian of the prophet's personal and spiritual

---

[7] Seder Olam Rabbah 14. See also R. Yisrael Yitzchak Yishai Chasidah, *Encyclopedia of Biblical Personalities,* 495.

[8] Sotah 48b. See also Chasidah, *Encyclopedia of Biblical Personalities,* 496.

[9] Otzar HaMidrashim 348. See also Chasidah, *Encyclopedia of Biblical Personalities,* 497.

[10] Chasidah, *Encyclopedia of Biblical Personalities,* 497.

education, a tradition that is still true today.[11] The anointing of Solomon by the priests and prophets reveals this lineage of training and counsel afforded anyone who turns to those endowed with divine insight and whose behavior is a model of purity.

> And Benaiah the son of Jehoiada answered the king, and said: "Amen; so say the LORD, the God of my lord the king. As the LORD hath been with my lord the king, even so be He with Solomon, and make his throne greater than the throne of my lord king David." So Zadok the Kohen and Nathan the prophet, and Benaiah the son of Jehoiada, and the Cherethites and the Pelethites, went down, and caused Solomon to ride upon king David's mule, and brought him to Gihon. And Zadok the Kohen took the horn of oil out of the Tent, and anointed Solomon. And they sounded the Shofar and all the people proclaimed: "Long live king Solomon." And all the people came up after him, and the people piped with pipes, and rejoiced with great joy, so that the earth rent with the sound of them. (1 Kings 1:36–40)

When Solomon becomes king, he does not have even a single horse; he rides a mule.[12] Later in his rulership, however, "Solomon had forty-thousand stalls of horses for his chariots, and twelve thousand horsemen (1 Kings 5:6). They were idle [i.e., not used for war]."[13] His indulgences in everything—some say at the expense of the peoples' labor—were well known. But whether it was his enormous harem or his love of bountiful feasts, his bodily indulgences did not diminish his prophetic endowments. In fact, the record shows that he was well aware of his actions, and that his cultivating this awareness of his faults ultimately served his own spiritual elevation: "Solomon said, 'I permitted myself [to amass wives, wealth, and horses]; for I thought I understood the Torah's reasons [for forbidding a king to do so, and I could therefore avoid the pitfalls]. This understanding and knowledge [of mine] was madness and folly.'"[14] We

---

[11] Some of us know our ancestors guide us from the spirit realms, even those we have never met; even souls who were our parents in other lifetimes can come to guide us now.

[12] Yalkut HaMechiri, Tehillim 71:9. See also Chasidah, *Encyclopedia of Biblical Personalities,* 497.

[13] Yerushalmi Sanhedrin 2:6.

[14] Shemos Rabbah 6:1. See also Chasidah, *Encyclopedia of Biblical Personalties,* 501.

are each asked to evaluate our actions with this kind of truthfulness—the inner nature of Yesod and the foundation of consecration demands this level of *emet,* the Hebrew word for truth, implying a basic sense of honesty in which truth is rooted.

Seeking Wisdom

Despite Solomon's indulgences on the material plane, he searched spiritually, asking, "Wisdom, where is it found?" (Job 28:12). He wanted to ascend to the ultimate heights of Keter, Chochmah, and Binah (the three upper Sefirot known by the acronym KaChaBa), as represented in the Tabernacle by the Holy Place and the Holy of Holies: "Solomon searched for the seat of wisdom: [he wanted to know if it] is in the head or the heart."[15] The climax of one's spiritual journey of coming into unity with the Creator and His Word, signified by His letters (i.e., the words of Torah) in the holy Ark of the Covenant, is like a lover anesthetized by pleasure: it is the joy of the soul. Yesod derives some of its light from the spiritual revelation attained in the Holy of Holies, that part of the Tabernacle that the High Priest enters once a year, on the Day of Atonement. In this annual return, and through the lifelong practice of softening one's heart to the pulse of the divine, the initiate experiences the ultimate bliss of divine consummation. This is the bliss expressed in Solomon's pure song of love between God and Israel, the Shir HaShirim, the Song of Songs, which is often called the greatest song in all of the Hebrew Bible.[16]

Solomon's Otherworldly Journeys

According to Talmudic literature, Solomon made many otherworldly journeys in search of wisdom; these journeys may be considered a form of multidimensional travel executed through the focused mind, part of all sacred traditions in which nonlocal consciousness functions and has dominion. The Zohar, in telling of such travels, describes how the Cloud of Glory and the Pillar of Fire would accompany the eagle that Solomon would ride to view the Tadmor, the mountain of darkness (the same

---

[15] Yalkut HaMechiri, Tehillim 51:15. See also Chasidah, *Encyclopedia of Biblical Personalities,* 499.

[16] The prophetesses Chanah and Devorah are credited with singing the greatest praises of all, which had never before existed. Solomon follows in their devotion to God.

manifestations of God that accompanied the Ark of the Israelites during their Exodus):

> This time a great eagle came on pillars of fire and cloud and bowed down before [Solomon]. Solomon put on his belt, took his ring on which the Holy Name was engraved, and mounted the eagle. He [flew] four hundred parasands and arrived in Tadmor in the wilderness, in the hills of darkness. There he alighted and learned all the secular realms of knowledge that he wished to know. When he had finished, he mounted the eagle and returned to his home. At that time he said, "I returned and contemplated."[17]

The eagle of flight, protection, and far-seeing; the mountain of darkness; the olive tree; the sacred ring of the king with his royal signet—all these elements are open to interpretation. The king's sacred ring reminds us of our own innate strengths and capacities if we surrender our seal of individualized personhood to God. Humility is the cornerstone of prophecy and divine wisdom. The olive tree and olive oil, according to the Kabbalistic teachings of the Arizal, are in fact the fruit of Yesod.[18] It is olive oil that burns in the sanctuary's eternal lamp as a sign of God's covenant with those who keep His teachings, who make of their lives a holy sanctuary like the one Solomon built, which is dedicated to the Divine Presence. When we dedicate our hearts to divinity, our own eternal lamps shine and can be felt, if not actually seen, by others. It is a lamp of joy and peace, which is the source of our singing out in devotion.

The instructions on the nature of joy that accompany those on prophecy can be understood in this wonderful teaching from the Mishnah:

> Blessed be you unto the Lord, ye heavens and ye who go down in the chariot, if you tell and declare to My children what I do when they pronounce the sanctification, saying, "Holy, holy, holy." Be sure to teach them to lift their eyes to their [heavenly] house of prayer and thus lift themselves to the region above. For I have no joy in the world

---

[17] Zohar 2:112b. See also Chasidah, *Encyclopedia of Biblical Personalities,* 499.
[18] See this author's *Kabbalistic Teachings of the Female Prophets,* 34–36.

like the joy in that hour when their eyes are lifted to Me on high and My eyes meet their eyes. In that hour I take hold of the throne of My glory, which is in the likeness of Jacob, hug them in My arms, kiss them, I am mindful of their exile and hasten their redemption.[19]

Solomon's adventures in other realms tell us that when we go in search of knowledge in the secular world we are cautioned to beware of the darkness that may be attached to it. When we are attached to the ego we can easily be misled by our desires, but when we alight on the wings of freedom—meaning when we live as a self-mastered person—we do not get attached but look with far-seeing perspective, as an eagle does. We move from an egotistic state of being self-focused to being altruistic, focused on the welfare of others. We are given sight (i.e., insight, or wisdom) and can return safely to the middle path, which is rooted in prayer. The Song of Songs has us crying out to God, and God crying out to us in the freedom of true devotion and desire. This desire (*ratzon*) is the essential fire of will that burns in the hearts of all humans; it is that which gives us the impulse to do, to act, to be in conscious relationship.

The desire for a mutual engagement with God is what Yesod represents. Notice that the ring of marriage is worn on the fourth finger, the finger of Yesod, of the left hand, the hand of *din,* judgment and restraint, Gevurah; and the engagement ring is worn on the fourth finger of the right hand, the hand of loving-kindness, Chesed (for an illustration of the sefirotic associations of the hands, see chapter 7, figure 7.1 on page 221). This tells us that marriage is a mixture of loving-kindness and discrimination, sorting out in the relationship what is good from what is not. Together these two qualities blend to make the middle pillar's guiding power of truth, justice, and beauty (Tiferet), which the prophetess Devorah reveals, as we shall see in chapter 7.

Solomon's Wisdom

There are many teachings about Solomon's soul being representative of Yesod and the Holy Spirit, or Ruach HaKodesh, which explains why he is filled with wisdom and prophetic vision. It is said that "when he

---

[19] Hayim Nahman Bialik and Yehoshua Hana Ravnitzky, *Sefer Ha-Aggadah,* 164, 524.

sought to do something improper, his wisdom would stand up against his [evil] inclination."[20]

Solomon became renowned in his own time for his reverence for God and his bringing Israel to Torah: "On every topic of the Torah, Solomon said 3,000 parables; for every rabbinic enactment, he offered 1,005 explanations" (Eruvin 21b). "He endeared the Torah to Israel."[21] Because of his level of spiritual attainment, Solomon was equally at home among the animal kingdom and displayed mastery over the evil spirits of the world as well:

> The Holy One, Blessed is He, made him king over the beasts of the earth, the birds of the sky, the crawling things of the ground, and the demons and spirits. He understood the language of them all, and they understood his language, as it is written, He spoke of the trees . . . (1 Kings 5:13). And when the king pleased, his scribes would call them by name, and they would all gather and come before him without chains or guards and dance before him in order to demonstrate his greatness [to the representatives of foreign nations who stood before him.]"[22]

Though notorious for amassing personal wealth, Solomon was nevertheless a charitable man: "Solomon Son of David was asked, 'How great is the power of charity?' He replied, 'Go see what father stated clearly: "He who scattered and gave to the needy, his righteousness endures forever"'" (Psalms 112:9).[23] Yesod, as the foundation and covenant between oneself and the Creator, reveals the sanctity of God's desire to help those in need, demonstrating that our acts of charity reflect this most basic aspect of God-like behavior.

The Inauguration of the First Temple

It took Solomon and the Israelites seven years to build the Temple; throughout this time the king refrained from drinking wine, the same prohibition observed earlier in history by the Nazarites, including

---

[20] Zohar, Pesikta Rabbasi 14:49.

[21] Shocher Tov 45:6. See also Chasidah, *Encyclopedia of Biblical Personalities*, 501.

[22] Targum Sheini, Esther 1:3. See also Chasidah, *Encyclopedia of Biblical Personalties*, 499.

[23] Bava Basra 10b. See also Chasidah, *Encyclopedia of Biblical Personalities*, 502.

the prophet Samuel. "When he [completed the Temple] and married Bithiah, daughter of Pharaoh, he drank wine that night. There were two celebrations: the rejoicing over the [completion of the] Temple and the rejoicing over the daughter of Pharaoh. Yet the sound of rejoicing over Solomon's marriage and new wife was greater than that heard over the Temple. Because of this, God 'considered destroying Jerusalem.'"[24]

This is a profound commentary by the sages: that in this climactic moment of having just completed the Temple, the physical, earthly vessel presenting the rectified Tree of Life that had been damaged since the fall from Eden and the sin of the golden calf, Solomon loses himself in wine and women. Are we to believe that the very man whose throne was said to be "made in the likeness of the chariot of the Holy One, Blessed is He"[25] was too busy celebrating with the latest addition to his harem to stay focused on his job of inaugurating the Temple the next morning?[26] Pharaoh's daughter puts gems and pearls above his bed in the canopy, so that when he awakens he thinks he sees the shining of the stars and falls back asleep. Oversleeping by four hours on the all-important day, thereby preventing the sacrifices from being made in a timely fashion, Solomon is finally awakened by his mother, Bathsheba, who strongly rebukes him.

The scenario is dramatic, yet it is said that Solomon did not sin, as his name, from the word *shalem* (the root of the word *shalom*, peace), means perfect, whole. His marriages and conversions of foreign women to Judaism was a practical way to keep peace in the land. After seven years of focused enterprise in the construction of the Temple, Solomon had refined his emotions (represented by the six Sefirot of Zeir Anpin); perhaps his bedroom celebrations merely reflected the First Temple's temporary nature. Just as Solomon was fooled by Pharaoh's daughter, who placed gems and pearls above his bed to simulate the heavens and thus made him think it was still nighttime, human beings are similarly deceived by the material riches. The loftiest of souls can be brought down precipitously, even overnight. In Solomon's case, his excesses in taking foreign wives "swayed his heart," and he

---

[24] Vayikra Rabbah 12:5. See also Chasidah, *Encyclopedia of Biblical Personalities,* 504.

[25] There are six steps to the throne (2 Chronicles 9:18), which correspond to the six firmaments (Esther Rabbah 1:12). See also Chasidah, *Encyclopedia of Biblical Personalities,* 504.

[26] Rabbah 1:12. See also Chasidah, *Encyclopedia of Biblical Personalities,* 504.

thereby enabled others in his kingdom to follow foreign gods, leading to his eventual downfall (1 Kings 11:7–21). In all these ways Solomon's life reflects the vicissitudes of our own lives, especially when it comes to temporal matters of lust, power, and wealth.

> All of Solomon's deeds were threefold. He had three ascents [in which the scope of his rulership increased until he ruled the whole world] and three declines [in which the scope of his rulership decreased until he ruled over just his own household]; he saw three worlds [having viewed life as a king, a commoner, and then again a king]; he committed three sins [having accumulated many horses, many wives, and much wealth]; composed three sets of proverbs [Proverbs 1, 10, and 25] and wrote three books [Proverbs, Ecclesiastes, and the Song of Songs]."[27]

The story of Solomon's life reminds us that any diminishment in life is for our eventual elevation, be it in this life or in the World to Come. We also learn that the measure of one's life, like the measure of one's deeds, is the result of the cumulative work a person does, both within and without. What we do and what we fail to do matters. Yesod is as much about what to do with one's devotion as what not to do with it. It is equally about crying out in joy *and* restraining from unholy deeds.

Solomon's Endowment of Yesod

Who better to pen the archetypal love poem than a man so capable of devotion and apparent abandonment in lovemaking, with both women and with God? Solomon composed the Song of Songs on the very day the Temple was completed—the same day he was to wed the woman who would become his favorite wife. For this reason we should perhaps see his marriage to Pharaoh's daughter and the celebration that followed not as a personal downfall but rather as a rectification of the earlier sin of the golden calf, which some sages say was caused by the presence of Egyptians in the mixed multitudes that came out of Egypt with Moses. Solomon's marriage to an Egyptian princess might have been a repair, or *tikkun,* in the spiritual worlds of the earlier misdeed of

---

[27] Shir HaShirim Rabbah 1:10. See also Chasidah, *Encyclopedia of Biblical Personalities,* 496.

worshipping a golden idol. Yet later in Solomon's life, he too was influenced by his foreign wives and was told by God that due to his failing to keep Torah in its entirety, his kingdom would be taken away during the lifetime of his son.

Just as the Temple rose after many years of exile for the Israelites, completing their cycle of obtaining freedom from Egypt, so too did Solomon elevate his own spiritual exodus on his wedding day. On one level he acted on the material plane, adding another wife to his retinue and completing the Temple; he also acted on the spiritual level, by bringing everything to completion and perfection in the holy place of worship. While his name means perfect, which can be a reference to Solomon's soul, his personal behavior was not perfect throughout his life, showing us that every person who elevates the world is not always completely perfect. Thus our task is to return, again and again, as many times as necessary, to correct ourselves and to keep our covenant.

It should be noted that though Solomon's marriages and conversions of foreign women to Judaism (he accumulated 1,000 women, including 700 wives and 300 concubines) has been criticized, considered in its historical context it was a practical strategy for keeping peace in his world. Creating political alliances through marriage is a time-honored royal tradition, and Solomon's actions bound many foreign territories together by bringing the daughters of foreigners into Israel's royal household. Some say the king reasoned that if he could sire at least one son a year per woman, in two decades he would have a personal familial army of 20,000. One could also say that bringing the Shechinah out of the veils of the kelipot (husks of evil) was made possible through the king's energetic coupling with so many women. Furthermore, his strategic accumulation of so many women suggests the desire he had to maintain constant contact with the Holy Spirit, the Ruach HaKodesh, for while it is not specifically stated, is it not possible, even probable, that many of these women had prophetic talents by which Solomon benefited?

Yet it can justifiably be asked how could a man said to have 300 concubines and 700 hundred wives write about fidelity, about being faithful to one's beloved? As Yesod is the Sefirah of sexuality and conjugality, it is notable that Solomon's obvious excesses in this area are a reflection of the energy of Yesod by which he was well endowed. Perhaps his consorting with so many women was God's way of facilitating the revelation of the Shechinah for the building of the Temple. The Song of Songs speaks to the fidelity between a man and woman in faithful marriage as extolled by Torah, as well as the fidelity between the worshipper and the Creator, between Israel and God. There is a courtship, a beginning, and a progressive growth of love; there is marriage and then a turning point, which may include issues of distance, apathy, and then later renewal of affections—a pattern reflected in many long-lived, mature marriages. It is of note that while "Solomon called himself a servant [of God], as it is written, 'Give your servant an understanding heart' (1 Kings 3:9), the Holy One, Blessed is He, however, did not call him a servant, but said [to him], 'For the sake of David my servant.'"[28] Is not the Shir HaShirim Solomon's own courtship of God? Is it not a call to His Holiness to come to their wedding bed, in effect a newly dedicated "temple"?

Taking into account all the emotions King Solomon expressed as a consequence of having so many women in his life, and the fact that he completed this love song on the day the Temple was to be consecrated, after seven years of single-minded devotion to building it—and the fact that it was on the eve of his marriage to a daughter of Pharaoh—he was well qualified to speak of perpetual seduction, spurning, and reunion. Also, because Solomon composed the song on the day the Temple was completed, the Song of Songs can, in my opinion, be called the First Temple's dedication song. This remarkable love song is the archetypal dedication we make when we consecrate our lives to serving the divine within us and all around us. We sing a love song to divinity; divinity responds, for its name is beloved.

The Ten Miracles

It is said that upon completion, the Temple—which may be considered the vessel of the ten Sefirot, just as the Tent of Meeting is such a vessel—was blessed by ten miracles. Here one can again see, as discussed in chapter 1,

---

[28] Shir HaShirim (Song of Songs) 1:6, 1:13. See also Chasidah, *Encyclopedia of Biblical Personalities,* 497.

how the Kabbalistic system of correspondences and the "ten-ness" of things unites many aspects of the Hebrew people's lives and religious practice.[29]

> Ten miracles were performed for [the Hebrews'] ancestors in the Beit Hamikdash [i.e., the Temple]: No woman miscarried because of the aroma of the sacrificial meat; the sacrificial meat never became putrid; no fly was seen in the place where the meat was butchered; no seminal emission occurred to the Kohen Gadol on Yom Kippur; the rains did not extinguish the fire of the wood pile on the altar; no disqualification was found in the Omer, the Two Loaves of the Shewbread; the people stood crowded together, yet prostrated themselves in ample space; neither serpent nor scorpion ever caused injury in Jerusalem; nor did any man say to his fellow, "The place is insufficient for me to stay overnight in Jerusalem."[30]

Stone into Song

Solomon's building and inauguration of the First Temple in Jerusalem, along with his devotion to the teachings of holy love, are his legacy. The Temple was a physical expression of stone turned to song, expressing the power of the B'nai Yisrael crying out to God in joy, its heart and body wedded to God. The first century Mishnaic scholar Rabbi Akiva (Akiba ben Joseph) reminds us that Solomon composed his great Song of Songs on the very day the First Temple was completed, and he goes so far as to say that the greatness of that day was that Solomon's written masterpiece came into the world, and that this manifestation of God was even more blessed than the building itself.

In Yesod, the heart of stone is turned to flesh made tender by God's divine effluence; the Song of Songs is a dedication to this truth. Solomon's Hebrew name, **Shlomo,** שלמה means both wholeness and peace; numerically it equals 375. The words **look,** שעה, **dwell,** השכן, and **astonishment,** לשמה, each have the same value, suggesting that Solomon's Temple becomes the dwelling place on which all the

---

[29] From the Sefirotic array, to the pathways and the worlds, Kabbalah, like a periodic chart, is the essential code to anything written in Hebrew.

[30] R. Yaakov Ibn Chaviv, *Ein Yaakov,* Yoma, 190.

world looks with astonishment as the place of the indwelling presence of God.

The Song of Yesod:
The Righteous Cry Out (Ranenu Tzaddikim)

*Tzaddik Yesod Olam—the righteous one is the
foundation of the world.*

PROVERBS 10:25

From quiet and deep self-evaluation in Malchut, where we praise God, we now light the fire of the emotions so that they blaze with the desire to serve our divine master and our own inner divinity. Here in Yesod we passionately declare our love of God. For the People of the Book, to be close to God means to act like God. Yesod represents the generative organs as well as the brit of the heart, the removal of any covering of the heart that would deny our intrinsic bond with God. The text of this Sefirah reveals the true greatness of King Solomon, the composer of the Song of Songs. Evoking the sense of being deeply in love with God, this sacred text reaches its crescendo as one cries out in joy, the emotional quality associated with Yesod. It is said "the righteous cry out" (*ranenu tzaddikim*) with all their hearts and souls, singing of their love for God.

Becoming the Beloved

As the song of Yesod, the Song of Songs uses vivid erotic, poetic, allegorical language to describe the way lovers relate to each other—how they speak, what they desire, and how they feel. The metaphor of lovers is at times sensual and at other times energetic; it is the story of love between God and Israel, each calling out to the other; it is the song of yearning, of each person calling out to the divine.

When we speak to the divine, we are the beloved of the Song of Yesod. When we share in this love, we increase and broadcast the goodness that is given to us to the whole world. In this sacred relationship, distance has no meaning and time no boundaries. In this love there are neither social norms nor political positions to take, and there are no family dynamics to navigate. One gives up nothing and everything. One is lost in the presence of the other, the beneficent Creator who sustains us with eternal love.

That the Song of Songs is considered by some to be the crowning achievement of Torah confirms that Solomon's "throne was made with Divine Inspiration, as it is written, Solomon sat on the throne of God."[31] Solomon is the perfected lover of God. His ability to reach this kind of union with God is a model for how each of us can sanctify our own sanctuary, our temporary bodily existence, turning it into a holy place of service and celebration, so that we can make all of life a love song to God and experience divine consciousness. That the Song of Songs is considered even greater than the Temple alludes to the fact that words are creative forces capable of going out into the world, while physical structures are stationary, requiring people come to them. This is why it is said it is the person who blesses the place—important to understanding the concept of holy place.

Crying Out in Love

Solomon's building of the Temple, and his composition of the Shir HaShirim to dedicate that act, embody both the lower and upper parts of the Tree of Life. We are reminded by the sages that nothing happens on this earth that is not decreed above, from a leaf falling, to a person rising in their station in life—in the Kabbalistic view, *As above, so below.*

> Rabbi Yosi began: "King Solomon was inspired to compose the Song of Songs when the Holy Temple was built and all the spheres, upper and lower, were completed with one wholeness . . . and the Holy Temple was built as a replica of the Holy Temple above. When the Holy Temple was built below [on earth], there was no greater joy before the Holy One, blessed be He, from the day the world was created than on that day."[32]

It took Solomon and the Israelites seven years to build the Temple. When it was finished there was great rejoicing and crying out in celebration. It is fitting that the Zohar correlates Yesod with the emotional quality of singing out, as in the crying out of the tzaddik who proclaims

---

[31] Chronicles 29:23; Midrash Esther, Otzar HaMidrashim, 52; Chasidah, *Encyclopedia of Biblical Personalities,* 504.

[32] R. Meir Zlotowitz and R. Nosson Scherman, *Shir HaShirim, Song of Songs,* introduction, xxxii.

his love of God. This is the central theme of Yesod. Solomon expresses this clearly at the dedication of the Temple:

> Would God truly dwell on earth? Behold, the heavens and the highest heavens cannot contain You, and surely not this Temple that I have built! But, may You turn to the prayer of Your servant and to his supplication, O God my God, to hear the cry and the prayer that your servant prays before You today: that Your eyes be opened toward this Temple night and day, to the place of which You said, 'My Name shall be there', to hear the prayer that Your servant shall pray toward this place. (1 Kings 8:27–29)

Here in Yesod, at the dedication of the house of prayer for the ancient Jewish people and their proselytes (converts to Judaism), Solomon expresses the fundamental quality and petition of Yesod: "to listen to the cry and the prayer" of each of God's devotees. Here we experience progressive ascent, combining Malchut, prayer, and Yesod, the covenant of love, for all of humanity and all generations. It becomes clear why speaking or singing the Song of Songs—or any prayer of love we choose—with great emotional feeling, crying out in joy, invigorates our lives with a beautiful sense of harmony and completion, just as the celebration at the dedication of the Temple honored the spiritual reality it reflected.

It is said that it takes seven years for us to rebuild our bodies at the cellular level, so we can say that every seven years we build a new physical sanctuary. This means that every seven years we can rededicate our own sanctuary, our own Temple, to serving divinity and unity, the foundation of all peace. There is good reason to cry out in joy and celebration when a person finds an inner-path calling. It is this inner light of renewal that is experienced and celebrated every seventh day of the week as well. The People of the Book call it the Sabbath.

In Malchut, our first rung of ascension on the ladder of light, prayer (tefillah) begins with praise of the Creator. In Yesod, the next rung, praise of God is the manifest destiny of humanity. We pledge to God that we, as well as our sons and our daughters and future generations, will always sing God's praises. This is why it is said that in messianic times all humanity will praise God and recognize the one Creator: "And the LORD shall be King over all the earth; in that day shall the LORD be One, and His name one" (Zechariah 14:9). Then humanity will truly be one.

The Song of Songs (Shir HaShirim)

1:1 The song of songs, which is Solomon's. 1:2 Let him kiss me with the kisses of his mouth—for thy love is better than wine. 1:3 Thine ointments have a goodly fragrance; thy name is as ointment poured forth; therefore do the maidens love thee. 1:4 Draw me, we will run after thee; the king hath brought me into his chambers; we will be glad and rejoice in thee, we will find thy love more fragrant than wine! Sincerely do they love thee. 1:5 "I am black, but comely, O ye daughters of Jerusalem, as the tents of Kedar, as the curtains of Solomon. 1:6 Look not upon me, that I am swarthy, that the sun hath tanned me; my mother's sons were incensed against me, they made me keeper of the vineyards; but mine own vineyard have I not kept." 1:7 Tell me, O thou whom my soul loveth, where thou feedest, where thou makest thy flock to rest at noon; for why should I be as one that veileth herself beside the flocks of thy companions? 1:8 If thou know not, O thou fairest among women, go thy way forth by the footsteps of the flock and feed thy kids, beside the shepherds' tents. 1:9 I have compared thee, O my love, to a steed in Pharaoh's chariots. 1:10 Thy cheeks are comely with circlets, thy neck with beads. 1:11 We will make thee circlets of gold with studs of silver. 1:12 While the king sat at his table, my spikenard sent forth its fragrance. 1:13 My beloved is unto me as a bag of myrrh, that lieth betwixt my breasts. 1:14 My beloved is unto me as a cluster of henna in the vineyards of En-gedi. 1:15 Behold, thou art fair, my love; behold, thou art fair; thine eyes are as doves. 1:16 Behold, thou art fair, my beloved, yea, pleasant; also our couch is leafy. 1:17 The beams of our houses are cedars, and our panels are cypresses.

2:1 I am a rose of Sharon, a lily of the valleys. 2:2 As a lily among thorns, so is my love among the daughters. 2:3 As an apple-tree among the trees of the wood, so is my beloved among the sons. Under its shadow I delighted to sit, and its fruit was sweet to my taste. 2:4 He hath brought me to the banqueting-house, and his banner over me is love. 2:5 "Stay ye me with dainties, refresh me with apples; for I am love-sick." 2:6 Let his left hand be under my head, and his right hand embrace me. 2:7 "I adjure you, O daughters of Jerusalem, by the gazelles, and by the hinds of the field, that ye awaken not, nor stir up love, until it please." 2:8 Hark! my beloved! behold, he cometh, leaping upon the mountains, skipping upon the hills.

2:9 *My beloved is like a gazelle or a young hart; behold, he standeth behind our wall, he looketh in through the windows, he peereth through the lattice.* **2:10** *My beloved spoke, and said unto me: "Rise up, my love, my fair one, and come away.* **2:11** *For, lo, the winter is past, the rain is over and gone;* **2:12** *The flowers appear on the earth; the time of singing is come, and the voice of the turtle is heard in our land;* **2:13** *The fig-tree putteth forth her green figs, and the vines in blossom give forth their fragrance. Arise, my love, my fair one, and come away.* **2:14** *O my dove, that art in the clefts of the rock, in the covert of the cliff, let me see thy countenance, let me hear thy voice; for sweet is thy voice, and thy countenance is comely."* **2:15** *"Take us the foxes, the little foxes, that spoil the vineyards; for our vineyards are in blossom."* **2:16** *My beloved is mine, and I am his, that feedeth among the lilies.* **2:17** *Until the day breathe, and the shadows flee away, turn, my beloved, and be thou like a gazelle or a young hart upon the mountains of spices.*

3:1 *By night on my bed I sought him whom my soul loveth; I sought him, but I found him not.* **3:2** *"I will rise now, and go about the city, in the streets and in the broad ways, I will seek him whom my soul loveth." I sought him, but I found him not.* **3:3** *The watchmen that go about the city found me: "Saw ye him whom my soul loveth?"* **3:4** *Scarce had I passed from them, when I found him whom my soul loveth: I held him, and would not let him go, until I had brought him into my mother's house, and into the chamber of her that conceived me.* **3:5** *"I adjure you, O daughters of Jerusalem, by the gazelles, and by the hinds of the field, that ye awaken not, nor stir up love, until it please."* **3:6** *Who is this that cometh up out of the wilderness like pillars of smoke, perfumed with myrrh and frankincense, with all powders of the merchant?* **3:7** *Behold, it is the litter of Solomon; threescore mighty men are about it, of the mighty men of Israel.* **3:8** *They all handle the sword, and are expert in war; every man hath his sword upon his thigh, because of dread in the night.* **3:9** *King Solomon made himself a palanquin of the wood of Lebanon.* **3:10** *He made the pillars thereof of silver, the top thereof of gold, the seat of it of purple, the inside thereof being inlaid with love, from the daughters of Jerusalem.* **3:11** *Go forth, O ye daughters of Zion, and gaze upon king Solomon, even upon the crown wherewith his mother hath crowned him in the day of his espousals, and in the day of the gladness of his heart.*

4:1 *Behold, thou art fair, my love; behold, thou art fair; thine eyes are as doves behind thy veil; thy hair is as a flock of goats, that trail down from mount Gilead.* **4:2** *Thy teeth are like a flock of ewes all shaped alike, which are come up from the washing; whereof all are paired, and none faileth among them.* **4:3**

Thy lips are like a thread of scarlet, and thy mouth is comely; thy temples are like a pomegranate split open behind thy veil. **4:4** *Thy neck is like the tower of David builded with turrets, whereon there hang a thousand shields, all the armour of the mighty men.* **4:5** *Thy two breasts are like two fawns that are twins of a gazelle, which feed among the lilies.* **4:6** *Until the day breathe, and the shadows flee away, I will get me to the mountain of myrrh, and to the hill of frankincense.* **4:7** *Thou art all fair, my love; and there is no spot in thee.* **4:8** *Come with me from Lebanon, my bride, with me from Lebanon; look from the top of Amana, from the top of Senir and Hermon, from the lions' dens, from the mountains of the leopards.* **4:9** *Thou hast ravished my heart, my sister, my bride; thou hast ravished my heart with one of thine eyes, with one bead of thy necklace.* **4:10** *How fair is thy love, my sister, my bride! how much better is thy love than wine! and the smell of thine ointments than all manner of spices!* **4:11** *Thy lips, O my bride, drop honey—honey and milk are under thy tongue; and the smell of thy garments is like the smell of Lebanon.* **4:12** *A garden shut up is my sister, my bride; a spring shut up, a fountain sealed.* **4:13** *Thy shoots are a park of pomegranates, with precious fruits; henna with spikenard plants,* **4:14** *Spikenard and saffron, calamus and cinnamon, with all trees of frankincense; myrrh and aloes, with all the chief spices.* **4:15** *Thou art a fountain of gardens, a well of living waters, and flowing streams from Lebanon.* **4:16** *Awake, O north wind; and come, thou south; blow upon my garden, that the spices thereof may flow out. Let my beloved come into his garden, and eat his precious fruits.*

5:1 *I am come into my garden, my sister, my bride; I have gathered my myrrh with my spice; I have eaten my honeycomb with my honey; I have drunk my wine with my milk. Eat, O friends; drink, yea, drink abundantly, O beloved.* **5:2** *I sleep, but my heart waketh; Hark! my beloved knocketh: "Open to me, my sister, my love, my dove, my undefiled; for my head is filled with dew, my locks with the drops of the night."* **5:3** *I have put off my coat; how shall I put it on? I have washed my feet; how shall I defile them?* **5:4** *My beloved put in his hand by the hole of the door, and my heart was moved for him.* **5:5** *I rose up to open to my beloved; and my hands dropped with myrrh, and my fingers with flowing myrrh, upon the handles of the bar.* **5:6** *I opened to my beloved; but my beloved had turned away, and was gone. My soul failed me when he spoke. I sought him, but I could not find him; I called him, but he gave me no answer.* **5:7** *The watchmen that go about the city found me, they smote me, they wounded me; the keepers of the walls took away my mantle from me.* **5:8** *"I adjure you, O daughters of Jerusalem, if ye find* *my beloved, what will ye tell him? that I am love-sick."* **5:9** *"What is thy beloved more than another beloved, O thou fairest among women? What is thy beloved more than another beloved, that thou dost so adjure us?"* **5:10** *"My beloved is white and ruddy, pre-eminent above ten thousand.* **5:11** *His head is as the most fine gold, his locks are curled, and black as a raven.* **5:12** *His eyes are like doves beside the water-brooks; washed with milk, and fitly set.* **5:13** *His cheeks are as a bed of spices, as banks of sweet herbs; his lips are as lilies, dropping with flowing myrrh.* **5:14** *His hands are as rods of gold set with beryl; his body is as polished ivory overlaid with sapphires.* **5:15** *His legs are as pillars of marble, set upon sockets of fine gold; his aspect is like Lebanon, excellent as the cedars.* **5:16** *His mouth is most sweet; yea, he is altogether lovely. This is my beloved, and this is my friend, O daughters of Jerusalem."*

6:1 *"Whither is thy beloved gone, O thou fairest among women? Whither hath thy beloved turned him, that we may seek him with thee?"* **6:2** *"My beloved is gone down into his garden, to the beds of spices, to feed in the gardens, and to gather lilies.* **6:3** *I am my beloved's, and my beloved is mine, that feedeth among the lilies."* **6:4** *Thou art beautiful, O my love, as Tirzah, comely as Jerusalem, terrible as an army with banners.* **6:5** *Turn away thine eyes from me, for they have overcome me. Thy hair is as a flock of goats, that trail down from Gilead.* **6:6** *Thy teeth are like a flock of ewes, which are come up from the washing; whereof all are paired, and none faileth among them.* **6:7** *Thy temples are like a pomegranate split open behind thy veil.* **6:8** *There are threescore queens, and fourscore concubines, and maidens without number.* **6:9** *My dove, my undefiled, is but one; she is the only one of her mother; she is the choice one of her that bore her. The daughters saw her, and called her happy; yea, the queens and the concubines, and they praised her.* **6:10** *Who is she that looketh forth as the dawn, fair as the moon, clear as the sun, terrible as an army with banners?* **6:11** *I went down into the garden of nuts, to look at the green plants of the valley, to see whether the vine budded, and the pomegranates were in flower.* **6:12** *Before I was aware, my soul set me upon the chariots of my princely people.*

7:1 *Return, return, O Shulammite; Return, return, that we may look upon thee. What will ye see in the Shulammite? As it were a dance of two companies.* **7:2** *How beautiful are thy steps in sandals, O prince's daughter! The roundings of thy thighs are like the links of a chain, the work of the hands of a skilled workman.* **7:3** *Thy navel is like a round goblet, wherein no mingled wine is wanting; thy belly is like a heap of wheat set about with lilies.* **7:4** *Thy two breasts are like* *two fawns that are twins of a gazelle.* **7:5** *Thy neck is as a tower of ivory; thine eyes as the pools in Heshbon, by the gate of Bath-rabbim; thy nose is like the tower of Lebanon which looketh toward Damascus.* **7:6** *Thy head upon thee is like Carmel, and the hair of thy head like purple; the king is held captive in the tresses thereof.* **7:7** *How fair and how pleasant art thou, O love, for delights!* **7:8** *This thy stature is like to a palm-tree, and thy breasts to clusters of grapes.* **7:9** *I said: "I will climb up into the palm-tree, I will take hold of the branches thereof; and let thy breasts be as clusters of the vine, and the smell of thy countenance like apples;* **7:10** *And the roof of thy mouth like the best wine, that glideth down smoothly for my beloved, moving gently the lips of those that are asleep."* **7:11** *I am my beloved's, and his desire is toward me.* **7:12** *Come, my beloved, let us go forth into the field; let us lodge in the villages.* **7:13** *Let us get up early to the vineyards; let us see whether the vine hath budded, whether the vine-blossom be opened, and the pomegranates be in flower; there will I give thee my love.* **7:14** *The mandrakes give forth fragrance, and at our doors are all manner of precious fruits, new and old, which I have laid up for thee, O my beloved.*

8:1 *Oh that thou wert as my brother, that sucked the breasts of my mother! When I should find thee without, I would kiss thee; yea, and none would despise me.* **8:2** *I would lead thee, and bring thee into my mother's house, that thou mightest instruct me; I would cause thee to drink of spiced wine, of the juice of my pomegranate.* **8:3** *His left hand should be under my head, and his right hand should embrace me.* **8:4** *"I adjure you, O daughters of Jerusalem: Why should ye awaken, or stir up love, until it please?"* **8:5** *Who is this that cometh up from the wilderness, leaning upon her beloved? Under the apple-tree I awakened thee; there thy mother was in travail with thee; there was she in travail and brought thee forth.* **8:6** *Set me as a seal upon thy heart, as a seal upon thine arm; for love is strong as death, jealousy is cruel as the grave; the flashes thereof are flashes of fire, a very flame of the* LORD. **8:7** *Many waters cannot quench love, neither can the floods drown it; if a man would give all the substance of his house for love, he would utterly be contemned.* **8:8** *We have a little sister, and she hath no breasts; what shall we do for our sister in the day when she shall be spoken for?* **8:9** *If she be a wall, we will build upon her a turret of silver; and if she be a door, we will enclose her with boards of cedar.* **8:10** *I am a wall, and my breasts like the towers thereof; then was I in his eyes as one that found peace.* **8:11** *Solomon had a vineyard at Baal-hamon; he gave over the vineyard unto keepers; every one for the fruit thereof brought in a thousand pieces of silver.* **8:12** *My vineyard, which is mine,* *is before me; thou, O Solomon, shalt have the thousand, and those that keep the fruit thereof two hundred.* **8:13** *Thou that dwellest in the gardens, the companions hearken for thy voice: "Cause me to hear it."* **8:14** *Make haste, my beloved, and be thou like to a gazelle or to a young hart upon the mountains of spices.*

The Holy of Holies in Words

The great eighteenth-century Chassidic master Baal Shem Tov ("the Master of the Good Name") says that the Song of Songs is the Holy of Holies in the Hebrew Bible. Our sages tell us that this spiritual masterpiece, in which the relationship between God and Israel is a declaration of selfless love, each for the other, is the ultimate goal of self-refinement for each and every person. This, we are told, is true love, each partner in the relationship wanting to bestow on the other all that he or she needs. We are to desire, with all our heart and soul, union with God and His creation. Whether one lives alone or in a partnership or in a family, the challenge is the same: to be aflame with desire for union with God in all life. This desire to give to others and the world ultimately becomes the highest desire, the desire to receive in order to give. In turn, the consecrated heart receives the illumination and bestowal from the sanctuary's Holy of Holies.

Malchut and prayer represent our ability to reflect out to the world all the blessings God has given us, using all of our talents in service to cultivating this divinity in our lives. Yesod refers to our covenant with God to form ourselves into holy beings. In Yesod, meaning foundation, we commit to this relationship as lovers commit to each other. There is an ecstatic surrender to the joy of the other, and this sweet nectar of losing oneself in the divine other is the call God makes to each one of us. When we answer the call, we are swept away by the grace of His love.

Ritual: The Necessity of Purification

Yesod marks our first step into the Outer Court, that portion of the Tabernacle devoted to communal sacrifices, where the priests offer sacrifices for acceptance of petitions of forgiveness as well as offering praise and thanksgiving. This field of consecration takes place through purification. Here in the Outer Court, just beyond the sacrificial altar where the ani-

mal and grain offerings are made, is the laver, or *kiyyor*, כיור (Caf Yod
Vav Reish) made of copper where the priests purify themselves with water
before entering the next station in the Tabernacle, the Holy Place, where
the shewbread (*lechem panim*) is placed on the holy table (*shulchan*), and
the incense (*ketoret*) and menorah are serviced for offerings: "And Aaron
and his sons shall wash their hands and their feet thereat; when they go
into the tent of meeting, they shall wash with water, that they die not; or
when they come near to the altar to minister, to cause an offering made
by fire to smoke unto the LORD. . . . And thou shalt bring Aaron and his
sons unto the door of the Tent of Meeting, and shalt wash them with
water" (Exodus 30:19–20; 40:12).

Purification is a journey we must sincerely want to undertake. Just
as Aaron and his sons, the first priests of the Tabernacle, had to wash
before entering the holy confines, so too must we purify our hearts
before we can sincerely offer service to the Lord. Like the penitent who
brings animal and agrarian sacrifices to offer up as a means of purification, the priests must also purify themselves before they can perform holy
rituals or enter a holier station in the Tabernacle. We must refine our
animal nature or animal soul, the yetzer hara, as a form of purification in
order to enter a higher state of awareness. The lower level of the soul, the
Nefesh, which is embedded in the blood, represented by the Outer Court
where the animals are sacrificed, becomes more and more refined as we
ascend into subtler and subtler soul dominions in our ascent toward wisdom. This is what Solomon shows us in his deliberate seeking of wisdom.

Stages of Self-Refinement

> *Speak to the Children of Israel, saying: When one brings his feast
> peace-offering to God, he shall deliver his offering to God from his
> peace feast-offering. With his own hands shall he bring the fire-
> offerings of God: the fat atop the breast shall he bring; the breast,
> in order to wave it as a wave-service before God.*
> LEVITICUS 7:29–30

Building, maintaining, and using our personal sanctuary in service to God
is what we are designed for. In our journey of ascending the ladder of light,
Yesod is the beginning of the six-part archetypal conglomerate called Zeir

Anpin, or the Son, when speaking of the partzufim.[33] The ground on which the Tent of Meeting stands is Mt. Moriah, called "the footstool of the Creator" (the present-day Temple Mount). The Outer Court represents the realms of Asiyah and Yetzirah (action and formation) and correspond to the stages of initiation and consecration. Consecration begins with a crying out in joy (Yesod) in the world (Malchut), and continues with humble thanksgiving and declaratory surrender, the theme of King David and Hod, the next Sefirah on our ascending ladder.[34]

Establishing One's Intention

Yesod is part of the six Sefirot that comprise Zeir Anpin and the emotions (middot), which are refined in the Outer Court rituals of fire and water. This Sefirah represents the realm of Yetzirah, or formation, where a person initially undertakes this kind of self-refinement by establishing the proper intention. To be aware of what one manifests in the world by investing one's thoughts, words, and actions with purposeful intent is the responsibility of each person and all of humanity. This is our shared covenant since the time of Creation: to become co-creators. This daily commitment to self-refinement reflects the realm of formation, where the purpose of "forming" the human being into a holy vessel can be seen in Solomon's inner and outer journey.

Our power in the world of Yetzirah is derived from our ability to make new things—to invent, produce, procreate, and co-create. A story from the Zohar tells of King Solomon's method for gaining wisdom. This essentially amounts to a Kabbalistic prayer guide honoring the distinct powers of each of the six directions of space and their corresponding Sefirot on the Tree of Life, by which we consciously make our lives aspects of divine service.[35]

---

[33] Zeir Anpin is referred to by the single, central Sefirah of Tiferet but assumed to include Yesod, Hod, Netzach, Tiferet, Gevurah, and Chesed, in ascending order.

[34] In most traditional teachings, King David is associated with Malchut, the origin of Moshiach. In this teaching, however, he is the exemplar of the servant, and thus his song text falls in the Sefirah of Hod, which we shall examine in chapter 5.

[35] The noted American Kabbalist and author Rabbi Aryeh Kaplan (1934–1983) writes extensively on this topic in his translation of the Sefer Yetzirah and in his book *Inner Space: Introduction to Kabbalah, Meditation and Prophecy,* for those interested in exploring further a three-dimensional exploration of the Tree of Life and related meditations.

The Work of Service

In Yesod we initiate the arena of consecration and the Ruach (spirit) aspect of the soul, that which is spirit within the body and soul. It is appropriate that the Outer Court where such consecration takes place includes the three Sefirot of Netzach, Hod, and Yesod (known by the acronym NeHiY). In the Zohar these three are called the Lower Chariot. The three Sefirot above this triad, Chesed, Gevurah, and Tiferet (as expressed by the acronym ChaGaT), are called the Upper Chariot, which complements the Lower Chariot, just as our arms do our legs; all are connected through the torso, where the heart is housed.

In the partzufim system, the six Sefirot of consecration, including the Lower Chariot and the Upper Chariot, are called Zeir Anpin, the Son. The Son's purpose is to mate with the female Nukvah, as represented by Malchut, just as the six days of the week do the Sabbath. Above the six Sefirot of Zeir Anpin are the attributes of the mind and intellect (*sechol*) as found in the triad of Chochmah, Binah, and Daat (ChaBaD) or in this work, the triad of Keter, Chochmah, and Binah (KaChaBa).[36] Keter is analogous to the light that illuminates the Holy of Holies and realm of Adam Kadmon (primordial man of earth), which, according to the Ramchal, is the root of the Third Temple.[37]

The light that shines on the High Priest on the one day of the year that he enters the Holy of Holies to make direct contact with God, Yom Kippur (as related in chapter 12), just as it shone on the people in the revelation at Mt. Sinai (as recounted in chapter 9), is the same light that emanates from Keter to each aspect and function of the ritual process within the Tabernacle. So too it is taught that the light of Creation shines inside the holy Ark, as it does in Torah. Thus when Torah's teachings are embodied, the outcome will be a perfected humankind, which is referred to as *Gemar Hatikkun* (the final redemption of Israel), symbolized by the coming Third

---

[36] In Kabbalistic frameworks one deals with ten Sefirot. As Keter is analogous with the unseen, concealed light of HaShem, one cannot know this Sefirah in direct experience as we do the other Sefirot. However, when examining Adam Kadmon, as we do in this work, Daat is understood to be the result of Chochmah (wisdom) and Binah (understanding), producing Daat (knowledge), so we speak instead of Keter, Chochmah, and Binah as the intellect (*sechol*).

[37] In classical Zohar, Chochmah is associated with Atzilut; Binah with Beriyah; and Daat with Yetzirah.

Temple. The Third Temple and world peace mark both the beginning and the end of the human story, making Keter the root of this perfection that comes down to us in stages. In Kabbalah, this personal and collective perfection comes from the realm of our own Holy of Holies, which receives the light of Creation directly from God.

Offering a Song of Love

Each person who brings God their prayer and song brings an offering to the Tent of Meeting. With prayer as the foundation—meaning the arena in which the Tent of Meeting stands—the offering of a song of love is our way of participating in the ritual process, standing just outside the Tent's single gate where the priests enter the Outer Court. That it is thirty feet wide suggests the letter Lamed, whose numerical value is 30. Often called "the queen of the Alef-Bet" (the Hebrew alphabet), Lamed is the teacher at the gate of life. Entering the Tent of Meeting is a life-long journey of learning and dedication, of coming into rapport with the Godhead and divinity in all life and in all life forms. When we dedicate our life to reverent service, we enter that holy gate.

In the Hebrew Bible, Solomon's Song of Songs, along with Ruth, Lamentations, Ecclesiastes, and Esther, comprise the five scrolls, or Five Megillot, read on various religious festivals of the Jewish year. The Shir HaShirim (also called the Canticle of Canticles) is read at the Sabbath service during Passover (Pesach), which celebrates the beginning of the Exodus of the Israelites from Egypt.

Fire and Water

Prayer, the first rung of our ascent of the ladder of light, grounds us in the earth from which we are made; this is the "kingdom" where we have sovereignty. When we pray, our decorum is a reflection of the wisdom and great brilliance that emanate from the crown (Keter) of the Divine Immanence. Our prayers reflect the emanations we receive from above, experienced as an emotional welling-up, which in Yesod leads to our crying out with desire from the heart. Our tears—for we may actually be moved to tears of longing and joy—are said to represent the water libations of the High Priest, while the experience of intense and arous-ing love (fire) in prayer and conversation with God is our fire ritual. In consecrating our lives to serving God in this way we burn away the ego, thereby removing any protective covering (brit) of the heart that might prevent us from feeling God's divine love for us. Then we bathe in the love we experience.

First there is the fire of ardor, of desire for the Other. After the intense experience of merging with the Divine Immanence, we purify our hearts and entire being. Might the cloud (or mist, or steam) that results from this inner alchemical process of fire on water be a sign of having made contact with the Divine Presence in the Holy of Holies, the personal experience of the Cloud of Glory within? The brit of the heart, like the circumcision of the phallus of the Jewish male baby on the eighth day of life, expresses the ways the People of the Book keep their covenant with God; this is the perfection of Yesod, the spiritual and physical foundation of the covenant between humankind and deity.

Lovemaking as a Metaphor

The Song of Songs has been likened to a record of the relationship between a man and a woman. It tells of early and mature love, seduction and conjugality, and it extols the benefits of lovemaking not only for human reproduction, but for increasing the flame of divine devotion as well. Prayer is compared to the ritual of coupling (zivug), which is why at the beginning of prayer one might sway with great motion, as in the initial stages of lovemaking, but then become very still. While the Song of Songs is both a symbolic and a literal story of love, it should also be considered an allegory of prayer, in which the initiate goes through various stages in the devotional practice. After the preparation of nullifying oneself in Malchut, we then focus on this joyful reaching out, to experience coupling with God and the Shechinah.

What comes from this spiritual intercourse is the birth of the love that has been invested in the prayer itself. The pleasure the ritual of prayer gives the body and soul can be as real and knowable as the pleasure a couple derives from the act of lovemaking. And just as in lovemaking between partners there is a momentary silence that comes after experiencing ecstatic pleasure, there is similarly a brief flood of light following any ecstatic experience of surrendering body and soul. When we take our leave from this kind of intense spiritual experience, there can arise a sense of distance and separation, a descent from the elevated state of ecstatic bliss. And just as we know this from the physical experience of the love bed, we must also know that such a state exists on the spiritual level—that spiritual ecstasy is attainable, as practitioners of the world's wisdom teachings know and experience.

The flame of devotion coupled with the healing waters of prayer, when spoken with great sincerity, are the rewards of prayer. These create a great spiritual fire and great luminous waters within us. This is how we create fire from water, an alchemical reality that can be re-created in one's personal life. This bestows on the initiate an ongoing capacity for emanation. When our brilliant inner fire reflects on our heart's waters, like sunlight reflecting on the surface of a lake, which looks like sparkling diamonds, we each become a gem of deity's being.

The Sacrificial Offerings

> And the LORD spoke unto Moses, saying: "Speak unto Aaron
> and to his sons, saying: 'This is the law of the sin-offering: in the
> place where the burnt-offering is slaughtered shall the sin-offering
> be slaughtered before the LORD; it is most holy. The priest who
> performs its sin offering service shall eat it; it shall be eaten in a
> holy place: in the Courtyard of the Tent of Meeting.'"
>
> LEVITICUS 6:17–19

The Outer Court is where the priests burn the offerings of the petitioner or their own offerings. The subject of sacrificial offerings made in the Outer Court is a vast one in Jewish law, with minute details regarding the specifics of the animal, grain, or fruit being offered, as well as the manner and time of offering it. For example, some of the free will offerings can be eaten by the penitent and community anywhere in Jerusalem, while the sin offerings made by the individual can only be eaten by the priests while in the Outer Court itself.

The details of the Levitical offerings, the main sacrifices used in rituals, are outlined in Leviticus 1 through 7. Burnt offerings, meal offerings, peace offerings, and sin and trespass offerings are the five basic kinds of sacrifices made in the Outer Court of the Ohel Moed, plus an offering related to the red heifer, each component of the various offerings is far more detailed than the scope of this work can provide, but suffice it to say that by making various types of offerings, the initiate and the community at large benefits. In some cases the remains of offerings are used to feed the priests (meal offerings, sin offerings); other sacrifices, such as burnt offerings, are entirely consumed by the fire; while still others, such as peace offerings, remain for the petitioner and the general community to share.

Various aspects of our own inner journey require that we make sin offerings, peace offerings, and so forth; the reader is invited to further explore this area in greater detail. In general, though, we concern ourselves in this work with the basic understanding that everything described as ritual inside the Ohel Moed (or Tent of Communion, as the Ohel is also called) can be found within our own life and life journey. Thus we find in the different kinds of sacrifices made in the Ohel the instructions for various kinds of personal repair (*tikkun*) that we can make through sacrifice, recalling that sacrifice means we give up something of our own property, inner nature, outer behavior, or attitudes. Some of these sacrifices concern our personal inner lives (sin offerings); some affect the welfare of our relationships (peace offerings); some are to express praise and gratitude (meal offerings); while trespass offerings are made for unintentional misdeeds.

The Song of Songs and the Holy of Holies

When Rabbi Akiva speaks of the Song of Songs as being analogous to the Holy of Holies, this suggests the holiday of Yom Kippur, when the High Priest makes his annual entry into the innermost sanctum of the Tabernacle, where the light of Creation is held. On that day the seal of Torah and life is made on every living being, it having been already decided who will flourish, or, God forbid, perish.

We have already learned in our study of Malchut that prayer is the process of bonding with our forefathers and foremothers, of accepting the reality of Resurrection, realization, and peace. Here, Yesod can be thought of as the glory that is concealed in the Outer Court rituals, which emanate from the Holy of Holies. It is this illumination from Keter and Chochmah that Yesod uses to bind us to our covenant with God, our desire for union with Him, to in fact be like Him, which is the seal on the human soul. This is our foundation; it is the meaning underlying Yesod and the purpose of our spiritual covenant.

Utilizing the Powers of the Tree of Life

In the Zohar, Solomon tells of visiting the oppression of the world and seeing those who die in childhood, in their mothers' laps. He also says, "So I returned, and considered all the oppressions that are done under the sun: and behold the tears of such as were oppressed, and they had no comforter: and on the side of their oppressors there was power: but they had no comforter."[38] Simply stated, he found that both the oppressed and their oppressors suffered. So thirsty was the king for wisdom and understanding that he looked to all parts of the world to gain knowledge to improve the world. "Daily Solomon would rise early, first face eastward, namely to Tiferet and the central column, and see what he saw. Later he would turn to the south, namely Chesed and the right column, and see what he saw. Later he would turn northward, being Gevurah and the left column, stand there, lower his eyes, and raise his head."[39]

Practical Kabbalah engages the practitioner in utilizing the primary powers and directions in space that each of the six Sefirot of Zeir Anpin (Chesed through Yesod) represent. In the passage above, which describes the Sefirot on the three pillars of the Tree of Life, one learns that Chesed is south; thus to pray for abundance one prays facing south. For discernment and courage one prays facing north, toward Gevurah. Tiferet, the Sefirah of truth, beauty, and mercy, is in the east, the orientation of the Tabernacle's entry gate. All six Sefirot describe a cube of space, including the remaining three Sefirot of Netzach (which is above us), representing our enduring will and attachment to what is eternal, namely God; Hod (which is below us), suggesting our humility and majesty; and Yesod, signifying our covenant with God and all that that implies (which is west and back behind us).[40]

Wisdom is the outcome of the awareness and intention we invest in all our actions. Practices such as these engage all parts of our being in the outer and inner dimensions of experience. The intention we invest in these kinds of activities facilitates our becoming a vessel for receiving divine insight.

---

[38] Zohar, Mishpatim 10:339.
[39] Ibid.
[40] For more information, see R. Aryeh Kaplan, *Sefer Yetzirah*, 82–87.

Spiritual Development:
Beginning Divine Service

Prayer and Malchut, our first rung on the ladder of light, represent the kingdom the soul inhabits energetically while we live. To pray is to nurture the body and the soul. Through daily self-evaluation and making an effort to renew our attachment to God, we are prepared to leave this realm of action, Asiyah, to enter Yesod and the realm of formation, Yetzirah, or what is sometimes called "making" (derived from the Hebrew word *yetzirah,* which means "formation"). Just as the generative organs are necessary for making life in the physical world, so is the longing for union with the divine crucial in making one an anointed human being.

In Yesod we are now able to commit with the totality of body, heart, and soul to divine service. We consecrate our body and soul to this purpose. We see everything in life through the lens of divine worship and devotion, including all of created life and all that we do, from keeping our homes or places of employment in harmony, to improving our own conduct a little each day. We are invited into the realm of eternity (Netzach) and majesty (Hod), where our covenant with God (Yesod) is turned into action (Malchut). In this practice we enter the river of timelessness, where all souls making this great commitment meet. Call it a community of meditators, worshippers, or people in prayer—all over the world, men, women, and children are committing time in their lives for these quiet and robust spiritual practices, including praise and thanksgiving for the field of life that we are all part of. Kabbalah says that what we give our attention to increases in power and presence.

Balancing Masculine and Feminine

Solomon and the Sefirah of Yesod represent the doorway to commitment, to consecrating our lives to God and the divine middle path. Here we cry out to God with joy for the divinity that is in fact shared between the Creator and created. Here in the sanctified Tabernacle we inaugurate our divine service. We conjoin our reason (male) and intuition (female); our desire to give (male) and our desire to receive (female). In so doing, we open the doorway for the Holy Spirit to rest upon us. This brings greater clarity, knowing what one should do in any situation.

Our sages tell us that we are in the age of Yesod, when all aspects of sexuality and sexual identity are rectified within the person, between the genders, and within society at large, as male and female aspects come into harmony. It is noteworthy that Yesod's song, the Song of Songs, is an allegorical love poem containing much erotic imagery. Just as the love bed facilitates the holy act of co-creation with God and enables a deeper kind of communication and pleasure for a couple, the Temple, a communal sanctuary, elevates the congregants simultaneously, their shared prayers energetically amplified.

Solitude, though, is also essential to communing with God, as the prophets show us in their wanderings in nature—in fields, forests, mountains, and near rivers, the places where they hear the voice of the Ruach HaKodesh. It was in such a state of rapport with the Holy Spirit that Solomon composed his Song of Songs, an expression of the illumination of the Holy of Holies and the wisdom of Chochmah. In this way Solomon "heard" the Song of Songs (through the voice of the Holy Spirit) and wrote it down. He knew the future exiles that Israel would suffer and knew the longing for return that would occupy their lives: "My Beloved is mine, he fills all my needs and I seek from Him and none other. He grazes me in rose like bounty" (Song of Songs 2:16–17).

The Importance of Humility

As we have seen, the kingdom of Malchut shows us the access we have to the wisdom and knowledge of the world through devoted study and service. Here in Yesod the initiate gains the glory of righteousness, which is not measured by one's perfection but rather by one's humility in admitting one's flaws and by making an effort to change, as Solomon demonstrates in acknowledging his excesses and his downfalls. We learn that righteousness is not an attained state; it is an ongoing occupation that a person undertakes as a lifelong devotional service.

Here we give up our limited selfhood—the attachments and concepts of the ego—and open to learning the sacred teachings the Holy Spirit imparts to the humble. The prayers of the humble initiate who has consecrated his or her heart and surrendered totally to God are returned in the form of divine light from the world of emanation (Atzilut) through the filters of creation (Beriyah) and formation (Yetzirah), which finally reach the physical world of action (Asiyah), giving the person great pleasure (ta'anug). This pleasure is a taste of Gan Eden, the garden celebrated in the Song of Songs.

Becoming God-like

All of Torah and all of Zohar direct the heart and soul to loving attendance of and union with God. Union means closeness, and closeness means likeness in Kabbalistic thinking. How is the human to become God-like? The Sefirot direct various degrees of light to our head, limbs, and torso (organs); when we pay attention to these measured sources of Godliness from each Sefirah, they can help us refine ourselves and make us more conscious and better able to fulfill our individual and collective destiny. Keter, Chochmah, and Binah (KaChaBa) represent an abundant overflow of the crowning light of God, or Keter, also referred to as Adam Kadmon (in his abode of Gan Eden), which we will discuss more fully in chapter 12. The soul is already complete; but when the individual desires change as a path of purification, a spiritual fire builds within, just as it does on the Outer Court's fire altar. It is this passion to do in the world that Solomon so beautifully embodies.

The legends of Solomon allude to the province of illumination available to us all when we innocently ask God to give us insight and a charitable heart, to remove the desire to receive for oneself alone, and implant in us a Creator-like desire to give, for this, as Rabbi Yehudah Leib Ashlag clarifies in his translation and commentary of the Zohar, is the essential teaching of God to his creation. God has no desire for Himself, no need to receive. He created humanity with the loving desire for us to become beings who desire most of all to give, to bestow, as He does. What parent does not want their child to have a bountiful, healthy, and joyful life and gives selflessly in order to foster these conditions?

Even more so than a dramatic change in one's actions, it is the disposition of the heart that is taught by Solomon, Yesod, and consecration. Yesod is the second step in the journey of refining the heart on the middle path. The middle path, the path of justice and truth that emanates from the Sefirah of Tiferet, brings together the right pillar of loving-kindness and mercy in Chesed and the left pillar of strength and judgment in Gevurah. As such it is the guiding power used by the Creator throughout the Tree of Life.

Our Interconnectedness

The Shechinah, or Divine Immanence, referred to in feminine terms as it represents the enveloping feminine essence of God, is said to illuminate all life to varying degrees. Whenever any one of us is sick, She is sick. Whenever we are in emotional turmoil, the Shechinah experiences this. All of life is interconnected in this way. The Torah teaches that we are a unity of individuals—that what any one of us does affects the world, and that our own lives and bodies reflect this interconnected reality. Kabbalah teaches that each of us is a sovereign kingdom arranged in octaves of relatedness. For example, while the eye is for seeing, it also represents the Sefirah of Chochmah, the Father, or wisdom. It is through this Sefirah and our own anatomical makeup that the greatest and purest light of the Or En Sof, from the realm of Adam Kadmon and emanation (Atzilut), illuminates the human being. This suggests the importance of guarding the holy gates of our eyes from seeing unholy things, as the body-soul experiences images as if they were actual events happening in real time. The Holy of Holies is related to the Mercy Seat and the two winged cherubim. It corresponds to the Yechidah aspect of the soul, that which resides entirely outside of the mortal body but which animates the soul. In other words, all physical parts of our anatomy have spiritual counterparts in the various worlds (Asiyah, Yetzirah, Beriyah, Atzilut, Adam Kadmon) and parts of the soul (the Nefesh, Ruach, Neshamah, Chayah, and Yechidah).

For this reason, illness, we learn, has its root in a spiritual component of the soul's development; the disrepair of the body is merely the last expression of a spiritual need. The Creator, in His mercy, allows us to heal and find peace in our health challenges by giving us the remedies we need and the understanding that makes our life's journey meaningful. It is heartening to learn from the sages that God creates the remedy before He creates the illness, reminding us that disrepair, or a diminishment in any aspect of our lives, is for our eventual elevation.

The Coming Third Temple

Solomon's Temple, called the *Beit HaMikdash,* "the house of that which is holy," was built in 960 BCE and destroyed by the Babylonians in 586 BCE, when the Israelites were exiled to Babylonian captivity. Construction of the Second Temple began in 535 BCE and was completed in 516

BCE and dedicated in 515 BCE.[41] The Second Temple stood until 70 CE, when the Romans destroyed Jerusalem and the Temple (ending the Great Jewish Revolt against Rome that had begun in 66 CE). From this point in history, without a temple in which to worship God, without a place honoring His presence, the People of the Book's 2,000-year span of homelessness and exile can be dated, their work considered not yet done.

As without so within: without a place of worship in our lives, in our hearts, our inner work is incomplete and we are, in effect, homeless, in spiritual exile. The loss of this focus in human culture has resulted in the spiritual diminishment so characteristic of the technological age. Multidimensional and intradimensional awareness is our legacy; we benefit from having a time of worship and a place for God's presence in our lives. Dedicating the use of our refined emotions, as expressed through our limbs, generative organs, and heart, to the spiritual divinity that pervades all of life is the field of consecration, that is, Yesod through Chesed, which the initiate enters after mastering prayer.

The building of the First Temple and then the Second Temple marked the stages of Israel's development and exile. Today people pray for the coming Third Temple, which some say will be built by human hands with God's help, while others suggest it will be built by God and placed here miraculously intact. I join with those who suggest it must be both: the collective desire of humanity to reach a place of peace and unity will be the vessel that will enable the hierarchal realms of God's legions to help us build the mirror reflection of the holy Temple that already exists in the supernal realms here on earth, and within each one of us.

The Sanctuaries Above

The Ramchal, in his *Mishkney Elyon* (meaning "Dwellings of the Supreme," titled *Secrets of the Future Temple* in an English translation), offers the premise of this book: that before a sanctuary can be built on

---

[41] This Second Temple was missing the Ark of the Covenant, the Urim and Thummim, the holy oil, the sacred fire, the Ten Commandments, the pot of manna, and Aaron's rod. The Kodesh Hakodashim (Holy of Holies) was separated by curtains rather than a wall, as in the First Temple. As in the Tabernacle, there was only one golden lamp for the Holy Place, one table of shewbread, and the incense altar with golden censers and many of the vessels of gold that had belonged to Solomon's Temple that had been carried to Babylon but restored by Cyrus the Great (Ezra 1:7–11).

earth it must be built above. The holy earthly Tent of Meeting is based on a heavenly Tent of Meeting. The vision of Ezekiel[42] regarding the building of the Third Temple—the subject of *Mishkney Elyon*—is possible because Ezekiel saw it in the upper worlds. The Chazal (sages) reflect that when the First Temple was destroyed, the template for the final, eternal Temple had already been created, showing the spiritual seeker future final outcome many centuries in advance, as the Ramchal makes clear:

> The Heavenly Temple is mentioned in a number of places in rabbinic literature. In the Talmud we find: "Rabbi Yochanan said: The Holy One blessed-be-He declared: 'I will not enter the heavenly Jerusalem until I enter the earthly Jerusalem.' Is there then a heavenly Jerusalem? Yes, as it is written (Psalms 122:3): 'Jerusalem will be built like the city that is joined to it together'" (Taanit 5a). The Zohar states that "the earthly Sanctuary depends upon the Upper Sanctuary, and that Upper Sanctuary depends in turn upon another Upper Sanctuary, which is the most exalted of all. All of them are included in one another, and this is the meaning of the verse (Exodus 26:6): 'And the Sanctuary was *one*.'" (Zohar Pekudey II, 235a)[43]

This Kabbalistic statement indicates that there are *two* heavenly sanctuaries, one above the other, which explains the phrase from Psalms that the Ramchal took as the title of his seminal work: "There is a river whose streams bring joy to the city of God, the holy place of the dwellings of the Supreme [Mishkney Elyon]" (Psalms 46:5). The Hebrew term *Mishkney Elyon* can be translated as "the sanctuaries above," alluding to the two heavenly sanctuaries mentioned in the Zohar.[44] Thus the Third Temple will be brought into being when each one of us is made whole, when we make our lives vessels in which the holy presence can dwell.

The song of Yesod, the Shir HaShirim, is a declaration between God

---

[42] Ezekiel 10:4: "Then the glory of the LORD rose up from upon the cherubim and rested upon the threshold of the Temple; and the Temple was filled with the cloud, and the courtyard was filled with the glow of His glory."

[43] R. Moshe Chaim Luzzatto, trans. R.A.Y Greenbaum, *Mishkney Elyon* (*Secrets of the Future Temple*), 20.

[44] Luzzatto, *Mishkney Elyon,* 20.

and the Temple, between humankind and God, and between God and His holy resting place. It is a love song of unity of one heart. The standard Jewish prayer book concludes with 2 Chronicles, where the king of Persia orders the construction of the Second Temple: "Thus saith Cyrus King of Persia: All the kingdoms of the earth hath the LORD, the God of heaven, given me; and He hath charged me to build Him a house in Jerusalem, which is in Judah. Whosoever there is among you of all His people—the LORD his God be with him—let him go up" (2 Chronicles 36:23). Here the Temple and the righteous person are one and the same. The Tabernacle, as well as the heart, is where one's offerings of humility and thanksgiving are made. One's very existence on earth becomes a unity with God—body and Temple, devotion and service of the heart combined.

> "And if thou wilt walk in My ways, to keep My statutes and
> My commandments, as thy father David did walk, then I will
> lengthen thy days." And Solomon awoke, and, behold, it was a
> dream; and he came to Jerusalem, and stood before the ark of the
> covenant of the LORD, and offered up burnt-offerings, and offered
> peace-offerings, and made a feast to all his servants.
>
> 1 KINGS 3:14 15

The Purpose of the Soul

The throne of the soul is the environment we make for it in our lives: how we live, what we do, who we reach out to, where we put our energy—all are signifiers of the sefirotic qualities that inform the body, the mind, the heart, and the soul. Life is ever changing, always in flux; yet our objective is constant: to refine our nature so that we do not lose sight (Chochmah) of our purpose, that of being a co-creator. The prophet Micah put it clearly: "What is the purpose of thee O man? To love mercy, to pursue justice, to walk humbly with thy God."[45]

As King Solomon is pivotal in the history of the Jewish people, so is Yesod the linchpin between our emotional nature (Zeir Anpin, the six Sefirot of Chesed through Yesod) and our willing desires (Malchut, the realm of action). What we do elevates the world. In consecration we take

---

[45] Micah 6:8.

the physical and spiritual talents we have and commit them to service of the divine. This is why Yesod illuminates the person who devotes him- or herself to loving God. Like the daily offerings that take place in the Outer Court of the Tabernacle, our daily actions can be offerings for the very same purpose of sacrifice and service. As it is said in the oral tradition: "**Let a beloved** (King Solomon; 2 Samuel 12:24–25), **the descendant of a beloved** (Abraham; Jeremiah 11:15) **come and build a beloved** [edifice] (the Temple; Psalms 84:2) **for a Beloved One** (the Holy One, Blessed is He; Isaiah 5:1) **in the territory of a beloved one** (Benjamin; Deuteronomy 33:12) **in which beloved ones** (the people of Israel; Jeremiah 12:7) **will be atoned for.**"[46]

Solomon and the Sefirah of Yesod teach us fervent surrender and abandonment of one's narrow sense of the self, necessary in loving God. In the next rung of our ascension of the ladder of light, his father, King David, whose lineage is the root of Moshiach, messianic consciousness, guides us in devoted humility as a servant to the Creator, showing us the true nature of nobility.

---

[46] Menachos 53b. See also Chasidah, *Encyclopedia of Biblical Personalities,* 502.

5
Sincere and Humble Heart of Majesty
Hod • Song of Thanksgiving

I will praise God's name in song and Glorify Him with thanksgiving.

PSALMS 69:30

Eighth Sefirot: Hod
Meaning: Glory, majesty, thanksgiving
Rung on Ascending Ladder: Three
Archetype: The Son (Zeir Anpin)
Symbol: The home and heart as sanctuary
Spiritual World: Yetzirah/formation
Spiritual Anatomy: Left leg/left hip
Inner Quality: Sincerity (temimut)

Historical Personage: King David
Text: 2 Samuel 22:1–51, and Tehillim (Psalms)
Key Words: Praise and piety; purity and sincerity
Key Emotion in Song: Majestic humility (hodu'ah)

Tent of Meeting: Outer Court
Spiritual Stage: Consecration; sincerely sanctifying one's life
Spiritual Practice: Humility and praise of God
Illumination: The illumination of the pure and humble heart

> With King David and the Sefirah of Hod, we discover our own
> inner majesty as part of a royal human family whose standard,
> humility, brings each of us to divine glory.

The Sefirah Hod: Humbled Majesty

As we continue the process of consecration, of dedicating our lives to serving the divine, King David, the father of King Solomon, teaches us about true service and humility. The Sefirah of Hod is about majesty and glory. Here we discover that our legs are not just for walking, but also for bowing, kneeling, and prostrating with complete sincerity. Hod, whose anatomical association is the left leg, is partnered with Netzach, the right leg, which is associated with victory and eternity.

Hod is an element of Yetzirah, the realm of formation; it corresponds to the emotions and mastery of one's impulses. In our ascension of the Tree of Life, we must first dedicate ourselves to divine service (in Malchut), centering ourself in prayer; and then express our deep love of God as the Beloved (in Yesod), crying out in joy in uniting with Him. At this, the third stage in the process of consecration, we must now focus on surrendering the ego to God and commit to serving His will, and so with complete sincerity we offer humble thanksgiving, totally relinquishing our desire to His will.

The offerings representing both earth (agrarian products) and fire (animals offered for sacrifice), as well as the water libations, all of which take place in the Outer Court of the Tabernacle, involve all six Sefirot of Zeir Anpin, the partzuf of the Son. *Zeir Anpin* is an Aramaic term meaning "the small face of God" (which can be a reference to the High Priest), while the term *Arich Anpin,* a reference to the uppermost Sefirah of Keter, refers to "the long face of God." These designations imply the stages of spiritual development as we ascend the ladder of light as well as the intensity of the light of God as reflected in each Sefirah. A son, as we know, is not as mature as his father, who is less mature than the grandfather (or "Ancient One," the alternative term in the system of the partzufim). In the very same way, our emotions, as signified by Zeir Anpin, are less developed than our intellect, represented by the uppermost Sefirot of Keter, Chochmah, and Binah (KaChaBa). Hod, which is part of the six-part construct of Zeir Anpin and which lies on the left pillar of the Tree of Life, shows us the great strength needed to surrender at this stage in our development. We must have great faith to give up our preconceived notions of who we are, what we have, what we are to do, and when we are to do it. As the Sefirah of Hod, as exemplified by the life of King David, reveals, the Holy Spirit comes to the one who makes himself an empty vessel in which the Divine Presence can reside.

Sincere Thanksgiving and Humility

Sincerity—of one's will, heart, and actions—is the quintessence of Hod. There is a seriousness of will, simplicity in surrender and trust, and an inner desire for union with God, which is said to be a God-given attribute. The word *temimut,* "sincerity" (also translated as "innocence"), appears in Torah in reference to Hod and Hod's right-pillar partner, Netzach, in the sense that the act of walking, which takes both the right and left legs, is coupled with this quality of the sincere heart.[1] To attain the sincere heart of King David means we must arrive at our own deep and personal holy relationship with supreme wisdom. This informs Hod's emotional quality of sincere thanksgiving.

Humility is required in any spiritual journey. It is this humble yet dignified procession that each of us makes as part of the royal court that will ultimately bring peace on earth. There is a quality of majesty in this kind of surrender, just as there is in the services that take place in this stage of consecration in the Tent of Meeting. Everything has its proper time and place. Humility facilitates our having this sense of timing because it makes us open to the Holy Sprit and the indwelling luminosity of the Holy One's love, which guides our hearts and souls. We act because we have an inner connection to something greater than that which is dictated by our own personal desires.

The Hebrew sages say that God made the world for us, each one of

---

[1] See the writings of R. Yitzhak Ginsburg, available at www.inner.org.

us. Our souls, like stone block hewed from a mountain, are taken from God's wholeness. Since the "thought of Creation was to give enjoyment to His creatures, it follows that He created with the souls an extremely great measure of the 'will to receive.'"[2] It is this will to receive *in order to give,* as the Creator does, that King David embodies in his rulership of Israel. This is why it is said that it is from King David's lineage that the Moshiach and unity consciousness will come. This also reminds us that it is through humanity's collective humility that peace on earth can be realized.

King David: Servant of God

King David's story is told twice in Torah: first in 1 Samuel and then in 1 Chronicles. The accounts vary, but the essential landmarks of the narrative remain the same.

Before the first kings of Israel, the prophets ruled the nation. Prior to King Saul, David's predecessor, the prophet Samuel, ruled and judged Israel. "He would travel year after year, circling to Beth-el, Gilgal and Mizpah, and judging Israel in all these places. Then he would return to Ramah, for his home was there, and there he would judge Israel. And there he built an altar to God" (1 Samuel 7:15–17).

As Samuel grew old, he appointed his sons as judges over Israel, but they perverted justice, requiring fees likened to bribery. It was in this state of national chaos and distrust that "all the elders of Israel then gathered together and came to Samuel, to Ramah. 'So now appoint for us a king to judge us, like all the nations have'" (1 Samuel 8:5). When the elders made this request, Samuel knew that it was a destructive desire, so he prayed to God. God answered, saying,

> Listen to the voices of the people in all that they say to you, for it is not you whom they have rejected, but it is Me whom they have rejected from reigning over them. Like all their deeds that they have done from the day I brought them up from Egypt until this day—they forsook Me and worshipped the gods of others, so are they doing to you, as well. And now heed their voice, but be sure to warn them and tell

---

[2] R. Moshe Chayim Luzzatto, *General Principles of Kabbalah,* preface, xv.

them about the protocol of the king who will reign over them. (1 Samuel 8:7–9)

Forsaking the Divine Ruler for a Worldly King

Despite his opposition to the idea of a king, Samuel proceeds as instructed by the Lord, warning the people that a king will take away their sons and put them into military service, use them to make the instruments of war, including the chariots they would have to manage, and require them to farm and harvest as well. He will take a tenth of their grain and vine, Samuel explains, and give them to the officers and servants. "He will take your servants and your maidservants and your best young men and your donkeys and press them into his service. He will take a tenth of your sheep and you will be his slaves. On that day you will cry out because of your king whom you have chosen for yourselves—but God will not answer you on that day" (1 Samuel 8:10–23). But having lost faith in their unseen divine ruler, the people want someone they can point to as their protector and arbitrator over the land, a king who will go out before them in battle. And so the background of David's appearance on the world stage is B'nai Yisrael's diminished state of faith.

According to Chassidut, the warnings God gives the people via the prophet Samuel are relevant in our own lives: when we let passing whims rule us we become slaves. All addictions, whether physical, emotional, or psychological, are rooted in this impulse of losing faith in one's own connection to divine right order, substituting desire for immediate gratification over enduring faith, just as the Israelites did when begging to have a human king rule over them. When we want what others have, we give up our freedom and autonomy, no longer steering our own course but imitating someone else's. A person who is not in control of his own life, who is guided by selfish or negative emotions and addictive tendencies, becomes a slave to the flux of desire rather than a master of the emotions and a humble servant of the higher heart-mind, where wisdom is found.

The Reign of King Saul

Enter Saul: more handsome, we are told, than anyone in Israel. At his father's request, Saul goes out to find his family's lost donkeys. After passing through various lands looking for them, to no avail, Saul's servant suggests they go find the seer, the prophet Samuel. Meanwhile, Samuel has been told by God that a young man will be coming "tomorrow from the land of Benjamin; you shall anoint him to be ruler over my people, Israel, and he will save My people from the hand of the Philistines" (1 Samuel 9:16).

Being from the smallest tribe, that of Benjamin, Saul doubts Samuel's praise of him upon their meeting. Nevertheless, after eating with Samuel and some thirty guests, Saul is anointed by the prophet, who kisses the young man, saying, "God has anointed you as ruler over His heritage" (1 Samuel 10:1).

So begins Saul's rule, and his eventual ruin. Samuel instructs Saul to wait for seven days and he will join him in Gilgal, the last station on the route of the Exodus (discussed in chapter 8), for the ritual sacrifice that comes with his public anointing. But mirroring an earlier time in biblical history,[3] Saul's impatience leads him to interfere with God's divine plan. And so instead of waiting as instructed for the right time and place for his official anointing, Saul decides his own will is more important than the Lord's, and he takes matters into his own hands, offering ritual sacrifices before the prophet's return. When Samuel does return a week later, he tells Saul he has disobeyed him and defied the Word of God. As a result, Saul's kingdom will not endure, Samuel says. Despite this inauspicious beginning, Saul is anointed anyway, and Samuel gives a stern warning to the people to follow the Word of God or else they and their king will perish.

Some time later, Saul is told by God to kill the Amalekite king, Agog, along with his people because they had slaughtered the Israelites' weak and infirm as they were leaving Egypt, but he fails to do so. Not only that, Saul lets Agog live and keeps the best of the Amalekite animals (and, some say, women). Since Saul consistently does what he pleases instead of following God's instructions, Samuel must be the one to carry out the will of God. He leaves Saul that day, never to see him again—making it clear that God has withdrawn his support of Saul, to the point where God says, "'I repent that I have set up Saul as king, for he has

---

[3] The Israelites, led by Aaron, became restless after Moses ascended Mt. Sinai and miscounted the forty days Moses said he would be on the mountain by a day. This resulted in their disobeying Moses' explicit instructions to wait for his return.

turned back from following Me, and has not performed My command-ments.' And it grieved Samuel, and he cried out to the Lord all night" (1 Samuel 15:11–29).

The Elevation of David ben Jesse

God tells Samuel to go to Bethlehem and inquire after the sons of Jesse, of whom David is the youngest. The prophet proceeds on God's instruc-tions and anoints Jesse's youngest son, the sheepherder David ben Jesse, who is brought back to Jerusalem. It is at this time Torah records that "the spirit of God passed over [i.e., rested with] David from that day on," and the spirit of God departed from Saul, who "was tormented by a spirit of melancholy from God" (1 Samuel 16:13–14).

As a result of Samuel's discovery of God's next chosen one, David is brought into Saul's court, at first to serve as the king's harp player, so that Saul's soul would be soothed, for when the king is possessed by what is described as an evil spirit he acts like a madman. We see in this sequence of events that Saul's initial elevation to the position of king was part of God's plan to eventually bring David to the throne; certainly Saul's ele-vated position did not come as a result of his own self-refinement—which shows us the danger of putting people not in control of their own emo-tions into positions of power.

After David plays his lyre, the sweet music does indeed quell the king's ill temper, and David is confirmed as the king's personal arms bearer and harp player. Thus God brings David into the king's house-hold. In David's story we observe God changing his mind, seeing in Saul's behavior the degree to which "the other side," that is, the sitra achra, has gotten hold of him; now God regrets having made him king.[4] Yet as an example of concealed good, this act of God placing an unworthy man on the throne is for the eventual elevation of the nation and the world.

---

[4] As a result of Saul's animosity toward David, David must both defend himself from Saul's nefarious intentions toward him as well as protect the people from their common enemies. David hides in a cave. This recalls the plight of the author of the Zohar, R. Shi-mon Bar Yochai (Rashbi), who was a student of R. Akiva at the time when the Romans ruled in Jerusalem during the first century CE. After his teacher was put to death, Shi-mon, along with his son Rabbi Eleazar ben Simeon, hid in a cave, where they remained for thirteen years, until the end of Roman rule.

David's Aliyah

David gains initial fame as a warrior when he slays the Philistine giant Goliath with a single slingshot to the head. David refused to wear armor on this dangerous mission, and so upon his victorious return, Saul's son Jonathan, who loves David dearly, gives him his own princely robe and weapons to use in battle. While celebrating and rejoicing the conquest of Goliath, the women called out, "Saul has slain thousands, and David his tens of thousands" (1 Samuel 18:7). We are told that as a result of the people's praise of David, Saul becomes angry and jealous.

Here begins the final downfall of Saul and the rise of David, thus demonstrating the truth of the saying "Pride before ruin."[5] Saul, who loved David originally, decides that David should marry his daughter Michal and tells his servants to tell David of this desire, and that no dowry is required except for 100 Philistine foreskins. David returns with a double portion, and the anticipated marriage goes forward. David would eventually acquire eighteen wives,[6] but it is his marriage to Saul's daughter that brings him to the threshold of worldly power.

The Downfall of Saul

Saul is now fully aware that the divine spirit rests with David, not himself, and despite his earlier affection for his nemesis, he tries to have David murdered. He enlists his son Jonathan, who not only refuses the odious task but manages to facilitate a temporary peace between the two adversaries. But then one day while David is playing his lyre for Saul, the king throws his spear, barely missing David, who now realizes the king's intentions. The greater Saul's enmity, the more focused are his efforts to kill David, and in turn the more powerful is God's protection of David. That is why humble thanksgiving for God's protection is the theme of David's song and the chief emotion of the Sefirah of Hod.

On two different occasions when Saul pursues David, David has the opportunity to kill the king but rejects the idea, knowing that whomever God makes king is God's appointee. When the prophet Samuel dies, David takes leave of the community for fear of his life, as Samuel had

---

[5] This same wisdom was used by Queen Esther in entrapping Haman in order to save the Jewish people from state-sponsored genocide.

[6] "Even when he was ill, he fulfilled his marital duty to his 18 wives" (Sanhedrin 107a).

been David's staunchest protector. He goes into exile among one of the five Philistine tribes. David is never trusted completely by them for fear he will trade sides in war and fight with the Israelites. It may seem odd that God puts the next king of Israel into exile among the very same people who had stolen the Ark of the Covenant, the very people against whom Israel would wage war. Yet David had already been placed by God in the personal retinue of the murderous Saul. And so as a story of succession outside of a royal bloodline, David's narrative is an example of God's concealed plan.

David's Kingship

It is only after Saul dies in battle,[7] taking his own life to prevent any Philistine claim of having killed him, that David is free to return home. Upon doing so, the people of Hebron, the tribe of Judah of which he is a member, announce that he is their king, as they have acknowledged all along. The other Israelite tribes choose Saul's right-hand man, Abner, who in turn makes Saul's son Ishbosheth their king.[8]

While king of Judah, David faces severe opposition from the other tribes of Israel. There are countless battles between the various tribes, suggesting our own inner battles with our many attachments and desires. Never does it seem that David has peace in his life; rather, it is wrought with conflict, war, deceit, family violence, and conspiracy.

David's familial and political relations are a drama of tragic dimensions that range beyond a single lifetime. Anytime there is extreme violence between people, one can assume lifetimes of such interactions are still at play in these situations. This shows us that patterns of imbalance generally underlie the relationships one carries forward from lifetime to lifetime. Each time a soul reincarnates, these patterns reemerge for rectification of the original harm that was set in motion. In David's case, he faced extreme challenges yet remained steadfastly attached to God's commands. For this reason he is called the greatest servant of all, the one God had chosen for the sacred task of uniting Israel and returning the Ark to Jerusalem.

---

[7] Saul's son Jonathan also dies in this same battle.

[8] Because of this, the tribes of Israel are divided for seven-and-a-half years. Ishbosheth is eventually assassinated by people trying to curry favor with David, after which David unites Israel and is crowned king.

The Ark Comes to Jerusalem

After Saul dies and David becomes king, he and his army march against the Philistines, and with God's help they emerge victorious. With his kingdom united, David summons all of Israel, each to a specific task of bringing the Ark of the Covenant to Jerusalem. It had been returned to the Israelites by the Philistines to Keriath-jearim and the house of the Hebrew tribesman Abinadab because the Philistines feared the power of the God of this Ark. The Ark is put on a wagon, and when the oxen dislodge it from the cart accidentally, Uzza, who guides the wagon, puts out his hand to stop it from falling and dies immediately. The Ark is then taken to the house of Obed-edom the Gittite (1 Chronicles 13:11–13), where it is kept for three months since David fears he cannot bring it home with him to Jerusalem, it being life-threatening for anyone but the Levite priests to handle it; as well, David wants to be sure the Ark's resting place is ready. After the three months pass, David assembles all of Israel to Jerusalem to bring up the Ark of God to the Tent he had prepared for it, commanding that it be carried only by the Levites, accompanied by the sons of Aaron, "for it was them whom God [had] chosen to carry the Ark of God and to minster before Him forever" (1 Chronicles 15:2–4).

> So David, and the elders of Israel, and the captains over thousands, went to bring up the Ark of the Covenant of the Lord out of the house of Obed-edom with joy. . . . And David was clothed with a robe of fine linen, and all the Levites that bore the ark, and the singers, and Chenaniah the master of the singers in the song; and David had upon him an ephod of linen. Thus all Israel brought up the Ark of the Covenant of the Lord with shouting, and with sound of the horn, and with trumpets, and with cymbals, sounding aloud with psalteries and harps. And it came to pass, as the Ark of the Covenant of the Lord came to the city of David, that Michal the daughter of Saul looked out at the window, and saw king David dancing and making merry; and she despised him in her heart. And they brought in the Ark of God, and set it in the midst of the tent that David had pitched for it, and David offered burnt-offerings and peace-offerings before God. And when David had made an end of offering the burnt-offering and the peace-offering, he blessed the people with the name of the Lord.

And he dealt to every one of Israel, both man and woman, to every one a loaf of bread, and a cake made in a pan, and a sweet cake. (1 Chronicles 15:25, 27–29; 16:1–3)[9]

The Planning of the Temple

> *Lo, children are a heritage of the LORD; the fruit of the womb is a reward. As arrows in the hand of a mighty man, so are the children of one's youth.*
>
> PSALMS 127:3–4 (WRITTEN BY
> KING DAVID FOR HIS SON SOLOMON)

While God does not permit David to build the First Temple of Jerusalem because "he is a man of war and has shed blood" (1 Chronicles 28:3), he is assured by God that his desire to serve Him in this way will be fulfilled by his son Solomon: "I will raise up your offspring to succeed you, who will come from your own body, and I will establish his kingdom. He is the one who will build a house for my Name. . . . I will be his father, and he will be my son . . . Your house and your kingdom will endure forever before me; your throne will be established forever" (2 Samuel 7:12–16). Thus David's greatest desire is denied him—just as his predecessor, Moses, was not permitted to enter the Promised Land. Yet David the prophet-king is allowed to participate in a significant manner: he draws the design of the Temple and gives the plans to Solomon (1 Chronicles 28:11) and collects the materials needed to build it. He purchases the site for the Temple, where he builds only an altar. He also arranges the priests who will serve in the Temple into divisions and designates the many weights and measures important in the Temple's various functions. As we have seen in our discussion of Yesod, King Solomon would complete the building of the Temple and dedicate it after his father's death.

The reader is encouraged to read the Torah's dramatic recounting of David's many escapes and the miracles God performs in his behalf, eventually bringing him to the throne of all of Israel. David's song, representing the Sefirah of Hod, speaks for itself: one gives thanks with sincere humility for being under the loving, protective shield of God.

---

[9] Some translations say "a loaf of bread, a portion of beef and a container of wine for each person" (Art Scroll, Stone Edition Tanakh).

The word **David** דוד (Dalet Vav Dalet), whose numerical value is 14, is the same value as the Hebrew words **beginning, beloved,** and **meditate,** underscoring King David's inner essence as the beloved of God, the originator of Tehillim (Psalms), and a teacher of devotional meditation.

The Song of Hod:
Majestic Humility (Hodu'ah)

The song of Hod, David's song of emancipation from his enemies, is the text recited as the haftorah (which means "concluding portion") and is a selection from the writings of the prophets recited at the close of the Torah reading on the seventh day of Pesach (Shevi'i Shel Pesach, or Passover), along with the Song at the Sea (which we will examine in chapter 11). Rabbi Menachem Mendel Schneerson (1789–1866), the third rebbe of the Chabad Lubavitch Chassidic movement, says that "on the seventh day of Pesach, the Haftorah is the Song of David [Hod] because on the seventh and final days of Pesach there is a revelation of Moshiach, who is a descendant of David, thus, it is to honor Moshiach that we recite the Song of David."[10] One can appreciate that both events—David's escape from the evil designs of Saul, and the Israelites' emancipation from Egypt and subsequent miraculous crossing of the Red Sea—commemorate God's protection of His people against their adversaries. It is suggested that David wrote this psalm while still a young man; its original version appeared in 2 Samuel 22:1–52. David would recite these verses in times of trouble; after his death it was amended into the Book of Psalms.[11]

The Song of David recounts God's mercy in saving him from King Saul, who has plotted to kill him. It is said that Saul was equivalent to all of David's enemies combined, putting the king's efforts to murder God's selected successor as a battle not just between the two men, but between God and the darker forces that had taken possession of Saul and Israel. One can therefore truly appreciate why the prophet Samuel prayed there

---

[10] R. Chaim Miller. *Chumash,* 1485.

[11] It is also known for being read on the Sabbath between the Jewish New Year, Rosh Hashanah, and the Day of Atonement, Yom Kippur. It is not read on Shabbas, between Rosh Hashanah and Yom Kippur. Though it is the haftorah for Parshas Haazinu, it is read only for Haazinu when Haazinu falls after Yom Kippur, otherwise a different haftorah is substituted.

would not be kings, knowing in advance the shortcomings of political monarchies.

Consecration: Humility of Heart

In Hod, humility of heart is expressed in the second stage of consecration; the first stage, as we learned from King David's son Solomon, is expressed through devotion. From the joyous crying out of the tzaddik in union with God in divine love, we progress to a union based on devoted servitude, without any desire for oneself at all. The Song of Hod is a majestic song in which the initiate arrives at the royal court of his or her own interior being. Selfless service becomes the hallmark of royalty and the essential inheritance of all of humanity as we ascend the Tree of Life. It is for this reason we know that the righteous are co-creators with God.

David's Song of Gratitude
(2 Samuel 22:1–51)

1 *David addressed the words of this song to the Lord, after the Lord had saved him from the hands of all his enemies and from the hands of Saul.* **2** *He said: O Lord, my crag, my fastness, my deliverer!* **3** *O God, the rock wherein I take shelter: My shield, my mighty champion, my fortress and refuge! My savior, You who rescue me from violence!*

4 *All praise! I called on the Lord, and I was delivered from my enemies.* **5** *For the breakers of Death encompassed me, the torrents of Belial terrified me;* **6** *The snares of Sheol encircled me, the toils of Death engulfed me.* **7** *In my anguish I called on the Lord, cried out to my God; in His Abode He heard my voice, my cry entered His ears.* **8** *Then the earth rocked and quaked, the foundations of heaven shook—rocked by His indignation.* **9** *Smoke went up from His nostrils, from His mouth came devouring fire; live coals blazed forth from Him.* **10** *He bent the sky and came down, thick cloud beneath His feet.* **11** *He mounted a cherub and flew; He was seen on the wings of the wind.* **12** *He made pavilions of darkness about Him, dripping clouds, huge thunderheads;* **13** *In the brilliance before Him blazed fiery coals.* **14** *The Lord thundered forth from heaven, the Most High sent forth His voice;* **15** *He let loose bolts, and scattered them; lightning, and put them to rout.* **16** *The bed of the sea was exposed, the foundations of the world were laid bare by the mighty roaring of the Lord, at the blast of the breath of His nostrils.*

17 *He reached down from on high, He took me, drew me out of the mighty waters;* **18** *He rescued me from my enemy so strong, from foes too mighty for me.* **19** *They attacked me on my day of calamity, but the Lord was my stay.* **20** *He brought me out to freedom, He rescued me because He was pleased with me.* **21** *The Lord rewarded me according to my merit, He requited the cleanness of my hands.* **22** *For I have kept the ways of the Lord and have not been guilty before my God;* **23** *I am mindful of all His rules and have not departed from His laws.* **24** *I have been blameless before Him, and have guarded myself against sinning—* **25** *And the Lord has requited my merit, according to my purity in His sight.* **26** *With the loyal You deal loyally; with the blameless hero, blamelessly.* **27** *With the pure You act in purity, and with the perverse You are wily.* **28** *To humble folk You give victory, and You look with scorn on the haughty.* **29** *You, O Lord, are my lamp; the Lord lights up my darkness.* **30** *With You, I can rush a barrier, with my God, I can scale a wall.* **31** *The way of God is perfect, the word of the Lord is pure. He is a shield to all who take refuge in Him.* **32** *Yea, who is a God except the Lord, who is a rock except God?* **33** *The God, my mighty stronghold, Who kept my path secure;* **34** *Who made my legs like a deer's, and set me firm on the heights;* **35** *Who trained my hands for battle, so that my arms can bend a bow of bronze!* **36** *You have granted me the shield of Your protection and Your providence has made me great.* **37** *You have let me stride on freely, and my feet have not slipped.* **38** *I pursued my enemies and wiped them out, I did not turn back till I destroyed them.* **39** *I destroyed them, I struck them down; they rose no more, they lay at my feet.* **40** *You have girt me with strength for battle, brought low my foes before me,* **41** *Made my enemies turn tail before me, my foes—and I wiped them out.* **42** *They looked, but there was none to deliver; to the Lord, but He answered them not.* **43** *I pounded them like dust of the earth, stamped, crushed them like dirt of the streets.* **44** *You have rescued me from the strife of peoples, kept me to be a ruler of nations; peoples I knew not must serve me.* **45** *Aliens have cringed before me, paid me homage at the mere report of me.* **46** *Aliens have lost courage and come trembling out of their fastnesses.* **47** *The Lord lives! Blessed is my rock! Exalted be God, the rock Who gives me victory;* **48** *The God who has vindicated me and made peoples subject to me,*

49 *Rescued me from my enemies, raised me clear of my foes, saved me from lawless men!* **50** *For this I sing Your praise among the nations and hymn Your name:*

51 *Tower of victory to His king, Who deals graciously with His anointed, with David and his offspring evermore.*

Ritual: To Make Holy

As an aspect of the Outer Court rituals and the realm of formation (Yetzirah), Hod shows us the deep surrender we must achieve in our devotional practice if we are to attain a higher state of consciousness. The Ruach, or spirit aspect of the soul, which corresponds to the Outer Court of the Tabernacle, inspires David in his writing of psalms. This tells us that a pure heart is the natural abode of the Ruach HaKodesh. When we can attain such a higher state of purity through surrender to God's will, especially when it seems that all has turned against us, we have a superior force at our disposal by which we can navigate through life. When we call out to God with specific requests, we will find that God answers.

The simple fact is that we live in a reflexive universe: what we focus on is formed of light before it materializes. Just as every idea begins as something immaterial, it later becomes concretized through the forming work we do with matter (the realm of Yetzirah). We form our own natures in exactly this fashion, and that is the importance of consecrating with sincere and humble love. This quality conditions our natures to receiving others of like vibration, which makes for a community engaged in prayer, devotion, and service. The disciple of devotion learns to invest intentional love into everything he or she does, every moment of life, not just on special holidays or in moments of prayer. Consecration must pervade one's consciousness and inform the limbs in action; it becomes one's focus in life, with everything else additional. This is what becoming a vessel for the divine means.

Refinement of the Emotions as a Form of Sacrifice

Who was the sweet singer of Israel? David son of Jesse.
SHOCHER TOV 1:6

As an aspect of the Outer Court, Hod is expressed through the sacrifices brought to the Ohel Moed to atone for one's sins and to offer thanksgiving and praise. This act of consecration purifies the emotions. Whether a bull, calf, dove, grain, or herb, the offerings are not handled by the initiate himself but are given to the priests to surrender to the altar, because the priests are considered God's assistants, held to higher standards of personal conduct than the average initiate. So too in our own personal sanctuary: when we consecrate an action we must act with focused intention, like the priests in the Tabernacle, as what we do in a sacred ceremony or an event of consequence such as a birth, holiday, healing, or loss can be transformed into an important moment of consecration and upliftment.

The Danger of Unrefined Emotions

David's life was full of war and loss; so too was his personal life marked by tragedy, especially as a result of the actions of his sons, whom he did not restrain properly. David's son Amnon falls in love with Tamar, his stepsister, and rapes her. Absolom, Tamar's brother, responds by waging revenge. Two years after the rape occurs, Absolom has Amnon murdered. After a period of forced exile, Absalom is allowed to return home, but upon reaching Jerusalem he attempts to oust David as king. It is eventually David's right-hand man, General Joab, who sees to Absolom's death after he tries to assassinate David. Toward the end of David's life, his fourth son, Adonijah, the heir apparent, attempts to overthrow his father and declare himself king, though it is his younger brother, Solomon, who is selected. After Solomon is anointed, Adonijah tries to marry one of his father's widows in a renewed effort to become king. Instead, Adonijah is seized by Solomon's military and put to death.

With this backdrop of family rivalry, political machination, and internecine strife,[12] one can easily see that David's life is a portrait of personal upheaval and national chaos. But he fulfills the desire of the people for a king, leads them in battle, and is victorious; moreover, he elevates the nation of Israel spiritually. What can we infer from a life filled with such conflict? It seems that if we let our emotions control us, we are capable, through our own supreme selfishness, of destroying others' lives, even to the point of affecting whole communities or nations. One sees this in cases where couples divorce with enmity, when people are fired from their jobs and bear grudges, and when people in power feel entitled to do things that are unethical or immoral, if not illegal. If we pursue power, position, control, and rewards, like King Saul and the sons of King David do, our holy soul goes into exile. The greater the arrogance and desire to

---

[12] Israel was forced to fight the neighboring Philistines and Amelakites, and on the East bank of the Jordan, the Moabites, Edomites, Ammonites, and Arameans.

receive for oneself alone, the more degraded becomes the vessel, whether the individual, the nation, or the world, whether a project, a business, or a government. The opposite can be said of a person or a community that surrenders its desires to the one supreme desire, that of being righteous, of being attached to God and helping those in need.

The more people pursue power and transient material pleasures and possessions, the greater is the exile of the Divine Immanence, the Shechinah. So we see that whether king or commoner, the same laws of spirit and matter govern us all. Generally those who have the desire or need to rule over others cannot rule themselves. If they are not self-refined leaders, they become brutish dictators. We see this on the world stage throughout history, all the way up to the present. We see it in homes and places of work. Unmitigated selfishness creates divisiveness that is antithetical to humanity's successful maturation, to our becoming one people of one planet, universal souls of the cosmos.

Difficulties Can Lead to Elevation

One might well wonder why God's chosen king, the person from whose lineage the Moshiach and divine consciousness will come, would experience such tragedy and hardship throughout his life, from a young age? It is said that God increases our difficulties in order to bring us closer to Him. This suggests that David's circumstances were necessary to effect his self-refinement—that his difficulties were part of his path of achieving his rightful throne before the Lord who had anointed him. His victories laid the groundwork for the coming Moshiach. Just as his trials were not punishments, neither are ours: they are opportunities for refinement.

David's great difficulties are the fire rituals of sacrifice that take place in the Outer Court, of which he and Hod, our left leg, is the guardian.[13] It was his deeper understanding of the need for self-refinement and his respect for Saul as a king appointed by God that prevented David from killing Saul, even in self-defense, after Saul had hatched various plots to

---

[13] In other Kabbalistic teachings that place the male leadership of patriarchs and prophets in the Sefirot of the Tree of Life, David is not positioned in Hod (which is associated with Aaron, the peacemaker), but in Malchut, as Moshiach. Because each Sefirah is composed of all ten Sefirot, it is possible to view each person through as many as ten qualities. As in life, at any one stage a particular quality is more evident, and at other times another attribute shines.

kill David. From this we can deduce that controlling one's anger, even in the face of death, is the sign of a tzaddik, a righteous one.

Despite all the hardships he endured throughout his seventy years of life, David's attachment to and sincere humility before God remained strong, as seen in his making full prostrations before the Lord:

> David came before the Divine Presence, stretched himself out full length on the ground, and said, "My Father in heaven . . . the Torah that I have studied before You is Yours [for the Torah is Yours], and the acts of kindness that I have done before You are Yours [for all the wealth is Yours]. Yet in reward for the little bit of Torah I have learned before You, You gave me possession of This World, the messianic era, and the World to come.[14]

Fearing God in Joy, Rejoicing in Fear

The three-part structure of one's practice in prayer, as first shown by an earlier prophetess, Chanah (see chapter 6), is also demonstrated by the prophet-king David: after first praising God, we then ask for what is most important, and then close by thanking God for answering us. David also teaches the importance of the disposition of the heart in prayer: in sincere humility. King David of Blessed memory said, "I feared God in joy and rejoiced in fear, but my love [of God] exceeded both."[15]

What does this mean, fearing God in joy and rejoicing in fear? It means that even our perception of God's greatness and our awareness of His awesome powers need not diminish our love of Him; rather, it should increase our joy in being made in His image and being in His presence. Why rejoice in fear? So that we do not forget who sustains our life, so that we might rejoice in happiness and awe. Each of these characteristics has something to do with humility and thanksgiving, just as these two qualities are deeply entwined in the state of piety that Torah tells us King David embodies.

We are at all times reminded to "know before whom we are pray-

---

[14] Tanna d'Bei Eliyah Rabbah 18. See also Chasidah, *Encyclopedia of Biblical Personalities*, 135.

[15] Tanna d'Bei Eliyahu Rabbah 3. See also Chasidah, *Encyclopedia of Biblical Personalities*, 135.

ing."[16] *Yirat HaShem,* "fear of God," derives from submission to the awesome cosmic order, which is seasoned with joy: "Serve the Lord with fear, and rejoice with Trembling."[17] Both of these qualities produce actual physical symptoms. The Ramchal tells us that we must recognize the majesty of God and our lowliness due to our material density and especially because of any sins that may have been committed during one's lifetime. It would therefore be impossible for our heart not to tremble and quake when we utter our words before God, "mentioning His name and trying to win His favor." That is why King David says in his praises, "I will bow down towards Your holy name in fear of You (Tehillim 5:8)."[18]

The Requirement of Humility

> *The most praiseworthy of kings was David.*
>
> SHOCHER TOV 1:2

While humility produces a particular biodynamic peace in the body, it also brings unity between the body and the soul through the heart's softened disposition. Emotional surrender and thanksgiving are actions we make with our heart and mind in unison, which creates a vessel for God's presence. They are acts of consecration. Humility creates a state where all life is bound together in harmony. It is our majesty and our glory, the very words associated with Hod. The glory (Hod) of victory (Netzach), then, whether in personal challenges or on the battlefield, as in David's time, must never be followed by arrogant jubilation, but rather by humble thanksgiving.

Humility is the foundation of prophecy. It is also a quality, as King David shows, befitting the majesty of the royal bloodline. The prophetess Avigail, in her marriage to King David, also reveals this quality of humility that is associated with royalty.[19] Here, as we ascend the ladder of light, we benefit by the cultivation of humility as the cornerstone of our eventual elevation and illumination.

David was so humble that when speaking about his place in the World

---

[16] Berakhot 28b.

[17] Tehillim 2:11.

[18] Luzzatto, *Mesillat Yesharim,* 448.

[19] As discussed in this author's prior work, *Kabbalistic Teachings of the Female Prophets.*

to Come, he said to the Lord, "It is not for me to sit with the great men; I will wait with lesser ones. Let Abraham, Isaac, and Jacob be in their room, and Moses and Aaron in the banquet room, and I will be on the threshold. If I am not worthy of sitting on the threshold, I will sit in the courtyard."[20] David's words refer to Malchut, which marks the threshold between the temporal world and the Outer Court of the Tabernacle.

In the tractate (book) of Talmud called Sanhedrin, we read: "The six blessings of the second of Ruth's descendants [Moshiach] are enumerated in the verse, 'The spirit of God will rest upon him—a spirit of wisdom [Chochmah] and understanding [Binah], a spirit of counsel [Tiferet] and strength [Gevurah], a spirit of knowledge [Daat] and fear of God' (Isaiah 11:2)."[21] In other words, the illuminations of the Tree of Life are given to each person, but the quality and intensity of light depends on the merit and needs of each soul. Each soul's destiny on earth is evident in its spiritual body, the Neshamah aspect, which a great tzaddik can read to determine a person's present life and past lives to discern the person's strengths and what he lacks. Similarly, when David's son Solomon builds the Temple of Jerusalem, it is a reflection of its spiritual counterpart in the heavenly realms. That is why God tells David, "Behold a son shall be born to you who shall be a man of tranquility; and I will give him rest from all his surrounding enemies. For Shlomo [Solomon] will be his name, and peace and quietness will I give to Israel in his days" (1 Chronicles 22:9). Because Solomon's soul was bound to David's, God foretold the future to David, for it was already written in their souls.

Humility, we learn over and over again, is the foundation for building a place for God's presence. "R. Yochanan said: Wherever you find the power of the Holy One, Blessed be He, mentioned in Scripture, you also find His humility mentioned. This is written in the Torah, repeated in the Prophets, and stated a third time in the Writings."[22] Consider the power of any kind of leader, which can be either self-motivated or altruistically rooted: in this context, King David's prayer is that of a human

---

[20] Shocher Tov 16:13. See also Chasidah, *Encyclopedia of Biblical Personalities,* 136.

[21] Sanhedrin, The Blessings of Mashiach. See R. Yaakov Ibn Chaviv, *Ein Yaakov,* 651.

[22] It is written in Torah, "God your Lord is the ultimate Supreme Being and the Master of all natural forces" (Deuteronomy 10:17). See also Meggillah 31a; and Chaviv, *Ein Yaakov,* 284.

who is keenly aware of the importance of humility in being able to receive the blessings of the light of God, not for himself alone, but for the welfare of the entire nation. Kabbalah says the desire to receive from God must be balanced by an even greater desire to give to others. Prophecy, as we have learned, reflects this two-way relationship between God's blessings and a person's humility.

> *Create in Me a Pure Heart, O God.*
>
> PSALMS 51:12

Cultivating Humility in the Outer Court

In the Outer Court, water libations are an expression of sincere humility. Before the priests can make any offerings they must go through various water purifications, of both their feet and their hands, which are called the "ministers" in Chassidut. Purifying one's feet and hands means to make pure one's intentions and desires. A humble spirit is the vessel for God's illuminating presence.

Even when told by God of the wonderful gifts he would receive, David remained aware of his role as the communal leader and spiritual enabler of Israel. For this reason, he continually cultivated humility, making it the hallmark of royalty. David says, "Master of the Universe, despise not my prayer, for Israel's eyes are raised to me in hope, and my eyes are raised to You in hope. If You hear my prayer, it is as if You heard theirs."[23] So humble is David that his "eyes were always lowered out of fear of the Master. When he walked among the people, there was no haughtiness whatsoever in him."[24]

So certain is David of his lowly place before God that even while king of Israel he refers to himself as God's servant. The conditions for prophecy, modeled on the life of Moses, stem from such cultivation of sincere humility. These conditions are also found in the life of David: "Might, Torah knowledge, and humility were all found in David."[25] These qualities are also found in the lives of the first prophet, Samuel, as well as in David's own son Solomon. In fact, David and Moses (the greatest prophet who ever was, is, or will be, whose song to the congregation is

---

[23] Shocher Tov 25:5. See also Chasidah, *Encyclopedia of Biblical Personalities,* 137.

[24] Zohar 2:101b. See also Chasidah, *Encyclopedia of Biblical Personalities,* 136.

[25] Shocher Tov 18:28. See also Chasidah, *Encyclopedia of Biblical Personalities,* 135.

our rung of light called Chesed), are equally regarded in their leadership of Israel: "Two good leaders stood by Israel: Moses and David."[26] It is also said, that "Moses was the teacher, David the disciple."[27]

We know that light descends the Tree of Life as well as ascends it, therefore wisdom, as represented by the Sefirah Chochmah, fills some of each Sefirah. Hod's wisdom is a bestowal from above in the form of prophecy, and prophecy depends on a person's humility. The Zohar reminds us that all of David's songs contain divine wisdom, "because they were all composed through Divine Inspiration. Divine Inspiration rested on David, and he composed songs of praise (Zohar 1:179a). David's psalms that begin with the words 'Of David—a song', first the Divine Presence rested upon him, and then he wrote the song of praise. [When it begins] A song of David, first he wrote the song and then the Divine Presence rested upon him."[28] The two different ways in which David was affected by the Holy Spirit is testimony to the various phenomenological experiences associated with the Ruach HaKodesh.

The Components of Piety

We learn in the Ramchal's eighteenth-century classic, *Mesilat Yesharim* ("Path of the Just"), that piety, a state of being, is comprised of three principal components: action, the manner in which we do mitzvot, and motivation. In this formula, Hod's achievement of piety is illuminated by the shine of faith; this creates an emanation to Tiferet, leading to the pure heart made of truth. The words of one's prayers are consecrated as an emotional investment in Hod as glory and thanksgiving. The soul and heart bow before the Shechinah, which illuminates the heart of the devotée. The act of doing what Torah instructs, doing it with devotion and with the desire only to serve humbly, is the epitome of King David's teachings and those of the Sefirah of Hod.

> *Halleluyah. Praise God in His sanctuary; praise Him in the firmament of His power.*
>
> PSALMS 150:1

---

[26] Yoma 86b. See also Chasidah, *Encyclopedia of Biblical Personalities,* 134.

[27] Shocher Tov, 14:6. See also Chasidah, *Encyclopedia of Biblical Personalities,* 134.

[28] Pesachim 117a. See also Chasidah, *Encyclopedia of Biblical Personalties,* 140.

Music in Ritual Service

David, the chief musician in King Saul's court and then later Israel's royal leader, institutionalizes the use of harps and other musical instruments as part of the services performed by the priestly Levites, whose task it was to make music around the Outer Court of the Tabernacle. Just as playing the harp helped David cultivate his own gift of prophecy, he saw that in the ritual services music is essential to uplifting the congregation.

> *Sing unto the* LORD *with thanksgiving; sing praise upon the harp unto our God.*
>
> PSALMS 147:7

The harp that the Levites played had seven strings. This was ordained for them by Samuel and David, who also decided how lyres, harps, and cymbals would be distributed among the Levites.[29] David also dictated that a Levite choir be assembled (1 Chronicles 15:16).

David loved God and had hoped to establish the Temple in His honor. So, though God told him that this task would be the honor of his son Solomon, David did participate in the creation of the Temple by having the Ark of the Covenant moved from Beit Shemesh, a territory of Judah on the outskirts of Jerusalem that had been set aside for the Levites and Kohanim to inhabit,[30] to Jerusalem, as we noted earlier in his narrative. David also designed many of the protocols of the future Temple in addition to its physical design. In so doing, he established the foundation of ritual worship for all of Israel in Jerusalem, the holy resting place of God. It was David himself who named Jerusalem, or Zion, "the city of David," after he had taken the city from the Jebusites (2 Samuel 5:4–12). He established his throne, transported the Ark of the Covenant, and set up the Tabernacle, building a great city to honor God.[31]

> *For the* LORD *shall comfort Zion: he will comfort all her waste places; and he will make her wilderness like Eden, and her desert*

---

[29] Bamidbar Rabbah 15:11. See also Chasidah, *Encyclopedia of Biblical Personalities,* 139.

[30] See Joshua 21:1–41 for the division of the lands of Israel between the tribes, the Levites, and the Kohanim.

[31] In Isaiah's time, Jerusalem was still the capital of Judah and the seat of the House of David.

like the garden of the LORD; joy and gladness shall be found
therein, thanksgiving, and the voice of melody.

ISAIAH 51:3

Ritual Singing

It is noteworthy that David's prayers were not just spoken words, for it was said that "David's voice was sweet,"[32] meaning his prayers were meant to be sung. The word *sweet* suggests the influx of Chesed (love) and Chochmah (wisdom). Singing is an element that helps create the conditions for prophecy and for receiving the Shechinah. "When he made a request of the holy One, Blessed is He, he would sing it. He would present the minor requests first, then the major ones."[33] We have already learned the importance of prayer and of song itself, of engaging God with our full heart. In chapter 3 we found within the structure of the Shemoneh Esrei the prophetess Chanah's three-part method for speaking to God: the petitioner praises God first; then petitions for His help, having identified one's greatest lack (which for Chanah was her childlessness); and then finally thanks God for having provided help. This is the vital structure of prayer in the People of the Book's tradition.

In our own practice we begin by declaring the greatness of this universal love field of which we are all part, infusing this declaration with great emotion. Then we humble ourselves, feeling our smallness in the larger scheme of creation. This process is reflected in the Outer Court fire rituals where we surrender our personal habits that inhibit holiness: arrogance, bullishness, flightiness, cowardice, deceitfulness, gluttony, and so forth. The sacrifices are consumed by the priests and the community, and the initiate feels the fullness that comes with the fulfillment of his request. Then, like the priest, we give thanks to the Creator for having been heard.

Simply put, we open up to God, and God fills us with His Divine Presence. Humility, a nullification of the personal ego, allows one to be saturated with holy harmony. Essentially, what one gives up is insignificant in terms of what one receives in return. The small *I* is replaced by the *I* that isn't. This is the big *I,* which is everywhere.

---

[32] Shir HaShirim Rabbah 4:4. See also Chasidah, *Encyclopedia of Biblical Personalities,* 134.

[33] Aggadas Bereshis, chapter 6. See also Chasidah, *Encyclopedia of Biblical Personalities,* 137.

Seclusion as a Means of Purification

Self-refinement is a lifelong process. It continues even after the body is cast off. Refinement then becomes the work of the soul from lifetime to lifetime. It is this process of purposeful development that makes it possible to understand the role of God in every person's life, even in the lives of those whom we might consider evil.

One method used by serious practitioners to achieve greater purification and self-refinement is seclusion. This seclusion can be literal, in the sense of withdrawing from the world and the community for a period of time, as most wisdom traditions advocate. Or it can refer to a person's inner ability, as the Ramchal teaches,[34] to separate our desires from worldly things beyond the simple, modest needs of food, shelter, clothing, and a place for education and religious practice. Beyond these basic needs are the desires for material indulgences and other worldly desires such as the pursuit of societal honors, prestige, or power, which should be avoided. "Dearer than all else is seclusion," writes the Ramchal, "for when a person removes worldly matters from before his eyes he removes the desire for them from his heart. King David, peace be on him, had spoken in praise of seclusion when he said, 'O that I had the wings of the dove! I would fly away, and find rest. Surely, I would wander far off, and lodge in the wilderness' (Psalms 55:7–8)."[35]

Spiritual Development: Sanctifying One's Life

The LORD is my shepherd; I shall not want. He maketh me to lie
down in green pastures; He leadeth me beside the still waters.
He restoreth my soul; He guideth me in straight
paths for His name's sake.

PSALMS 23:1–3

To summarize our progression thus far toward an illuminated state of awareness: We begin in Malchut, the very bottom of the Tree of Life,

---

[34] R. Moshe Chayim Luzzatto of Padua's magnum opus was *Mesillat Yesharim,* which details the proper service of God. This is why I draw from it in this chapter related to the subject of piety, which is also a hallmark of the righteous of Yesod.

[35] Luzzatto, *Mesillat Yesharim,* 425. The Ramchal notes that the prophets Eliyahu and Elisha designated a place for themselves in the mountains because of their practice of seclusion.

where we are engaged in deep self-reflection and bonding with our ancestors and God. Next, in Yesod, we declare our devotion to God with a great crying out in joy, like one in love. Now in Hod we praise God in a majestic way, with heartfelt sincerity, for His constant protection as we choose the path of selfless service. David shows each person what it means to be a member of God's royal family—to be devoted, humble, and full of praise and thanksgiving, acting not only for oneself but for one's entire generation. This emancipates us from a limited, self-oriented approach to life. Here, David leads the singer of his song through dangerous journeys, narrow escapes, and ultimately to complete trust in God.

Hod draws us deeper into the mystery of the heart as it is purified. At this stage, adding another element to consecration in the Outer Court, we learn that the Hebrew word for consecrate, *kadosh,* means "to make holy." This tells us explicitly that when we approach our service to God with complete devotion, selflessness, with intensely focused desire, we become instruments of holiness, making it possible for the Holy Spirit to rest where such consecration occurs. The Outer Court is where the community brings their sacrifices to the priests to burn; the priestly rituals of purification, necessary before the priests' entry (aliyah, or elevation) into the Holy Place, are also part of this process. In Hod we are absorbed into the light of majesty. This is the robe of royalty we can each don. It is available to all humans, for it is the garment of the pure and sincere heart.

Achieving Purity of Heart

In chapter 4 we saw that the six Sefirot comprising Zeir Anpin, the Son or "the small face," represent the spiritual advancement of the initiate in the Outer Court. Having gained in Yesod our first step into the Outer Court, along with the devotion of the Beloved and the covenant of spiritual marriage, we now, in Hod, develop a greater capacity for humility and therefore a greater attachment to the divine light emanating from above. This stage in our spiritual growth is a refinement that adds a type of purity of heart to the disposition of the initiate.

As a quality of consecration, piety elevates an offering, enabling it to receive from its superior root of Binah, at the top of the left pillar of the Tree of Life, the essential emanation of understanding, an aspect of faith, or *emunah* in Hebrew. Binah, which in the partzufim system is the Mother, expresses the quality of acting without wanting anything for oneself; this is the inherent selfless nature of an aliyah. Malchut, being the Daughter of the Mother, can be this way as well, which is why it is said that like the moon, the Daughter has no light of her own but rather reflects the light of others. Essentially Hod derives from Binah the capacity for total selflessness, but at this less mature stage of ascension its quality is more personal than universal. It is a personal accomplishment to achieve piety; from it arises "the perfection of the heart and thought."[36]

This is the reason why God spoke of David as His servant, mentioned in the previous chapter on Solomon. David makes clear the outcome of this kind of purity, the next station of the covenant in which our consecrated lives are endowed: "Whom have I in heaven but You?" he says to God. "And having You, I need no one on earth" (Psalms 73:25). In the same vein, he says, "Your word is very pure; therefore Your servant loves it" (Psalms 119:140). For in fact the true service of God must be much more refined than gold and silver; as it is stated regarding the Torah, "The words of the Lord are pure words, as purified silver, clear to the world, refined seven times" (Psalms 12:7).[37]

Making Daily Life Holy

As we go about our daily lives, our activities, whether working, making meals, or helping someone in need, can become gifts we give to our community, to our workplace, to the people in our lives, and to where we live our lives. By refining our own behavior—how we talk to others, how we think of them, what we are willing to do and what we are rightfully restrained from doing—we make offerings in the Outer Court of our life, just as the Hebrews made their sacrificial offerings in the Ohel Moed and later in the Temple. Every day we have things to be grateful for and, most likely, we also become aware of aspects of ourselves that could be improved. Attending to the fire altar of our desire to purify our hearts, and to the water rituals of immersion in the Divine Presence and to the teachings of the holy traditions, is the way we learn that our life is meant to be a sacred dwelling place for God.

---

[36] Luzzatto, *Mesillat Yesharim*, 427.

[37] Ibid., 430.

Cultivating Loving-Kindness

We also consecrate through the practice of loving-kindness. David "did kindness for all, for he said, 'Whether he be killer or victim, pursuer or pursued, I will still do kindness for him.'"[38] David's remark that "it would be sacrilegious before God for me to send forth my hand against God's anointed one" (1 Samuel 26:11) explains why he refuses to kill Saul, even in self-defense. We are not to forget that our enemies also share our own human potential for spiritual refinement: "For the Holy One, Blessed be He, takes no pleasure in the destruction of the wicked. Rather the pious are commanded to strive for their vindication and Atonement."[39]

David's statements reflect the essence of the inner aspect of Hod, sincerity. They also suggest that surrender to the higher will of God can lead to one being filled with God's emanations. Under certain circumstances this could even enable a person to act on behalf of God for the greater good, as David does. In such cases a great leader will then serve as an example of a holy teaching, inspiring others to emulate his or her behavior.

The prophet's lives and teachings remain vibrant and applicable to our lives today—the passage of time does not alter holy truths. What we learn from David's life and attitude as recorded in Torah, and in Psalms in particular, is that humility is the foundation for building a personal holy Tabernacle for God to occupy. "Though He was king but he said, 'I am not king; God is King and He has crowned me.' He was powerful, but he said, 'I am not powerful'; he was rich, but he said, 'I am not rich, Yours, God, is the wealth and the power' (1 Chronicles 29:11). He went to war and won, but he said, 'I did not win because of my might; [God] helped me and granted me victory.'"[40] In other words, one does not think "all that I am"; one instead should think, "All that I have is yours on loan to me." This is the traditional Chassidic perspective.

---

[38] Yalkut HaMechiri, Tehillim 13:6. See also Chasidah, *Encyclopedia of Biblical Personalities*, 136.

[39] Luzzatto, *Mesillat Yesharim*, 470.

[40] Shocher Tov 144:1. "He who sees David in dream can expect to attain piety" (Berachos 57b). See also Chasidah, *Encyclopedia of Biblical Personalities*, 134–35.

Personal Inheritance and National Goodness

In Chassidut it is taught that every nation is rewarded or punished based on its good works—in particular, some say, relative to their treatment of the nation of Israel and the Jewish people. It is also said that an individual living within a nation is given only his fair share of the nation's apportioned good fortune, making one's place in life dependent on the nation's overall goodness. The exception is the person who lives a holy life, the tzaddik, who is apportioned good fortune on his own merit, as governed by God's direct involvement. But the average person is judged both as an individual and as a member of his or her nation. That is why even the very best of people, along with immoral people, die in the flames of war or the tragedy of natural disasters like earthquakes, floods, and fires.

We are one world, consisting of many nations and people, having a shared relationship in time and space when we incarnate. There are groups of souls, from century to century, who incarnate together: one time one will be the aggressor, another time the victim. We cannot know the depth and complexity of the balancing and rebalancing that takes place throughout our many lifetimes, but we do know that all of it eventually leads to completion of the human soul's journey of becoming God-like.

The Practice of Opening the Heart

In the beautiful, eleventh-century teachings of Rabbi Bachya ben Joseph ibn Paquda, "Rabbeinu Bachya," as found in the classic work *Duties of the Heart,* we are told exactly how each person can reach a state of unity with God and all of life. These Jewish wisdom teachings make it clear that peace in the world is dependent on each person's devotion to the divine celestial light present in each one of us; this is what unites us all. Humanity's evolution depends on our ability to act with wholehearted devotion—to be of one heart, or *lev echad,* לב אחד (Lamed Bet Alef Chet Dalet). In the Judaic tradition this begins with love of God. "What constitutes wholehearted devotion of acts to God?" asks Rabbeinu Bachya. "It is the intention, in public and private acts of worship, for the sake of His Name, to do His Will alone and not to win the favors of human beings."[41] The devotion one feels to God and therefore the love

---

[41] R. Bachya ben Joseph ibn Paquda, *Duties of the Heart,* 477.

of His entire creation is attainable by every single person by "virtue of ten attributes. If a person internalizes them and comprehends truly that they are the foundations of worship and the roots of his works, then his devotion of acts to God's Name will be complete. He will turn to no one else, rely on no one beside Him, and the sole aim of his works will be to please Him."[42] This, we now know, is considered the hallmark of the righteous person. As well, the "Lord our God is wheresoever we call upon him" (Deuteronomy 4:7).

Rabbeinu Bachya counsels us to assiduously cultivate these ten attributes if we are to open our hearts entirely to God and to the love that is our legacy, which is to be shared with the world. In a certain sense these attributes represent the entire Tree of Life as reflected in the single Sefirah of Hod (i.e., the Keter of Hod, the Chochmah of Hod, etc.); together these produce the inner light of the *keli* (vessel) called Hod.

The ten attributes of the open-heart practice include:

1. Wholeheartedly acknowledging God's unity
2. Reflecting on God's graces, which are continually bestowed on us
3. Taking on the practice of service of God
4. Embracing reliance on Him and not on human beings
5. Believing that it is not within the power of any created being to help or harm without the permission of the Creator
6. Cultivating indifference to people's praise or insults
7. Refraining from currying favor with other people
8. Clearing one's heart of worldly matters when working for the World to Come
9. Being in awe of God and diffident before Him
10. Consulting the intellect whenever evil thoughts enter the heart, and accepting the counsel of the intellect rather than that of one's baser instincts

The Importance of Joy

There is another requisite for the gift of prophecy, one King David so ably demonstrates, and that is joy. A prophet needs to be emotionally

---

[42] Paquda, *Duties of the Heart*, 477.

elevated, as we see in the description of the Ark's return to Jerusalem, when David danced before the Lord "with all his might" (2 Samuel 6:14).

> Just what did he do? He was dressed . . . in glistening garments embroidered with fringes shining like fine gold (paz), and he struck his hands one against the other, clapping them. As he danced, crying, "[Hail], exalted Lord (kiri ram)!" the glistening gold fringes that he wore made tinkling sound (pozez). More! He pulled up his skirts [thus baring his legs] and cavorted as Israel cheered loudly, sounding horns and trumpets and all kinds of musical instruments. When he reached Jerusalem [cavorting thus], all the women looked at David from roofs and windows, and he did not mind.[43]

In this scene of jubilation, David shows us that true humility means not only bowing before the King (i.e., God) but that it is also a disposition of the heart in which one wants to honor the Creator with great, joyful devotion. Who has matured in heart to know the importance of praise in prayer also knows the responsibility each person holds for the entire generation. King David, the author of the prophetically inspired Book of Psalms, best describes the feeling of Hod and its song: "That I may publish with the voice of thanksgiving, and tell of all thy wondrous works" (Psalms 26:7).

The Illumination of the Heart

The opening and illumination of the heart in Hod allows the person to make his entire life a totally consecrated act—not for any gain he might receive, but rather for the joy of glorifying in the Divine Presence. Rising from our place in personal prayer with great self-reflection in Malchut, we arrive in Yesod in joy, in consecrated union with our Beloved, devoting our lives to divine service. Then in Hod we discover that elevation requires total selflessness, humility, and piety, and so we dedicate ourselves to doing good deeds and refraining from wrong action. The initiate is then safely prepared to inherit from Netzach, the next Sefirah in our ascent of the ladder of light, a sense of victory through the application of physical and spiritual will.

---

[43] Hayim Nahman Bialik and Yehoshua Hana Ravnitzky, *Sefer Ha-Aggadah,* 119:92.

King David learned during his forty-year reign that it was not for him to complete the task of building the Temple and bringing Moshiach, but he was to make an effort in that direction. In the same way, while we may not be able to accomplish total peace in our lives or complete and perfect love of God and attachment to Him at all times, we should not fail to make an effort to do so, for it is effort and intention that are the hallmark of the soul's development. In the long run it is neither the rank nor the station that one can name as having reached, but rather the desire, the aim, and the hope in one's heart to grow more perfect, and the effort one makes to form a pure place for the Divine Presence that allows Him to write His will on us. We must always remember that humans are created from love in order to love.

> *The way of God is perfect.*
>
> PSALMS 18:31

As we conclude the second aspect of consecration, piety (the first being devotion), we experience components of the world of formation, Yetzirah. In general this informs us that when we form an idea, an object, or an act of devotion, it is made sacred by the emotion and intention we invest in it. Thanksgiving for the opportunity to act is the foundation of humility. Combining devotion and sincerity as aspects of formation makes the Ruach—the spirit, the breath, the air of our worldly body—primary. The sustaining inhalation and exhalation of our breathing, our everyday actions, our everyday words and demeanor—all these affect whether we hear the voice of spirit or drown it out.

The Service of Devotion

The Holy Spirit is expressed and experienced by us when we are united in mind and heart, fully engaged in devotional service. It is this same spirit, the Ruach, which animates our words of prayer and our songs of praise, our crying out in joy and great thanksgiving, qualities associated with the Outer Court and the persona of Zeir Anpin, of which Hod is a part. When David sought refuge in a cave while hiding from Saul, "He came to realize that a person is sustained neither by his wealth, nor by his wisdom, nor by his might, but by his prayer."[44] Just as the Sefirot are composed of a smaller inner light and a larger outer or surrounding light, David recognized that his inner and outer light was dependent on God.

> *The word of the Lord is pure.*
>
> PSALMS 33:4

We leave our study of the Sefirah of Hod with our majesty aroused and our piety established. Consecration becomes more complete when we merge the humble heart (Hod) with enduring commitment (Netzach) and cleave to God in body and soul (Yesod). "David's greatness is that he composed songs of praise that raised him to sublime heights where Divine Inspiration came to rest upon him. He achieved this exalted spiritual level at the end of his life, when he had reached extraordinary perfection."[45]

We continue our ascent of the ladder of light, moving back in time, arriving at Shiloh, where Chanah the prophetess is our guide, showing us what it means to have an enduring commitment to spiritual teachings. Discipline, she demonstrates, is the liberator of the human spirit.

---

[44] Shocher Tov 142:1. See also Chasidah, *Encyclopedia of Biblical Personalities,* 145.
[45] Zohar 3:285a. See also Chasidah, *Encyclopedia of Biblical Personalities,* 140.

6
Uplifting Praise
Netzach • Song of Victory

*And Hannah prayed, and said: my heart exulteth in the
Lord, my horn is exalted in the Lord: my mouth is
enlarged over mine enemies: because I rejoice in Thee.*

1 Samuel 2:1

Seventh Sefirot: Netzach
Meaning: Victory, eternity, endurance
Rung on Ascending Ladder: Four
Archetype: The Son (Zeir Anpin)
Symbol: The prayer book
Spiritual World: Yetzirah/formation
Spiritual Anatomy: Right leg
Inner Quality: Confidence (bitachon)

Historical Personage: Chanah the prophetess
Text: Chanah's Song (1 Samuel 2:1–10)
Key Words: Strong attachment
Key Emotion in Song: Victorious praise (nitzuah)

Tent of Meeting: Outer Court
Spiritual Stage: Consecration
Spiritual Practice: Victory over one's lower nature
Illumination: The illumination of devoted will

The prophetess Chanah leads all of Israel in vigorous prayer and attachment to God's teachings.

Netzach:
Cultivating Spiritual Discipline

Now therefore, our God, we thank thee, and praise thy glorious name.

1 CHRONICLES 29:13

We enter now the Sefirah of Netzach, the right-pillar attribute of enduring in our efforts, which leads one to sing an uplifiting song of victory (nitzuah) and form a deeper level of attachment to God's teachings and presence. We learn that constant practice and energetic commitment to doing what we can to achieve what is holy is Netzach's role. Like a mighty engine of will, Netzach allows us to take all that we have acquired in qualities so far—attachment to ancestors, devotion to God, humility before His kingship, and now, enduring desire to do—to carry out the will of God as revealed through His Divine Presence.

Here we acquire a level of self-mastery important for our continued ascension. This Sefirah's inner attribute of confidence tells us why the saying "practice makes perfect" is true not only in regard to physical activities, but to our spiritual work as well. We should not expect perfection, but we should endure and never give up trying, for we can be confident that we will become the better for it. This means that in the Outer Court rituals of daily and seasonal sacrifices, the regular practice of ritual law leads to refinement of both the person and the community. In our own lives we must put into action what we learn and refine our behavior with a rigorous willingness to change.

The Prophetess Chanah:
Vigorous Attachment to God

The LORD maketh poor, and maketh rich;
He bringeth low, He also lifteth up.

1 SAMUEL 2:7

The prophetess Chanah, the wife of Elkanah, an exceptionally kind and devoted spouse and observant man, is barren. For nineteen years she petitions God to conceive a child, trying many schemes to engage God's mercy to accomplish her goal. Her story is a dramatic telling of vigorous attachment to God, Torah, and the ritual sanctuary. Her determined will (*ratzon*) and knowledge of Halacha, Jewish law, and how to apply it in pursuit of her heart's desire are the hallmarks of endurance and victory, the essence of Netzach's spiritual function. She knows when, where, and how to apply her will, and above all, that it must be surrendered completely to God, to one's divine purpose.

Enduring Obstacles

One of Chanah's strategies to conceive is based on her notion that jealousy might arouse her womb to conception. And so after her first ten years of barrenness, she tells her husband to bring another wife, Peninah, into their household so that Elkanah will not be deprived of the opportunity to father offspring and increase the family. Chanah thinks that by bringing another woman into the home God will grant her wish, since it is forbidden to deliberately create rivalries between women. In fact, there are prohibitions against two sisters being married to the same man; the Bible is replete with accounts of how much anguish this can cause women. Yet if all is God, then these kinds of polarizations eventually lead to the rectification of both the individuals involved and the community, and this is exactly what happens in Chanah's case.

After Peninah enters the household, she gives birth to a total of ten children, during which time Chanah remains barren. This is a time of severe testing of Chanah's will. In addition to all the various remedies she pursues for her barrenness (including the idea of pretending to have committed adultery), she never stops praying, she never stops trying, and she remains steadfast in her faith in God. Her spiritual practices center on her daily prayers and her annual pilgrimage to the ancient city of Shiloh, in the Ephraim hill country near the present-day West Bank, for the spring festival of Shavuot, when the first fruits of the wheat harvest are brought as thanksgiving offerings.

"Requested of God"

Shiloh was the religious capital of Israel during the time of the judges. The desert Tent of Meeting built under Moses' direction, which contained the Ark of the Covenant, had been installed there, a stone wall replacing the Tent of Meeting's outer fabric walls. Ritual pilgrimages were made here by the faithful. The three required pilgrimage festivals for men (both then and today, where the pilgrimage is made to Jerusalem) included Passover (Pesach), Weeks (Shavuot), and the Tent of Booths (Sukkot). Chanah would annually go to this sanctuary in Shiloh to offer sacrifices and to petition God's help in fulfilling her desire. It was on one such occasion that events would take a dramatic turn.

While Chanah prays at Shiloh, "She spake in her heart; only her lips moved, but her voice was not heard" (1 Samuel 1:13). The sanctuary's High Priest, Eli, later to become the tutor and spiritual master of Samuel, Chanah's first-born son, mistakenly accuses her of being drunk and tells her to leave the sanctuary at once. At this, Chanah speaks her mind: "And Hannah answered and said, 'No, my lord, I *am* a woman of a sorrowful spirit: I have drunk neither wine nor strong drink, but have poured out my soul before the Lord'" (1 Samuel 1:15). Furthermore, she tells Eli that the presence of the Holy Spirit does not rest on him if he has mistaken her for an inebriated person. Seeing his error, realizing she was praying with complete devotion, Eli begins to petition God on her behalf. As a result of Eli's prayers and Chanah's tears, the gates of mercy are opened for her, as it is said that the gate of tears is never closed to those who pray with a sincere heart and cry out for God's help. In turn, mercy is bestowed.

As a result of Chanah's declaration of God's preeminence and her steadfast devotion to Him at the Tabernacle at Shiloh, combined with the auspicious intervention of the High Priest who is to play such an important role not only in Chanah's life but her son's, she finally gains God's favor. We are told that at the age of 129, Chanah conceives Samuel, whose name means "requested of God"—the very prophet who later would anoint both Saul and David as kings. She later bears four more children. In thanksgiving, Chanah (like Sarah, another prophetess associated with the right pillar of Chesed and its attribute of loving-kindness, who is childless until the advanced age of eighty-nine) gives her first-born son to the service of God.[1]

In the process of investing confidence in her prayers and offering the song associated with the emotional quality of Netzach, uplifting praise, Chanah leads Israel in its spiritual evolution, showing the way of victory as she teaches the Israelites the virtue of performing sacred rituals and making constant, determined prayer rather than waiting passively for miracles to happen. Chanah, as mentioned in chapter 3 on Malchut, was the progenitor of the formula for the foundational Shemoneh Esrei, commonly known as the Amidah, or Standing Prayer. As well, Chanah was the first person on earth to call God the Host of Hosts—in Hebrew, *Tsvaot,* expressing the fundamental awareness that the Lord is the progenitor of all and that what we praise increases in spiritual power.

So new was this to the world that even God took note of the event.[2]

The Benefits of Spiritual Partnership

Our prior sefirotic representatives King Solomon (Yesod) and King David (Hod) each had multiple wives and concubines.[3] Chanah, who reveals for the generations to come the benefits of spiritual partnership, prospers in part due to her husband's status as a prophet. It was said of Chanah's husband, Elkanah, "There was one man (1 Samuel 1:1). Wherever it says one, [it indicates] a great man . . . there was no one else like Elkanah in his generation."[4] Here, the prophetess's only husband, as the insemina-

---

[1] For a complete exploration of Chanah as a prophetess, see this author's *Kabbalistic Teachings of the Female Prophets,* 196–233.

[2] See this author's *Kabbalistic Teachings of the Female Prophets,* 207.

[3] It is possible that King Solomon's brilliance of wisdom (Chochmah, or *Abba,* the Father) was due in part to the many women with whom he consorted, some of who may have had prophetic talent. This kind of activity, represented in its own way of Yesod as a spiritual arousal from below, resulted in the construction of the holy Temple (which included a women's courtyard).

[4] Bamidbar Rabbah 10:5. See also R. Yisrael Yitzchak Yishai Chasidah, *Encyclopedia of Biblical Personalities,* 95.

tor, endows his child Samuel with the supernal wisdom (Chochmah) of the Father (Abba), while Chanah endows him with the understanding (Binah) of the Mother (Imma); this accounts for the loftiness of Samuel's soul and the fact that he too is a prophet.

The connection between Chanah and the matriarch Sarah, both on the right pillar, extends to a comparison of their husbands. "He [Elkanah] was the outstanding righteous man of his entire generation. In all his deeds, Elkanah resembled Abraham [Sarah's husband]. . . . He was called a prophet."[5] Elkanah, so moved by Chanah's suffering over her childlessness, would generously give her double portions at the table, despite the fact that Peninah, the wife Chanah brought into their household hoping to make her womb jealous, bore Elkanah ten children (all of whom but two would die during her lifetime).

"Every year, Chana and Elkhana go up to Shiloh together to make their annual offerings, at which time Eli blesses them. 'May God grant you offspring from this woman', because of the request that he [Elkanah] had made of God . . . For God remembered Chanah and she conceived and gave birth to three sons and two daughters. And the boy Samuel grew up with God" (1 Samuel 2:20–21).[6] Just as it is said that God closed Chanah's womb, He opened it, and she conceived Samuel on the Jewish New Year, Rosh Hashanah. Torah records this moment: "They arose early in the morning and prostrated themselves before God: then they returned and came to their home, to Ramah. Elkanah knew Chanah his wife and God remembered her" (1 Samuel 1:19).

Chanah's Mercy

While Chanah is childless, Peninah taunts her for her barrenness. Later, as a result of Peninah's cruelty,

> whenever Chanah would give birth to one son, Peninah would bury two sons. [By the time] Chanah had given birth to four children, Peninah had buried eight. [Now] Chanah was expecting the fifth, and Peninah was afraid lest she bury her two remaining sons, so she went to

---

[5] Aggadas Bereshis 50. See also Chasidah, *Encyclopedia of Biblical Personalities,* 95.
[6] See also this author's *Kabbalistic Teachings of the Female Prophets,* 205.

Chanah and said, "I know I have sinned against you, please forgive me so that the two sons I have left will live." Thereupon Chanah prayed before the Holy One, Blessed is He: "Forgive her and let her two sons live." Said the Holy One, Blessed be He, "By your life, they should have died, but because you prayed for them they will live. I will consider them your sons." Therefore it says, a barren woman bore seven (1 Samuel 2:5) [although Chanah herself bore only five].

We are told that in addition to the five children that Chanah bore herself, the two children of Peninah's that survived were considered hers as well.[7]

The prophets Chanah and Elkanah demonstrate the significance of holy matrimony, wherein both male and female are devoted to God. Not only did they have five children together as a result of their good deeds and prayers, they regarded all of Israel as their family. When we learn that Chanah and Elkanah took the whole community up to Shiloh, this is a reference to spiritual elevation, aliyah, not merely to the physical act of traveling to Shiloh. That Elkanah never took the same route twice, as we are told, tells us that every spiritual journey is a new journey. Each time we embark in the service of doing good deeds it is a new moment. Each day is a return, or for some a first-time encounter, with the ways of the ancient teachings. Like their predecessors on the right column, Abraham and Sarah, who had many proselytes, Elkanah and Chanah teach us how to convert our many misdeeds into good deeds.

"Holy, Holy, Holy"

Though Torah tells us of Chanah's annual ascent to Shiloh, there is one time we learn of her absence, and this occurs when Samuel is too young and delicate to go with them. "Until the child is weaned," Chanah announces, "I will not come to Shiloh" (1 Samuel 1:22). The Zohar instructs us that it was for Samuel's soul that Chanah prayed, hoping he would serve God when he grew up, a promise she had made to God in

---

[7] Pesikta Rabbasi 44:7. See also Chasidah, *Encyclopedia of Biblical Personalities,* 197. As we have already learned, all numbers in Torah are meaningful. Though she gave birth to five children, and the number 5, like the letter Hay, stands for God's living presence, the addition of Peninah's surviving two children is on account of Chanah's merit.

beseeching His mercy for conception. "She made a vow and said, Lord, Master of Legions, if you take note of the suffering of Your maidservant, and You remember me, and do not forget Your maidservant, and give Your maidservant male offspring, then I shall give him to God all the days of his life, and a razor shall not come upon his head" (1 Samuel 1:10–11).[8] This is the historic moment when Chanah first expresses God's true nature as Tsvaot, the Host of Hosts (i.e., "Master of Legions") about which the oral tradition says that "God responded saying, 'You have multiplied my Hosts [by calling me Host], I will multiply yours,' thus it is written, all these were the sons of Chanah."[9]

In the oral tradition, Chanah's biblical narrative is interpreted through the lens of her prophetic talents. As a prophetess she is tested for nineteen years before giving birth to Samuel. She prays, "Give your handmaid seed of men (1 Samuel 1:11): a man [distinguished] among men, [Shmuel said:] a son who will anoint two men: Saul and David. [R'YoChanahn said:] A son who is equivalent to two men: Moses and Aaron. [Our sages say: A son] who will be average among men, neither tall nor short . . . [so the people should not speak about him and place an evil eye on him (Rashi)].[10] This Torah text, as interpreted by the sages, gives us a sense of Chanah's gift of prophecy: we see in her prayer both the future kings of Israel and the lineage of prophets of which Samuel is part. Another time, "Hannah prayed with prophetic inspiration." She said, "My son Samuel is destined to be a prophet in Israel, and in his days Israel will be miraculously saved from the Philistines. My great grandson Heman, son of Joel, together with his fourteen sons, is destined to sing hymns with lyres and harps among their fellow Levites in the Temple."[11] The prophetic inspiration that emerges from the sages' commentary on the People of the Book's teachings reveals why it is taught that every time one reads these sacred stories, new insights can be gained—just as our daily routines can be understood as new holy opportunities. As Chanah teaches, it depends primarily on one's enduring attachment to God and the Word of God and to doing holy deeds.

---

[8] Those dedicated to God, that is, Nazarites such as Samuel, did not cut their hair.

[9] Chasidah, *Encyclopedia of Jewish Personalities,* 196. See also this author's *Kabbalistic Teachings of the Female Prophets,* 208.

[10] Berachos 31b.

[11] Targum Shmuel 1:2:1. See also Chasidah, *Encyclopedia of Biblical Personalities,* 198.

Like many talents, prophecy runs in bloodlines. Here we have a unique three-part constellation of a prophetess, Chanah, and a prophet, Elkanah, giving birth to the prophet Samuel. Chanah, by whom all of Israel benefits, is an emanation from the right-hand pillar of Chesed,[12] like Sarah and Abraham[13] before her, and Chochmah above Chesed.

The Value of Communal Aliyah

During the time that Chanah and Elkanah are leaders of their community, Shiloh is the first semipermanent center of worship since the days of the Exodus and the Tabernacle's location at Gilgal (discussed in chapter 8). It is here in Shiloh that the Tent of Meeting rests for 369 years before it is relocated to Jerusalem by King David (as described in chapter 5). Four times a year, Elkanah would "go up" to Shiloh. He would take his entire household, as well as his relatives, and eventually all of Israel to worship there. Three of these occasions were for the three pilgrimage festivals, as directed by Torah, and one visit was for a private vow Elkanah had made. Chanah and Elkanah's enduring commitment to prayer and to serving God inspires their community; each year more and more people would go up to honor God during the sacred holidays:

> "Where are you going?" [the people would say. Elkanah would reply,] "To the house of God in Shiloh, why don't you come with us and we shall go together?" Thereupon [the people] would shed tears and say, "We shall go up with you." The following year five households would go up, the next ten, and the year after all would assemble to go up, until about sixty households were going up with him. Elkanah did not go up by the same route twice. Finally, all of Israel would go up [to Shiloh].[14]

---

[12] For full elaboration on this, see this author's *Kabbalistic Teachings of the Female Prophets,* 199.

[13] Traditionally, when we speak of Abraham as Chesed, Sarah is Gevurah (judgment). In the stories of the seven prophetesses of Israel, the Ramak (Rabbi Moshe Cordovero) placed Sarah in Chesed (see *Kabbablistic Teachings of the Female Prophets*). Again, we see that depending on the constellation or situation, a person can occupy more than one Sefirah. So too in our own lives—sometimes we demonstrate one particular quality or Sefirah, and at other times we exhibit another essential energy.

[14] Tanna d'Bei Eliyahu Rabbah 8. See also Chasidah, *Encyclopedia of Biblical Personalities,* 95.

Netzach, as represented by the Tabernacle at Shiloh, brings strength and enduring commitment to personal and communal worship. Note that "going up" also refers to aliyah, spiritual elevation, the next stage of the initiate's development after consecration. As one climbs the Tree of Life, one inherits humility from Hod and King David, whom Chanah's son, the prophet Samuel, anoints. In terms of the interrelationship between the Sefirot, Netzach, as the right leg, combines with Hod, the left leg, giving us the lower limbs of our personal Lower Chariot, as Kabbalah describes the three Sefirot of Netzach, Hod, and Yesod (NeHiY). Taken together: one bows in humble supplication (Hod), while also acting with zealous imperative (Netzach), to consecrate one's covenant of devotion to God (Yesod).

As we ascend the Tree of Life in the reverse order from which the light descends, Netzach is the stage of consecration represented by the animal and agrarian sacrifices as well as the water rituals in the Outer Court. Everything that takes place in the holy sanctuary can be taken back to its roots in the Sefirot. Even the "ten curtains that form the inner covering of the Tabernacle, closest to the holiness of the Ark, and the other vessels"[15] express the relationship between the life force of God and the ten Sefirot, which absorb this life force in the form of light, just as we do.

Song of Netzach:
Victorious Praise (Nitzuah)

God is my strength and power: and he maketh my way perfect.

2 SAMUEL 22:33

In chapter 3 we focused on the formula of the Shemoneh Esrei, which the elders composed based on Chanah's three-part method of prayer. We will now consider the song that Chanah chants for guidance in refining the emotions.

Recall that all of the Sefirot from Yesod to Chesed comprise the partzuf of the Son, Zeir Anpin. These six Sefirot represent the emotions (middot). Thus far we have examined the role of our feelings in our covenant with God (Yesod) and in our marriage to humility and royalty (Hod). Now we declare

---

[15] R.Yitzchak Luria, *Apples from the Orchard*, Tavo, 992.

our spiritual fervor in a tone of eternal upliftment, producing the feeling of spiritual victory that is the hallmark of Netzach. That Netzach's quality of song is one of uplifting praise tells us that when we sing our praises to God we are making offerings in the Outer Court. Like the smoke from the sacrifices that goes up and the aroma, which is pleasing to God, our prayers at this stage of consecration rise up when we offer up an aspect of ourselves that we burn off with enduring will. This is the meaning underlying the song of Netzach. It is said that there is nothing more pleasing to God than the prayers of the righteous, particularly when they are offered with a great sense of arousing spiritual love.

Netzach embodies spiritual will and the quality of spiritual discipline required of every initiatic path. When examined in the context of the partzufim system, as part of the six Sefirot that make up the archetype of the Son (Zeir Anpin), Netzach is part of a constellation that deals with the spiritual development of the emotions. Zeir Anpin is synonymous with the soul's quality of Ruach, or spirit. To consecrate our emotions, to make our feelings tools of holiness, is to do the work of the priests in the Tabernacle. In this way we elevate ourselves and everyone we meet. We create a resting place for the Holy Spirit, the Ruach HaKodesh, the medium of prophecy. This is how the prophets were able to receive the Word of God; this is how Chanah composed her song. We are reminded that "although all the prophets begin their books with recitals of Israel's guilt, they end them with words of comfort"[16]—a warning to people that their feelings of separation from holiness is a false path, and reminding them of humanity's divine purpose, which is unity. All prophets are assigned this duty of helping humanity recover its God-like nature.

Chanah's Song (1 Samuel 2:1–10)

Taking Samuel up to Shiloh for the first time when he turns two, Chanah dedicates him to the priesthood and sings this song:

🌿**1** *And Hannah prayed, and said: my heart exulteth in the LORD, my horn is exalted in the LORD; my mouth is enlarged over mine enemies; because I rejoice in Thee.* **2** *There is none holy as the LORD, for there is none beside Thee; neither is there any rock like our Godly salvation.* **3** *Multiply not*

---

[16] Hayim Nahman Bialik and Yehoshua Hana Ravnitzky, *Sefer Ha-Aggadah*, 8:90, 478.

exceeding proud talk; let not arrogance come out of your mouth; for the LORD *is a God of knowledge, and by Him actions are weighed.* **4** *The bows of the mighty men are broken, and they that stumbled are girded with strength.* **5** *They that were full have hired out themselves for bread; and they that were hungry have ceased; while the barren hath borne seven, she that had many children hath languished.* **6** *The* LORD *killeth, and maketh alive; He bringeth down to the grave, and bringeth up.* **7** *The* LORD *maketh poor, and maketh rich; He bringeth low, He also lifteth up.* **8** *He raiseth up the poor out of the dust, He lifteth up the needy from the dung-hill, to make them sit with princes, and inherit the throne of glory; for the pillars of the earth are the* LORD'S, *and He hath set the world upon them.* **9** *He will keep the feet of His holy ones, but the wicked shall be put to silence in darkness; for not by strength shall man prevail.* **10** *They that strive with the* LORD *shall be broken to pieces; against them will He thunder in heaven; the* LORD *will judge the ends of the earth; and He will give strength unto His king, and exalt the horn of His anointed.* **11** *And Elkanah went to Ramah to his house. And the child did minister unto the* LORD *before Eli the priest.*

Vigorous Attachment

Chanah's song includes a statement about the ruination that comes to those who are arrogant: having acquired from Hod (the left leg) a genuine understanding of humility, she tells others, that "by Him actions are weighed," that is, God evaluates our actions and intentions and from this judgment the conditions of our lives are created. Fundamentally, what we sow, we reap, from lifetime to lifetime. We are co-creating our life circumstances, even when we are unaware of the influence we can have in changing them. So complete is Chanah's devotion and attachment to God that for her there is nothing *but* God. From this we can infer that it is not by our individual will that we will prevail, but by loving and honoring God and all of creation, and by surrendering our personal will to God's.

Inner Quality: Confidence

In the emotional fervor of glorifying the divine root of all life, Chanah reveals in her song an inner quality of Netzach: a form of certainty and confidence, or *bitachon*. It is said there are two kinds of confidence, one active and the other passive. Chanah shows us both. Active confidence consists of trust in our ability to accomplish our goals, the will to do. Passive confidence does not mean nonaction; it rather describes a great ability to surrender one's personal will to the higher will. The passive form of confidence is trust that God and universal law will guide and bless one's life at all times and that events will unfold in accord with the greatest revealed and oftentimes concealed good. It is associated with the Sefirah of Hod and its action or effect on Netzach. This combined energetic state of being is beautifully demonstrated by both King David, a person with a humbled will, and Chanah, who demonstrates confident will in action by doing everything she can to persuade God to give her a child to benefit Israel. At the same time Chanah glorifies God with uplifted feelings, displaying a passive form of bitachon, surrendering to God, exhibiting Hod's more inward form of confidence.

There is a stark, no-nonsense quality to the prophetic text of Chanah's song. There is good and evil, and the ways of both are known. The results of our choices are also known. This is the spiritual discipline Netzach instills in the initiate when he consecrates his life to God. This aspect of consecration is a willing attachment that endures, which is why Netzach is also called Eternity. Looking at other elements of consecration, one begins to see that by using the Tree of Life model as Kabbalists do to explain life's circumstances, we discover that there are at least ten aspects in holiness and in all holy things.

Ritual: Netzach in Partnership with Hod

And if ye offer a sacrifice of peace offerings unto the LORD,
ye shall offer it at your own will.

LEVITICUS 19:5

Netzach is always partnered with Hod and referred to in the Zohar as the thighs, which our walking through life, both literally and metaphorically, depends on. This pair is also called the groom (Netzach) and the bride (Hod), inasmuch as the right pillar on which Netzach stands is masculine and active, and the left-pillar position of Hod, with its quality of majestic humility, is receptive.[17] We are each both masculine and

---

[17] The right-sided Netzach is on the masculine pillar of Chochmah, the Father, and Hod is on the left, feminine side of Binah, the Mother. See chapter 1, figure 1.3, page 15.

feminine in our inner nature. Learning to balance our male and female qualities, our active and receptive tendencies, our rational and intuitive talents, is to make peace in one's own inner household (body) and in one's life and to sanctify the holy marriage between ourselves and God.

Chanah and her son, the prophet Samuel, represent Netzach, which partners with King David and Hod. To gain additional insight into the importance of Netzach's quality of spiritual discipline and its manifestation in the lives of Chanah and Samuel, the Zohar (in Naso, 124–125) tells us that a Nazarite (from the Hebrew word *nazar*, "to dedicate") such as Samuel is not only prohibited from drinking wine,[18] which is Malchut as it is the produce of the physical world and considered a mind-altering substance, but from eating grapes as well. According to tradition, the Nazarite must keep himself far away from evil and away from the harsh judgment (Gevurah) that attends misdeeds, so that he may maintain a standard even higher than that of the High Priest, who is allowed wine. Chanah's discipline, as we have seen, is evident in her prayers and petitions to God to become a mother and in her dedication to the Tabernacle. After Samuel is entrusted to the care of the High Priest Eli, who trains him for his spiritual role, Chanah makes Samuel a new cloak to wear each year, taking it to him every time she makes her annual journey to Shiloh. In this sense she literally and figuratively wraps Samuel in her love of God as well as in her enduring motherly love.

Netzach on the Right Column

As a Sefirah of the right column, Netzach is directly related to the Sefirah immediately above it, Chesed, which is represented by Moses' final communication to the people of Israel, the song of Chesed we will study in chapter 9. Notably, the Zohar often equates **Moses** (משה) with **Shiloh** (שילה), and in Hebrew both of these words have the same number value, 345, as do the Hebrew words for **pomegranate** (הרמנים); the **Book** (הספר), referring to the Hebrew Bible; and **HaShem** (השם), which translates as "the name," referring to the name of God. All these words are holy aspects of the devotional path. Whether it is a holy fruit of the land of Israel (the pomegranate is associated with the Sefirah of Hod), a

---

[18] Vayikra 10:9 says, "Do not drink wine or strong drink."

person (Moses/Chesed), a holy place (Shiloh/Netzach), or the holy Book (the Word of God/Malchut and Keter), we see that all material vessels are holy when we elevate their purpose to service of the divine.

Rabbi Moses ben Jacob Cordovero (1522–1570), a.k.a. Ramak, the sixteenth-century Kabbalist who was an older colleague of the Arizal, points out that Netzach and Chesed are also related through Chanah and the first prophetess and matriarch, Sarah. Thus Shiloh, the location associated with Netzach, is endowed with the light that shines on it from the right-pillar Sefirah above it, Chesed. Shiloh therefore holds the blessings of the emancipator and greatest prophet, Moses, as well as the blessings of Sarah, the mother of the Jewish people (who, like Chanah, surrendered her son, Yitzchak, to the service of God). This also points to the fact that the Ten Commandments, which Moses brought down, are housed in the Tabernacle, or Mishkan, which is later brought to Shiloh, the place where the Ark of the Covenant rests for 369 years before its establishment in Jerusalem—all of which is an illustration of how the inner light of created spiritual reality (the realm of Beriyah) is revealed via humans' thought forms, wherein a person first has the idea for something (the realm of Yetzirah), then finally manifests this as a material reality in the world through physical action (the realm of Assiyah).

Drawing the light of Binah, the supernal Mother, from the left pillar, and the light of Chochmah, the supernal Father, from the right is a process of melding. It takes Chanah and Sarah many years of supplication before God, of serving in the community, before either of them is granted a son. The result was Isaac (Yitzchak) with Sarah, and Samuel (Shmuel) with Chanah—two great men who led Israel and emerged from the right pillar of kindness. One finds in this a hidden truth about battles and why we must sweeten them with mercy (Tiferet), for our greatest battles are won by enduring love and surrender to God's will and through our effort to persevere no matter what.

The Luminosity of Creation

Kabbalah teaches that there are different kinds of light; each refers to a different aspect of the Creator's presence in the workings of the universe. As the source of brilliance that Moses emanated, this light was so luminous that people could not gaze at the prophet's face. This great light is also associated with the Ark in the Tabernacle, hence the special precautions needed for moving and serving it. We know the Ten Commandments hold this light, that of Creation itself, while this same illumination is described as coming from the protective, hovering Cloud of Glory that follows the Ohel Moed. So, like the Ark, which is made of three box encasements, one inside the other, all of which are inside the Tabernacle, which in turn is surrounded by the enveloping Shechinah, these envelopes of light, one inside the other, are much like the original depiction of the Sefirot of the Tree of Life, in which one realm encompasses another. Like the layers of an onion, they are a sacred unity. In the same way, Torah describes the attachment between the Creator and Israel through the Ten Commandments, the Ark, and the Tabernacle, each a container of the original light of the Tree of Life and its ten-part spiritual architecture. As human beings, we contain all of these elements in our spiritual and physical makeup. The many ways that life fields encapsulate and inhabit one another is a fascinating area of Kabbalistic study that the reader is encouraged to pursue.

Ritual Consecration and Illumination

That Chanah makes offerings annually for nineteen years at the Tabernacle at Shiloh is akin to the progression each person goes through, described in this book, as we ascend the ladder of light. We are to understand that it was only after nineteen years of disciplined self-refinement, with deeper and deeper reliance on the reflexive universe between created and Creator, that Chanah was able to reach such a great place of luminosity that she was able to consecrate the Tabernacle for all of Israel with the conception of the prophet Samuel. Samuel would eventually anoint both King Saul and King David, and would even co-rule, along with David, the nation of Israel for several years. Samuel, like his mother, knew with certainty that what we do while alive determines our afterlife, which is why everything we do matters. "The righteous Samuel feared the judgment [of the World to Come]."[19]

---

[19] Chagigah 4b. See also Chasidah, *Encyclopedia of Biblical Personalities*, 513.

The Outer Court Offerings

When Chanah "goes up" (aliyah) to Shiloh each year, she goes for the first fruits of the spring, a time of birth and thanksgiving. This marks the station of the Outer Court of our Tabernacle where people bring offerings of thanksgiving, atonement, and elevation, which are taken to the altar by the priests to facilitate this consecration.

The subject of the laws regulating the offerings made in the Outer Court is too vast to include in the scope of this book; the Talmud dedicates many pages to the minute details of protocol surrounding sacrificial offerings. For example, there are instructions on which direction the priest walks with the burnt-bird offering, as opposed to other types of offerings (Succah 48b); there are laws regarding the gender of the offering (Temurah 14a, 17b, 18b); laws saying what to do if one accidentally eats a bird that is intended as a burnt offering (Succah 42a); and whether one may bring a bird offering if his vow is a generic "I will bring a burnt offering" (Temurah 20a). So numerous and detailed are these descriptions, with deeper meanings attached to each law, that one could make a marvelous journey of scholarly inquiry in this direction. For our purposes, though, we will deal with the very basic components of the ritual process.

Historically there were six basic categories of offerings made in the Outer Court of the Tent of Meeting. Within each of these categories are rules so specific as to be a large portion of Halacha. Though these Temple rituals are no longer performed as in biblical times, to study them, it is said, takes the place of actually doing them, since the celestial roots are the same, it being only a matter of degrees of separation. As we continue our climb up the ladder of light, we shall see just how these sacrifices fit in with the Outer Court's correspondence to the partzuf of Zeir Anpin, the Son, and what it means to refine the middot and bring them into wholeness.

The Sacrificial Offerings of the Outer Court, *Qorbanot,* קרבנות (Kof Reish Bet Nun Vav Tav)

The following are the primary categories and substances used in the Outer Court ceremonies, though there are subcategories of offerings which are not addressed in this work:

Burnt offerings, *Olah*, עלה (Ayin Lamed Hay): A male animal, ram, bullock, or pigeon, all without blemish, was offered. It was entirely burned on the altar, and no part was eaten.

Peace offerings, *Zebach Sh'lamin*, זבח שלמים (Zayin Bet Chet Shin Lamed Mem Yod Mem): This category includes the idea of thanksgiving, free will, and offerings for a vow. A portion of the offering (a male or female of herd or flock) was burned on the altar, a portion given to the priest to eat, and the rest was consumed by family and community. It is said that in the time of Moshiach, this will be the only type of offering that will be made.

Sin offerings, *Chatat*, חטאת (Chet Tet Alef Tav): A bull, male and female goats, doves, or fine flour for the very poor was offered. This was eaten in part only by the Kohanim (priests); the rest was burned on the altar.

Guilt offerings, *Asham*, אשם (Alef Shin Mem): This was different from sin offerings in that it was generally made for acts in which one is uncertain of having sinned, where one has sinned unintentionally, or as compensation for a trespass. An unblemished ram was partially burnt and the rest was consumed by the priest.

Meal offerings (Food and Drink), *Minchah*, מנחה (Mem Nun Chet Hay): A portion of the meal offering was burnt and the rest given to the Kohanim. These are also called thanksgiving offerings, in which case they consisted of grain offerings: cooked grain, baked cakes, or raw grain offered along with frankincense and oil. All grain offerings were made with oil and salt.

Red Heifer, *Para Adumah*, פרה אדמה (Pey Reish Hay Alef Dalet Mem Hay): The purpose of this ritual involving the ash of the red heifer was to purify those who made contact with the dead or elements of the dead (i.e., open graves, bones, battlefield remains, objects of the dead) (see Numbers 19).

As we proceed through the coming chapters on the Upper Chariot Sefirot of Tiferet, Gevurah, and Chesed (in ascending order), we will discover more about the subject of making sacrifices in the Outer Court. As rituals of fire and water, these sacrifices have particular associations with the processes of refining the emotions, fire being associated with the letter

Shin, which is the pathway on the Tree of Life between Chochmah and Binah (as seen in chapter 1, figure 1.1, page 11), suggesting the fire of action and choice in all that we do. The water ablutions are associated with the mother letter Mem, the pathway between Netzach and Hod. So while Mem is a more internal feeling, Shin is a more external display, such as when we feel love for a person but don't demonstrate it visibly (Mem), as compared to when in another situation we might reach out to hug that person (Shin). Regardless of the display, the inner fire of that love is felt; the embracing of the other is the purity of that feeling expressed openly.

Keeping Our Practice Fresh

We are told that even though we may say the same prayers as part of our regular practice, we should try to find new ways of presenting our hearts to God, such as in the meal offering:

> Of the meal offering. R'Yiztchak said: Why is the meal offering different in that the term Nefesh [soul] is used in connection with it? The Holy One, Blessed be He, said who is it that usually brings the meal offering? A poor man [because he cannot afford to bring an animal]. I consider his meal offering as if he had offered his soul. R. Yitzchak said also: Why is a meal offering different in that it may be prepared in any of five ways? You can compare it to a human king for whom a friend had prepared a meal. Knowing that his friend was poor [and could only afford inexpensive food], the king said to him, "Prepare it for me in five different ways, so that I will enjoy what you are offering me."[20]

This tells us that creatively pursuing how we refine ourselves is not only acceptable, but preferable. The sages simply remind us not to make the same mistakes twice, whether they be unintentional errors in judgment or, God forbid, whether they involve participating in acts one knows are wrong.

How the Worlds Are Impacted by the Outer Court Rituals

As noted in chapter 1, the Sefirot are often referred to as vessels, that which holds the light (similarly, we created beings are also vessels that

---

[20] R. Yaakov Ibn Chaviv, *Ein Yaakov,* Menachot 104b, 763.

hold the light of Creation). When God made the world, Kabbalah teaches, he deliberately made vessels that would break, and indeed they did. "R. Hanina bar Isi said: At times the world and its fullness cannot contain the glory of His Godhead, and at other times He speaks to a man of [a space as tiny as] that between the hairs of his head."[21] In one of the many designs God experimented with before Creation as we know it, the vessels did not receive the light in gradual stages that minimized the descent of the light, hence the vessels each received all the light from the prior Sefirah. This would be like several people handing one person ten boxes all at once; the person cannot hold them all and hence drops some of them, and what is in them consequently breaks. In the same way, the descending vessels could not hold the quantity or quality of light, and so they shattered. This created what is referred to in Kabbalah as the "breaking of the vessels," which in turn created the "fallen sparks" of light, giving humanity the task of elevating them back to holiness.

In chapter 1 we discussed the concept of the five worlds in Kabbalah. All the worlds below En Sof, the highest realm, are made from the shattered parts of this event called "the breaking of the vessels," or in Hebrew, *Shevirat HaKelim*. It is for this reason, the Ari says, that the sacrifices in the Temple or Tent of Meeting elevate the other worlds and the corresponding aspects of ourselves. "R. Yudah said: Very wise in the power of language are the prophets, who [in order to make the children of Israel aware of His Presence] speak of the form of the Almighty as though it were like the form of a man."[22]

What is most delightful to discover, as figures 1.4 and 1.5 (see pages 23 and 31) reveal, are the correspondences that exist in Kabbalah, such as between the five worlds we exist in, the five different aspects of the soul, and the five realms (including the mineral, vegetable, animal, human, and the soul's/heavenly root). Regarding the sacrifices in the Outer Court, the Ari says, "Salt is a mineral, and through it the mineral kingdom was rectified, the wine and oil offered with the sacrifices rectified the vegetable kingdom. The animals rectified the animal kingdom. The confession of the animal's owner recited over the animal corresponds to the articulate

---

[21] Bialik and Ravnitzky, *Sefer Ha-Aggadah,* 8:57, 473. See also Genesis 4:4.

[22] Bialik and Ravnitzky, *Sefer Ha-Aggadah,* 8:58.

kingdom, that is, man. The intention of the priest (*kohen*) while he [is] offering the sacrifice corresponds to the soul within man. Through these five aspects of the sacrifice, the four 'kingdoms' are elevated."[23]

Here we have a precise Chassidic interpretation of Kabbalistic elements and their relationships, explaining the spiritual effect of a physically consecrated action. What we consecrate and give up (i.e., sacrifice) is elevated, an aliyah, showing us why our conscious sacrifices attain a greater spiritual significance than when we simply do things without thought or attachment to the divine root in everything. The sacrifices we make in life to benefit others and our good deeds are like a banner waving above our soul: each mitzvah adds effluence and power to the various parts of the soul and therefore to the body it inhabits.

Consecration Requires Right Intention

As Netzach shows so well, if the intention of the priest is not focused, the initiate's sacrifice can be invalidated. When we offer up something as a sacrifice—a quality of our behavior or a way of speaking or way of doing things that does not bring benefit—our intention to bring about change is the single most important aspect of this process of consecration. The word *consecrate* in Hebrew literally means "to make holy." How is something made holy? By our willingness to attend to it with reverence, to give meaning to that thing's purpose beyond its mere physical attributes.

Consecration involves a spiritual dimension; it is a sacred act, as opposed to a profane, temporal act. This shows that when our bodies are used for divine service in a reverent fashion, we are elevated. When we use Hod, humility, and Netzach, victorious will—the left and the right legs together—to overcome our lower inclinations, we walk soundly, in the same way that King David teaches, with a sincere heart.

Aspects of the Soul and the Outer Court Rituals

In the rituals of the Tabernacle, Keter (the crown) is said to be found in the intention of the priest; it corresponds to the Yechidah level of the soul, the spark of God in the soul. The confession corresponds to Chochmah, the Father, corresponding to the Chayah aspect of the soul, the

---

[23] Luria, *Apples from the Orchard*, 521.

living presence of God. The animal itself represents the Neshamah aspect and the Sefirah of Binah, the discrete soul in each person. The Ruach, the spirit that animates each person, is represented by the wine and oil offerings and the Sefirot of Zeir Anpin (Chesed through Yesod, sometimes referred to by the single Sefirah of Tiferet). Nefesh is the blood of the person and is seen in the blood of the animal sacrifices and the Sefirah of Malchut. (Though like the blood in all mammals, it pervades the entire living creature.) Salt, representing Malchut and the partzuf of Nukvah, the Woman, complete this composition.

The correspondences shown in chapter 1, figure 1.5 (see page 31), are represented in the single service of the Outer Court and the arena called consecration in this work.[24] The word for sacrifices in Hebrew is *qorbanot,* קרבנות (Kof Reish Bet Nun Vav Tav) a word whose root (Kof Bet Reish) means "to bring close" or "to draw near," which is why it is said in Kabbalah that the mystery of the animal sacrifices lies in their ability to bring close those who are far away. This reflects in our personal lives as well: when we give up any kind of improper or selfish behavior, others naturally want to be around us. A refined personal nature leads to a refined spiritual life as well, meaning we draw nearer to the Creator.

A Microcosm of Creation

Just as the person of biblical times brought an offering for God to the Ohel Moed, so too are we instructed to do the same. The prototypical example of this process of spiritualizing matter by elevating whatever we commit ourselves to "is the sacrificial service in the temple."[25] The Arizal teaches that the Temple is a microcosm of Creation—the very premise of this book. Put in more modern terms, "The rites performed within them [the sanctuary] are vital symbolic actions of the wider Divine service that mankind performs in the world at large."[26]

---

[24] Luria, *Apples from the Orchard,* 521. The animal sacrifices were salted before being offered, and wine and oil were used in most animal sacrifices. As for confession, before the animal is slaughtered a person must confess his or her sins; in the case of a sin offering the penitent must express his or her joy and thanksgiving. The power of speaking as the soul's expression is what makes the human elevated above all other aspects of God's creation.

[25] Luria, *Apples from the Orchard,* VaYikra, 521.

[26] Ibid.

Chanah understood this. Having a child was not for herself alone, but for God and the world. Even before her son Samuel was conceived, Chanah had committed his soul to divine service. The words of her song reveal the depth of feeling of Netzach, which is the sensation of being attached to God, to eternity, and to the vastness of the divine light, in an effort to serve the perfect created world in which we have existence. It is a feeling of total immersion in life, a confidence in the path and journey that gives one bearings. It is not ultimately theological, though this is the lens through which humankind has often experienced divinity; it is rather the awareness that there is a divine landscape that consecrates consciousness.

Kabbalah is a spiritual science of correspondences and layers. Each Sefirah contains all the other Sefirot. The Zohar speaks in Kabbalistic detail, using terms that for the most part have been eliminated from this work. For instance, the sages in the Zohar discuss Zeir Anpin (the Son) of Beriyah (the realm of creation), or the Imma (the Mother/Binah) of Atzilut (the realm of emanation), and so on. As each Sefirah contains all ten Sefirot, we are dealing with a minimum of 100 combinations in any one of the four realms, or 400 unique sefirotic qualities, or 500 unique combinations when we include the Or En Sof, the Adam Kadmon realm. Note that the final letter of the Alef-Bet is the letter Tav, equal to the number 400, suggesting that in the Tree of Life is all of Torah's teachings. Under every condition the emanation is slightly different from any other. But for the sake of keeping our sefirotic focus simpler in this work, we speak only in terms of the general nature of the Sefirot, and in particular where the individual Sefirah applies to the correspondences as traditionally set forth.

Spiritual Development: "Going Up" to the Tabernacle

Also in the day of your gladness, and in your solemn days, and
in the beginnings of your months, ye shall blow with the trumpets
over your burnt offerings, and over the sacrifices of your peace
offerings; that they may be to you for a memorial before your God:
I am the LORD your God.

NUMBERS 10:10

To review our progression from the bottom of the Tree of Life: we perfect our speech in Malchut, then join King Solomon in Yesod in perfecting the use of our procreative gifts; next, King David guides us in humble thanksgiving in Hod, showing us our true majesty; and now, in Netzach, Chanah teaches us about enduring victory over our challenges through persistent, vigorous attachment to God.

From our initiation in prayer, to our acts of consecrating our commitment (or covenant), to humbling ourselves and giving thanks, and now to consecrating our enduring commitment to being victorious over our own ungodly inclinations, it is now possible, like Chanah and Elkanah, to "go up" to the Tabernacle. Every aliyah suggests a new level of spiritual attainment: in this case it is an ascension of the Son (Zeir Anpin), who goes up to the Mother (Binah, understanding), from which the Daughter (Malchut, the world of action) gets its supernal influx. It is also an ascension to the Father (Chochmah), which emanates knowledge and wisdom. Thus the entire family within and without is elevated by this spiritual refinement.

It is noteworthy that Moses, in the Sefirah of Chesed on the right pillar above Netzach, and the prophet Samuel are both right-pillar vessels. While we know Moses to be the greatest prophet who ever was, is, or will be, it is also said that "Moses and Samuel are equal," despite certain distinctions: "Moses came to the Holy one, blessed be He, to hear the Divine communication; whereas the Holy one blessed is He, came to Samuel. Said the Holy One, Blessed is He, 'Let Moses, who sits in one place to judge Israel, come to Me, but [as for] Samuel, who goes to the people of Israel in their towns to judge them, I will go and speak with him.'"[27] We also discover that "when the people of Israel saw the [Glory] cloud suspended between heaven and earth, they knew that [God] was speaking with Moses. So it was also with Samuel."[28] The main point is that in the Zohar, the character of the personages of the right pillar—Chanah, Moses (chapter 9), and the children of Israel after crossing the Red Sea (chapter 11)—are all connected to aspects of love in an ascending path of spiritual development.

---

[27] Shemos Rabbah 16:4. See also Chasidah, *Encyclopedia of Biblical Personalities,* 514.

[28] Sifri Zuta, Bamidbar 12:5. See also Chasidah, *Encyclopedia of Biblical Personalities,* 515.

The Refinement of the Will

We see in the shine of Netzach, as shown by Chanah, a determination, a will that does not flatter, even before the authority of a High Priest, even before the authority of God Almighty. While never rude, Chanah simply and directly protests being mistaken for someone who would arrive at the holy Tabernacle at Shiloh drunk. She firmly places her faith in God and discharges her duties as a Jewish woman, never ceasing to petition God for the one thing she lacks: the opportunity to bear children. The oral tradition interprets the prophetess's comments in 1 Samuel 1:13, where we find Chanah speaking from her heart: "Master of the universe," she says, "nothing which you created in woman is superfluous. For what are these breasts that you placed on my heart if not to nurse with? Give me a son to nurse!"[29] This is the essence of Netzach's will to action; it is the focused will to a specific task, as well as the enduring attachment to the holy within each act, which is the essence of consecration. This is why this addition to our spiritual development is so essential.

We are told, "She was granted conception in the merit of [her] prostration [before God]."[30] It is also said of her husband, that in reward "for Elkanah's deed [of leadership and kindness to Chanah], Samuel was born [to him]."[31] This tells us that our will is the source of our rewards as well as the source of our actions. Our acts, our good deeds, as well as our physical children, are all our offspring. Beseeching God for the privilege of serving Him is an act of consecration. While Yesod shows us our love of God, and Hod our humility before Him, Netzach and Chanah the prophetess remind us of the importance of the will, of attaching to God in all that we do. This is the essence of consecration. As an aspect of Zeir Anpin, the Sefirot ruling the emotions, Netzach brings courage and commitment to a level of communal worship, as the Tabernacle at Shiloh did. Shiloh, the place where the Tabernacle rests for 369 years, and Chanah, the prophetess associated with this sacred locale, are keys to understanding this Torah progression.

---

[29] Berachos 31b. See also Chasidah, *Encyclopedia of Biblical Personalities,* 197.
[30] Yalkut Shimoni, Shmuel 80. See also Chasidah, *Encyclopedia of Biblical Personalities,* 197.
[31] Tanna d'Bei Eliyahu Rabbah 8. See also Chasidah, *Encyclopedia of Biblical Personalities,* 95.

Orienting Everything to Divine Service

Chanah shows us that the will, ratzon, is a reflection of the soul's desire. Chanah states, "Master of the universe, there is a host in heaven and a host on earth, and I do not know to which I belong, if [I belong] to the host of heaven, I should not eat, drink, procreate, or die and I should live forever. And if I am of the earthly host, I should eat, drink, and also procreate!"[32]

The bodily will, represented by the right leg, and the spiritual will that is expressed in our enduring attachment to God and service to God and the world, is a story about the unity of the body and soul. One appreciates that the spirit of God cannot rest in someone who has too weak a will to hold this presence—much the same way the sefirotic vessels broke at the time of Creation when they could not hold the effluence of the Creator's light. But when, like Chanah, we orient all that we do to divine service, we acquire a surrendered will.

When one can surrender the ego and cultivate closeness to the Creator, one becomes like the holy priest who offers the sacrifices in the Outer Court of the Tabernacle; we walk in balance, between the left leg of Hod/humility and the right leg of Netzach/victory and enduring will. When we consecrate something, as the initiate does when making sacrifices that the priests then offer up, we are offering up our prayers to God. There is a natural desire on the part of the soul to want to repair one's emotional nature. This suggests the necessity of cultivating the individual will in order that it can be surrendered it to the higher divine will. We cannot give up what we do not have to begin with, therefore acquiring this enduring will that Chanah and Netzach demonstrate is requisite to true surrender in Hod. This is borne out in Tanya, a centerpiece of Judaic esoterica in the wisdom tradition, where we are told, "The side of holiness is nothing but the indwelling and extension of God's holiness. Now, God dwells only on that which is surrendered to Him, whether [the surrender is an] actual [one] (and visible even in that surrendered being's external aspects) as is the case with the supernal angels whose entire being is constantly and openly surrendered to God."[33]

---

[32] Pesikta Rabbasi 43:3. See also Chasidah, *Encyclopedia of Biblical Personalities,* 196.

[33] Tanya, chapter 6, part 2, 23.

The Unity of Body and Soul

Many centuries after the time of Chanah, toward the end of the second century CE, the Roman emperor Marcus Aurelius became a good friend of the renowned rabbi Yehudah Hanasi, an important leader of the community of Judea. One day the emperor posed a question to the holy sage that touched on the nature of the connection between the body and the soul:

> The body and the soul have an alibi to free themselves from punishment on Judgment Day. How so? The body can say: the soul is the one that has sinned. For from the day it left me, I have been lying like a silent rock in the grave, [unable to sin]. And the soul can say: It is the body that has sinned, for from the day I left it, I have been flying in the air like a bird [unable to sin].

The rebbe responded to the emperor's question with a wonderful parable about a king who had a luscious garden full of figs, the fruit associated with Chanah and Netzach:

> He posted in [the garden] two guards, one lame and the other blind. Said the lame one to the blind one: "I see luscious figs in the orchard. Come, put me on your shoulders and together we will pick the figs and eat them." The lame one climbed on the blind one's back and the picked the figs and ate them. A while later, when the king, the owner of the orchard, came [and found that his figs were gone, he] said to the guards, "What happened to my luscious figs?" Said the lame one, "Do I have feet to take me to the fig trees?" Said the blind one, "Do I have eyes to see where the figs are?" What did the owner do? He placed the lame one on the shoulders of the blind one, and judged them jointly. So, too, on the Day of Judgment, the Holy One, Blessed be He, brings the soul, puts it back into the body, and judges them jointly. As it says, "He will summon the heavens above and the earth, for the trial of His people" (Psalms 50:4). "He will summon the heavens above"—this refers to the soul; "and the earth, for the trial of His people"—this refers to the body.[34]

---

[34] Sanhedrin, after 89b. See also Chaviv, *Ein Yaakov*, 643.

In Netzach one becomes acutely aware of this partnership between body and soul, for it is here that the soul's desire is expressed in the will, which the body then carries out. In the Tabernacle schemata this corresponds to Netzach, the third stage of consecration in the Outer Court, where the sacrifices of communal worship are performed. Here the animal sacrifices of our offerings of sin, the peace offerings, and other types of offerings are made. The priests preside over the communal worship and make requests for forgiveness. In Netzach the body is mastered by the spiritual will of the soul. This stage of our spiritual development is referred to as spiritual discipline, with Chanah the quintessential example of this attribute refined.

Attaining Balance

Netzach teaches us about surrendering our emotions, Zeir Anpin, the six Sefirot above Malchut. While the Tabernacle itself can be thought of as Malchut, Shiloh is the place of refining the spiritual will, showing us that we are victorious when we conquer our own selfish, animalistic natures. To do this we make sacrifices, giving up things that are precious to us. Chanah shows us that the ego must be surrendered if one is to serve the divine plan that we are all part of. We must use all of our skills, both physical and spiritual, to accomplish our work in the world. What we do in the world impacts the supernal worlds as well. Thus when a person is boastful, the consequences are more than simply unbecoming behavior; it reflects in the spiritual realms, too.

The most important aspect of this process of gradually changing oneself is our effort and our intention to do so. While we cannot eradicate overnight an emotional, physical, or spiritual habit, we must try to do so, for it is the effort we put into the process that determines the impact it has, not only in our own lives but in the spiritual worlds of which our soul is part. One way we can change ingrained behavior is to do the opposite of the bad habit. For instance, a selfish person is advised to perform countless acts of kindness toward others until a balance can be achieved between giving and not giving. A person who constantly argues is not permitted to argue with anyone, about anything, for a period of time until he has developed the faculty of reasoning and self-control that enables him to know when an argument will be for the betterment of everyone, versus arguing needlessly on behalf of himself alone. Like the sacrifice of the bull made on the fire altar, a person learns to surrender personal stubbornness, of standing one's ground in fury, to the fire of a will committed to the world's elevation.

The behavioral patterns that prevent us from being at peace are usually rooted in some aspect of selfishness, which is desire born not of a person's sense of wholeness, but from some sense of inner lack, which can be traced to a lack of connection to God. The Tree of Life is a model for how to balance between receiving and giving; its three pillars of judgment (left), truth (center), and love (right) guide us on our own self-correcting path of refinement. We must ask ourselves if we lean too far to the left or the right and then practice the opposite path until we are spiritually and emotionally mature enough to act in a balanced way, walking the most revered path, the middle path. When a person arrives at such a balanced disposition, he does not react emotionally to either praise or criticism, but comes only from the middle pillar of seeking truth, mercy, and beauty. Such a response is an elevation, not just for the individual but for the world. Chanah accomplishes this after her long ordeal with Peninah.

When Chanah saw that she was not producing children, she thought that by bringing another woman, Peninah, into her household she could make her womb jealous and arouse it to fertility. In the difficult relationship between Chanah and Peninah we see something akin to the relationship between the prophetess Sarah and Hagar and their complex situation.[35] Why do both of these holy female prophetesses on the right pillar experience the struggle not only to bear children, but of sharing their husbands with other women that have been invited into their households to become surrogate wives? Here we see the right pillar drawing from the severity of the left; this is what underpins both Chanah's and Sarah's suffering, and their eventual joy—illustrating the key point: that all diminishments are for our eventual elevation.

Of course, most of us would rather not endure any suffering at all, but life is made up of both revealed and concealed good, the concealed good being in the experience of suffering and the outcome of the suffering. When given opportunities to serve God that may include some hardships, some

---

[35] See this author's *Kabbalistic Teachings of the Female Prophets*, 76.

people choose not to do what is required. For example, when we encounter an injured person, do we help him because we must always choose life, or do we fail to help for fear of the legal ramifications or because we do not want to get involved with a stranger's situation? It is for this reason that when the prophets were told to perform some act in the world and they hesitated, they were reminded that there were other vessels willing to serve the divine plan: "The Holy One said to the Prophets: 'What do you suppose—if you refuse to go on a mission of Mine, I have no other emissary? With the superfluities of the earth, with all (Ecclesiastes 5:8)—I can have My mission carried out with all, even by means of a serpent, even by means of a scorpion, even by means of a frog.'"[36]

God makes it clear that humans are not the only vehicles for expressing divine will. All of life is a vessel for the divine will, as all of creation is the holy Tabernacle of the Creator. The Bible is full of stories revealing how animals and nature obey the Word of God. Again and again we learn that our animal nature or evil inclination, the *yetzer hara,* is designed to be elevated to serve the divine will of God. This is each person's lifelong inner work.

As Above So Below

When we are in harmony with the archetypal pattern that emanates from above, we return the signal, thereby creating a pathway for the energies to unite. In this way what we create on earth, when in harmony with celestial patterns, can be maximized for the benefit of all life, all people, and all nations. This is the journey of the soul. This, then, is the key to refining our personal, collective, and universal Tabernacle, represented by the earth, on which all life in our physical world depends. In the context of Netzach, we are describing our enduring will as applied to self-refinement and right action in the world: "Within and without shall you overlay it" (Exodus 25:11). Indeed, these very words were used by God to instruct Moses in building and designing the Tabernacle.

Shiloh describes a state of enduring spiritual discipline, making it clear that to complete the stage of consecration represented by Netzach we must use all of our might to eradicate our own ungodly impulses. To

---

[36] Bialik and Ravnitzky, *Sefer Ha-Aggadah,* 8:101, 480. See also Exodus 10:1 and Leviticus 22:3.

show how the emanations from a Sefirah show up in the events of its representative personage's life, consider that Shiloh is the necessary precedent to the building of the First Temple. Just as Samuel the prophet preceded King David, so connected are Shiloh and Jerusalem that it is said that it was "David who gave Samuel a scroll"[37] containing the plans for the construction of the Temple. Of the Shechinah we learn She rested in Shiloh[38] but Her inheritance is Jerusalem—the former being more impermanent, while Jerusalem represents the eternal contract between God and Israel.

Concluding Consecration

As we shall see in the course of this book, the left column of judgment (din) and fear (yirah) is comprised of David, Joshua, and the people singing to the well. The middle column of truth (emet) and mercy (rachamim) consists of the personages of the Moshiach, Devorah, and Adam, making the central Sefirah of Tiferet the integrating axis for the individual person, Israel, and the spiritual world. The Israelites in the Song of the Sea, Moses' end-of-life song, and Chanah's own song are our right-pillar songs of love (ahavah).

Zeir Anpin is referred to by the single Sefirah of Tiferet, which in the Zohar's teachings is occupied by the prophetess Devorah, who with General Barak, sings a hallel (a song of praise and thanksgiving) after the Israelites' victory over the Canaanites.[39] As the next Sefirah in our ascent of the ladder of light, Tiferet continues our progression through the Outer Court of the Tabernacle and the realm of Yetzirah, or formation, which includes the Lower Chariot, comprised of the locations of Shiloh (Netzach), Jerusalem (Hod), and the Temple (Yesod), each being a progression of the downward light and chronological history of Israel. The Ari shows us that the Sefirot correspond not only to our body parts, to the worlds that we are made of and exist in, and to the emotions that

---

[37] Yerushalmi Megillah 1:1. See also Chasidah, *Encyclopedia of Biblical Personalities,* 515.

[38] Joshua 18:1: "The entire assembly of the children of Israel gathered at Shiloh and erected the Tent of Meeting there." Also, 1 Samuel 1:3: "And this man went up out of his city from year to year to worship and to sacrifice unto the Lord of hosts in Shiloh."

[39] Devorah maintains this position in Tiferet in this author's prior work, *Kabbalistic Teachings of the Female Prophets,* this author's previous work.

we experience while living, but as well to the areas of our lives that need rectification through the sacrifices made in the Outer Court of the Tent of Meeting. When we go to consecrate something, we must first reaffirm our eternal covenant with God (Yesod), then be humble (Hod), and then, with great willing devotion (Netzach), we attend to self-refinement though our sacrifices. What we are willing to give up from within ourselves and in relation to our actions in the world are those things that need to be elevated, which contribute to our own spiritual development and capacity for being a resting place for the Divine Immanence. Once we discern the changes we must make in our lives, we must add those qualities and behaviors that are proper to our path of spiritual growth.

Our next song and quality of spiritual development is revealed by the Sefirah of Tiferet and the teachings of the prophetess Devorah. The reader will begin to notice that the songs are becoming increasingly fuller in terms of their emotional welling-up, said to produce an arousal from below, which in turn fosters a response of bestowal from above. When we express an intention through our actions, we create a mold for the spiritual world to fill. Matter, the material realm of Malchut, is simply the last in this chain of descent of the light; the idea, the intention, is the shape of the light. So we see that what actually manifests is a lot more involved than simply our own will, vision, or plan.

As our emotions become filled with more and more joy as we ascend, our devotional service produces a greater impact. Since the destruction of the temples, we are told that to read and study the prayers about the rituals of the Tabernacle takes the place of actually performing them. We see then how the roots of every form go back to our awareness, our consciousness, and our willing attendance. It is the consciousness invested in each action, expressing the essence of each Sefirah, that causes a rectification of whatever we are paying attention to. It is in this manner of living life as a holy act that over time allows us to build our sanctuary of the Divine Presence, a harmonic unity of body, mind, and soul.

7

The Beauty of Truth
Tiferet • Hallelujah, Radiating Joy

My heart is with the lawgivers in Israel who are
devoted to the people, [saying] "Bless God."

JUDGES 5:9

Sixth Sefirah: Tiferet
Meaning: Beauty, splendor, truth
Rung on Ascending Ladder: Five
Archetype: Zeir Anpin (the Son)
Symbol: Throne of Truth
Spiritual World: Yetzirah/formation
Spiritual Anatomy: Torso
Inner Quality: Mercy (rachamim)

Historical Personage: Devorah the prophetess
Text: Judges 5:1–31
Key Words: Truth, beauty, mercy, justice
Key Emotion in Song: Radiating joy, hallelujah (hallel)

Tent of Meeting: Outer Court
Spiritual Stage: Sanctifying one's life with truth

Spiritual Practice: Radiating praise in all directions
Illumination: The illumination of the heart of justice

> Devorah leads Israel as prophetess, judge,
> and warrior, showing the initiate how to elevate
> every situation to its greatest benefit.

The Sefirah Tiferet: Zohar's Middle Path

In the Zohar, the single Sefirah of Tiferet also refers to the entire middle pillar, the place where the right and left pillars meld, analogous to the torso, which connects the arms and legs. This is the central point of the Tree of Life around which the five other Sefirot of Zeir Anpin revolve. Ascending the Tree of Life from Chanah in Netzach (the right leg) to Devorah in Tiferet (the torso), we leave the realm of consecrating what we do through our lower limbs and organs, which is likened to making sacrifices in the Outer Court, and we now begin the spiritual practice that leads to elevation in Binah by consecrating what we do with our hands, as in the Tabernacle ritual of water purification.

Tiferet is an integrator and elevator. After we consecrate something we draw all of the parts together and elevate them in the singular objective of service. Our limbs, our arms and legs, and our generative organs are all dedicated to the task of refining and repairing the world. This is the deeper meaning of *tikkun*, repair, and *tikkun olam*, repair of the world: that which is repaired is elevated to a state even better than when we found it and consequently its holiness is brought out. This is the essence of elevated law-making, which the prophetess and judge Devorah, and the Sefirah of Tiferet that she represents, show us.

> *Open the gates of justice for me that I may enter them and praise*
> *God. This is the gateway to God—the just shall enter through it.*
> PSALMS 118:19–20

As a judge (ruler), Devorah was also responsible for creating gates and walls around the Israelites' cities, to protect them from the many assaults they suffered at the hands of neighboring peoples, who attacked them relentlessly. As we will examine more fully in chapter 10, these gates and walls refer not just to the cities erected in Devorah's time or to the gates to the holy Tabernacle through which the priest entered the Outer Court; they also refer to what the sages show us to be the "gates" to our own lives. We have seven such holy gates: the two openings each of the eyes, the ears, and the nose, plus the mouth. We are instructed to guard these gates, to be vigilant about what goes into them and what goes out of them. We must be careful about what we look at and be honest about what we see in ourselves. We are to be careful in our judgment of what is holy and what is not, in what we listen to or what we say. We must guard our speech from gossip or malice—our ears from listening to it, and our mouths, God forbid, from originating it. "Open up, O gates, that a righteous nation may enter" (Isaiah 26:2): when we guard ourselves from doing wrong, we become the "righteous nation." Tiferet's nature is one of equilibrium between all parts of the whole, endowing the person with righteousness.

Devorah: Judge and Prophetess

Devorah was an extraordinary woman: the third prophetess of seven holy women of ancient Israel, she was the only female judge of pre-monarchic Israel. She was also a successful businesswoman, owning four enterprises: apple orchards, white-earth quarries (white earth was used in ceramics), palm trees, and olive oil. She was independently wealthy, which meant she could not be bribed—a vital quality for a judge or political leader in any era. That Devorah was the only female judge at the time is remarkable, but especially significant is the fact that she was the only Israelite judge of her time that God chose to actually sentence people for their crimes. This was in part because her judgments occurred through prophecy; it should also be noted that women, who possess extra Binah, or intuitive understanding, tend to be more merciful than men.

Devorah's seat of justice was on top of a hill under a palm tree in Ephraim, between Beit El and Ramah. Traditionally it is held that "a woman must not secure herself with men in the house,"[1] making Devorah's open forums proper and, more importantly, enabling large numbers of people to benefit from hearing how she discerned truth and adminis-

---

[1] Yalkut Shimoni, Shoftim 42.

tered justice. Also, as the Rambam points out in his classical description of the eleven types of prophecy (in *Guide of the Perplexed*), prophecy, a gift of the Holy Spirit, is more easily accessed in nature.

In addition to her renown as a judge, Devorah was also a celebrated military leader who fought a war of liberation to win her people's independence from Jabin (Yavin), the king of Canaan (the historical name of the Levant, roughly corresponding to the region encompassing modern-day Israel, the Palestinian territories, Lebanon, and the western parts of Syria).

Partnership between Male and Female

In the Hebrew Bible story,[2] Devorah is instructed by a divine voice to wage war against the Canaanites. She calls on General Barak, who some suggest is her husband, telling him the outcome of the divinely directed war they are about to wage. But the outcome "will not be for your glory" (Judges 4:9), she tells him, for a clanswoman, Yael, will be the one to actually kill the Cannanite king. Seeing their victory in the coming battle, Devorah reveals to Barak that the enemy commander, General Sisera, will not return home. General Barak says he will go to war only if she will go with him—an acknowledgment that the Holy Spirit rests with the prophetess. Thus in partnership, male and female, right and left, they together go out to vanquish their enemy.

One sees such a partnership between a man and a woman in many of the important biblical stories. In each of the seven prophetess's narratives, if there is not a husband there is usually a man with whom the prophetess has a vital spiritual relationship, or the prophetess works in tandem with other men in addition to her husband: Sarah with her husband, Abraham, Miriam with her husband, Caleb, as well as with her brothers Aaron and Moses; Chanah with Elkanah, her husband, as well as Eli the Kohen Gadol of the Tabernacle at Shiloh; Chuldah and King Yosiah; Avigail and King David; Queen Esther and her uncle Mordechai. So too in our examination of the ten songs corresponding to the ten Sefirot we find a similar melding of male and female qualities. For example, in chapter 8, a study the Sefirah of Gevurah, we have the story of Joshua stopping the sun (male) and the moon (female). There, with the help of God, Joshua becomes the master of nature, knowing how to arrest natural cause and effect. From this kind of

---

[2] Recounted in detail this author's *Kabbalistic Teachings of the Female Prophets,* 168–71.

balancing of opposites we learn that it is possible to become fully awake to our own divinity, overcoming the laws of nature and the ever-fluctuating tides of our emotions.

The Pillar of Adjustment

Tiferet and the prophetess Devorah represent the development of moral order among the Israelites. This is the purpose of the middle pillar, the pillar of adjustment, just as the scales of justice are a balance between judgment, *din,* as expressed by the Sefirah of Gevurah, and love, *ahavah,* as expressed by Chesed. Mercy, or *rachamim,* is the outcome of these two opposites blended and in balance and is the inner quality of Tiferet, producing the attributes of beauty and compassionate justice. This balance is also evident in the method by which justice is meted out to a person. "We leaned in Baraita: Rabbi Meir used to say, 'From where do we know that the measure a person uses in regard to his own actions is the measure God uses to determine what will happen to him?' Because it says, 'With the same measurement that a person sinned, he will receive his punishment'" (Isaiah 27:8).[3]

The Song of Tiferet:
Praise and Thanksgiving (Hallel)

The Song of Tiferet is a hallel, a song of praise, in which Devorah and Barak extol God's might and His protection and rescue of Israel. A commemorative song used to accentuate this historical event's sense of celebratory gratitude, Devorah's song exudes the same emotional quality of radiating thanks as the formal Hallel[4] sung in ritual services today. So

---

[3] Sotah 8b. See also R. Yaakov Ibn Chaviv, *Ein Yaakov,* 443.

[4] The formal Hallel, which expresses a quality of praise derived from Devorah's song, is composed specifically of Psalm 113, Psalm 114, Psalm 115:1–11,12–18, Psalm 116:1–11,12–19, Psalm 117, and Psalm 118. It is chanted as part of the morning prayer service (the Shacharit) following the Eighteen Benedictions, or Shemoneh Esrei, the song of Malchut we studied in chapter 3. It is recited during the evening prayers the first night of Passover and following the Grace after Meals (Berakhot) in the Passover Seder service. It is also recited as a signifier for the three pilgrimage festivals: Passover, Shavuot, and Sukkot. In addition, the formal Hallel is recited during Hanukkah and on Rosh Chodesh, at the beginning of the new month. Some people recite the Hallel on Yom Ha'atzma'ut, Israeli Independence Day, and others recite it on Yom Yerushalayim, which commemorates the reunification of Jerusalem in 1967. On Rosh Hashanah and Yom Kippur, the Hallel

important is the Sefirah that emanates this celebratory quality, Tiferet, that we call it Torah.

> *Sow to yourselves according to righteousness, reap according to*
> *mercy, break up your fallow ground; for it is time to seek Adonai,*
> *until God comes and causes righteousness to rain upon you.*
>
> HOSEA 10:12

The word *hallel* translates literally as "praise." That the Hallel, the aforementioned formal prayer, is derived from the type of song associated with Tiferet, and that both repeat a pattern of six (i.e., the formal Hallel is comprised of six psalms; the Sefirah of Tiferet refers to the entire six-part Zeir Anpin) shows us once again that the Etz Chayim pattern is reflected in the rituals and texts of the People of the Book.

A Dedication of the Holy Land

The occasion for the singing of Devorah's song, derived from Judges 4, occurs after the prophetess and General Barak lead the Israelites to victory in the battle against the Canaanites and their leader, Sisera:

> And Deborah said unto Barak: "Up; for this is the day in which the
> LORD hath delivered Sisera into thy hand; is not the LORD gone out
> before thee?" So Barak went down from mount Tabor, and ten thou-
> sand men after him. And the LORD discomfited Sisera, and all his
> chariots, and all his host, with the edge of the sword before Barak; and
> Sisera alighted from his chariot, and fled away on his feet. But Barak

---

is not recited because, as the Talmud (Arachin 10b) states, "Is it seemly for the King to be sitting on His Throne of Judgment, with the Books of Life and Death open before Him, and for the people to sing joyful praises to Him?" Passover (Pesach), like Sukkot, has the structure of a main holiday, followed by intermediate days (Chol ha-Moed), followed by a main holiday. Because Passover involves only a partial redemption of the Jews and the destruction of Egypt, only half—i.e., partial Hallel—is recited on all of the last six days of Pesach. Full Hallel is recited for the entirety of Sukkot. The ten days between the holiday of Rosh Hashanah, when the Book of Life is opened, and Yom Kippur, the day of Atonement, when the Book of Life is closed, are so monumental in the annual life cycle, when fates are sealed for the coming year, that deep introspection rather than jubilation, such as that of the Hallel, is required. It should be noted that the ten-day journey between these last two holidays engages the penitent's attention through each of the ten Sefirot, one each day.

pursued after the chariots, and after the host, unto Harosheth-goiim; and all the host of Sisera fell by the edge of the sword; there was not a man left. (Judges 4:14–16)

Assisted by Devorah's prophetic insights prior to going into battle, the Israelites emerge victorious. Devorah's predictions come to pass, and the Israelites gain their freedom in the land that God has promised as theirs.

And, behold, as Barak pursued Sisera, Jael [Yael] came out to meet him, and said unto him: "Come, and I will show thee the man whom thou seekest." And he came unto her; and, behold, Sisera lay dead, and the tent-pin was in his temples. So God subdued on that day Jabin the king of Canaan before the children of Israel. And the hand of the children of Israel prevailed more and more against Jabin the king of Canaan, until they had destroyed Jabin, king of Canaan. (Judges 4:22–24)

With this sign that their enemy has been completely subdued, the victorious song of heartfelt praise that follows demarcates the period when the Israelites gain their freedom to establish their religion and culture in the Holy Land. One could call the song of Tiferet a dedication of the land song, much the way we consider the Song of Songs, as described in chapter 4, a song of dedication of the First Temple.

The Song of Tiferet (Judges 5:1–31)

🌿*1 Devorah Sang—as well as Barak Son of Abinoam—on that day saying: 2 When vengeances are inflicted upon Israel and the people dedicates itself to God—Bless God. 3 Hear, O Kings; give ear, O Princes! I, to God shall I sing; I shall sing praise to God, God of Israel! 4 God, as You left Seir, as You strode from the fields of Edom, the earth quaked and even the heavens trickled; even the clouds dripped water. 5 Mountains melted before God—as did Sinai—before God, the God of Israel. 6 In the days of Shamgar, son of Anath, in the days of Jail, highway travel ceased, and those who traveled on paths went by circuitous roads. 7 They stopped living in unwalled towns in Israel, they stopped; until I,*

Devorah, arose; I arose a mother in Israel. **8** *When it chose new gods, war came to its gates; was even a shield or a spear seen among forty thousand in Israel?* **9** *My heart is with the lawgivers in Israel who are devoted to the people, [saying] "Bless God."* **10** *O riders of white donkeys, [you] who sit in judgment, and you who walk the roads, speak up!* **11** *Rather than the sound of arrows [aimed] at the water-drawers, there they will recount the righteous deeds of God, the righteous deeds for His open cities in Israel. Then the people of God descended [again] to the [open] cities.* **12** *Give praise, give praise, O Devorah! Give praise, give praise, utter a song! Arise, O Barak, and capture your prisoners, O son of Abinoam!* **13** *Now the survivor dominates the mightiest of the people; God has given me dominion over the strong ones.* **14** *From Ephraim, who root [fought] against Amelek; after you came Benjamin with your people. From Machir descended lawgivers; and from Zebulun, those who ply the scribal quill.* **15** *The leaders of Issachar were with Devorah, and so was [the rest of] Issachar with Barak; into the valley he was sent on his feet. But in the indecision of Reuben there was great deceit.* **16** *Why did you remain sitting at the borders to hear the bleatings of the flocks?*

The indecision of Reuben demands great investigation. **17** *Gilead dwelled across the Jordan; and Dan—why did he gather [his valuables] onto ships? But Asher lived by the shores of seas and remained [to protect] his open [borders].* **18** *Zebulun is a people that risked its life to the death, so did Naphtali, on the heights of the battlefield* **19** *Kings came and fought—then the kings of Canaan fought, from Taanach to the waters of Megiddo, without accepting monetary reward.* **20** *From heaven they fought, the very stars from their orbits did battle with Sisera.* **21** *Kishon Brook swept them away—the ancient brook, Kishon Brook—but I myself trod it vigorously.* **22** *Then the horses' heels were pounded by the gallopings, the gallopings of their mighty riders.* **23** *"Curse Meroz," said the angel of God, "Curse! Cursed are its inhabitants, for they failed to come to aid [the nation of] God, to aid [the nation of] God against the mighty."* **24** *Blessed by women is Jael, wife of Heber the Kenite; by women in the tent will she be blessed.* **25** *He asked for water, she gave him milk; in a stately saucer she presented Cream.* **26** *She stretched her hand to the peg and her right hand to the laborers' hammer. She hammered Sisera, severed his head, smashed and pierced his temple.* **27** *At her feet he knelt, he fell, he lay. At her feet he knelt, he fell; where he knelt there he fell, vanquished.* **28** *Through the window she gazed; Sisera's mother peered through the window. "Why is his chariot delayed in coming? Why the hoofbeats of his carriages so late?"* **29**

The wisest of her ladies answer her, and she, too, offers herself responses. "Are they not finding [and] dividing loot? A comely [captive]. Two comely [captives], for every man; booty of colored garments for Sisera, booty of colored embroidery, colored, doubly embroidered garments for the necks of the looters." **30** *"So may all Your enemies be destroyed, O God! And let those who love Him be like the powerfully rising sun. And the land was tranquil for forty years.*

Ritual: The Middle Path of the Tabernacle

Just as it represents all of Zeir Anpin, Tiferet represents all of the Outer Court rituals, but its nature is best understood through the specific ritual of water purification, a purification of the emotions in order to integrate them into a unity, making one's deeds purely motivated. This is a central point of ritual consecration, as seen in chapter 2, figure 2.1, on page 40, which shows the laver on the Tent of Meeting's central axis.

Looking at this image, one notes that the priest enters the arena through a central gate. The sacrificial offerings are made on the central altar of the Outer Court. The priest then approaches the laver of water purification before entering the Holy Place, where the incense is directly in front of him to administer. As he enters the Holy of Holies, the Mishkan proper and the central position of the Ark of the Covenant, he completes the middle axis. This gives the sanctuary of the Divine Presence four central items that, like the four worlds, engage the practitioner stage by stage until reaching the place of illumination. As seen in chapter 1, figure 1.2, on page 13, the holy sanctuary resembles the anatomy of the human being. This progressive development, as seen through the different places and practices in the sanctuary, imparts specific information about our own spiritual nature, as the specific sefirotic associations are the roots of our anatomical and eternal makeup.

Like the Israelites who come to worship at the Tabernacle, the Levites who sing the holy ritual songs, and the Kohanim who perform the ritual ceremonies, we unite all these aspects of ourselves in the sanctuary of our own inner kingdom. We are the ones who strive to refine ourselves (the Israelites); we are the ones who sing to elevate the soul (the Levites); and we are, as well, the ones who offer sacrifices for the elevation of the people (the Kohanim). We fulfill all three roles, and when we bring them together in our daily service, we commit our holy Tent of Meeting—

our lives—to service of the divine within and without. We can thus be assured that our daily acts of devotion, sacrifice, and elevation will lead to the experience of enlightenment.

"R. Elazar further said in the name of R. Chanian: In time to come, the Holy One, blessed be He, will be a crown on the head of every righteous person. For it says, 'In that day, the Lord of Hosts shall become a crown of beauty, a diadem of glory to the remnant of His people' (Isaiah 28:5)."[5] Here we are told that when we do God's will and remain humble, we are able to judge ourselves properly, thus overcoming our inclinations that are destructive to us or others or the community as a whole. Then, like Devorah, we can sit in judgment with the presence of God.

The Laver of Purification

The purifying laver, or kiyyor, the symbol of the essence of Tiferet, prepares us for the remaining stages of spiritual development in the Tabernacle rituals. Ritual acts of ablution, as in the water-purification rituals performed by the priests, express the cleansing of our emotions. This ritual immersion of hands and feet, the ministers of the will, is also a method used to rid the body of kelipot, the husks or shells of evil (i.e., selfishness), making the body a sacred tool fit to render spiritual service in the material and supernal realms. After the sacrificial fire rituals of strengthening what in the Zohar is called the Lower Chariot (Netzach, Hod, and Yesod), in which we consecrate our will to divine service, we can now approach the kiyyor with great joy and thanksgiving in our hearts for this opportunity to purify ourselves in readiness for elevation. Through this progression, the Upper Chariot of Chesed, Gevurah, and Tiferet is activated.

> And the LORD spoke unto Moses, saying: "Thou shalt also make
> a laver of copper, and the base thereof of copper, whereat to wash;
> and thou shalt put it between the tent of meeting and the altar,
> and thou shalt put water therein."
>
> EXODUS 30:17–18

---

[5] Megillah. See also R. Yaakov Ibn Chaviv, *Ein Yaakov*, 272.

Washing both hands and feet before performing particular parts of the Tabernacle ceremony reminds us that there are necessary times for purifying our bodies, our intention, and our awareness. We must remember what we are doing and why we are doing it. Washing our hands means reorienting ourselves to the holy in all; this allows us to let go of unnecessary mental and emotional habits before carrying out a holy act. In the washing of hands before partaking of bread, it is the recitation of a blessing, or *beracha,* that creates the sacred vessel for the actual fulfillment of the act. In the People of the Book's rituals, all deeds are sanctified by such a blessing attached to the act itself. The blessing is the vital force of soul seen in the action, therefore the blessing and the act are inseparable, just as a thought and a deed, an idea and an action.

Hands That Form

That our two hands and two feet are each comprised of ten elements reminds us that they represent the Tree of Life, the hands being in the realm of Yetzirah (formation), and the feet in the realm of Asiyah (action). So while one person might excel at running (Malchut/Asiyah), another might excel in painting (Tiferet/Yetzirah), and yet another may show talent for writing (ChaBaD: Chochmah, Binah, and Daat/Atzilut). The potter's use of clay to make pots is a good metaphor for the use of the hands in the realm of Yetzirah/formation. Like the potter, we use our will, as expressed through our hands, to make vessels to be filled with spiritual sustenance, thereby allowing us to nourish our own soul and thereby benefit the world.

> *I wash my hands in purity and walk around*
> *your altar, O God.*
>
> PSALMS 26:6

As illustrated in figure 7.1, the two hands represent a microcosm of the Tree of Life, with each finger corresponding to a Sefirah. When we wash our hands with a blessing (beracha), as in the water purification ritual of the Outer Court, our hands become sacred instruments because we are consecrating them for holy service. This intentional act can confer healing powers through the hands relative to the Sefirot of the Etz

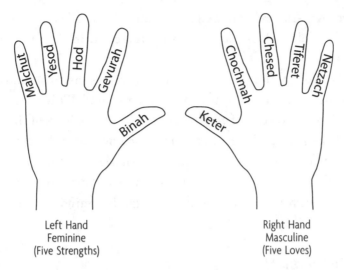

Figure 7.1. Holy Hands of Creation
(Based on teachings by R. Aryeh Kaplan, drawn by Amy Ford)

Chayim.[6] There are many stories in the Chassidic tradition that tell of healing through the laying on of hands, as well their use as a means of conferring power through anointment, as in the case of both King David and King Solomon, as well as in Moses' transference of power to Joshua.

Helping Hands of the Creator

The Sefirot are arranged in three columns, as shown in chapter 1, figure 1.3, on page 15. The light travels downward in a zig-zag fashion, beginning with Keter at the top, then, from right to left: Chochmah to Binah, (through an attribute of Daat), to Chesed on the right, to Gevurah on the left, and so forth, as the arrows in the illustration show. When arranged into purely masculine and feminine energies, the Sefirot are referred to

---

[6] In the Western mystery paths it is taught that magnetic as well etheric passes can be used to help revivify a person. This is accomplished by a practitioner who connects the mind, the hands, and the heart. This triangle then acts as a carrier of the life force to the person being treated, who borrows in part from the sender, much the way a car with a dead battery can be jump-started by another running car. Because all life force is one life force that is differentiated, the more advanced healer does not have any energy drained from his or her own essence, but acts only as a bypass for the universal energy current to pass through to the person being treated. This is the goal of every true healer: to be an empty vessel through which God's love can pass and be used to benefit other living forms.

as the five loves (the masculine right column) and the five strengths (the feminine left column), as can be seen in figure 7.1, in the image of our two hands.

The field of tension between these two arrays, as two hands, produces a middle field called "the unifying covenant." This refers to the transformational practice of Kabbalah and Torah study itself, including mastery of the Hebrew letters as accomplished by Adam, Moses, Joshua, and Betzalel (the chief artisan of the Tabernacle). It also refers to the keeping of the covenant of the brit milah, the act of circumcision incumbent on all Jewish males.[7] Essentially, though, it reminds the initiate to stay on the middle path.

Blessing with the Hands

In the various blessings using the hands—in anointing, as Moses does Joshua in the Tent of Meeting; in the priestly blessings (the *Nesiat Kapayim,* or "Raising of the Hands") of Aaron and the Kohanim; in the raising of the hands in battle, as Moses and Joshua do; and as well when we wash our hands with a beracha, or make a blessing on the bread—we transform them into sacred instruments, and what we bless is made holy. The ten Sefirot of the Etz Chayim, each present in one of our ten fingers as the above illustration shows, gives us clues about how our hands are rooted in the power of Creation and confer qualities derived from the Tree of Life we are rooted in. This underscores that Kabbalah is a universal hermetic science of correspondences, designed for the world's benefit. By applying its components in an orderly fashion we can clarify any field of inquiry, from physics and the economy, to social action and environmental restoration.

> *I Bless You all my life; I lift up my hands invoking your name.*
>
> PSALMS 63:5

Human beings may be considered the helping hands of the Creator. In this, the significance of the pattern of ten is evident. "Just as the Book of Psalms was composed by ten men [with David], so was it composed in ten different forms of song [zemer and mizmor are analogous]: zemer,

---

[7] R. Aryeh Kaplan, *Sefer Yetzirah,* 32–35.

nitzuach, nigun, mizmor, shir, hallel, tefillah, beracha, hoda'ah, halleluyah, and ashrei. The greatest of all is halleluyha (lit. 'praise of God'),
which includes the Names of God and His praise in a single word. Rav
called the entire Book, Halleluyah."[8] Here we are told that there are ten
different kinds of psalms as well as the ten songs (i.e., Torah texts) representing the ten Sefirot.[9] This work uses the ten songs, the ten emotions,
and the ten Sefirot, and houses them, as Torah is housed, within the Ark,
which rests inside the Tabernacle, which is inside the Ohel Moed, the
Tent of Meeting.

Conditioning the Field for the Divine Presence

Let us not forget that all of the work (avodah) we do to refine ourselves
is in order to receive the Shechinah into our lives. Where is this Divine
Immanence found? The Talmud tells us that where ten are gathered in
prayer, where three sit in judgment, where two are learning, and where
one sits alone studying holy words, the Shechinah is present; She rests
in all four situations. In composing his psalms, King David would sometimes write the song first and then the Holy Spirit would descend upon
him, and at other times the Holy Spirit would come first and then inspire
his prayers.

Regardless of whether we are alone in prayer or part of a communal
prayer, we are preparing the field for the holy presence. The longer one
conditions a field, the more prone it is to elevating a person's consciousness. Anyone who has a special place of prayer set aside for their daily
practice will find that over time this sacred space is energized by their
consistent work. So, too, many people will sit in the same place of prayer
in communal sanctuaries for this very same reason.

Unless we are focused on consecrating our activities, we can expect
nothing special to occur in our spiritual development or in our awareness
of the multidimensional phenomena around us. On the other hand, refined
attention and elevated intention attracts the help of angelic beings, which
some people are able to see and even name. The seventy-two names of God
(see appendix 4) are an expression of these various powers and attributes to

---

[8] Shocher Tov 1:6. See also R. Yisrael Yitzchak Yishai Chasidah, *Encyclopedia of Biblical Personalities,* 140.

[9] Shocher Tov 1:6. See also Chasidah, *Encyclopedia of Biblical Personalities,* 140.

which are attached angelic beings. The sacred art of talismanic protection also derives from these correspondences as well.

What we put our attention on changes it, as physics shows in what is called the "observer effect." Hence the blessing and the intention attached to an action elevates even the simple task of making food to a sacred art of devotion. When our attention focuses on seeking the refinement of the self and serving the community, it draws to us people, situations, and opportunities of a similar nature. Adding the qualities of a particular Sefirah to our dedicated acts draws from a particular root of the Etz Chayim. This special influence is part of the conditioned field we each develop as life branches out, with our prayers becoming the fruit of our practice. In this manner we each, like the prophetess and judge Devorah, own orchards of fruit-producing trees, or like Adam and Eve, have access to the fruits of the Garden of Eden.

Spiritual Development: Singing the Truth

Thine is the day, Thine also the night.

PSALMS 74:16

To review our development thus far: We come to prayer in self-reflection, the place where we begin our journey and where we always return; then we develop the will and the skills needed to consecrate our lives and actions to divine service. As we begin consecration, learning from King Solomon's Song of Songs in the Sefirah of Yesod, we sing a joyous song; then King David's prayer of gratitude to God in Hod brings us to a sense of our global inheritance in our shared majesty and thanksgiving. Chanah's prayer for conception in Netzach, as a song of victory and eternity, is the foundation on which Tiferet's hallel, a song of exuberant joy, is built.

And so, progressing from a feeling regarding a need for one's own repair and change, to declaring one's love, to crying in joy at the experience of oneness, we shift slightly into the feeling of gratitude, giving thanks for what we receive, declaring God sovereign over all things, all time, all nations. Here in Tiferet, the truth is sung out, radiating thanks and joy. If we allow ourselves to really feel this sequence of emotions, we will experience in prayer the same sequence shown in chapter 4 in King Solomon's Song of Songs. If we trace the middle path in our ascension of the ladder of light, we go from inward repentance (Malchut), to declared adoration (Yesod), to radiant gratitude and joy (Tiferet). Each stage represents a development in prayer and in the process of our own self-refinement. Emulating this progression of feelings furthers our own spiritual development.

Cultivating a Pure Heart

We seek truth as our divine purpose in order to help create peace among others based on this same truth. Tiferet emanates this power. We note that the entire six-part Zeir Anpin is also referred to by the single Sefirah of Tiferet, which suggests that when our emotions are brought into orderly service of the divine, both within and without, we are ready to enter the Holy Place and the Holy of Holies. When our hearts are pure, we are prepared to enter the place of elevation and illumination.

While the fire rituals of the Lower Chariot (Yesod, Hod, Netzach) enliven the blood (Nefesh) and the world of action (Asiyah), fire also calls in the spirit of God, the Ruach aspect of the soul and the corresponding realm of Yetzirah. Here, the Upper Chariot of Tiferet, Gevurah, and Chesed refine the drive to do into the desire to be, to consecrate what we do, to give it purpose and meaning, so that we become holy parts of holy action—in effect, holy instruments.

The legs (Netzach and Hod) take us where we need to go; the hands (Chesed and Gevurah) carry out the activities we do. The heart is housed in the torso (Tiferet), though its seat is in Binah. All of the bodily organs that are served by the heart are brought into coherence in the Outer Court rituals of fire, water, and earth. Here in Tiferet we gain the heart's place as the supreme benefactor, judge, and healer; in fact, Tiferet is often the Sefirah associated with healing, as its purpose is to make a refined mixture of the left and right pillars, so that as we walk the middle path, we lean neither too far to the left nor too far to the right. Such a person, like the prophetess Devorah, is able to sit in judgment properly, finding what elevates any situation.

> *I have taught thee in the way of wisdom;*
> *I have led thee in paths of uprightness.*
>
> PROVERBS 4:11

The Song of Tiferet is a declaratory arrival at the center of this exquisite system of chambers and paths that is the Tree of Life, which, like our body, is regulated by the crown/Keter and by our Creator. Just as the prophetess Chanah offers sage advice about the vitality of prayer, Devorah demonstrates through her life what each of us must do: we must judge our own actions honestly and judge others with mercy.

A Triad of Consecration

In the triad composing the Upper Chariot—Tiferet, Gevurah, and Chesed—Tiferet is central. Here we join Devorah, Joshua, and Moses. All three of these prophets command armies and serve as judges of the people. Together they form an epochal period in the Israelites' lives and hence in our own experience.

As we shall see in the coming chapters, with Moses and Chesed we experience God's greatest love in the crossing of the Red Sea; in Joshua's song of stopping the sun and moon to win a battle, Gevurah reveals that a restriction at one end of a moment can produce the greatest freedom and opening at the opposite end—something we see in childbirth and in the Kabbalistic description of how God withdrew himself (*tzimtzum*),[10] creating a contraction in order to create the world. When we humble ourselves, eradicating the desire for ourselves alone, we arrive at the greatest freedom: the desire to serve others, to benefit them. This desire becomes the consecrating seal on our will. Selflessness is the reward for the sacrifice of the ego.

As a prophetess, judge, and military leader, Devorah shows us this state of being. The Upper Chariot's fantastic triumvirate of Moses, Joshua, and Devorah reminds us that our organs, arms, hands, and torso are a miraculous unity that, when consecrated to God, is capable of overcoming all obstacles. Moses shows us how to do this in the parting of the Red Sea; Joshua demonstrates this in overcoming nature with the help of God; and Devorah, our inner judge of balanced decision-making, shows

---

[10] Tzimtzum is a lurianic (from R. Yitzchak Luria, i.e., the Ari), Kabbalistic explanation of existence. In order to create the world, HaShem withdrew Himself in order to reveal Himself below. This tzimtzum, or contraction, was also a concealment of HaShem, creating the empty space needed to give birth to the diversity of form. This is much like the way a teacher must conceal his brilliance and knowledge of a subject in order to teach his student, who may have no knowledge of the subject.

us that we can administer our intentions and our actions by this same code of selfless devotion made of strong boundaries (Gevurah/Joshua), truth telling (Tiferet/Devorah), and complete surrender to God's love (Chesed/Moses).

Exuberant Joy on the Middle Path

Tiferet is the center of the Ruach (spirit) aspect of the soul and the world of Yetzirah (formation). It is called Torah, and as Torah Tiferet is the central organizer of all six parts of Zeir Anpin and the refinement of our emotions. We are shown how to elevate whatever we come in contact with. This is the charge of Tiferet, Devorah, and any person on the middle path.

As a type of song, a hallel instructs us that our praise and thanksgiving, our exuberant joy, should be the center around which everything we do revolves, for by cultivating this attribute we can make each act one of purpose and elevated harmony. Joy, the emotional quality of hallel, is our emotional center, the place where all other emotions are blended in unity.

The Seat of the Soul

> R. Ishmael said: "He who studies in order to teach is afforded adequate means both to study and to teach."
>
> AVOT 4:5

Devorah sits on top of a hill under a palm tree in Ephraim and teaches the people. In this image we discern the development of Zeir Anpin's journey to its climax in Chesed. First, in Yesod (foundation), there is a declaration of love; then in Hod (majesty), a bowing before the beloved; in Netzach (victory), a perpetual pursuit of the beloved; and now in Tiferet (beauty), a recognition of the Tabernacle's beauty, harmony, and truth. Resolving all doubt, we gain entry to the holy place within ourselves, where truth is learned. At this stage in our spiritual development we radiate from the seat of the soul and the throne of truth. We become more self-aware and see more readily the whole that we are part of. One might even say that Tiferet *is* the seat of the soul, just as the Torah is the living throne of God for the People of the Book. While this holy teaching is rooted in Judaism, its inner message is of value to every person.

Devorah teaches the people about true justice, which must be sweetened with mercy. When the moon (Malchut, Nukvah/Female [daughter]) and the sun (Zeir Anpin, the Son) become partners, justice (the rectified Zeir Anpin) is administered fairly on earth, glorifying in the bounty of the Nukvah/Female/Kingdom. In the same way, the male aspect within the individual and within society needs to be rectified with the female aspect for there to be balance within our own makeup as well as true partnership between men and women worldwide.

This coupling between Zeir Anpin, the male aspect, and Nukvah, the female, is much of the day-to-day work we do in our lives, balancing intellect and feelings, generosity and restraint, the desire to do versus the impulse not to. In terms of the Tabernacle metaphor, it is the work of uniting prayer and consecrated service. This work leads to elevation, illumination, and revelation. We refine our emotions, Chesed through Yesod, and cultivate our intellect, Keter through Binah, for the express purpose of creating peace, as we have seen on the first rung of the ladder in the song of Malchut, the Shemoneh Esrei. Balancing passive and active tendencies, the rational and the intuitive, giving and receiving, is the accomplishment of the refined Tiferet. In the Tabernacle schemata, the triad of Tiferet, Gevurah, and Chesed, the Upper Chariot, refers to the carrying out of divine will through the use of the hands and the heart.

Beauty, the Essence of the Middle Path

Joy, the quality of Tiferet and its song of praise, is the feeling we must generate when we make something beautiful. As well, justice that is merciful balances all parts in a beautiful way, thus resolving conflict and restoring balance between people and events. Indeed, beauty is often defined in terms of harmony and balance. This is the essence of the middle path in life: to make a beautiful life balanced between all of these sefirotic qualities and skills; to make of our lives a holy Tent of Meeting, a place full of reverence, awe, and joy. Becoming a tent of peace is the outcome of being a fully developed human.

The Shechinah dwells, as does Torah, in Tiferet. As mentioned earlier, both of these manifestations of God are sometimes called Tiferet. Sometimes the Tabernacle is called Malchut. Both Malchut and Tiferet are on the middle pillar of the Tree of Life. The Shechinah and the Ruach HaKodesh are present when there is balance between parts, which is the meaning underlying the word *shalom,* peace, whose root is *shalem,* wholeness.

As seen in figure 7.2, Devorah emanates and receives the influx from five other Sefirot of Zeir Anpin: Yesod and King Solomon from below; Hod and King David from the left side; and from the right, Netzach and

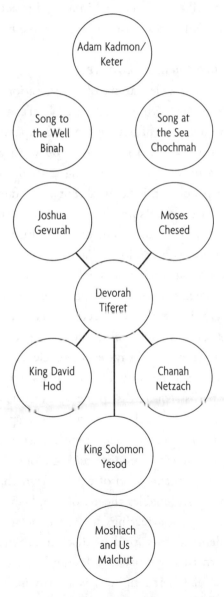

Figure 7.2. Sefirotic emanations to Tiferet

Chanah. The left above Devorah is Gevurah and Joshua; and the right above Devorah is Chesed and Moses.

In a civil and just society, all citizens are elevated, from the highest to the lowest, and ideally the same laws apply to everyone equally. In our own lives we strive for a balance between one's own needs and the service one renders to others. In all of these day-to-day activities and dispositions, our intentions, like a banner held in a royal procession, wave above us. These intentions call in responsive energy of like kind from above.

Moving Everything toward Balance

This stage in the Tabernacle's arena of consecration requires that we imbue our daily activities with a consecrated heart, a clear intention of serving, and a thorough will of devotion and compassion. In Tiferet we discern how to improve, whether inwardly or outwardly, any situation we are part of, learning how to move anything toward balance, whether it involves a group of people, an idea, an activity, our families, or our own inner life. We recognize when something, whether a situation, a person, or a trait of our own, needs to be cut off or minimized. This requires the administration of compassionate action. We administer justice between those parts of ourselves that steal our time and energy and, like thieves, take from us what is not theirs. Once we see that all things come from the same origin, it is wise to concentrate on making life balanced, allowing our inner voice, the voice of the soul, its place in our daily lives.

The soul is a pure vessel always eager to elevate and cleave to the divine. The body can also be brought into this service once shown the path. All spiritual paths require discipline and effort, and teachers have a responsibility not to usurp either the will or the spirit of the student, but to skillfully guide him toward acting with discernment and the ability to do what is just even if it requires acting alone. Every prophet and every great leader displays this kind of courage, which, along with great imagination and humility, enables the art of prophecy. The path of righteousness is a narrow path affecting the body, the soul, and the world. All sacred paths demand this kind of discipline, within and without. Being able to discern this truth with a loving heart is the great accomplishment of the refined Zeir Anpin; it is a refinement of feelings more than thought.

Cultivating Humility

Words of Torah are life to those who find them.

PROVERBS 4:22

Oppression is not only a force exerted from the outside: our own emotional patterns can act as tyrants in our lives. Unrefined anger is easily understood as an out-of-control parent, spouse, child, or boss, whose temper tantrums are hurtful to those around them and to the very person exhibiting the rage. Anger held within harms us, and God forbid that we direct it toward others. Anger is the root of all terrorism. It makes everyone an enemy and everyone's life expendable. It is the expression of extreme selfishness and arrogance. We can see why the Ramban reminds us that anger is the cause of judgment in Gehinom, Hell. In fact, anger causes the most harm to others as well as to ourselves.

Anger derives from not getting what one wants in a situation. Cultivating humility, as King David so ably demonstrates, is the necessary antidote to overcoming anger. Humility regards every situation as an opportunity to offer service. In fact, anger and humility are opposites. If we do not speak gently to all people, we need to examine why this is so. Have we overcome our own prejudices and the intolerances that affect our household and our community? Do we suspend judgment or judge prematurely? A fair inner judge considers that everyone has something to offer or teach.

Moral Development

The emotive experience of radiating thanks and joy requires a certain inner confidence, or bitachon, a word we saw associated with the Sefirah of Netzach. Tiferet's inner quality in Chassidic teachings is mercy, rachamim, so it is fitting that our prophetess Devorah, the exemplar of justice, should fulfill this element for the Israelites' development as a people and as an example for each one of us.

Devorah shows us the importance of justice administered with mercy, as God instructs. Before Jerusalem and the building of the Temple, before Shiloh, there was Devorah on Mt. Ephraim, sitting under a palm tree, teaching and judging the people. In a previous work, *Kabbalistic Teachings of the Female Prophets,* I showed that this is akin to the stage of moral development of B'nai Yisrael. So let us now ask ourselves:

Are we moral people? Are we fair? Do we know what justice really is?

Sweetening justice (Chesed added to Gevurah) produces mercy, which in turn reflects what is true. When we evaluate ourselves, are we able to see what is good, what needs to be changed, and how to do this in a way that is merciful? Do we act with awareness and with humility, or do we rather act like a cruel taskmaster, with severity and deprivation? How do we behave when we are responsible for other people? How do we treat co-workers, family members, strangers? The way we treat others is the reality of what we inherit throughout our lives and in our afterlife. We are dressed in our own conduct: the garment the soul wears in the afterlife is made of a person's words, thoughts, and deeds. Thus mercy, Devorah teaches, is the basis of law and order. This is what leads to personal and societal peace and beauty.

Honest Self-Reflection

Tiferet, like its exemplar, the prophetess Devorah, shows us balanced judgment, discernment, and restoration. The essence of justice is to make a balance between things—the victim and the accused, the crime and the restitution. In our own lives we balance our inner nature between the things that may do us harm, our attachment to people, places, or things that are unhealthy, and the outcome of these bonds. Freeing ourselves from these inner enemies sometimes requires intervention by friends, professionals, or loved ones. There is also, of course, the path of prayer and selfless service, as selflessness, Kabbalah teaches, builds a person's strength in overcoming adversity.

Just as God desired to manifest on earth and therefore created the human being's body for the soul to inhabit, so too the "Torah possesses a body and a soul. The body, i.e., the legal aspect of the Torah, acts as its garments and in fact is referred to by the sages as 'the bodies of the Torah.'. . . [The] spiritual dimension of the Torah assumes the garb of the laws in order to make it applicable to this world."[11] So our body is meant to serve the soul in order to serve God, just as law serves Torah. Finding the inner lawmaker and the inner judge is one aspect of consecration and spiritual development. Truth-seeking persons must have courage and

---

[11] R. Yitzchak Luria, *Apples from the Orchard*, 884.

compassion for themselves as well as the world, for honest self-reflection as a daily practice is a spiritual devotion.

Transforming Ourselves

Being able to discern with compassion the difference between what is good and what is not is the first step in transforming ourselves. The easiest path to take is to pray for help and guidance. Most chronic emotional patterns, which can manifest in physical ailments, are rooted in some unconscious aspect of a person's identity. Trying to figure it out is, of course, the path of psychology. Another option is to dedicate our attention and intention to elevating our whole self by generating positive actions each day, refining our inner nature according to the practical teachings of Kabbalah. Change like this, which is incremental, often brings about more permanent change anyway. It may be so gradual as to go unnoticed until one day we say to ourselves, "I don't get angry the way I used to about things," or "I know how to set boundaries with people so that I do not take part in things that are not helpful to myself, others, and the world." Most of life is a mixture of both gradual and sometimes, out of necessity, immediate change. This blessing of free will and the beauty of becoming self-managed and victorious over our unhealthy impulses is the signature of Tiferet. Justice is the outcome of a balanced inner life.

In Tiferet, the skills one has acquired facilitate being able to see what each situation needs in order to elevate the divine light in everyone. It is an ability to synthesize even polar opposites in such a way that a peaceful settlement between different elements is possible. This is what the middle path demands of the initiate.

The lateral groupings of three, a Sefirah from each of the three different pillars of the Tree of Life, are, as the Zohar teaches, spiritual groupings that reveal how to structure organizations, an economy, and especially one's own life. As well, there is a spiritual sequence reflected through the Torah songs associated with these Sefirot that serves as the basis of this work; like a mirror, it shows us our own soulful journey as a human being.

The Development of the Soul

As we ascend the ladder of light, seeing the sanctuary reflected in our own bodies, it becomes apparent that there is a higher spiritual body, which is called by different names in the various wisdom traditions of the world, but which is called the soul in Judaism. As noted in chapter 1, it is comprised of five parts, each specialized for a particular capacity. The body's various parts facilitate the soul's work of action, formation, creation, emanation, and revelation thus the body and soul work in partnership. Just as the mind can do what the hands cannot, the hands depend on the mind for direction, though they do seem to develop their own innate awareness in any craft in which they are employed.

In the Zohar we learn that God created man with the Nefesh, or animal soul; the Ruach, or spirit; and the Neshamah, the holy breath given to us by God at birth. He created man at the place where the holy Temple would stand and drew the breath for the Neshamah from there. Traditionally this is said to be the rock of Mt. Sinai on which Abraham laid his son Isaac; it is the rock of the Temple in Jerusalem (currently housed in the Dome of the Rock on the Temple Mount in Old Jerusalem). When a person is born, the Nefesh is granted. Only by personal refinement does he go on to receive a Ruach, and only after he has refined himself in the service of God does he receive the Neshamah. These are qualities we acquire through purposeful self-development. Even though an unconscious element of all parts of the soul is in us as well, when we access these parts through our proper actions and intentions, we can consciously, willfully embody the qualities of each Sefirah and the worlds to which they correspond.

While each person's soul is made of five parts, it takes great effort and self-refinement to become aware of the level of existence from which each emanates. Just as there is an inner spiritual aspect to food that we call a vital force, so too in every commandment there is a vital force. The prayers we recite before performing a deed activate the mitzvah. In every deed there is a thought, speech, and action: "The intention is the thought, the blessing is the speech and the action is the conclusion. Therefore scripture refers to 'all the commandment,' meaning the entire commandment, including its intention."[12] Our intention is the vital force of the soul acting through the body.

---

[12] Luria, *Apples from the Orchard*, 888.

God is the rock, my heart, and my portion forever.

PSALMS 73:26

The full development of all five levels of the soul's makeup is the potential of each person, and in the coming messianic times this will be granted to all. The very reason why a person is born is to refine his will, his heart, and his actions. As seen in figure 1.5 in chapter 1 (see page 31) and in a more simplified version below in figure 7.3, the highest two aspects of the soul, the Chayah (the living presence) and the Yechidah (the divine spark of God), are aspects of the soul that are eternal and do not reside within the physical body. They emanate and inform our soul from above and maintain the person's connection to the World to Come, imparting that which is immortal in our soul and in our awareness while we are incarnate.

World	Soul
Or En Sof (Limitless Light)	Yechidah
Atzilut (Emanation)	Chayah
Beriyah (Creation)	Neshamah
Yetzirah (Formation)	Ruach
Asiyah (Action)	Nefesh

Figure 7.3. Correspondence of the five worlds and the parts of the soul

The Soul's Ascension

The Nefesh (the animating life force in the blood) and Ruach (the spirit) sustaining that life force is refined in the initiate, the one who prays. One benefits by the prior sefirotic work one has done. In Malchut one gains a sense of lowliness (shiflut), along with a deep and glad return to God. In Yesod, one's love is declared without any hesitation, without any restraint; it is a crying out from the heart of the soul's sense of its contract with God, the cry of the righteous for the world's repair (tikkun olam). In Hod, one gains a great sense of servitude in the highest meaning of the word, as in surrendering one's personal will to the divine will; it is a feeling of great loyalty and devotion to something greater than oneself, producing sincere thanksgiving. In Netzach, one acquires the practice, the persistence, and the ability to appreciate that each act contributes to the much-larger scheme of things. Arriving now in Tiferet, the initiate reaches an emotional balance between reflection and crying out in joyous praise, with the desire to bring balance among others through proper action.

As Within, So Without

As we have already learned, the directive God gave Moses to build a place for Him to meet with His people is attended by the numerous details He describes. At the same time, despite the specific technical instructions for the Tent of Meeting's components, ritual objects, and worship requirements, its fundamental purpose is made clear: it is for the refinement of B'nai Yisrael, the children of Israel. As the oral tradition asserts, humanity's development is judged by their actions and inner nature. Just as God and His presence are one and the same, so too what we do and who we are remain inseparable and determine the judgment each person receives during life and at the time of the death of the body.

> The sages of the Mishnah teach: "Not the expounding of the Law is the chief thing, but the doing of it" (Zohar: Pinchas; 332). For the Holy One, blessed be He, is concealed by the secrets of the Torah. In what, then, can He be known? In the precepts, for they are the Shechinah, which is His form. Just as the Holy one, Blessed is He, is humble, so is His Shechinah humble. He is pious and She is pious. He is valiant, and She is valiant over all the nations of the world. He is truth and She is faith. He is a prophet and She is a prophetess. He is righteous and She is righteous. He is King and She is kingdom. He is wise and She is wisdom. He understands and She is His understanding. He is a crown, and She is His diadem, "a crown of glory" (Yeshayah 62:3). This is why the sages taught: "No disciple whose inside does not correspond to his exterior may enter the house of study." That is, the disciple will be as the form of the Holy One, Blessed be He, who is his inside and the Shechinah is his outside. He is the inside within and the Shechinah is His exterior on the outside. And She that is on the outside has not changed from Him who is on the inside, that it should be known that She is His Atzilut, and there is no separation there whatsoever, this

being the secret of the verse: ". . . within and without shall you overlay it" (Shemot [Exodus] 25:11).[13]

Tiferet, where the male and female, the right and left pillars co-mingle in balance, reveals the deeper meanings behind the instructions God gave Moses when He first told him to erect the Tent of Meeting; in fact, the whole purpose of creating the Ohel Moed is revealed here. The harmony the rituals impart to the community is the same harmony each person achieves by emulating the meaning of all the parts and practices, which together comprise our own personal sanctuary of the Divine Presence. It is this very process that this book explores as the main tenant of Kabbalah: As within, so without; as above, so below.

Declaring the rank of prophet as being akin to the Shechinah, as the quote from Zohar above tells us, reminds us of the purpose of song, meditation, chant, recitation, and study of sacred writings: it is through these consecrated (Yetzirah) actions (Asiyah) that we create a field of harmony capable of receiving and holding the Holy Spirit. The Zohar states that our great prophetess Devorah is among the heavenly instructors who guide us in these consecrated activities on our human journey. The Zohar speaks of several sanctuaries, including Devorah's:

> The emissary tells Rabbi Shimon about the sanctuary where Batyah, the daughter of Pharaoh lives, and how she goes out to see Moses's image three times a day. Batyah and the other women are clothed in light bodies and study the Torah. In another sanctuary there is Serach, [the daughter of Ashur], with many other women who study the Torah; she goes three times a day to see a light in the image of Joseph. In another sanctuary lives Yocheved, the mother of Moses, with many other women, and three times a day they all thank and praise God, and they sing the Song of the Sea. The fourth sanctuary of the Matriarchs is that of Deborah the prophetess. The emissary talks about the nightly coupling of the souls—soul-to-soul, light-to-light. Those unions produce the souls of those who get converted; this is the secret meaning of "The fruit of the righteous is a Tree of Life."[14]

---

[13] Zohar, Pinchas 332.
[14] Zohar, vol. 18. Shlach Lecha 26:195–205, 123.

Cultivating a Place for the Holy Spirit

In the beautiful classical work *A Letter for the Ages (Iggrees HaRamban)*, the Ramban, in this letter to his eldest son, inspires many parents to write letters to their children to be read after their death as living testimony to what is important and what one hopes for one's children, grandchildren, and the future generations. The Ramban's letter to his son Nachman has been a gift to millions since it was first written in the thirteenth century. A few of its principal teachings are included in this work. It is of value for people of all faiths and is the definitive teaching on the middle path, which includes all of Zeir Anpin, and in particular the Sefirah of Tiferet, which stands, like the centrally placed laver in the Tabernacle, as a place of mercy and humility.

The Ramban begins his missive:

> Heed my son, the discipline of your father, and do not forsake the guidance of your mother. Accustom yourself to speak gently to all people at all times. This will protect you from anger—a most serious character flaw which causes one to sin. . . . Once you have distanced yourself from anger, the quality of humility will enter your heart, through humility the fear of God will intensify in your heart, for you will always be aware of from where you have come and to where you are destined to go. You will realize that in life you are as frail as the maggot of the worm—all the more so in death.[15]

The holy sage goes on to detail the numerous traits one must develop for the Holy Spirit to enter one's life: "When your actions display genuine humility—when you stand meekly before man, and fearfully before God; when you stand weary of sin—then the spirit of God's presence will rest upon you, as will the splendor of His Glory, you will live the life of the World to Come." He tells his son to be humble before all people, to cast his eyes downward, to consider everyone else above himself. As all the prophets and prophetesses teach, as Chanah and Devorah declare, it is God who raises up and brings down, it is God who makes one wealthy or poor, but it is the individual

---

[15] R. Avrohom Chaim Feuer, *A Letter of the Ages, Iggress Ramban,* 16–20.

person who must acquire the traits of humility and loving-kindness.

"Review your actions every morning and evening, and in this way live all your days in repentance," says the Ramban. So particular is his choice of words that earlier in the letter he tells Nachman, "In all your words, actions and thoughts—at all times—imagine in your heart that you are resting in the presence of the holy One, Blessed is He, and that His presence rests upon you. Indeed, the glory of God fills the universe."[16] Here, stated eloquently, is the outcome of humility and reverence for God and all of His creation, including every human being on earth: the cultivation of a place where the Holy Spirit resides, an idea that has been expressed in different ways in all the different wisdom traditions of the world.

Millions of readers of this living letter written by a father to his son are likely to have taken this statement about the Holy Spirit as a simple metaphor, something perhaps to know but not to believe is meant for each one of us. Yet this explains precisely why we study and "do" the Word of God. In this remarkable letter, the Ramban describes the significance of preparing a place for God's glory and the Divine Presence through the Holy Spirit. Furthermore, he says that our rituals, prayers, repentance, and good deeds help us cultivate the kind of deep humility required for the Holy Spirit, the glory of God, to rest upon us and enlighten us.

Rabban Simeon ben Gamaliel II, the leader of the Great Sanhedrin after the fall of the Second Temple, said: "The world stands on three things: on truth, on justice, and on peace, as is said, 'Execute truth, justice and peace within your gates' (Zech 8:16). These three are interlinked: when justice is done, truth is achieved, and peace is established."[17]

Understanding now a bit more about the connection between the Tent of Meeting, our own lives, and the Tree of Life, we will continue our ascent of the Tree of Life, moving from the center pillar of Tiferet to the left pillar and the Sefirah of Gevurah, where strength and *din*, judgment, allow us to discern what is holy from what is not.

---

[16] Feuer, *A Letter of the Ages, Iggress Ramban*, 16–20.
[17] Avot 1:18. See also Hayim Nahman Bialik and Yehoshua Hana Ravnitzky, *Sefer Ha-Aggadah*, 5:128, 733.

8
Mastery of the Emotions
Gevurah • Song of Cutting Through

Moses received the Torah at Sinai and transmitted it to Joshua, Joshua to the elders, and the elders to the prophets, and the prophets to the men of the great assembly.

AVOT 1:1

Fifth Sefirot: Gevurah
Meaning: Strength, judgment
Rung on Ascending Ladder: Seven
Archetype: Zeir Anpin (the Son)
Symbol: Sword
Spiritual World: Yetzirah/formation
Spiritual Anatomy: Left hand
Inner Quality: Awe or fear (yira), protection of one's gifts

Historical Personage: Joshua the warrior-prophet
Text: Joshua 10:1–15
Key Words: Discernment, sword of holy separation
Key Emotion in Song: Cutting through (zemer)

Tent of Meeting: Outer Court

Spiritual Stage: Consecration, rising above limitations, making all holy
Spiritual Practice: Breaking through, separating the holy from unholy
Illumination: Illumination of discernment, choosing between good
and evil

> *Joshua shows how to use the strength of*
> *discrimination to protect what is holy,*
> *including oneself.*

The Sefirah Gevurah: Strength and Discrimination

The Sefirah of Gevurah teaches us how to use the discerning heart and mind. As an energetic process, Gevurah sorts, dissects, separates, and eliminates. This takes courage and strength. Gevurah is innately motivated to ask, "What is good, what is important, and what is essential?"

In the Outer Court rituals, Gevurah represents our immersion in the waters of the copper laver of purification, the *kiyyor,* which is represented by the *mikvah,* the ritual bath used by Jewish men and women in each community worldwide today. It also represents the sword of protection, tempered on the fire altar of the animal sacrifices. On the Tree of Life, Gevurah sits on the left pillar, directly under Binah, representing the Mother and the quality of understanding. This configuration informs Gevurah's intelligence of discernment. As we shall see, the power of this Sefirah can be the difference between life and death. Using the will to protect what is holy requires daily decisions, whether it is choosing the best food for the body or the best thoughts for the mind and soul; this requires using the sword of discrimination to discern the pure from the impure, and then consecrating what is holy.

In our Tabernacle progression, we are now only one step away from entering the Holy Place. On the Tree of Life, Gevurah is the last of the left-pillar-influenced Sefirot of the persona of the Son, Zeir Anpin, and the next-to-last step in our ascent of the Upper Chariot (Tiferet, Gevurah, Chesed). Like the sword of Joshua the prophet, who leads the Israelites into the Promised Land, Gevurah is burnished by the fire of sacrifice and cleansed and sanctified by water and the love of Moses and Chesed, which lie opposite it on the right pillar. In the human realm, it is the balance between the qualities of these two Sefirot—between unconditional love and the will to sustain it with discipline and proper boundary-making in our lives—that is constantly sought yet oftentimes seems so elusive.

Here, as we near the final stages of consecration in the Outer Court of the Tent of Meeting that is our life, we can sense the climax of this progression in the story of Joshua, who refines himself by decisively removing all darkness from his heart. His mighty sword represents the action of cutting through. A fearless leader, Joshua shows us that we must be willing to separate the holy from the unholy, both within and without, but that this kind of decisiveness must be sweetened with mercy. His long apprenticeship with Moses is a process of initiation that eventually allows him to assume leadership of his people, closing the chapter on the forty-year Exodus, during which time his teacher, Moses, served as initiator and guide.

The Prophet Joshua:
The Initiate as Warrior and Leader

Joshua, trained by the greatest prophet to ever live, Moses, is considered every bit as great a leader as his predecessor. Their lives, as we shall see, are bound closely together, just like the two Sefirot of Gevurah and Chesed, or the way our left and right hands are a working pair. Joshua was the first in the lineage of oral transmission of the law, receiving it directly from Moses and subsequently transmitting it to the elders of Israel. He was also the first leader of the Israelites in their own land.

Joshua and Moses

Joshua was a constant fixture in Moses' life. His relationship to his master and his future greatness is signaled early on in his story:

> Now Moses used to take the tent and to pitch it without the camp, afar off from the camp; and he called it the tent of meeting. And it came to pass, that every one that sought the LORD went out unto the tent of meeting, which was without the camp. And it came to pass when Moses went out unto the Tent that all the people rose up, and stood, every man at his tent door, and looked after Moses, until he was gone into the Tent. And it came to pass, when Moses entered into the

Tent, the pillar of cloud descended, and stood at the door of the Tent; and [the LORD] spoke with Moses. And when all the people saw the pillar of cloud stand at the door of the Tent, all the people rose up and worshipped, every man at his tent door. And the LORD spoke unto Moses face to face, as a man speaketh unto his friend. And he would return into the camp; but his minister Joshua, the son of Nun, a young man, departed not out of the Tent. (Exodus 33:7–11)

As the attendant of the Ohel Moed, Joshua remains in the Tent's vibratory holiness long after everyone else has left. Within its sacred confines the limitless light of the Creator illuminates Moses and his apprentice, Joshua.

This description of Joshua's devotion not only to his master, Moses, but to the holy Shechinah, speaks volumes: Joshua becomes king over his own kingdom—i.e., he masters all his emotions—by completely submerging himself in the limitless light of God, which removes all darkness from his heart. This is what allows him to become the leader of the people, with all his organs and limbs engaged in that service as he guides the Israelites into the Promised Land, the land flowing with milk and honey, which in Kabbalah represents the divine sustenance of the soul and body in union.

Meeting Joshua at the Tent

That we first meet Joshua as Moses' student suggests his vital role in protecting the Tabernacle and the teachings held within its design and various functions. Moses' tent, the original place of meeting, is later replaced by the formal Ohel Moed, which becomes the initiatory vehicle for the Hebrews throughout the Exodus before they enter the Holy Land under Joshua's leadership. Kabbalah teaches that this is the story of each human being's exodus from limitations and doubts. The historical transformation wrought by the Exodus takes forty years. According to the sages, the process of our own inner transformation also takes forty years—meaning that it takes this amount of time to develop the brain (*mochin*) to the point that it allows the person to separate from Egyptian worship's dependence on many idols and gods, which Kabbalah says is akin to doubting the oneness of God and the light of His holiness that shines within us. In Torah studies it is said that until a person is at least forty years old, he should not advise others and should seek counsel from the elders, for this is the amount of time it takes to transform oneself. It is only when we are mature enough spiritually to use freedom wisely, for the elevation of the entire world—the next stage of development in our initiatory journey—that we are transformed. Until then, one has not completely overcome one's selfishness, arrogance, and material lust, including the desire for wealth or power, which is the equivalent of the idol worship of the Egyptians.

While Moses leads the children of Israel and teaches them the Word of God, Joshua devotedly attends his teacher, meaning he humbles himself before the teachings and develops his nature to the point of manifesting such supreme humility (Hod) that he can be trusted to use the will of victory (Netzach) and the sword of discrimination (Gevurah) combined with wisdom (Chochmah) as a warrior. His teacher, Moses, is called the most humble person on earth; Joshua is called "son of Nun," a simple tribesman of Ephraim. His humility is further indicated by the fact that the letter Nun (נ) is the first letter of the root of the Hebrew word for prophecy, prophet, and prophetess, נביא (Nun Bet Yod Alef [Navi]). This shows us that a prophet must be willing and able to bow in supplication to the truth of God's teachings.

The Battle Against Amalek

At the start of the Exodus, after the Israelites have gone through the miracle of the bitter waters turned sweet, and after the manna has fallen and a portion of it saved for the Ark of Testimony, it falls to Joshua to lead a battle against the Amalekites, the very same people who had savagely attacked the old, the weak, and the infirm at the rear of the Israelites' tribal entourage as they fled Egypt. Moses tells Joshua, "Choose people for us and go do battle with Amalek; tomorrow I will stand on top of the hill with the staff of God in my hand" (Exodus 17:9).

And so while Joshua leads the Israelites into battle, Moses, his brother Aaron, and Hur, the grandfather of Betzalel, go to the top of a nearby hill to pray for God's help. What follows is yet another demonstration of God's protection of the people:

> It happened that when Moses raised his hand [the one that held the staff], Israel was stronger, and when he lowered his hand, Amalek was

stronger. Moses' hands grew heavy, so they took a stone and put it under him and he sat on it, and Aaron and Hur supported his hands, one on this side and one on that side, and he remained with his hands in faithful prayer until sunset. Joshua weakened Amalek and his people with the sword's blade. (Exodus 17:11–13)

Here, the self-mastered leader and prophet Moses must stay completely attached to faith in God's power and protection, as must Moses' military commander, Joshua. When Moses raises his heart of attachment to the divine, symbolized by raising his staff above his head, a gesture representing love and mercy combined with strength, Joshua raises his sword and eliminates the enemy, representing the extremes of cruelty and selfishness as shown in the recent slaughter of the living treasure of women and children and infirm. Together thus, Moses and Joshua open the door to the Hebrews' ascension as a nation of priests and as the People of the Book. Their living collaboration teaches us to use our will with guarded strength seasoned by loving-kindness, producing the quality of mercy. To inherit the Promised Land—the state of being free and balanced—we must overcome our own selfish, intractable tendencies and try our best to change those aspects of ourselves that need refinement. To do this, we learn to use our sword (Gevurah) and our staff (Chesed) in proper measure.

The Sinatic Revelations

The next time we encounter Joshua is when he is accompanying Moses during the dramatic revelations that occur on Mt. Sinai. Joshua is described as "a young man (Exodus 33:11) of almost sixty years old at the time."[1] He and the elders walk with Moses partway up the mountain, where Joshua remains, waiting for his teacher as instructed until his return forty days and forty nights later:

Moses stood up with Joshua, his servant; and Moses ascended to the Mountain of God. The glory of God rested upon Mount Sinai and the cloud covered it for a six-day period. He called to Moses on the

---

[1] Midrash Aggadah, Shemos 24:1. See also R. Yisrael Yitzchak Yishai Chasidah, *Encyclopedia of Biblical Personalities*, 215.

seventh day from the midst of the cloud, the appearance of the glory
of God was like a consuming fire on the mountaintop before the eyes
of the Children of Israel. Moses arrived in the midst of the cloud and
ascended the mountain; and Moses was on the mountain for forty days
and nights. (Exodus 24:16–18)

Moses makes three such ascensions of Mt. Sinai; Joshua plays a role
in each.[2] During this pivotal moment in the spiritual development of the
Hebrews, when God transmits his law to Moses, we are not told what
Joshua does—only that he waits for his teacher further down the mountain. "When Joshua left the camp of Israel to wait at the bottom of Mt.
Sinai [for the return of Moses], manna fell for Joshua just as it fell for
the whole community of Israel."[3] That he is the only figure mentioned in
Torah who waits for Moses at this crucial time indicates that he is essential to Moses' task. In this we again see the unity of Moses and Joshua,
the right and left hands of God, who together lead the children of Israel
out of the Exodus and into the Promised Land.

The Transmission of God's Laws

On his first ascent of the mount, Moses receives oral teachings from God:
the Ten Commandments, how to keep the holidays, the Sabbath, and
more. He descends the mountain, having recited these oral instructions
into the ears of Joshua, and now speaks God's commandments within
"earshot of the people," who respond enthusiastically, saying, "All the
words that God has spoken, we will do and we will obey" (Exodus 24:7).
After the people agree to these obligations, God tells Moses to go back
up the holy mountain a second time, to be given the "stone tablets of

---

[2] Just as there are varying accounts of Creation, there are different accounts of the three
forty-day sojourns Moses makes on Mt. Sinai. One perspective says that the Torah's order
is not chronological. Another interpretation says that the second ascent was made to ask
God for forgiveness for the Israelites, their having received the Ten Commandments on
the first ascent. Yet another account is the chronology presented in this chapter: the first
ascent occurs when Moses receives Torah orally; on the second ascent he receives the first
set of stone tablets, which he subsequently breaks upon reentering the camp and finding
the people worshipping a golden calf. On his third ascent of Mt. Sinai, Moses receives the
second, replacement set of tablets.

[3] Yoma 76a. See also Chasidah, *Encyclopedia of Biblical Personalities,* 215.

the law," called the HaEven V'HaTorah. "Ascend to Me to the mountain and remain there, and I shall give you the stone Tablets and the teaching and the commandment that I have written, to teach them" (Exodus 24:12). Significantly, in addition to the stone tablets, Moses receives God's instructions for building "a sanctuary for Me, so that I may dwell among them" (Exodus 25:8). So begins Torah's detailed description of all of the parts and purposes of the Tabernacle and its vessels, as described in Exodus 25–30 and as discussed in chapter 2.

After Moses' second forty-day sojourn on the mount, Joshua accompanies his master down the mountain. They hear loud sounds coming from camp. Joshua fears it is the sound of an attack; Moses correctly says it is rather another kind of distress: the people have fallen back into old ways, worshipping a golden calf made during Moses' absence. God tells Moses that his people have corrupted themselves, and that He plans to eliminate them and start a new people from Moses' own line. Moses argues and pleads with God for mercy for the people, thus exhibiting Chesed's quality of mercy, saying they should be spared (Exodus 32:11), and God relents. But upon reaching the camp and seeing for himself the idol the people are worshipping, Moses becomes angry. He throws down the tablets God has inscribed on sapphire, destroying them. He then takes the statue and burns it and grinds the gold into a fine powder, which he then sprinkles over water, creating a homeopathic treatment that he orders the Israelites to drink. Moses then confronts his brother, Aaron, whom he had left in charge: "What did this people do to you that you brought a grievous sin upon it?" (Exodus: 32:21). Aaron explains that they had asked him to make a god for them, as Moses was late in coming down the mountain; after throwing all their gold into a fire, the calf emerged, he says. In other words, if we fail to honor a particular restriction, as the Hebrews disobeyed the restriction on worshipping false gods and did not await Moses' return, we can lose faith in ourselves and our relationship with God, allowing negative forces to engulf our lives. From Aaron's actions we learn that when we do not make some effort to stop people from making bad choices when we are in a position to do so, or are party to them in some other manner, we are held accountable, as was Aaron.

At this point Moses declares to the people, "Whoever is for God, join me!" (Exodus: 32:26). Many of the Israelites step forward, including the entire tribe of Levites—the Hebrew tribe of Levi, to which Moses and Aaron belong, and from whose ranks the priestly class would later be designated. It is thus left to the Levites to go through camp and kill, according to Torah, 3,000 of their own people, said to be part of the mixed multitudes that came out of Egypt with Moses.

It is hard for any of us to imagine being in this situation ourselves. Even though these kinds of uncivil slaughters go on throughout the world today, it seems illogical to interpret this kind of killing as Godly. But in the narrative of the People of the Book, eliminating those who were not ready to live the Word of God, as well as stripping the children of Israel of the precious gold that they had given to create the calf, was to be the final separation from idol worship.

The Establishment of the Ohel Moed

The third time Moses ascends the mountain for forty days and nights he is given the second, replacement set of stone tablets and is, appropriately (given the purification that recent events required), shown the Thirteen Attributes of Mercy (Exodus 34:5–7).[4] Called the Shelosh-'Esreh Middot, these attributes are drawn from the way God describes himself to Moses:

> The Lord (Adonai) descended in a cloud and stood with him there, and he [Moses] called out with the Name Adonai. Adonai passed before him [Moses] and proclaimed: Adonai, Adonai, God, Compassionate and gracious, Slow to Anger, and Abundant in Kindness, and Truth; preserver of Kindness for thousands of generations, Forgiver of Iniquity, Willful Sin, and Error, and Who Cleanses—but does not cleanse completely, recalling the iniquity of parents upon children and grandchildren, to the third and fourth generations. (Exodus 34:5–7)

At this point the Israelites are finally ready to formalize their faith and devotion to God and to

> make everything that God has commanded: the Tabernacle, its tent, and its cover, its hooks, its planks, its bars, its pillars, and its sockets; the Ark and its staves, the Cover, the Partition-curtain; the Table, its

---

[4] See appendix 6, "The Thirteen Attributes of Mercy and Thirteen Principles of Faith."

staves, and all its utensils, and the shew-bread; the Menorah of Illumination, its utensils, and its lamps, and oil for the illumination, the incense Altar and its staves, the anointment oil and the incense species, and the entrance screen for the entrance of the Tabernacle; the Elevation-offering Altar and the copper netting for it, its staves, and all its utensils, the Laver and its base; the curtains of the Courtyard, its pillars, and its sockets, and the screen of the gate of the Courtyard; the pegs of the Tabernacle, the pegs of the Courtyard, and their cords; the Kohane's vestments to serve in the Sanctuary, the sacred vestments for Aaron the Kohen and the vestments of his sons to minister. (Exodus 35:1–19)

The Israelites gather all their gold, silver, copper, wool, linen, and cotton—in short, all their wealth—and they each put their hands to some task in creating the Ohel Moed. After the recent revelations, so great is their desire to contribute to this fulfillment of the covenant that Moses has to stop them from bringing more of their belongings. Moses tells the people that "Betzalel, Son of Uri, son of Hur, of the tribe of Judah" has been filled with the "Godly spirit, with wisdom, insight, and knowledge" (Exodus 35:31) of every craft, therefore he is appointed chief artisan of the Tabernacle. The creation and erection of the Tent of Meeting is subsequently described in Exodus. When the work is completed,

> the Cloud [i.e., the Shechinah] covered the Tent of Meeting, when the Cloud was raised up from the Tabernacle, and the Children of Israel would embark on their journeys. If the cloud did not rise up, they would not embark until the day it rose up. For the cloud of God would be on the Tabernacle by day, and fire would be on it at night before the eyes of all of the House of Israel throughout their journeys. (Exodus 40:34–38)

Guarding the Inner Dominion

Following the creation of the Ohel Moed, the people request that Moses send out a group of scouts to see what lies ahead in the land promised them by God. Joshua, Caleb (the prophetess Miriam's husband and the grandfather of Betzalel, the Tabernacle's chief artisan), and ten other men, each representing his own tribe, are chosen by Moses to secretly infiltrate Canaan and inspect the land while the Israelites are camped in nearby Kadesh-Banea.

After an absence of forty days, the scouts return with their report. They are awed by the size and strength of the Canaanites. They have brought back the choicest fruits of the land to show its incredible bounty. But the account they give is nevertheless discouraging: ten of the spies say it will be impossible to confront such formidable foes, who are a race of giants against whom the Israelites are like grasshoppers. Only Joshua and Caleb insist that with God's help they will succeed. Once again, the people are despondent. Joshua and Caleb try to allay their doubts and fears by reminding them of God's promise, but this only angers the people, who are on the verge of killing them when the Shechinah descends over the Ohel Moed, saving them and as well demonstrating Joshua's connection to the Divine Immanence.

Like Joshua and those he led, we learn to stand as guardian over the Ohel, our inner dominion. It takes both our right and left hands—our disciplined refinement and sense of compassion—to clear a path in life that is balanced, to make a middle road for the world and for each of us to inhabit. It is from this middle path that peace can be sustained.

The Passing of Moses

Nearly forty years later in the Israelites' journey, as they stand ready to enter the Promised Land, God gives Moses his last instructions: he is told to go up to the mountain and look out over the land of Canaan as far as he can see, and to know that his descendants will inherit all that God has promised. Moses, in seemingly perfect health in body, mind, and soul—we are told at the advanced age of 120—is then informed that he will soon be "gathered to your people," that is, that he will die. We later learn that his body is secretly buried in a place no one to this day has found.

This mysterious ability of Moses to leave his body at the appointed time tells us that there is a time to come in and there is a time to leave. We do this every day of our lives—leaving our homes and returning, leaving our bodily consciousness in sleep and returning upon waking. This is preparation for the way in which we will leave our physical bodies after we have completed the work done in our allotted time.

Joshua's Ascension

As Moses' end of life approaches, God tells him who he must choose as the next leader: "Take yourself Joshua son of Nun, [who is] a hero like yourself" (Numbers 27:18).[5] The two prophets are compared in other ways, as well. The Talmud says, "Before the sun of Moses set the sun of Joshua rose."[6] Even Moses' own sons do not inherit his position, but Joshua does: "'He who waits on his master will be honored' (Proverbs 27:18). Joshua attends Moses day and night [and thereby] merited Divine inspiration and prophecy."[7] As we shall learn, just as God parts the Red Sea for Moses, He parts the Jordan River for Joshua. Both were great military leaders; both were prophets in whom the people put their faith. Yet it is clear that while Moses lives, "Joshua constantly stood and guarded the Tabernacle that Moses had built."[8]

This suggests Joshua's place in Torah, and also serves as a guide for our own spiritual development: that what is built through love and with love must be guarded with discernment and strength. Joshua receives the ultimate ordination as the Hebrew nation's leader from his predecessor, Moses, at God's command. Having been told by God that he is about to pass away, Moses is concerned that God's will be realized, and that the children of Israel are not left without someone to lead them, understand them, protect them, inspire them, and comfort them.

> And Moses spoke to the Lord, saying, "Let the Lord, the God of the spirits of all flesh, set a man over the congregation. Who may go out before them, and who may go in before them, and who may lead them out, and who may bring them in; that the congregation of the Lord be not as sheep which have no shepherd." And the Lord said to Moses, "Take Joshua the son of Nun, a man in whom is spirit, and lay your

---

[5] Sifri Vayeilech, 305. See also Chasidah, *Encyclopedia of Biblical Personalities,* 215.
[6] Bereshis Rabbah 58:2.
[7] Bamidbar Rabbah 12:9. See also Chasidah, *Encyclopedia of Biblical Personalities,* 218.
[8] Zohar 2:16a. See also Chasidah, *Encyclopedia of Biblical Personalities,* 218.

hand upon him. [Have him] stand before Elazar the Kohen [priest] and before the entire assembly, and command him before their eyes. You shall place some of your majesty upon him, so that the entire assembly of the Children of Israel will pay heed. Before Elazar the Kohen shall he stand, who shall inquire of the judgment of the Urim before God; at his word shall they go out and at his word shall come in, and he and all the Children of Israel with him, as God has spoken through Moses." (Numbers 27:15–21)

Joshua's importance is signaled when Moses asks God for a successor who is a statesman as well as a person of courage and power. Joshua was exactly that: he was not the kind of person who would send others out to fight battles—he went first. He thus inspired in them the confidence to be successful and thus come back ("and come in before them"). Joshua's leadership would last twenty-eight years. Like his teacher, Moses, who only ever wanted to serve by going out in the fields in Egypt and ease the suffering of the Hebrews toiling there as slaves, Joshua never asked to be a leader; he only wanted to serve by devoting himself to Moses and God.

The act of Moses placing his hands on Joshua in the presence of all the people is a gesture that confers authority to his successor, as we know from our discussion of blessing with the hands in chapter 7. As their newly anointed leader, Joshua must lower his head in submission to receive this transmission—a gesture emblematic of the initiate's posture of humility in many of the world's wisdom traditions, and which describes the countenance required for the experience of prophecy.

Joshua remains in his master's service up through the very last days of Moses' life, learning statecraft from him, speaking to the people as the teacher, with Moses standing at the doorway listening. That Moses shares his majesty with Joshua suggests Moses as the sun and Joshua as the moon, the former radiating its luminosity, the latter reflecting his light, and both expressing the equal importance of the right pillar (of gold) and the left pillar (of silver) in the people's development.

God spoke to Moses: "Behold, your days are drawing near to die; summon Joshua, and both of you shall stand in the Tent of Meeting, and I shall instruct him." So Moses and Joshua went and stood in the Tent of Meeting. God appeared in the Tent, in a Pillar of Cloud, and the Pillar of Cloud stood by the entrance of the Tent. God said to Moses, "Behold, you will lie with your forefathers, but his people will rise up and stray after the gods of the foreigners of the land, in whose midst it is come, and it will forsake Me and annul My covenant that I have sealed with it." (Deuteronomy 31:14–16)

God goes on to tell Moses of the hardships the people will know and then tells Moses, "To write this song for yourselves and teach it to the children of Israel, place it in their mouth, so that this song shall be for Me a witness against the children of Israel" (Deuteronomy 31:19).[9] Then God initiates the final transference of authority and responsibility to Joshua:

> And he [the Lord] gave Joshua the son of Nun a charge and said, "Be strong and of good courage: for thou shalt bring the children of Israel into the land which I swore unto them: and I will be with thee. . . ." And Joshua the son of Nun was full of the spirit of wisdom; for Moses had laid his hands upon him: and the children of Israel hearkened unto him, and did as the LORD commanded Moses. (Deuteronomy 31:23, 34:9)

And so just as Joshua never left Moses' side, God and Torah will never leave Joshua.

After the ceremonial transfer of leadership to Joshua, Moses offers the Hazeinu, the Song of Chesed (Deuteronomy 32:1 43) that we will examine in chapter 9. As Moses' legacy to the children of Israel, the Hazeinu offers a concise recapitulation of all of Torah's precepts in the context of the Israelites' history. In this act of prophecy and revelation, Moses, as Chesed, is the recipient of the flow of the Divine Immanence from Keter above. With Joshua now consecrated and anointed as leader—representing the near-completion of our journey through Zeir Anpin—his teacher, Moses, departs his mortal body.

With the conclusion of the second of the five books of Moses and the

---

[9] The ninth chapter of this book features the song Moses chants prior to his death.

account of the consecration of Joshua as the new leader of the Israelites, the People of the Book's Exodus comes to an end, and the era of rulership by prophets, and later kings, begins. Near the end of the Exodus, the people's material consciousness has been transformed by the experiences they have had throughout the forty years of their ordeal. They know that whatever they do on the physical plane is already manifest on the spiritual plane; they also know that what man does on the material plane affects the spiritual worlds. With Joshua initiated as the new leader and guide, the Hebrews are ready to embark on the next stage of their journey. Like the ancient Israelites, we too are now prepared for the next stage of our journey through the Ohel Moed, as we prepare for the experience of the Holy Place and Holy of Holies in our lives.

Crossing the Jordan

In chapter 9, which picks up at an earlier period in the Israelites' chronology, at the beginning of their Exodus, we will see how with God's help, Moses raises his staff and the Red Sea is parted. Here, in the story of Joshua, we find that this event is in effect reenacted at the very end of the Exodus when Joshua, with his emblematic sword aloft, leads his people across the Jordan River into the land God has promised as an inheritance:

> And it was after the death of Moses, the servant of the LORD, that the LORD spoke to Joshua, the son of Nun, Moses' minister, saying, "Moses my servant is dead; now therefore arise, cross over the Jordan, you, and all this people, to the land which I give to them, to the people of Israel. . . . Be strong and courageous; for you shall cause this people to inherit the land which I swore to their fathers to give them. Only be strong and very courageous, that you may observe to do according to all the Torah, which Moses my servant commanded you; turn not from it to the right hand or to the left, that you may prosper wherever you go. This Book of the Torah shall not depart from your mouth; but you shall meditate on it day and night, that you may observe to do according to all that is written on it; for then you shall make your way prosperous, and then you shall have good success. Have I not commanded you? Be strong and courageous; be not afraid, nor be dismayed; for the Lord your God is with you wherever you go." (Joshua 1:1, 2:6–9)

The story of the inheritance of the land under Joshua's leadership is replete with accounts of battles and miracles. Just as God parts the Red Sea for Moses and the children of Israel, He parts the Jordan River for the Israelites to cross over so that they may bring the Ark, the Tent, the Tabernacle elements, and all their belongings with them.

Two days before Joshua is to lead the Israelites across the Jordan into the Promised Land, two of his men, having been sent out to spy on the land of Jericho, return and approach him: "And they said unto Joshua: 'Truly the LORD hath delivered into our hands all the land; and moreover all the inhabitants of the land do melt away before us'" (Joshua 2:24). Like Moses, who had to prepare the stones on which the Ten Commandments were inscribed, Joshua must also make certain preparations for bringing the people and the Holy Ark and its sacred contents across the Jordan:

> And Joshua rose up early in the morning, and they removed from Shittim, and came to the Jordan, he and all the children of Israel; and they lodged there before they passed over. And it came to pass after three days that the officers went through the midst of the camp; and they commanded the people, saying: "When ye see the Ark of the Covenant of the LORD your God, and the priests, the Levites, bearing it, then ye shall remove from your place, and go after it. Yet there shall be a space between you and it, about two thousand cubits by measure; come not near unto it, that ye may know the way by which ye must go; for ye have not passed this way heretofore." (Joshua: 3:1–4)

In these instructions, God is absolutely clear: this is to be a collective ritual process, a journey requiring the participation of *all* of the people, not just the priests who bear the Ark. "And Joshua said unto the people: "Sanctify yourselves; for tomorrow the LORD will do wonders among you" (Joshua 3:5). He then tells the priests,

> "Take up the Ark of the Covenant, and pass on before the people." And the LORD said unto Joshua: "This day will I begin to magnify thee in the sight of all Israel, that they may know that, as I was with Moses, so I will be with thee. And thou shalt command the priests that bear the Ark of the Covenant, saying: 'When ye are come to the

brink of the waters of the Jordan, ye shall stand still in the Jordan.'"
(Joshua 3:6–8)

Next comes the promised miracle so reminiscent of Moses' parting of
the waters in an earlier age, as Joshua tells the Israelites,

"Behold, the ark of the covenant of the LORD of all the earth passeth
on before you over the Jordan. Now therefore take you twelve men out
of the tribes of Israel, for every tribe a man. And it shall come to pass,
when the soles of the feet of the priests that bear the ark of the LORD,
the Lord of all the earth, shall rest in the waters of the Jordan, that the
waters of the Jordan shall be cut off, even the waters that come down
from above; and they shall stand in one heap." And the priests that
bore the ark of the covenant of the LORD stood firm on dry ground
in the midst of the Jordan, while all Israel passed over on dry ground,
until all the nation were passed clean over the Jordan. (Joshua 3:11–17)

After the entire nation crosses over the river in this way, Joshua tells
the people from each of the twelve tribes to choose one man, who he
then instructs to take a stone from the middle of the Jordan, "at the station of the feet of the Kohanim" (Joshua 4:3), and to carry it across with
him to their camp on the other side. Joshua himself then places twelve
other stones, each one at the foot of the High Priests still standing in the
dry riverbed with the Ark, to commemorate this event for all the generations to come. The Ark of the Covenant, the holy model of our own
inner sanctuary, is then borne across the river by the twelve priests, each
wearing a breastplate with twelve stones.

Becoming a Conscious Co-Creator

The Israelites' crossing of the Jordan under Joshua's direction is the final
moment in the nation's separation from Egypt, marking the end of the
Exodus. The waters of the Jordan are parted, allowing the Hebrew tribes
to cross over. The twelve tribes are represented by the twelve priests, who
each wear a breastplate with twelve stones, with each tribe bearing a stone
gathered from the river bottom. Kabbalah says that this entourage represents the "crossing over" of all of humanity, for everyone is born under the

influence, to greater or lesser extent, of the twelve signs of the zodiac. The strong hand of Elokhim, the name of God relating to might, judgment, courage, and fear, as expressed by Joshua and the Sefirah of Gevurah, is evident in the crossing of the Jordan River with the holy Ark, an event that marks yet another stage of the alchemical transformation of the people, linked in space and time to the parting of the Red Sea by Moses.

In the same way, a person's two births—one from ancestral bonds that influence one's familial DNA and history; the other from the enslavement that results from self-created doubt—is accomplished by the use of both mercy (Chesed) and purposeful strength (Gevurah). That Joshua commemorates this crossing-over ritually as he does suggests that we should try to cross over planetary influences, becoming completely free-willed humans acting as co-creators, beyond the power of the celestial bodies, which affect all life on earth. Chassidut teaches that the only way to transcend the daily influence of planetary aspects is to become a conscious co-creator through self-refinement. Joshua, in Gevurah, accomplishes this: at Gibeon, he is able to buy the Israelites enough time to guarantee their victory by commanding the sun and the moon to be still. He is able to accomplish this because he has mastered both his mind (the sun) and his emotions (the moon) in the course of his long apprenticeship with Moses. This level of refinement allows him to be infused by the Ruach HaKodesh, the Holy Spirit.

Kabbalists say that prayer, ritual action, and right intention can bring the Sefirot into balance. We call on God to help us, we follow our inner voice, and we carry out our tasks, even if others abandon the work. This is the role of Gevurah. It is the disciplined inner warrior who sets aside what is unholy to accomplish for the greater good. It is the power of this Sefirah that enables a person to be strong enough as an individual to march to the beat of a different drummer.

The infinite Chesed of God is intended for finite creatures who are unable to absorb the infinite loving-kindness of God and still remain in physical existence. For this reason the attribute of Chesed is limited by Gevurah's restrictive power. Thus Gevurah is also an aspect of God's love, for if the outpouring of infinite love were to remain unrestrained, finite creatures would be nullified by the revelation of the limitless light of God's love. Therefore Gevurah restricts and conceals the light, so that each of God's creatures can receive His loving-kindness according to his individual capacity. This quality of restraint enables a person to appreciate that there are proper and necessary boundaries for receiving the light of God in good measure, in correct proportion. As Moses' protégé, Joshua was the inheritor of the entire guidebook for operating the inner temple of the human being, the Torah's inner teachings. It is Joshua who teaches this hidden aspect of Torah—restraint and discernment—to all the elders of Israel.

Cutting Through to Freedom

On the western bank of the Jordan was a place called Gilgal, where Joshua erects a monument of the twelve stones brought by the representatives of each of the tribes to commemorate the miracle of the crossing. Here the priests erect the Tent of Meeting, which remains there during the entire fourteen years of the conquest and partition of the Promised Land.

> It happened when the entire people had finished crossing [the Jordan] that the Ark of God and the Kohanim passed in front of the people. The Children of Reuben, the children of Gad and half the tribe of Manesseh crossed, armed before the Children of Israel. . . . On that day God exalted Joshua in the eyes of all Israel, and they revered him as they had revered Moses all the days of his life. God spoke to Joshua, saying, "Command the Kohanim, bearers of the Ark of Testimony, that they should ascend from the Jordan." (Joshua 4:11–13)

When they reach the opposite bank of the miraculously parted river, the waters resume their flow.

> And the people . . . encamped in Gilgal, on the east border [end] of Jericho. And these twelve stones that they had taken from the Jordan, Joshua erected at Gilgal. And he spoke unto the children of Israel, saying: "When your children shall ask their fathers in time to come, saying, 'What mean these stones?' then ye shall let your children know, saying, 'Israel came over this Jordan on dry land.'" (Joshua 4: 19–22)

When the kings of the Canaanite and Amorite tribes hear about the miracle of the Jordan's parting, "their hearts melted, and there was no longer any spirit [within them to fight] because of the children of Israel" (Joshua 5:1). Because of their reticence to engage the Hebrews, Joshua gives the Canaanite kings three choices: he tells them that those willing to evacuate the land could do so, and he would not pursue them; those willing to remain and make peace with Israel on such terms as to not endanger the spiritual commitment of the Hebrews would receive his peace terms; finally, those desiring nothing but war would have to fight those who, in the name of God, had been promised the land of Canaan. Thus we see in the miraculous crossing of the Jordan and in this subsequent demonstration of Joshua's diplomacy Gevurah's ability to cut through, as in cutting through the waters of the Jordan River as well as the lands of Canaan.[10]

The Israelites had moved about in the desert for forty years until, some teachings recount, all the men who were of military age when they left Egypt had died. Because the remaining men who had been born in the desert during the long journey had not been circumcised, God next commands Joshua to make flint knives so that all the men can fulfill the covenant of circumcision. This explains why in the Torah Gilgal is also called the Hill of Foreskins (Gibeath Haaraloth).

After this covenant ritual takes place, "The LORD said unto Joshua, 'This day have I rolled away the disgrace of Egypt from upon you,' wherefore the name of that place was called Gilgal, unto this day" (Joshua 5:9). Gilgal (גלגל) means "wheel," "rolling," or "rolled away." The zodiac, the ongoing wheel of cause and effect, is rolled back, as it would be later when Joshua sings the song associated with the Sefirah of Gevurah.[11] We are endowed with free will so that we may make the choice to take ourselves across the division between the mind and heart, putting our faith in God and living according to His Word. This is the path that enables us to live beyond the influence of other people, other nations, and even the cosmic wheel of planetary influences over our emotions.

Following the ritual act of circumcision, the children of Israel

---

[10] Looking at the record of Joshua's conquest, we note that his strategy was to cut through the middle of the country and then to open up its eastern and western corridors.

[11] The seven years of conquest of the land promised the Israelites and the seven years of apportioning that land to the Hebrew tribes accounts for the fourteen years the Ohel Moed was stationed at Gilgal.

celebrate Passover (Joshua 5:10), and the manna that had given them sustenance throughout the Exodus ceases (Joshua 5:12) on the day after they eat from the grain of the land, on Pesach.

A Place of Decisiveness and Clarity

While scholars are of differing opinions about the location of Gilgal and which places may in fact be called Gilgal, in our context it refers to the place where the Israelites and their leader, Joshua, settle after crossing the Jordan River and where they placed the twelve standing stones drawn from the river. Gilgal is also the place where it is said that in the final battles of humanity, during the days of Moshiach, eternal peace will be given.

Metaphorically, Gilgal is considered a place of decisiveness and clarity, where one eliminates evil from one's heart and life, the place where God "rolled away the disgrace [reproach] of Egypt." In this we are being told that when we cross moments of uncertainty and conjoin with divine right order, the ability to overcome destructive habits and behavior is strengthened.

From Gilgal, Joshua and the Israelites succeed, over the course of many battles, including the famous siege of Jericho recounted in Joshua 6:1–27, in taking the land of Canaan to settle in. In the battle at Gibeon, as described in Torah, Joshua, with God's help, is able to stop the sun and the moon, which remain stationary for twenty-four to thirty-six hours, allowing the Israelites to defeat their enemy in daylight.[12] "There has never been a day like it before or since, a day when the LORD listened to a human being. Surely the LORD was fighting for Israel!" (Joshua 10:14). In Kabbalah we may understand this as meaning that when we are able to master our emotions and our mind—the moon being the emotions and the sun the mind—the natural progression of worldly influences can be overcome. Joshua demonstrates this kind of alchemy in this historic moment in biblical history.

The Passing of Joshua

Two years before his death, Joshua gathers the people at Shechem, the Canaanite city that became the first capital of the nation of Israel. Here,

---

[12] R.Yitzchak Luria, *Apples from the Orchard,* 531.

just as Moses did prior to his death, Joshua recounts their long ordeal and success in entering the Promised Land. Before Joshua's passing, the borders of each tribe's lands are decided by the casting of lots. Only a few tribes had taken full possession of their lands, and so the tribe of Judah, which was then joined by its adjacent tribe of Simeon, became the designated leaders of the people. Finally, after having fought battles against thirty-one kings of the lands, and after leading Israel for twenty-eight years, Joshua takes leave of the physical realm at the age of 110.[13]

The Song of Gevurah: Cutting Through (Zemer)

Zemer, a type of song made by instrumental music, is associated with Gevurah. Both zemer and the Hebrew word for song, *shir,* mean "to cut," though one is done with the voice and the other with musical instruments. When we sing praises to God we cut through our doubts and feelings of separateness from holiness. When we use our musical tools, the things we make to hold the Divine Presence such as a harp or a horn, these vessels represent our will to glorify divinity, and as such they are an extension of our voicing this splendor.

In the context of Joshua's life, the Sefirah of Gevurah is also called *din,* or judgment. Having learned in our first chapter that music elevates the soul of the prophet in preparation for hearing the Word of God and is thus a tool of prophecy, we are reminded that the power of our sword of Gevurah to cut off from ourselves that which is destructive of holiness is in itself a prophetic action. Therefore, Joshua's song, a zemer, cuts through the *kelipot* (the husks of evil) attached to living forms.

The emotional quality of a zemer suggests a conservation of energy, an energetic restraint, before a final, full emergence. This is precisely the emotional quality of the song of Gevurah. It is explicitly associated with fear and awe of God and a supreme attachment to His holiness and power, as witnessed when Joshua, with God's help, takes command of the

---

[13] "Three were crowned with the titles of 'age' and 'days,' and all three were heads of distinguished houses, Avraham, Yehoshua [Joshua], and David. Avraham was the head of the Patriarchs, Yehoshua the head of the Kingship of the Tribe of Ephraim, and David the head of the Kingship of the Tribe of Judah" (Bereshit Rabbah 59:6). See also Chasidah, *Encyclopedia of Biblical Personalities,* 215.

sun and the moon at the Battle of Gibeon. Joshua expresses this same quality in his life and actions, redeeming lands at God's command from the enemies of Israel, allowing the people to finally emerge victorious from their Exodus.

The word *zemer* is comprised of the letters Zayin (7), Mem (40), and Reish (200). It can mean harvesting produce, pruning a juice-producing vine, singing a wordless melody, or it can simply refer to a knife and the idea of cutting through. God told Moses to instruct Joshua in the ways of Torah in preparation for his future role. Joshua's ability to stop the natural course of the sun and the moon reveals the notion that the Tent of Meeting is where one refines one's sefirotic qualities and learns to control the natural elements of the mind and the emotions. In the Tent, one is infused with the radiating light of the Godhead, which comes from gaining a heart of courage and mastering the alchemical rites of the Israelites as expressed in the Tabernacle rituals, which have their roots in the Sefirot of the Tree of Life.

The Sword of Gevurah: The Blade of Discrimination

The Hebrew word for sword, *cherev,* חרב (Chet [8] Reish [200] Bet [2])—can be interpreted as meaning using our mind (Reish) to choose life (Bet) over death (Chet). This expresses the essential nature of Gevurah and describes the emotional quality of this Sefirah's song, a *zemer,* which translates as "cutting through." The numerical value of the Hebrew word for **sword,** 210, is the same as that of the word for **the mountain** הרה (Hay Reish Hay) (Genesis 14:10); **bone,** עצמי (Ayin Tzadee Mem Yod) (Genesis 29:14); **choose,** בחר (Bet Chet Reish) (Genesis 46:17); **left-handed,** אטר (Alef Tet Reish) (Judges 3:15); and **overthrow,** מסלף (Mem Samech Lamed Fey) (Proverbs 21:12). The gematria of this sequence suggests we have the ability to overthrow our lower inclinations by using our discrimination and strength, as signified by the left hand.

The modern person may find it difficult to fully grasp the reality that the Israelites faced after escaping from slavery to wander homeless in the desert for forty years, having to fight for their very survival and trust that God would provide for their most basic needs. Yet even when the Israelites waged war it is important to recall that Joshua balanced (Tiferet) discernment (Gevurah) with loving-kindness (Chesed). When facing a foe, Torah records that he offered alternatives: "When you draw near a city to fight against it, you must first proclaim peace terms to it" (Deuteronomy 20:10). The sages further clarify: "Who fulfilled this verse? Joshua son of Nun. At each place God told him to conquer, he issued the following written proclamation: 'whoever wants to leave should leave; whoever wants to make peace should make peace; whoever wants to fight should fight'"[14]

His Song of Victory over the Enemy (Joshua 10:1–15)

The short prophetic text associated with the Song of Gevurah, detailing the events at Gilgal described above, is found in Joshua 10:12–14, but the event includes verses 1–15 as well. The event described in this text comes immediately after the familiar story of the battle of Jericho, as described in Joshua 6:1–27, in which the walls "come tumbling down" after the Kohanim, while carrying the Ark, blow their shofars in a certain order while encircling the city for seven days.

At this point the Hebrew people know their leader, Joshua, is capable of channeling God's miracles: they have already witnessed the Jordan River parting; then they see the walls of Jericho collapse. One can only imagine their state of awe, a signal quality of this Sefirah. Joshua's song describing the stopping of the sun and the moon at Gibeon suggests the conjoining of Moses' soul in heaven with Joshua's soul on earth—the sun and moon together, standing in their associated sefirotic positions of mastery, thereby meriting the assistance of God and His heavenly hierarchies.

Gevurah, as Joshua, sits beneath the Sefirah of Binah, the Mother (and its associated Song of the Israelites), showing us that mercy is available in even the most desperate situations. The dramatic story of the battle at Gibeon is accentuated by the power God manifests in fulfillment of Joshua's need to create a window of opportunity to manifest the Israelites' victory. Here, set in its larger context, we can better appreciate Joshua's alchemical mastery over life:

1 *Now it came to pass, when Adoni-zedek king of Jerusalem heard how Joshua had taken Ai, and had utterly destroyed it; as he had done to Jericho and her king, so he had done to Ai and her king; and how the inhabitants of Gibeon had made peace with Israel, and were among them;* **2** *that they feared greatly, because*

---

[14] Devarim Rabbah 5:14. See also Chasidah, *Encyclopedia of Biblical Personalities*, 223.

Gibeon was a great city, as one of the royal cities, and because it was greater than Ai, and all the men thereof were mighty. 3 Wherefore Adoni-zedek king of Jerusalem sent unto Hoham king of Hebron, and unto Piram king of Jarmuth, and unto Japhia king of Lachish, and unto Debir king of Eglon, saying: 4 "Come up unto me, and help me, and let us smite Gibeon; for it hath made peace with Joshua and with the children of Israel." 5 Therefore the five kings of the Amorites, the king of Jerusalem, the king of Hebron, the king of Jarmuth, the king of Lachish, the king of Eglon, gathered themselves together and went up, they and all their hosts, and encamped against Gibeon, and made war against it. 6 And the men of Gibeon sent unto Joshua to the camp to Gilgal, saying: "Slack not thy hands from thy servants; come up to us quickly, and save us, and help us; for all the kings of the Amorites that dwell in the hill-country are gathered together against us." 7 So Joshua went up from Gilgal, he, and all the people of war with him, and all the mighty men of valor. 8 And the Lord *said unto Joshua: "Fear them not; for I have delivered them into thy hand; there shall not a man of them stand against thee." 9 Joshua therefore came upon them suddenly; for he went up from Gilgal all the night. 10 And the* Lord *discomfited them before Israel, and slew them with a great slaughter at Gibeon; and they chased them by the way of the ascent of Beth-horon, and smote them to Azekah, and unto Makkedah. 11 And it came to pass, as they fled from before Israel, while they were at the descent of Beth-horon, that the* Lord *cast down great stones from heaven upon them unto Azekah, and they died; they were more who died with the hailstones than they whom the children of Israel slew with the sword. 12* **Then spoke Joshua to the** Lord **in the day when the** Lord **delivered up the Amorites before the children of Israel; and he said in the sight of Israel: "Sun, stand thou still upon Gibeon; and thou, Moon, in the valley of Aijalon." 13 And the sun stood still, and the moon stayed, until the nation had avenged themselves of their enemies. Is not this written in the book of Jashar? And the sun stayed in the midst of heaven, and hasted not to go down about a whole day. 14 And there was no day like that before it or after it, that the** Lord **hearkened unto the voice of a man; for the** Lord **fought for Israel.** [Bold indicates lines from which the Chazal divined the song type] *15 And Joshua returned, and all Israel with him, unto the camp to Gilgal.*

Ritual: Completing the Upper Chariot

The Upper Chariot of our being, comprised of Tiferet, Gevurah, and Chesed, and as exemplified by their associated historical personages, shows us how to consecrate anything, how to make it holy. This is accomplished through the use of the hands and the heart, the mighty warriors that cleanse the lands of one's inner and outer life from unhealthy tendencies.

In the Outer Court of the Tent of Meeting, as in the Upper Chariot of our being, we engage the water rituals of the hands and feet, for it is the hands and feet that carry out a person's will. The world of Yetzirah (formation) rules the hands, which act on or form the ideas that come from the mind (KaChaBa, the three Sefirot above Zeir Anpin) and the heart. To immerse one's hands in water before performing a ritual, as the priests do in the Outer Court before performing a ritual offering, means to immerse oneself in the teachings of truth (Tiferet) with clear intentions. Balance comes from keeping our hands pure, that is, from not participating in things that are wrong. Just as anger, which is purified through the fire altar sacrifices, can come out of a person's mouth and express itself through the hands, generosity and compassion—the hallmark of Chesed—must refine a might that is fierce and swift (Gevurah) or it can result in tyranny, as much within the individual as within society.

A militarized dictatorship is an example of the manifestation of the dark side of Gevurah—the abuse of power through heavy restraint unseasoned by mercy. Gevurah refined manifests in knowing how to find the light concealed in the darkness; the person influenced this way is capable of changing the world within and without. Such a person may be a leader or a role model for others, or a pioneer who fights against destructive tendencies in society and becomes adept at using the power of discernment. Note that the right pillar and the right hand represent the loving Adonai (Chesed), while the left pillar and the left hand the more reproving disciplinarian Elokhim (Gevurah). We each possess both of these qualities. Balancing them, becoming this balance, is the lesson of Joshua and his teacher, Moses.

The Temple Sacrifices and the Worlds

The sacrifices made in the Tabernacle represent the manner in which we refine ourselves in word, thought, and deed. These rituals offer us explicit instructions about the orderly way in which we can go about refining the animal soul, the yetzer hara, and elevating the divine soul, the yetzer tov, as we are made of both, the former inevitably attempting to dominate the latter. This lifelong struggle began with Adam's sin, which resulted in a mixing of evil with good, and, as the Arizal tells us, the "forces of evil gained power, in other words, he caused a blemish in all worlds, which now need to be purified anew."[15] The midrash adds, "Know, that when the sparks for the light from the world of Tohu (chaos) fell into the realm of evil, some fell into the inanimate kingdom, some into the vegetable kingdom, and into the articulate animal kingdom. Thus, our Sages stated 'there is no blade of grass below that does not have its spiritual angel above it, which activates its growth.'"[16] The sparks that fell "are agents that assure everything to grow until a human being comes along and elevates them by separating the good from the evil."[17]

As noted in chapter 1, each human being takes part in this elevation of the worlds, including the mineral, vegetable, animal, and human realms of existence, which correspond to the four worlds of action (Asiyah), formation (Yetzirah), creation (Beriyah) and emanation (Atzilut), as well as to the stations and rituals of the Tent of Meeting. So, for example, when God consecrates Joshua, he is told he must walk the middle pillar of the Tree of Life, as this is the method that elevates the fallen sparks and strips away the husks of evil and elevates them to good: "Be strong and of good courage; for thou shalt cause this people to inherit the land which I swore unto their fathers to give them. Only be strong and very courageous, to observe to do according to all the law, which Moses My servant commanded thee; turn not from it to the right hand or to the left, that thou mayest have good success whithersoever thou goest" (Joshua 1:6–7).

In the Outer Court of the Tent of Meeting, as exemplified by Joshua and the Sefirah of Gevurah, along with the other five Sefirot of Zeir Anpin, we note that God "commanded man concerning the sacrifices,

---

[15] Luria, *Apples from the Orchard,* 531.
[16] Bereshit Rabbah 10:6.
[17] Ibid.

that he bring, together with himself, something from all four fundamental elements, so that they can all be rectified."[18] The rituals of the Ohel Moed represent this individual and collective rectification.

The chart below summarizes the Arizal's correspondences, showing how the specific ritual elements used in the Tent of Meeting each correspond to a letter in God's unpronounced name of HaVaYaH as well as to the four worlds of existence that we each take part in rectifying.

World, Sefirot, and Name of God	Place of Ritual and Corresponding Elements
Atzilut – Emanation – Chochmah human kingdom Yod '	Outer Court prayers, songs, offerings, rituals
Beriyah – Creation animal kingdom Hay ה	Outer Court animal sacrifices
Yetzirah – Formation vegetable kingdom Vav ו	Outer Court flour, oil, wine offerings
Asiyah – Action mineral kingdom Hay ה	Outer Court salt and water fire rituals and laver of purification

Figure 8.1. The name of God and the elements in the Tabernacle rituals (based on the teachings of the Arizal from R. Moshe Wisnefsky, Apples from the Orchard: Mystical Teaching of Rabbi Yitzchak Luria on the Weekly Torah Portion, *532)*

The Arizal explains these correspondences in great detail, showing how the Outer Court rituals elevate all of the worlds:

The mineral kingdom ascends by means of salt and water; it derives from the world of Asiyah [action]. The vegetable kingdom ascends by means of flour, oil and wine; it derives from the world of Yetzirah [formation]. The animal kingdom ascends by means of the animals—the

---

[18] Luria, *Apples from the Orchard,* 531.

flock, i.e., sheep and goats and the herd, i.e., cows—and the birds—turtledoves and pigeon; it is derived from the world of Beriyah [creation]. Those who exert the effort to offer all these—the priest in their service, the Levites on the dais where they sing, the laymen on watch, and the people who offer themselves through the sacrifice—elevate the human kingdom, which is derived from the world of Atzilut [emanation]. Furthermore: the consumption of the sacrifice by fire elevates the world of Asiyah. The fragrance the sacrifice produces elevates the world of Yetzirah. The satisfaction this fragrance produces, elevates the world of Beriyah. The divine revelation the satisfaction causes expresses the world of Atzilut.[19]

When the Temple of Jerusalem stood, the rituals performed there caused the sparks to ascend, rectifying the body and soul of a person and the spiritual worlds attached to each part of the anatomy. Today, without a physical temple in our midst (though prophecy says it will be rebuilt in the coming time of Moshiach) our prayers, which are composed of action (that we pray), and speech (that we speak our prayers), replace these Temple sacrifices. These are represented in both the content and order of the daily and Sabbath prayer ceremonies. Thus the Hebrew liturgy and the sacrifices in the Outer Court, as enacted through our prayers, enable the ascent of the soul through the worlds.

The subject of the Tabernacle is so vast that one can only hope to clarify some small aspect of its relevance to our lives today. Our purpose in this book is simply to show that all of these elements from the ancient Hebraic teachings are still applicable to our modern era. How each one of us performs these purifying processes is our own choice. But when we devote ourselves entirely to seeking the divine in all of life, as Joshua does in his role of service and leadership, we are anointed with the strength, the courage, and the ability to manifest our vision.

The Hands: Uniting Gevurah and Chesed

Our hands, represented by Gevurah and Chesed, and as employed in the rituals of the Outer Court, are capable of making peace, projecting the

---

[19] Luria, *Apples from the Orchard,* VaYikra, 532.

heart into the world as we act. Our hands can embrace and love others and provide for and nurture ourselves. They can protect those we love, heal the sick, care for the widowed, help the needy, bury the deceased, build cities, and make it possible to travel to the moon.

Hands can take the direction of the mind and heart, whether for good or for wrong doing, for as we know they can surely cause death and destruction. The hands (Yetzirah/formation) express the heart (Beriyah/creation) through doing (Asiyah/action). Moral order and beauty—Tiferet, representing the union of the hands working together in harmony—is evidenced when we allow the feelings of the heart, the compassion in the heart (Binah), to flow through our hands (Chesed and Gevurah) as we do good works (Malchut). This contributes to the betterment of the world. Our hands are made for loving and protecting. Joshua teaches us all about protecting what is holy within and without and shows us that protecting what is holy is not for the weak of heart or for one lacking courage and fortitude.

Cultivating a Direct Experience of God

After the Tabernacle is created, after the Shechinah is a recognizable, regular presence in the lives of the Israelites, the second of the five books of Moses, Exodus, concludes. Moses' role as the chief prophet of the people then shifts: the people themselves must now assume responsibility for their own prophetic insight, that is, for their own spiritual development. It is no different than when an initiate leaves his teacher. The entire book of Leviticus, which follows Exodus in Torah, deals exclusively with the individual's service and the observance of Torah and the Tent of Meeting and its Tabernacle.

In discovering that Torah was given and required a special place to rest in, one sees why the Exodus from Egypt facilitated the building of the holy alchemical formula for personal revelation. Once Moses is told by God to build "a Sanctuary for Me, so that I may dwell among them, like everything that I show you, the form of the Tabernacle and the form of all its vessels; and so shall you do . . . they shall make an Ark" (Exodus 25:8), it is clear that we are witnessing an important historical transition that affects us both collectively and individually.

In the act of creating the Tent of Meeting is the transition from enforced worship and foreign gods to a community of people told to trust their own direct experience of God, which becomes a cornerstone of Judaism. "Make me a holy sanctuary to dwell in" is a directive for communal worship and the communal sanctuary. It is also a mandate for the individual: God is saying, in effect, "Make a place in your life, in your heart, for me; find out where I am in you. Allow Me to be present in your life." This is no less a spiritual revolution for the people of biblical times as it is for us today. Any person of sincere heart can enter into a conversation with the one God inside the Tent of Meeting, and can do so without an intermediary. Our emotions, our many thoughts, like idols and autocratic rulers, must be stilled in order that we may hear the clear voice of God as manifest in the blessed Shechinah and the Ruach HaKodesh.

When, upon completion, the Tent is illuminated by the Divine Presence, only Joshua remains there after Moses leaves. Joshua, the son of Nun, the exemplar of Gevurah and its song, the zemer, thus experiences the enduring Glory Cloud in the Ohel Moed. That Joshua does not leave suggests that God's presence endows him with perseverance, strength, and holiness.

A Place of Formal Immersion

As the Tabernacle inside the Ohel Moed comes to life, so too does formalized worship. This is a place of holiness through which the people's donations of sacrifices and prayers support the many priests and Levites who act as God's right and left hands at the altar of communal refinement. This is why only certain people, the Levites, are permitted to carry the Ark; and why only certain others, the Kohanim, can light the menorah and perform the holy ritual functions of the inner sanctum. This tells us that only those dedicated to serving God, to becoming God-like, are able to light the seven lamps of their being and preserve the shewbread from Sabbath to Sabbath, reflecting the light Sabbath gives to the world. Each activity in the Ohel Moed and later, in the two temples in Jerusalem, describes a process that each of us can reenact within our own inner sanctuary.

The aspect of externalized communal worship shows us how the supernal kingdoms emanate to the physical world and to the individual. Everything is related in octaves of similars: this is the foundation of hermetic understanding in all the wisdom traditions of the world. The sacred Tree of Life and the paradigm of the Tabernacle provides the model of each person's life, with the temple of worship being the united body and soul of the person dedicated to divinity. The priests are our conditioned, refined behaviors, dedicated to the service of unity in life, peacemakers within and without. For the Israelites, the stage of building a specific place of worship was a necessary step in the development from idol worship (as represented by the desire for power, wealth, and domination), as was common in biblical times, to developing their own faith in and direct connection with God, as facilitated by the priests.

While "no spot on earth is devoid of the Presence,"[20] it is also true that there is a great advantage to cultivating a special place for one's devotional practice. This is what is meant by "conditioning the field." Conditioned fields, places we ritually use over and over again for prayer and meditation, facilitate the movement of brainwave activity from the lowest alpha level to the highest theta level more quickly and thoroughly than, say, a busy street corner. In the same way one is counseled to put a fence around Torah—meaning to protect it from diminishment or harm in one's life and in the world. So we also need to put a fence around our lives and its holy activities. The Sabbath is that fence for the Jewish people, commemorating, as it is taught, Creation itself.

All Is One

We are told that the children of Israel (the descendants of Jacob, who are called Israel, which means "the straight path to El," that is, to God, as well as meaning "over whom God prevails"), upon reaching the Promised Land, were comprised of a new generation, most of whom had never experienced either enslavement by the Egyptians or its idolatrous practices. These young men and women were the children of the desert, the offspring of the Exodus in the Sinai, and had grown up witnessing awesome miracles in which seas split, rocks provided water, manna fell from heaven, and whole lands were turned over to them by means of God's intervention through hail, rain, and other natural phenomena. This was a people who knew only that when the pillar of cloud (i.e., the Shechinah) arose, they had to dismantle the Tabernacle, pack their belongings, and leave. So ritualized and

---

[20] Hayim Nahman Bialik and Yehoshua Hana Ravnitzky, *Sefer Ha-Aggadah,* section 6, fn. 5, 421.

well-orchestrated was this process, announced each time by the blowing of silver trumpets by each of the twelve tribes in a specific order (Numbers 10:1–10), that the departure was always the same: each leader or prince gathered behind his particular tribe's banner—a pattern reflected in the High Priest's breastplate, with gemstones corresponding to each tribe said to represent their various spiritual qualities. Then some 600,000 men of military age and their families would rise up and follow the pillar of cloud as one would the leader of an expedition, a request Moses made of God that was fulfilled, showing through this manifestation of His presence that He was with the Israelites.

The disengagement from relying on multiple external deities to relying on the power of prayer to the one power from which all life springs is a development of one's true inner self. A person is, at first, a stranger to his own spiritual nature, as the Hebrews were to theirs while in Egypt. Once a person finds his inner voice, though, he delights in being aware of and close to the oneness within and without. This is the Sinatic—or perhaps even the neurological synaptic—revelation available to each of us today. All is One. All hear the same voice of God. All hear the same and feel the same thing. "Yes," is the answer, "yes, we will do and we will hearken." We will do what God commands even before we intellectually understand *why* we are to do it. This is the hallmark of Joshua's faith, as well as that of each prophet or person who follows the Word of God as imparted by the Ruach HaKodesh and the Shechinah.

Protecting What Is Holy

That Joshua led Israel for twenty-eight years[21] after the death of Moses gives us a clue about the nature of his power. The Hebrew word for **power** or strength, *koach,* כֹּחַ (Caf Chet), has a numerical value of 28. Joshua led Israel with strength, power, and might (Gevurah) for twenty-eight years. He was God's left hand, the hand of God's might in delivering the Holy Land to His people. Our power, koach, in emancipating ourselves, along with our abilities and resources—the will applied to certain tasks—tells us that to consecrate is to protect what is holy. The rabbis teach that to cut through, one must use one's power, which is sourced in awe of and reverence for the greater power of God. "Four things require strength,

---

[21] Seder Olam Rabbah 12. See also Chasidah *Encyclopedia of Biblical Personalities,* 216.

namely, [study of] the Torah, good deeds, praying, and one's worldly occupation. Whence do we know this of Torah and good deeds? Because it says, *Only be strong and very courageous to observe to do according to all the law.* Be strong in Torah."[22]

The middle path, radiating from Tiferet upward through Chesed and Gevurah on the right and left pillars, shows us that truth is the outcome of using both the sword and the staff to manifest the qualities of mercy, beauty, strength, and love. This is the outcome of consecration, the extraordinary journey reflected in Joshua's life. He leads us into the Holy Place, as he leads all of Israel into the Promised Land.

When Joshua and the people finally arrive in Canaan and camp at Gilgal, where they will remain for fourteen years, the men perform, as already described, the rite of brit milah, the covenant of the circumcision, followed by the celebration of Pesach (Passover) on the fourteenth of the month of Nisan (Aires the lamb). On the second day of the covenant ceremony, the manna ceases, having already diminished the day before. Afterward comes a sublime prophetic moment in the life of Joshua, as he stands at the walls of Jericho. God is ready to tell Joshua that He has sealed the city, preventing anyone from leaving or entering. Joshua, seeing what he believes to be a man standing opposite him with a drawn sword in his hand, walks toward him and asks, "Are you with us or with our enemies?" The stranger replies, "'No, for I am the commander [Metatron] of God's legion; now I have come.' Joshua fell before him to the ground and prostrated himself, and said to him, 'What does my master say to his servant?' The commander of God's legions said to Joshua, 'Remove your shoe from upon your foot, for the place upon which you stand is holy.' And Joshua did so" (Joshua 5:13–15).

This tells us that when we are victorious over our challenges in life, we are to humble ourselves, nullify our sense of selfhood entirely, for the sanctuary of our lives and where we each stand is holy.

Cutting Off What Is Unholy

As seen in the song of Joshua and in the meaning underlying the word *zemer,* Gevurah refers to the compassionate but decisive removal from

---

[22] Brachot 32b.

our inner and outer lives of those things that do not assist us in becoming independent, holy, God-like humans, whether this is someone in our life, some habit we have, some place we frequent, a limited view of ourselves and our potential, or a personal point of view or world view that is crippling our progress, personally and/or collectively. This is the strength of Gevurah. This action is also reflected in what the priests must do with their knives in preparing offerings for the ritual fire.

Mastering one's inner life is the purpose of all sacred traditions. To do this, we must cut off and remove that which is unholy. This must be accomplished before we can fully consecrate our lives. Is it any wonder that in all of Torah, Moses had only one successor? Joshua removes all obstacles and doubts from his inner self and his outer world, enabling him to receive the *shefa,* the flow of divine light from the Sefirah directly above, Binah, the Mother, the source of all life, which in turn draws from Keter (the crown) through Chochmah (wisdom), the Father.

The Mother (Binah) sits directly above Gevurah on the left pillar of the Tree of Life, showing us why mothers are more often than not the disciplinarians of their children; they have the understanding—the quality of Binah—to know what each child needs and why. Placing boundaries on our children's actions helps keep them safe, teaches them right action, demonstrates proper decorum, and shows them how to choose between what is good and what is not, keeping them safe from choosing things that will harm themselves or others. We must be our own mothers, guiding our own conduct in this manner as well.

Holy Consecration and God's Name

To consecrate, kodesh, קדיש (Kof Dalet Yod Shin), means "to make holy" or sanctify. The work of consecration tells us that the intention we bring to our actions, our understanding of what we are doing and why, is what makes something holy. Our consciousness makes it holy through our awareness. The letter Kof, which equals 100, is the value represented by the Hebrew words for **time, days,** and **year.** We can infer that God's presence is manifest at any time—at any hour, day, season, or year. Kof also represents the eagle, which in biblical times was said to live a hundred years and refers to all of the secrets held within the Alef-Bet, the building blocks of Creation. The act of consecration, the stage of Tabernacle worship Gevurah is part of in the Outer Court, including the fire and water rituals, gives us long life and farsightedness as well as collaborative power with God over the building blocks of Creation. This is what Joshua learned to master inside the Ohel Moed.

The letter Dalet is the doorway between all things material and spiritual, in and out, above and below, just as the door of our house separates what is in the world from what is in our home. It is why we call our home our castle or sanctuary. The word *sanctuary* in Hebrew suggests two other words, *place* and *holy*. A holy place is a sanctuary, a *Mikdash* (מקדש). This is the exact command God gives the Israelites, which Moses and Joshua faithfully carry out. They are the instructors for the Israelites as they are for us, teaching how to erect the holy place within. It is a place over which only we can exercise control, whether to refine it or to diminish it.

In terms of our inner lives, the door and the letter Dalet (ד) allow us to change states of awareness and consequently our experiences. In the physical world, the observant Jewish person consecrates the doorways to the house with a mezuzah (מזוזה), which in Hebrew means "doorpost." The letters Shin, Dalet, and Yod, forming the word for God's divine name, Shaddai (שדי), "Guardian of the Doors of Israel," are written on the back of the parchment of the mezuzah itself, along with the words *Adonai, Elokeinu, Adonai*: "The Lord our God the Lord."[23]

Consecration transforms the experience of the material realm into something spiritual. We see this when we examine just one word of the mezuzah observance, which, like Joshua's sword, protects the household from harm. The letters that make up the word and meaning of God's divine name, Shaddai, שדי, begin with the mother letter Shin, ש, which connects the upper

---

[23] Moses commanded that the Word of God should be written on the doorposts of every house in order to keep them constantly in their minds and hearts. This commemorates the protection God afforded the Hebrews during the last of ten plagues that He cast on the Egyptians before the Exodus, when the first-born son of every Egyptian family and their livestock was killed. To prevent the death of the Hebrew children, God told them to mark their doorposts with the blood of the lamb so that the angel of death would pass over their homes (Exodus 11:1–10). Some time later, the Jewish people took this directive further by inaugurating the practice of placing scripture (Deuteronomy 6:4–9 and 11:13–21, and Numbers 15:37–41) on a small parchment scroll within a special cover, attaching it to the right side of the main door into the home, and for some, not only at the entry but also on the right side entryway of every room in the home.

Sefirot of Chochmah and Binah on the Tree of Life (see chapter 1, figure 1.1, page 11). The brilliance of the light, the fire of the Shechinah, is the wisdom of the heart (Binah) and the mind (Chochmah) unified in a single purpose. The three pillars of the Tree of Life represented by the three vertical lines in the letter Shin stand for the perfectly balanced human being that informs our conduct. Dalet, ד, is traditionally a door through which we experience different states of being, enabling the Holy Spirit and its teachings to enter us, by which we are changed. The letter Yod, י, in Shaddai, is the revelation of God's presence. Yod means oneness, a unity, containing everything that lives, even in potential, as expressed by the numerical equivalent of this letter, 10. Thus in consecration we see in each act, in each material or spiritual form, the God within—within ourselves and within everything around us. Each person and thing is blessed in the single purpose of serving divinity.

The mezuzah, the handwritten parchment protected inside of its special covering, contains the first two paragraphs of the Shema, the ancient prayer that is the first prayer a Jewish child is taught even today. This prayer is taken from two books of the Hebrew bible. Deuteronomy 11:13–21 describes how God will bless the people with rain in its proper amount and season, providing a bountiful harvest if a person observes His commandments and does not stray after other gods; and Numbers 15:37–41 details the proper observance of the *tzitzis,* the fringes on the corners of the prayer shawls of the men. The Shema begins with text from Deuteronomy 6:4–9, Judaism's defining statement: "HEAR, O ISRAEL: The LORD our God, the LORD is one. You shall love the LORD your God with all your heart and with all your soul and with all your might" (see appendix 3 for the entire text of the Shema).

The Waters of Awareness

We human beings are predominantly water. When a newborn enters the world, 85 percent of that baby's body is water, while in the adult water decreases to between 50 to 75 percent, depending on the individual. In Kabbalah, "upper waters" refers to our intellect, "lower waters" to our emotions. "Parting the waters" signifies the possibility of manipulating the material circumstances of one's life. If, like the Israelites, we can wade into the waters without fear, surrendering our heart in love and trust of God, the waters will part and we can walk on dry land and not risk drowning in our emotions and thoughts. This is the purpose of consecration in the Outer Court: it is a commitment we make to refine our behavior, particularly our feelings, learning to control the power of the emotions and how we respond to them, so that they become tools of divine service, thereby benefiting ourselves and the world.

As described earlier, the ritual act of gathering up twelve stones from the river Jordan's bottom after the waters have miraculously parted, and then placing them at Gilgal, where the people settle after crossing the river, makes this act a memorial. That the people reestablish the Mishkan, the sanctified Tabernacle and Tent of Meeting, on the other side of the river is symbolic of the demarcation of the stages of our own inner development: we go from a lack of awareness and self-mastery before the waters are parted, to a state that transcends even the influence of natural elements. Note that the High Priest's breastplate is made of twelve stones, representing each of the twelve tribes' heavenly origins as expressed by the zodiac's twelve constellations. The twelve zodiacal influences surrounding us and within us is the same pattern found in the encampments of the Israelites, whose twelve tribes surround the Tent of Meeting (see chapter 9, figure 9.3, page 329). This pattern is symbolic of God's ability to help us transcend the natural forces, just as God, through Moses and Joshua, helps the Israelites. This is an exhibition of the potential power of co-creation that exists within each human being; it is what we are designed to do. Once the river stones are ceremonially placed in Gilgal and the Mishkan reestablished, this location becomes God's breastplate of the earth; what is commemorated there, in my opinion, holds a portion of the blessings for the prophesied messianic times.

Spiritual Development: Completing the Refinement of the Emotions

In the Zohar, the six Sefirot of Zeir Anpin are sometimes called the Lad. In part this differentiates the more turbulent emotions (middot) of youth from the calm, even disposition of the elders, who have mastered their emotions and are directed by the higher qualities of intellect and wisdom, as exemplified by the upper Sefirot of KaChaBa (Keter, Chochmah, Binah). That Joshua is sixty and called "the lad" when we first meet him as Moses' attendant in the Tent of Meeting tells us that he has not yet attained the level of development of his teacher, Moses; it also tells us another story about the nature of the six Sefirot of which he is a constituent, Zeir Anpin, the Son: Joshua is, in effect, the spiritual son of Moses.

Chassidut says that it takes ten years to refine a Sefirah. Recall that Zeir Anpin includes Chesed, Gevurah, Tiferet (the Sefirah that refers to Zeir Anpin), Netzach, Hod, and Yesod. This six-part constellation encompasses our right and left hands, our torso (where the heart is housed), our two legs, and our procreative organs. Also recall that each Sefirah contains the entire Tree of Life, which means that each Sefirah has ten aspects. If one were to take one year to refine each of ten aspects of one of the Sefirah of Zeir Anpin, then the process of completing the entire cycle of refinement for all six Sefirot would take sixty years, and it would take 100 years to complete the cycles of all ten Sefirot of the Tree of Life.

Joshua's age of sixty, the age at the time he becomes the attendant to the Tent of Meeting, represents his completion of the process of consecration and the work of refining the emotions. At the age of sixty he is finally humble and strong enough to receive the upper light from God through Moses. "His servant, Joshua, Son of Nun, a lad, would not depart from within the Tent" (Exodus 33:11): in other words, Joshua is Moses' protégé and successor; until he completes the entire cycle of refining his emotions, he cannot lead the nation of Israel.

Recall that light descends the Tree of Life, zigzaging down like a lightning strike, from right to left (see chapter 1, figure 1.3, page 15), which, of course, is the complement to our ascending process in this book. This pattern is evident in the chronology of the Bible as well: the transmission of the teachings goes from the right pillar of Chesed (Moses) to the left pillar of Gevurah (Joshua) to the middle pillar of Tiferet (Devorah), and so on. God adds sweetness (Chesed/Moses) with judgment (Gevurah/Joshua) to produce law and truth and beauty (Tiferet/Devorah). This biblical journey contains a Kabbalistic formula for everyone, not just B'nai Yisrael.

The Sword of Discernment

When Moses called on God for help as the Hebrew people, under the military command of Joshua, faced the fierce Amalekites, the Israelites were successful. The meaning is clear: when the children of Israel looked heavenward—meaning when they focused on their trust and faith in God—they were victorious. But when they doubted His presence and protection, they failed. The Jewish sages teach that when we surrender our situation to God, asking for His help through our petition, we gain access to the power of the one law and the law of One, which unites all of life.

After the battle, God admonishes Moses to never forget Amalek: "And God said unto Moses, 'Write this as a remembrance in the Book (of the Covenant) and recite it in the ears of Joshua, that I shall surely erase the memory of Amalek from under the heavens.' Moses built an altar and called its name 'God is my miracle'; and he said, 'For the hand is on the throne of God: God maintains a war against Amalek, from generation to generation'" (Exodus 17:14–16). In God's instructions to Moses to never forget Amalek[24] we are being told how to eliminate from our inner lives that which tries to wipe out the soul that is illuminated by freedom. Indeed, the Jewish people are commanded to read aloud the Parshat Zachor, the account of the victory over the Amalekites, in synagogue once a year, on the Sabbath that precedes Purim, when one is reminded that it is only through awe and love of God that we can confront Amalek—our cruel or selfish tendencies within—and emerge victorious.[25] As long as we glorify violence and force, as represented by Amalek, these destructive qualities will remain within us and without, manifesting in our own actions and in world affairs. But when divine law and ethical action are the sole criteria of humankind, then the reign of Amalek will cease and we will be truly free.

It is not an easy journey to this sort of self-mastery, for even in the lives of the Israelites, who had God's visible protection, we see their doubts arise. Here was a nation that had experienced unceasing miraculous activity: protection from the ten plagues, the splitting of waters, and the daily provision of manna and fresh water. And yet still they doubted God's omnipotence. Amalek thus represents all doubts, all limitations

---

[24] Son of Eliphaz by his concubine Timnah, grandson of Esau, and progenitor of a tribe of people in southern Canaan; descendants of Amalek.

[25] In biblical times, King Agog, who lived during King Saul's reign, whom Samuel the prophet slew; and Haman, the anti-Semitic viceroy of Persia who tried to annihilate the Jews but who was prevented from doing so by Mordechai and Queen Esther; and in modern times, Adolph Hitler, are all said to be reincarnations of Amalek.

one imposes on oneself, and all roadblocks to internal and external growth created by the relentlessly spinning wheel of the mind and the unrefined emotions directing our thoughtless reactions. Amalek seeks to tamper with our pure faith, and in so doing it represents the voice of the ego, which we must cut through and slay with the sword of discrimination. Yes, these are actual battles. Joshua was a mighty warrior trained by his predecessor, Moses, who was also a mighty warrior. Both of these leaders learned to master their emotions and refine their minds, and as a result they were able to control their willpower, cut through all that was not holy, and put themselves to the task of holiness. But how does one inherit peace from war?

Within each one of us is the programming of war, of exclusion. The fight-or-flight tendency is an inborn survival mechanism. Aggression can be expressed in intolerance, prejudice, or outright violence. When the will is used for purely selfish reasons—as in the will to power without regard for those who are impacted either directly or indirectly—we are counseled to put down this "sword" until we can regain composure. Fighting for justice, equality, or sanctuary, on the other hand, is a will to do for the benefit of all, which is ultimately not aggression but compassion in action. It can be a fine line, though. Joshua was trained by his master, Moses, to vanquish the lower aspects of aggression and to resort to fighting only as a last means, and only then in order to achieve a greater end that would benefit all. He reached the highest level of Gevurah—the ability to cut through to the holy that exists in potential in everything and everyone, in order to bring about peace. He had many adversaries and fought many battles to do so.

Would this great initiate and prophet Joshua want to harm another person? Was Joshua a violent person? Joshua understood that he had no choice but to take up the sword. In fact, when the Israelites traveled under Joshua's leadership, Joshua and his men would announce their arrival for the express purpose of avoiding battle if at all possible. If there was no concession made for the large refugee population of Israelites to settle some portion of each area's unused land, the Hebrews would have to fight. They lost limbs and lives. So what does this mean for each one of us? What does Joshua show us about our own self-refinement?

Balancing Discernment with Love

Moses, on the right pillar of the Tree of life, represents the flow of loving-kindness, of helping anyone who comes our way. Joshua represents our necessary inner discretionary self that sorts and chooses, that knows and does not hesitate to act swiftly, to serve properly at the right time, even by refusing to do something. When we say "no," we must mean no. When we say "yes," we should mean yes. There should be no confusion within our own minds or with others about this clear and necessary distinction, since ambivalence can only lead to a great deal of conflict in relationships, enabling abusive situations, whether in the household, in the business place, or between nations.

Our society has lost this sense of balance. We use unnecessary force against the wrong people, and we are soft when we should be firm. We equate personal limitations with unfairness and decisiveness with cruelty. A society that does not honor life above all and does not seek to support all living from this place of merciful judgment will give to the wrong people, take from the wrong people, and destroy many in the process. Such is the course of history, but it need not be our personal history.

As our right and left legs are partners, so too are our right and left arms and hands. We all know this from life experience. While one may be more proficient or dominant, right-handed or left-handed, anyone who has ever injured an arm, wrist, or hand knows how difficult it is to get things done without the partnership of both hands. So too in our inner life and outer behavior, where Joshua and Moses, as the anatomical left and right hands on the Etz Chayim, teach us how to combine the use of the sword of strength and discernment with the staff of love and compassion.

The Middle Path of the Initiate

Integrating Gevurah with Chesed, the next Sefirot in our ascension of the Tree of Life and journey through the Tent of Meeting, is integral to the middle path. Moses' end-of-life song, called the Hazeinu, tells of the Israelites' efforts to inhabit the lands God has promised them as an inheritance. It is noteworthy that even Joshua's strategy for conquering the lands, fulfilling what Moses had prophesied, includes a route up through the middle of the territories. This, as we shall see, is discrete advice for each person's path in life: we should follow the middle path.

This is the divinely designated avenue that all wisdom traditions point to as the path to illumination. The middle path is advocated in many passages in Torah:

> Let me pass through the land: I will go along the highway, I will neither turn unto the right hand nor to the left (Deuteronomy 2:27).

> Ye shall observe to do therefore as the Lord your God hath commanded you: you shall not turn aside to the right and or to the left (Deuteronomy 5:32).

> And though shalt not go aside from any of the words which I command thee this day, to the right hand, or to the left, to go after other gods to serve them (Deuteronomy 6:14).

> According to the sentence of the law, which they shall teach thee, and according to the judgment, which they shall tell thee, thou shall do; thou shall not decline from the sentence which they shall shew thee, to the right hand, nor to the left (Deuteronomy 17:11).

> This heart be not lifted up above his brethren, and that he turn not aside from the commandment, to the right hand, or to the left, to the end that he may prolong his days in his kindred, he, and his children in the midst of Israel (Deuteronomy 17:20).

Our swordlike discrimination and ability to refrain from acting in an imbalanced fashion, as exemplified by Joshua, is a description of the middle-path practice.

The Ascent to Higher Awareness

The two Sefirot of Chesed and Gevurah, on the right and left pillars respectively, form the gateway to the next stage of the initiate's path inside the Ohel Moed, the Holy Place, as represented by the Sefirah of Binah. After the battle with the Amalekites, God tells Moses to come meet him on Mt. Sinai: "And Moses stood up with Joshua, his servant; and Moses ascended to the mountain of God" (Exodus 17:13). A mountain is higher than the surrounding terrain, suggesting a more elevated state of consciousness than the one in which we battle within, all that is negative, limiting, and doubting.

Joshua's act of erecting the twelve stones at Gilgal to commemorate the miracle of the Jordan River pulling back, demarcating their arrival in Canaan, represents the refinement of all the twelve tribes of Israel, including Joshua himself. The Hebrew word for stone, אבן, also means "precious stone," "penetrate," "weight," and "scale." From this we may extrapolate that the humble heart and the inner scales of justice allow the initiate to ascend to receive divine life teachings, as Moses, Joshua's holy teacher, ascended the mount to receive the two stone tablets. The quality of devotion and love of truth that both of these prophets embody show us that we are compelled to weigh our choices carefully. The heart is where the teachings of the Ten Commandments are written, and the ten Sefirot are inscribed in the body and soul. When we consciously attach ourselves to God, the heart is transformed into a personal place of elevation and illumination—an Ark within the Holy of Holies of the sanctuary of our being. The prophet Joshua shows us how to master the Sefirah of Gevurah and its cutting sword as a prerequisite to using the powerful staff of Moses' loving-kindness—both necessary elements in self-refinement before we can safely enter the Holy of Holies in Binah.

To complete the Outer Court process of self-refinement and mastery over our emotions, we next join Moses, said by the People of the Book to be the greatest prophet who ever was, is, or will be. Moses reveals the mystery of compassionate love and commitment, on which the continuity of the generations in the pursuit of peace on earth depends.

9
Abundant Love
Chesed • Soaring Melody

Rav and Samuel both said: "Fifty gates of understanding were created in the world, and all of them but one were opened for Moses at Sinai, as is said, 'Thou hast made [Moses] but little lower than God' (Psalms 8:6)."

SEFER HA-AGGADAH, 8:78

Fourth Sefirah: Chesed
Meaning: Loving-kindness
Rung on Ascending Ladder: Seven
Archetype: Zeir Anpin (the Son)
Symbol: The Book of Teachings, the Five Books of Moses
Spiritual World: Yetzirah/formation
Spiritual Anatomy: Right hand
Inner Quality: Love (ahava)

Historical Personage: Moses the Prophet
Text: The Hazeinu (Deuteronomy 32:1–43)
Key Words: Charity, good deeds, loving all
Key Emotion in Song: Sublime awe in love of God (nigun)

Tent of Meeting: Outer Court
Spiritual Stage: Consecration, conferring holiness, consecrating others
Spiritual Practice: Conferring loving intention; the hand of anointing
Illumination: The illuminated heart

> *Moses, the greatest prophet who ever was, is, or will be, shows us how unity with God is rooted in supreme love of the Creator and the created.*

The Sefirah Chesed: Loving-kindness, Mercy

The Sefirah of Chesed is the essence of the flow of divine love into the world and the power that sustains the universe. Representing the right hand, which most people in fact favor, Chesed reflects the need for love in all that we do. Balanced by the qualities of judgment and strength as represented by Gevurah, the left hand, Chesed administers to the world with God's eternal kindness and mercy, the words often used to describe Chesed. God's name of Adonai is assigned to this Sefirah and to the right pillar overall. We are instructed to invest love even in those things we do that seem harsh or eliminating, as we learned in our study of Gevurah. So vital is this energy of love in our lives that without it life will not thrive.

As the last of the Sefirot comprising the persona of the Son in our ascent of the Tree of Life—or from the traditional perspective of descending the Tree, the first Sefirah of the six-part cluster of Zeir Anpin—Chesed is the root of our emotions. We feel all the other kinds of emotions, but love is the root of holiness in them all. We were made in love, from love, with love, to love. Chesed's exemplar, Moses, brings down the Word of God to the people and stewards the Exodus generations with loving-kindness.

The Prophet Moses: "Moses Our Teacher"

Moses Rabeinu, "Moses our teacher," is how the People of the Book refer to Moses, for he is considered the greatest teacher and prophet who ever existed or ever will. It is traditionally said that God gave Moses all of Torah, both oral and written, on Mt. Sinai; Moses, in turn, gave it to the Israelites. But it should be understood that Torah was already written in the spiritual realms, as the name of the Creator. Moses is shown how to build and establish the Ohel Moed, the holy sanctuary of our story, which serves as the model for human beings' progressive development in holiness.

Moses' Birth

Moses' birth, to Yocheved, a daughter of Levi, is announced in Exodus 2:1–3:

"A man went from the house of Levi and he took a daughter of Levi. The woman conceived and gave birth to a son. She saw that he was good and she hid him for three months." Fearing that the Egyptian soldiers would find her newborn child, as Pharoah has decreed that all firstborn sons of the Hebrew slaves be killed, Yocheved and her daughter Miriam, Moses' older sister, conspire to have him found by the royal household. To do this, they place him in a little ark made of bulrushes near the marshes of the Nile, where Pharaoh's daughter bathes. Finding the "Hebrew child" (which was evident, we are told, because he was "born circumcised"— signifying a heart connected to God), she is moved to compassion for the baby (Exodus 2:6). The plan is fully executed when Miriam comes forward and innocently suggests a wet nurse she knows in the community. This, of course, is her own and Moses' mother, Yocheved.

> *The Holy One, Blessed is He, appointed Moses over all Israel, over*
> *all the hidden treasures of Torah and [all forms] of wisdom, and*
> *over all the hidden treasures of the garden of Eden.*
>
> Osios d'Rabbi Akiva, 90

Even before Moses is born, Miriam, at the age of five, announces, "My Mother is destined to bear a son who will redeem Israel,"[1] thus demonstrating that she too is a prophet. This explains Miriam's complete confidence, from an early age, in her brother's destiny. That Moses is breastfed by his mother for the first three years of life suggests that at the age of three a child can be properly weaned (Exodus 2:7–10); breastfeeding can also be likened to providing a total education through a mother's love (i.e., milk), signified by the Sefirah of understanding, Binah (the

---

[1] Megillah 14a. See also R. Yisrael Yitzchak Yishai Chasidah, *Encyclopedia of Biblical Personalities,* 338.

Mother), which emanates to Chesed, the Sefirah of unconditional love.

Yocheved instills in Moses, as all mothers can in their children, a sense of belonging and value in the world. The child is schooled in the three pillars of Judaism: charity, justice, and mercy. Moses thus gains an inner experience of his heritage through his mother's presence in his early life, during which time he lives in the royal house of Egypt as an adopted prince of the land. We see that the love of his people is a constant, not just during the first forty years of his life, but throughout his entire earthly existence.

Moses the Shepherd

Little is known about Moses' youth as a prince; the five books of Torah written in his name tell us nothing specific beyond his prophesied birth and engineered adoption into the royal household. And so the next we learn of his life occurs forty years later, when he kills an Egyptian taskmaster for beating a Jewish slave (Exodus 2:11–12).[2] Leaving the royal household and fleeing to Midian (an area some scholars believe to be in northwest Arabia, on the east shore of the Gulf of Aqaba and the northern Red Sea) for his own safety, Moses meets Zipporah, the daughter of Jethro, a Midanite priest (Exodus 2:16–21), and marries her. She gives birth to Moses' two sons, Gershom (Exodus 2:22) and Eliezar (Exodus 18:4).

For the next forty years, Moses is keeper of his family's flock in Midian, where he learns stewardship, loving-kindness, and management of the various needs of all. Forty represents a unit of time that signifies maturation, just as we see in Noah's forty days and nights of the Flood and Moses' forty days and nights on Mt. Sinai. The number 40 is also equivalent to the letter

---

[2] One traditional story tells that when he was a child sitting on Pharaoh's knee, Moses took the crown off Pharaoh's head and put it on his own. The court magicians assumed this was a bad sign, and they demanded that he be tested: they put before Moses a brazier full of gold and a brazier full of hot coal to see which he would take. If Moses took the gold, he would have to be killed. An angel guided Moses' hand to the coal, and he put it into his mouth, leaving him with a life-long speech impediment (Exodus 4:10). Esoterically, we can say that Moses slew the part of his persona that was an Egyptian taskmaster, which enslaved the soul. He thereby eliminated the doubts and narrow world view he had had; this caused him to flee from Egypt (Exodus 2:14–15), the place of idol worship—that is, ego worship—where Pharaoh (his own ego) is treated as one's god instead of the one God that rules over all.

Mem, the letter that begins Moses' name, suggesting a leader who is mature. There is a beautiful and well-known teaching that takes place during this period of Moses' life, in which he finds a lamb far from the the rest of the flock, having strayed in search of water (prefiguring the Israelites' later search for water, i.e., the teachings of truth). Realizing what has happened, Moses carries the lamb on his shoulders back to the flock out of consideration for its weariness rather than, perhaps, his own. The sages remind us that this act shows Moses' magnificent quality of mercy and compassion for all life, a signal quality of the spiritually mature person.

Moses' forty years as a shepherd is to be his singular preparation for leading more than 600,000 men and their families out of Egypt, an act about which it is said that "Moses was equivalent to 600,000 of Israel"[3] and that he "acted in place of a seventy-one member Sanhedrin."[4] These statements reveal that Moses' earthly presence was spiritually equal to the merit of all of those whom he led, and his wise counsel was equal to that of the legal assembly formalized during the time of the Temple called the Great Sanhedrin (a kind of Supreme Court of ancient Israel), which consisted of seventy-one elders. Most importantly, though, we are told that "no generation is without someone like Moses,"[5] meaning that even though he or she may not come to public prominence as a worldwide leader, such a person can be found in every generation.

Moses, the Emancipator

At the age of eighty, following the pastoral forty-year period that Moses has spent in Median, he is selected by God to be the emancipator of the Jewish people, fulfilling his older sister Miriam's prophecy.

The scenario is dramatic: tending to his father-in-law's large flock, Moses nears Mt. Horeb when he sees what appears to be a bush on fire. He goes to examine more closely when God, seeing Moses' inquisitiveness, calls out to him, "Moses, Moses," to which Moses responds, "Here I am" (Exodus 3:1–4). Seeing that the bush has not been consumed by the fire, Moses recognizes the supernal nature of this phenomenon. God tells him to first take off his sandals, for the ground where he stands is

---

[3] Tikkunei Zohar 19:40. See also Chasidah, *Encyclopedia of Biblical Personalities,* 341.
[4] Sanhedrin 16b. See also Chasidah, *Encyclopedia of Biblical Personalities,* 341.
[5] Bereshis Rabbah 56:7. See also Chasidah, *Encyclopedia of Biblical Personalities,* 341.

holy; He then informs him that He is the God of his father, "the God of Abraham, the God of Issac and the God of Jacob" (Exodus 3:6). God then goes on to instruct Moses in his responsibilities as the emancipator of the Jews enslaved in Egypt, telling him that he must return to Egypt, where those who once sought his death are now themselves dead, making it safe to return.

Moses does not reveal this miraculous encounter with God to his father-in-law, Jethro; instead, he tells him that he is returning to his birthplace to see if his birth family still lives. Moses takes his wife, sons, and brother, Aaron, (and, one assumes, many of their relatives' households) with him, and upon arriving in Egypt, Moses and Aaron go to meet Pharoah to request that they be allowed to go on a on three-day journey with all of the Israelites in Egypt, in order to worship their God. Their request is denied, as Pharoah fears they will all run away. So begins God's deliberate hardening of Pharoah's heart, which brings on the ordeal of the ten plagues.

The many miracles that characterize Moses' narrative explain why the sages have said that "Moses was Israel's Banner [for miracles were done for Israel in his merit and often it appears as if Moses himself had performed the miracle]. And who was Moses' banner? The Holy one, Blessed is He [for He effected the miracles for him].[6] Considered the father of all prophets as well as the foremost prophet, Moses is able to see the future as though he was gazing through clear glass—meaning his prophetic vision was crystal clear: "The [other] prophets saw [their prophetic visions] through nine glasses; Moses saw through one. All the [other] prophets saw through a dim glass; Moses saw through a polished one."[7] Just as Moses is said to be the only prophet who was conscious of his prophecy, God's method of meeting and speaking to Moses was unique from the very start. For example, when God first comes to Moses in the burning bush, this did not transpire in just a single moment, as is often portrayed, but rather over a period of seven days: "For seven days the holy one Blessed is He, spoke with Moses at the bush, arranging that [the climax of] this revelation occur on the fifteenth of Nissan [April,

---

[6] Bereshish Rabbah 59:5. See also Chasidah, *Encyclopedia of Biblical Personalities,* 348.

[7] Vayikra Rabbah 1:14. See also Chasidah, *Encyclopedia of Biblical Personalities,* 346.

the Constellation of Aires the Ram], at which time, the following year the Children of Israel would go forth from Egypt."[8]

The story of Moses' efforts to win Pharoah's release of the Jewish slaves is well-known. The Egyptian ruler's heart is deliberately hardened by God in order to bring about an eventual elevation. The more entrenched Pharoah becomes in his denial of Moses' requests, the more severe are the plagues God visits upon the Egyptian nation, from the first plague of water being changed to blood; to frogs taking over the land; to plagues of gnats, wild beasts, pestilence, boils, hail, locusts, and darkness; to the final plague, that of the death of all firstborn Egyptian male babies. Moses tells his people God's instructions for how to avoid having their own firstborn sons eliminated: by painting the blood of a lamb on the doorposts of their houses, the angel of death would fly over (i.e., "pass over," Passover) them. This becomes a sign of the month of their emancipation, telling us of a greater archetypal story—that of the rebirth of every person, every nation, every world, in the springtime; and that there is a spring for everything, just as there is a winter that precedes it. We too can be coldhearted, ignoring God's will for us, until we soften our hearts, which warm in the rebirth of His grace.

Crossing the Red Sea

After the succession of ten plagues has wreaked complete havoc across Egypt, Pharoah finally agrees to allow the Israelites to go. But as they depart Pharoah has second thoughts, and he sends his army and a fierce group of local tribespeople, the Amalekites, after them. The Amalekites kill many of the Israelites, including women and children and the old and infirm at the rear of the fleeing population in the Sinai desert.

As we saw in chapter 8, the subsequent crossing of the Red Sea is significant for many reasons of faith and divine protection; but it also marks the beginning of the time when Joshua, Moses' successor, witnesses all of the miracles that occur under his teacher's leadership. The Israelites are chased to the edge of the sea, with nowhere to turn but into the surging waves; God tells Moses to raise his staff, that the waters will part and it will be safe for the children of Israel to cross over (Exodus 13:18). At first hesitant, several Hebrews wade into the waters, which then part, allow-

---

[8] Seder Olam Rabbah 5. See also Chasidah, *Encyclopedia of Biblical Personalities,* 340.

ing a passageway, and soon hundreds of thousands of people follow. The Egyptian horses and chariots close in on them (a part of the narrative that we will explore in greater detail in chapter 11), but the sea turns back and they all drown. Thus the people collectively witness another miracle: they had been spared from the ten plagues, and now they are again delivered from certain death.

In Kabbalistic thinking, the crossing of the Red Sea signifies the moment when a person (or a community) overcomes all doubts in his own holiness, in his ability to rise above the natural course of events, and surrenders body and soul to God. In the biblical narrative, the Israelites do cross over, while the Egyptians drown in the sea. Indeed, people all over the world attest to the personal and collective miracle of being saved from death and injury, doing everything they can and then being saved through divine intervention, as a result of having surrendered completely to divine right order, to God's divine will.

The Sinaic Revelations

The next epic event in this saga occurs when God instructs Moses to ascend Mt. Sinai to receive Torah. First, the people are prepared through purification rites for three days and instructed not to ascend or even touch the mountain. Then Moses makes his first of three ascents of the mountain, each time for a period of forty days and forty nights. During the first sojourn, on Shavuot (Pentecost), Moses goes up with the elders and Joshua, who wait for him below while he makes the final ascension alone to receive the Torah orally, which subsequently all the people hear and agree to. This sojourn includes God's instructions for establishing the Tent of Meeting and its Tabernacle, as recounted in chapter 2. During his second ascent, Moses is engulfed in the Cloud of Glory on the lower part of the mountain for six days, then, on the seventh, he is told to ascend alone to the top of the mount, where he again stays for forty days and nights. This time he is given the Ten Commandments engraved on a set of stone tablets. Meanwhile, below, in camp, the people, growing uneasy as they await their leader's return, miscalculate his forty days and nights, thinking he might be dead. Fearful, they make a golden calf to worship. Upon his descent, Moses sees this and in anger throws the tablets down, breaking them. He returns to Mt. Sinai a third time to entreat God on the people's behalf, something we might expect of the progenitor of Chesed. He then receives the second, replacement set of tablets.

Establishment of the Tent of Meeting

> And thou shalt make the boards for the tabernacle of acacia-wood, standing up. Ten cubits shall be the length of a board, and a cubit and a half the breadth of each board. Two tenons shall there be in each board, joined one to another; thus shalt thou make for all the boards of the tabernacle. . . . And their forty sockets of silver: two sockets under one board, and two sockets under another board.
>
> EXODUS: 26:15–17, 21

When God gives Moses the instructions for building the Tabernacle at the time Moses makes his first forty-day journey up Mt. Sinai, it comes when the Hebrew people, having endured slavery by the Egyptians and a harrowing escape, must wander the desert in search of food, water, and basic safety. Knowing of their need for spiritual support in this difficult time, God commands Moses to "build a sanctuary for Me, so that I may dwell among them" (Exodus 25:8). In *Basi Legani* ("I Have Come to my Garden"), R. Yosef Yitzchak Schneersohn (1880–1950), the sixth rebbe of Chabad-Lubavitch, explains that creating a sanctuary is for the express purpose of the "subduing of man's physical nature, which brings one to the yet loftier goal of transforming darkness into light."[9] In the Mishnaic teachings, the method God used to teach Moses is discussed:

> R. Levi (Joshua b. Levi) [a renowned Mishnaic sage], said: When the holy One said to Moses, "Make the Tabernacle for Me," Moses might simply have brought four poles and stretched skins over them to form the Tabernacle. Since he did not do so, we may infer from the verse cited below that while Moses was on the mount, the Holy One showed him red fire, green fire, black fire, and white fire, and said to him: Make the Tabernacle of Me. Moses asked the holy One: Master of the universe, where [on earth] am I to get red fire, green fire, black fire and

---

[9] R. Yosef Y. Schneersohn, *Basi Legani*, 8.

white fire? The holy One replied, "after the pattern, which is shown thee in the mount."(Exodus 25:40).[10]

The subject of the establishment of God's holy sanctuary is vast, and many aspects of the story are miraculous, unexplained, and hidden. One finds in the Hebrew Bible that the event is prepared for many years before Moses is commanded to build it, in fact, before Moses is even born. Some of the wood the Hebrews used in its construction came from trees planted decades earlier, specifically for this purpose:

> Where did the boards come from? Jacob our father had planted them. When he came down to Egypt, he said to his sons: "My sons! You are destined to be redeemed from here, and when you are redeemed, the holy One will tell you that you are to make a Tabernacle for Him, Rise up and plant cedars now, so that when he tells you to make a Tabernacle for Him, these cedars will be on hand." So Jacob's sons set to planting cedars, doing just what he had told them. Hence scripture speaks of the "the boards," [so that] the boards their father had arranged should be on hand.[11]

In this description of the kind of wood to be used in building the Ohel Moed we find a teaching about continuity from one generation to the next, from one year in our lives to the next. Sometimes what we are guided to do is not only for the present, but the future as well, just as Jacob saw prophetically that the wood would be needed for the future sanctuary and he thus instructed the people to plant trees that would be available for the coming generations to use.

A Gift of Love

After the Ohel Moed is established, Moses takes the Tent some distance outside of camp, and "all who sought God would go out to the Tent of Meeting" (Exodus 33:7). This caused celebration on the part of all the heavenly hosts: "The ministering angels came to sing hymns

---

[10] Hayim Nahman Bialik and Yehoshua Hana Ravnitzky, *Sefer Ha-Aggadah,* 5:69, 86.
[11] Bialik and Ravnitzky, *Sefer Ha-Aggadah,* 5:70, fn. 8, 86.

before the Holy One, Blessed is He, and He was with Moses. The sun, moon, and stars, came to bow before Him. They asked the Chayos [meaning the order of angels called the Ofanim, among which are the wheels of His chariot made of the wild animals that have four faces, twelve wings, and one leg], "Where is the Throne of Glory?" The Chayos replied, "Go to Moses."[12] In this description, Moses, a human being, is stationed even higher than the most elevated of the celestial beings, showing us that all humans are designed for this purpose. Later, the Tent, like Moses himself, becomes the center of the Israelites' encampment, showing its central role in their Exodus and spiritual development—and ours as well.

Our teacher Moses loved the people of Israel.

MENACHOS 65A

Moses is so completely joined to the Creator in love and obedience that it is not surprising that he is the one to establish the holy Ohel Moed for all of humanity, showing the Israelites, and us, how to attend God with complete love and devotion: "All seven days of inauguration, Moses erected the Tabernacle and disassembled it twice daily, without anyone's help. All seven days of the inauguration [of the priests and the Tabernacle], Moses would erect the Tabernacle, and each morning he would anoint it and [then] disassemble it. On the [the eighth] day he erected it and anointed it, but did not disassemble it."[13]

For the entire forty-year period that Israel wandered in the desert, Moses served as High Priest, along with his brother, Aaron, and Aaron's sons, Gershom and Eliezar, who were consecrated by Moses. Moses would assist Aaron, disrobing and dressing him, anointing him with oil between his eyes. This act of anointing his older brother shows us that the prophetic power that comes with sancitification is available to anyone who humbles his heart and surrenders his mind to divine right order. As the chosen prophetic leader of the Exodus, Moses is so holy that even the archangels "Michael and Gabriel were in awe of Moses. [Yet] when [Israel] sinned, Moses could not look even at the smallest

---

[12] Shemos Rabbah 45:2. See also Chasidah, *Encyclopedia of Biblical Personalities,* 346.
[13] Sifri Naso 44. See also Chasidah, *Encyclopedia of Biblical Personalities,* 379.

of the angels."[14] Moses had direct interface with God, face to face, and acted on God's behalf. His profound humility and kindness remain vibrant examples for people today.

The classical teachings about prophets and prophecy originate with Moses as the archetype. We see in his behavior that which every person should try to emulate. He sacrificed his personal desires in place of that which would benefit the community. He had faith in the divine voice that guided him and spoke kindly to all of the people he guided. He argued with God when he was afraid for the community's survival, and he remained entirely devoted to bringing humanity into union with divinity, even though he himself was not permitted to enter the Promised Land at the conclusion of the Exodus. From Moses we learn of our individual journey out of the slavery of fear and narrow-mindedness, and we are shown how to dedicate our hearts to the pursuit of wisdom and peace.

> The Holy One, Blessed is He, rests His presence only on one who is mighty, rich, wise, and humble. All of these [traits] are [learned] from Moses; mighty, from the verse "He spread the tent over the Tabernacle" (Exodus 40: 19), [or] from the verse "I took hold of the two Tablets, cast them out of my two hands, and broke them" (Deuteronomy 9:17); rich, [from the verse] "Carve yourself two tablets of stone" (Deuteronomy 10:1)—the remnants [of the precious stone] are for you; wise, [as] Rav and Shmuel said: "Fifty gates of understandings were created in the world and all but one were presented to Moses, as it is written, You have made him only a little less than the angels" (Psalms 8:6); [and] humble, as it is written, "the man Moses was exceedingly humble" (Numbers 12:3) (Nedarim 38a).[15] Yet it also said of his position in the world that "[Moses] was close to heaven and distant from earth."[16]

The Song of Chesed: Soaring Melody (Nigun)

The type of song associated with Chesed is called a nigun (נגון), which is a wordless and soaring melody to which the singer can put his own

---

[14] Bamidbar Rabbah 11:3. See also Chasidah, *Encyclopedia of Biblical Personalities,* 346.

[15] Chasidah, *Encyclopedia of Biblical Personalities,* 346.

[16] Targum Yonasan, Devarim 32. See also Chasidah, *Encyclopedia of Biblical Personalities,* 346.

words. Chesed is an uplifting Sefirah of supreme belovedness, both the end and the beginning of Yesod's calling out in love to God. Here in Chesed there is only unity—between oneself and God, with family and loved ones, and even with strangers near and far.

The prophetic text associated with Chesed and the song of Moses is the Hazeinu, found in Deuteronomy 32:1–43. It is Moses' final call to all of creation to hearken to the words and divinity of God. While in general a nigun is a worldess song, its inner dynamic, that of a soaring melody, is the essence of Moses' last words and testament, the song of Chesed.

The word *nigun* is composed of the letters Nun Gimel Nun, meaning one who prostrates (the first Nun) and stands up righteously (the final Nun). Between these two is the letter Gimmel, suggesting a movement from a mood of supplication to one of great ascension. The music of the nigun moves from a state of bowing to the Creator's majesty at the beginning, and then the melody seems to fly upward as it reaches the closing aspect with a declaration of attachment to God—almost as though the melody stands vertically, as the final Nun stands. Did not Moses' entire life portray this process? He began life as the son of a slave woman and became one of world's greatest leaders, whose name and actions are glorified to the present day, thousands of years after he lived.

The three-letter root of **nigun, נגן**, plus the one who sings it, is equal to 104. **Midian, מדין**, the place where Moses flees at the age of forty, also equals 104. So does the expression **to teach, ללמד**, which appears in Deuteronomy 4:14.[17] Nigun can also mean **foundation, ליסד**, and has the additional meaning of protecting and preserving music.

A nigun is a melody that anyone can create, and many people have their own special tunes for their various mitzvot that they perform. Just as when each person expresses love for another in their own unique way, love is still at the core of the action. So too with the composition of a nigun, whose melodic feeling is one of upliftment, as its core in Chesed is expressed in terms of songs of love and adoration that elevate the spirit. Chesed prepares the soul for understanding, Binah, the next Sefirah we will encounter on the ascending ladder of the Tree of Life.

---

[17] "And the LORD commanded me at that time to **teach** you statutes and judgments, that ye might do them in the land whither ye go over to possess it."

The Five Books of Moses

There are a total of fifty-four chapters in the five books of Moses that comprise Torah (Genesis, Exodus, Leviticus, Numbers, Deuteronomy, sometimes called the Pentateuch). As we know, every number, every word, every letter in Torah is significant. In the last book of Torah, which marks the final days of Moses' life, his song, the Hazeinu, begins with Deuteronomy 32:1. The number 32 refers to the Hebrew word for **heart**, *lev,* לב, (Lamed Bet). The number 1 refers to God Himself, to all of creation and the created, the inherent design of oneness from which all diversity springs. From this we may conclude that Moses' last words, including their placement in Torah, are the words of the spiritual heart of humankind, the illuminated prophet each of us is designed to become. This song is one of unity with God, making these words an activator of the heart. This is the culmination of the story of initiation, consecration, elevation, illumination, and revelation; it is the story of being of one heart, *lev echad.*

"Incline an Ear"

When Moses would speak to the congregation of Israel, he would always remind them that these were not his words, but the Word of God. "When our teacher Moses prophesied amidst the congregation of Israel, he used the term *Hazeinu,* incline an ear (Deuteronomy 32:1) for heaven, and hear for earth because he was close to the heaven and far from the earth."[18] The Hebrew word *hazeinu* האזינ (Chet Alef Zayin Yod Nun) includes in it the Hebrew word for ear, *ozen,* אזן (Alef Zayin Nun), thus making Moses' last song a directive to listen to the Word of God. Also, the ears, in Kabbalah, represent the Sefirah of Binah, conferring on the one who listens with an open heart complete understanding, and as our next chapter on Binah demonstrates, elevation, an aliyah in body and soul. As we subdue our own voice, which reveals personal issues, needs, and desires, and focus instead on the eternal voice our soul possesses, we too can hear the divine voice within. This is one level of prophecy. However, while most prophets and other ordinary humans depend on God speaking to them, Moses was

---

[18] Targum Yonatan, Devarim 32:1. See also Chasidah, *Encyclopedia of Biblical Personalities,* 346.

able to speak directly to God and receive His answers, any time he needed to. He could literally converse with God.

Prophecy is commonly thought of as an extremely rare or occasional encounter, but the record shows that in one day the Holy One spoke to Moses fifteen times: "That was the day on which the Tabernacle was erected."[19] "All of God's calls were, 'Moses, Moses!' and to each he would reply, 'Here I am.'"[20] Oftentimes a prophet is not certain at first that what he hears is actually God's voice. "[When] Moses was a novice in prophecy, the Holy one, Blessed is He, said, 'If I appear to Him with a loud voice, I will frighten him; if with a low voice, he will hold prophecy in low esteem.' What did the holy One, blessed be He, do? He appeared to him with the voice of his father. 'Has my father come from Egypt?' asked Moses. [God] replied, 'I am not your father, but the God of your father.'"[21]

A sanctuary of the Divine Presence is a place of transformation and prophetic reception. God, taking the form of the Shechinah that descends, covers, surrounds, and envelops the Ohel Moed, indicates the proper time to enter the holy vessel of illumination, the Ohel Moed. In Moses' narrative, once the cloud departs the Ohel, it is a signal for Moses to enter in order to hear the voice of God: "As long as the Cloud was [upon the Tent of Meeting,] Moses would not enter. When the Cloud departed, he would enter [and God] would speak with him . . . A voice would descend from heaven like a duct of fire between the two keruvim [cherubim], and he would hear the voice speaking to him from within [the tent]."[22] This kind of receptivity requires total surrender of heart and mind. The point at which we have no doubts or projections of thought is like the departure of the cloud; it is a quietness that comes from pure devotion in silent listening. Then we, too, can hear the voice of God.

Moses' Parting Words

The song of Chesed consists of Moses' parting words to the Israelites, sung just before he dies. The story of Moses' death, like that of his birth, is bound to prophecy and the manifestation of the Divine Presence. God

---

[19] Mishnas R'Eliezer 6. See also Chasidah, *Encyclopedia of Biblical Personalities,* 347.

[20] Sifra 1:1. See also Chasidah, *Encyclopedia of Biblical Personalities,* 347.

[21] Shemos Rabbah 45:6. See also Chasidah, *Encyclopedia of Biblical Personalities,* 347.

[22] Bamidbar Rabbah 14:19. See also Chasidah, *Encyclopedia of Biblical Personalities,* 347.

Himself announces Moses' immanent death in his 120th year: "And the Lord said unto Moses: 'Behold, thy days approach that thou must die'" (Deuteronomy 31:14).

There are beautiful and loving stories told of Moses' efforts to be allowed more time on earth so that he might enter the Promised Land, or, barring that, to have his bones taken there to be buried after his death. Upon his death, the entire world, including God, weeps for the loss of Moses, and the archangels are too grieved to bring Moses' soul to the Almighty. Here, in the prelude to Moses' parting words, God tells him what to do:

> And the LORD said unto Moses: "Behold, thy days approach that thou must die; call Joshua, and present yourselves in the tent of meeting, that I may give him a charge." And Moses and Joshua went, and presented themselves in the Tent of Meeting. And the LORD appeared in the Tent in a pillar of cloud; and the pillar of cloud stood over the door of the Tent. And the LORD said unto Moses: "Behold, thou art about to sleep with thy fathers. . . . Now therefore write ye this song for you, and teach thou it to the children of Israel; put it in their mouths, that this song may be a witness for Me against the children of Israel. . . ." So Moses wrote this song the same day, and taught it to the children of Israel. And he gave Joshua the son of Nun a charge, and said: "Be strong and of good courage; for thou shalt bring the children of Israel into the land which I swore unto them; and I will be with thee." And it came to pass, when Moses had made an end of writing the words of this law in a book, until they were finished, that Moses commanded the Levites, that bore the ark of the covenant of the LORD, saying: "Take this book of the law, and put it by the side of the ark of the covenant of the LORD your God, that it may be there for a witness against thee. . . . And Moses spoke in the ears of all the assembly of Israel the words of this song, until they were finished." (Exodus 31:14–16, 19, 22–26, 30)

From this poignant description of the finale of Moses' life, we learn how in fact we each sing our own song of departure at the time of death. This occurs when we do a life review from beginning to end, just as Moses reviews the journey of the Hebrews from slavery to freedom. For each of us life is a journey from limitation to freedom. It is a freedom that can only be won through constant devotion to truth, mercy, and justice, and all the other sefirotic qualities, both in our inner lives and in our outer actions. Being a nigun, a wordless melody, the song of Chesed describes the life review process precisely through the emotional quality of the melody, in which we experience the emotions we caused others as well as our own in the course of our review. We thus can leave our bodily incarnation with our story clearly understood, rising up in perfection into the light of eternity from which we originate, like the melody of the nigun.

The Song of Chesed: The Hazeinu (Deuteronomy 32:1–43)

We now come to the final chapter of Moses' life with the recitation of the Hazeinu. This is Moses' final teaching to his people before he is "gathered up" to the house of God. This song is, in effect, the historical root of an ethical final will that is a charge and directive to Moses' descendants.

1 Give ear, ye heavens, and I will speak; and let the earth hear the words of my mouth. 2 My doctrine shall drop as the rain, my speech shall distill as the dew; as the small rain upon the tender grass, and as the showers upon the herb. 3 For I will proclaim the name of the LORD; ascribe ye greatness unto our God. 4 The Rock, His work, is perfect; for all His ways are justice; a God of faithfulness and without iniquity, just and right is He. 5 Is corruption His? No; His children's is the blemish; a generation crooked and perverse. 6 Do ye thus requite the LORD, O foolish people and unwise? Is not He thy father that hath gotten thee? Hath He not made thee, and established thee? 7 Remember the days of old, consider the years of many generations; ask thy father, and he will declare unto thee, thine elders, and they will tell thee. 8 When the Most High gave to the nations their inheritance, when He separated the children of men, He set the borders of the peoples according to the number of the children of Israel. 9 For the portion of the LORD is His people, Jacob the lot of His inheritance. 10 He found him in a desert land, and in the waste, a howling wilderness; He compassed him about, He cared for him, He kept him as the apple of His eye. 11 As an eagle that stirreth up her nest, hovereth over her young, spreadeth abroad her wings, taketh them, beareth them on her pinions—12 the LORD alone did lead him, and there was no strange god with Him.

13 He made him ride on the high places of the earth, and he did eat the fruitage of the field; and He made him to suck honey out of the crag, and oil out of the flinty rock; **14** Curd of kine, and milk of sheep, with fat of lambs, and rams of the breed of Bashan, and he-goats, with the kidney-fat of wheat; and of the blood of the grape thou drankest foaming wine. **15** But Jeshurun waxed fat, and kicked— thou didst wax fat, thou didst grow thick, thou didst become gross—and he forsook God who made him, and contemned the Rock of his salvation. **16** They roused Him to jealousy with strange Gods, with abominations did they provoke Him. **17** They sacrificed unto demons, no-Gods, Gods that they knew not, new Gods that came up of late, which your fathers dreaded not. **18** Of the Rock that begot thee thou wast unmindful, and didst forget God that bore thee. **19** And the LORD saw, and spurned, because of the provoking of His sons and His daughters. **20** And He said: "I will hide My face from them, I will see what their end shall be; for they are a very froward generation, children in whom is no faithfulness. **21** They have roused Me to jealousy with a no-god; they have provoked Me with their vanities; and I will rouse them to jealousy with a no-people; I will provoke them with a vile nation. **22** For a fire is kindled in My nostril, and burneth unto the depths of the nether-world, and devoureth the earth with her produce, and setteth ablaze the foundations of the mountains. **23** I will heap evils upon them; I will spend Mine arrows upon them; **24** The wasting of hunger, and the devouring of the fiery bolt, and bitter destruction; and the teeth of beasts will I send upon them, with the venom of crawling things of the dust. **25** Without shall the sword bereave, and in the chambers terror; slaying both young man and virgin, the suckling with the man of gray hairs. **26** I thought I would make an end of them, I would make their memory cease from among men; **27** Were it not that I dreaded the enemy's provocation, lest their adversaries should misdeem, lest they should say. 'Our hand is exalted, and not the LORD hath wrought all this." **28** For they are a nation void of counsel, and there is no understanding in them. **29** If they were wise, they would understand this, they would discern their latter end. **30** How should one chase a thousand, and two put ten thousand to flight, except their Rock had given them over and the LORD had delivered them up? **31** For their rock is not as our Rock, even our enemies themselves being judges. **32** For their vine is of the vine of Sodom, and of the fields of Gomorrah; their grapes are grapes of gall, their clusters are bitter; **33** Their wine is the venom of serpents, and the cruel poison of asps. **34** "Is not this laid up in store with Me, sealed up in My treasuries? **35** Vengeance is Mine, and recompense, against the time when their foot shall slip; for the day of *their calamity is at hand, and the things that are to come upon them shall make haste. 36 For the LORD will judge His people, and repent Himself for His servants; when He seeth that their stay is gone, and there is none remaining, shut up or left at large. 37 And it is said: Where are their gods, the rock in whom they trusted; 38 Who did eat the fat of their sacrifices, and drank the wine of their drink-offering? let him rise up and help you, let him be your protection. 39 See now that I, even I, am He, and there is no God with Me; I kill, and I make alive; I have wounded, and I heal; and there is none that can deliver out of My hand. 40 For I lift up My hand to heaven, and say: As I live for ever, 41 If I whet My glittering sword, and My hand take hold on judgment; I will render vengeance to Mine adversaries, and will recompense them that hate Me. 42 I will make Mine arrows drunk with blood, and My sword shall devour flesh; with the blood of the slain and the captives, from the long-haired heads of the enemy." 43 Sing aloud, O ye nations, of His people; for He doth avenge the blood of His servants, and doth render vengeance to His adversaries, and doth make expiation for the land of His people.*

The Essence of Love

We are told that "Moses came and spoke all the words of the song in the ears of the people, he and Hoshea [Joshua] the son of Nun" (Deuteronomy 32:44). Moses' song reminds us of God's ultimate loving-kindness, which sustains all. Love—the love of God for his prophet Moses, Moses' love of God and all of creation, and creation's love of Moses—is the inner aspect of Chesed. This Sefirah expresses at least thirteen different qualities of love, reflecting the thirteen attributes of mercy, or Shelosh-'Esreh Middot (see appendix 6). It is this love that flows through all the Sefirot below Chesed on the Tree of Life, sustaining them and enriching them, just as Moses does the tribes of Israel. Love, we discover, in life and in Torah, is the essential energy of divinity.

After Moses gives his final will and testament to his people in the form of the Hazeinu, God again speaks to him:

> Ascend to this mount of Abarim, Mount Nebo, which is in the land of Morad, which is before Jericho, and die on the mountain where you will ascend, and be gathered to his people because you trespassed against Me among the Children of Israel at the water of Meribath-kadesh in the wilderness of In, because you did not sanctify Me among

the Children of Israel. For from a distance shall you see the Land, but you shall not enter there, into the land that I give the Children of Israel. (Deuteronomy 32:49)

It seems incredible to most readers of the Hebrew Bible that after all Moses had done on behalf of God and the Hebrew people he was denied what so many common people were permitted: the gift of entering the Promised Land. But God held Moses to a higher standard relative to his elevated station as a prophet. God told Moses it was because of what he had done after the Hebrews left Egypt, on the fifteenth day of the second month of the Exodus. At that time God had just provided the miraculous manna and quail to eat, but the people lacked water. The Mishnah tells us that when God told Moses to speak to the rock to bring forth water, he chose instead to strike the rock two times with his staff. In this, we are being told that it was as if he had struck the Shechinah, and thus it was for this error that God forbade him from entering the Promised Land.[23]

Moses' death was preceded by the deaths of his older sister, the prophetess Miriam, followed by his older brother, Aaron. Thus three great leaders died in the same year, in their birth order. They had all three gained merit in behalf of the people: the Cloud of Glory (Aaron), the manna (Moses), and the portable rock-well (Miriam). These divine gifts had sustained the nation throughout their forty-year maturation in the desert. Each of these prophets performed different roles during the Exodus. Moses, the father of his people, was aided by Miriam, who acted as both a medical and spiritual midwife; Aaron complemented the work of his siblings by nursing the spirit of peace among the people. Together they helped the Hebrews overcome their feelings of rootlessness. The "home" each of these prophets was given consisted of a personal relationship with God. We learn that it is in the spiritual sanctuary of the self that one is truly at home with the divine.

Even in readying themselves for their deaths, Moses and his brother

---

[23] "'You shall speak to the Rock' (Numbers 20:8). The Shechinah was present on that rock for [when] the holy One, Blessed is He, wishes to perform a miracle, the Shechinah precedes Him to the site. [Moses] should not have hit the rock, for [doing so] was disrespectful [toward the Shechinah]" (Tikkunei Zohar 21:44a). See also Chasidah, *Encyclopedia of Biblical Personalities,* 387.

spoke of God. During Aaron's preparations, Moses said to him, "'Just think, Aaron my brother, when Miriam died, you and I attended her. Now that thou are about to die, who will attend me?' The Holy One said to Moses, 'As you live! I will attend you.'"[24] To really understand Moses is to know that he is part of a larger constellation of previous prophets, as his parents, Amram and Yocheved, as well as his two siblings, Miriam and Aaron were prophets as well. Every human being is born of parents and has family relations. But that all three of these holy prophets left the temporal world in the same year suggests that they had completed their purpose of guiding, overseeing, birthing, stewarding, healing, and teaching the Israelites in preparation for entering the land promised them by God. From this we can infer that to enter the Promised Land of illumination, we must each do our fair share of spiritual and material work to become a worthy vessel for the presence of God and the experience of God's miracles.

The Death of Moses

In the oral tradition of Torah, after Moses gives his final teaching from God to the assembled Hebrews, recounting the miracles God granted the Israelites as well as reviewing their own obligations in serving Him, Moses asks God for more time on earth, showing that he too is a mere mortal: he knows some commandments can only be fulfilled in the Holy Land, and for this reason he begs God for the opportunity to fulfill all of them by asking Him to extend his life. Also, he wants to leave Bnai Yisrael with some final blessings and words of peace.

A divine voice came forth and said, "The time has come for you to depart from the world." Moses pleaded with the holy One, "Master of the universe, for my sake, remember the day when You revealed Your-

---

[24] Bialik and Ravnitzky, *Sefer Ha-Aggadah,* 5:108, 94–95. "Then Moses said to Aaron, 'My brother, go up [and lie] on this couch,' and he went up. 'Stretch out your arms,' and he stretched them out. 'Shut your eyes,' and he shut them. 'Close your mouth,' and [he] closed it. At once the Presence came down, and as it kissed him, his soul departed. Then, as Moses and Eleazar kissed him on his cheeks, the cloud of Glory rose up and covered him. The holy one commanded them, 'Go hence.' The moment they left [the cave where Aaron's body lay], the cave sealed up."

self to me at the bush; for my sake, remember the time when I stood on Mount Sinai forty days and forty nights. I beg You, do not hand me over to the angel of death." Again a divine voice came forth and said, "Fear not, I Myself will attend you and your burial." Moses pleaded, "Then wait until I bless Israel. On account of the warnings and reprimands I heaped upon them, they never found any ease with me." Then he began to bless each tribe separately, but when he saw that time was running short, he included all the tribes in a single blessing. Then he said to Israel, "Because of the Torah and its precepts, I troubled you greatly. Now, please forgive me."[25]

The people, in grief over Moses' imminent departure, replied, "Our master, our Lord, you are forgiven." They then turned to this prophet who had been their guide and initiator all these years and said:

"Moses our teacher, we troubled you even more, we made your burden so heavy. Please forgive us." Moses replied, "You are forgiven," Again a divine voice came forth: "The moment has come for you to depart from this world." Moses replied, "Blessed be His Name! May He live and endure forever and ever!" Then he said to Israel, "I implore you, when you enter the Land, remember me and my bones, and say, 'Alas for the son of Amram, who had run before us like a horse, yet his bones fell in the wilderness.'" Again a divine voice came forth and said, "Within half a moment you are to depart from the world." Moses lifted both his arms, placed them over his heart, and called out to Israel, "Behold the end of flesh and blood." Moses arose and washed his hands and feet, and thus became as pure as the seraphim. Then, from the highest heaven of heavens, the Holy One came down to take the soul of Moses, and with Him the three ministering angels, Michael, Gabriel, and Zagzagel. Michael laid out his bier, Gabriel spread a fine linen cloth at his head, with Zagzagel spread it at his feet. Michael stood at one side and Gabriel at the other. Then the Holy One said to Moses, "Moses, close your eyes," and he closed his eyes. "Put your arms over your breast," and he put his arms over his breast. "Bring your

---

[25] Bialik and Ravnitzky, *Sefer Ha-Aggadah* 5:137, 104.

legs together," and he brought his legs together. Then the Holy One summoned Moses' soul, saying, "My daughter, I had fixed the time of your sojourn in the body of Moses at a hundred and twenty years. Now your time has to come to depart. Depart. Delay not." She replied, "Master of the universe, I know that You are God of all spirits and Lord of all souls, You created me and placed me in the body of Moses one hundred and twenty years ago. Is there a body in the world more pure than the body of Moses? I love him, and I do not wish to depart from him." The Holy One exclaimed, "Depart, and I will take you up to the highest heaven of heavens, and will set you under the throne of glory, next to the cherubim and seraphim." In that instant, the Holy One kissed Moses, and took his soul with that kiss. At that, the Holy Spirit wept and said, "There hath not arisen a prophet since in Israel like unto Moses" (Deut. 34:10). The heavens wept and said, "The Godly man is perished out of the earth" (Michah 7:20). The earth wept and said, "The upright among men is no more" (Micah 7:2). The ministering angels wept and said, "he executed the righteousness of the Lord" (Deut. 33:21). Israel wept and said, "and His ordinances are with Israel" (Deut. 33:21). These as well as those said together, "Let him enter in peace and rest on his couch" (Isa 57:2).[26]

At the very moment of Moses' death, the miraculous well, the Cloud of Glory, and the manna ceased.[27] "And he was buried in the valley in the land of Moab over against Beth-peor" (Deuteronomy 34:6).

The Hidden Burial Place

Torah tells us that Moses' burial site was deliberately concealed. Even though his servant and successor, the prophet Joshua, attended him at the time of his death, Moses' body was carried on the wings of the Shechinah[28] to its burial place, a phenomenon akin to the Pillar of Fire that preceded the Tabernacle in its journey at night, and the Cloud of Glory that preceded it by day.

---

[26] Bialik and Ravnitzky, *Sefer Ha-Aggadah* 5:137, fn. 4, 104.
[27] Bereshis Rabah 62:4.
[28] Sotah 13b.

So Moses the servant of the LORD died there in the land of Moab, according to the word of the LORD. And he was buried in the valley in the land of Moab over against Beth-peor; and no man knoweth of his sepulchre unto this day. And Moses was a hundred and twenty years old when he died: his eye was not dim, nor his natural force abated. And the children of Israel wept for Moses in the plains of Moab thirty days; so the days of weeping in the mourning for Moses were ended. And Joshua the son of Nun was full of the spirit of wisdom; for Moses had laid his hands upon him; and the children of Israel hearkened unto him, and did as the LORD commanded Moses. And there hath not arisen a prophet since in Israel like unto Moses, whom the LORD knew face to face; in all the signs and the wonders, which the LORD sent him to do in the land of Egypt, to Pharaoh, and to all his servants, and to all his land; and in all the mighty hand, and in all the great terror, which Moses wrought in the sight of all Israel. (Deuteronomy 34:5–12)

We learn from Moses that the soul of a person, while eternal, cleaves to a body made pure by righteousness. Each life is holy, and in each person's life there are angels who plead for mercy on our behalf. We each have an allotted time in life to be of loving service to the divine and to all of creation, to refine our natures and to lend our expertise to younger generations.

Ritual: Protection of the Dead

Returning briefly to Moses' narrative: the night before the Hebrews begin their Exodus, while they are preparing their household goods for travel and collecting gold and silver from the Egyptians who by now are practically begging their slaves to leave after experiencing the ten plagues—Moses sets out on a mission to find the bones of Joseph, the son of Jacob, which he intends to carry to the Holy Land for burial there.[29]

While hundreds of thousands of Hebrews hastily prepare to leave

---

[29] According to Genesis, Joseph was the eleventh of Jacob's twelve sons and Rachel's firstborn. He was sold into slavery by his jealous brothers, yet became the most powerful man in Egypt next to Pharaoh, saving many Hebrew lives from a seven-year famine. He eventually reconciled with his brothers and lived to the age of 110. Before he died, he made the children of Israel swear that when they left the land of Egypt they would take his bones with them, and upon his death his body was embalmed and placed in a coffin in Egypt.

Egypt, Moses goes to Serah, daughter of Asher, to inquire where Joseph's remains are. Moses then goes to the banks of the Nile, having learned from Serah that the Egyptians made him a metal casket and put it in the Nile in the hopes that it would bring blessings. Moses calls out, "Joseph, Joseph, now is the time that the Holy One, Blessed is He, is fulfilling His oath to redeem Israel. Now is the time for fulfilling that oath that you adjured Israel. If you appear, fine, if not, we are released from your oath." Forewith, Joseph's coffin floated to the surface.[30] Having thus discovered the bones of Joseph, Moses makes ready to take them with him on the night he is to lead the people out of Egypt:

> And it came to pass, when Pharaoh had let the people go, that God led them not by the way of the land of the Philistines, although that was near . . . But God led the people about, by the way of the wilderness by the Red Sea; and the children of Israel went up armed out of the land of Egypt. And Moses took the bones of Joseph with him; for he had straitly sworn the children of Israel, saying: "God will surely remember you; and ye shall carry up my bones away hence with you." And they took their journey from Succoth, and encamped in Etham, in the edge of the wilderness. And the LORD went before them by day in a pillar of cloud, to lead them the way; and by night in a pillar of fire, to give them light; that they might go by day and by night: the pillar of cloud by day, and the pillar of fire by night, departed not from before the people. (Exodus 13:17–22)

The Bones of Life

We are told that during all the years that the Israelites were in the wilderness, the arklike casket of Joseph, as well as the Ark of the Divine Presence, moved side by side. "When passersby asked, 'What is the significance of these two arks?' they were told, 'This one is the coffin of a mortal, and that is the Ark of the Presence.' 'But is it proper that a corpse move side by side with the Presence?' Israel replies, 'The corpse in this ark fulfilled all that is written in that ark.'"[31]

---

[30] Sotah 13a. See also Chasidah, *Encyclopedia of Biblical Personalities,* 363.
[31] Sotah 13a. See also Bialik and Ravnitzky, *Sefer Ha-Aggadah* 4:71, 71.

The People of the Book believe that the bones of a person carry the record of what that person has done in life—where he went and how he carried out the will of God and that of his own soul.[32] As the story above suggests, we are always two arks in procession on the way to the Holy Land: we are the body of teachings (the Ark of the Covenant) and we are the physical body that carries them out. It is not enough to study the holy Word of God; we must live it. It is not enough to understand spiritual law; we must embody it. The teachings themselves and becoming them are of equal and interdependent value.

> *The Holy One, Blessed is He, showed Moses all the leaders who were destined to serve Israel from the day they went out of the desert until the time the dead are resurrected.*
>
> SIFRI PINCHAS 139

Joseph's bones thus come full circle, as they return to the place of his birth, Canaan, the designated Promised Land. This is commensurate with other initiatory acts of marking sacred precincts, such as when Abraham purchases the Cave of Malchpeah for the Israelites' matriarchs and patriarchs to be buried there along with Adam and Eve. That Moses is the one to fulfill the oath between Israel and Joseph is a story of lineage: the book of Genesis, the first book of Torah, ends with the death of Joseph; the book of Deuteronomy, the final book of Torah, closes with the death of Moses. Thus these two figures are connected from the beginning to the end of Torah—which illustrates the importance of revering our ancestors and the teaching lineages they impart. The oath to which Joseph binds the sons of Israel, and which is executed by Moses, is found in Genesis:

And Joseph said unto his brethren: "I die; but God will surely remember you, and bring you up out of this land unto the land which He swore to Abraham, to Isaac, and to Jacob." And Joseph took an oath of the children of Israel, saying: "God will surely remember you, and ye shall carry up my bones from hence." So Joseph died, being a hundred

---

[32] I think of it as the first people of Alaska, whose art of scrimshaw preserved their own histories, which were inscribed on the bones of whales.

and ten years old. And they embalmed him, and he was put in a coffin in Egypt. (Genesis 50:24–26)

Forty years after Moses brings Joseph's bones out of Egypt, Joshua presides over the nation's mourning following the death of Moses. Later, when Joshua dies, "They buried him in the land of his inheritance, at Timnath Serah in the hill country of Ephraim, north of Mount Gaash" (Joshua 24:30). God chastises the people for failing to mourn his death properly with an official period of mourning. Yet right after we learn of Joshua's burial, we learn of the interment, in Shechem, of Joseph's bones, as well as the burial of Aaron's two sons, Gibea and Phineas.

In this sequence of burials lies a deeper mystery. The burials of these three prophets, Moses, Joshua, and Joseph, represent a triumvirate of living testimony to receiving the holy presence of God. Their bones and lives are like pillars in the Jewish people's history: they mark the going down to Egypt (with Joseph); the coming out of Egypt (with Moses); and the arrival in the Promised Land (with Joshua), where the burial of Joseph's bones completes the cycle. Thus the end is included in the beginning, as the Sefer Yetzirah describes.[33]

Over and over again we learn that the death of a person is a sacred time of passage and transition for the entire community. Moses' song, the Hazeinu, is the epitome of a soul's final instructions to the living, inviting each person into the messianic phenomena of communal prophecy.

The Eyes of History

To explore further the significance of ancestral bones in the Bible of the Hebrews, we turn to gematria. As we know, finding words that share the same number value is a basic tool that Kabbalistic gematria uses to reveal hidden meanings, as explained in chapter 1. The Hebrew word for **bone**, עצם (Ayin Tzadee Mem), has a numerical value of 200. The Hebrew word for **eyes** is also equal to 200. This shows us that the bones of our ancestors are more than simply the remains of the elders; they are

---

[33] Sefer Yetzirah, chapter 1, section 6: "The decade of existence out of nothing has its end linked to its beginning and its beginning linked to its end, just as the flame is wedded to the live coal; because the Lord is one and there is not a second one and before one what wilt thou count?"

in fact the "eyes," עיניכם (Ayin Yod Nun Yod Caf Mem), of history: "For God doth know that in the day ye eat thereof, then your **eyes** shall be opened, and ye shall be as Gods, knowing good and evil" (Genesis 3:5). The Hebrew word for bone is also numerically equivalent to **tree,** עצם (Ayin Tzadee Mem), as in the inner nature of the Tree of Life: "And the LORD God said, 'Behold, the man is become as one of us, to know good and evil: and now, lest he put forth his hand, and take also of the **tree** of life, and eat, and live for ever'" (Genesis 3:22). The bones are the bearers of a person's history and powers, thus they are the pillars of the people. Remarkably, the word for **pillars,** לעמודים (Lamed Ayin Mem Vav Dalet Yod Mem) also equals 200: "And of the thousand seven hundred seventy and five shekels he made hooks for the **pillars** and overlaid their chapiters, and filleted them" (Exodus 38:28).

Facilitating the eventual Resurrection of the Dead, that is, from their interred bones,[34] Moses demonstrates complete adherence to God's instructions, assuring the continuity of the people into the Holy Land, by bringing forth the bones of Joseph and transporting them back to the land of his birth. It is now completely understandable why the People of the Book do not cremate the dead, for it destroys the integrity of the record of that soul's body. Refusing the soul's story from the soil through cremation in place of burial means discarding the spiritual and physical imprint in the bone, rejecting the holy place in the land from which the body for that soul was formed and from which it is said that person's final Resurrection will occur. While Joseph's bones go to Israel, Moses' bones might be revealed during messianic times, when the prophetic story of the Jewish people will conclude. We learn, though, that Moses' body is carried to his secret grave on the wings of the Divine Immanence after Moses died in the land of the tribe of Reuben and was buried, the Torah tells us—our only clue as to his general burial location—in the territory of the tribe of Gad.

---

[34] There are many opinions regarding the meaning of Resurrection. One is that a body properly interred in the ground in burial will have preserved an indestructible bone at the base of the skull called the luz bone. It is said by some of the Chazal that this is the source of a person's DNA as well as their bodily history. Using this bone remnant, God will be able to reconstitute each deceased person into the body they inhabited during life, only perfected, that is, the lame will walk, the blind will see, the deaf will hear.

R. Hama bar Hanin asked: Why was the sepulcher of Moses hidden from the eyes of mortals? And answered: because it was revealed and known to the Holy One that the temple was to be destroyed and Israel banished from the Land; hence [the spot was hidden], lest at that time Israel should come to the sepulcher of Moses and stand there, weeping and beseeching Moses, saying, "Moses our teacher, rise up for prayer in our behalf." Then Moses would rise and nullify the decree [of banishment]. For after their death, the righteous are even more beloved by God than while alive.[35]

Even though Moses was prevented from entering the Holy Land, he advocated for every righteous person's admittance. This tells us that when we are unable to fulfill a desire or even a duty, it is incumbent on us to hope for another's success where we may have failed. Moses' end-of-life song affirms what we do in the Outer Court of our life by refining the emotions and consecrating our lives to holy service. The Tent of Meeting is both personal and collective, individual and global. Each person who is able to come into self-mastery liberates the world a little more from the chaos of negativity, doubt, wrongful judgment, and imbalance.

The Bones of the Patriarchs and Matriarchs

The Cave of Machpelah, where Adam and Eve, Abraham and Sarah, Issac and Rebecca, Jacob and Leah are buried—the same cave that Caleb seeks for refuge and counsel—is a cave of sacred records as well as a cave of revelation. Many sages have described the holy convocations that take place between the ancestors buried in the Cave of the Double Tombs (מערת המכפלה), that is, Machpelah.

This sacred site, located in the heart of Hebron's old city, is said to have been purchased by Abraham from a Hittite for 400 silver shekels. Both Judaism and Islam (which calls it the Sanctuary of Abraham) venerate this burial site, where the People of the Book say Adam and Eve are buried. Housed inside a large, Herodian-like structure, the cave consists, according to one teaching, of a tunnel connecting Moses' grave with the graves of the patriarchs.[36] It is not coincidental that the People of the

---

[35] Bialik and Ravnitzky, *Sefer Ha-Aggadah,* 5:14, 105.

[36] Sifri Berachah 34:51. See also Chasidah, *Encyclopedia of Biblical Personalities,* 398.

Book have such a sacred burial grounds for their ancestors, for it reminds us that these holy men and women were actual physical human beings. The Cave of Machpelah is called a double cave, as it houses the remains of the patriarchs and matriarchs (some say one above the other); in this we see the equality of souls in death, despite the culture's diminishment of those who incarnate in female bodies. This is an important teaching: our eternal natures are best consecrated by showing this kind of balance and equality in life—between male and female, rationality and intuition, love and discipline.

People from all over the world, from various traditions, come to visit this sacred site. This universal reverence for preserving this place of ancestral burials in part explains why respect for the dead and their burial places is such an important aspect not only of the People of the Book's ritual process, but of other sacred traditions of the world as well. For Jewish people, this means guarding the soul and the physical remains from the time a person dies until the remains are interred. In Jewish tradition, the body is never left unattended until the time of burial, so that the soul might be given companionship and guidance through the praying of psalms. The attention the deceased person's soul and its temporal parts receive from the living prior to burial, the burial ritual itself, and yearlong period of praying by the living that follows burial, assists the soul in its journey. During this year-long process, the two lower aspects of the soul (the Nefesh and Ruach) completely detach with the body's full disintegration, while the three other components of the soul (the Neshamah, the Chayah, and Yechidah, which are already attached to the supernal realms) are released at the time of the person's last breath (although these aspects are said to visit the grave of the deceased body they inhabited at certain times). But all five components of the soul leave their imprint in the bones of the deceased person.

Bone, in fact, lies at the very root of the Hebrew Creation story: "This *is* now bone of my bones, and flesh of my flesh: she shall be called Woman, because she was taken out of Man" (Genesis 2:23). While some say this describes a kind of divine genetic engineering by the Creator, others suggest a different tale of epic extraplanetary intervention by extraterrestrial travelers, as described in Sumerian creation stories. One of the most important lessons we learn from the description of why Adam and Eve are banished from the Garden of Eden, as Moses is from the land of Israel, is that their eyes were opened to their own individualities. In both instances a sort of rebellion that comes with free will occurred. Both Adam and Eve as well as Moses did things they were not supposed to do. The Mesopotamian stories of Creation detail a similar rebellion by the newly created Adamah, the "men of earth."[37]

> *Since Moses prayed on behalf of the public, he was*
> *considered the public.*
>
> TA'ANIS 9A

Using our free will wisely is, of course, the lifelong path of the seeker. If each person is said to have his own staff of Moses, that is, if he becomes upright yet humble, strong but compassionate, then we are all capable of overcoming fear, doubt, and worry, and our lives will consequently sing God's glory with a soaring melody. This kind of uplifting emotion is recorded deep within the bones of a person. The more frequently we allow ourselves to reach this elevated state, the more deeply ingrained will be its effect on our bones. This kind of connectedness to divinity can actually be seen by others. The luminosity afforded Moses when in direct contact with God through the Shechinah and the Ruach HaKodesh is the same light available to each one of us.

The Initiator of the People

The rituals of the Outer Court, which are designed to unite the body and the soul in one sanctuary, are reflected in the life of Moses. The Sefirah of Chesed marks the completion of the Outer Court ritual process in our ascension of the Tree of Life. Here we see the fire rituals, the water rituals of purification, and the air rituals of incense combining with Moses, the man of earth, standing in bare feet on holy ground, the image of the holy, rectified person. The fire represents the blood and vitality, or Nefesh aspect of the soul, which is strengthened through prayer and in consecrated action when we sacrifice the ego and all selfishness. The water purifications undertaken by the priests during their ritual services express our own

---

[37] For a fascinating examination of the Sumerian and Mesopotamian stories of Creation, see the works of Zechariah Sitchin, including the works of the Earth Chronicles series.

emotional refinement of the Ruach aspect, the vital spirit that animates the body. The special incense used to consecrate the Holy Place elevates the Neshamah of the soul, representing the "I" that is eternal.

When we say that Moses led the children of Israel out of Egypt, we can understand this as meaning that this is the story of each person's emancipation from fear, cold-heartedness, and lack of faith; it is the arrival of each person in their own Holy Place of the self, where from the mountain of one's divinity one can see and thus go to the Holy Land, that is, the place of divine unity in the heart.[38] There we will each arrive at peace. Chesed, as the Sefirah from which Moses' life and these teachings emanate, displays itself in Moses' refined, consecrated temperament: "For the entire forty years [in the desert], Moses was careful not to lose his temper with [Israel]."[39]

In our journey up the ladder of light, we have seen the challenges of bringing the emotional body to stillness, so that when it is conjoined with the quiet mind it can reflect wisdom (Chochmah), by which all truth is found. Through the rituals of the Outer Court, the two stone (אבן) tablets of the cold heart are turned to living flesh (בשר), meaning we are consecrated and can now become God-like co-creators. Thus have we crossed the *yarden* (garden) safely, no longer tempted by anything, including any desire greater than that of oneness with God, unity within. Simply stated, we experience nonduality. This is exactly what Moses accomplishes, setting clear the course for the rest of humanity.[40] Moses removes any obstacle that would prevent his heart and soul from becoming attached to the inner voice, the voice of God, to which he is privy. At any moment chosen either by Moses or God, the two cherubs sitting on the top of the Ark on the Kapporeth (כפרת) can facilitate this dialogue.

When Moses is first told by God exactly how to construct the Ark of the Tabernacle, there is no doubt what the Ark and its Mercy Seat are for: "And there I will meet with thee, and I will speak with thee from

---

[38] It is what Jacob meant when he said, "How holy is this Place [Heb. *maqomb*]. This is none other than the abode of God, and this is the gate of the heavens" (Genesis 28:17).

[39] Yalkut Shimoni, Chukas 763. See also Chasidah, *Encyclopedia of Biblical Personalities,* 385.

[40] In the Jewish tradition, as in many other traditions of the world, we find that the most realized beings seem to grow up in wealth and opulence. Buddha, Krishna, Moses—to name only a few—are each founding fathers of world religions, and each came from great wealth and higher education. Material splendor seems to afford the soul an opportunity to learn quickly that the material world is not what nurtures the soul.

above the ark-cover, from between the two cherubim which are upon the ark of the testimony, of all things which I will give thee in commandment unto the children of Israel" (Exodus 25:22). As Moses and the children of Israel show us through their historical narrative, once we have done the preparatory work of self-refinement by offering up destructive thoughts, feelings, or actions, we are then prepared for direct communication with God. At this point, sufficiently endowed with the Holy Spirit, we are able to engage God directly, without injury to body or soul, just as Moses did inside of the Holy of Holies.

Moses' Prepartion for Spiritual Leadership

Moses' life shows us why it is often only in our senior years, after cultivating family and community involvements in the early part of our lives, that we come closest to God. This explains why the judges of Israel were all over seventy years of age, and why Moses wasn't called to serve the Lord until he reached the age of eighty.

> *The holy One, Blessed is He, gave strength and might to Moses,*
> *and He assisted his voice. With the [same] melody that*
> *he learned [Torah], he would teach Israel.*
>
> MECHITA BECHODESH 4

Like most of the prophets, Moses spent much of his life in the open wilderness, learning from nature all the mysteries of creation. Just as Adam knew the names of all the animals by their inner essence, Moses, it is said, could look backward and forward in time, and he praised future generations that would survive a spiritual darkness greater than in his own times, such as the age we live in now. As a person immersed in nature, as were most of the prophets, Moses was sensitive to all life forms. He knew the language of the sea and the language of the birds, just as he knew the heartfelt cries of human beings. Coming into rapport with all of life eliminates the barriers of time as well, making it possible to see "everywhere and everywhen," as the late American dowser Terry Edward Ross taught his students. In listening to all of life, a person becomes a luminous vessel of spirit. So radiant was Moses with the Shechinah that people longed to look at him to absorb his warmth, as one basks in the rays of the sun: "From the day Moses was born the Shechinah never departed from him."[41] Significantly, the sages say, that "the holy One, Blessed is He, concurred with all that Moses ordained."[42] Moses is the one who ordains not only his successor, Joshua, but all of Israel and beyond, as at the end of his life he ordains the entire world, both in his own time and for the future.

Spiritual Development in Chesed: Cycles of Refinement

Moses' life is characterized by three periods of forty years: he lives in Egypt as a member of the royal household of Pharoah for four decades; he leaves the royal life and lives simply with the people in Midian for forty years; and then, at the age of eighty, he is called on by the Lord to lead the Hebrews out of Egypt, which begins the forty-year period of wandering in the desert. According to the sages, Moses' death, on his birthday, at the age of 120, defines the natural lifespan of the human being; we are intended by the Creator to live long and fruitful lives.

This recurring pattern of the number 40 translates in terms of our own lives. Until a person reaches the age of forty, he may worship every "idol" there is: himself, his accomplishments, his possessions. We all yearn for recognition and want to build our castles and—hopefully—do some occasional good works as well. Then, at the age of forty, and for the next forty or so years, we face the hard work of freeing ourselves from our attachment to the edifice of the ego and the parts of ourselves that are unbalanced and unholy, which we formed in the first forty years.

In the Hebrew alphabet, there are three mother letters: Alef (1), Mem (40), and Shin (300). Mem, the mother letter equal to 40, represents something that is fully developed, incubated, and prepared for birth. It also signifies water and our emotions. Hence we find that all three times Moses stands on the mountain it is for a period lasting forty days and nights, and that his life was comprised of three segments of forty years. In the last forty years of a person's life, we are finally—God willing—at peace in the inner kingdom. This explains why the Great Sanhedrin, the supreme court of ancient Israel formed in the time of the Temple,

---

[41] Zohar 1:120b. See also Chasidah, *Encyclopedia of Biblical Personalities*, 345.

[42] Devarim Rabbah 5:13.

was comprised of the elders from each community, all aged seventy and older. Before they were formally structured as the Great Sanhedrin, the elders of all the tribes were selected as judges of the people. This group of elders comprised the first tribunal of Israel, which was a forerunner to the formal body that in later times became known as the Great Sanhedrin. They had the wisdom to hear the prophecy of a child, Miriam, predicting the birth of the redeemer Moses. They knew, as we know today, that prophecy occurs through women, children, and even those considered not of "normal" mind.

There were seventy-one members of this judicial council, which in his own time came to include Moses. God, as the first and foremost member, made for seventy-two members, a number that reflects the seventy-two different names of God and the corresponding seventy-two God-like attributes we are each comprised of (see appendix 4, "The Seventy-Two Names of God"). These unique seventy-two names express various qualities and powers possessed by the Creator. Knowing them allows a person to pray in the proper name of God, depending on one's circumstances. Of course we can each simply call on the Creator with a loving heart and joyful countenance, but it is also true that knowing God's many attributes allows us to call Him and his legions by names appropriate to our request. Two names the reader is now familiar with are Adonai, which represents the attribute of Chesed and loving-kindness, and Elohkim, which stands for Gevurah and judgment. The names of God are used in reference to His actions, which is why Moses' staff is an example of the power of the names that were encoded in it.

The Staff of Moses

Moses' staff, the Zohar states, is inscribed with the letters of the names of the ten plagues as well as the formula for God's divine name, making it a causative agent when used by its proper operator. Like the Arthurian legend of Excalibur, Moses' staff, a gift from Adam, is a symbol for us as well, indicating that we each have such a power object at our disposal. Might this staff represent our attaining full consecration, when we have become masters over our emotions? When the Son, Zeir Anpin, is in good working order, the resulting unity of the Upper Chariot and Lower Chariot gives us an upright spine—an image suggesting a staff. Might a staff be the outcome of the initiate who goes up and down the ladder and who knows how to use it properly?

So holy is Moses' staff that tradition teaches that it was one of ten things God created at twilight before Sabbath:

> The staff was created at the end of God's works, after he had created heaven and earth and all their hosts, the seas and river and all their fish. When Adam was banished from the Garden of Eden, he took the staff in his hand and went out to work the land. The staff came into the possession of Noah, who entrusted it to Shem and his descendants, until it reached the hands of Abraham the Hebrew, who gave it to Issac. When Jacob fled Paddanaram he took it along, and when he went down to Egypt he took it along and gave it to Joseph. The staff came into the hands of Reuel (Jethro) the Midianite. When he left Egypt he took it along and planted it in his garden. All the mighty ones of Keinan (Canaan) tried to uproot it, for they sought to marry his daughter Zipporah. But they were not able to. It remained in the garden until Moses came and took it . . . and Reuel (Jethro) gave his daughter Zipporah to Moses.[43]

The staff, or rod, as the Hebrew word is sometimes interpreted,[44] is a symbol of authority in many Semitic cultures. Used to shepherd livestock, the humblest of professions, it is also a tool of emancipation. Moses' staff was involved in many acts of liberation; with it he parted the Red Sea (Exodus 14:16), helped Israel win victory in battle (Exodus 17:9), and brought forth water from a rock (Exodus 17:6, Numbers 20:11). His brother, Aaron, had a similarly miraculous staff, and at Moses' command he extended it to bring on the first of three plagues in Egypt, turning the water of the river Nile to blood (Exodus 7:19, 8:1, 12). Scripture claims that in preparation for leading the Jews out of bondage, God had Moses practice the skillful use of his staff: at God's command, Moses could transform the staff into a serpent that could both inflict

---

[43] Yalkhut Shimoni, Shemos 168. See also Chasidah, *Encyclopedia of Biblical Personalities,* 356.

[44] In scripture, the word *staff,* used in reference to Moses' power object, is spelled with the Hebrew letters for *mateh,* "rod" (מטה, Mem Tet Hay).

and heal leprosy; God told Moses that he could pour river water on dry land to change the water to blood (Exodus 4:3–9). It was Moses' staff that, when outstretched, drew divine wrath upon Pharaoh and his subjects (Exodus 7:17; 8:5; 8:16–17; 9:23; 10:13–22). After the Ohel Moed was established and the priesthood delineated, Aaron's staff miraculously bloomed (Numbers 17:8), testifying to Aaron's status as the living tree of the high priesthood. Some sources suggest that, like Aaron's staff, Moses' was made of wood; others say that Moses' rod was sapphire and weighed about ten pounds. Various scholars say that the staffs of both prophets were kept inside the Ark of the Tabernacle following their deaths, hidden until the coming of the Moshiach.

What is important to note here is that some tradition is being passed down—from Adam, to Moses, to King David. The power in the staff and the person using it represents a complete, rectified human, who reflects the rectified Tree of Life. The words **staff, tree,** and **eyes,** as we learned earlier, all have the numerical value of 200, therefore it is said they share the same root. All three terms are facilitators of dramatic transformation: the staff is an element in the miracles performed for the people of Israel and the world; the Tree of Life represents one's personal sanctuary; and our eyes are vehicles of wisdom, witnessing both mundane and sacred events in our own lives and in events that occur in the world. We should also remember that for every physical implement there is a counterpart to it in the supernal realms: "There were two staffs: that of Moses and that of the Holy One, Blessed is He."[45]

Power Objects

Power objects are integral to the Exodus story. Just as there were three redeemers—the siblings Miriam, Aaron, and Moses—there were three holy implements that accompanied them: the well of Miriam and the two rods of Aaron and Moses. Rods, of course, are vertical, upright objects, much like the spine of a person or the phallus of a man (reflecting Yesod, ruling the generative organs). Miriam's well, a feminine symbol of life and birth, much like a womb (also represented by Yesod), displays God's restorative, creative, and protective powers. When taken together, the

---

[45] Zohar 2:272a . See also Chasidah, *Encyclopedia of Biblical Personalities,* 356.

staff and the well represent the inner covenant between a strong intellect and a compassionate heart, the sacred tools of the human odyssey. The mind is our staff of deliverance, and the heart our portable well of life. Just as the Tabernacle, of which Moses was guardian, was sanctified by God's Glory Cloud, the Divine Presence manifested through these power objects, making them archetypes of divine guidance. But there was another power object that Moses was steward of, in addition to the Tabernacle and Ark and its holy contents, and that was the bones of his ancestors, as described earlier in this chapter.

Completing the Refinement of the Emotions

Completing in Chesed the refinement of the emotions as represented by Zeir Anpin, we have now reached a certain developmental stage of luminosity within and without. In several places in Moses' life story we learn about his brilliant emanation. At his birth, the entire household shines with his presence. So luminous was his countenance after being in God's company, Torah says, that he needed to wear a mask to be in the company of his people. From where does it say that Moses received his divine luminosity? One teaching says that it came from the "cave, as it is written, When My glory passes, I will place you in a cleft of the rock (Exodus 33:22)."[46] Yet another source tells us his luminosity came "from the sparks that emanated from the mouth of the Shechinah when the Holy One, Blessed is He, taught him Torah, he had rays of glory."[47] Torah describes it this way:

> And it came to pass, when Moses came down from mount Sinai with the two tables of the testimony in Moses' hand, when he came down from the mount, that Moses knew not that the skin of his face sent forth beams while He talked with him. And when Aaron and all the children of Israel saw Moses, behold, the skin of his face sent forth beams; and they were afraid to come nigh him. And Moses called unto them; and Aaron and all the rulers of the congregation returned unto him; and Moses spoke to them. And afterward all the children of Israel

---

[46] Yalkut Shimoni, Ki Sisa, 406. See also Chasidah, *Encyclopedia of Biblical Personalities,* 351.

[47] Tanchuma, end of Ki Sisa. See also Chasidah, *Encyclopedia of Biblical Personalities,* 351.

came nigh, and he gave them in commandment all that the LORD had spoken with him in mount Sinai. And when Moses had done speaking with them, he put a veil on his face. But when Moses went in before the LORD that He might speak with him, he took the veil off, until he came out; and he came out; and spoke unto the children of Israel that which he was commanded. And the children of Israel saw the face of Moses, that the skin of Moses' face sent forth beams; and Moses put the veil back upon his face, until he went in to speak with Him. (Exodus 34:29–35)

As well as being a vivid description of the surrounding light of the holy Shechinah, this is a description of the physical countenance of holy men and women as described in wisdom traditions the world over. Refinement leads to an actual glow emanating from within. Moses embodies the Shechinah and is himself a radiant being. In the same way, "Moses ascended in a cloud, was covered with a cloud, and was sanctified with a cloud in order to receive the Torah for Israel in Sanctity."[48] We learn at the very beginning of the Israelites' Exodus that Moses asks God to accompany the Israelites on their journey, which is why the Cloud of Glory rests on the Tent of Meeting and guides them throughout their forty years of wandering in the desert. This shows us that we can create our own portable inner sanctuary for the Shechinah to inhabit, just as Moses and Chesed reveal the glory that love of and attachment to divinity brings:

And Moses said unto the LORD: "See, Thou sayest unto me: Bring up this people; and Thou hast not let me know whom Thou wilt send with me. Yet Thou hast said: I know thee by name, and thou hast also found grace in My sight. Now therefore, I pray Thee, if I have found grace in Thy sight, show me now Thy ways, that I may know Thee, to the end that I may find grace in Thy sight; and consider that this nation is Thy people." And He said: "My presence shall go with thee, and I will give thee rest." And he said unto Him: "If Thy presence go not with me, carry us not up hence. For wherein now shall it be

---

[48] Yoma 4a. See also Chasidah, *Encyclopedia of Biblical Personalities,* 365.

known that I have found grace in Thy sight, I and Thy people? Is it not in that Thou goest with us, so that we are distinguished, I and Thy people, from all the people that are upon the face of the earth?" And the LORD said unto Moses: "I will do this thing also that thou hast spoken, for thou hast found grace in My sight, and I know thee by name." (Exodus 33:12–17)

But Moses goes one step further and asks God to show him his face:

And he [Moses] said: "Show me, I pray Thee, Thy glory." And He [God] said: "I will make all My goodness pass before thee, and will proclaim the name of the LORD before thee; and I will be gracious to whom I will be gracious, and will show mercy on whom I will show mercy." And He [God] said: "Thou canst not see My face, for man shall not see Me and live." And the LORD said: "Behold, there is a place by Me, and thou shalt stand upon the rock. And it shall come to pass, while My glory passeth by, that I will put thee in a cleft of the rock, and will cover thee with My hand until I have passed by. And I will take away My hand, and thou shalt see My back; but My face shall not be seen." (Exodus 33:18–23)

When the ministering angels saw that the Holy One had given the Torah to Moses, they gave him letters from the Hebrew alphabet that contained cures for human beings. All of these beautiful teachings about Moses' particular heavenly and earthly blessings are lessons for the living.[49] As we learn to master our emotions and arrive at a state of equilibrium, we can elevate the community simply through our presence. In short, we become vehicles of the Divine Presence.

The Purpose of Self-Refinement
While Torah tells us there is one Glory Cloud escorting the Israelites, the oral tradition asserts there were actually seven:

"And the Lord went before them by day in a Pillar of Cloud to guide

---

[49] Yalkhut MaMechiri, Mishlei 21:22. See also Chasidah, *Encyclopedia of Biblical Personalities*, 367.

them" (Exodus 13:21). How many clouds of glory encompass Israel in the wilderness? Seven clouds: one at each of the four sides; one above them; one beneath them; and one that advanced before them, raised every lowland, lowered each highland, and thus turned them all into level ground. As that cloud advanced, it also killed snakes and scorpions, and swept and sprinkled the road before them.[50]

Each of these seven clouds are said to have derived from one of the seven heavens, telling us that the array of the six directions of space—East, West, North, South, above and below—with ourselves in the center, is the basic operating vehicle for human awareness. This makes it possible for us to navigate the world in a multidirectional way, allowing the soul, which is spherical, to be present under any circumstance in life.

In a certain sense this tells us that when we are enveloped by the Shechinah, something—a presence, an energetic consciousness—goes out in front of us, in the same way that the Cloud of Glory and the Pillar of Fire advanced before the Israelites in their Exodus journeys. If we ever want to know who or what is directing us into an action, look to see who or what is leading. What is the driving force? Is it charitable, selfish, or questionable? Or is the motivating factor to do good for others? Or are we motivated simply for fun or pleasure? For the Israelites, the driving force was God. The Shechinah, the Divine Presence, was within their collective awareness and was a sign of God's intervention.

Each of us is influenced by the intentions and actions of the culture in which we live. In addition, we are impacted by what we do within our own makeup and inner life, for it is this drama that we create, maintain, and participate in. This is the compelling story that can be written with purpose through the exercise of free will. Using all of our aptitudes, all of the six Sefirot of Zeir Anpin in complete harmony, makes us a vessel for the Holy Spirit to direct and protect.

The Ohel Moed's purpose as a model is to tell us that everything we do with our bodies, our minds, our hearts, and our souls is for one common purpose: to create harmony between the parts. Just as the cosmos has a harmony of its parts, the harmonized person has

---

[50] Bialik and Ravnitzky, *Sefer Ha-Aggadah*, 5:15, 76.

a part in the greater cosmic harmony of existence. It is a privilege to have a body, to be able to refine one's own nature and thereby refine the world we live in. Moses shows us this in his holy relationship with God's presence. He spoke to and for God at all times, whether he was coming or going, sitting down or standing up. Moses realized the idea that here, where we stand right now, in this very place, is holy ground. It is the person who blesses the place, the sages teach, therefore each place we go to can be elevated by our awareness, our intention, and our physical presence.

The Enveloping Shechinah

The oral tradition's account of the way in which the Hebrew encampment would proceed is a fascinating description of the descent of the Divine Presence, suggesting our own life's journey:

> How did Israel's journeying in the wilderness proceed? A sign would appear in the cloud for Moses when it was about to move. When he saw by this sign that the cloud was about to move, he would say, "Rise up, O Lord, and Thine enemies be scattered" (Numbers 10:35). Then the cloud moved. As the cloud moved, all made preparation for the journey and began loading their utensils. Whoever had an animal would load the utensils on it, and the cloud would take on the rest. After all the utensils were loaded, the trumpets sounded and Judah, led by his standard, set out: first Judah's prince, and then his tribe. The other tribes followed in the same order—"every man to his own standard, according to the emblems" (Numbers 2:2).[51]

Each prince had his own emblem and his own color corresponding to his tribe's precious stone on the breastplate of Aaron. In this manner, the movement of the twelve tribes represented the movement of the cosmos, the twelve months of the year, and the twelve zodiacal signs of the heavens.

---

[51] Bamidbar Rabba 2:7. Each stone and tribe represents a zodiacal sign as well (Exodus 28:15–20). There are various teachings regarding what the stones actually were, based on the color we are told they possessed.

Month (Eng)	Month (Heb)	Tribe list #1	Zodiac	Element	Tribe list #2
1. April	Nissan	Yehuda	Aries	Fire	Yehuda
2. May	Iyyar	Reuben	Taurus	Earth	Yissachar
3. June	Sivan	Efriam	Gemini	Air	Zebulon
4. July	Tamuz	Dan	Cancer	Watr	Reuben
5. August	Av	Yissachar	Leo	Fire	Shimon
6. September	Elul	Shimon	Virgo	Earth	Gad
7. October	Tishrei	Menashe	Libra	Air	Efriam
8. November	Cheshvan	Asher	Scorpio	Water	Menashe
9. December	Kislev	Zebulon	Sagittarius	Fire	Binyamin
10. January	Tevet	Gad	Capricorn	Earth	Dan
11. February	Shevat	Binyamin	Aquarius	Air	Asher
12. March	Adar	Naftali	Pisces	Water	Naftali

Figure 9.1. Two sequences of the encampment of the tribes with corresponding months, zodiacal signs, and elements (Based on research and drawings by Rabbi Noah Shavrick and Akiva Shavrick; see also Sefer Yetzirah)

The Twelve Tribes and the High Priests' Breastplates

The twelve tribes each represent one of the signs of the zodiac, as well as a stone and its color, as described by the instructions they are given for the creation of the High Priest's breastplate:

> And thou shalt make a breastplate of judgment, the work of the skilful workman; like the work of the ephod thou shalt make it: of gold, of blue, and purple, and scarlet, and fine twined linen, shalt thou make it. Four-square it shall be and double: a span shall be the length thereof, and a span the breadth thereof. And thou shalt set in it settings of stones, four rows of stones: a row of carnelian, topaz, and smaragd shall be the first row; and the second row a carbuncle, a sapphire, and an emerald; and the third row a jacinth, an agate, and an amethyst; and the fourth row a beryl, and an onyx, and a jasper; they shall be enclosed in gold in their settings. And the stones shall be according to

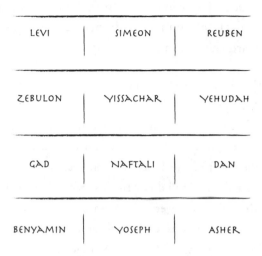

HIGH PRIEST'S BREASTPLATE AND
THE TRIBES OF ISRAEL

LEVI	SIMEON	REUBEN
ZEBULON	YISSACHAR	YEHUDAH
GAD	NAFTALI	DAN
BENYAMIN	YOSEPH	ASHER

*Figure 9.2. The High Priest's breastplate and the tribes of Israel
(Drawing by Amy Ford, based on the Torah)*

the names of the children of Israel, twelve, according to their names;
like the engravings of a signet, every one according to his name, they
shall be for the twelve tribes. (Exodus 28: 15–21)

Applying these correspondences, the Hebrews were able to readily
identify each tribe and its specific role during the Exodus (e.g., Moses
camped among the Levites, the priestly caste). To this day, traditional
people wear small amulets designed like the breastplate In an effort to
stay connected to serving God daily. Others wear a precious stone corresponding to the month of their birth, and still others who can trace
their family lineage wear the stone representing the tribe they come from.
(There are many opinions concerning what stone corresponds to which
tribe, yet these kinds of small rituals evoke a set of corresponding powers
and thus are of benefit to the wearer.)

Israel's Pattern of Encampment

As Kabbalah says, for every physical manifestation on earth there is a
counterpart in the spiritual realms, as we see in the example of the High

Priest's sacred breastplate, reflecting the twelve zodiacal signs that corresponded to the twelve tribes. The Israelites also enacted this pattern in their method of setting up camp, as seen in figure 9.3, and as indicated by this description of Miriam's well (discussed in our next chapter), as they traveled toward their ultimate destination:

> What was the form of Israel's encampment? They were encamped around the Tabernacle in a circle whose perimeter was four thousand cubits. Moses, Aaron and his sons, and their families were to the east of the Tent of Meeting. The well that was near the Tent of Moses, at the entrance to the court of the Tabernacle, indicated to the tribes where to encamp. How did the well do it? In this way: After the hangings for the court of the Tabernacle were put in place, the twelve princes (tribal leaders) stationed themselves at the well and uttered the song that is the song of Binah, "Spring up, O well." At that, its waters would spring up and presently form many streams. At first, only one stream encircled the camp of the Presence [i.e., the Tabernacle]. Out of this one stream, four streams flowed toward the four corners of the court of the Tabernacle, where they joined, thus encompassing the entire camp of the Levites, as well as coursing in between the areas to be occupied by the Levite families. Each of these areas—squares of dry land encircling the camp of the Presence—was thus set apart for occupancy. . . . A larger stream encompassed the perimeter of Israel's entire camp, its waters formed themselves into a number of streams, which flowed between every two tribes, encompassing them inside and out, marking off throughout the area squares of dry land, this indicating the bound areas of each tribe. The stream made all kinds of good things to grow for Israel, their cattle grazed just beyond the encampment—the cloud that spread over Israel separated them from their cattle. Because of the cloud's radiance of blue, the streams sparkled with the reflection of dawn, of the moon, and of the sun. Hence the people of the world, sighting them from many miles away, would extol them, saying, "Who is this shining like the dawn, beautiful as the moon, clear as the sun?"[52]

---

[52] Bialik and Ravnitzky, *Sefer Ha-Aggadah*, 5:82, plus fn. 10, 89.

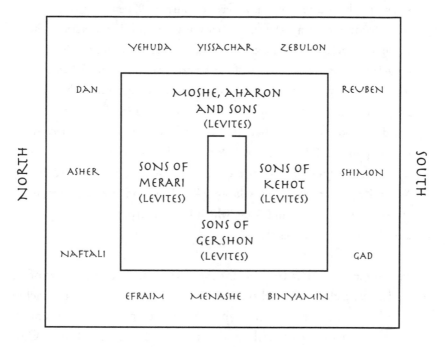

EAST

YEHUDA	YISSACHAR	ZEBULON

DAN

REUBEN

MOSHE, AHARON
AND SONS
(LEVITES)

NORTH   SOUTH

ASHER

SONS OF
MERARI
(LEVITES)

SONS OF
KEHOT
(LEVITES)

SHIMON

SONS OF
GERSHON
(LEVITES)

NAFTALI

GAD

EFRAIM	MENASHE	BINYAMIN

WEST

*Figure 9.3. The camp of Israel (Based on research and drawings by Rabbi
Noah Shavrick and Akiva Shavrick; drawn by Amy Ford)*

The miracle of the Israelites having fresh water that issued from Miriam's well, a portable rock that provided hundreds of thousands of people with fresh water even in the parched desert, reinforces the truth that our prayers bring us sustenance, both physical and spiritual. Acting in accord with our nature and being mindful of the natural cycle of seasons (i.e., the zodiac), planting and harvesting at the right time, allows us to travel through life safely, under God's protection. We become, with great, determined effort, both the protected Tabernacle and a valued member of the larger global community that we are each part of. In the description of how a moveable sanctuary functions in the wilderness, a metaphor for the human being walking through life, the various phenomena described are achievable inner states of awareness.

Thus did Israel proceed—with the clouds over them. Now and then a beam of light would issue from one of the clouds, by which they knew in which direction they were to journey. When [it was God's] wish that they encamp, the cloud that was above the Tabernacle, in the center of Israel's camp, halted. Then the Levites would set up the Tabernacle first, before the camps of the several tribes arrived. When they did arrive, they would halt, and each one would encamp in the place assigned to it, with the clouds of glory hovering above them. Such was the distinction of Moses that the cloud of the Presence did not come down upon the Tabernacle until Moses said, "Come to rest, O Lord, upon the ten thousands of the families of Israel" (Numbers 10:36). When Israel journeyed, the Ark preceded them, and from between its staves sparks of fire would issue, which burned serpents and scorpion, and slew Israel's enemies.[53]

Having learned that the ancient Israelites believed in the law of correspondences, a classical teaching describes how Jerusalem, the Israelites, and the Tabernacle share a three-part system of meaningful hierarchy. Jerusalem, the Israelites overall, and the outer altar in the Outer Court are connected. So too, the Temple Mount, the Levites, and the overall Tent of Meeting are related to each other. Proceeding from a more general set of properties, the Temple, the High Priest, and the Holy of Holies are meaningfully connected to one another.

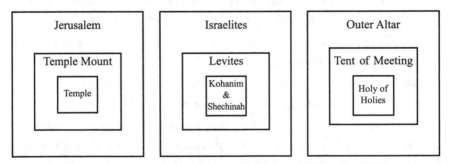

Figure 9.4. Corresponding patterns showing the relationship between the Ark, Israel, and the Temple Mount (Based on research and drawings by Rabbi Noah Shavrick and Akiva Shavrick; drawn by Amy Ford)

---

[53] Sifra 1:1. See also Chasidah, *Encyclopedia of Biblical Personalities,* 347.

Concluding Consecration: The Gateway to Elevation

One of the prayers attributed to Moses explains why in the oral tradition of Judaism it is said that the world exists because of him. "Master of the World," Moses prayed, "when you see your children in distress and there is no one to plead for mercy on their behalf, answer them immediately."[54] This plea for God's compassion reflects the essence of Chesed, the illumination that comes from the consecrated human being, the consecrated nation, the consecrated earth. It happens when all of the sparks in the six Sefirot from Yesod through Chesed are elevated, and we are gathered up in the essential love of our eternal bond with God. Here in Chesed, we are no longer for ourselves alone, but for service to all of creation. This is the portal that makes aliyah possible; it is a combination of humility, prophecy, and peace.

The Son, Zeir Anpin, our emotional body, has been refined and integrated into the pinnacle of the higher mind, the seat of supernal wisdom from which our "ten-ness" derives. The throne's illumination is summarized in Moses' glorious and hopeful declaration. The human model is Moses (Moshe), משה (Mem Shin Hay). Even the letters of his name tell a story: of incubation (Mem, water); purification (Shin, fire); and initiation through breathing/acting properly (Hay, air). Fire, water, air, and earth, when combined in our heart, makes a united kingdom—left, right, and center, one with God, one with the world, without separation, without want for the self, but for the One and the All.

In the Tree of Life pathways, the three mother letters, Shin, Alef, and Mem (in descending order on the Tree), represent the three parallel paths by which the three pillars of the Tree of Life are connected (see chapter 1, figure 1.1, page 11). The letter Shin and the fire it represents connect Chochmah and Binah, or Mother and Father, eyes and ears. The letter Alef and the property of air connect Chesed and Gevurah, love and judgment, right and left hands. The letter Mem, as water, is the bridge between Netzach and Hod, right and left legs, enduring will and complete humility. One can see in these patterns the clues to self-refinement found in the Tabernacle rituals. In some way the rituals of fire, Shin, help us balance Chochmah and Binah, wisdom and understanding. The

---

[54] Devarim Rabbah 2:11.

rituals of air, Alef, improve our ability to act justly in the world, balancing our desire to love and to give, and our instinct to withhold or give in measured portion. All breathing exercises, singing and spoken prayer, along with the ritual of incense, elevates this aspect of our nature. Finally, Mem, the letter of development and incubation, connects our right and left legs, making it possible for us to purify every action with holy intention and humility, so that we give birth to holy acts. One can see in the act of ecstatic dancing an empowering of Mem, or one's emotions.

Moses shows us that the world we live in and the worlds our souls are immersed in are blessed by this process of consecrating our lives in the Ohel Moed. This is what leads to divine awakening. We can better understand now how Moses, as the exemplar of Chesed, in leading the children (our limbs and body parts) out of Egypt (a sense of duality in consciousness), helped them transcend their individual identities and feeling of separation from divinity. Moses' life shows us that by surrendering our own life to divine guidance, we can obtain the source of our inner freedom and peace. But he also reveals in his life the full development of Zeir Anpin, which in the descent of the light begins with Chesed and in its ascent is its pinnacle. This makes Moses the source of love for all the descendants of Israel, further amplifying why Chesed, and the love of all people and all of nature, is a mature love, and why consecration, the process of making all acts in life holy, begins and ends with unconditional love and love of the Divine.

Moses could look backward and forward in time. He was called the most humble man on earth. In Chassidut it is said that he was humbled by the age that would deliver the Moshiach. This is our holy charge: to consecrate every moment of our life for the world's elevation. Elevation is the next part of the holy journey of body and soul, Tabernacle and ritual, as we each become the High Priest who enters the Holy Place, the Promised Land, and eventually the Holy of Holies, the Jerusalem that exists within each one of us.

Elevation

10
The Well of Understanding
Binah • Drawing Down Blessings

> *"A well of living waters" (Song 4:15)—such is the Torah in Israel's Land.*
>
> YALKHUT, SONG 537

Third Sefirot: Binah
Meaning: Understanding
Rung on Ascending Ladder: Eight
Archetype: The Mother (Imma)
Symbol: The well
Spiritual World: Beriyah/creation
Spiritual Anatomy: Ears and the faculty of hearing
Inner Quality: Joy (simcha)

Historical Representatives: B'nai Yisrael singing to the well
Text: Numbers 21, in particular 21:16–18
Key Words: Drawing down to cause elevation
Key Emotion in Song: Elevated joy; drawing down blessings (beracha)

Tent of Meeting: The Holy Place (incense, menorah, shewbread)
Spiritual Stage: Elevation of the holy gates (eyes, ears, nose, mouth)

Spiritual Practice: Elevating the senses for joyous service
Illumination: The illuminated heart of joy in total service and unity

> The Israelites' communal song to the well represents an evolution,
> from dependence on the merit of the prophetess Miriam alone for
> water, to unity and one-heartedness in drawing down God's blessings.

The Sefirah Binah:
Understanding and Joyfulness

The Sefirah of Binah is the uppermost point of the left pillar of the Tree of Life. Called the Mother, she stands for understanding. Binah gives a person the ability to sense what is best in any situation and to discriminate with the strength of Gevurah below her and the wisdom of her partner, Chochmah, the Father, who emanates to her from the right pillar. Intuition filled with divine wisdom leads one to making wise choices for the community, the family, and oneself.

Binah, with its quality of understanding, represents joy and happiness, *simcha,* in our emotional experience. The entire community of Israel sings the song of Binah, calling out to God to manifest a supply of water.

When we meet the Israelites in the Sefirah of Binah, they are still in the wilderness of their journey. It is the final part of the Exodus. At this time, having experienced the miracle of redemption from Egypt, with all of its attending trials in coming to Canaan, their lives are physically arduous yet spiritually potent. As we climb the Tree of Life in our study of the Sefirot, we are going in reverse chronological order of historical events; in fact, the higher one goes in the ascent of the Tree of Life, the less important is the material realm, as we become increasingly spiritualized. We find this reflected in the biblical narrative as well: as the children of Israel come into possession of their land, their religion becomes institutionalized in the form of buildings and cities. Until then, these hundreds of thousands of desert nomads wander from territory to territory, strangers in a strange land, on their way to the place God has promised them. It is only through sheer faith in the one God who has delivered them from Egypt and sustained them throughout the Exodus that they remain strong, oriented to the higher states of initiation that God and their prophets have taught them.

At this stage in our journey, we note that the further down the ladder and timeline we go, the more the various parts of the self become engaged, until we reach Malchut (the kingdom), the bottom Sefirah, where the entire physical world and the physical body of the person emanates the one true light of God from above. "Israel is more beloved by the Holy One than the ministering angels . . . for the ministering angels do not utter song above until Israel first utters it below."[1] Once again we acknowledge that each Sefirah imparts some aspect of the Hebrews' spiritual evolution, as it does our own as we too become a nation of priests.

B'nai Yisrael: Singing Collectively to the Well

When we meet the children of Israel immediately before their historic elevation in Binah, they are exhausted from recent battles with the Edomites. Moving camp several times until coming to the border of the land of the Amorites, the people are anxious about their day-to-day survival—worried about the availability of food and water and grieving the recent deaths of two of their beloved prophets, Miriam and Aaron. Nearing the end of their Exodus, poised to enter Canaan (as discussed in chapter 8), the people are called to the passion of the heart and the well of faith that sustains the soul.

The prophetess Miriam has died, at the age of 126, leaving the people without the bounty of her miraculous well, for it was in her merit that God gifted the Israelites with this water wherever they went during the Exodus. Miriam's brother Aaron, the High Priest, in whose merit the Cloud of Glory has guided the people, has also just died, having been called by God to Mt. Hor, stripped of his priestly vestments, and prepared for death (Numbers 20:22–25). This leaves only Moses, assisted by Joshua, to lead the people. Miriam and Aaron have been buried, and now the community experiences doubts concerning their ability to merit God's protection and care in the form of a miraculous supply of water. They overcome their fears by singing a song of elevated joy. In Binah, each person is called to the heart, as are the Israelites in this situation. It

---

[1] Hayim Nahman Bialik and Yehoshua Hana Ravnitzky, *Sefer Ha-Aggadah*, 1:5, 333.

is a spiritual state of illuminated will wherein one is entirely attached to God's presence, praying with joy and gladness for life itself.

The Song of Binah:
Drawing Down Blessings (Beracha)

R. Yohanan said: The well used to water all kinds of garden herbs, all kinds of seeds for planting, and all varieties of Trees. You can see for yourself that it was so, for after Miriam died and the well stopped watering plants. The people said, "This is no longer a place of seed, of fig, or of vines" (Numbers 20:5).

SEFER HA-AGGADAH, 5:76

The well, which is central to this prophetic text, refers to "the well of which God said to Moses, 'assemble the people and I shall give them water'" (Numbers 21:16). This, according to some scholars, is Miriam's well, which, having stopped at the time of her death, is restored in the merit of all the people, led by Moses. Various commentators suggest that earlier in the Exodus Moses could not find this well, which is why he struck the rock with his staff, in order to find it,[2] the very act he was penalized for by being forbidden from entering the Promsied Land.

The text of the song of Binah is preceded in Torah by an account of the people's desperation as a result of endless wars and their uncertainty over the many factors that govern their lives, particularly the basic survival needs for water and food. As a song to hidden water, this beracha, a type of song meaning the drawing down of blessings, is a symbolic act of calling on the feminine presence of God, the Shechinah. Water represents the Mother principle, that which sustains life, which is relevant to our experience of Binah as the realm of Beriyah, creation, to

---

[2] Prior to this event of singing to the well, Miriam's well sustained the people during their Exodus. In Rephidim, following the miracle of Manna and quail, Moses was pressed by the people to bring them water. God told him to speak to the rock as testimony to God's power, as he did earlier in their journey. Instead, perhaps thinking that the crowd needed a ritual performance, Moses struck the rock; only a trickle of water resulted, and so the people complained. So Moses hit the rock a second time, some say in anger, which Aaron did not prevent, and the water gushed forth (Exodus 17:5–6 and Numbers 20:8). It was for this indiscretion—striking the rock rather than speaking to it as God had directed—that Moses was prevented from entering the Holy Land, as was Aaron for his complicity in this misdeed.

which the soul is eternally connected. The well directs our attention to the creation of the world and in this case to the people's elevation and re-creation as a new community, chastened and purified by the ordeal of coming to the border of the land promised them by God.

There is a fascinating teaching that says that "At the beginning of the world's creation, the praise of the Holy One ascended only from the water, as is said, 'From the voice of many waters' (Psalms 93:4). And what did they proclaim? 'The Lord on high is mighty' (ibid.). The holy One said: If these, which have neither mouth nor the capacity of utterance or speech, praise Me, how much more and more when Adam will be created?"[3]

Here, the people said to preserve the lineage of teachings that Adam was originally given must now collectively demonstrate their love of and faith in God. Regardless of their physical circumstances and their anxieties, they are required to sing with their entire being, hearts open, singing a glad song to God, knowing their prayers are already answered in the act of praising God. This is the nature of blessings, beracha. This is the secret of prayer we learned in chapter 3 in our study of Malchut, the realm of action, or Asiyah; it is the treasure the prophetess Chanah gives us, as discussed in chapter 6 on Netzach: that prayers are answered in the very act of praying.

Praising with gratitude is a state of elevation of mind in union with heart. As we bring focused intention to being one with God to the heart center, just as the Shechinah is one with all of creation, our feelings are elevated, for it is here we attain the state of oneness. Petitioning God with a feeling of humble thanksgiving, knowing that they have already received His mercy and support, the people sing to the well that Miriam has bequeathed them; as a result, the miraculous flow of water is restored. In simple, nontheological terms, desire creates a vessel for the light to fill. It is only by creating a vessel through words, thoughts, and deeds that the immaterial can become material. One cannot have a pitcher to hold water only by imagining it, though this is the first step in manifesting a physical vessel. In the spiritual realms, we are what we believe we are. Our thoughts create a vessel for the light to fill. This makes the mind, when conjoined with the heart, a fully endowed co-creator. Having unshakeable faith in the divine source of all is the experience of arriving in the Holy Place of our own sanctuary of life—as the Israelites experienced at

---

[3] Hayim Nahman Bialik and Yehoshua Hana Ravnitzky, *Sefer Ha-Aggadah*, 8:120, 482.

this historical moment, exhibiting a belief in the deep interconnectedness between spiritual desire and physical manifestation.

As we know, in Kabbalah it is taught that there are different levels of prayer. The daily prayer structure is designed to allow us to progress through these levels, as exemplified in the Tabernacle and its ritual stages, to produce in the initiate the same experience as that of the Israelites, their priests, and the Kohen Gadol (the High Priest). As the American scholar Rabbi Aryeh Kaplan (1934–1983) outlines, to enter the realm of Binah in Beriyah, one recites the holy Shema (discussed in chapter 3; see also appendix 3 for the full text of the Shema): "Hear O Israel, The Lord our God, the Lord is One." After reaching a state of inward and outward unity, a person can hear with the ears of Binah, deriving from each moment in life an understanding of our parallel existence in the spiritual realms. That is why even without a formal sanctuary to worship in, the one who prays in a certain order performs the very same functions as are found in the Tabernacle rituals. This process facilitates the experience of divine unity with God.

Levels of Prayer

Prayer, endowed with faith, is the service of the heart that is represented by Binah and the well. The water from the well sustains and purifies the physical body, just as prayer purifies and sustains the soul. The stages in the daily prayer sequence describe the ascent of the Tree of Life, a reflection of the Hebrews' ritual process in the Tent of Meeting as described in this book. This sequence is explored in the charts below. It begins with the sacrificial reading and ends with the recitation of the Standing Prayer, which we studied in chapter 3 in our discussion of Malchut. Traditionally, all of these stages occur prior to reading the Torah portion of the week.

Worlds	Quality	Sefirah	Service
Asiyah	Action	Malchut	Sacrificial reading (Karbanoth)
Yetzirah	Formation	Zeir Anpin	Biblical songs of praise (Pesukey De Zimra)
Beriyah	Creation	Binah	The Sh'ma and its blessings (Birkat Sh'ma)
Atzilut	Emanation	Chochmah/Keter	The Amidah

Figure 10.1. Levels of prayer (Based in part on Aryeh Kaplan's Meditation and Kabbalah, *285).*

Rabbi Kaplan further reveals how the Zohar's system of worlds relates to our own refinement by showing the connection between the realms, the stages of the Tabernacle, and how we engage particular faculties that spring from specific spiritual roots, as seen in figure 10.2.

World	Manifestation	Sefirah	Tabernacle
Atzilut	Nothingness	Chochmah	The Holy of Holies/the Ark
Beriyah	Thought	Binah	The Holy Place/ Menorah, shewbread, incense
Yetzirah	Speech	Zeir Anpin	Outer Court/ Animal sacrifices and water rituals
Asiyah	Action	Malchut	Prayer at the threshold of the Outer Court

Figure 10.2. Correspondences: the Tree of Life and the Tabernacle rituals (Based in part on Aryeh Kaplan's Meditation and Kabbalah, *301).*

Appreciating the elevated state of joy and spiritual well-being the Israelites proclaim in their song to the well, this being a reflection of perfected thought, it is apparent that this moment provides a personal and collective experience of holiness, the very station in the Tabernacle—the Holy Place—that is illuminated by Binah. The People of the Book thus take us to a place within where we experience divine unity of the upper waters of the mind as reflected in the heart, as Binah is where the heart and the mind unite, producing an elevated spiritual consciousness—the intelligence of the heart.

I have placed God Before me at all time.

PSALMS 16:8

When we pray, we must merge the heart, the physical organ associated with Binah, with the mind. We can then elevate prayer as a vehicle of transcendent consciousness. When we pray, we should leave behind the physical world and its demands, at least for the duration of our prayer. Focusing our attention solely on the words of the prayer, we experience the vibrant light contained within the words in such a way that this spiritual root shines into each word we utter. This allows us to enter into a heightened state of awareness—as though entering the

Holy Place in the Tabernacle, where our senses of taste (shewbread), sight (menorah), and smell (incense) become potent actualizers of cosmic forces. If we are distracted by worldly concerns when we pray, we are counseled to take those thoughts and elevate them to divine service; for example, concerns about one's livelihood can be transformed by blessing one's work as a service to God. This elevates even distractions. In this way we understand Binah's song to the well as being the divine service of the purified heart.

In the biblical narrative, this is how, no longer dependent on individual prophets for everything they needed, the Israelites managed to "cross over" their separation from God. As a result of the merit garnered through their collective effort and intention, their prayer was answered, and they were bestowed with the gift of precious water. They had to do (the world of Asiyah), to act, to use their entire beings—body, mind, and soul consciously united in the divine (Yetzirah and Beriyah)—to affect an outcome in the natural, physical world.

This is the same formula for any person or generation working in the manifest world. The Israelites' situation required, as does our world today, the collective purification of the heart, making the community of one voice, singing out with great praise to the one God. The lack of water (or in the modern era, lack of fresh water due to large scale pollution) required a communal engagement; through the inner growth experienced as a result of their prayer for blessings, that which was not yet manifest was made manifest. We can learn something from every moment in the Hebrew Bible; here we see our own and future generations' relationship to the Divine Immanence through this bestowal of water—the collective nature of the people's prayer represents a spiritual essence, while the water itself is the physical element on which all life depends.

This event of singing to the well reflects an earlier time in the Hebrews' experience, when they were of one heart and one voice at the time of the Sinatic revelations. From that experience the people learned the spiritual reality of what it means to have faith in the supreme Creator. Binah is associated with the quality of emunah, or faith, required of a person in order to receive divine bestowal. We must know that even in the worst situations there are blessings available.

Joy, Faith, and Peace

The three letters that comprise the Hebrew word for **well,** באר, Bet, Alef, and Reish, indicating a place from which water is drawn, equals 203. If we rearrange these letters we get other words of the same value: the Hebrew words for **create,** ברא; **lay (in wait),** ארב; and **great,** רבא. Other words with the same numerical value include **stranger,** גר; **wings,** אבר; **laugh,** צחקה; **and together,** ונאספו; and **to the elders,** ולזקני. The gematria of the word *well* thus reveals a concealed story about the Israelites' sojourn as strangers in a strange land, and in this instance, the community and its elders coming together to pray (an act of creation) for the water needed for their survival. The inner qualities of joy, faith, and peace that illuminate the song of Binah are also present in this analysis. It is quite powerful that the three-letter root of the symbol of this Sefirah, the well, is also found in the meaning of the word *Beriyah,* creation, the realm of Binah. Humanity's existence depends on spiritual benefits that come from our right stewardship of creation, including the waters of the earth. Similarly, life depends on the ability of the archetypal Mother within each person to nurture with wisdom and understanding, giving life the joyous encouragement and support it needs. This eighth song of our ascent, though referred to as "singing to the well," actually signifies singing to the source of life itself. Here, the word *singing* suggests the state of cultivating prophecy through joyous song.

The Song of Binah: Numbers 21

1 *And the Canaanite, the king of Arad, who dwelt in the South, heard tell that Israel came by the way of Atharim; and he fought against Israel, and took some of them captive.* **2** *And Israel vowed a vow unto the Lord, and said: 'If Thou wilt indeed deliver this people into my hand, then I will utterly destroy their cities.'* **3** *And the Lord hearkened to the voice of Israel, and delivered up the Canaanites; and they utterly destroyed them and their cities; and the name of the place was called Hormah.* **4** *And they journeyed from mount Hor by the way to the Red Sea, to compass the land of Edom; and the soul of the people became impatient because of the way.* **5** *And the people spoke against God, and against Moses: 'Wherefore have ye brought us up out of Egypt to die in the wilderness? for there is no bread, and there is no water; and our soul loatheth this light bread.'* **6** *And the Lord* *sent fiery serpents among the people, and they bit the people; and much people of Israel died. 7 And the people came to Moses, and said: 'We have sinned, because we have spoken against the LORD, and against thee; pray unto the LORD, that He take away the serpents from us.' And Moses prayed for the people. 8 And the LORD said unto Moses: 'Make thee a fiery serpent, and set it upon a pole; and it shall come to pass, that every one that is bitten, when he seeth it, shall live.' 9 And Moses made a serpent of brass, and set it upon the pole; and it came to pass, that if a serpent had bitten any man, when he looked unto the serpent of brass, he lived. 10 And the children of Israel journeyed, and pitched in Oboth. 11 And they journeyed from Oboth, and pitched at Ije-abarim, in the wilderness which is in front of Moab, toward the sun-rising. 12 From thence they journeyed, and pitched in the valley of Zered. 13 From thence they journeyed, and pitched on the other side of the Arnon, which is in the wilderness, that cometh out of the border of the Amorites. For Arnon is the border of Moab, between Moab and the Amorites; 14 wherefore it is said in the book of the Wars of the LORD: Vaheb in Suphah, and the valleys of Arnon, 15 And the slope of the valleys that inclineth toward the seat of Ar, and leaneth upon the border of Moab.* **16 And from thence to Beer; that is the well whereof the LORD said unto Moses: 'Gather the people together, and I will give them water.' 17 Then sang Israel this song: Spring up, O well—sing ye unto it—18 The well, which the princes digged, which the nobles of the people delved, with the sceptre, and with their staves. And from the wilderness to Mattanah;** [Bold indicates lines from which the Chazal divined the song type] *19 and from Mattanah to Nahaliel; and from Nahaliel to Bamoth; 20 and from Bamoth to the valley that is in the field of Moab, by the top of Pisgah, which looketh down upon the desert. 21 And Israel sent messengers unto Sihon king of the Amorites, saying. 22 'Let me pass through thy land; we will not turn aside into field, or into vineyard; we will not drink of the water of the wells; we will go by the king's highway, until we have passed thy border.' 23 And Sihon would not suffer Israel to pass through his border; but Sihon gathered all his people together, and went out against Israel into the wilderness, and came to Jahaz; and he fought against Israel. 24 And Israel smote him with the edge of the sword, and possessed his land from the Arnon unto the Jabbok, even unto the children of Ammon; for the border of the children of Ammon was strong. 25 And Israel took all these cities; and Israel dwelt in all the cities of the Amorites, in Heshbon, and in all the towns thereof. 26 For Heshbon was the city of Sihon the king of the Amorites, who had fought against the former king of Moab, and taken* *all his land out of his hand, even unto the Arnon.* **27** *Wherefore they that speak in parables say: Come ye to Heshbon! let the city of Sihon be built and established!* **28** *For a fire is gone out of Heshbon, a flame from the city of Sihon; it hath devoured Ar of Moab, the lords of the high places of Arnon.* **29** *Woe to thee, Moab! thou art undone, O people of Chemosh; he hath given his sons as fugitives, and his daughters into captivity, unto Sihon king of the Amorites.* **30** *We have shot at them—Heshbon is perished—even unto Dibon, and we have laid waste even unto Nophah, which reacheth unto Medeba.* **31** *Thus Israel dwelt in the land of the Amorites.* **32** *And Moses sent to spy out Jazer, and they took the towns thereof, and drove out the Amorites that were there.* **33** *And they turned and went up by the way of Bashan; and Og the king of Bashan went out against them, he and all his people, to battle at Edrei.* **34** *And the* LORD *said unto Moses: 'Fear him not; for I have delivered him into thy hand, and all his people, and his land; and thou shalt do to him as thou didst unto Sihon king of the Amorites, who dwelt at Heshbon.'* **35** *So they smote him, and his sons, and all his people, until there was none left him remaining; and they possessed his land.*

The emphasized part of this biblical entry from Numbers, from which the song of Binah is derived, begins with verse 16, in which God prevails by making the well rise up, revealing the aliyah, the elevation, of the water itself. That it arises by the collective efforts of the collective will and effort of everyone in the community, from the most elevated prophet (Moses) and the priests, to the tribal princes and elders, to the very youngest children, declares that this is an endeavor created by the merit of *all* the people. That this water is a gift, a bestowal, does not go unnoticed: commentators vary regarding the source of this water, but they all agree that the water from this well is the physical manifestation of God's love and sustenance bestowed on the Hebrews as a result of their collective prayer and merit. It is the group's petition and disposition that makes a dwelling place for the Shechinah, which comes in the form of this sustenance.

It is taught of Hillel the Elder: When he celebrated during the rejoicing at the place of water drawing, he used to recite, "When I am here, everyone is here; but when I am not here, who is here? To the place that I love, there my feet lead me." The holy One's response: If you

come into My house, I will come into your house; if you come not into
Mine, I will not come into your house; In every place where I cause
My Name to be mentioned, I will come to thee and bless thee" (Exodus 20:21).[4]

The Properties of Miriam's Mysterious Well

While Jewish sages and commentators are of differing opinions regarding
the well of the Israelites being in fact Miriam's well, knowing the root of
its creation supports the conclusion that it is indeed Miriam's, and that its
function is restored through the merit that arises from the people's unity
following her death, when it stopped working. It is said that the mouth of
Miriam's well, which provided the Israelites with water throughout the Exodus,
was one of ten things created at twilight before the Sabbath of Creation.
That it was created just prior to the first Sabbath on earth, and that
the rituals of the Holy Place welcoming the Divine Immanence into one's
household are replicated on the eve of every Shabbat by the woman of the
household, makes the well a holy midwife, an expression of the water from
the holy Mother. We find in the Talmud and in midrashim fascinating
descriptions of this miraculous stone well that rolled, which is the symbol of
Binah, just as the staff of Moses is the symbol of Chesed (loving-kindness)
and the sword of Joshua (strength and judgment) is the symbol of Gevurah:

> The well that was with Israel in the wilderness has extraordinary properties.
> It resembled a rock the size of a beehive, from which, [like] a
> narrow-necked jug, water coming out in a trickle shot high up into the
> air like a geyser. The well rolled up mountains with Israel and went
> down into valley with them. Indeed, wherever Israel encamped, the
> well rested close by on an elevated spot opposite the entrance to the
> Tent of Meeting. The princes of Israel would come and walk around
> the well with their staves as they chanted the song "Come up, O well,
> sing ye unto it" (Numbers 21:17). At that the water welled up, rising
> high like a lofty pillar; and each of the princes, digging [into the
> ground] with his staff, channeled water toward his tribe and toward
> his family as it said: "The well, which the princes dug, which the

---

[4] B. Suk 53a. See also Bialik and Ravnitzky, *Sefer Ha-Aggadah,* 9:86, 183.

nobles of the people delved, with maces, with their own staffs" (Numbers 21:18). This miraculous well, which was actually a stone said to be in the Sea of Galilee waiting for Moshiach in order to be found, ". . . flowed in all directions throughout Israel's camp, watering all the surrounding wasteland. It branched out into streams so large that the Israelites would seat themselves in small boats and go visiting one another. [There was no need to row.] For a man who went upstream on the camp's right side would [as the current reversed itself] return downstream on the right side; and so it was with the man who set out on the camp's left side. Even the overflow of drinking water spilled on the ground became a wide river, which coursed toward the Great Sea and, upon its return, brought back from there all the things in the world that were desirable.[5]

Each story in Torah, in both the oral and written traditions, is a story about oneself. This marvelous description can be read as a metaphor of the blood going out from the heart to all the body parts and its return; it is also like the tide, or like our inhalation and exhalation. An archetypal story of the People of the Book, this pattern manifests in the dynamics of historical events. Kabbalah, as a system of correspondences, shows us how we are both earthly and heavenly beings; all the descriptions found in the Hebrew Bible apply to our own life experiences. The sages tell us that Torah speaks to us on various levels: literal, metaphorical, symbolic, and allegorical. Like the teachings on the five aspects of the eternal soul discussed at the beginning of this book, there is in each case a physical, emotional, intellectual, spiritual, and eternal aspect to the teachings of the holy book of truth that is Torah.

Spiritual Development in Binah: Becoming the High Priest

To fully grasp the dramatic stage of elevation in our personal and communal development and the essential joyousness we experience in being close to God as we reach the Sefirah of Binah, let us recall all that has been accomplished prior to this pivotal moment:

---

[5] Bialik and Ravnitzky, *Sefer Ha-Aggadah*, 5:14, 76.

In Malchut, at the bottom of the Etz Chayim, we pray, binding to all that has come before us in our individual lives and in the world's existence. This marks a departure from the past, giving us the desire to bow with thanksgiving and humility and the desire to attach to God. And so we begin with prayer and self-nullification in the world of action as symbolized by the feet and mouth. Speaking holy words of the heart is the foundation of humanity's sanctuary.

Next, we enter the Outer Court of the Ohel Moed to begin the process of consecrating our lives. Here we experience a six-part process of uniting our personal and collective attributes, the kingdom and its members: the generative organs, Yesod, representing our fundamental commitment to unity; the two legs, Netzach and Hod, the balance of enduring will and dedicated humility; the heart's throne, Tiferet, where beauty, justice and truth reign. We instruct the ministers we call our arms and hands, Gevurah and Chesed, to act with power and love, mercy and proper judgment. Upon completion of this process we are a united kingdom at peace, having crossed over the experience of doubt about our holy essence.

The initiate arrives in Binah fully consecrated, devoted to making each moment in life an act of sacred intention and attention. Now the initiate is prepared for the elevation that precedes illumination and total revelation. We are consecrated beings dedicated to the temple of body and soul. We have learned moderation—how to walk the middle path. We know how to use the practice of ritual animal sacrifice in the form of giving up our brutish, animalistic behavior, our arrogance, selfishness, and anger, our cowardice, dishonesty, and greed. We have dedicated our hearts and cleave to the Creator, as the fire does the coals upon which the incense of our prayers is offered at this stage in the Tabernacle ritual. We have practiced using our emotions in good measure for bringing harmony to all that we engage, both in our inner being and in the outer world. We have learned to eliminate that which is not holy from our lives, in the manner expected of the Levites and Kohanim who serve the holy Tabernacle. We know what it is to live with kindness and the desire to elevate ourselves and benefit others. Now, after the fire rituals of sacrifice and the water rituals of purifying our hands and feet, and having perfect motivation, we enter the Holy Place.

Refining the Senses

Binah is the Sefirah of elevation, the place where we engage the ritual instruments of shewbread, menorah, and incense inside the Holy Place. Having mastered our limbs, our ministers and workers, in the preceding seven Sefirot, we now progress to refining our senses and the talents they impart relative to divine service.

The senses are the tools through which the soul experiences pleasure from life in the body, in addition to their providing joy through service to divinity. Prophecy reveals itself though various sensorial experiences as well—for some through hearing, others sight, still others smell and touch. We see this in the different ways the various prophets received information from God:

> Some such as Ezekiel, prophesied through seeing, "I saw visions of God" (Ezekiel 1:1); Habakkuk, through hearing: "I have heard that which Thou hast made heard" (Habakkuk 3:2); Jeremiah, through the mouth: "The Lord touched my mouth . . . 'Behold, I have put My words in thy mouth'" (Jeremiah 1:9). Some, through the nose; "and spirit entered into me" (Ezekiel 2:2). Some though the hand: "By the hand of the prophets have I used similitude's" (Hoseah 12:11). Some prophesied in enigmas, and some in enigmas within enigmas."[6]

In Binah we encounter that aspect of our development in which we must perfect the guarding of our seven holy gates: what we see with our two eyes, or Chochmah (wisdom); what we hear with our two ears, or Binah (understanding); what we speak and eat with our mouth, or Malchut (sovereignty); and even what we smell with our nose, or Daat (knowledge). We use these holy gates as one does the rituals of the Holy Place—for elevating the body and soul. These sensory faculties are our garments of the priesthood. Having learned how to properly manage our emotions, which affect the organs they are attached to, we are now able to elevate the entire community along with ourselves, as all of our senses are anointed. The joy of the Mother, Binah, comes from receiving blessings *in order to share them with others*. It is a complete and

---

[6] Bialik and Ravnitzky, *Sefer Ha-Aggadah*, 8:73,476.

total nullification of the self that leads to higher forms of prophetic experience, where one's desire to receive is entirely the result of the desire to give. One becomes an emanatory, a shining light to others, at all times. Under this influence, men, women, and children become a nation of priests, the mandate God has given not just to Israel but to all of humanity.

Elevation in the Holy Place

The Holy Place and the corresponding Sefirah of Binah facilitates aliyah. What are we causing to ascend? It is the soul and the body united, inseparable until death. Each refined action of the body expresses the soul's effluence, which becomes, through our thoughts, words, and deeds, the revealed light. Just as the act of creation involved a withdrawing of the Creator from visibility, called the tzimtzum,[7] and resulted in a filling light that extended from the contracted point of light to create the world of form, so too our body holds within it a concealed light that is later revealed in our willed actions and in the functions of every body part, which are animated by the hidden life force within it. In other words, we are made in the image of God and are at any given moment of life a co-creator—whether we are consciously aware of this or not.

The encoded system of revelation inside the Holy of Holies (Chochmah) attaches itself to a vessel or receiver—in the Tabernacle metaphor, to the High Priest, or in the case of the individual initiate, to his or her elevated state of awareness and being. The refinement necessary to be such an adequate vessel for the filling light that emanates from the realms of Atzilut, so that we do not shatter from its intensity, can only be made possible by the spiritual awakening we have undergone in Binah and in the corresponding world of creation, Beriyah. Mastering our will and body in Malchut, our emotions in the six Sefirot of Zeir Anpin, we now discover, in Binah, the sublime root of our senses. Here, having discovered the spiritual root of the soul and the physical world through the intellect and its faculties, everything makes sense. And then, finally, in Chochmah, we become the Ark of the Covenant itself, embodying the

---

[7] See chapter 7, fn. 10, on page 226. This was necessary for the sake of Creation itself, for the bestowal of free will to mankind, and for the fulfillment of God's ultimate will in Creation, that is, to reveal Himself below.

teachings that are held therein. We and the Divine Immanence are collaborators, and the Holy Spirit uses the intuitive mind and sensory faculties of the intiate, the heart and the emotions, to broadcast divine light.

"Make Me a Sanctuary and I Will Dwell among Them"

Rebbe Menachem Mendel Schneerson (1789–1866), the third Rebbe of the Lubavitch dynasty, was a great leader of the Jewish people in Russia and the world. His epithet, Tzemach Tzedek, translates as "righteous sprout" or "righteous scion." One of the many works he authored is the *Derech Mitzvosecha* ("Way of Your Commandments") to explain the mystical reasons for the obligation of mitzvot, including the need for building a physical temple (Beit Hamikdash, "House of the Holy," בית המקדש) in Israel as well as the need for making one's own life a holy sanctuary. So first, let us examine the directive given by God to make a dwelling place for Him:

> And the LORD spoke unto Moses, saying: "Speak unto the children of Israel, that they take for Me an offering; of every man whose heart maketh him willing ye shall take My offering. And this is the offering which ye shall take of them: gold, and silver, and copper; and blue, and purple, and scarlet, and fine linen, and goats' hair; and rams' skins dyed red, and sealskins, and acacia-wood; oil for the light, spices for the anointing oil, and for the sweet incense; onyx stones, and stones to be set, for the ephod, and for the breastplate. And let them make Me a sanctuary, that I may dwell among them. According to all that I show thee, the pattern of the tabernacle, and the pattern of all the furniture thereof, even so shall ye make it." (Exodus 25:1–9)

The Tzemach Tzedek explains with great clarity that just as the will is not visible in the body except by its action, so too the concealed light of God is not known or seen except through the countenance of our presence and conduct. Building a temple, that is, making a holy place, whether it is a physical building or one's personal awareness, facilitates the redemption of humanity. Making one's life holy is a daily process of refinement for each human being. The will, the ratzon, expresses the soul's nature through love and the desire to be close to divinity, the desire to draw down the greater light from God so that we can be full of His glory. We see this as a divine life force that reveals itself in each world through its proper vessels. Our own actions determine the quality of the spiritual light we are invigorated by. When the people gathered together as a unified community just outside the Tent of Meeting for a holy purpose, it was the same as when they gathered together to request water of the well: they created a single vessel that the Creator then filled. This is like the individual's desire to come to God: in the realm of Yetzirah, that of formation, which corresponds to the Outer Court of the Tent of Meeting, it is in how we use our emotions to celebrate this relationship with deity; in the realm of Beriyah, the Holy Place, an even higher state of creation, it is in how we use our intellect and the faculties of the senses. While formation (Yetzirah and the Outer Court) takes what exists and refines it in a new way, creation (Beriyah and the Holy Place) takes an idea and manifests it out of nothing. This is the elevation that occurs at this stage. This is the power of co-creatorship. That is why until one has done the work of refining one's emotions, the power of co-creatorship by means of using the intellect to create in the world can be misused—as is so often seen in world history and in our modern world today.

The Tzemach Tzedek writes, "The fundamental intention [motivating the] the construction of the Sanctuary is that Godliness should be revealed within the . . . people. As it is written: 'And I will dwell among them': [Therefore] we were commanded to make [the Sanctuary] in a manner that corresponds to the pattern in which the different phases of influence within the spiritual cosmos are drawn from the essence of [God's] infinite light."[8] It is in exactly this fashion of observing correspondences that we are studying the various stages of initiation, consecration, elevation, illumination, and revelation, each being rooted in the worlds described by Kabbalists as interpenetrating fields of action, formation, creation, emanation, and limitless light. That which is above us is within us, and vice versa. The design of the Tent of Meeting and its Tabernacle is, as we know, a pattern designed specifically to reflect cosmic realities that in turn are represented by the various parts and purpose of the body, mind, and soul. This spiritual-physical connection is therefore found in all parts of a person's life. We know a person's will through what he does, which is the revealed light of God's infinite presence,

---

[8] Rabbi Menachem Mendel Schneerson of Lubavitch, *Derech Mitzvosecha*, 295.

even though we cannot completely see the concealed light surrounding the will of that person.

> The holy One, blessed be He, desired to have a dwelling in the lower realms that parallel the beginning of the downward progression of existence from the essence of God's infinite light, therefore He commanded that the Sanctuary (and similarly the Beit Hamikdash) be made following such a paradigm. "The curtains and the beams of the Sanctuary are representative of [both the sublime encompassing lights that transcend Atzilut and] the encompassing lights of Atzilut. The utensils reveal the inward lights that descend from the kav [the rays of light that emanate from God's original contraction before creation]. They represent the actual revelation of Godliness in every world. Thus with regard to the Ark, it is written (Shemos [i.e., Exodus] 25:22) "And I will make Myself manifest . . . between the two cherubs." Similarly, with regard to the [outer] Altar, Divine fire would descend upon it, and the Menorah is described (Shabbos 22b) as "testimony to all the inhabitants of the world that the Divine Presence rests within Israel."[9]

The Light of God

We can see the reality of the spiritual light and the material vessels that hold it in all of the Tabernacle's components. The light each part holds is determined by the purpose and design of the object itself:

> And thou shalt make a candlestick of pure gold: of beaten work shall the candlestick be made, even its base, and its shaft; its cups, its knops, and its flowers, shall be of one piece with it. And there shall be six branches going out of the sides thereof. . . . Their knops and their branches shall be of one piece with it; the whole of it one beaten work of pure gold. And thou shalt make the lamps thereof, seven; and they shall light the lamps thereof, to give light over against it. And the tongs thereof, and the snuff dishes thereof, shall be of pure gold. Of a

---

[9] Schneerson, *Derech Mitzvosecha*, 295. There is an inward light, or *penimi,* referring to the revelation of Godliness in every world according to its level, and an encompassing light, *Or makif,* referring to that which remains hidden and does not come into revelation but rather surrounds each person on all sides equally.

talent of pure gold shall it be made, with all these vessels. And see that thou make them after their pattern, which is being shown thee in the mount. (Exodus 25:31–32, 36–40)

We are told that the seven holy gates we master in Binah—the two openings of the eyes, ears, and nose, plus the mouth—correspond to the heavenly realms: "These seven eyes which are the eyes of the Lord, that run to and from through the whole earth" (Zech. 4:10)—"the seven lamps of the lamp stand correspond to the seven planets, which range over the whole earth."[10] Our senses, in other words, range over our entire lives. Just as the shewbread on the table remains warm from Sabbath to Sabbath as an expression of God's presence,[11] what we eat should be consecrated to God from week to week. The Tzemak Tzedek continues with his beautiful insights, telling us about the commonality in all encompassing lights (meaning that the source of the light is shared by all its different forms): "They are not entirely the same, for the form of encompassing light is determined by the nature of the inward light that emerges from it."[12] Both are needed. "All that God desired, he made" (Tehillim 135:6) refers to the encompassing light, and "the heavens were made through God's speech" (Tehillim 33:6) refers to the inward light. The inward light distributes itself in different parts of the body, in the limbs and organs, but the encompassing light holds the entirety as a single unit and is considered the primary source of life energy. The inward light is not revealed in a direct way in the human being; rather, it is concealed equally from the head to the foot, and part of it is revealed only indirectly through our thoughts, speech, and actions.

Divine Revelation and the Concealed Light

In Binah, corresponding to creation, one's entire being is present, awake, aware. This is the clear, reflective surface of the peaceful mind and heart,

---

[10] Bialik and Ravnitzky, *Sefer Ha-Aggadah,* 5:73, 86. The seven gates correspond to the seven planets of Mercury, the Moon, Saturn, Jupiter, Mars, the Sun, and Venus.

[11] Placed anew before Sabbath each week, the shewbread, when consumed just before the new loaves are brought in, remains as fresh and warm as when they were baked the week prior.

[12] Schneerson, *Derech Mitzvosecha,* 298.

wherein every movement, at all times, reflects the Divine Presence. At this point in our ascent of the Tree of Life, our appreciation for Adam Kadmon's archetypal design deepens. We see this inner light hidden in the body, in all its constituents, referred to as the ray that emanates from the soul. This ray of light in each soul affects the body and world in the same manner as the Creator affects His creation. The various elements of nature and the world each came into being for specific purposes. The brain, heart, and liver, called the "supreme regulators" of the human being, are created by the nature of our soul and are vitalized by the life we lead, whether positively or negatively. The rituals of the Hebrews reflect this dynamic of co-creatorship in terms of what we do with the body and soul. The life energy invested by the soul in a particular limb or organ depends on the qualities of that soul and its physical constituents, or inner vessels. Hence the inner vessels are transformed—either weakened or strengthened—by a person's actions.

The intellect of Binah rests within the brain, just as the emotions of Tiferet (including Chesed through Yesod) originate in the heart, which is Binah. The power of movement in the external limbs is done through the action of the blood (i.e., the liver) and the will. What we think, say, and do is processed through these organs, which are the vessels that hold the inner light emanating from Atzilut. Therefore the concealed light of Atzilut, and higher still, the Or En Sof, is revealed because there is a medium suitable for receiving it and a human being capable of utilizing it.

The Supreme Regulators

The three essential organs of life, the brain, the heart, and the liver, have their correspondences in the soul and in the worlds of Asiyah, Yetzirah, and Beriyah. This explains today's health-care crisis—meaning our spiritual crisis—as seen in the level of brain cancers, heart attacks, and liver diseases. This expresses an even deeper illness, in the soul-life of humanity, in the same way the demise of the bee from the earth at the beginning of this century tells us of a radical disassembling from the middle of the Tree of Life.[13] Might it be that humanity does not appreciate the holiness with

---

[13] Interestingly, the Hebrew word for bee, *devorah* (דבורה), appears only once in Torah, and it is in reference to the prophetess Devorah, who, of course, represents the middle pillar and the very center of the Etz Chayim.

which we are endowed, the great gifts emanating to us and from within us? Do we underestimate the power of our minds and hearts to improve the world, the power each of us has to become the High Priest? Don't we see that every place is made holy by our reverent natures?

It is the mind and heart brought together in praise and blessing that elevates everything in the holy place we call life. That is why among observant People of the Book one makes an effort to say a hundred blessings a day. The number 100 represents holiness as well as completion. Words with the value of 100 reveal some of the other hidden qualities of the Holy Place: **redeem,** יגאלנו; **dedicate,** ויחנכו; **king,** מלכי; **vessels,** כלים; **the waters,** המימה; **praise,** מודים; and **of thy bread** בלחמך. All these words are elements of the holy story of Binah.

In the historical progression from the Ohel Moed to the Beit Hamikdash (the First and Second temples and the prophesied Third Temple), the Ohel Moed, the tent of initiation, becomes the first Mikdash, the sanctified place where the elements of elevation—incense, menorah, and shewbread—are used, and where the Ark and its implements are installed. Later, the Temple in Jerusalem becomes the holy resting place of God. Once a person sanctifies his life in devoted service to God, he becomes a sanctified place of this indwelling presence, the Mikdash, a person in whom the Tabernacle and its constituent parts are housed.

The Ritual: Approaching the Inner Sanctum

Receiving an aliyah is like graduation: we go from being the Ohel Moed itself to being the Tent's inner sanctum, the Mikdash, the Holy Place, where the *rosh,* or head, the master of the kingdom, reigns over his kingdom, and the queen, the *lev,* or heart, reigns with charity and justice over her subjects.

Before and after presiding over the Outer Court rituals of fire and the offerings of thanksgiving, the Kohanim use the laver to purify their hands, that which does the ritual offering, and their feet, so that the holy ground they stand on is not contaminated. Thus their ministers, that is, their hands and feet, are purified, as is their speech by means of the prayers said during the purification rituals. The High Priest is then ready to enter the Holy Place (i.e., the initiate moves into the place of the heart), which is open only to the priests (our sanctified selves). Here is found the holy menorah that Betzalel made from one piece of gold, modeled on the exact image shown to Moses on the mount, which Betzalel could see in his heart's mind with perfection, as he had mastered the use of letters and was a man filled "with the spirit of God, with wisdom, with understanding, and with knowledge" (Exodus 31:3).

As we learned earlier, the Outer Court rituals invigorate the Nefesh aspect of the soul, the will that is in the blood and fibers of the person. It is the blood that comes to and from the four rivers (i.e., the four chambers of the heart), the Eden from which flows the vital animating life force sustaining the kingdom of the person. God's perpetual light feeds the soul through its physical vessels the same way partaking in Sabbath bread and other Sabbath ritual elements invigorate the soul of the person for the work of the week to come. As we shall see, the Sabbath itself is the embodiment of the entire Ohel Moed, as well as being the time of meeting God face to face in the inner sanctuary of one's own consciousness.

Lighting the Lamp of Devotion

The Holy Place is concealed by a special barrier called the Curtain of Testimony. The mind and heart are similarly concealed by the body in which they are hidden. By taking care that everything we do is done with careful attention and intention—the way the High Priest goes about his specific duties in the Holy Place—we can elevate anything we take part in, raise it up, and present this aliyah as an offering. In the same way, the mind and heart are revealed through our proper actions; in this way, when we keep the lamp of our devotion alive in our hearts, we come into the holy place of the sanctuary of our being.

After the seven-day period during which Moses erected the Tabernacle for the first time, the responsibilities of the High Priest fell upon Aaron. At this point, the Lord says to Moses, "Command the Israelites to bring you clear oil of pressed olives for the light so that the lamps may be kept burning continually [just outside the Curtain of the Testimony, separating the High Priest from the Holy of Holies], Aaron is to tend the lamps before the Lord from evening till morning, continually; an eternal decree for your generations" (Leviticus 24:1–3).

So too are we advised to light the lamp of devotion in our heart and limbs every single day and night, our prayers and consecrated actions taking the place of the actual rituals. Elevating our words, thoughts, and deeds by consciously intending to be of service allows the initiate to make his life a vessel for the Divine Immanence. This is the meaning of creating a sanctuary for the filling light that emanates from God's infinite light; this is the entire reason for our existence in the material world we co-create, just as it is the reason for the soul's temporary housing in a sacred body: to revel in the light of the divine.

The Instruments of the Holy Place

What do the sages say about the menorah, shewbread, and incense, the ritual instruments engaged by the High Priest in the Holy Place of Binah? These rituals are to prepare us for making direct contact with God in the Holy of Holies, between the wings of the cherubim, on the Kaporeth—analogous to ascending to Chochmah, the wisdom center, and then to Keter, the crown of our being.

The constant flames of the candelabra, the pleasing aroma of sweet incense, and the placing and eating of shewbread are ritual elements of the refined body and soul experienced through the sanctification and elevation of all the senses. In Chassidut it is said that a Jewish woman's Sabbath mitzvot includes all of these sanctifications, meaning Binah, the Mother, is their proper home. Lighting the menorah is akin to lighting Shabbat candles, which commemorate the light of Creation. The lamp stand is placed outside the Curtain of the Testimony of the Most Holy Place. Aaron, along with his sons, keep the lamps burning in the Lord's presence day and night. This ritual practice as a permanent law for the people of Israel is a teaching about the flame of our hearts being constantly kept alive to God's presence.

> It shall be a statute forever throughout your generations. He shall order the lamps upon the pure candlestick before the LORD continually. And thou shalt take fine flour, and bake twelve cakes thereof: two tenth parts of an ephah shall be in one cake. And thou shalt set them in two rows, six in a row, upon the pure table before the LORD. And thou shalt put pure frankincense with each row, that it may be to the bread

for a memorial-part, even an offering made by fire unto the LORD. Every Sabbath day he shall set it in order before the LORD continually; it is from the children of Israel, an everlasting covenant. And it shall be for Aaron and his sons; and they shall eat it in a holy place; for it is most holy unto him of the offerings of the LORD made by fire, a perpetual due. (Leviticus 24:4–9)

The shewbread ritual in the Holy Place, which represents the heavenly manna that sustained the Israelites, corresponds to the blessings of making and eating challah, Sabbath bread. In some families this consists of twelve braided small breads. Our sweet prayers, along with the aroma of Sabbath foods with their added spices, the scent of which we experience during the closing ritual of Shabbat, Havdallah, are pleasing to the Neshamah aspect of the soul, which is connected to the breath the Creator breathes into us at birth.

> *May my prayer be set before you like incense; may the lifting up of my hands be like the evening sacrifice.*
>
> PSALMS 141:2

The fragrance of the sacred incense of the Holy Place, which corresponds to the realm of Beriyah, the world of creation, invigorates the sense of smell and in turn facilitates aliyah. It burns continually throughout the day and night. Made of equal parts of four precious substances, the mixture is considered so holy that God forbids the Israelites from using the same formula outside the Tabernacle to make perfumes for their own use. In fact, doing so is reason to be excommunicated or cut off from the people (Exodus 30:34–38).

God said to Moses: "Take yourself—stacte, onycha and galbanum—spices, and pure frankincense: These shall all be of equal weight. You shall make it into a spice compound, the handiwork of a perfumer, thoroughly mixed, pure and holy. You shall grind some of it finely and place some of it before the Testimonial-tablets in the Tent of Meeting, where I shall designate a time to meet you; it shall remain holy of holies to you." (Exodus 30:34–37)

Symbolic of the Neshamah aspect of the soul in Beriyah, the incense also represents the smoke that rises from the fire of our devotion.

Once in the Holy Place of Binah, and further, in the Holy of Holies of Chochmah, we are able to access the part of the soul that arises after death. So like the Neshamah aspect of the soul that rises after bodily death, the smoke that comes from the fire rises above the ash of the burned incense. The seven holy gates of the soul are sanctified first by the Outer Court sacrifices, then by the priestly water ablutions, and then by the menorah, shewbread, and incense. Only then is the initiate prepared to engage the full glory of His name inside the Holy of Holies, represented by Chochmah, the upper Sefirah of the right pillar of the Tree of Life. At that point, by means of the filling light of His name, we can enter Keter and the Mercy Seat, the very apex of our journey back to our inherent Godliness.

Communal Elevation through Sabbath Rituals

By performing the Sabbath rituals in communal worship, by reading the Torah prayers about these holy rituals from the bimah (the elevated central platform in the synagogue from where Torah is read), the entire congregation is elevated. Sabbath, like a queen among women, is honored by Israel. In the same manner we are instructed to honor our father and mother: "Our Masters taught: There are three partners in a man: the Holy one, his father and his mother. When a man honors his father and his mother, the holy One says: I account to them as though I were dwelling among them, and they were honoring me."[14] This is a reference not only to the oral Torah of women and the written Torah of men, but to the union of the archetypal Father/wisdom and Mother/understanding. In this respect, the Holy Place and the Holy of Holies are inseparable, the Holy Place standing for the Mother and the Holy of Holies the Father.

In the union of Abba and Imma, Father and Mother, our eyes and our ears, our wisdom and our understanding, the rest of the house of Creation—our inner kingdom—is at peace. Life shows us how in families disunity between the mother and father can cause harm to their children and to others in the family, and this impacts the community. Once again we are

---

[14] Bialik and Ravnitzky, *Sefer Ha-Aggadah,* 2:638, 267.

reminded that Torah is a practical system of personal and collective guidance, and that all of Kabbalah guides one to self-observation and self-management as the chief method for embodying God's holy laws and wisdom teachings.

The Vestments of Soul and Priest

> And of the blue, and purple, and scarlet, they made plaited garments, for ministering in the holy place, and made the holy garments for Aaron, as the LORD commanded Moses. And he made the ephod of gold, blue, and purple, and scarlet, and fine twined linen. And they did beat the gold into thin plates, and cut it into threads, to work it in the blue, and in the purple, and in the scarlet, and in the fine linen, the work of the skilful workman. They made shoulder-pieces for it, joined together; at the two ends was it joined together. And the skillfully woven band that was upon it, wherewith to gird it on, was of the same piece and like the work thereof: of gold, of blue, and purple, and scarlet, and fine twined linen, as the LORD commanded Moses. And they wrought the onyx stones, enclosed in settings of gold, graven with the engravings of a signet, according to the names of the children of Israel. And he put them on the shoulder-pieces of the ephod, to be stones of memorial for the children of Israel, as the LORD commanded Moses. (Exodus 39:1–6)

The Kohen Gadol is attired in elaborate vestments and corresponding implements while performing the menorah, shewbread, and incense rituals in the Holy Place—just as we adorn ourself in the great and powerful garb of the elevated soul in the Sefirah of Binah. Following these Tabernacle rituals, he removes these vestments to don simpler garb as he enters the Holy of Holies. In the same manner, we go simply, without any sort of adornment, when we enter the Holy of Holies of the self, so that we may meet the eternal soul that is known through the heart and the mind.

Binah's partnership with Chochmah—it is said they never separate—is evident in the attire of the High Priest. While inside the Holy Place of Binah, where his body, mind, and soul are endowed with the Creator's joy and blessings as garments of splendor and beauty (Tiferet), the priest wears an elaborate and regal eight-part dressing called "the golden garments." This consists of the breast plate, ephod, robe (all three being unique to the High Preist), and the tunic, turban, belt, crown, and pants (Exodus 28:4). These are the eight special components that confer the station of Kohen Gadol on the one who wears them. Thus attired, the High Priest is the groom, and Binah, the Holy Place, the chamber of the Shechinah, is the bride. He then engages Her in performing the rituals of incense, menorah, and shewbread. Through our refined senses we too engage the Holy Spirit and the Divine Presence.

> In the tent of meeting, without the veil which is before the testimony, Aaron and his sons shall set it in order. . . . And thou shalt make holy garments for Aaron thy brother, for splendour and for beauty. And thou shalt speak unto all that are wise-hearted, whom I have filled with the spirit of wisdom, that they make Aaron's garments to sanctify him, that he may minister unto Me in the priest's office. . . . And thou shalt gird them with girdles, Aaron and his sons, and bind head-tires on them; and they shall have the priesthood by a perpetual statute; and thou shalt consecrate Aaron and his sons. (Exodus 27:21, 28:2–3, 29:9)

Year-round the High Priest ministers in the Tabernacle wearing the golden garments whenever he enters the Holy Place. On the Day of Atonement, Yom Kippur, however, the one day when he enters the Holy of Holies, he must change out of the golden garments and don "the white garments," described in Torah: "He shall put on the holy linen tunic, and he shall have the linen pants upon his flesh, and he shall be girded with a linen belt, and with the linen turban he shall be attired" (Leviticus 16:4). This simple white linen garb, consisting of tunic, belt, pants, and hat, is the same as that worn by the other priests who minister in the Outer Court. The High Priest is then ready to enter God's inner sanctum as a humble, barefooted man, his entire being—body, mind, and soul—united to serve the Creator, whose sublime essence resides within the holy Ark. So too with ourselves: when the heart and mind are united in the purity of devotion, our senses, being the soul's physical faculties, are heightened and sensitized. Every action, every perception, everything we engage in becomes an expression of divinity. After the Kohen Gadol's rituals inside the Holy of Holies are completed, and he emerges from the sanctum, his white garments are buried so that they are not reused by any other person.

> *Aaron will wear this robe whenever he enters the Holy Place to*
> *minister to the LORD, and the bells will tinkle as he goes in and*
> *out of the LORD's presence. If he wears it, he will not die.*
>
> EXODUS 28:35

There are many books and essays on the significance and composition of all the priestly items and implements, the study of which the reader is encouraged to pursue.[15] Like the eight-part priestly garb, our souls wear the eight-part powers of sight, hearing, and smell, which are each two-part vehicles, along with the singular vehicles of taste and touch. These are our garments of light. When we master our emotions, we can dress in the holy vestments of the High Priest.

Serving Divinity in Body and Soul

In the Holy Place of Binah, where we gain understanding that is illuminated by wisdom (the Holy of Holies and Chochmah), we use our limbs and heart as well as all of our senses in serving divinity. Whether it is what we see, eat, smell, or listen to, we are counseled to make sure the content is pure, holy. Here, the practice of seclusion of our senses becomes as important as seclusion of the body. We are to be selective when it comes to what we expose ourselves to, how we use our soul's sensory faculties—just as selective as the High Priest, who must use great care in serving the community through the duties of the Holy Place. Blessing everything we do before we do it is the secret to elevating our temporal experiences, as the essential power of Binah is to draw down God's blessings. Bless the present moment, and this simple act of consecration (Zeir Anpin) elevates anything we focus on.

The High Priest is secluded and consecrated for seven days prior to entering the Holy of Holies, which he does, as noted previously, only once a year. He evidences the eight-part refinement of the body and soul in the Holy Place of Binah in wearing the full regalia of the golden garments. But once he has entered the Holy of Holies, corresponding to Chochmah, he wears only the four pure-white linen garments, which correspond to the mastery of the four worlds of action (Asiyah),

---

[15] The Temple Institute, www.templeinstitute.org, has comprehensive writings on this subject.

formation (Yetzirah), creation (Beriyah), and emanation (Atzilut).

The High Priest is elevated by the golden garments; through these vestments God's presence is with him. The design of the breastplate, which details the twelve tribes, reflecting their birth order and placement in the camp surrounding the Ohel Moed (as discussed in the previous chapter) has divine origins. Behind the article called the ephod, (a richly embroidered vest or apron having two onyx gemstones on its shoulders and engraved with the names of the tribes of Israel) are the mysterious oracle stones called the Urim and Thummim, which are worn in a pocket over his heart. Thought to be an oracle of a binary sort, answering questions framed for yes and no, neither its physical makeup nor its operation is known for certain; nevertheless it is an integral aspect of the power that comes with the station of the High Priest, who is able to divine the truth in Binah.[16] As these oracle stones have never been found, their usage debated for centuries, what is important here is the notion that the High Priest had a divination tool helpful to those permitted to ask questions of it. For our purposes what this means is that we too are capable of divining any question's answer, especially if we frame it as a yes or no choice. Learning to listen to the voice of the Holy Spirit, a sympathetic participant in our lives established via the law of vibrational sympathy (like attracts like), is an art requiring that we attune to the energy of life all around us. In this way we are our own divining tool. Our senses, elevated in Binah, become a source of information for the intellect united with the heart, which is then capable of discerning meaning. When we elevate the body and soul, applying the senses and mental faculties to divine service as we do in Binah, we experience divine consciousness and the ability to thus divine the answers to our questions.

The Priestly Elevation

Returning to our focus on Binah's song of singing to the well, we note that it was not just Moses who was called on to speak to the well; it was necessary for *all* the people to speak together, in harmony, in order to

---

[16] Rabbinic tradition records that through the Urim and Thummim certain letters would light up on the breastpiece of the High Priest who could then form these letters into an answer to his questions. Some scholars believe that this was a form of divination by the use of lots.

create the merit needed to draw down God's blessings. In this sense the Israelites collectively performed the function of the High Priest. Just as this experience transformed the Hebrews, the Holy Place transforms the High Priest who performs the rituals that are secluded from public view, as he becomes a conduit for God, elevating the entire community to prepare them for direct contact with the divine in the Holy of Holies. This is why a person's ability to become God-realized is an aliyah for the entire community, and why prayer serves as that universal conduit.

For my house will be called a house of prayer for all nations.

ISAIAH 56:7

The word for elevation, **aliyah** עליה (Ayin [70] Lamed [30] Yod [10] Hay [5]), the central theme of the world of Beriyah (creation) and the Sefirah of Binah, has a numerical root of 115. So does the Hebrew word for "in their ears," באזניהם (**ozen**) . Remarkably, so does the word for the High Priest's **ephod** לאפד (Exodus 25:7). These kinds of beautiful inner correspondences discerned through gematria show us the concealed light shared by seemingly disconnected people, places, things, and events. In Kabbalah, the ears correspond to the Sefirah of Binah. That Binah and *in their ears/ozen* share the same numerical root tells us of their concealed relationship, since numerical values, the sages say, reveal the deeper teachings of Torah.

We know from our own experience that being able to say what we feel allows someone else to hear and then understand us. In general, Kabbalah shows us that women have extra Binah, the archetypal Mother—meaning greater intuition—than men. Such an endowment implies that women tend to have a higher level of understanding derived from heightened intuition, which explains why women have always assisted in bringing God's divine message to the world. During this time of birthing a new stage for humanity, the time of the Moshiach, their status as world leaders will become self-evident.

Other terms sharing the value of 115 are: **the people,** העם (Genesis 14:16); and **we,** אנחנו (Genesis 13:8). It is noteworthy that in the stages of prayer described earlier, the Shema brings the person into the Holy Place of him- or herself. Its very first words are an instruction: "Shemah Yisrael" (Hear, O Israel). This summons the Neshamah, the part of the soul that corresponds to Binah and the ears, inviting it to come to the Holy Place, so that we can bring the breath of God into harmony with our own breath in joyous prayer. This makes a person **strong,** חזק—another word with the numerical value of 115. Thus, by saying the blessings of the Shema, by listening to God in our life journey of self-refinement, guarding our soul's holy gates, we become an Israelite, the one over whom God prevails; we become the High Priest, who performs the rituals in the Holy Place.

In this stage of ascending the Tree of Life, the Israelites who sang to the well were collectively elevated. *Aliyah* refers not only to high places, but to stations of highest power such as that held by the High Priest. When we cultivate a holy meeting place for God within, when we enter our holy heart through prayer, cultivating a desire to attach to God, the entire world benefits by the spiritual strength that results from this effort. This teaching is, in fact, the conclusion of each of the five books of Moses, where the word *chazak,* "strong," is repeated: "Chazak, chazak! Venischazeik! Be Strong, be strong! And may we be strengthened!" This declaration emphasizes the will and desire that each person must exert to stay on the straight path to the One God of Israel, leading to personal and, ultimately, collective illumination.

From Consecration to Elevation

The Outer Court of the Ohel Moed, the place where we center ourselves and practice receiving the Holy Spirit inwardly, refines the flesh and the blood within us, the Nefesh, or life force and the spirit force, or Ruach. In consecration we make each action a holy action, committing ourselves to the good within, to elevating the sparks from the fire rituals and the self-sacrifices we make. By this the Ruach is strengthened. As we progress to the next level, the Holy Place, we elevate the Neshamah part of the soul, the part that is eternal and represents our higher sense of hearing or intuitive understanding. Representing Beriyah, the realm of creation, the Holy Place rituals are a link between our eternal soul and our mortal body. The Chayah aspect of the soul (related to acquiring wisdom) from the realm of Atzilut is perfected in the Holy of Holies, where once a year we experience the Yechidah, as the Or En Sof, the limitless light of Creation, which shines into the heart of the individual initiate, the congregation, or the nation.

The curtains that separate the Outer Court of consecration from the Holy Place of elevation are a resting place for the Shechinah's encompassing light. In fact, they are said to glow with this light. Likewise, our clothing can act as a place for the encompassing light to rest, the same as the vestments worn by the priests. From this we are to conclude that our clothing should be modest and protective of the holy body and soul housed within. We are to wear regal clothes for sanctification, such as those worn on the Sabbath, the day of the week reflecting the Holy of Holies and the Garden of Eden, toward which we are ascending.

In Tanya, chapter 53, it is said of the tablets housed inside the Ark that Godliness was revealed above; from there comes a downward progression of spiritual worlds, from Atzilut (emanation) to Asiyah (action). When we examine the deeper meanings underlying the many diverse elements of the Mishkan, we are being given a method for our own entry into the Garden of Eden, the "promised land" of a sanctified earth and reverent personal life. Arriving in this land means to arrive at the holy place of one's own heart. The land of Israel is called the Holy Place, the heart of the soul. Described in the oral teachings as the place where the world begins, with the rest of the world branching out and encompassing it, much like the way the tribes of Israel surrounded the Tent of Meeting in their encampments (see chapter 9, figure 9.3, page 329), the Promised Land is likened to the planetary heart, the Holy Ark of the earth. The heart is the source of the life force that invigorates the organs and limbs, which is why the heart is called Binah, the Mother. Thus the Mother—our intuition—is seated in the heart, on her throne, happy and in balance among all the other parts of the body. It is said, "The mother is happy seated among her children,"[17] which include her Son (Zeir Anpin, Chesed through Yesod) and her daughter, Nukvah (Malchut). In the Tree of Life, as in ordinary family life, the Mother is the connector between her children (all the Sefirot below her) and the Father (Chochmah). So too in the ritual practices of the Tent of Meeting: the Outer Court represents our outer actions, which spring from our inner emotions; once they are refined, we can enter the Holy Place of the heart, Binah. After we center ourselves through prayer, we consecrate our lives by steadily removing from it anything that is unhealthy for our

---

[17] Sotah 19a. See also this author's *Kabbalistic Teachings of the Female Prophets,* 116.

own, others', and the world's refinement. Then and only then are we are ready to use the intellect and heart in an elevating way, to uplift every person, idea, feeling, and moment.

The Power of Understanding

Beriyah, Binah, and the Holy Place instruments of menorah, shew-bread, and incense are all expressions of the power of understanding, the literal meaning underlying Binah בנה (Bet Nun Hay). The letter Bet suggests a container of some sort; that which holds life and death, and duality in general, as in up and down, day and night, in and out, and so on. Nun, in the middle of the word *Binah,* tells us of the proper nature of this vessel: its humility is its ability to make space for something to occupy it, as a pregnant woman does for her growing child within. The final Hay regards Binah as the life giver, as Hay always signifies the animator of life, the breath, and the Neshamah. Hay's numerical value of 5 is like our hands and feet, each with five digits, but when brought together in prayer make ten, showing us the elevation of our hands and feet through prayer. This value also points to the ten Sefirot, which are animated by the concealed light, and suggests why in Jewish law it says that ten men must be gathered together to form what is called a minyan, the minimum requirement for men, when reciting prayers—though it should be noted that a woman can pray effectively alone, once again showing the elevated status of women spiritually in the Jewish tradition.

And so we see that by performing the rituals that have correspondences in the body and soul, our neural networks and bodily fluids are invigorated. Like rivers and streams giving moisture to dry land in the proper season, hydration of the body is as essential as hydration of the land:

> Words of Torah are likened to waters: "Ho, everyone that thirsteth, come ye to waters" (Isaiah 55:1). As waters reach from one end of the world to the other, so Torah reaches from one end of the world to the other. As waters gave life to the world, so Torah gives life to the world. As water is given without cost to the world, so Torah is given without cost to the world. As water is given from heaven, so is Torah given from heaven. Waters are given to the accompaniment of powerful thunder.

So was Torah given to the accompaniments of powerful thunderings. As waters restore a man's spirit, so Torah restores a man's spirit. As waters cleanse a man from uncleanness, so Torah cleanses an unclean person from his uncleanness. As waters come down in myriad of drops and become a multitude of brooks, so are words of Torah.[18]

In Beriyah and the Holy Place, we see that the soul's vehicles in the material world—the ears, eyes, nose, mouth, and sense of touch—are juncture points by which the body and soul show themselves in unity. What we see, hear, taste, and smell can be experienced by others at the same time. What will not be the same is the way in which each person's body and soul responds to that sensory input. Here in the Holy Place, we practice using our intellect and refined senses and emotions for service in the world. In our own lives this manifests as a compassionate understanding of what each situation calls for, so that we may elevate its parts. This reflects a refined understanding of the living well, the Shechinah, which provides the essential waters of life.

The Song to the Well is the song we sing to God, our body and soul asking for His divine sustenance. We draw down blessings by performing our lives with joyful and holy intent. We leave Binah and the Holy Place having found the seat of wisdom that the prophet-king Solomon sought. Here in our heart, through our consecrated actions, we become the High Priest whose reverent nature, a combination of intellect and sensitive heart, is capable of elevating all of life. Safely prepared for the auspicious event of entering the Holy of Holies in Chochmah, we once again join the People of the Book as they leave Egypt behind, singing a song of jubilant revelation, having just crossed the Red Sea.

---

[18] Bialik and Ravnitzky, *Sefer Ha-Aggadah,* 7:22, 405.

Illumination

11
Crossing Over
Chochmah • Jubilant Song of Illumination

Second Sefirah: Chochmah
Meaning: Wisdom
Rung on Ascending Ladder: Nine
Archetype: The Father (Abba)
Symbol: The Ark of the Covenant and the staff of Moses
Spiritual World: Atzilut/emanation
Spiritual Anatomy: The eyes in the head
Inner Quality: Self-nullification (bitul)

Historical Representatives: B'nai Yisrael crossing the Red Sea
Text: Song at the Sea: Exodus 15:1–29
Key Words: Bestowal, the Ark
Key Emotion: Jubilation (shir)

Tent of Meeting: Holy of Holies
Spiritual Stage: Illumination
Spiritual Practice: Direct conversation with God
Illumination: The illumination of vision

Demonstrating complete and total trust in God, the Israelites, led by Moses, wade into the sea, eliminating all doubt in God's providence and supreme rulership.

The Sefirah Chochmah: The Wisdom of the Father

A man's wisdom maketh his face to shine.

ECCLESIASTES 8:1

Chochmah, the Father, or Abba, stands for wisdom. Anatomically, this Sefirah is represented by the eyes. Chochmah receives the shine of God's limitless light, the Or En Sof, directly from the crown/Keter and thus is in the realm of Atzilut, emanation, where being enveloped in the direct shine of the Creator's presence, one experiences enlightenment.

Chochmah is the partner of Binah, the Mother; the two do not separate. These two Sefirot balance the all-knowing, instantaneous perception that is the spark of origination (Chochmah) with intuitive understanding (Binah). From this we discover that it is the combination of both whole seeing and intuitive perception, male and female attributes, that leads to knowledge (the Sefirah of Daat, which represents the knowable aspect of Keter). Like the High Priest who enters the Holy of Holies to be illuminated by the presence of the Shechinah that settles on the Ark and the veil surrounding it, the initiate enters the inner sanctum of the Tabernacle of the self to come into direct contact with God, to be filled by His Holy Spirit. This is in essence the betrothal chamber of God and humanity, male and female, Shechinah and Ruach HaKodesh, for the purpose of serving the Creator and the created.

It is through the wisdom of Chochmah, as manifest in the radiant Cloud of Glory and Pillar of Fire that guides the Hebrews throughout their Exodus, that Israel is protected during the crossing of the Red Sea. This crossing marks the end of the Hebrews' exile in Egypt and the beginning of their consecration as a nation, which prepares them for their sacred journey and the receiving of Torah. This process of transformation represents the spiritual phenomenology being studied in this book: the Israelites go from a 430-year period of enslavement to freedom, with the turning point represented by their jubilant Song at the Sea, in which the women, led by Miriam, and the men, by Moses, sing out after the miracle of crossing the Red Sea.

Torah, the teachings lived and studied by the People of the Book as received by Moses, is equated with water. Moses' own relationship with God is described by a short parable that uses water as a metaphor: "How may the give-and-take between Moses and the Lord be illustrated? By the parable of a cave situated at the edge of the sea. The sea rises and fills it. Henceforth, the waters of the sea flow freely into the cave, and the waters of the cave into the sea. So, too, [was the give and take between Moses and the Lord]: 'The Lord said unto Moses.'"[1]

Just as water sustains our physical life, Torah nurtures and protects the observant person's spiritual life. Just as Moses was the central axis during the Exodus, around whom the peoples' lives were prophetically guided, the Tabernacle where Torah was housed stood at the epicenter of the twelve tribes of Israel wherever they camped, and its teachings directed their way of life as they do the observant Jewish person of today. From Moses and the Ark, both Torah and divine water come forth.

They [Israel] were encamped around the Tabernacle in a circle whose perimeter was four thousand cubits. Moses, Aaron and his son, and their families were to the east of the Tent of Meeting. The well, which was near the tent of Moses at the entrance to the Outer Court of the Tabernacle, indicated to the tribes where they were to encamp. How did the well do it? In this way: After the hangings for the court of the Tabernacle were put in place, the twelve princes stationed themselves at the well and uttered the song "Spring up O well." At that, its water would spring up and presently form many streams. At first, only one stream encircled the camp of the Presence [i.e., the Tabernacle]. Out of this one stream, four streams flowed toward the four corners of the court of the Tabernacle, where they joined, thus encompassing the entire camp of the Levites, as well as coursing in between the area to be occupied by the Levite families. Areas—squares of dry land circling

---

[1] Hayim Nahman Bialik and Yehoshua Hana Ravnitzky, *Sefer Ha-Aggadah*, 5:128, 100.

the camp of Presence—[were] thus set apart from living occupancy. Then a larger stream encompassed the perimeter of Israel's entire camp. Its waters formed themselves into a number of streams, which flowed between every two tribes, encompassing them inside and out, marking off throughout the areas squares of dry land, thus outlining the boundaries of each tribe. The stream made all kinds of good things to grow for Israel. Their cattle grazed just beyond the encampment— the cloud that spread over Israel separated them from their cattle. Because of the cloud's radiance of blue, the streams sparkled with the reflection of dawn, of the moon, and of the sun. Hence the peoples of the world, sighting them from many mil [miles] away, would extol them, saying, "Who is this shining like the dawn, beautiful as the moon, clear as the sun?" (Song of Songs 6:10).[2]

Exactly like the way the shining water encircles the Israelite encampments in this description, Chochmah, the Sefirah of wisdom, emanates as a brilliant radiance seen in the countenance of the initiate, hence the names of Kabbalah's great books: the Bahir, "The Shining Light," and the Zohar, "The Radiant Light."

The emotional quality of the Song of Chochmah is jubilation. And how could it be otherwise? Like the jubilee that occurred every fifty years in Eretz Yisrael, when land was returned to its prior owner and slaves set free, it is an accomplishment of arrival, of coming to the fiftieth gate of wisdom, forty-nine of which Moses opened for the world. Kabbalah teaches that these fifty "gates" are represented by the seven weeks between the time the Israelites left Egypt and fifty days later, when they received Torah on Mt. Sinai. During these seven weeks, the lower seven Sefirot of the Tree of Life were the framework for self-refinement. These forty-nine aspects of self-refinement are reflected in the traditional forty-nine-day practice called the Counting of the Omer (Sefirat HaOmer), during which Jewish people count seven weeks—seven times seven days—to refine themselves individually for the receiving of Torah to commemorate the historial event this ritual honors. As a Kabbalistic practice, all forty-nine days are represented in the Tree of Life. Using the seven middot, or Zeir Anpin plus Malchut, the practitioner

<hr>

[2] Bialik and Ravnitzky, *Sefer Ha-Aggadah,* 5:82, 89.

counts in this manner, beginning on the second night of Pesach. Thus the first night and day is the Chesed of Chesed, the second is Gevurah of Chesed, the third Tiferet of Chesed, and so on through Malchut of Malchut on the forty-ninth night and day.[3] The observant person is to meditate on the qualities expressed by these sefirotic combinations (i.e., the Chesed of Chesed is supreme beneficent love, whereas the Gevurah of Chesed would be restricting that love with proper limits). This ritual counting, with its opportunities for reflection, self-refinement, and associated blessings, culminates on the holiday of Shavuot, when the congregation of Israel reaccepts Torah. In such a manner, year after year, century after century, the Jewish people celebrate the receiving of Torah on Mt. Sinai by their own annual reacceptance of its teachings and obligations.

Crossing the Red Sea, departing the realm of doubts and fears represented by Egypt, and arriving at Mt. Sinai, the place of reveling in the light of God's presence, mark two connected events that are represented by Chochmah and its song and its corresponding aspect in the Tabernacle, the Holy of Holies. In Chochmah, the initiate inherits the illuminated treasures of God-consciousness. One earns one's freedom and gains the bestowal of God's emanation. At this point, with a balanced mind and heart, a holy marriage having been made between the body and soul, one has but one last rung of the ladder to ascend to become a completely God-realized human being. Jubilation, indeed, the quality of song (shir) attributed to Chochmah, is the appropriate emotional quality, but one whose foundation is made through total self-nullification, or bitul, in this Sefira.

The Value of Wisdom

Chochmah, or wisdom, חכמה (Chet Caf Mem Hay), has the same numerical value, 73, as the word **prophetess,** הנביאה (Hay Nun Bet Yod Alef Hay), as referenced in Exodus 15:20: "Miriam the **Prophetess,** sister of Aaron, took the drum in her hand and all the women went forth after her with drums and with dances. Miriam spoke up to them, 'Sing to HaShem for He is exalted above the arrogant, having hurled horse with its rider into the sea.'" Here, the numerical connection between these two words can be found in the very situation described in the

---

[3] See this author's *Kabbalistic Teachings of the Female Prophets,* 64, fn. 38.

song of Chochmah. Miriam's wisdom, therefore, and the well water that was bestowed in her merit (as described in chapter 10) is connected to the time when she leads the women in song after crossing the Red Sea. This tells us that we must master our emotions, the lower waters, and our intellect, the upper waters, before we are properly prepared to receive the direct illumination of God. Just as we do not stare directly at the sun or it will blind us, the brilliant prophetic luminosity of Moses as he descended Mt. Sinai required that he cover his face, for it was too bright for the people to gaze at. This analogy suggests one reason why the High Priest does not linger inside the Holy of Holies, under the direct emanation of the Mercy Seat illuminated by Keter, where the prophet is given wisdom and is filled with the light of the Godhead. Chochmah, in the realm of Chayah, that part of the soul related to our ability to see, to acquire wisdom, and which does not reside within the body but rather remains connected to the body from its supernal root, is a bridge to transcendence in the realm of Yechidah (corresponding to Keter and Adam in the Garden of Eden). It enables each person to "cross over" to their divine inheritance in the World to Come as well as in the world now.

My son, be wise, and make my heart glad.

PROVERBS 27:11

The power of the Divine Immanence is experienced in Chochmah, conferring on the person divine insight. The entirety of God's angelic kingdom depends on this emanation as well: "Samuel said to Hiyya bar Rav: . . . Each and everyday ministering angels are created from the fire river, utter song, and then cease to be, as is said, 'Because they are new every morning, [the praise of] Thy faithfulness is great'" (Lam. 3:23).[4] It is also said that the angels are kept alive by their prostrations before the splendor of the Presence. If this is so for the angels, how much more so for the human being.

The Seventy-two Names of God

One of Kabbalah's most profound alchemical formulas, which describes Moses' mastery of himself and nature, can be found in three crucial

---

[4] Bialik and Ravnitzky, *Sefer Ha-Aggadah,* 1:73, 513.

verses from Exodus. This text is composed of 216 Hebrew letters, including three verses each of seventy-two letters:

> **19** And the angel of God, who went before the camp of Israel, removed and went behind them; and the pillar of cloud removed from before them, and stood behind them; **20** and it came between the camp of Egypt and the camp of Israel; and there was the cloud and the darkness here, yet gave it light by night there; and the one came not near the other all the night. **21** And Moses stretched out his hand and his staff over the sea; and the LORD caused the sea to go back by a strong east wind all the night, and made the sea dry land, and the waters were divided. (Exodus 14:19–21)

Through a particular way of combining these Hebrew letters, the seventy-two names of God[5] are derived. I believe that these seventy-two names represent the dominions that preside over the twelve signs of the zodiac and the twelve tribes of Israel.[6] The 72-letter name of God, Shem ha-Mephorash (שם המפורש), or Tetragrammaton, plus the one Creator that it represents makes for the number 73, the numerical value of Chochmah, as described above, suggesting that in wisdom we find the presence of God fully articulated. The reader will marvel at how the entirety of God's presence, known through these seventy-two alchemical processes, is expressed in the description in Exodus of the crossing of the Sea of Reeds (i.e., the Red Sea). That the alchemical source of Creation, the seventy-two names of God, can be found in that part of the Israelites' narrative that we are now exploring in Chochmah, and that this story combines the power of the Cloud of Glory and the staff that Moses uses to split the sea shows us that all the wisdom, from the moment of Creation, rests in Chochmah. The light of Creation shines on the High Priest and each one of us when we make sincere atonement, as on Yom Kippur, when we participate in reuniting with the divine emanation that illuminates our minds and hearts, rectifying our lives and bringing us closer to the Garden of Eden.

---

[5] See appendix 4, "The Seventy-two Names of God."
[6] Since the 1980s I have developed a correspondence system between astrology, color, sound, the dimensions of space, and the 72 names of God, with plans for future publication.

Wisdom is beyond mere faith, as one can see with one's own eyes the light of the Divine Presence inside the Holy of Holies. It is likened to the inner spiritual eye that is open: once we engage divinity in its wholeness and splendor, we know it is possible to attain this experience again. Having discovered that our senses are tools of the soul, that they are refined in the the Holy Place and in the world of creation, Beriyah, we now no longer need to rely on either our senses or our intellect, but can totally immerse ourselves in the essence of God. So in Chochmah, rather than studying God, perceiving Him through some kind of intellectual filter, we experience direct contact with Him in the corresponding part of the Tabernacle, the Holy of Holies. Not every person can have this kind of prophetic experience, but for some it is a very real and vital part of one's life experience. Though it seems all people have some kind of awakening at the time of their death, what a person experiences depends on whether one chooses to live a reverent life full of divinity, strengthening the divine soul, or a limited, egoic life, shaped primarily by the desires of the animal soul in the material world.

The Song of Chochmah: Jubilation in Song (Shir)

He led them through the depths as through the wilderness.

PSALMS 106:9

The parting of the Red Sea is so momentous for the Israelites and the world of its time that even to this day men, women, and children study this historical event, which shows the omnipotent power of the Creator to alter the course of natural phenomena.

Recall that at this point the Israelites have just embarked on their Exodus. God has directed them to take a roundabout route out of Egypt to avoid a confrontation with the Philistines, as well as to transform and educate them by testing their faith, teaching them a new way of life and its attending obligations. Pharaoh regrets having allowed them to leave and personally leads a massive army of Egyptian cavalry and war chariots. He closes in on hundreds of thousands of Hebrew men, women, and children assembled at the banks of the Sea of Reeds (a.k.a. the Red Sea), pressing them to the water's edge. The sages teach that the tribes began fighting over the dangerous privilege of being the first to enter the sea. While they were arguing, the Mishnaic sage Rabbi Meir Baal Hanes, (the miracle maker) and student of Rabbi Akiva, says that Benjamin (the matriarch Rachel's youngest son and the brother of Joseph [Yosef]) sprang forth and "won the privilege of becoming host for the Almighty [in the holy of Holies], as is said, 'He dwelleth between the shoulders'" (Deut. 33:12). Another sage of the same stature and time period of Roman rule, R. Judah (also known as Judah the Prince), claims that the entire tribe of Judah sprang into the sea, explaining their later heightened inheritance in Judea and why "Judah became his Sanctuary, Israel His dominion" (Psalms 114:2).[7] What is certain, though, is the manifestion of God's presence: the Pillar of Fire separates the Israelites from the pursuing Egyptians during the night before crossing the sea, and then the Cloud of Glory goes before the people and hovers over them in this dramatic moment, casting them in radiant light, while spreading a veil of darkness over the Egyptians. The Israelites are entirely hemmed in as the waves crash at the water's edge, when God speaks to Moses, ordering him to split the sea with his staff. Then, as the last of the Israelites cross through what is described as two glass walls—referring to the passageway made in the middle of the sea by waters held back—the first Egyptian warriors follow in hot pursuit. At this moment, the waters of the sea rush back in, as Moses again holds out his staff at God's command, swallowing the entire army. On the opposite shore, the awestruck Israelites, led by Miriam and Moses, offer a humble yet jubilant song of praise and thanksgiving as they sing the Song at the Sea, the song of Chochmah.

Surrendering Completely to God

We will do and we will hearken.

Exodus 24:7

Wading into the rough seas at the decisive moment when Moses raises his staff is the ultimate act of trust required of the Israelites. This shows us that at some point in our own development we must overcome the

---

[7] Bialik and Ravnitzky, *Sefer Ha-Aggadah*, 4:82, 73.

compelling power that our emotions and our rational mind have over us in order to surrender completely to God. With our faith unwavering, with fear no longer in control of us, God becomes our true leader. For the ancient Hebrews, passing this test was a necessary preparation for the trials and the miracles to come.

We too are capable of parting the waters, separating our emotions, the lower waters, and the upper waters of the intellect, and walking between them, free of their influence. The Holy of Holies is the still place in our awareness that is undisturbed by any emotion, desire, or thought. In this state we are both present to and immersed in the radiance of the Divine Presence. It is where we and the Shechinah become one, making it possible, as Joshua shows us in chapter 8, to collaborate with God as a master over nature. In this state of bestowal, we receive the single filling light of God, as occurred in the tzimtzum, or contraction that took place before God created the world, which produced a single ray of light that extended downward through the worlds. It is this same ray of light that the Cloud of Glory issues to indicate the direction in which the tribes are to travel or where they are to camp; this is also the light that separates the Israelites from the Egyptian army the night before they cross over the Red Sea. This holy shine penetrates and illuminates the entire human anatomy, both physically and spiritually, in the Kadosh HaKadoshim (the Holy of Holies), elevating us above the influence of nature—the true meaning of freedom and free will.

Chassidic tradition says that each event in the Hebrew Bible expresses an aspect of the Creator and likewise an aspect of the human being. The crossing of the Red Sea is said to be a "garment" that God put on to make His presence known. As the Jewish sages teach,

> "For he hath clothed me with garments of salvation" (Isaiah 61:10), with the seven garments that, according to scripture, the Holy One will have put on successively from the day the world was created until the day He requites wicked Edom. When he created the world, He put on glory and majesty. When he appeared to us at the Red Sea, He put on pride. When He gave the Torah to His people, He put on strength. When He requited the Chaldeans, He put on vengeance. When He will have forgiven the iniquities of Israel, He will put on a

white garment. And when the Messiah appears, God will be clothed in righteousness.[8]

The holy garments of righteousness, like the golden and white garments worn by the High Priest, are not gained without sacrifice. In this Sefirah, one gives up any preconceived notion of what is or is not possible in the manifest world. What if the Hebrews, standing at the edge of the sea, were immobilized by their initial logical questions such as, "How can we cross over with the waters over our heads?" or "How is it possible to walk through water?" or "Why should we risk drowning?" These are the kinds of questions that arise from a mind of doubt, which Chochmah overcomes. Chochmah is the ineffable experience of knowing with inner certainty. It knows experientially, not through an intellectual lens. Just as seeing oneself in a mirror one knows instantly that the reflection is of oneself, so too in Chochmah we instantly recognize the truth in its entirety, absent either inductive or deductive reasoning.

God's Instructions to Moses

Traditionally it is said that the "children of Israel were redeemed from Egypt because of four meritorious acts: they did not change their names, they did not change their language, they did not reveal their secrets,[9] and they did not abandon circumcision."[10]

Here, at the edge of the Sea of Reeds, with the Egyptian army and its chariots closing in on the 600,000 Hebrew men and their families, Moses calls out to God for help. The Lord responds, telling Moses, "Why do you cry out to me? Speak to the children of Israel and let them journey forth! And you—lift up your staff and stretch out your arm over the sea and split it; and the children of Israel shall come into the midst of the sea on dry land" (Exodus 14:15–16).

---

[8] Bialik and Ravnitzky, *Sefer Ha-Aggadah,* 4:79, 386.

[9] "Secrets" refers to their having been told they would leave captivity with some of Egypt's gold and silver, which they did because the Egyptians gave it to them to encourage their departure. They collectively refined their male (the sun, gold, rational) and their female (the moon, silver, intuitive) aspects; through this process, male and female were to be equal (balanced).

[10] Bialik and Ravnitzky, *Sefer Ha-Aggadah,* 4:73, 71.

When we are afraid to do something unknown, we can prepare ourselves first by becoming centered in our breathing. Then with the mind we can still our emotions, knowing with absolute certainty that everything is in divine right order—including and perhaps especially difficult situations. The truth is that everything is for our elevation. Having cultivated humility, we can form a clear intention to do what we are being called to do, face what we are being asked to face, using our powers of observation to determine the best way to proceed. To do this we must first surrender to the will of the Creator by attaching to His presence. We can see the reflection of God's beneficence in the clear and shining sea of the heart and mind. We use Torah's holy guidance to overcome fear, knowing that if one stays attached to the truth of God's holiness within, all obstacles will be overcome. Our fears and doubts will sink to the bottom of the sea, and we will arrive at our destination safely. Is this not in fact what God promises the Israelites? Do His holy instructions in Torah not tell us what the reward will be for believing in Him and His Word?

> But when you cross the Jordan and settle in the land the Lord thy God is giving thee as an inheritance, He will give thee rest from all thy enemies around thee so that ye will live in safety. Then there shall be a place which the Lord the God shall choose to cause His name to dwell there. There ye shall bring all that I command thee; thy burnt offering, and thy sacrifices, thy tithes, and the offering of the hand, and all thy choice vows which ye vow to the Lord, And ye Shall rejoice before the Lord the God, ye and thy sons, and thy daughters, and thy menservants, and thy maidservants. (Deuteronomy 12:10–12)[11]

A Song of Crossing Over

The declaratory praise and thanksgiving of the Song at the Sea, Shabbat Shira ("Sabbath Song"), sung by the people after the miracle of the crossing of the Red Sea, is recited annually on the Sabbath that falls before or on the minor holiday of Tu B'Shevat, the New Year for Trees

---

[11] After Moses receives instruction from God about the law and how to interpret it, he comes back down to the people and starts hearing cases and judging them for the people, but this quickly becomes too much for one man. Upon the advice of his father-in-law, Yitro (Jethro), Moses institutes a judicial system (Exodus 18:13–26).

(the season in which the earliest-blooming trees in the land of Israel emerge from their winter sleep and begin a new fruit-bearing cycle). On this occasion, the Torah portion that includes this song of crossing over is an assurance that God will reward the people with peace. When we unite our inner kingdom with our outer life, we become the holy nation, the holy kingdom, the holy place. The one law, or the Law of One, is an awakening for all of humanity and the essence of the messianic age we shall inherit, which is represented by Adam in the Garden. By first gaining wisdom, we are prepared for this eventuality: "The world endures because of three activities; study of Torah, divine worship, and deeds of loving-kindness."[12]

Traditionally it is said that this song was taught by Moses, who sang it phrase by phrase to the people, who, like students, would then repeat the words after him. In this fashion, every phrase was repeated twice. It is also said that even an unborn child in his mother's womb, upon hearing these verses, can also sing this song, and like the rest of Israel, can thus experience the Divine Presence hovering above.[13]

The Song at the Sea (Shirat HaYam): Exodus 15:1–27

🌿1 *Then sang Moses and the children of Israel this song unto the* Lord, *and spoke, saying: I will sing unto the* Lord, *for He is highly exalted; the horse and his rider hath He thrown into the sea.* 2 *The* Lord *is my strength and song, and He is become my salvation; this is my God, and I will glorify Him; my father's God, and I will exalt Him.*

3 *The* Lord *is a man of war, The* Lord *is His name.* 4 *Pharaoh's chariots and his host hath He cast into the sea, and his chosen captains are sunk in the Red Sea.* 5 *The deeps cover them—they went down into the depths like a stone.* 6 *Thy right hand, O* Lord, *glorious in power, Thy right hand, O* Lord, *dasheth in pieces the*

---

[12] Avot 1:2.

[13] Bialik and Ravnitzky, *Sefer HaAggadah*, 4:89, 74. "R. Akiva expounded: When Israel came up from the Red Sea, the holy spirit rested on them, and they sought to utter song, How did they utter their song? In the manner of an adult who leads in reciting the Hallel in the synagogue, while the congregation responds by repeating each verse of each psalm. Thus Moses said, 'I will sing unto the Lord.' (Exod. 15:1), and Israel responded, 'I will sing unto the Lord.' Moses said, 'The Lord is my "strength and song"' (Exod 15:2), and Israel responded, 'I will sing unto the *Lord*.'" (Sefer Ha-Aggadah 8:129, 483; Yalkut Be Shallah 241)

enemy. **7** *And in the greatness of Thine excellency, Thou overthrowest them that rise up against Thee; Thou sendest forth Thy wrath, it consumeth them as stubble.* **8** *And with the blast of Thy nostrils the waters were piled up—the floods stood upright as a heap; the deeps were congealed in the heart of the sea.* **9** *The enemy said: "I will pursue, I will overtake, I will divide the spoil; my lust shall be satisfied upon them; I will draw my sword, my hand shall destroy them."* **10** *Thou didst blow with Thy wind, the sea covered them; they sank as lead in the mighty waters.* **11** *Who is like unto Thee, O* LORD, *among the mighty? Who is like unto Thee, glorious in holiness, fearful in praises, doing wonders?* **12** *Thou stretchedst out Thy right hand—the earth swallowed them.* **13** *Thou in Thy love hast led the people that Thou hast redeemed; Thou hast guided them in Thy strength to Thy holy habitation.* **14** *The peoples have heard, they tremble; pangs have taken hold on the inhabitants of Philistia.* **15** *Then were the chiefs of Edom affrighted; the mighty men of Moab, trembling taketh hold upon them; all the inhabitants of Canaan are melted away.* **16** *Terror and dread falleth upon them; by the greatness of Thine arm they are as still as a stone; till Thy people pass over, O* LORD, *till the people pass over that Thou hast gotten.* **17** *Thou bringest them in, and plantest them in the mountain of Thine inheritance, the place, O* LORD, *which Thou hast made for Thee to dwell in, the sanctuary, O Lord, which Thy hands have established.* **18** *The* LORD *shall reign forever and ever.* **19** *For the horses of Pharaoh went in with his chariots and with his horsemen into the sea, and the* LORD *brought back the waters of the sea upon them, but the children of Israel walked on dry land in the midst of the sea.* **20** *And Miriam the prophetess, the sister of Aaron, took a timbrel in her hand; and all the women went out after her with timbrels and with dances.* **21** *And Miriam sang unto them: Sing ye to the* LORD, *for He is highly exalted: the horse and his rider hath He thrown into the sea.* **22** *And Moses led Israel onward from the Red Sea, and they went out into the wilderness of Shur; and they went three days in the wilderness, and found no water.* **23** *And when they came to Marah, they could not drink of the waters of Marah, for they were bitter. Therefore the name of it was called Marah.* **24** *And the people murmured against Moses, saying: "What shall we drink?"* **25** *And he cried unto the* LORD; *and the* LORD *showed him a tree, and he cast it into the waters, and the waters were made sweet. There He made for them a statute and an ordinance, and there He proved them;* **26** *and He said: "If thou wilt diligently hearken to the voice of the* LORD *thy God, and wilt do that which is right in His eyes, and wilt give ear to His commandments, and keep all His statutes, I will put none of the diseases upon*

thee, which I have put upon the Egyptians; for I am the LORD that healeth thee."
27 *And they came to Elim, where were twelve springs of water, and three score and ten palm-trees; and they encamped there by the waters.*

The Ritual: Entering the Holy of Holies

Chochmah corresponds to the Holy of Holies, where the Ark of the Covenant containing the Ten Commandments, the Torah, Aaron's staff, and a container of manna are protected. This is where God tells Moses to come in order to speak to Him, and where the Kohen Gadol, on Yom Kippur, makes restitution for the transformation of the entire community. The priestly facilitator, having previously sacrificed a male goat in the Outer Court, having performed water purification rituals and the Holy Place rituals of menorah, shewbread, and incense, is now prepared to enter the innermost sanctum of the Tabernacle.

This is a sacred mission fraught with potential danger should the High Priest arrive unprepared or harboring any impure thoughts or incorrect motives. For this reason he is guarded, fed, and taken care of for an entire week prior to entry. As well, there is a back-up priest available just in case the designated High Priest is unable to enter the Holy of Holies because of ill health, or, God forbid, that he dies before entering or while inside the holy precinct, preventing the proper offerings and prayers from being made. The priest is instructed to be brief in his prayers while inside the Holy of Holies so that the community outside will quickly know that their High Priest lives, that their atonement is acceptable to God, and that their intercessor has not died inside the sacred chamber from the impact of the intense, penetrating light emanating there.

It is true that God is our partner, protector, and leader, but in times of danger we are counseled not to expect miracles without our own willing participation. Essentially, we each have our own part to do, while God has His.[14] In the signal historical occasion of Moses splitting the Red Sea, he is told that he has the ability to change the world of nature by using

---

[14] The deeds of loving-kindness are analogous to the worlds of action; we "do the deed" (the realm of Asiyah); we form the deed with right intention, the world of formation (Yetzirah); we act with the purpose of elevating the world, as in elevation (Beriyah); and illumination and emanation (the realm of Atzilut) is the shine that comes to the world, the doer, and the beneficiary of the good deed.

his staff. In other words, the light of wisdom (Chochmah), understanding (Binah), love of truth (Tiferet), strength and courage (Gevurah), love and compassion (Chesed), will to victory (Netzach), humility and glory (Hod), devotion to God's covenant (Yesod), and spoken prayers (Malchut), once combined, are much more mighty than the forces of nature. In the same way, the initiate, as the High Priest, must enter the Holy of Holies—his innermost sanctuary—completely elevated as a humble, purified being. Once he attains divine revelation he should not try to remain in this state for long, for the power of the limitless light is so great it can overcome a person and force the soul to eject from the body. We understand that there is a purpose for this level of illumination: it is not for our personal enjoyment, something for our ego to become attached to, but for the benefit of all others. Once we are completely nullified of any selfish desire or need, we become the empty vessel, a suitable conduit for the highest powers to fill. One speaks to God and God answers. One basks—but not indefinitely—in the glorious light of His presence. In this way the person is completely remade in His image.

Atonement as a Form of Wisdom

The Day of Atonement, Yom Kippur, occurs on the tenth day after, but including, the New Year, Rosh Hashanah, and marks the time when an observant Jewish person takes inventory of his life's actions and those things he might have done but chose not to do, for better or worse. It is a day reserved for atonement and repentance, making peace with God and honoring God's presence in all other people and in all of creation. It is preceded by a week plus three days of atonement—a time of reckoning, of returning borrowed things, of apologizing for hurtful words or actions to others. Taking responsibility for oneself in this manner confers the wisdom that allows us to know how to behave in all situations. We know that all is one, and that we are connected to all wherever we stand, for where we stand is holy. We also know that the eternal divine soul is housed inside a temporal body. The physical body, like the Ohel Moed, is a reflection of God and is called the Tzelem Elo-him, or "Form of God." This form of God is reflected in the Sefirot of the Tree of Life within us.

The inner soul and the rituals of the Tent of Meeting fill us with God's infinite light from the Or En Sof (Keter/crown), illuminating the

Sefirot that constitute our physical and spiritual anatomy. This inward illumination is called the Demut Elohim, the "image of God." Chochmah endows us with the pleasure of divine union, which the Chayah aspect of the soul, the living essence within us, is native to. Chayah allows us to love God with all of our being, the foundational declaration in the Shema prayer: "You shall love the LORD your God with all your heart, with all your soul, and with all your might " (Deuteronomy 6:5). This living presence of God is near to us. In Moses' final instructions to the people, as we learned in chapter 9, there is a renewal of the covenant, warnings against idolatry, the prophesied repentance and redemption of the people, and a reminder that the teachings and commandments God gave the Israelites are not kept in the skies or across the seas, but rather "this thing is very near to you, in your hearts and in your soul, to observe it" (Deuteronomy 30:11). Following this clue to our inner sanctum of worship, Moses continues: "See—I have placed before you today the life and the good, and the death and the evil, that which I command you today, to love the Lord, your God, to walk in His ways, to observe His commandments, His decrees and His ordinances; then you will live and you will multiply. And the Lord, your God, will bless you in the land to which you come, to possess it" (Deuteronomy 30:15–16).

Here in Chochmah we learn that the eternal Chayah part of the soul that is never in the material body but attached to it, surviving the body's death (unlike the Nefesh and Ruach aspects, which do not), is like the initiate's experience in the Holy of Holies, which is an eternal experience meant for every living person to know—that it is near to us; in fact, it is already within us. Therefore, each human being is a potential Holy of Holies. The unity of mind and heart, body and soul, the individual ego entirely nullified, allows us to cultivate the right conditions for this sort of divine illumination and prophecy of the highest degree. Recall that the realm of Nefesh (Malchut) represents our instincts and actions; the Ruach (Chesed through Yesod) our emotions and how they are reflected in our actions; and the Neshamah (Binah) our intellect and hence our thoughts. In Chochmah and the realm of Chayah we experience wisdom's truths. This is the bridge to complete transcendence in Keter, the realm of Yechidah, where the initiate is entirely transformed into an ascended master in ecstatic oneness, Creator and created united. In that ultimate place of illumination, one becomes Adam Kadmon, completely self-nullified and completely self-realized.

The Ladder of Light

In biblical times, the sanctified High Priest, before entering the Holy of Holies, would go through an elaborate routine of dressing and undressing, ritually immersing himself, and redressing (see Leviticus 16). On the occasion of Yom Kippur he would wear five different sets of garments, including three golden and two white linen sets of vestments, alternating in sequence between the Outer Court, the Holy Place, and the Holy of Holies for the performance of the various rituals associated with each chamber (see chapter 10, figures 10.1 and 10.2, pages 339–40). He would immerse himself in the mikvah five times and wash his hands and feet ten times during the day-long ritual. The sacrifices made on this day prior to his entering the Holy of Holies would include two daily lambs, one bull, two goats, and two rams, with accompanying *mincha* (meal) offerings, wine libations, and three incense offerings (the regular two daily offerings and an additional one for Yom Kippur). The priest would then enter the Holy of Holies three separate times. Surrounded by the reflective surfaces that curtain the golden Ark, the High Priest would then be at the very center of a radiant cube formed by the symmetrical dimensions of the holiest place in the sacred Tabernacle. Each of the priest's visitations into the innermost sanctum is likened to climbing a rung higher on the ladder of light, because each encounter leads the priest to greater and greater holiness, purity, and intensity of emanation.

Note that the word for ladder, *sulam,* סלם (to lift up, to exalt), occurs only once in Torah: "And he dreamed, and behold a ladder set up on the earth, and the top of it reached to heaven; and behold the angels of God ascending and descending on it. And, behold, the LORD stood beside him, and said: 'I am the LORD, the God of Abraham thy father, and the God of Isaac. The land whereon thou liest, to thee will I give it, and to thy seed'" (Genesis 28:12–13). As a description of the process of revelation from the bottom of the Tree of Life to the top, we see this as an ongoing process of going up and down, between the soul below and the heavens above, and that this ladder, the metaphor often used for the Tree of Life, unites heaven and earth; thus the ladder (*sulam*) of light (*ohr*) is a process of ongoing descent and ascent. In our physical anatomy, the spine is this ladder of light, the central path, the middle cord of balance. Thus our anatomy shows us how every aspect of the Israelites' experience can also be seen as a description of our many incarnations and life journeys.

The middle way is the path that Moses teaches. In the Ohel Moed, as we saw in chapter 7 on Tiferet and the prophetess Devorah, the middle path is the path of balance that enables us to climb the ladder of light; leaning to either side creates an imbalance, making the ladder—that is, ourselves—unstable. This is moral instruction, physical instruction, and spiritual guidance.

Our spine, like the ladder Jacob dreamt of when he called the place he was standing holy, reaches the bowl of heaven, that is, the cerebellum. While we live we are at all times a body and soul designed to speak directly to our Creator, who is both within us and all around us. The function of the cerebellum, like the Ark that houses the Ten Commandments, is to protect the contents of His inner chamber. When we can climb above our personal dramas, we gain clarity about our holy place in the world, finding that where we stand is holy and that what is around us and within us is holy, and that this—this being alive—*is* the journey to the Promised Land that each soul desires.

A Time to Be Brief

There is a parallel relationship between the biblical splitting of the Red Sea and the High Priest's performance inside the Holy of Holies: just as the High Priest is instructed to keep his prayers brief, so too is Moses. Standing on the banks of the Red Sea, fervently praying to God, the prophet is nudged by the Holy One: "My beloved[s] are on the verge of drowning in the sea, and you spin out lengthy prayers before me." Moses replies, "But Master of the Universe, what else can I do?" God answers, "Speak unto the children of Israel, that they go forward, and lift up thy rod."[15]

Our sages tell us that God's directive to Moses to be brief, to "speak unto the children of Israel, that they go forward," speaks for our own lives. While we draw down the light from the realm of Atzilut in the Holy of Holies, we are to stand in this powerful emanation only long

---

[15] Bialik and Ravnitzky, *Sefer Ha-Aggadah,* 4:82, 72.

enough to benefit from the presence of God so that we can turn this into action, because an illuminated one takes action for the benefit of the whole community. The example of Moses also tells us that in times of calamity, do not stand around praying and waiting for miracles, but rather take action and know with certainty that God manifests through our limbs and our hearts.

Ritual Tool: The Staff of Deliverance

Moses' power object, his staff, which also translates as "rod," accompanies him throughout his journey of leading the Israelites. After using it to split the Sea of Reeds, we find Moses, with the help of his brother, Aaron, and Hur (Moses' companion, the grandfather of Betzalel), holding up the staff in the war against the Amalekites, as described in chapter 8. This is the same staff Moses uses when he strikes the rock for water, as described in chapter 9, which causes him to be banned from entering the Promised Land. It is also the same staff that Elisha uses to resurrect a child (2 Kings 4:29) and the staff carried by David when he slays Goliath. And so we see from the oral tradition in Judaism, this staff has a long and illustrious history, having been handed down through the millennia since it was first bestowed on Adam when he left the Garden of Eden.

The word for staff, or rod, *matteh,* מטה (Mem Tet Hay), is also translated as "tribe," suggesting that the staff of Moses is a scepter of power over the tribes, just as our own enlightened connection to the God within enables us to come into harmony with divine right order in all parts of ourselves. This sacred staff is a specific form of God's providence that is invested in each one of us. In a certain sense, the staff is an instrument for separating and controlling the upper and lower waters, the mind and emotions. When we are in union with the divine, everything we act on can be made holy and complete.

We learn of this holy power object in the oral tradition when Moses comes into possession of it; he is the only one who is able to retrieve it from the ground in Jethro's garden. The next time it is highlighted is when Moses encounters the burning bush, and God tells the prophet of his duty to emancipate the people from Egypt (Exodus 3:16–20). Moses fears that the Hebrews will not know he has been empowered by God's orders, and so God, demonstrating the power of this staff, tells Moses to throw it down, and it subsequently turns into a snake. Told to grab its tail, Moses does, and the snake (said to be the same snake as the one in the Garden of Eden) returns to its form as a staff, which some sages suggest was made not of wood, but of sapphire (Exodus 4:3–4).

This power object was inscribed, according to Kabbalists, with the forty-two names of God (different from the 72-name sequences), as well as the names of the ten plagues, six of which Moses intiated with his staff, and four of which were cast by God directly. It is said that this staff was created at twilight before the first Sabbath, making it a tool of Creation. It was given to Adam by God as he left the Garden, and Adam gave it to Enoch, followed by a succession of holders, vital biblical figures who each mastered the alchemical formulae inscribed on it. It eventually came into the possession of the Midian priest Jethro, who was to become Moses' father-in-law, who, after taking it from Pharaoh with his permission, carried it home and planted it upright in his garden. Thereafter only Moses was able to read its insignia and its operating instructions; he was thereby able to remove it from the garden—a prerequisite for being granted Jethro's daughter Zipporah in marriage.

The staff represents our own anointed consciousness; when we are illuminated by the light that is the source of Creation, as in Atzilut, we inherit the power of life and death that is guarded by the cherubim and the flaming sword on the east side of the Garden of Eden that protects the Tree of Life. We become immortal souls in a resurrected, eternal body of light. As a facilitator of transformation, this holy staff comes from Adam, the progenitor of all the prophets (whom we will encounter in our next chapter on Keter). Here in Chochmah we learn that the two tablets God gave Moses, which are housed inside the Ark of the Tabernacle, the supreme transformer, are also inscribed in our own hearts. Likewise, the two hemispheres of the brain are inscribed with the names of the Creator and the powers of Creation. Each one of us, like Adam, Moses, and the High Priest, is thus fully equipped with God's blessings for self-mastery and mastery over nature.

Kabbalah shows us that all that is externalized in the journey of the Israelites is internalized in every human being. In this historical narrative we see the influence of the majesty of the Creator's design, from the supernal realms to the atoms that comprise the cells of His created beings. The Ark and its tablets symbolize the mind and the heart in union. The emotions are refined through the ritual acts performed in the Ohel Moed. In Chochmah we receive the direct presence of God, the Yod in his divine name, HaVaYaH (Yod Hay Vav Hay). The Ten Commandments and the numerical value of Yod, which is also 10, are both commensurate with the perfection of Creation, with which the High Priest makes direct contact on Yom Kippur. Every power object and power place, every person and every drama in the Hebrew Bible are states of being that we each embody. Whether we are righteous or selfish determines the course of each person's life story. This lesson is the legacy of all the prophets. Freedom can be gained by using all of the tools the Creator has put at our disposal. The staff of our endowed vision—that which we rest on, over which we have command, from which we gain our royalty and our prophetic insight, is a miraculous tool of divinity.

Spiritual Development in Chochmah

At this stage in the initiate's spiritual development, progressing into the Holy of Holies, we begin to grasp all the preparation that has gone into strengthening the initiate for illumination. Here in the Sefirah of Chochmah, marking the next-to-last stage of the initiate's progress up the ladder of light, the Israelites are about to face their greatest test of faith as a people at the beginning of their journey. Can they put aside their fears, trust in God and their leaders, and wade into the rough currents of the sea, even though life experience tells them they will surely drown?

Water refers to divine energy or beneficence. The letter Yod in the name HaVaYaH (Yod Hay Vav Hay, or YHVH), the most sacred of the names of God—which is unpronounceable—is synonymous with the Sefirah of Chochmah, the inseminating Father. The Father (Abba) issues forth, and the first repository of his holy seed of Yod is his partner, the Mother (Imma, the Sefirah of Binah), represented by the first Hay in God's name. Therefore, Chochmah, as manifest in the light of the Holy of Holies, illuminates Binah, the realm of creation, with the direct shine of the Creator from the realm of Atzilut (Chochmah and Keter), the realm of emanation where one experiences complete enlightenment. This is the illumination of the mind and heart. Wisdom, Chochmah, is a deep inner knowing of the whole that requires no analysis. It illuminates Binah, the intellect, giving us divine insight. We then take these teachings and apply them to our emotional development as expressed by the Vav in God's holy name and the archetypal persona of the Son. The Chazal tell us that God's presence at the Sea of Reeds is represented by the final Hay in the name HaVaYaH. It is produced by the gathering of the water of the seas through Malchut, the daughter of Binah.[16]

Such a Kabbalistic interpretation shows us how we find deeper, hidden meanings in biblical stories by looking at the inner components. Crossing the Red Sea is synonymous with rectifying the Tree of Life, an immersion by all of the people into the holy waters, the mikvah of the Creator's beneficence. It is a unification of His name, YHVH, which enables a person to enter into a state of perfect unity consciousness in Chochmah, which in turn is made eternal when we enter Gan Eden in Keter and the realm of Yechidah. Crossing the Red Sea is thus the illumination of the body, mind, and soul that has been brought into direct contact with God consciousness. That the song of Chochmah, the crossing of the Red Sea, and the Holy of Holies are all connected in this way tells us that the Ark and its contents represent the receiving of Torah that will occur fifty days after the Israelites leave Egypt, and that the three boxes comprising the Ark, one inside the other, house the Shechinah. The Torah, the tablets, the manna by which the Israelites survive, and Aaron's rod are held together within the Ark as four divine objects, suggesting the perfection of the four worlds of Asiyah, Yetzirah, Beriyah, Atzilut—or the perfection of the observant person in his Ohel Moed.

Heavy is the burden of exile; it outweighs
all other divine afflictions.
SEFER HAAGADDAH, 4:1

The Israelites show us that wading into the engulfing waters of the sea means being willing to surrender entirely to the overwhelming power of God. Exile, like all concealments of the light, is for a purpose. When we surrender entirely to the loving and wise care of the Creator, we open to the miracle of becoming an enlightened human being. We leave the

---

[16] R. Yitzchak Luria, *Apples from the Orchard,* 357.

enslavement of attachment, doubt, and personal desire and arrive at the truest inner freedom, the freedom that comes from being attached to the eternal Divine Presence.

In their Song at the Sea, the Hebrew people did not celebrate the drowning deaths of the Egyptians and their horses. Rather, they sang to God for His victory. They had witnessed the miracle done in their behalf, and their jubilation was mixed with a humble reverence for being spiritually and physically attached to God in this way. This is what is also asked of the High Priest as he enters the Holy of Holies on Yom Kippur. We too are asked to metaphorically cross the waters—the Red Sea, as the Israelites did in this case, and the Jordan River at the end of their Exodus. Both events represent the two stages of the Israelites' birth as a nation; both are water purifications that bring about a new state of consciousness—that of complete trust in being one with God.

Making God Contact

Reaching this stage of our spiritual development requires a long and specific course of practice. To review: We begin in prayer in Malchut, entering into an intimate relationship with God. In Yesod we cry out to the beloved in this covenant. In Hod one gains a certain luminary position from being humble, which makes prophecy possible. Netzach confers on the one learning consecration the willing endurance it takes to stay the course. In Tiferet the initiate learns greater balance, that of sweetening judgment with mercy. In Gevurah we further separate ourselves from all that is unworthy of our higher goals and assets. In Chesed we are bound up in loving union with the Creator. All this preparation leads to what comes next: in a single leap of faith, emunah, which we gain from Binah, we enter the Holy Place of understanding, with the menorah, the shewbread, and the incense representing the soul's sense faculties, which are engaged and enlivened in order to elevate the body and soul in preparation for the illumination and bestowal in the Holy of Holies, and after that, for revelation at the Mercy Seat.

The Holy of Holies is both an arrival and a departure point. It is an arrival in the realm of Atzilut, emanation, telling us of its lofty nature. It is a departure point into the deeper sanctum of the Holy of Holies, a secret kept by Moses and the High Priests—or the one who makes contact with the Divine Immanence through progressive self-refinement. When we are prepared properly in body, mind, and soul, the gateway is opened for us and we enter the inner sanctum, a holy meeting place within that is protected by our soul's guardians. Here we are one with God. We are not attached to either image or idea; instead, a loving breath on the wave of the supreme deity's waters of loving-kindness envelops us. This is what is referred to as enlightenment, the "land flowing with milk and honey" (Exodus 3:8) each human is intended to inherit.

Enlightenment

Certainly on the day of one's death one experiences a certain kind of enlightenment: the sense of knowing what one's life was for, what was gained, what was lost. In this way the personal revelation about one's embodied life is made clear. This is a death-born revelation. Yet, such a state of transcendental awareness is also available to us while we live in the body if we make a conscious ascension. Such a divine insight into the deeper mysteries of the eternal within the mortal can be realized when the initiate becomes the illuminated High Priest. It is this pursuit that has been the preoccupation of people in all the world's various sacred traditions over many centuries. It is the soul within that seeks to connect with the source of its creation while the body lives. It is this effort that charges the atmosphere of one's life, invigorating the fields of Asiyah, Yetzirah, Beriyah, and Atzilut where we each have multidimensional existence, making God-contact possible. These continuous interpenetrating realms of existence of body and soul, consciousness and heart, wisdom and action together represent the supreme chariot of God. This is our own interstellar and intercellular odyssey, with departures and arrivals, short trips and long ones, explorations and restorations. Life's adventures have a purpose, and when we direct them toward closeness with divinity, we are given the great privilege of discovering and living our destiny.

In Chochmah, the next-to-last Sefirah in our ascent to Gan Eden, we are but one step away from total and complete absorption in the holiness of the Divine Immanence. In Beriyah, the realm of creation as expressed by the Sefirah of Binah, we experience the importance of the bestowal from above to below in the form of Miriam's well, with its life-giving waters available wherever the Israelites travel. Here in Chochmah we declare ourselves the beneficiary of the emancipator, God Himself, the King in whose presence we now stand. As fully consecrated guardians of the Ark, we have been initiated into the inner sanctum of our being, the holy temple of the mind and heart united, where truth is like a king and queen sitting side by side on their thrones. We have graduated from our initiation through prayer; from the six stages of consecration in the Outer Court activated in the fire sacrifices of animal and agricultural products and water purifications; and from the Holy Place and its elevation of the senses through the menorah, shewbread, and incense. Each stage is an aliyah. Now the entry into the Holy of Holies, the last chamber, is open to us; it is the gateway to our own inner wisdom, the portal to our own Sanhedrin, our own inner circle of sages illuminated by the teachings of God. This is the overflow of the concealed light becoming the revealed light in all that we do. The Ark housing the Ten Commandments, Moses' scroll, the jar of manna, and Aaron's rod comprise a holy record of a life lived close to God. All of these attributes, refined, elevate the initiate to the place of being at one with God and God's Word.

Preparing for Illumination

Moses is told that God will come to speak to him inside the Holy of Holies, from behind the veil, and that His voice will come from above the lid of the Ark, between the wings of the two cherubim. Through this example of Moses we are being instructed on how to speak to God: we must do all the necessary preparatory work revealed by the ten Sefirot of the Tree of Life, as explored in each chapter of this book. By diligently making an effort at self-refinement, the body-soul field of the initiate is conditioned, making one fit to receive and reveal the Divine Presence.

Upon offering the jubilant Song at the Sea, the Israelites and the mixed multitudes,[17] everyone who has survived the passage out of Egypt, embark together on the next stage of their spiritual evolution, entering an unknown land with an unknown plan. They have been told that God has promised them an inheritance of land, but that is not a lot to go on for a people so hard-pressed for survival. Nevertheless, they continue their journey, and later, as beneficiaries of many miracles, they experience

---

[17] This refers to Egyptians and others who chose to leave Egypt with the Hebrew people, who were circumcised per Joseph's orders. Moses calls them "his people."

collective revelation at Mt. Sinai, when all of the people hear the Word of God. Yet only Moses at the mountaintop, like the High Priest in the Holy of Holies, is called into direct, face-to-face contact with God.

Arrival at Divine Consciousness

This stage of ritual in the Tabernacle, represented by Chochmah, occurs when the High Priest—that is, the individual initiate—enters the Holy of Holies, the smallest, innermost chamber of the Tabernacle where the golden Ark is stationed. Here the person experiences the radiance of the crown (Keter) illuminating the Holy Place veil that separates it from the Holy of Holies. The veil conjoins the seven gates of Binah (the eyes, ears, nose, and mouth) with the Ark, which is akin to the higher mind linked to the soul of the initiate. The person now stands directly before the Ark, the conductor of the higher holy emanation of Atzilut. The Ark is protected by the shining veil on which the Shechinah rests. Like the face of Moses that shone from his encounters with God, the Ark is the face of the Tent of Meeting; like Moses' face, it requires a veil to protect the viewer from the intense luminosity. In fact, the Veil of Testimony, as it is called, as well as the curtains on the other three sides of the Ark, separate the Holy of Holies from view on all four sides. In a similar way, our soul is surrounded by its protective sheath, which is the body of each person. Standing before the Ark, the initiate experiences the holy presence behind the veil and is suffused with light. It is an illumination that comes from the tablets contained within it and from the spark of lightning-like fire that arcs between the wings of the two cherubim.

The living human being's soul is filled with the light of God's divine spirit, which animates the Nefesh, the vital force in the blood; the Ruach, the spirit; the Neshamah, or soul of breath; the Chayah, the living presence; and then finally the Yechidah, the spark of God each soul originates from. Like a stellar alignment in the cosmos, this is an alignment of all the parts of a person's body, mind, and soul. Just as the Holy of Holies is separated from the Holy Place by the Veil of Testimony, so too, our higher consciousness is always near us yet hidden behind a veil imposed by our sense of being an individual self, separate from others. Here in the holiest domain of the Tabernacle, the finger of God writes on each soul the ten utterances of Creation, the ten Sefirot and all that they confer on humankind. The anointed human experiences divine consciousness.

And it came to pass, when Moses came down from mount Sinai with the two tables of the testimony in Moses' hand, when he came down from the mount, that Moses knew not that the skin of his face sent forth beams while He talked with him. And when Aaron and all the children of Israel saw Moses, behold, the skin of his face sent forth beams; and they were afraid to come nigh him. And Moses called unto them; and Aaron and all the rulers of the congregation returned unto him; and Moses spoke to them. And afterward all the children of Israel came nigh, and he gave them in commandment all that the LORD had spoken with him in mount Sinai. And when Moses had done speaking with them, he put a veil on his face. But when Moses went in before the LORD that He might speak with him, he took the veil off, until he came out; and he came out; and spoke unto the children of Israel that which he was commanded. And the children of Israel saw the face of Moses, that the skin of Moses' face sent forth beams; and Moses put the veil back upon his face, until he went in to speak with Him. (Exodus 34:29–35)

When we arrive at the Holy of Holies in our own sanctuary of being, it is a place of communication with God. While there, we do not need to hide any part of ourselves—represented by the fact that the High Priest enters the Holy of Holies in bare feet, wearing the simple white linen garb of the Outer Court priests, though the garments woven for the High Priest and used by him on just this one day a year, the Day of Atonement, are buried following the ritual. We too can bury our past errors, making them the source of our "at-one-ment," the condition of absolute, loving harmonization between individual consciousness and God's presence. But when we come out of this state of consciousness, oftentimes the truths learned are teachings that should be veiled, if revealed at all to others. Some inner experiences are meant to be private engagements between oneself and God; but when we return to the community and daily life, the change that experience has effected within us, the wisdom gained, is meant to be used to benefit others. In this way the initiate who has ascended to the heights of Chochmah becomes like the Ark in the Holy of Holies inside the Tabernacle wherever he or she goes—a portable sanctuary of the Divine Presence, like that of the ancient Hebrews.

The Anatomy of "Crossing Over"

There are many physiological counterparts to the various parts of the Tabernacle, which I leave to others to elucidate. Certain striking correlations between our body elements and the Tabernacle are the overall structure of this book, but a few others are worth noting as well, such as the fact that the hypothalamus, pituitary, and other glands are activated through particular hermetic practices. The two lobes of the brain, whose separate functions, like two walls of water, are "crossed over" with something akin to arc lighting, are like the sparks of fire between the wings of the cherubim atop of the Ark, whose influence results in ecstatic joy and divine revelation. As all things from world to world are related in octaves of similar form, and since we human beings reflect the supernal pattern, then our physiological processes, down to each cell and atom, should reflect a similar divine holy template as described by the People of the Book's spiritual and physical odyssey.

Guarding the Sacred Essence

Having entered the Holy of Holies, the initiate accepts the sacred honor of guarding the Holy Ark and its contents: the tablets, Torah, the rod of Aaron, and the jar of manna. In this way the now-illuminated initiate, invigorated by the glow of the Shechinah and the shine of Her love, is able to protect the holy heart of truth and its wisdom. Here, the heart, mind, body, and soul cross the sea together as the water rises up like a wall, pulling back the dim lens associated with lesser levels of prophecy. God speaks to the prophet, and the prophet speaks to God.

Gates can block the view, but once they are opened one can see clearly the path ahead. Our every action is part of creating and then illuminating a clear path. Our every thought, word, and deed is part of the soul's record in the body. That we use our soul's faculties of seeing (Chochmah) and hearing (Binah) to do this work of self-refinement reflects certain teachings about our lives: "Rabbi [Judah I, the third-century patriarch] said: Consider three things, and you will not fall into sin. Know what is above you: a seeing eye, a hearing ear, and all your deeds recorded in a book."[18]

---

[18] Bialik and Ravnitzky, *Sefer Ha-Aggadah,* 2:241, 562; Avot 2:2.

The Song at the Sea, sung in triumphant jubilation by the nation of Israel at having been spared death, at nature having changed its course as a result of God's intervention, becomes a public testimony, a consecration of everyone who made it out of Egypt. It is an acknowledgment of the bestowal of God's presence. Here the Israelites are sanctified on dry land as the sea closes up behind them. From here they embark on the journey to the Promised Land, having taken ownership of their hard-won freedom. From this we learn that with autonomy comes responsibility: the free person has an obligation to master the self. With elevation and illumination comes an even greater degree of self-nullification.

Gaining Wisdom through Self-nullification

So what do we do with freedom when we gain emancipation from our fears, our hesitations, our frailties, and our habits? According to the sages, we turn to the wisdom of the Holy Book: "Ben Bag Bag said: Turn to it, and turn to it again, for everything is in it. Pore over it, grow old and gray over it. Do not budge from it. You can have no better guide for living than it."[19] When we integrate wisdom, we are inseparable from it: "Rava said: All bodies are sheaths. Blessed is he who is privileged to be a sheath for Torah."[20]

> *O Lord my God, Thou art very great.*
>
> PSALMS 104:1

Wisdom, the Sefirah we arrive at as we enter the Holy of Holies, is acquired through a process of cultivating the ground of our being: "The following three are of equal importance: wisdom, fear of God, and humility."[21] Self-nullification, bitul, is the essential inner experience of Chochmah. To receive wisdom, we must humble ourselves completely, giving up our fear and our belief in anything except for the power of the Creator. "R. Joshua ben Levi said: Humility is greater than all other virtues, for it is said, 'The spirit of the Lord God is upon me; because the Lord hath anointed me to bring good tidings unto the humble' (Isaiah

---

[19] Avot 5:25.
[20] Bialik and Ravnitzky, *Sefer Ha-Aggadah*, 7:28, 405; Sanhedrin, 99b.
[21] Bialik and Ravnitzky, *Sefer Ha-Aggadah*, 4:208, 708.

61:1)—not 'unto the saintly,' but 'unto the humble.' From this you learn that humility is greater than all other virtues."[22]

Chochmah and its accompanying song of jubilation embody the revelatory experience of oneness that cannot be known other than by direct experience. One cannot learn it from another, even a teacher; it is a direct engagement with the Divine Immanence in a way that is instantaneously recognizable. Experiencing the limitless light of God's divinity that comes through the process of self-nullification, one is no longer an observer of the divine; rather, the initiate and the Divine Presence become a unified field, without any separation. In genuine self-nullification, in which one completely surrenders one's attachment to self and to the voice of the ego, one becomes absorbed in the luminous light that flows down from the crown of Creation: this is Chochmah, the realm of Atzilut, the realm of emanation. It is only the completely self-nullified person, without any sense of a personal "I," who can enter this pure realm. This kind of selflessness brings a sense of joyous brilliance, like an eternally burning flame in the elevated heart.

The Light of Wisdom

And he went out unto his brethren, and he looked
on their burdens.

EXODUS 2:11

Chochmah, wisdom, is illuminated by the limitless light, the Or En Sof, above it. Like the High Priest inside of the Holy of Holies on Yom Kippur, the light of Creation illuminates consciousness. As with Creation, when God withdrew Himself into a finite point, the tzimtzum, from which He issued Creation out of His desire only to give, the qualities each person needs to develop to withstand this limitless light are made clear:

> The way of the disciple of the wise: humble, meek, eager, full of goodwill, submissive to discourtesy, loved by all people, undermanding [not demanding] even with the people in his own house, fearful of sin, appraising each person according to his deeds, ever saying, "All that is in this world I have no desire for, because this world in not mine": he

---

[22] Bialik and Ravnitzky, *Sefer Ha-Aggadah,* 4:211, 708.

keeps studying and is ever ready to throw his robe on the ground and sit on it, at the feet of other disciples of the wise, and no man ever espies him anything evil.[23]

Here in Chochmah, the Holy of Holies of the self, one becomes an illuminator for others, just as Moses was for the Israelites. This is the fulfillment of God's directive for the people of Israel: to become a kingdom of priests—the very words used when God first calls Moses to Mount Sinai.

In the third month after the children of Israel were gone forth out of the land of Egypt, the same day came they into the wilderness of Sinai. And when they were departed from Rephidim, and were come to the wilderness of Sinai, they encamped in the wilderness; and there Israel encamped before the mount. And Moses went up unto God, and the LORD called unto him out of the mountain, saying: "Thus shalt thou say to the house of Jacob, and tell the children of Israel: Ye have seen what I did unto the Egyptians, and how I bore you on eagles' wings, and brought you unto Myself. Now therefore, if ye will hearken unto My voice indeed, and keep My covenant, then ye shall be Mine own treasure from among all peoples; for all the earth is Mine; and ye shall be unto Me a kingdom of priests, and a holy nation." (Exodus 19:1–6)

This is a directive for each person: to be full of the light of His glory, which requires a refined vessel capable of holding such light. Refinement, we now see, implies being strengthened, burnished, put through the kiln of life to increase one's strength and endurance so that we may be an adequate vessel to hold the light of God. To be a water bearer for others, to be the sea of His shining light unto others—our own family and our community—in whatever way we can, is a gift of anointment. It is this countenance that becomes the great addition we make to wherever we are, making that place a holy sanctuary of the Divine Presence, elevating the sparks in all the created world we make contact with.

---

[23] Bialik and Ravnitzky, *Sefer Ha-Aggadah*, 7:310, 435.

Cultivating Wisdom

A wise man has his eyes in his head.

ECCLESIASTES 2:14

Moses was the initiator of all the sons of Yaakov (Jacob), who are also called Israel.[24] His preeminence is clear. God speaks to Moses as one does a friend, face to face, which means Moses was able in any given moment to hear the voice of God, to know the right action, to know the right words, to know the right way to direct his emotions, balancing them with love for the purpose of guiding the people. "When Moses was angry with Israel, the holy One, Blessed is He, appeased him; and when the holy One, blessed is He, was angry with Israel, Moses appeased Him."[25]

Moses is credited with having a partnership with God unlike any other. As the Israelites' advocate, he reminds God, "Even if You destroy heaven and earth, You cannot destroy Israel for You have made them a promise."[26] He frequently intercedes for them: "Master of the world, whenever the people of Israel sin before You and then repent, consider their willful transgressions as unintentional ones."[27] He even argues with God. When the Lord tells him, "Your people have corrupted themselves" (Exodus 32:7), Moses replies, "When they sin, they are my children, and when they are righteous they are yours?"[28] Every request that Moses made of God, except for his dearest wish, to go to the Promised Land with the flock he had stewarded for forty years, was granted. "Moses asked the Holy One, Blessed is He, for three things, and they were granted him [and these were] that the Divine Presence dwell in Israel; the Divine Presence not dwell among idol worshippers; and that the 'ways' of God be revealed to him."[29]

Our selfish desires in the material world are the "idols" the people are admonished to reject. But when we desire only closeness to the divine,

---

[24] Yisrael (Israel)—Yod Sheen Reish Yod Lamed (ישריל)—the teachers of God's Word are guided by Moses and his ability to transfer his wisdom and understanding in such a way as to be guidance for all time.

[25] Shemos Rabbah 45:2.

[26] Devarim Rabbah 3:15.

[27] Yoma 36b.

[28] Pesikta d'Rav Kahana 16:101. See also R. Yisrael Yitzchak Yishai Chasidah, *Encyclopedia of Biblical Personalities,* 381.

[29] Berachos 7a. See also Chasidah, *Encyclopedia of Biblical Personalities,* 380.

explained in the beginning of this book as being the delight of every soul, we receive the light of God and inner peace. "R. Yohanan said: Words of Torah endure only with one who is willing to make himself as nothing, for it is said, 'Wisdom shall be found in nothing' (Job 28:12)."[30] In Beriyah, the realm of creation, the person must completely nullify himself, surrendering his personal wishes in favor of "Thy will be done." Just as the High Priest is the instructor and transformer of the people, so are each of us transformers of our own inner kingdom when we fulfill our priestly duties, which means helping and guiding others—provided we have attained the genuine wisdom to do so. But good deeds require only a loving heart, thus no one is exempt from serving the world in this way. Benefiting others by Torah wisdom is itself a Godly duty.

> Where is the proof that he who teaches Torah to his fellow man is deemed as though he had formed him, articulated his limbs, and brought him the world? The verse "If though bringest forth the noble of that which is worthless, though shalt be as My mouth" (Jeremiah 15:19). Whosoever brings even one person under the wings of the Presence is deemed as though he had formed him, articulated his limbs, and brought him into the world.[31]

The sages tell us there are fifteen characteristics of a disciple of the wise:

> He is pleasant when he comes in and pleasant when he departs. He is unassuming in his academy, resourceful in bringing about fear of God, prudent in awareness, wise in his ways. He collects [the words of Torah] and remembers them well, takes pains to reply properly, makes his questions relevant and his replies to the point, listens carefully before replying, adds something novel of his own to each and every chapter, goes to a sage [to minister to him], and studies in order to teach and to practice.[32]

---

[30] B. Sotah 21b. See also Bialik and Ravnitzky, *Sefer Ha-Aggadah,* 7:68, 410.
[31] Bialik and Ravnitzky, *Sefer Ha-Aggadah,* 7:127, 415. See also B. Sanh 105b.
[32] Bialik and Ravnitzky, *Sefer Ha-Aggadah,* 7:307, 434.

A Story of Freedom

The air of Israel's Land makes one wise.

SEFER HA-AGGADAH 2:52

The center of our being is the heart; it signifies the middle of the world; when purified it is like the Tabernacle in the middle of Israel. The heart requires that we come out of Egypt, that is, our fears and limitations, in order to inherit the new land—our completely sanctified being. Just as the Exodus is the archetypal freedom story, the crossing of the Red Sea is everyone's personal story—the story of earning, and then protecting, one's own holy place in the world.

> Even as the navel is in a man's middle, so the Land of Israel, it is said, "dwells in the middle of the earth" (Ezekiel 38:12). It is situated in the world's middle, and from there the foundation of the world extends. Now, Jerusalem is in the middle of the land of Israel, and the Temple area in the middle of Jerusalem, the Holy of Holies in the middle of the Temple, the Ark in the middle of the Holy of Holies, and the foundation stone out of which the world was founded in the front of the Ark.[33] [See figure 9.4 on page 330.]

The word *Israelite* means "one who walks a straight path to God" and "one over whom God prevails." When we become an Israelite, we add to the illumination that peace brings to the world, recalling that the greatest blessing the Creator wants to give Israel is peace. Peace, therefore, is the result of union with God.

Once we have arrived in the Holy of Holies, we receive direct emanations from the root of Creation. Having refined one's emotions and intellect, one is now a vessel fit for illumination and therefore for becoming an emanator by which the entire community benefits. Here the initiate serves as the High Priest in the community's redemption, modeling closeness to God. We are now prepared for the final revelation, where we become enveloped by Almighty God in His entirety, and where Adam, our final guide, reveals the source of the light of revelation.

---

[33] Bialik and Ravnitzky, *Sefer Ha-Aggadah,* 2:61, 365. See also Tanhuma, Kedoshim 10.

Revelation

12

Or En Sof, Bestowal in the Garden of Eden

Keter • Adam's Song of Divine Unity

You open Your hand and satisfy the desire of every living thing.
PSALMS 145:16

First Sefirah: Keter
Meaning: Crown
Rung on Ascending Ladder: Ten
Archetype: Adam Kadmon
Symbol: The Garden of Eden
Spiritual World: Or En Sof/limitless light of the Creator (En Sof)
Spiritual Anatomy: The human body and soul in union
Inner Quality: Faith (emunah)

Historical Personage: Adam, the first "man of earth"
Text: Adam's song (Psalms 98)
Key Words: Revelation, divine awareness, Sabbath
Key Emotion in Song: Uplifting praise (ashrei)

Tent of Meeting: The light illuminating the Holy of Holies

Spiritual Stage: Revelation, bestowal
Spiritual Practice: Complete union with the Divine Presence
Illumination: The revelation of union with God

Joining Adam at the gates of Eden just before we incarnate in earthly form, we reflect on the splendor of the Garden we are leaving; this is sealed within us as truth, as we say, "How awesome are you, O Lord."

The Sefirah Keter: The Crown

R. Eleazar said: The holy One will form a circle of righteous men in the garden of Eden with Himself in the center, so that each of them will be able to point with his finger and say, "Lo, this is our God for whom we waited, that He might save us; this is the Lord, for whom we waited, we will be glad and rejoice in His salvation (Isaiah 25:9)."

SEFER HA-AGGADAH, 6:17

Keter, the crown, is the very top Sefirah of the Tree of Life from which all the Sefirot below receive their originating light. Its corresponding aspect in the Tabernacle metaphor is the light that emanates from the Ark between the wings of the cherubim. This represents the realm of Adam Kadmon, the Or En Sof, the limitless light of the Creator (En Sof). It is said we do not experience this light directly: just as the holy Ark is veiled, we experience the light through various veils and levels, through the descending and ascending of the spiraling light from the remaining nine Sefirot that comprise the Tree of Life.

Keter's shine is the source of the Holy of Holies said to exist within each of the five worlds: the Holy of Holies of Asiyah (Malchut/Nukvah), Yetzirah (Chesed through Yesod/Zeir Anpin), Beriyah (Binah/the Mother), Atzilut (Chochmah/the Father), and the Or En Sof (Keter/Adam Kadmon). This is the place where the initiate reaches divine consciousness in the Holy of Holies of the self—the place where heart and mind, body and soul are one, and one with all creation. This holy light emanates through our actions in the world, elevating the sparks of holiness in matter. In Keter, we are each members of the priesthood that serves in Holy of Holies; here we are touched by the Ruach HaKodesh and the Shechinah and we thus experience the perfection of the Garden, Gan Eden.

As we develop the qualities of each Sefirah—that which brings us to act in the world, to love divinity, to be humble, to be enduring in our commitments, to love justice, to show mercy, to serve our fellow humans and God—we acknowledge that the spiritual path elevates the physical world. Kabbalah teaches that we are intended to be co-creators, re-creating society and civilization in the image of the balanced middle path. Yet this is not a solitary journey of only our own individual inner refinement; it is an inner refinement that leads to robust outer action *for the benefit of others and the world.*

Keter represents the originating vessel of man, known as Adam Kadmon, our primordial template, according to the Hebrew story of Creation. This also represents our own personal creation story as described by our journey through life and even through the afterlife. Just as the left and right pillars of the Tree of Life represent loving-kindness and judgment, seemingly two opposites, the admixture of good and evil first occurred, we are told, with Adam and Eve's eating from the forbidden tree—the first instance of the use of free will in the human experience. It is taught furthermore that the first couple's actions were already known by God before He created them, such that their flawed use of human free will enabled Him to give humankind the task of nurturing and elevating the world outside the perfection of the Garden.

Adam's sense of separation from God came about essentially as a result of his lack of humility: Adam desired what the Creator had forbidden. This is why we are told not to chase after what our eyes desire. Just as there is the light of wisdom (Chochmah), there is its opposite, the sitra achra, the "other side," meaning the side of impurity, which is attached to every spinning atom in the physical universe, resulting in a type of moral heads-or-tails choice for us. Just as this positive-negative polarity is present physically, both on the individual level and in the world at large, this same polarity exists within our spiritual makeup. Choosing between good and evil is thus the job of the conscious co-creator.

Adam Kadmon: The Heavenly "Man of Earth"

Then the LORD God formed man of the dust of the ground, and breathed into his nostrils the breath of life; and man became a living soul. And the LORD God planted a garden eastward, in Eden; and there He put the man whom He had formed.

GENESIS 2:7–8

Tradition states that "the Holy One, Blessed is He, molded every human being with the die of Adam, yet not one is identical with another."[1] In Kabbalah this refers to Adam Kadmon, the primordial man of earth, the template on which an entire cosmology and theology are based. When applied to human life processes, this template produces a heavenly being, a God-like man or woman of earth. One teaching tells of Adam's—and therefore each human soul's—native universality: "The dust from which Adam was created was gathered from all over the earth: his body from Babylon, his head from Eretz Yisrael, his limbs [i.e., his arms and legs] from other lands, his rump from Akra d'Agma [in Babylon]."[2] It is also taught that "while Adam was still a shapeless mass lying before the Holy One, blessed be He, He showed him each generation and its sages."[3] The fact that Adam was given this ability to see "beyond time" suggests each soul's ability to see its previous lifetimes, future lifetimes, and how the intermediate stage between incarnations is an actual state of existence in which the soul is steeped in learning from the previous lifetime and making plans for the next lifetime. Some say all of this takes place in realms that precede the soul's reaching the perfection of Gan Eden, while it is in Olam HaBa, the World to Come, or, God forbid, due to improper conduct, in Gehenim, a fiery hell-like place where the soul is cleansed of its imperfections before being able to ascend. Yet, overall, humanity's purpose is made explicit in the writings of the People of the Book: "And God said, 'Let us make Man in Our image, after Our likeness. They shall rule [have dominion] over the fish of the sea, the birds of the sky, and

---

[1] Sanhedrin 37a. See also R. Yisrael Yitzchak Yishai Chasidah, *Encyclopedia of Biblical Personalities,* 47.

[2] Sanhedrin 38b. See also Chasidah, *Encyclopedia of Biblical Personalities,* 46.

[3] Bereshis Rabbah 24:2. See also Chasidah, *Encyclopedia of Biblical Personalities,* 46.

over the animals, the whole earth, and every creeping thing that creeps upon the earth.' So God created Man in His image, in the image of God He created him; male and female He created them" (Genesis 1:26–27).

Another beautiful teaching about our roots in the Creator's plan for humanity's ultimate perfection as stewards of the earth is revealed in the description of how God made Adam: "The Holy One, Blessed is He, took one full measure [of earth] from the site of the [future Temple's] altar, and from it He created Adam."[4] This suggests that the future Third Temple in the age of the Moshiach and messianic consciousness will not only be an actual physical structure; it will also manifest as the temple of a spiritually mature humanity, in which we will collectively become the perfected vessel on earth that the Divine Presence already fills and illuminates in the supernal realms. Kabbalah teaches that, in this time that will come, humanity will finally become fully aware that it is the living, holy Ark of the Covenant, and that its superconductor, the Ark's lid, the holiest of altars that exists within each us, is the source of this divine intelligence. This is our designed purpose; how we succeed in accomplishing this and when we accomplish this depends on the elevation of each individual, a process described in this book.

The Creation of Adam

Adam's genesis was preceded by three other creations: "the making of the world: water, wind (spirit) and fire. Water conceived and gave birth to thick darkness, fire conceived and gave birth to light, wind (spirit) conceived and gave birth to wisdom. The world is maintained by means of these six creations: by wind (spirit), wisdom, fire, light, darkness and water."[5]

The oral tradition in Judaism is not vague about the creation of this heavenly earth man. Not everyone in the spiritual kingdom was supportive of the Creator's plan. Tradition says the station and rank that Adam would be afforded as God's most cherished creation was disputed in heaven:

---

[4] Nazir 7:2. See also Chasidah, *Encyclopedia of Biblical Personalities*, 46.
[5] Hayim Nahman Bialik and Yehoshua Hana Ravnitzky, *Sefer Ha-Aggadah*, 17:70. All six creations are also mentioned in Psalms 104:1–7.

R. Simon said: When the Holy One was about to create Adam, the ministering angels formed themselves into groups and complained, some of them saying, "Let him be created," while others urged, "Let him not be created." Thus it is written, "Love and truth fought together, righteousness and peace combated each other" (Psalms 85:11). Love said, "Let him be created for he will perform acts of love." Truth said, "Let him not be created, because all of him will be falsehood." Righteousness said, "Let him be created, because he will do righteous deeds." Peace said, "Let him not be created, because he will be all strife." What did the Holy One do? He took truth and cast it to the ground, as is said, "Thou didst cast down to the ground" (Daniel 8:12). The ministering angels dare said to the Holy One, "Master of the universe, why do You humiliate Your Seal? Let truth arise from the earth." Hence it is written, "Let truth spring up from the earth" (Psalms 85:12). The Elder R. Huna Sepphoris said: While the ministering angels were parleying with one another and disputing with one another, the Holy One created Adam and then said: "What are you parleying about? Man is already made."[6]

After earth and its many life forms were created, "a mist ascended from the earth and watered the whole surface of the soil. And God formed the man of dust from the ground and He blew into his nostrils the soul of life; and man became a living being" (Genesis 2:6–7).

Torah's story of humankind's creation describes how everything in the world comes to life after the creation of Adam, who prays to God for mercy in the form of rain. God sends down rain and everything on earth flourishes. God also plants two trees in Adam's abode, the Tree of Life, which is in the middle of the Garden, and the Tree of Knowledge of Good and Evil. Then God "took the man and placed him in the Garden of Eden, to work and to guard it. And God commanded the man, saying

---

[6] Bialik and Ravnitzky, *Sefer Ha-Aggadah,* 2:46, 13. There is a shorter version of this story in which God tricks the angels by distracting them in order to create Adam in the first place: "When the holy One, blessed is he, was about to create Adam, [the attribute of] kindness said, 'Let him be created,' but [the attribute of] Truth said, 'Let him not be created.' [God] took Truth and cast it to the ground. Said the ministering angels before the Holy One, Blessed is He, 'Why do you scorn Truth?' While the ministering angels were debating [the issue], the holy One, blessed is He, created [Adam]."

'Of every tree of the garden you may freely eat; but of the Tree of Knowledge of Good and Evil, you must not eat thereof; for on the day you eat of it, you shall surely die'" (Genesis 2:15–17). The light that illuminates and fills all of the material forms in the Garden is the same light that shines in the Holy of Holies; it is the light of Creation that sustains each person and all life on earth.

As Adam's story unfolds, God creates Eve, his companion, who is persuaded by a snake in the garden to eat of the forbidden tree. Eve persuades Adam to share in this delight with her. As a result, "the eyes of both of them were opened and they realized that they were naked; and they sewed together a fig leaf and made themselves aprons" (Genesis 3:7). At this point, Adam and Eve's narrative confirms that all of our deeds are noted by God:

> They heard the sound of God manifesting Itself in the garden toward evening; and the man and his wife hid from God among the trees of the garden. God called out to the man and said to him, "Where are you?" He said, "I heard the sound of You in the garden, and I was afraid because I am naked, so I hid." And He said, "Who told you that you are naked? Have you eaten of the tree from which I commanded you not to eat?" The man said, "The woman whom You gave to be with me—she gave me of the tree, and I ate." And God said to the woman, "What is this that you have done!" The woman said, "The serpent deceived me, and I ate." (Genesis 3:8–13)

Despite disobedience, Adam was full of wisdom and could call all living entities by their names, for he perceived their essence, and from their essence, their purpose. This is one reason why he is sometimes referred to as the first Kabbalist, for he was a master of the Creator's language, ancient Hebrew, the foundation of all languages, from which came the seventy languages of the world and countless thousands of dialects. Though Adam is called king of earth, he is also the first person to be described as having God's presence given to him—and taken away, as in this description of Adam's clothing (which some Chazal state was like the raiment of angels): "Adam's clothing was the skin of fingernails, and a Cloud of Glory covered him. After he ate the fruit [of the forbidden tree] the nail skin was removed and the Cloud of Glory departed from him, and he saw that he was naked."[7]

Temptation

Quickly realizing the error he has made by eating of the Tree of Knowledge of Good and Evil, Adam is not able to admit his own role in this transgression. Here is God's first created human son, who after doing what he was explicitly told not to do, first insinuates that it is God's fault for giving him a wife, and then goes even further, blaming Eve for coercing him instead of acknowledging his own free will in making a bad choice. Hence both Adam and Eve succumb to the temptation of not taking responsibility for their actions: Adam easily condemns his wife, and likewise Eve tells Adam to do something she herself would not do alone, and as well, she blames the snake for her choice. Thus Adam and Eve are partners in their desire for forbidden things from the very start of their cohabitation, and both deny responsiblity for the exercise of their own free will.

Adam and Eve's disobedience represents the energy of temptation and sometimes immoral collaboration that is inbred in the Nefesh, that part of the human that correlates to the source of the animal soul and is portrayed as the serpent in this narrative. As a representation of the inborn energy of light that travels up and down the spine, this inner serpentine presence can control us by stimulating improper desires. By learning to manage this Nefesh power, much in the way one speaks of controlling the animal soul, through conscious self-refinement and self-discipline, we can elevate it, ourselves, and all that we encounter and do.

The Eternal Body

God's intention for humanity is that it rectify all of creation.[8] Humankind is God's intended collaborator and thus only humankind can do this work. After Adam and Eve's rebellion in the Garden, we are told that a fiery sword was placed by the Garden's gate, "lest Adam eat from

---

[7] Yalkut Shimoni, Bereshis 27. See also Chasidah, *Encyclopedia of Biblical Personalities,* 50. "How much labor did Adam invest before he had a garment to wear! He sheared, whitened, hatchelled, dyed, spun, wove, washed and sewed—and [only] then did he have a garment to wear" (Berechos 9:1).

[8] See this author's *Kabbalistic Teachings of the Female Prophets,* 42.

the Tree of Life and live forever." This suggests that it is possible for a human being to acquire an immortal physical body in union with his eternal spiritual body: "God banished Adam from the Garden of Eden, to work the soil from which he was taken. And having driven out the man, He stationed at the east of the Garden of Eden the Cherubim and the flame of the ever-turning sword, to guard the way to the Tree of Life" (Genesis 3:22–24).

One has to ask, though, given that the Creator does everything with forethought (as do we when we create): Is not the Tree of Life being guarded by the cherubim on the Kapporeth (the Ark's top)? Isn't this what they are protecting in the Ark—the holy wisdom teachings of the Etz Chayim that enable one to read the future, control nature, and raise the dead? They are guarding the The Tree of Life from all but the High Priest who, if exposed to its wisdom, will not die or be destroyed by it. Such powerful knowledge, God makes clear, cannot be accessed by humans unless they are properly prepared. As above, so below. The cherubim in Gan Eden and the cherubim of the Ark guard the same secret, in my opinion—that of Resurrection. For is not the inheritance of an eternal body and an eternal soul the final step in humankind's spiritual evolution? Is not the entire subject of the Resurrection of the Dead, that which can best describe this knowledge of life that the Israelites inherited, telling us that we can live forever?

The potential inheritance of an eternal body is interpreted in different ways. One interpretation is based on the idea that our good deeds live on after us in the world and in the lives of those whom we benefited; these good deeds can also be thought of as the garments of life that we put on in Gan Eden, making our good works an aspect of our eternal raiment. This, then, is the "body" that survives physical death, showing that our incarnate influences live on forever.

Another perspective says that this eternal body is given a material sheath—a dense material body—that is like a garment one puts on and takes off at will, like an act of materialization. "In the school of Elijah it was taught: The righteous whom the Holy One will quicken will not return to the dust. You may ask, 'In the thousand years during which the Holy One will renew His world, what will they do?' [The answer is that] the Holy One will provide them with wings like eagles, and they will fly above the water."[9] In the modern era this eternal body might be seen as a type of intradimensional materialization and dematerialization, which can be done at will, as shown in some popular films.

Another viewpoint describes this eternal body as the body of light that can never be destroyed, and which accompanies the eternal soul in the work that earth beings are undertaking, whether consciously or unconsciously, throughout their many incarnations. It is also said that this eternal life refers to Gan Eden, the higher realm of consciousness after one goes through various stages of the World to Come, Olam HaBa. The Zohar says that if Adam had not sinned, he would have begotten children from the side of holiness "who would have been as holy as the ministering angels and they would have been immortal."[10] So what then is the purpose of the body's death if we are designed to live, at least in spirit, forever?

In dying, and in the process of incarnating and then dying again, in the cycle of reincarnation, we are refined by stages, from lifetime to lifetime, suggesting a gradual enlightenment that is earned and sealed into the very bones of a person. So that rather than repeating Adam's mistake and again taking what is not ours to take, we are protected from having the powers of creation too soon, when we are not yet ready, by the fiery sword and the cherubim. The cherubim, being the alchemical witnesses and guardians of the contents of the holy Ark, guard the knowledge of life and death in the form of the Torah. Resurrection, then, might refer to the creation of this eternal body, which is prophesied for all of humanity as its inheritance from the Garden when each human being is completely self-nullified and has united with the perfection of all Creation—the predicted time of messianic awareness. "Great is Torah, which in this world as well as in the world-to-come gives life to those who obey it, as is said, '[Words of Torah] are life to those that find them'" (Proverbs 4:22).[11]

While the ultimate plan might be for humankind's perfection, we, like Adam and Eve, experience times in our lives when we make decisions that are not only hurtful to ourselves but to others as well. The result of Adam and Eve's indiscretion, which subsequently affected all of humanity, teaches us that we are all one; individually and collectively we are affected by the

---

[9] Bialik and Ravnitzky, *Sefer Ha-Aggadah,* 6:27, 402. See also B. Sanh, 92a–b.

[10] Zohar 1:161a.

[11] Avot 5:25.

choices and actions of everyone else in the world. It is for this reason that each of us represents the *entire* world, not simply our own individual self. We also learn from Adam's return to God, made clear in the song of Keter, that when we say or do something that is wrong, we should always remember that every moment is endowed with the light of Creation; this allows us to re-create our life—to return again to God.

The Mind of Separation

"When God banished him [Adam and Eve] from the Garden of Eden (Genesis 3:23), [Adam] settled on Mount Moriah to work the soil from which he was taken."[12] It was to this very same holy place that the patriarch Abraham took his son Isaac for the test of sacrifice, an act that elevated all of B'nai Yisrael. The sin of Adam and the later sin of the golden calf are considered two parts of the same fall from grace: a separation from God (sin) that leads to repentance, self-refinement, and ultimately a return to God.

The mind of separation can come from a sense of entitlement, a sense of feeling special, such that a person views himself as being more important than another person, or above the laws of right conduct and the law of return (i.e., "What ye sow, so shall ye reap"). The darkness of selfishness, of personal desire, which descended on the world as a result of this sense of separation, is the root cause of why the First and Second temples that were later built on Mt. Moriah (where the Temple Mount stands today) were destroyed. But as we know, the root contains the fruition, for as it is prophesied, the final, Third Temple, which each of us is part of bringing into form, will be built at this same sacred site in Jerusalem.

Most important, we learn from Adam and Eve's narrative a basic lesson that applies to our own conduct: Adam and Eve were judged not according to their specific act of disobedience, but according to their desires, their motivation, and their intention. While it is said they were spared death because God did not think their sin was premeditated, their choice and their subsequent actions were. They did not, out of ignorance, eat from the forbidden tree. They wanted to do what they were

---

[12] Targum Yonasan, Bereshis 4:23. See also Chasidah, *Encyclopedia of Biblical Personalities,* 52.

told not to do—as children so often do—in order to gain something that was not theirs to possess. They saw something that delighted their eyes (Chochmah, or wisdom), which they wanted, but which was forbidden to them. In this sense it was the first theft on earth. This explains why all sacred traditions have guarded knowledge in secrecy: wisdom is earned, not given, and certainly not stolen.

Adam was created on the sixth day, on the eve of Sabbath, but by the day's end of this very first Sabbath we are told that "six things were taken from Adam: his radiance, his life, his stature, the produce of the earth, the fruits of the tree, and the luminaries,"[13] revealing the reason for the saying that "first the serpent was cursed, afterwards Eve and finally Adam."[14]

Lighting the Fire of Devotion

Following the fall from grace, we are told that after enjoying the great wonders of the effluence of the Creator in the form of the Sabbath's light and love, the sun goes down, and for the first time Adam knows darkness. He wonders if he has brought this darkness to the world through his forbidden actions, and for the first time fear arises:

> Adam retained his glory [throughout the Sabbath]. When the Sabbath departed, his radiance left him and he was banished from the Garden of Eden. When the sun set with the departure of the Sabbath and darkness approached, Adam was frightened, [for] he thought, "The [serpent] of whom it is written, 'He will pound your head, and you will bite his heel' (Genesis 3.15) is coming to attack me." The Holy One, blessed is He, caused [Adam] to find two flints, which he struck against each other, thereby producing fire, then he pronounced a blessing over [the fire].[15]

The power over evil or over the desire for things we know are not for our betterment is the fire in the heart and soul that burns like a

---

[13] R. Yaakov Ibn Chaviv, *Ein Yaakov,* Shab 152b–153a, 128.

[14] Eiruvin 18a. See also Chasidah, *Encyclopedia of Biblical Personalities,* 52.

[15] Bereshish Rabbah 11:2–3. See also Chasidah, *Encyclopedia of Biblical Personalities,* 53. At the close of Sabbath, the Havdalah prayer is said with this event in mind.

lamp of devotion to unity consciousness and holiness, over which we pray. This shows us, once again, the primacy of prayer as a tool for staying close to God and His manifestations as the Holy Spirit and the Divine Immanence. Adam's lessons are our own. The light of Creation is our invitation to union and communion with God. Our separation is represented by the darkness that Adam and Eve experience when the sun goes down after the Sabbath. Here, in Keter, the crown of our being, where we revel in the Divine Presence, we become fully conscious of the truth of our unity with God and the light of Creation. Inside the Holy of Holies is where God's Presence is said to rest, between the wings of the cherubim on the Ark's cover, enabling transcendent God-consciousness. Repentance, teshuvah, owning up to our own shortcomings and offering sublime praise and thanksgiving for God's assistance in our success, is that process by which we renew our contact with the Creator. Like the High Priest's ritual on the Day of Atonement, this is how we reunite our mind and body, heart and soul. This gives credence to the old adage that "God gives the cure before the ailment." Prayer, like the Sabbath, is that cure.

The Song of Keter: Sublime Insight (Ashrei)

In Adam's song of praise, an ashrei, meaning a sublime song of insight and thanksgiving to the Creator, we hear his heart's attachment to the oneness of Creation, not his own self-importance. In his declaration of the day of God's glory, the Sabbath, the greatest of all days of the Creation story, we hear not of his own entry into the world on the sixth day as the greatest of all days; rather, Adam declares that the Sabbath is the mirror of Eden. This is the revelation of Adam and of every single person: to honor the Sabbath, for it is holy; it is the Mercy Seat of Creation, the place where God comes to speak to each one of us. Sabbath is to the week what Yom Kippur is to the year. In this way one understands that Shabbat was created before the world, and it is the salve for the world's woes. When humanity is cognizant of its united roots in the one Creator, the world will be as Sabbath. Such is the quality of life prophesied for the messianic thousand years of peace.

Adam's Song (Psalms 92:1–16)

🌿**1 A Psalm, a song. For the Sabbath day. 2 It is a good thing to give thanks unto the LORD, and to sing praises unto Thy name, O Most High; 3 To declare Thy loving kindness in the morning, and Thy faithfulness in the night seasons, 4 With an instrument of ten strings, and with the psaltery; with a solemn sound upon the harp.** [Bold indicates lines from which the Chazal divined the song type] *5 For Thou, LORD, hast made me glad through Thy work; I will exult in the works of Thy hands. 6 How great are Thy works, O LORD! Thy thoughts are very deep. 7 A brutish man knoweth not, neither doth a fool understand this. 8 When the wicked spring up as the grass, and when all the workers of iniquity do flourish; it is that they may be destroyed forever. 9 But Thou, O LORD, art on high for ever more. 10 For, lo, Thine enemies, O LORD, for, lo, Thine enemies shall perish: all the workers of iniquity shall be scattered. 11 But my horn hast Thou exalted like the horn of the wild-ox; I am anointed with rich oil. 12 Mine eye also hath gazed on them that lie in wait for me, mine ears have heard my desire of the evil-doers that rise up against me. 13 The righteous shall flourish like the palm-tree; he shall grow like a cedar in Lebanon. 14 Planted in the house of the LORD, they shall flourish in the courts of our God. 15 They shall still bring forth fruit in old age; they shall be full of sap and richness; 16 To declare that the LORD is upright, my Rock, in whom there is no unrighteousness.*

Tears of Joy

As we reach the upper branches of the Tree of Life, we sing Adam's song, the song of Keter, with uplifting, abundant praise and an overwhelming sense of joy, such that it can bring one to tears, as in this noteworthy example: "R. Akiva sat weeping on the Sabbath. His disciples said: 'Our Master you taught us: call the Sabbath a delight' (Isaiah 58:13). R. Akiva: 'This is my delight.'"[16]

There is a connection, according to scholars, between Adam, the first man of earth, and Rabbi Akiva, the famous first-century (95–135 CE) Tanna known as "the head of all the sages." Resh Lakish, that is, Simeon ben Lakish, the third-century amora (Aramaic for "those who say," that is, an oral teacher), notes this connection: "What is meant by 'This is

---

[16] Bialik and Ravnitzky, *Sefer Ha-Aggadah*, 1:159, 235.

the book of the generations of Adam' (Genesis 5:1)? It intimates that the Holy One showed him each generation and its expounders of Scripture, each generation and its sages. When He reached the generation of R. Akiva, Adam rejoiced in R. Akiva's Torah but grieved over his death and protested, 'How precious to me Thy friends [each sage, each expounder of scripture], O God'" (Psalms 139:17).[17]

When we join Adam in Keter it is both our individual and our collective anointing. Just as "Adam was King over the whole world,"[18] we too are to be rulers over our own actions in the world and over the inner kingdom of life. Just as "Adam's place was closer [to God than that of] the ministering angels,"[19] we too are to be conscious of our place among these angelic helpers and guides who assist us throughout our many incarnations. Just as "Adam was the first born of the world, when he offered his sacrifice, he wore the vestments of the High Priesthood,"[20] our decorum serves as our vestments, like those worn by the High Priest.

Ritual: Arrival at the Innermost Sanctuary

Here, as we experience the last stage of our ascension of the ladder of light, we come into direct contact with the limitless light, the Or En Sof, as it streams down into Atzilut, the realm of emanation, where we experience complete enlightenment. While our physical body has arrived at the innermost chamber of the Holy of Holies, our consciousness reaches beyond the physical realm. This is the Eden-like paradise, the origin of spirit and soul, where the Divine Presence is known to us and speaks directly to us. In Jewish ritual tradition this can occur whenever we pray or perform a mitzvot in utter joy, but this elevated state of consciousness is especially available to us on Yom Kippur (or in any other moment of profound, sincere repentance). This is the day the High Priest enters the innermost chamber of the Tabernacle—beyond the Outer Court of animal sacrifices and water libations; beyond the Holy Place of the menorah, shewbread, and incense; beyond even the Holy of Holies' curtain, to arrive at the Ark itself. This inner sanctum is so sacred that death

---

[17] Bialik and Ravnitzky, *Sefer Ha-Aggadah*, 1:139, 232.
[18] Zohar 2:150a.
[19] Bereshis Rabbah 21:1.
[20] Bamidbar Rabbah 4:8. See also Chasidah, *Encyclopedia of Biblical Personalities*, 47.

comes to anyone unfit to enter—those with any blemish of attachment to an idea or to a notion of an individual self, or anyone not holy enough to be a pure vessel for the light of God to fill. Only the completely self-nullified person can become the staff, the Ark, and the testimony of the earthly community in which one has habitation, that is, an instrument of God. This level of refinement offers a unique yet dangerous exposure, one that can either give divine life or take it away.

The possibility of the death of the High Priest in this innermost part of the sanctuary is of such great concern that it is said he has a red cord tied to his waist (some say ankle) so that if he dies inside the Holy of Holies he can be brought out by the cord to avoid risking the death of anyone who might otherwise have to enter the chamber to retrieve him. In the same way, when we risk saving a drowning man we are counseled to tie a line around our own waist and attach it to something above water, lest the drowning man pull us down as well. These are moral and ethical, as well as practical, instructions: we must attach to God above, or else we risk death.

So what, then, do Adam and Eve really do for us, what do they show us? What exactly is death (for that is what came from eating from the Tree of Knowledge of Good and Evil)? What does Adam, the final prophet in our journey homeward, teach us? In life we are given choices about what we can do. Each decision affects not only oneself but the world as well. When we nullify the ego and come into complete faith and trust in God, surrendering to His will, we inherit the bounty of life in the Garden of Eden, no longer experiencing any illusory sense of separation between ourselves and God and God's creation. In short, we overcome death, which is represented as separation consciousness.

We can call out to God at any moment in life, and at any moment we are rescued by His call back. Adam turns to God upon realizing what his expulsion means. Leaving the glory of the Sabbath in Gan Eden, Adam "opened his mouth and said, 'A Psalm, A Song for the Sabbath Day,'" the song of Keter found in Psalm 92. This is the psalm that was recited by the Levite priests in the Temple and is still recited by observant People of the Book to this day, on the Friday-evening service called Kabbalat Shabbat ("Welcoming in the Sabbath") and during the Sabbath morning services. Reading it, one understands how it summarizes all that we have learned about the importance of prayer, song, praise, and above all, humility and devotion, as conditions for revelation.

Sabbath as Tonic

We succeed in life by supporting what is holy in ourselves and others. Those things forbidden to us are forbidden for a good reason. The knowledge of good and evil—for example, humanitarian actions and other acts of compassion, versus war and exploitation—is the preoccupation of humanity. So what does God give us as a healing tonic? He gives us Sabbath. He gives us the ability to stop and think, to meditate, to pray for divine insight. Within our daily framework, Sabbath represents the awareness that we must stop before we speak or act; ultimately we must master our own thoughts. We must always intend and make the effort to stay connected to the Divine Presence that surrounds and fills us. If we do so, then whatever action we undertake will be correctly motivated for the benefit of all and it will thus be elevated to the highest good. Recall that truth, the Sefirah of Tiferet, the middle of the Tree of Life, elevates all the parts, making it greater than the sum of the parts.

Activation of the Divine Spark

We see the path into the inner sanctuary activated through Adam and Eve's experience. God has already created the Sabbath, the holy day of rest from the work of Creation. While in the Garden, Adam and Eve basked in the light of God's radiance and peace. Sabbath and its holy light of emanation, the light of the Or En Sof in Atzilut, is the light of the entire Tree of Life, all being rooted in His divine being.

The importance of honoring the Sabbath is, of course, part of the Ten Commandments given to Moses on Mt. Sinai; this directive is still honored millennia later by the Jewish people:

> Observe the Sabbath day, to keep it holy, as the LORD thy God commanded thee. Six days shalt thou labour, and do all thy work; but the seventh day is a Sabbath unto the LORD thy God, in it thou shalt not do any manner of work, thou, nor thy son, nor thy daughter, nor thy man-servant, nor thy maid-servant, nor thine ox, nor thine ass, nor

any of thy cattle, nor thy stranger that is within thy gates; that thy man-servant and thy maid-servant may rest as well as thou. And thou shalt remember that thou was a servant in the land of Egypt, and the LORD thy God brought thee out thence by a mighty hand and by an outstretched arm; therefore the LORD thy God commanded thee to keep the Sabbath day. . . . And it came to pass, when ye heard the voice out of the midst of the darkness, while the mountain did burn with fire, that ye came near unto me, even all the heads of your tribes, and your elders; and ye said: "Behold, the LORD our God hath shown us His glory and His greatness, and we have heard His voice out of the midst of the fire; we have seen this day that God doth speak with man, and he liveth." (Deuteronomy 5:11–14, 19–20)

The Ten Commandments are housed in the Ark, illuminated inside the Holy of Holies by the limitless light, the light without end, which corresponds to Keter and the completely rectified human being. The observance of the Sabbath acts as an energetic reality capable of radiating to the soul a light greater than on any other day of the week. Sabbath activates the divine spark of God, the realm of Yechidah, protected by the cherubim who are also our inner guardians, hovering over our personal Tree of Life. Sabbath prayers and rituals bring us to the divine revelation of unity, exposing us to the holy light of Creation, the act of God that the Sabbath commemorates.

The Tabernacle of Peace

As we know, once the Ohel Moed was erected, Sabbath became institutionalized for the Jewish people as the axis of their lives. The Zohar calls Sabbath "the Tabernacle of Peace," and as such it is the final outcome of the initiate's journey:

Come and behold: When the day is sanctified on the evening of Shabbat, a Tabernacle of Peace descends and settles on the world. He asks: What is this Tabernacle of Peace? And He answers: It is the Shabbat. On Shabbat all the evil spirits, stormy sprits, demons and the defiled hide behind the millstone of the chasm of the great abyss. For when the Sanctity spreads over the world, the spirit of defilement does not waken; one runs from the other. Holiness shuns the unclean, and the unclean shuns holiness.[21]

The Zohar continues by explaining that on the Sabbath this Tabernacle of Peace spreads over the entire world and protects it from all directions.[22] Just as the Mother, Binah, protects her children, that is, all the Sefirot below (Chesed through Malchut), the Sabbath illuminates the world with holiness. The People of the Book speak of the extra Neshamah (the aspect of the soul that is eternal and represents our higher sense of hearing or intuitive understanding) that is endowed on the Sabbath: "And because this Tabernacle of Peace dwells upon and spreads her wings over her children, she sheds new souls upon each and every one of them."[23]

The great quality of light that issues from the wings of the two cherubim on the cover of the Ark is part of divine re-creation. Similarly, when we arrive at divine consciousness, the peace that comes from honoring, remembering, and keeping the laws of divinity, the Divine Presence fills and surrounds us and we become endowed with the ability to hear God speak. It can even be said that a person becomes the Sabbath itself when fully awake in this way. At such a time one can say, as Jacob did upon awakening from his own dream of the ladder of light on which the angels climbed up and down, "How holy is this place!" In the realm of Or En Sof illuminating Atzilut, as in the other realms, God and his attributes are one; we too, as emanations of His light, are one with His essence. Here, where righteous souls receive the light of wisdom, one learns, as Adam, Abraham, Moses, and Joshua did, how to combine the twenty-two letters of the Alef-Bet. Therefore God's holiness is revealed to us in the letters of Torah and in the ten utterances of Creation, the ten Sefirot, the Tree of Life within each one of us.

At-one-ment at the Mercy Seat

The Mercy Seat, or Kapporeth, the top of the Ark, is called an atonement piece. This is where the High Priest places the offering on Yom Kippur, after sprinkling blood from the Outer Court animal sacrifices as an atonement (for Israel's sins collectively) on the altar, which the holy

---

[21] Zohar 2:192.
[22] Ibid., 2:193.
[23] Ibid., 2:195.

incense covers in smoke. The Ark is made more powerful by its gold makeup and the transformative power between the two cherubim, who face each other and whose wings touch, enclosing the area on the cover of the Ark for this holy meeting: "From the lid [of the Ark] you shall make two Cherubs at its ends. Their wings will spread upwards, sheltering the lid with their wings" (Exodus 25:19). Each cherub has the face of a child,[24] one with the likeness of a male and the other a female.[25] As conductors of the source of God's light of revelation and bestowal, they facilitate communication between God and humans. We understand this as meaning the childlike innocence within us is the guardian of our oneness with God until we are spiritually mature, that is, realized.

Rosh Hashanah, the day of Adam's creation, marks the beginning of a ten-day ritual process during which time we perfect each sefirotic aspect of ourselves. This culminates in Yom Kippur, the Day of Atonement, which can also be thought of as the day of at-one-ment, oneness in God-consciousness, which takes place on the Mercy Seat. This is also a place of judgment, or Gevurah, where the soul faces its moment of reckoning, and a place of loving-kindness, Chesed, showing us that when manifest beings use their gift of free will to support original divine intention, the state of at-one-ment can be known and embodied while within the earthly experience. Put another way: as seeming opposites are blended in balance, it is through this elevation of all of matter and thus of one's own inner nature and one's outer actions that humanity accomplishes its purpose and joy, divine union with God. This is a co-resonance, a conscious union between God and the initiate. Through the state of at-one-ment (atonement) brought about through selflessness, ceaseless service to others, devotion to God, and complete humility, genuine love can be known. Adam's repentance reminds us that we always have this possibility of reunion with God, for as Chassidut teaches, we are not in fact separate from God at all. All of creation *is* God. It is in taking a body at birth that we experience duality, the veil of separation, an illusion that the soul guides the body in overcoming. Once the soul and the intelligence, clothed in a body that comes to nullification, comes into union, we can revel in the Divine Presence while on earth. This is what the Mercy Seat facilitates. When we sacrifice our illusory sense of separation,

---

[24] Sukkah 5b.

[25] Zohar 2:227b.

we come into prophetic relationship with God. This is what Adam and Eve learned; it is what each of us must learn as well. This is the message of each Sefirah: unity with divine consciousness, within and without. "No person leaves this world without seeing Adam, who asks him why he left the world and how. The person replies to [Adam], 'Woe, because of you I left the world!'"[26] Learning from Adam by taking complete responsibility for one's individual free will is the maturation that leads to the person's and eventually all of humanity's collective refinement.

While Adam is considered the first man of earth, it is also said that "three righteous men were the foundation of the world: Adam, Noah, and Abraham."[27] It is even stated that the "patriarch Abraham was worthy of being created before Adam, but the Holy One, blessed is He, said, 'I will create Adam first, so that if he sins, Abraham will come and make amends.'"[28] This reveals that God had foreknowledge of what Adam and Eve would do, and that he had a back-up plan in preconceiving the patriarch of the People of the Book. Just as Adam settled on Mt. Moriah, Abraham brought his son Isaac there to sacrifice him; seeing Abraham's complete devotion to Him, God replaced Isaac with a sacrificial goat instead. Therefore, connecting Adam's expulsion and the rectification brought about through the later act of Abraham once again reflects why it is said that like Adam himself, the messianic Third Temple will be made by the two hands of God, thereby connecting the beginning, Creation, with the sucessful revelation of divinity in all of humankind. Mt. Moriah is a sanctified consciousness of service, and our return to Edenic paradise is as preordained as was Adam and Eve's expulsion. Therefore, we are free to leave and we are free to return to Eden.

The Jewish Ritual of Burial

> *Your dead shall live; carcasses shall arise—awake and sing,*
> *dwellers of the dust.*
>
> ISAIAH 26:19

Burial is an obligation in Jewish tradition, considered a tithing to God's created earth, showing honor to the body God has fashioned for us. We

---

[26] Zohar 1:57b. See also Chasidah, *Encyclopedia of Biblical Personalities,* 55.

[27] Shocher Tov 34:1. See also Chasidah, *Encyclopedia of Biblical Personalities,* 45.

[28] Shocher Tov. 34:1. See also Chasidah, *Encyclopedia of Biblical Personalities,* 45.

are each, through our body, connected to the earth, as we are connected to heaven through our soul, making us heavenly earth-humans.

Cremation, according to the Judaic esoteric writings, is considered an offense against the Creator; it is hurtful to the soul's refinement of its five aspects (Nefesh, Ruach, Neshamah, Chayah, Yechidah) and five corresponding worlds (Assiyah, Yetzirah, Beriyah, Atzilut, Adam Kadmon [Or En Sof]). For those who believe in a final Resurrection that is dependent on the interred bones of the dead, a boneless remnant cannot be resurrected: "We have been taught: For a full twelve months, the human body remains in existence while the soul ascends and descends [to join the body]. After twelve months, the body ceases to exist, and the soul ascends [to the treasury of souls] and descends no more."[29] Another perspective allows that even a cremated person has the opportunity for Resurrection in certain cases. There is a bone in the back of the skull (some say the seventh vertebra) called the luz bone, "which is never destroyed and remains intact forever,"[30] thus making it possible for those who died in the crematoriums in the Holocaust, or for others whose interment decisions were out of their control, to be included in the final Resurrection.

An exploration of this subject through gematria, a tool for understanding the hidden story revealed in every Hebrew word or letter, explains why the patriarchs and matriarchs followed Adam in the holy ritual practice of burial.[31] The Hebrew word for **bones, עצם**, has a value of 200: "And Adam said, this *is* now **bone** of my **bones**, and flesh of my flesh; she shall be called Woman, because she was taken out of Man" (Genesis 2:23). Other Hebrew words sharing the same numerical value are found in the story of Adam and Eve and reflect the lessons learned from them:

Your eyes, עיניכם: "For God doth know that in the day ye eat thereof, then **your eyes** shall be opened, and ye shall be as Gods, knowing good and evil" (Genesis 3:5).

Tree, מעץ: "And the LORD God said, Behold, the man is become as one of us, to know good and evil: and now, lest he put forth his hand, and take also of the **Tree** of Life, and eat, and live for ever" (Genesis 3:22).

---

[29] Chaviv, *Ein Yaakov*, B. Shabbat 152b–153a, 128.

[30] Zohar 3:22a.

[31] The Cave of Machpelah was purchased by Abraham for Sarah's burial, and he joined her there upon his death. Also buried there are Adam and Eve, Isaac and Rebecca, and Jacob and Leah.

Wings, כנפים: "And the cherubim shall stretch forth their **wings** on high, covering the Mercy Seat with their **wings,** and their faces shall look one to another; toward the Mercy Seat shall the faces of the cherubim be" (Exodus 25:20).

In each of these examples, the context in which we find these words whose value equals 200, the same as that of *bones,* is part of Adam's story. In the verse containing the word *eyes* we find Adam's personal story of knowing good and evil. The Tree of Knowledge of Good and Evil that is guarded as a result of their deed contains certain secrets that are already in our bones: that is, that our bones can be resurrected and we can thus live forever. In the word *wings* we find a reference to the wings of the cherubim guarding the Mercy Seat and the idea that Adam is suffused with God's mercy after his expulsion from the Garden of Eden, that is, the Holy of Holies. Adam and Eve's bones, buried in Machpelah along with other ancestors' bones, represent the stories of their times. We learned with Moses how sacred and important the bones of the ancestors are regarded in the story of his bringing Joseph's bones out of Egypt. This explains why Adam was so careful to hide his own bones, for they contained the Tree of Life and all of its teachings: "When [the time] came for Adam to leave this world, he said, 'If I do not make myself a resting place deep inside the earth now, all the generations will take my bones and make them an object of idolatrous veneration.' What did he do? He dug crooked caves very deep inside the earth and called [them] the Cave of Machpelah."[32]

Using gematria to look at the name **Adam** in Hebrew, אדם (Alef Dalet Mem), we find it has a number value of 45. Looking at other words of equal value, we discover more about the purpose of each human being. For example, the words **praise, יהל** (Job 31:26); **redeem, הגואל** (Psalms 103:4); **and mourn, ואבלו** (Isaiah 3:26); and **live, ויחיהו** (Psalm 41:2); suggest Adam's praise of God and Sabbath; that death brings mourning to our hearts; and that we live as Adam does, hoping for redemption,

---

[32] Midrash HaGadol, Bereshis 5:5. See also Chasidah, *Encyclopedia of Biblical Personalities,* 54. More than 300,000 people visit Ma'arat HaMachpelah Me'arat HaMachpela (the Cave of the Double Tombs, מערת המכפלה, or Machpelah) annually. The structure is divided into three rooms: Ohel Avraham, Ohel Yitzhak, and Ohel Ya'akov. Presently, Jews have access to Ohel Yitzhak, the largest room, only ten days per year.

which our actions effect. We each, like Adam, learn that God created us as pure and perfect human beings. Leaving Eden—that is, once we receive an incarnate body—means we must choose between right and wrong, good and evil. Thus through free will we work in the world to redeem ourselves and others from the sitra achra, the other side, the side of selfishness and egoic attachment, the very root of separation consciousness.

Emanating Light upon Death

Adam was designed to live forever, but eating from the tree brought about his mortality, and ours. "God gave him a lifespan of one thousand years, but Adam took seventy years off his own life and gave them to David, son of Jesse. Thus Adam lived only 930 years when he could have lived a thousand."[33] Unlike most modern funerals, which are somberly oriented to the grief of the survivors, the death of the first man of earth was a celebration: "They made the day of Adam's death a festival, a day of drinking and rejoicing."[34]

It is said that the day of a person's death is far greater than that of one's birth. Why? Because at the time of death we emanate to the world all the good we have done. Depending on the amount of benefit we have created, so great is this illumination that people feel the presence of the departed one's soul. This confirms the principle that when we put our ego to rest we are a far greater messenger and vessel of God's holy light. In this same way, at the time of our birth, we are a recipient of God's light of Creation, by which the Neshamah aspect of the soul is breathed into the body. Just as Adam was made from the light of Creation on the sixth day, this same light illuminates our earthly odyssey. It is this light that, upon death, is returned to its source, when one is reunited with the Godhead. This great light of the soul is known to illuminate the living after a person's bodily death.

As discussed earlier in this book, the vital force, or Nefesh (corresponding to the realm of Asiyah), that is carried in a person's blood and nerves leaves the body at its death, and within a year of burial, the spirit

---

[33] Bamidbar Rabbah 14:12. See also Chasidah, *Encyclopedia of Biblical Personalities*, 53.
[34] Tanna d'Bei Eliyahu Rabbah 16. See also Chasidah, *Encyclopedia of Biblical Personalities*, 54.

force, or Ruach (realm of Yetzirah) also departs the body. The Nesha-mah (and corresponding realm of Beriyah) stores the record of one's good deeds and the wisdom one has gained and becomes the "credentials" we carry with us into our next life. It is the breath breathed into a person at birth, and it hovers around the body of the deceased until the body is buried, and afterward it lingers over the grave of the deceased until the body's complete decay a year later. In Jewish tradition, at that point the headstone is unveiled and the yearlong ritual process of remembering the departed ends, other than annual prayers said on the anniversary of the person's death.

The Traditional Practice of Burial

I will overturn their mourning to joy, I will comfort them, and I will give them joy that will be greater than their former pain.

JEREMIAH 31:12

Traditionally, from the moment of death until the body is buried, the community keeps a vigil over the body called *shemira,* "watching or guarding," during which the Book of Psalms is read until the time of burial, the constant presence of the living giving comfort to the deceased's soul while the body awaits burial, before the soul's transition to Olam HaBa, the World to Come. These ritual vigils are generally per-formed by each community's Chevra Kadisha, or Burial Society, which consists of Torah-observant members of the community; they perform the same function for the sanctuary of the body as the people's prayers in Malchut do for the soul. For this reason, those living recite psalms for the deceased.

Before the newly departed's life is offered up at burial, the body is cleansed and purified. Called *tahara,* this aspect of the burial rites can be likened to the High Priest's preparations, in which he must cleanse and purify himself in the Outer Court before he can proceed to the Holy of Holies. The deceased's body is washed and dressed for its day of return. Men prepare men for burial, and women care for women who have died. In this way, the living pay respect to the holy vessel of life and help the departed soul pay honor to the temple in which the Divine Presence once rested. Then comes the dressing of the body in traditional garments, which do not distinguish between men and women; both are provided white burial shrouds, called *tachrichim,* which consist of a shirt, pants, a head covering, and a belt. These white shrouds, often made of linen but also of muslin, are made by hand and are without buttons, zipper, or any fasteners. They represent the sacred garments worn by the High Priest when he enters the Holy of Holies, where the soul faces its moment of judgment. Like the High Priest on the Day of Atonement, it is said that each departed soul hears the living in praying for the welfare of the deceased's soul and family, community, and world. After this, the shrouded body, which is not embalmed or shown publicly, is placed in a simple wooden box that disintegrates along with the body in the soil it is buried in.

In the Tent of Meeting, the High Priest (the vessel of God's light, Asiyah) who has been cleansed in the Outer Court (Yetzirah) by water and fire is dressed in the garments of light to offer sustenance and incense in the Holy Place (Beriyah); afterward he is prepared to enter the Holy of Holies (Atzilut), where he wears simple garb, without any worldly ornamentation. This ritual process is reflected in the burial rites as well. The body inside of the casket, which is also called an ark, or *aron,* is given an in-ground burial (Kvura BiKarka). The record of that person's life is in their bones—much the way the tablets rest inside the Ark, making the union with God complete: "For dust you are, and dust you are to return" (Genesis 3:19). The soul is now free to begin its journey through the vehicles of the Chayah, the living breath, and the Yechidah, the divine spark, the two eternal aspects of the soul that never reside in the body during life at all but are connected to it like a spiritual umbilical cord. Now the soul is ready for judgment and eventually, for ascension to the perfected souls' abode of Gan Eden, the stage above that of Olam HaBa.

The beauty of this correspondence between the Tent of Meeting and its Tabernacle and the deceased person's initiation (prayers over the body), consecration (ritual cleansing), and sanctification (proper burial in the arklike coffin in the earth) tells us that the work of spiritual development as practiced on the path of the Tree of Life during one's life prepares the soul for its journey at the time of the body's death. In this fashion, the prophets we have learned from went to their deaths totally awake and prepared to go.

Adam's decision to locate a burial place for himself while he still lived is a custom followed to this day by Jewish people, who select where one's family will be buried. The People of the Book have such regard for each person's spiritual purpose that regardless of one's station or deeds in life, upon seeing the grave of a Jewish person one says, "'Blessed be He who fashioned you in justice, Who maintained you in justice, Fed you in justice, And in justice gathered you in, And in justice will raise you up again.' Mar, son of Ravina, citing R. Nahman, used to conclude the blessing thus: 'And he knows the number of all of you, And he will bring back to life and preserve you. Blessed be He who bring the dead back to life.'"[35]

Spiritual Development: The Edenic Return at the Mercy Seat

Adam shows us the journey we embark on at birth and complete upon death—our journey back to Eden. It is the universal spiritual path. What one searches for is already within us but is concealed from us until we desire unity with God. Sometimes it takes whole generations—if not whole lifetimes—of exile for this desire to be activated. Sometimes it takes but a single illness or personal tragedy for a person to generate awareness of his innate love of God and the purpose of life. Sometimes it takes many years of living to discover the essential oneness of all life. Sometimes a person realizes unity with God only upon physical death.

Adam's song, the twelfth and final song in our ascent of the Tree of Life, tells us of this lifelong spiritual journey. It sings of the redemption available to each person who seeks in earnest. It represents the pinnacle of the prophetic experience of directly encountering God in the Holy of Holies, the most concealed chamber holding the light of the unknowable Creator, the source of all light, the immaculate Or En Sof, where the eternal aspects of the soul are rooted and nurtured. The Mercy Seat is an enigma, as very few people are allowed to service it or even come near it. During the Exodus, those few included Moses, Joshua, and Aaron and his sons. Mercy, being an attribute of the right-pillar Sefirah of Chesed, reflects the idea that God tilts the scales toward mercy when our life's actions are weighed and our soul is judged.

[35] Bialik and Ravnitzky, *Sefer Ha-Aggadah,* 1:264, 536.

It is here at the Mercy Seat that Adam shows us that we praise God for His mercy and for giving us Sabbath. Sabbath is the healing water for all that ails us. It is the light of the Or En Sof, the light of Creation that enables Adam and Moses and all subsequent generations from age to age, until final Resurrection, to see. These great prophets were able to see within themselves the scope of humankind's odyssey, and in this way they themselves achieved the unity consciousness that is the quest of the human journey.

Becoming Adam Kadmon

We become like Adam Kadmon upon death, experiencing union with God; but we are to discover our inner holy origins while we live. Arriving now at our final destination, having refined each and every aspect of our being, from the feet to the head, we come into self-mastery. This is ultimate freedom. When we are no longer controlled by any impulse or desire other than to serve God, we are free. When we cross over, from the desert of doubt, ignorance, and fear that separation consciousness and exile creates, to the holy Promised Land, at-one-ment, we are at home in God's kingdom within. This is not a matter of any one religion; it is the archetypal pattern reflected in all sacred traditions, which describe the ultimate state, that of enlightenment, in terms of this kind of oneness.

To reach the ultimate revelation through speaking with God directly, as Adam does inside the gates of Eden, we must die to our material, temporal view of the world and to all our attachments to it. Doing so makes the actual physical death of the body no different than putting on or taking off a cloak, as one sees in the deaths of Moses, Aaron, and Miriam, the three sibling prophets who were all taken by a kiss from God, and over whom the power of the angel of death did not exist.

Cosmic Beings in Mortal Bodies

Adam was created on the sixth day of Creation; tradition states this is because of God's desire to give all that He had created up until then to man, so that he might have dominion over it, that is, use it, protect it, refine it, and preserve it. As we are earth people, this is our destiny.

Adam's appearance in the Garden with Eve was despoiled by defying the Creator's admonition to "eat freely of everything in the garden but do not eat from the Tree of Knowledge of Good and Evil" (Genesis 2:17). We too are counseled to beware of egoistic pride, which engenders the consciousness of separation. We must be faithful to the natural unity between the mind and the heart and work toward inner peace. Above all, we must be secure in the sense of who we are: cosmic beings clothed in mortal bodies who are capable of becoming immortal and heavenly.

Humans are capable of refining matter, elevating the sparks in matter, and refining the holy light that is held within—even within evil. Thus humanity is the elevator by which creation is honored and celebrated. Adam's legacy and God's gift to humanity is the Tree of Life, which exists within each one of us. The Tree teaches us how to elevate our inner and outer composition. The earth man is a perfect duplicate of the heavenly realms, just as the constellations of the zodiac and the natural elements are reflected in our own makeup, physically, emotionally, and spiritually.

> Our masters taught: six things are said concerning human beings. In regard to three, they are like ministering angels: in regard to three others, like animals. Three like ministering angels: they have understanding like the ministering angels, they walk erect like the ministering angels, they can use the sacred tongue like the ministering angels. Three like animals: they eat and drink like animals, they procreate like animals, and they excrete like animals.[36]

Kabbalah teaches that we are cosmic beings in mortal bodies, elevating each atom into the light of Creation. From this perspective, every organ in our body has a purpose beyond its mere physical nature. The Sefer Yetzirah as well as other holy works explore our cosmic anatomy and our soul's benefiting by the informed body. The reader is encouraged to reflect on these ancient teachings from the People of the Book. The following is a short reference to this ancient wisdom, concerning the inner functions of the body's parts, which have spiritual correlates in the rituals performed in the Tent of Meeting and its Mishkan:

---

[36] Bialik and Ravnitzky, *Sefer Ha-Aggadah,* 1:266, 786.

Our masters taught: The kidneys counsel, the heart discerns, the tongue shapes [words], the mouth articulates. The windpipe produces the voice, the gullet takes in all kinds of foods, the lungs absorb all kinds of moisture [from the stomach], the liver is the seat of anger, the gall lets a drop fall in the liver and allays anger, the spleen produces laughter, the large intestine grinds foods, the maw produces sleep, and the nose awakens. Should the organ that induces sleep awaken, the awakener fall asleep, the man would pine away. The sages taught; should both organs cause sleep or both keep awake, the man would die at once.[37]

The organs and limbs of the human body are the spiritual components of the Tent of Meeting and its sanctuary, as described in this work. When we examine this idea from the perspective of the Book of Formation (Sefer Yetzirah), we see that physical and spiritual health go hand in hand, and that personal and collective evolution are inseparable. Heaven and earth are the multidimensional landscapes in which we have beingness. As ten-dimensional beings, we are always experiencing the interpenetrating fields and realms of which the body and soul are comprised: from the blood in our Nefesh (the vital force); to the will in the spirit (Ruach) of the body; to the breath in our Neshamah (the eternal aspect of the soul as represented by our higher sense of hearing or intuitive understanding), the light force invigorates the Chayah (the living presence) and Yechidah (originating spark), which are all connected as the spiritual and material dimensions of our existence.

To Receive in Order to Give

Sometimes we make choices that have unintentional consequences, like Adam and Eve, who did not intend to create misery for all of humanity, and from a traditional perspective they did not: God knew before creating Adam and Eve what would happen. Their disobedience was already known in the supernal realm before they were created. So why then, we might ask, did God design the ability for disobedience in His created human?

---

[37] Bialik and Ravnitzky, *Sefer Ha-Aggadah,* 1:277, 788.

We must earn our place in Gan Eden. We must use our free will to make choices that are for the betterment of the world. Revelation is the result of self-refinement and self-mastery. As the greatest pleasure one can have is to revel in the Divine Presence, God realizes that if everything is given easily to human beings, without their having to do anything but receive such gifts, they can become gluttonous, lazy, selfish, and depressed. This is because the greatest, deepest desire in the human soul is to receive *in order to give*. For this reason, when a person works to accomplish something in life, it is not reaching one's goal that counts; it is the effort and the intention one applies in accomplishing the task that matters the most for the soul. This is the teaching of Keter, the teaching of divine revelation and the Mercy Seat. God evicts us from formlessness when He gives us form. When we are thoughtless about the impact of our deeds and aspire only for our own personal benefit, we are cast out of the holy Garden of Eden into separation consciousness. But when we are merciful toward others and aspire most of all to benefit them, we are in conversation with creatorship. This creates unity consciousness, which is the path to divine revelation.

As truth is the seal of God, Adam discovers the one truth that all humanity must embrace: that separation consciousness is death, death to the possibility of the Divine Presence coming to a place of rest within us. Once Adam became aware of his own uncovered self he was cast out of the Garden, for duality is the state that engenders violation of all of the Commandments of God. But when a person comes into loving oneness, our origination point, truth is revealed by the souls of all times. This is the prophesied messianic era. It is said that forty years after its onset, the Resurrection of the Dead will come to pass.

Life and Death

> *Death will be swallowed up forever, and Lord God will wipe the*
> *tears off every face. He will remove the insult against His people*
> *from the entire world. God, the merciful One, has declared.*
>
> ISAIAH 25:8

In Adam's story we have the same lesson that is later taught by the prophets and prophetesses and by the Israelites as a nation in their journey toward self-realization: that of becoming one with God and all of creation. The consciousness of separation is a wall between the Holy Spirit's presence and our own. For Adam and Eve, separation came as the outcome of wanting to know that which was forbidden, which shows us the reality of what happens when we desire what we should not have. Is the earthly consciousness of the human being inherently a consciousness of separation? Does being born into physical form engender this experience of duality?

Life in a human body means having to choose between good and evil. This life-and-death cycle is the legacy of the descendants of Adam and Eve. Rather than being a curse, however, might it be the only way each person can come to God, irrespective of what others might do? We must do our best to don the robes of the High Priest in order to carry out our charge of becoming obedient to our highest nature, to our innate template of heavenly perfection. These are, of course, matters of choice. Yet still, the Torah tells us that immortality is our rightful inheritance, as it was Adam and Eve's when they were created.

Spiritual Development as Toil

As has been pointed out over the centuries, God's plan all along was that the man of earth should work, earning his rewards through effort, for if this had not been the divine plan God would not have created in Adam the ability to sin, to choose of his own free will, including things strictly forbidden to him. Adam had been told of six things he could not do: "Idolatry, desecration of the Name, establish courts, murder, adultery, and theft."[38] As punishment for Adam and Eve's disobedience, not just Adam, but all humankind would have to labor for its rewards, and woman would have to suffer childbirth:

> Unto the woman He said: "I will greatly multiply thy pain and thy travail; in pain thou shalt bring forth children; and thy desire shall be to thy husband, and he shall rule over thee." And unto Adam He said: "Because thou hast hearkened unto the voice of thy wife, and hast eaten of the tree, of which I commanded thee, saying: Thou shalt not

---

[38] Devarim Rabah 2:25.

eat of it; cursed is the ground for thy sake; in toil shalt thou eat of it all the days of thy life. (Genesis 3:16–17)

The toil referred to here is experienced globally. "How much labor did Adam invest before he had bread to eat? He planted, sowed, harvested, cut, piled up, threshed, winnowed, removed the chaff, ground, sifted, kneaded and baked—and [only] then did he eat."[39] These are the things we must do metaphorically to refine ourselves: we plant our seeds—our thoughts, words, and deeds; we sow them in the world; we harvest them, cutting and piling them up, threshing and winnowing them; and then we remove the chaff from ourselves, grinding our egos, sifting what is holy from what is not; then we knead and bake until we are done. Finally, we partake of the supernal mysteries.

Adam's engineered fall from grace, and God's subsequent forgiveness of him, was to enable Adam to ask for God's help, and to thus enable each one of us to seek this relationship with the living God within us and all around us. This reflexive nature of God and His creations shows us once again the interrelationship between the spiritual development of the person and that of the world, between the inner temple of the individual and humanity's collective spiritual refinement: "R. Alexandri said: He who studies Torah for its own sake makes peace in the household below. Rav said: It is as though he built the Temple above and the Temple below. R. Yohanan said, he shields the whole world all of it, [from the consequences of sin]. Levi said: he also brings redemption nearer."[40]

The End in the Beginning

While Adam and Eve began life in the Garden of Eden, our destinies end in the Garden, that is, the Holy of Holies of our body-soul temple. While the destiny of the primordial human being involved a descent from holiness, ours is an ascent. Each generation has contributed to the perfection of some realm, along with its corresponding Sefirah and archetype (partzuf).

According to Kabbalah, at this time in the history of humanity we

---

[39] Berachot 58a.
[40] B. Sanh 99b. See also Bialik and Ravnitzky, *Sefer Ha-Aggadah,* 7:113, 414.

stand in Yesod, the next-to-last Sefirah in our timeline of descending the Tree; we are therefore at the point of near completion of the descent of the light. We are beginning to see what this means in terms of the world: ecological cataclysm, warfare, terrorism, economic upheaval, and other forms of global instability. In these times, considered the precursor or the "heels" of the age of Moshiach of which we are all the midwives, we will experience the birth pangs of messianic consciousness and transformation. Trials and tribulations can spur humanity's good hearts to greater and more vigorous work and prayer, as the harder it gets, the more we must do to bring balance to the world situation. This can bring us into unity consciousness.

Humanity's descent through the worlds is no different from Adam's eviction from a state of perfection. We must earn back this original, innate perfection through our labor and commitments. By so doing, we inherit and maintain elevation from lifetime to lifetime. We are the inheritors of this holy planet. We are its stewards. The Tree of Life tells us that reverence for all life is the teaching of this holy Tree. All sacred wisdom lineages teach this basic holy truth, which is God's seal on Creation.

Attaining Paradise

Imagine we are the freshly created royal couple of perfection, born already mature, as it is said, in our early twenties, enjoying, as vegetarians, all the fruits of the Garden: the lush oasis, the fresh water, the spiraling brooks, the singing birds—a kingdom at peace. It is perfect, idyllic wholeness—an image every soul is stamped with and can imagine, telling us that it is an inherent part of our human makeup. I refer to it as a piece of paradise, something the soul has known from the beginning. We know this is our possible inheritance and rightful inheritance, that all of earth was created to manifest this, even though our "civilization" is part of earth's despoilment. Yet we are also capable of being the solution to the current crisis, elevating earth and all of humanity.

To accomplish this refinement of life on earth, we must take responsibility for our own inclinations. If we fail to do so, we will be acting as the first couple did, claiming someone or something outside of ourselves tricked us, as Adam blames Eve; and then we will encourage others, as

Eve did Adam, to join in our misdeeds. War follows this beguiling pattern, as does all intolerance and injustice, contributing to our downfall as individuals and as a planetary whole. All forms of systematic abuse depend on collaborative sins of severe selfishness and callousness as seen in the horrendous treatment of animals and minorities worldwide, including women and children. When the collective will is applied to exclusivity and domination rather than inclusiveness and compassion, division and destruction follow.

The metaphorical nakedness that Adam and Eve knew is the state of separation that we know as a feeling of obliviousness to the pulse of the divine. It is right, therefore, that the soul fears such a state, as Adam feared the darkness and his separation from God. Humankind has an obligation to protect the earth and all life forms. We have an obligation to improve the world, not destroy it. This charge is for each person. We all know that this is so—when we do something wrong, we feel remorse. When Adam and Eve realized that they were naked—unprotected—and later after the Cloud of Glory had departed from them, they were aware of having fallen from their higher level of perfection. This protective glory, however, returns every week of the year in the form of Sabbath.

Each of us has to struggle to regain the original, primordial unity consciousness. We can spend lifetimes in pursuit of this noble truth, which takes us back to the Garden, our origination point. God gives us Sabbath as His resting place for our body and soul; it signifies a time and place for restoring our relationship with divinity, with family, with community, and with all of life. So holy is Sabbath that it is called Israel's partner. Its special radiance is different from that of the other six days of Creation, and it is Adam who declares for each soul that this is so.

Final Integration

In Keter, through the light that illuminates the Mercy Seat, we attain the body of Adam Kadmon, the fully realized primordial man of earth, one who is united with the Divine Presence. While said to be a state of being only the tzaddik accomplishes, we are also told that this is the state that all of humanity will one day achieve. In this state of perfection, there is no separation between what one desires for oneself and what one desires for others and the world. Divine realization is the state of coherence that comes as a result of self-mastery. Talking to God means finding God's voice within us, the voice of prophecy.

All sacred wisdom lineages have their spiritual leaders and mediums, people open to the divine spirit, able to hear and translate messages from the supernal realms. This exists in potential in each person. Hearing the inner voice of the divine is the experience of the Mercy Seat, suggesting that Adam Kadmon—that is, each one of us—is by design a ten-dimensional being operating simultaneously in ten different fields, all interconnected, as Kabbalah teaches. This holy Tree of Life teaches us how to integrate the body and soul in order to live by the wisdom hidden inside our own holy Tent of Meeting, the Tabernacle of Peace, the sanctuary of the Divine Presence, as described in the teachings of the People of the Book, beginning with Adam and Eve.

A Sanctuary
for
God's Presence

13
The Holy Temple of Body and Soul
The Illuminating Path of Peace

And God Saw the light, and it was good.

GENESIS 1:4

Becoming a Tabernacle of Peace

Having climbed the ladder of light rung by rung, we now have a complete set of tools to use in pursuit of inner and outer peace. The self-refined person is a person at peace. Such a person can bring others to this same sense of wholeness. There is no more perfect abundance than peace. We can now see that the Israelites were given a method for achieving inner peace and communal harmony that anyone in the world can use freely. The journey is the same for all of humanity, and it is described by the workings and meaning of the Tent of Meeting and the Sabbath, the Tabernacle of Peace. We are each a Tent of Meeting—the place of initiation, consecration, elevation, illumination, and, ultimately, revelation and Godliness.

Concealed and Revealed Good

We began our ascent of the Tree of Life by seeing it in terms of being a life journey, wherein one goes up and down this sacred Tree every day of every year, from lifetime to lifetime. Additionally, we now understand how to use the body, its specific abilities and senses, as expressions of the divine qualities that each Sefirah embodies within its parts. We have also looked at this journey of light from the narratives, rituals, and songs of biblical personages. In our own lives as in theirs, the holy journey from emancipation to revelation includes two kinds of goodness: the concealed good and the revealed good. One might ask is one greater than the other?

Revealed good is the goodness we experience in our lives when things go well—when we are happy, loving, and healthy. This might be called the Chesed of God's presence. When we are confronted by sorrow, loss, pain, and all the things we associate with demise, this is called the concealed good or the Gevurah of the Creator. Just as we now know that these two sefirotic aspects, like our two hands, are partners, and that God manifests in many ways, we are reminded that our lives are for the purpose of growth and refinement. Therefore we are counseled that each hardship holds within it something even more precious than the kind of happiness that comes when things go well, for within life's challenges is the great light of blessings. This is concealed good. Handling our difficulties from the perspective of looking for the good in them, we are shown the concealed good that is a more refined light, held, as it is, in a concealed situation, which is our blessing to discover. Both revealed and concealed good are the ingredients of life, and when we find the purpose of each, we arrive at peace. Having faith that there are truths hidden in each moment is the priestly duty of humankind, for only the children of Adam and Eve can elevate the mixture of good and evil, joy and sorrow, and all other opposites, to pure goodness.

The Ten Emanations of Creation

Now that we have completed our ascent of the Tree of Life, recall that the historical representatives of the ten Sefirot and the Ten Songs of Creation are either individual prophets or B'nai Yisrael acting collectively. The ten Sefirot and their historical representatives connect us, as initiates, to the ten emanations of Creation that comprise our body and soul. Adam, Moses, Joshua, Devorah, Chanah, King David, and King Solomon are each both singers and composers of the prophetic texts of their associated Sefirah's song. Reading and contemplating these sacred texts over and over again, will, over time, bring much deeper insights, as conditioning oneself to receiving the Ruach HaKodesh and the Shechinah is made possible by diligent practice.

Reviewing the Process

Sanctuary of the Divine Presence has taken the reader up the ladder of light, telling the Israelites' story in reverse chronological order. Reviewing this sequence, then, this time in chronological order—from the top to the bottom of the ladder of light—is a fitting close to this spiritual odyssey.

Sefirah: Keter (crown)
Quality: Emunah (faith)
Archetype: Adam Kadmon (primordial man of earth)
Realm: Or En Sof emanating to Atzilut (emanation)
Soul: Yechidah (divine spark of God)
Anatomy: The entire skull
Tent of Meeting: The Mercy Seat
Biblical Personage: Adam outside the gates of Eden (Psalms 92:1)
Type of Song: Ashrei (sublime insight)

Looking at Adam and Eve's story, we begin with the primordial couple's eviction from paradise. When we look at the deeper meaning underlying this story, which can be read literally, metaphorically, and esoterically, we find wise instructions for the creation of the new Eden: it is not in heaven but rather on earth. In fact, the new Eden—what some have called the New Jerusalem, which is represented by Malchut and Moshiach—is the state of humanity's perfection, of being in unity with one another and with God. This suggests that inner peace is the final and necessary step each member of humanity must achieve to bring about global revelation and harmony. This begins with creating well-being of body, mind, heart, and soul. What facilitates this peace? In Torah, we are told that peace is based on love of God *and* personal humility. Without both we are unable to properly discern what is best for everyone in any given situation. How are we to know what leads to peace? Our right actions and generosity of spirit, talents, and possessions are also part of this gradual development. Our actions should bring us closer to our own holy nature and shared divinity. Sabbath, Adam declares, is this God-given peace, which will one day be the quality of perfect light and protection for all the days of Creation.

Sefirah: Chochmah (wisdom)
Quality: Bitul (self-nullification)
Archetype: Abba (Father)
Realm: Atzilut (emanation)
Soul: Chayah (living presence)
Anatomy: Eyes
Tent of Meeting: Holy of Holies
Biblical Personages: The Israelites at the Sea
Type of Song: Shir (praise and thanksgiving)

In the next stage of the descent of light into matter, we are greeted by the entire nation of Israel, led by Moses and Miriam. In the Song at the Sea, the great miracle of the parting of the Red Sea and the escape from Egypt is acknowledged. The wisdom imparted at this stage of development enables our emancipation from any form of enslavement. Here the descendants of Adam and Eve, under the leadership of Moses, learn to overcome doubt, thus gaining the power of faith and understanding and learning that the laws of the universe are balanced: "As we sow, so shall we reap." What we experience makes us living witnesses to history. Our quality of presence is the greatest gift we can give the world, for it permeates all that we think, say, and do.

Sefirah: Binah (understanding)
Quality: Simcha (happiness)
Archetype: Imma (The Mother)
Realm: Beriyah (creation)
Soul: Neshamah (hearing and understanding)
Anatomy: Ears
Tent of Meeting: The Holy Place
Biblical Personages: The Israelites collectively singing to the well
Type of Song: Beracha (blessings)

We next meet the nation of Israel following the death of Miriam the prophetess. The Israelites no longer have a supply of water and thus are compelled to sing to Miriam's miraculous well, whose flow has ceased, to draw down its blessings. It is the first time since the revelation at Sinai that we witness the Israelites acting as a unified whole to merit, through their collective prayer, the blessing of water. Prior to this event, the miracles of the Cloud of Glory, the manna, and fresh water were in the merit of specific individuals: Aaron, Moses, and Miriam. The quality of emotion associated with the song of Binah is that of a mother petitioning on behalf of her children. It is also a song of joy. When we are thirsty, when we are in need of spiritual sustenance, we must, like the Israelites at the well, communally bring down God's life-giving blessings, both as groups of individuals and as a planetary whole. In total joy we give thanks, knowing our prayers are heard. Also, we should not be concerned that our good deeds will not return to us in the form of good—they will. Just as Torah is called water and nurtures us, we learn that "all the streams run into the sea" (Eccles. 1:7). All of man's wisdom is nowhere other than in the heart. "Yet the sea is not full" (ibid.), the heart is never filled to capacity. You might suppose that when a man lets his wisdom go forth from his heart, it will never flow back to him. Hence Scripture says, "Yet the stream flows back again."[1]

Sefirah: Chesed (loving-kindness)
Quality: Ahavah (love)
Archetype: The Son (Zeir Anpin)
Realm: Yetzirah (formation)
Soul: Ruach (spirit)
Anatomy: Right hand
Tent of Meeting: Outer Court
Biblical Personage: Moses, offering his final words to Israel
Type of Song: Hazeinu (soaring melody)

After singing to the well, the Israelites gather together to hear Moses' final song and admonition to the people to teach these truths to their children and all subsequent generations. The song of Chesed, Moses' end-of-life song, is a soaring melody expressing the qualities of loving-

---

[1] Hayim Nahman Bialik and Yehoshua Hana Ravnitzky, *Sefer Ha-Aggadah,* 8:14, 470.

kindness and mercy. From this we gain appreciation for the teachings of truth as being a demonstration of God's love for His people, which ultimately means all of humanity, and the created worlds' love of God and His creation in return.

Sefirah: Gevurah (judgment, strength)
Quality: Yira (fear and awe of God)
Archetype: The Son (Zeir Anpin)
Realm: Yetzirah (formation)
Soul: Ruach (spirit)
Anatomy: Left hand
Tent of Meeting: Outer Court
Biblical Personage: Joshua, who stops the sun and the moon
Type of Song: Zemer (cutting through)

The next sefirotic exemplar in our descent down the ladder of light and in Torah chronology is Moses' successor, Joshua. Here we experience an emotional cutting through—a breakthrough—which can refer to our own inner enemies of holiness and the idea of overcoming the egoic inclinations of the yetzer hara (animal soul) in order to show God's ultimate power over every manifest form. This Sefirah signifies cutting through our sense of duality, our feelings of separateness as either a male or female, and in particular our illusory sense of separateness from God, which we struggle to overcome. In Gevurah we can better see why judgment and restriction is not a punishment, but rather an opportunity for radical transformation, taking each person beyond even the influence of the stars (i.e., fate), thus allowing one to be truly sovereign. Moses' consecrated successor, Joshua, knows the secret of the Hebrew language. With God's help he stops the natural order of the sun and the moon for thirty-six hours, enabling the Israelites to achieve victory over their enemy. As the Israelites get closer to Jerusalem, their opponents multiply and their battles increase; in the same way, as we get closer to overcoming our animal nature, it seemingly gets even stronger in asserting itself.

Sefirah: Tiferet (beauty, truth)
Quality: Rachamin (mercy)

Archetype: The Son (Zeir Anpin)
Realm: Yetzirah (formation)
Soul: Ruach (spirit)
Anatomy: Torso
Tent of Meeting: Outer Court
Bibical Personage: The prophetess Devorah
Type of Song: Hallel (praise and thanksgiving)

Following the descent of light on the Tree of Life, we join the prophetess Devorah, along with her counterpart, General Barak, as they wage a successful battle against the Canaanites on Mt. Tabor. Mountains are places of far-seeing and deep inner hearing, as we saw with Moses on Mt. Sinai. Historically and geographically, Mt. Tabor, in Lower Galilee, at the eastern end of the Jezreel Valley, was a crossroads: at the bottom of the mountain was an important road junction, and the mountain's bulgy formation above its environment gave Mt. Tabor a strategic value; consequently wars were conducted in this area in different periods in history. Mt. Tabor is much like the Sefirah it represents, Tiferet, which signifies the middle path, balancing the right and left, male and female sides of the Tree of Life. Meditation and prayer is the foundation for knowing what to do when our opposition challenges us. When we are victorious, we sing the great praise of the song of Tiferet, a hallel, radiating thanks and joy for our triumph. The Tabernacle shows us that the heart, the seat of the soul, radiates the light of God's joy for us, and ours for the Creator. We are designed to overcome obstacles. We do this by centering ourselves in God and the truth and beauty of Tiferet, where we await the Ruach HaKodesh, for the Ruach of one's soul speaks to the inner person as the Holy Spirit does Devorah, telling her the outcome of the battle before it even takes place.

Sefirah: Netzach (victory, eternity)
Quality: Bitachon (confidence)
Archetype: The Son (Zeir Anpin)
Realm: Yetzirah (formation)
Soul: Ruach (spirit)
Anatomy: Right leg

Tent of Meeting: Outer Court
Biblical Personage: The prophetess Chanah at the Tabernacle of Shiloh
Type of Song: Nitzuah (victory)

We next follow the Israelites to the Tabernacle's location at Shiloh, the holy place of ritual for some 400 years prior to its relocation to the City of David. Here the Israelites learn to pray to God in a new way, formally. It is here that the prophetess Chanah teaches the people the three-part method of praying: first, praising the Creator; then petitioning Him; and finally thanking Him for fulfilling our specific request. This is a victory over our own natures, where we come to a true attachment to God in our actions. Shiloh represents the station of development that tells us that praying to God is what gives us a sense of eternity in our temporal lives.

Sefirah: Hod (glory, the humble heart of royalty)
Quality: Temimut (sincerity)
Archetype: The Son (Zeir Anpin)
Realm: Yetzirah (formation)
Soul: Ruach (spirit)
Anatomy: Left leg
Tent of Meeting: Outer Court
Biblical Personage: King David
Type of Song: Hoda'ah (majestic humility)

As B'nai Yisrael moves toward the ultimate task of building the First Temple as a permanent dwelling place for God, they first join King David in establishing the "City of David," Jerusalem. Thanks to God, David has survived the murderous plots of King Saul and arisen to the pinnacle of power. Here in Hod, a place of thanksgiving and majesty, we arrive at the holy city. In moving from Shiloh to Jerusalem, we are moving from a place that is less permanent in our relationship with God to a place meant to be a permanent locus of thanksgiving and unity. Until all live in the holy city in a state of caring for one another—that is, until each person lives in his or her own illuminated heart—no one on earth can experience the complete deliverance God intends for human beings. This is why, in Kabbalah, the contemporary term "peace in the Middle East" should not be interpreted as signifying peace in just this one place;

rather, it means something much more: it is about the fulfillment of our shared destiny as the spiritual descendants of Adam and Eve. Recall that Adam was made from the soil taken from Mt. Moriah, said to be the very place of the Temple, where the final Third Temple will be built in the era of messianic consciousness, when there will be world peace.

Sefirah: Yesod (foundation)
Quality: Emet (truth)
Archetype: The Son (Zeir Anpin)
Realm: Yetzirah (formation)
Soul: Ruach (spirit)
Anatomy: Generative organs
Tent of Meeting: Outer Court
Biblical Personage: King Solomon
Type of Song: Ranenu tzaddikim (crying out of the righteous)

King David teaches us about fostering humility in our heart, which is the holy city; his son, King Solomon, shows us the covenant we all share: to make our life a holy sanctuary. In the end, each person builds his own temple of the body and soul. Learning from each stage of the Israelites' journey what it is to make a sanctuary of one's life, we now see that this Edenic quest is part of our human nature: we are in fact rooted in the Garden. It is neither too much to expect nor too much to want this paradise, which is the natural path of humankind. Here are the desires we each have: for freedom, for a good and meaningful life, for closeness to the divine, and for health and peace. By fulfilling the nature of each Sefirah and through service, we delight in the Divine Presence. As we continue to do our spiritual work, we enter the Temple of King Solomon and sing his love song to God. This tells us that when we make sacrifices and pay homage to the source of all, our Lord Almighty, we cry out joyfully for this holy marriage. Ultimately, each person arrives at his or her own understanding of the world and place in it. We also learn that while people are different from one another, these different ethnicities or religions are unimportant. "We have been taught that R. Meir said: 'A man differs from his fellow in three ways—in voice, in appearance, and in understanding.'"[2]

---

[2] R. Yaakov Ibn Chaviv, *Ein Yaakov.* "Why no two people look alike," Sanhedrin 38a, 616.

Sefirah: Malchut (kingdom)
Quality: Shiflut (lowliness)
Archetype: The Daughter (Nukvah/female)
Realm: Asiyah (action in the world)
Soul: Nefesh (vital force)
Anatomy: Feet and mouth
Tent of Meeting: The ground on which the Ohel Moed stands
Historical Personage: Moshiach and all of humanity
Type of Song: Amidah (self-reflection)

In Malchut, the kingdom of the physical world, we finally arrive at our individual and collective epochal fulfillment by design. Here on earth is the restoration reflected in the end, of which we are each part. Here, our primary task of self-evaluation prepares us for the highest good God intends for us, that of attaining the happiness and insight of Keter. Here, as we await the Moshiach and messianic consciousness, the time when world peace will be the natural state of being, we are shown that the Tabernacle is not just a place in the desert, or in Shiloh, or in Jerusalem, but is located within each one of us. In the ten Hebrew Bible texts representing each Sefirah can be found a discrete teaching for each person's life: that each of us is designed to be a holy sanctuary, a dwelling place for the Divine Presence. When each of us can fulfill our own individual part in this inner and outer transformation, the outcome will be unity consciousness. One can see why it is said that Jerusalem's borders will extend to all of Israel proper, and Israel's borders will extend to the rest of the world. This is not to say the boundaries of individual nations will be obliterated, but rather that all nations, all people, will respect one another's sovereign inheritance as representatives—indeed, prophets—of God.

And so we descend the ladder: from Eden with Adam and Eve; to the Red Sea with the Israelites; to Beer and Miriam's well; to Mt. Nebo with Moses; to the Jordan with Joshua; to Mt. Tabor with Devorah; to Shiloh with Chanah; to the City of David with King David; to the First Temple in Jerusalem with King Solomon; and finally, to where we each stand, right now, to our own unique place in the world.

The Holy Architecture of Light:
From Here to Gan Eden

Like the angels Jacob saw ascending and descending the ladder, we too continually ascend and descend Kabbalah's holy architecture of light. Having just recapitulated our journey down the ladder, let us undertake an ascent through the five realms of our soul as we do during life and on the day that we die, as described in our discussion of Adam.[3]

Combining all of the elements detailed in our journey—the worlds, the Sefirot, the partzufim, the aspects of the soul each is connected to, as well as the bodily components in which the holy light is housed—we can see how we are each an entire kingdom comprised of all of the archetypal family members found in the traditional family setting of the ancients: grandparents, father, mother, son, and daughter. As we have learned, each rung of the ladder represents an aspect of our own anatomy, both physically and spiritually, and each Sefirah's song brings us both the content and the emotional quality associated with it.

First Stage
Initiation—Daughter—Asiyah (action)—Prayer—Malchut

Recall that we begin in Malchut with our own prayer and a sincere effort to speak to God, that is, with that part of oneself that is the soul's voice while it resides within the physical body. It is a quality of reaching upward, signaling our intention to undertake divine service. Our first service is prayer. Here we learn an eighteen-step process for creating the conditions that will allow us to receive the highest light of the Godhead. Malchut, like our feet, takes us where we need to go and, like our mouth, speaks holy words of petition and praise. In this way we each stand in any given moment as living testimony to all of creation, both witnesses and actors. In the framework of the Ohel Moed, the Amidah, the prayer of Malchut and Asiyah, is said to stand for the sacrificial offerings made in the Tabernacle in the morning and afternoon. These are embodied by Israel (the daughter), Sabbath, and the

---

[3] Ascending the ladder of light is the same process the soul experiences during the death of the body.

Shechinah. We now know that we meet God everywhere we go. God is always with us should we choose to acknowledge the Divine Presence that infuses, vitalizes, and sustains us and the world around us. Our prayers take the place of the ritual offerings in the Tabernacle, making each of us an initiate of the middle path, while our actions are also part of this sacred service of making offerings.

Second Stage

Consecration—Son—Yetzirah (formation)—Refining the Emotions—Zeir Anpin (Chesed through Yesod)

Having prayer as the primary tool around which we orient our lives, we then move into a six-step integration of our emotions, or middot, in the six Sefirot of Chesed through Yesod. This group of six is called the Son, or Zeir Anpin, which in Kabbalah is represented by the single Sefirah of Tiferet. Representing our arms, legs, and generative organs, as well as the torso in which our bodily organs are housed, the Sefirot of the emotions are the various unique energies available to us on our journey of learning how to consecrate our lives and everything we do to sacredness. Revisiting these six emotional attributes from the last to the first, the bottom to the top, we begin in the ninth Sefirah of Yesod with King Solomon and his Song of Songs. We express in this pure, joyous song our desire to cry out to God in total devotion and our wish to use our generative powers for good and holy acts, for coming closer to God.

King David, in the eighth Sefirah of Hod, shows us how we take this cleaving to God and elevate it further, with David's psalm of thanksgiving showing each one of us our own genuine royalty, which is the state of supreme humility. Humility, our left leg, is partnered, as the bride to the groom, with our right leg.

Netzach, the seventh Sefirah, which the prophetess Chanah demonstrates as the invigorated will, is where we attach our lives to divine service, where we are victorious over our selfishness, arrogance, and sense of separation. Like Chanah, we learn that eternity is scripted into our makeup, and our victory over our lower impulses is what binds us to the Creator in whose image we are made.

The sixth Sefirah of Tiferet, being in the middle of the Tree of Life, is like a radiant sun; here we emanate joy, truth, and thanksgiving in all directions, toward every person we meet and in everything we do. Through the prophetess and judge Devorah we learn not only how to elevate our own emotions, singing out in this song's hallel, but as well how to elevate each situation we are part of. She shows us that right action takes discernment and the strength to eliminate anything injurious to oneself or to others.

Joshua, in the fifth Sefirah of Gevurah, shows us how to properly eliminate that which is destructive from our lives. We must break through our own habitual tendencies and desires in order to discover our inherent sacredness. Knowing oneself better than anyone else does, we must discern what in ourselves, whether emotionally, mentally, spiritually, or physically, needs to be changed. Joshua shows us that we are partners with God, capable of rising above our own inclinations as we discover how to re-create our lives by transforming the old into the new.

In Moses' end-of-life review in Chesed, the fourth Sefirah, love is the theme, the message, and the story. Here, with a soaring melody called a hazeinu, our right hand becomes the hand of loving-kindness; we receive from God in order to benefit others, and we give to others in order to heal and love.

All six of these Sefirot, of Zeir Anpin, the "small face" (or impatient one), are members of our consecrating team that helps us make a daily occupation of holy involvement. Everything we do is a part of the divine life we are immersed in from day to day, lifetime to lifetime. Impatience, the Kabbalistic quality of the Hebrew *Zeir Anpin,* explains why our emotions can spur us to act in selfish or thoughtless ways. Patience, therefore, is a holy attribute we must cultivate on the journey of spiritual refinement.

Third Stage
Elevation—Mother—Beriyah (creation)—
Understanding—Binah

After refining our emotions, we learn how to use our intuition and intellect. As we leave the realm of the emotions and the Outer Court, as signified by the fire and water rituals, we enter the Holy Place and become an expert at drawing down blessings, just as the Israelites learned in singing to the well. Here we encounter the archetypal Mother in the form of the third Sefirah, Binah. This is where our ability to listen, hear, and understand is emphasized. Here the Israelites sing to the well, proving how bestowal from above, and therefore our spiritual elevation, occurs. Here in Binah, where a sense of feeling is combined with the intellect, we gain a sense of being cared for, protected, and nurtured. We develop our intuition, which is often described as having a hunch. Mothers are said to have extra intuition, just as traditionally it is said that all women have extra Binah. The Mother aspect of every human being is a deep, feeling quality that can "hear" what is unspoken as well as "understand" in a feeling way what is said.

Fourth Stage

Illumination—Father—Atzilut (emanation)—
Wisdom—Chochmah

The combination of skills we have acquired thus far makes it possible for us to graduate from a focus on our emotions to a focus on our wisdom center as we enter Chochmah, the second Sefirah from the top, where we sing a jubilant song, thanking God for saving us from the enemies of doubt and our own mind games, which spring from unbalanced emotions like fear and anger. Here God illuminates each person with wisdom and jubilation, experiences we are conscious of and witness to, seeing with our own eyes the glory of God all around and within us. We cross over all doubts in God and leave material and emotional enslavement behind.

Fifth Stage

Revelation/Revealed Essence—the Ancient One—
Or En Sof (limitless light of the Creator) emanating to Atzilut
(emanation)—Godliness—Keter

As we reach the apex of our journey of self-mastery, we encounter a still higher realm of experience, one that leads to sublime insight and thanksgiving. At this point, so thoroughly immersed are we in the Divine Presence that there is only one thing remaining: to be grateful for this holiness we are comprised of and able to reveal. No longer separate from God, we are united in body, mind, and soul with the universal source of life and love, the state of oneness. We are no longer made of parts; we are a completely re-created person, re-created consciously in God's image. While few people may reach such a sublime level of refinement, we do not lack the knowledge of or the instructions for how to do this. This is the gift of the Hebrews' ancient teachings on how to make a dwelling place for the Divine Presence within the sanctuary of one's own individual life.

Resurrection: Making Eden on Earth

Arriving at our own perfection, like Adam and Eve in the Garden of Eden, we are resurrected, not just spiritually, but physically, too. Infused with the light and love of God, every cell of the initiate's body is charged and changed. Engaging the supreme, eternal roots of our soul, the levels of Chayah (life force) and Yechidah (spark of God), we find that it is not the soul that needs refinement, for it is already perfect; rather, it is the temporal body we occupy that is given the task of making Eden on earth.

While most traditions speak of the eternity of the soul, the Chassidic tradition speaks of the body being designed to accompany the soul as an eternal partner in the time of messianic consciousness. Just as the cherubim on the top of the Ark are made of the same piece of gold as its lid, so too our experience of God on earth is not separate from what the People of the Book call Olam HaBa, the World to Come, and Gan Eden, the ultimate state of perfection. This world we live in is the world that is always coming into being. Yet the afterlife's supernal realms are accessible to us while we live, we need die only to the sense of separation we experience between body and soul. Having done so, we embody the eternal light of God that illuminates the heavenly realms and earthly creations. The same light suffuses all; the same surrounding and filling light of the Divine Presence enables us to live as Adam was designed, for a thousand years. In this sense, the longstanding quest for longevity is but an echo from ancient times.

Illumination through the Rituals of the Tabernacle

It must be emphasized that the body is not less important than the soul, for we are each a temple of the body *and* the soul. The body is a temporary vessel by which the soul can participate in refining the material world. In whatever place the Tent of Meeting is pitched, that is, wherever we live and in each lifetime we are given, we must act with loving-kindness, for the benefit of others, praying, studying holy texts, and singing, as did the Levites in ancient times. Proper actions nurture the body and vitalize the Nefesh of the soul. Then, by making the animal sacrifices in the Outer Court, representing the Ruach, or spirit in the body, we are strengthened as we nourish ourselves with proper food and proper deeds.

As we proceed into the Holy Place and the rituals of the menorah, shewbread, and incense, we engage the faculties of the mouth, nose, ears, and eyes, as tasting, smelling, hearing, and seeing are brought into harmony, elevating the senses to divine purpose and stimulating the soul's ability to commune with God directly. This corresponds to the Neshamah, that part of the soul that is eternal and represents the higher sense of hearing, or intuitive understanding.

Upon entering the Holy of Holies and approaching the Mercy Seat, the initiate who has done avodah, the work of self-improvement through selflessness, is able to receive direct illumination from God to those aspects of the soul that are eternal and that reside outside the body: the Chayah, the living presence of God, and the Yechidah, the spark of God from which each soul originates. Here we join the cherubim who guard the eternal wisdom of life and death, knowing this is the province of the Creator. Until we each stand on the verge of perfection as Adam and Eve do, praising God for the holy Sabbath, the ability to reflect, to think, to ask God's help in all that we do, we are but mere mortals. Once we enter the divine consciousness of unity, though, we become immortal. We no longer identify as just a body; rather, our body and soul are particles reveling in the Divine Presence. This, as we learned in the beginning of this book, is the greatest pleasure of all for the created human being. This is the intention God has had all along for humankind, as made clear when He tells the People of the Book to make a dwelling place for Him.

The ten songs of transcendence that the prophets and prophetesses give us, when meditated on, studied, or chanted, can assist us in cultivating the experience of the light that illuminated Moses as he descended Mt. Sinai with the Ten Commandments. This is the light our soul cherishes, for it is the illumination of God's Word, the creative powers of the universe written in our souls, as they are on the tablets in the Ark of the Tabernacle.

Final Review: Climbing the Tree of Life

By reviewing yet one last time the ten songs and ten emotions we have just explored, we gain the clear, integrated perspective on how progressive self-refinement through the Tree of Life and its Sefirot illuminates each person with the holy light of Creation, and how each one of us can soar like the eagles, as our resurrected nature of perfection is characterized by the Chazal. Through the prayers and songs presented in this book, the reader is given the traditional tools used for self-refinement by the People of the Book; however, one can develop one's own personal rituals, prayers, and songs, applying the pure intention and sincerely expressed emotional qualities of each Sefirah. What is of utmost importance is that one's heart and mind, body and soul are open to serving the divine; if other ways of praying and singing facilitate this process, then the reader should follow his or her own intuition in composing personal prayers and songs.

And so, one final ascent in our journey to revelation:

- We begin as the speaking human being in Malchut, making life a kingdom of prayer, returning to divinity every single day. Prayer is the foundation of the sanctuary of our being and establishes the conditions within the global community for messianic awareness and Moshiach.
- Entering the Outer Court of life, we make sacrifices in order to refine our emotions and come closer to God. We cry out in loving joy, as the righteous holy servants of God do in Yesod, as we make life a dedicated temple like the one built by the prophet-king Solomon. We consecrate our entire being to this purpose.
- Ascending to Hod, we enter the holy city of the prophet-king David with great, majestic thanksgiving and humility, acknowledging that humility is the source of each person's greatness. It is humility that allows the body and soul to sing a soaring melody, dedicating one's entire life to service and surrendering entirely to God's divine plan.
- Humility is joined by enduring will, as the next Sefirah, Netzach, the partner of Hod, and its exemplar, the prophetess Chanah, show us what it means to be victorious, to serve God with unwavering attachment—like God's eternal attachment to His creation.

- The prophetess Devorah reveals that truth, justice, and beauty, the qualities of Tiferet, combine in each of us, leading to a life of balance, the middle path. It is this privilege of integrating everything in harmony that causes light to radiate in all directions, inspiring a person to sing Tiferet's song, a hallel, in great joy.
- The prophet Joshua shows us how to use our inner and outer strength and self-discipline to cut away anything that is not holy. In Gevurah we must separate the holy and the unholy, allowing us to break through the darkness of our doubts and fears to cross over into unity with God.
- Moses, the emancipator, completes the six-part consecration of one's life to divine service by bringing us out of the tyranny of old habits, showing us that love, above all else, is God's holy presence. We are reminded that this quality of love, or Chesed, is why our right hand of loving-kindness is for doing good deeds.
- Entering the Holy Place, the inner arena of guarding our senses from harm, we learn to draw down God's blessings as we gain deeper understanding; this allows us to be a source of living spirit. Here, in Binah, everything is elevated by our ability to hear the essence of each moment.
- Just as the High Priest enters the Holy of Holies once a year, we receive divine wisdom and illumination through repentance each day. By honestly correcting ourselves, we are able to receive the direct light of our soul's higher nature in Chochmah, and thus gain clarity aided by wisdom.
- At the climax of our journey back to the Garden, we reach the crown of our being in Keter, the Godhead. Here, in completion, the divine human receives revelation leading to sublime unity with God, unity consciousness. The Sabbath, we learn, is the crowning achievement of Creation and the source of God's most refined light. We attain a sense of Godliness from the Or En Sof, the limitless light of divinity that surrounds us and fills us.

The Sefirot of the Tree of Life, from Malchut to Keter, as expressed in the work we do, the refinements we undertake, the effort we apply to our good deeds, and the restraint from wrong action we apply to our lives, all help each of us to make our life a sanctuary of the Divine Presence.

It is said that one can attain oneness, holy peace within, without complicated systems and practices. This is true. It is said that prophecy through the Ruach HaKodesh can illuminate any person anywhere in the world as long as he or she is deserving of receiving the Holy Spirit. It is said that prophecy on the higher levels occurs not only when a person is deserving of this kind of intimate relationship with God, but if his or her entire generation is worthy.

Since we are both individuals and members of a community, each one of us takes responsibility for society's development. Kabbalah's system of correspondences is a well-tried and proven strategy for the refinement and elevation of humanity and of each person of sincere heart who desires "the straight path to God," the legacy of B'nai Yisrael.

Closing Prayer

"R. Yohanan said: 'The day of the gathering of exiles will be as momentous as the day heaven and earth were created.'"[4] What is above is below; what is at the end is rooted in the beginning. May each person, as a sanctuary of the Divine Presence, appreciate the preciousness of life and gain an awareness that the inner work and outer actions we do are vital to the peace that all of humanity craves and will one day experience. Peace is the final outcome of Creation, the final accomplishment of humanity. May each of us become a holy Tent of Meeting, and may we gather together like our guides, the People of the Book, to share in the blessings of God's presence.

> *According to all that the LORD commanded Moses, so the children of Israel did all the work. . . . And it came to pass in the first month in the second year, on the first day of the month, that the tabernacle was reared up. And Moses reared up the tabernacle, and laid its sockets, and set up the boards thereof, and put in the bars thereof, and reared up its pillars. And he spread the tent over the tabernacle, and put the covering of the tent above upon it; as the LORD commanded Moses. And he took and put the testimony into*

---

[4] B. Pes 88a. See also Bialik and Ravnitzky, *Sefer Ha-Aggadah*, 5:44, 394.

*the ark, and set the staves on the ark, and put the ark-cover above
upon the ark. And he brought the ark into the tabernacle, and set
up the veil of the screen, and screened the ark of the testimony; as
the* LORD *commanded Moses. And he put the table in the tent of
meeting, upon the side of the tabernacle northward, without the
veil. And he set a row of bread in order upon it before the* LORD;
as the LORD *commanded Moses. And he put the candlestick in the
tent of meeting, over against the table, on the side of the tabernacle
southward. And he lighted the lamps before the* LORD; *as the*
LORD *commanded Moses. And he put the golden altar in the tent
of meeting before the veil; and he burnt thereon incense of sweet
spices; as the* LORD *commanded Moses. And he put the screen of the
door to the tabernacle. And the altar of burnt-offering he set at the
door of the tabernacle of the tent of meeting, and offered upon it
the burnt-offering and the meal-offering; as the* LORD *commanded
Moses. And he set the laver between the tent of meeting and the
altar, and put water therein, wherewith to wash; that Moses and
Aaron and his sons might wash their hands and their feet thereat;
when they went into the tent of meeting, and when they came
near unto the altar, they should wash; as the* LORD *commanded
Moses. And he reared up the court round about the tabernacle and
the altar, and set up the screen of the gate of the court. So Moses
finished the work. Then the cloud covered the tent of meeting, and
the glory of the* LORD *filled the tabernacle. And Moses was not able
to enter into the tent of meeting, because the cloud abode thereon,
and the glory of the* LORD *filled the tabernacle. And whenever the
cloud was taken up from over the tabernacle, the children of Israel
went onward, throughout all their journeys. But if the cloud was
not taken up, then they journeyed not till the day that it was taken
up. For the cloud of the* LORD *was upon the tabernacle by day, and
there was fire therein by night, in the sight of all the house of Israel,
throughout all their journeys.*

EXODUS 39:42, 40:17–38

Hebrew Alphabet Chart

ט	ח	ז	ו	ה	ד	ג	ב	א
Tet	Chet	Zayin	Vav	Hay	Dalet	Gimel	Bet	Alef
(T)	(Ch)	(Z)	(V/O/U)	(H)	(D)	(G)	(B/V)	(Silent)
9	8	7	6	5	4	3	2	1

ס	ן	נ	מ	ם	ל	ך	כ	י
Samech	Nun	Nun	Mem	Mem	Lamed	Chaf	Caf	Yod
(S)	(N)	(N)	(M)	(M)	(L)	(Kh)	(K/Kh)	(Y)
600/60	500	50	40	40	30	20	20	10

ת	ש	ר	ק	ץ	צ	ף	פ	ע
Tav	Shin	Reish	Kof	Tzadee	Tzadee	Fey	Pey	Ayin
(T)	(Sh/S)	(R)	(Q)	(Tz)	(Tz)	(F)	(P/F)	(Silent)
400	300	200	100	900	90	800/80	800/80	700/70

Hebrew alphabet chart with corresponding numeric values. For letters with two numbers listed, the smaller number is the usual value. When the letter is a final letter, it may have either of the values listed.

Eleven Degrees of Prophecy

According to the Rambam's writings on the subject, there are eleven distinct levels of the prophetic experience. Following are brief summaries of these identifiable and distinct processes in the Judaic tradition by which the prophetic experience occurs.[1]

1st Degree. At this level of experience, an individual is moved to great, righteous, and important action by the spirit of God and is referred to as being moved by the spirit of the Lord.

2nd Degree. Another force descends on the person or community and makes him or her speak about the nation (government) or divine matters while awake. It is said that in this way King David composed Psalms and King Solomon composed Proverbs, Ecclesiastes, and the Song of Songs. In addition, Daniel and Job composed their writings in a state of the second degree of prophecy. In cases of this prophecy, an individual or the community as a whole "speaks through the Holy Spirit."

3rd Degree. At this level the prophetic experience occurs through seeing images: Parables in a dream are made clear in the dream itself. It is identified by the saying "The word of the Lord came to me."

---

[1] R. Moses ben Maimon (Maimonides; the Rambam), *The Guide of the Perplexed,* chapter 45, book 2, 396, 403.

4th Degree. Here the person hears a parable in a dream without seeing the speaker.

5th Degree. In this case the prophet is addressed by a man in a dream, much like Ezekiel was: "And a man said unto me." In other words, an individual is aware of who it is that is imparting information, and this information is not in parables.

6th Degree. At this level, the prophetic experience involves angels appearing to an individual in a wakened state. It is often stated in Torah as: "an angel of God said to me . . ."

7th Degree. The prophet at this level has a dream in which the messenger is identified "as the Lord," as is attested by Isaiah's record.

8th Degree. Here the development of the prophet's clairvoyance and clairaudience increases. The prophet's revelation comes to him in a "vision of prophecy" in parable form, as Abraham saw "in a vision during the day." Here the prophet is not asleep, but is fully conscious and is shown a vision of parables.

9th Degree. Here the person's clairaudience and clairvoyance are equal—he hears speech in a waking vision.

10th Degree. Joshua at Jericho demonstrated this degree in seeing a man who addressed him in his prophetic vision. At this level, a prophet is awake and has a vision and is aware of being addressed by a human being.

11th Degree. The prophet sees an angel in a dream, as the patriarchs experienced at various times.

The Rambam has differentiated between waking and sleeping states and information brought by messengers and by direct communion with God. Some degrees of prophecy seem more attainable than others, making it easier to interpret the divine messages. For a more developed examination of the subject, turn to the Rambam's work *The Guide of the Perplexed,* from which this summary is taken.

The Shema

Cover your eyes with your right hand and say:
Hear, O Israel, the Lord is our God, the Lord is One.

Recite the following verse in an undertone:
Blessed be the name of the glory of His kingdom forever and ever.

You shall love the Lord your God with all your heart, with all your soul, and with all your might. And these words which I command you today shall be upon your heart. You shall teach them thoroughly to your children, and you shall speak of them when you sit in your house and when you walk on the road, when you lie down and when you rise. You shall bind them as a sign upon your hand, and they shall be for a reminder between your eyes. And you shall write them upon the doorposts of your house and upon your gates.

And it will be, if you will diligently obey My commandments which I enjoin upon you this day, to love the Lord your God and to serve Him with all your heart and with all your soul, I will give rain for your land at the proper time, the early rain and the late rain, and you will gather in your grain, your wine and your oil. And I will give grass in your fields for your cattle, and you will eat and be sated. Take care lest your heart be lured away, and you turn astray and worship alien gods and bow down to them. For then the Lord's wrath will flare up against you, and He will close the heavens so that there will be no rain and the earth will not yield its produce, and you will swiftly perish from the good land which the Lord gives you. Therefore, place these words of Mine upon your heart and upon your soul, and bind them for a sign on your hand, and they shall be for a reminder between your eyes. You shall teach them to your children, to speak of them when you sit in your house and when you walk on the road, when you lie down and when you rise. And you shall inscribe them on the doorposts of your house and on your gates—so that your days and the days of your children may be prolonged on the land which the Lord swore to your fathers to give to them for as long as the heavens are above the earth.

The Lord spoke to Moses, saying: Speak to the children of Israel and tell them to make for themselves fringes on the corners of their garments throughout their generations, and to attach a thread of blue on the fringe of each corner. They shall be to you as tzizit, and you shall look upon them and remember all the commandments of the Lord and fulfill them, and you will not follow after your heart and after your eyes by which you go astray—so that you may remember and fulfill all My commandments and be holy to your God. I am the Lord your God who brought you out of the land of Egypt to be your God; I, the Lord, am your God. True. (Source: Kehot Publication Society, Brooklyn, New York)

The Seventy-two Names of God

8	7	6	5	4	3	2	1	
כהת	אכא	ללה	מהש	עלם	סיט	ילי	והו	1
הקם	הרי	מבה	יזל	ההע	לאו	אלד	הזי	2
חהו	מלה	ייי	נלך	פהל	לוו	כלי	לאו	3
ושר	לכב	אום	רייי	שאה	ירת	האא	נתה	4
ייז	רהע	חעם	אני	מנד	כוק	להח	יחו	5
מיה	עשל	ערי	סאל	ילה	וול	סיכ	ההה	6
פוי	מבה	נית	ננא	עמם	החש	דני	והו	7
מחי	ענו	יהה	ומב	סצר	הרח	ייל	נמם	8
מום	היי	יבמ	ראה	חבו	איע	מנק	דמב	9

The seventy-two names of God (or the 216-letter name of God)

As described in chapter 11, these holy names or attributes of the Creator are derived from Exodus 14:19–21, the portion of the Hebrew Bible that describes Moses parting the Red Sea with his staff.

19 And the angel of God, who went before the camp of Israel, removed and went behind them; and the pillar of cloud removed from before them, and stood behind them; **20** and it came between the camp of Egypt and the camp of Israel; and there was the cloud and the darkness here, yet gave it light by night there; and the one came not near the other all the night. **21** And Moses stretched out his hand over the sea; and the LORD caused the sea to go back by a strong east wind all the night, and made the sea dry land, and the waters were divided.

The tools for calling in the Cloud of Glory and the Pillar of Fire suggest mastery over one's own nature and that these aspects of God are articulated in these names, which are not vocalized. Made of three letters each, these seventy-two triads offer us aspects of ourselves and Creation that are formulated into Hebrew letters. Meditating on them, seeing them written in the mind, using gematria to derive deeper meanings, or focusing on how each one affects one's feelings and insights, are all good ways to come into rapport with the vibratory tools used in re-creating ourselves and co-creating the world.

Summary of the Eighteen Aspects of Initiatory Prayer Based on the Shemoneh Esrei

The following summary can be used to create your own structured ritual and prayer.

Step One: binding oneself to God and our ancestors

Step Two: recognizing God's power to sustain the living and raise the dead, that is, to return to holiness by choice

Step Three: proclaiming the holiness of God, the source of all

Step Four: requesting the Holy Spirit to descend, that is, to be bestowed on oneself

Step Five: understanding that repentance is a daily action enabling reception of the divine emanations of bestowal

Step Six: asking for forgiveness, which requires humility and a sincere heart

Step Seven: seeing all people's redemption as one's own

Step Eight: asking God to bless us with health, to heal us

Step Nine: asking God to bless the Year and our world with bounty; we serve the world.

Step Ten: assembling others of like mind and heart in service to God

Step Eleven: committing to becoming an agent of justice in our world

Step Twelve: removing from the self all that is not holy in word, thought, and deed, and thus overcoming of sense of separateness

Step Thirteen: honoring the righteous, honoring one's teachers

Step Fourteen: committing to building our sanctuary of self and community through greater humility

Step Fifteen: knowing that salvation/freedom is the outcome of prayer, the prayers of the righteous initiate benefit the world

Step Sixteen: speaking directly to God, asking that our prayers be heard

Step Seventeen: feeling one's heart and mind united, the culmination of initiation

Step Eighteen: thanking God for all the miracles of life

Summary/Formal Close: asking God for peace

The Thirteen Attributes of Mercy and Thirteen Principles of Faith

The Thirteen Attributes of Mercy or Shelosh-Esreh Middot (Exodus 34:6-7)

1. *Adonai*—compassion before a person sins;
2. *Adonai*—compassion after a person has sinned;
3. *El*—mighty in compassion to give all creatures according to their need;
4. *Rachum*—merciful, that humankind may not be distressed;
5. *Chanun*—gracious if humankind is already in distress;
6. *Erech appayim*—slow to anger;
7. *Rav chesed*—plenteous in mercy;
8. *Emet*—truth;
9. *Notzer chesed laalafim*—keeping mercy unto thousands;
10. *Noseh avon*—forgiving iniquity;
11. *Noseh peshah*—forgiving transgression;
12. *Noseh chatah*—forgiving sin;
13. *Venakeh*—and pardoning.

Maimonides' Thirteen Principles of Faith
or Sheloshah-Asar Ikkarim
(Tractate Sanhedrin, Chapter 10)

1. The existence of God

2. God's unity

3. God's spirituality and incorporeality

4. God's eternity

5. God alone should be the object of worship

6. Revelation through God's prophets

7. The preeminence of Moses among the prophets

8. God's law given on Mount Sinai

9. The immutability of the Torah as God's Law

10. God's foreknowledge of human actions

11. Reward of good and retribution of evil

12. The coming of the Jewish Messiah (Moshiach)

13. The resurrection of the dead

Glossary

Adam Kadmon: The primordial man of earth.

ahavah: Love.

Alef-Bet: The Hebrew alphabet, composed of twenty-two letters.

Aliyah: Elevation, going up, to rise up.

Arich Anpin: "The long face of HaShem"; partzuf referring to the Sefirah Keter.

Aron HaBrit: The Ark of the Covenant, the traveling container (or box) that held the Ten Commandments.

ashrei: A song of sublime insight.

Asiyah: Realm of action, the material world in which we live, lowest of four worlds beneath the En Sof.

Atzilut: Realm of emanation, highest of the four worlds beneath the En Sof.

avodah: Work, in particular, spiritual effort.

avot: Ancestors, forefathers.

bahir: Literally "brightness" (of God).

beracha, pl. berachot: Blessing(s); the quality of blessing.

Beriyah: Realm of creation, the next to the highest realm of the four worlds beneath the En Sof.

Bet Hamikdash: "The house of that which is holy," or the Temple.

bimah: Elevated area in the synagogue where the Torah is read.

Binah: Sefirah of understanding.

Binyin Yerushalyim: Rebuilding Jerusalem (or the Third Temple)

Birkat HaMamin: Uprooting heretics, that is, those who undermine refinement.

bitachon: Confidence (associated with Netzach).

bitul: Self-nullification.

B'nai Yisrael: The children of Israel, the People of the Book.

bohu: Desolation.

brit: Covenant.

brit milah: Circumcision

ChaBaD: Acronym referring to the upper Sefirot of Chochmah, Binah, and Daat.

ChaGaT: Acronym for the Upper Chariot Sefirot of Chesed, Gevurah, and Tiferet

Chayah: Living presence or life force of the soul.

Chazal: An acronym (from Hakhameinu Zikhronam Liv'rakha) meaning "Our Sages, may their memory be blessed."

Chesed: Sefirah of loving-kindness.

Chochmah: Sefirah of wisdom.

Daat: Sefirah of knowledge.

Demut Elohim: The image of God.

din: Judgment, strength.

emet: Truth.

emunah: Faith.

En Sof: The Creator as infinity, formless and boundless, without end.

Eretz Yisrael: Land of Israel.

Etz Chayim: Tree of Life.

galut: Exile or captivity.

Gan Eden: The Garden of Eden.

gematria (gematriyah): "Numerology" systems of converting words into number values.

geulah: Redemption.

Gevurah: Sefirah of judgment and strength; might.

haftorah: "Concluding portion," a selection from the writings of the prophets, recited at the close of the Torah reading.

Halacha: The body of Jewish law.

hallel: A song radiating praise and joy.

HaShem: Literally, "the name"; refers to the Creator's ineffable name.

HaVaYaH: Four-letter name of God (Yod Hay Vav Hay).

Hod: Sefirah of glory and majesty.

hodu'ah: A song of majestic humility.

Holy of Holies: Most inner chamber of the Tabernacle, and later the Temple, reserved for the High Priest.

Kabbalah: Received tradition of correspondences.

KaChaBa: Acronym referring to Keter, Chochmah, and Binah.

kadosh: Holy, to make holy.

Kadosh HaKadoshim: The Holy of Holies in the Tabernacle.

Kapporeth: The cover of the Ark with the two cherubim, also known as the Mercy Seat.

kavanah: Intention.

Kedushat HaShem: The holiness of God's name.

kelim: Vessels (referring to the Sefirot).

kelipot: Shells, or husks, of evil encasing the fallen sparks.

Keter: Crown, the highest Sefirah in Etz Chayim.

ketoret: Sweet incense.

Kibbutz Galuyot: Gathering in of the righteous, or exiles.

kiyyor: Laver of water purification.

Kohanim: Priests.

Kohen Gadol: High Priest.

lechem panim: Shewbread.

lev echad: Of one heart, as in one people of one heart.

Lower Chariot: The three Sefirot of Netzach, Hod, and Yesod, sometimes referred to by the acronym NeHiY.

Malchut: Sefirah of kingdom and sovereignty, the lowest of the Sefirot in the Etz Chayim.

middot: "Measured flows," representing our emotions; the six Sefirot of Chesed through Yesod.

midrash, pl. midrashim: A haggadic exposition of the underlying significance of a Bible text.

Mikdash: A sanctuary.

mikvah: "Collection" or "gathering" of water for ritual immersion; laver of purification.

minyan: "Number," referring to the traditional requirement of ten men over the age of thirteen to pray in assembly in order to bring the Shechinah.

Mishkan: Tabernacle, Tent of Congregation (i.e., Meeting).

Mishnah: Literally, "teaching" or "instruction"; the first written collection of oral law (20–200 CE).

mitzvah, pl. mitzvot: commandment, good deeds, meritorious acts.

Moshiach: "Anointed One"; the prophesied redeemer of Israel and the world, whose arrival is imminent.

Nefesh: Vital force of the soul.

NeHiY: An acronym referring to the three Sefirot of Netzach, Hod, and Yesod.

Neshamah: Breath of the soul.

Netzach: Sefirah of victory and eternity.

nigun: A soaring, wordless melody.

nitzuah: A song of victory.

Nukvah: female (woman); Sefirah of Malchut.

Ohel Moed: Tent of Meeting, gathering; original Hebrew place of worship.

Olam HaBa: The World to Come.

omer: "sheaves" (as in the Counting of the Omer).

Or En Sof: Limitless light of the Creator (En Sof).

Or Makif: God's hidden light that does not come into revelation but rather surrounds each person on all sides equally.

partzufim: Family archetypes or personae in the Tree of Life that have correspondences to the Sefirot.

Penimi: God's inward light, the revelation of Godliness in every world.

Pentateuch: The five Books of Moses that comprise Torah.

Pesach: Passover, the celebration commemorating the Exodus from Egypt.

qorbanot: Sacrifices.

rachamim: Mercy, compassion (in Tiferet).

ranenu tzaddikim: A devotional song of the righteous.

ratzon: Will.

rebbe: A rabbinic teacher and/or spiritual leader.

Rosh Hashanah: Holiday of the Jewish New Year.

Ruach: Spirit of the soul.

Ruach HaKodesh: The Holy Spirit, the level of prophecy any righteous person can attain.

Sanhedrin: Sitting council of seventy-one elders.

Sefer Yetzirah: The Book of Formation, a Kabbalistic text attributed to Abraham.

Sefirah, pl. Sefirot: Ten vessels in the Etz Chayim that hold the light of God.

Shabbat: Sabbath.

shalom: Peace.

Shavuot: Holiday of receiving of Torah at Mt. Sinai; one of three pilgrimage holidays.

Shechinah: The Divine Immanence, a feminine aspect of the Creator.

Shema: Prayer said at least twice a day, to be the last words on a Jewish person's lips at death.

shemira: The vigil of "watching" or "guarding" the deceased's body before burial.

Shevirat HaKelim: The "breaking of the vessels," an event that resulted in the creation of the fallen sparks or the kelipot, the husks of evil.

shewbread (showbread): Bread of the Presence, ritual bread offered in the Tabernacle.

shiflut: Lowliness.

shir: A song (of jubilation).

Shir HaShirim: Song of Songs.

shulchan: Table on which shewbread is placed.

simcha: Joy.

sitra achra: "The other side" (i.e., that which opposes holiness).

sukkah: Booth used on Sukkot.

Sukkot: Holiday of the Booths, celebrating God's pillar of glory during Israel's Exodus from Egypt.

tachrichim: Traditional burial shroud.

tahara: Ritual cleansing and purification of the deceased.

Talmud: Central body of Jewish law and folklore comprising the Mishnah and Gemara (rabbinical commentary on the Mishnah), accumulated between 200 and 500 BCE.

Tanakh: The Hebrew Bible.

Targum: An Aramaic translation of the Hebrew Bible (Tanakh) written or compiled from the Second Temple period until the early Middle Ages.

tefillah: Prayer; a song of self-reflection.

Tehillim: The Book of Psalms.

temimut: Sincerity.

teshuvah: Repentance, return.

Tiferet: Sefirah of truth, mercy, and beauty.

tikkun; tikkun olam: Repair; repair of the world.

tohu: chaos.

Torah: Literally, "to teach"; teaching, instruction, all of Judaism's teachings, more commonly referred to as the Five Books of Moses, or the Pentateuch.

Tsvaot: "Host of Hosts" (Master of Legions), a reference to God.

tzaddik, pl. tzaddikim: A righteous one, the righteous.

tzimtzum: "Contraction," referring to the concept of the "removal" of God's infinite presence in order to allow His light (or En Sof) to be channeled into the creation of independent realities (Sefirot).

Yechidah: Divine spark of the soul.

Yesod: Sefirah of foundation and covenant.

yetzer hara: Evil inclination or the animal soul; our animal nature.

yetzer tov: Good inclination or divine soul.

Yetzirah: Realm of formation, the next-to-last realm of the four worlds beneath the En Sof.

yira; yirat HaShem: Awe or fear; fear of God.

Yom Kippur: Holy day of repentance.

Zeir Anpin: "Small face," "impatient one," the partzuf of the Son, comprised of the six middot (emotions) from Chesed to Yesod.

zemer: A song of breaking through; cutting through, harvesting with a knife.

zivug: Coupling, as in coupling with the divine in prayer.

Zohar: Book of Splendor, the foundational Kabbalistic work transmitted orally and then written down by R. Shimon bar Yochai (Rashbi) (80–160 CE). In the twentieth century the Zohar was translated from Aramaic into Hebrew by R. Yehudah Leib Ashag (Baal HaSulam, Master of the Ladder as in the Tree of Life, the ladder of light that all of the Zohar pertains to).

Bibliography

Abohav, R. Yitzchak. *Menoras Hamaor, The Ten Days of Teshuvah*. Lake Wood, N.J.: Torah Script Publications, 1983.

Ashlag, R. Yehudah Leib. *Shamati*. Edited by R. Avraham Mordechai Gottleib. Bnei Brak, Israel: Or Baruch Shalom, 2003.

Avital, Samuel Ben-Or. *The Invisible Stairway: Kabbalistic Meditations on the Hebrew Letters*. Boulder, Colo.: Kol-Emeth Publishers, 2003.

Baal Shem Tov, R. Israel. *The Testament of Rabbi Israel Baal Shem Tov*. Translated by R. Jacob Immanuel Schochet. New York: Kehot Publication Society, 1998.

The Bahir (Illumination): Translation, Introduction and Commentary. York Beach, Maine: Samuel Weiser, 1979.

Bar-Lev, R. Yechiel. *Song of the Soul, Introduction to Kabbalah*. Jerusalem: Book Distributors Ltd., 1994.

Basser, R. Tuvia. *Pirkei Avos, Maharal of Prague: A Commentary Based on Selections from Maharal's Derech Chaim*. New York: Mesorah Publications, 1997.

Bialik, Hayim Nahman, and Yehoshua Hana Ravnitzky. *The Book of Legends, Sefer Ha-Aggadah*. Translated by William G. Braude. New York: Shochen Books, 1992.

Birnbaum, R. Mayer. *Pathway to Prayer: A Translation and Explanation of the Shemoneh Esray*. New York: Feldheim Publishers, 1997.

Blumberg, Raphael, trans. *The Blueprint of Creation: The Chofetz Chaim on Torah Study*. Jerusalem: Bais Yechiel Publishers, 1990.

———. *The Chofetz Chaim Looks at Eternity*. Jerusalem: Bais Yechiel Publishers, 1989.

Bokser, Ben Zion. *The Maharal (1512–1609): The Mystical Philosophy of Judah Loew of Prague.* Northvale, N.Y.: Jason Aronson, 1994.

Brandwein, R. Avraham. *Classical Kabbalah: The Hidden Teachings of Torah and the Zohar.* Translated by R. Noah Shavrick. Owings Mills, Md.: Zohar Press, 2005.

Buxbaum, Yitzhak. *Jewish Spiritual Practices.* Northvale, N.J.: Jason Aronson, 1990.

Chasidah, R. Yisrael Yitzchak Yishai. *Encyclopedia of Biblical Personalities, Ishei HaTanach, Anthologized from the Talmud, Midrash, and Rabbinic Writings.* Jerusalem: Shaar Press Publications, 1994.

Chaviv, R. Yaakov Ibn. *Ein Yaakov: The Ethical and Inspirational Teachings of the Talmud.* Translated by Avraham Yaakov Finkel. Lanham, Md.: Rowman and Littlefield Publishers, 2004.

Clark, Matityahu. *Etymological Dictionary of Biblical Hebrew.* New York: Feldheim Publishers, 1999.

Cordovero, R. Moshe. *The Palm Tree of Devorah (Tomer Devorah).* Translated by R. Moshe Miller. New York: Targum/Feldheim, 1993.

Davis, R. Menachem, ed. *The Pirkei Avot: Ethics of the Fathers.* New York: Artscroll, Mesorah Publications, 1995.

De Fano, R. Menachem Azariah. *Asarah Ma'amarot, Ma'amar Em Kol Hai.* Venice, 1597.

Encyclopedia Judaica. Jerusalem: Keter Publishing, 1971.

Feuer, R. Avrohom Chaim. *A Letter of the Ages, Iggeres HaRamban: The Ramban's Ethical Letter.* New York: Artscroll, 1989.

———. *The Shemoneh Esrei.* New York: Artscroll, Mesorah Publications, 1990.

Finkelman, R. Shimon, and R. Nosson Scherman, eds. *Lag Ba' Omer: Its Observance, Laws and Significance.* New York: Artscroll, Mesorah Publications, 1999.

Frankel, Ellen, and Betsy Platkin Teutsch. *The Encyclopedia of Jewish Symbols.* Northvale, N.J.: Jason Aronson, 1992.

Ginsburgh, R. Yitzchak. *The Alef-Beit: Jewish Thought Revealed through the Hebrew Letters.* Northvale, N.J.: Jason Aronson, 1991, 1995.

———. *Living in Divine Space: Kabbalah and Meditation.* Jerusalem: Linda Pinsky Publications, Gal Einai Institute, 2003.

Glazerson, R. Matityahu. *Building Blocks of the Soul: Studies on the Letters and Words of the Hebrew Language.* Northvale, N.J.: Jason Aronson, 1997.

———. *Sparks of the Holy Tongue: The Secret Behind Words and Letters in the Hebrew Language.* New York: Feldheim Publishers, 1980.

Greenbaum, Avraham, trans. *Rabbi Nachman's Tikkun: The Comprehensive Remedy (Tikkun Hakali with Shemot Hatzaddikim) (Names of the Tzaddikim)*. New York: Breslov Research Institute, 1984.

Haralick, Robert M. *The Inner Meaning of the Hebrew Letters*. Northvale, N.J.: Jason Aronson, 1995.

Hieronimus, J. Zohara Meyerhoff. *Kabbalistic Teachings of the Female Prophets*. Rochester, Vt.: Inner Traditions, 2008.

Jacobson, Simon. *The Counting of the Omer*. New York: Vaad Hanochos Hatmimim, 1996.

———. *The Spiritual Guide to Counting the Omer*. New York: The Meaningful Life Center, 2007.

Kaplan, R. Aryeh. *Handbook of Jewish Thought,* two volumes. Edited by R. Avraham Sutton. New York: Maznaim Publishing Corporation, 1979.

———. *Immortality, Resurrection, and the Age of the Universe: A Kabbalistic View*. Hoboken, N.J.: KTAV Publishing House and Association of Orthodox Jewish Scientists, 1993.

———. *Inner Space: Introduction to Kabbalah, Meditation and Prophecy*. New York: Moznaim Publishing Corporation, 1990.

———. *Meditation and Kabbalah*. York Beach, Maine: Weiser Books, 1982.

———. *Sefer Yetzirah: The Book of Creation in Theory and Practice*. Boston: Red Wheel/Weiser, 1997.

Kramer, R. Chaim, and R. Avraham Sutton. *Anatomy of the Soul: Rebbe Nachman of Breslov*. New York: Breslov Research Institute, 1998.

Lieber, R. Moshe, and R. Nosson Scherman, eds. *The Pirkei Avos: Ethics of the Fathers, The Sages Guide to Living*. New York: Mesorah Publications, 1995.

Locks, Gutman. *The Spice of Torah—Gematria*. New York: Judaica Press, 1985.

Luria, R. Yitzchak. *Apples from the Orchard: Gleanings from the Mystical Teachings of the Rabbi Yitzchak Luria*. Translated with commentary by Moshe Wisnefsky. Malibu, Calif.: Thirty Seven Books, 2006.

———. R. Mordechai Scheinberger, ed. *Sefer Halikutim*. Jerusalem: R. Avraham Brandwein, 1988.

Luzzatto, R. Moshe Chayim [Chaim]. *General Principles of Kabbalah*. New York: Samuel Weiser, 1970.

———. *Mesillat Yesharim, Path of the Just*. Edited, translated, and annotated by R. Avraham Shoshana. Euclid, Ohio: Ofeq Institute, 2007.

———. *Mesillat Yesharim*. Based on MS Guenzburg 1206, Russian State Library, Moscow first edition, Amsterdam, 1740. Edited, translated, and annotated by R. Avraham Shoshana. Euclid, Ohio: Ofeq Institute, 2007.

———. *Mishkney Elyon, Secrets of the Future Temple.* Translated by R. Avraham Yehoshua ben Yakov Greenbaum. Jerusalem: The Temple Institute and Azmara Institute, 1999.

———. *Secrets of Redemption.* Translated by R. Mordechai Nissim. New York: Feldheim Publishers, 2004.

———. *The Path of the Just (Mesillas Yesharim).* Translated by R. Yosef Leibler. New York: Feldheim Publishers, 2004.

———. *The Path of the Just (Mesillat Yesharim).* Translated by R. Shraga Silverstein. New York: Feldheim Publishers, 1966.

———. *The Way of God (Derech HaShem).* Translated by R. Aryeh Kaplan. New York: Feldheim Publishers, 1983.

Maimonides (R. Moses ben Maimon). *The Guide of the Perplexed.* Translated by Shlomo Pines. Chicago: University of Chicago Press, 1963.

———. *Mishneh Torah.* Translated by R. Eliyahu Touger. New York: Moznaim Publishing, 1990.

———. *Mishneh Torah: Hilchot Yesodei HaTorah, vol. 1, Hilchot Teshuvah, vol. 4, and Shaarei Kedusha.* Translated by R. Eliyahu Touger. New York: Moznaim Publishing, 1989.

Menzi, Donald Wilder, and Zwe Padeh, trans. *The Tree of Life: The Palace of Adam Kadmon, Chayyim Vital's Introduction to The Kabbalah of Isaac Luria.* Northvale, N.J.: Jason Aronson, 1999.

Meyers, R. Dovid. *The Mishkan Illuminated.* Wickliffe, Ohio: self-published, 2010.

Miller, R. Chaim. *Chumash, the Five Books of Moses with commentary from Classic Rabbinic Texts and the Lubavitcher Rebbe.* The Gutnick Edition. New York: Kol Menachem, 2009.

Miller, R. Moshe, trans. *The Chofetz Chaim on Awaiting Mashiach.* Southfield, Mich.: Targum Press, 1993.

Nachman, R. of Breslov. *Rabbi Nachman's Tikkun (The Comprehensive Remedy, Tikkun Haklai).* Compiled and translated by R. Avraham Greenbaum. Jerusalem and New York: The Breslov Research Institute, 1984.

Naor, Betzalel. *From a Kabbalist's Diary: Collected Essays.* Spring Valley, N.Y.: Orot, 2005.

———. *Lights of Prophecy.* New York: Union of Orthodox Jewish Congregations of America, 1990.

Paquda, R. Bachya ben Joseph Ibn. *Duties of the Heart*. Translated by R. Yehudah Ibn Tibbon and Daniel Haberman. New York: Feldheim Publishers, 1996.

Rosenblatt, R. Yaakov. *The Maharal, Emerging Patterns: Ten Representative Essays Culled from the Works of Rabbi Yehudah Loew of Prague*. New York: Feldheim Publishers, 2001.

Scherman, R. Nosson. *Shabbos, The Sabbath: Its Essence and Signficance*. New York: Artscroll, Mesorah Publications, 2002.

———. *The Song of the Universe*. Edited by Perek Shira. New York: Artscroll, Mesorah Publications, 2005.

———. *Tanach: The Torah, Prophets, Writings—The Twenty-Four Books of the Bible*. New York: Artscroll, Mesorah Publications, 1996.

Scherman, R. Nosson, and R. Meir Zlotowitz, eds. *The Complete Artscroll Siddur*. New York: Artscroll, Mesorah Publications, 1985.

———. *Shir Hashirim, Song of Songs: An Allegorical Translation based on Rashi with a Commentary Anthologized from Talmudic Midrashic and Rabbinic Sources*. New York: Mesorah Publications, Ltd., 1977.

Schneersohn, Rabbi Menachem Mendel of Lubavitch (Tzemach Tzedek). *Derech Mitzvosecha: A Mystical Perspective on the Commandments, Vol. 1*. Translated by Eliyahu Touger. New York: Kehout Publication Society, 2004–2007.

Schneerson, R. Shalom Dov Ber of Lubavitch. *Forces in Creation, Yom Tov Shel*. New York: Kehot Publication Society, 2003.

Schneerson, R. Yosef Y. of Lubavitch and R. Menachem M. Schneerson. *Basi Legani*. Chassidic Discourses. New York: Kehout Publication Society, 1990.

Schneider, Sarah. *Kabbalistic Writings on the Nature of Masculine and Feminine*. Northvale, N.J.: Jason Aronson, 2001.

Sivan, Reuven, and Edward A. Levenston. *Hebrew and English Dictionary: The New Bantam-Megiddo*. New York: Bantam, 1975.

Sokolovosky, Meir Simcha. *Prophecy and Providence: The Fulfillment of Torah Prophecies in the Course of Jewish History*. New York: Feldheim Publishers, 1991.

Steinberg, Rabbi Shalom Dov. *The Mishkan and the Holy Garments*. Translated by R. Moshe Miller. Jerusalem: Toras Chaim Institute, 5752 (1992).

Tanakh, The Holy Scriptures. Philadelphia, Pa.: Jewish Publication Society, 1917, 1985. Also available online at www.mechon-mamre.org.

Trugman, R. Avraham. *The Mystical Nature of Light: Divine Paradox of Creation*. New York: Devora Publishing, 2008.

———. *The Mystical Power of Music*. Southfield, Mich.: Targum Press, Inc., 2005.

Volozhin, Rav Chaim ben Yitzchak. *Nefesh HaChaim*. Translated by R. Avraham Yaakov Finkel. New York: The Judaica Press, Inc., 2009.

Wigoder, Geoffrey. *The Student's Encyclopedia of Judaism*. New York: New York University Press, 2004.

Wisnefsky, R. Moshe, translation and commentary. *Apples from the Orchard, Gleanings from the Mystical Teachings of Rabbi Yitzchak Luria (the Arizal) on the Weekly Torah Portion*. Malibu, Calif.: Thirty Seven Books, 2006.

Yoshor, R. Moses M. *The Chafetz Chaim: The Life and Works of Rabbi Yisrael Meir Kagan of Radin*. New York: Artscroll, Mesorah Publications, 1994.

Zalman, R. Schneur of Liadi. *Likkutei Amarim Tanya*. New York: Kehot Publication Society, 1993.

Zaloshinsky, R. Gavriel. *The Ways of the Tzaddikim*. Edited and translated by R. Shraga Silverstein. New York: Feldheim Publishers, 1995.

Zlotowitz, R. Meir, ed., R. Nosson Scherman, trans. *Shir HaShirim, Song of Songs: An Allegorical Translation Based upon Rashi with a Commentary Anthologized from Talmudic, Midrashic and Rabbinic Sources*. New York: Artscroll, Mesorah Publications, 1977.

Index

Page numbers in *italics* indicate illustrations.

Books of Related Interest

Kabbalistic Teachings of the Female Prophets
The Seven Holy Women of Ancient Israel
by J. Zohara Meyerhoff Hieronimus, D.H.L.

The Temple of Solomon
From Ancient Israel to Secret Societies
by James Wasserman

Qabbalistic Magic
Talismans, Psalms, Amulets, and the Practice of High Ritual
by Salomo Baal-Shem

The Woman with the Alabaster Jar
Mary Magdalen and the Holy Grail
by Margaret Starbird

14 Steps to Awaken the Sacred Feminine
Women in the Circle of Mary Magdalene
by Joan Norton and Margaret Starbird

The Gospel of Mary Magdalene
by Jean-Yves Leloup

Feminine Mysteries in the Bible
The Soul Teachings of the Daughters of the Goddess
by Ruth Rusca

Kabbalah and the Power of Dreaming
Awakening the Visionary Life
by Catherine Shainberg

INNER TRADITIONS • BEAR & COMPANY
P.O. Box 388
Rochester, VT 05767
1-800-246-8648
www.InnerTraditions.com

Or contact your local bookseller